Gourmet's BASIC FRENCH COOKBOOK

TECHNIQUES of FRENCH CUISINE

Louis Gray

Gourmet's
BASIC FRENCH COOKBOOK

TECHNIQUES of FRENCH CUISINE

BY
LOUIS DIAT

ILLUSTRATED BY
GEORGETTE DE LATTRE

WEATHERVANE BOOKS
NEW YORK

This 1990 edition is published by Weathervane Books, distributed by Crown Publishers, Inc., 225 Park Avenue South, New York, New York 10003, by arrangement with Alfred A. Kopf Inc.

Gourmet is a registered trademark of Conde Nast Publications.

Printed and bound in the United States of America

Library of Congress Cataloging-in-Publication Data

Diat, Louis.
    Gourmet's basic French cookbook / Louis Diat.
        p.   cm.
    Reprint. Originally published: New York : Knopf, 1961.
    ISBN 0-517-01475-0
    1. Cookery, French.   I. Title.
TX719.D49   1990   89-48695
641.5944—dc20   CIP

8 7 6 5 4 3 2 1

CONTENTS

CONTENTS

FOREWORD

By

HELEN E. RIDLEY

EVEN BEFORE his death a few years ago, Louis Diat of the Ritz had already become something of a gastronomic legend in the tradition of the great chefs who left behind them written records of their culinary achievements. He wrote his first book in 1941, and it was my privilege to be invited to work with him on this and on his later books, as well as on the articles he contributed to GOURMET Magazine over a twelve-year period, beginning in 1946. GOURMET'S BASIC FRENCH COOKBOOK, subtitled Techniques of French Cuisine, is the natural and fitting culmination of Monsieur Louis' lifelong career as a chef and teacher of chefs.

Montmarault, the small Bourbonnais town where Louis Diat was born in 1885, lies very close to the vineyards that produce some of the finest wines in the world, and boasts as neighbors such famed centers of gastronomy as Dijon, Lyons, and Moulins. In this milieu, it was almost inevitable that every man should be a connoisseur of fine wines and fine food and every woman a good cook, and that every second young boy should aspire to become a great chef. The road to such culinary heights was not open to everyone. The boy had to have genuine talent, and he had to undergo an arduous apprenticeship at no small expense. The ambitious young Louis was fortunate; his father could afford to pay the fee for his two years' training as an apprentice at the Maison Calondre in Moulins. And that he did have genuine talent is a matter of record.

From Moulins the young chef-in-training went to Paris to begin his career in earnest, at the Hôtel Bristol and the Hôtel du Rhin. Subsequently he served at the Ritz Hotels in Paris and in London.

The years around the turn of the century were unique in *haute cuisine*. The fantastically elaborate dishes and extravagant feasts of the eighteenth and nineteenth centuries were all but out of fashion. Nuances of flavor and texture had become more important than sculptured effects, and although young chefs worked just as hard as their predecessors, they worked to produce results that were exquisite, rather than exotic.

César Ritz, mentor of the Ritz hotels, was a leading spirit in this gastronomic reformation, and when he planned the Ritz-Carlton in New York, to open in 1910, he spared nothing that might be needed to carry out his theories. As Monsieur Louis, who became *chef de cuisines*, explained, " Our bakery and ice cream plants were as well equipped as any shop's. We had a huge tank to keep live trout in. When I say we did everything for the kitchen right on the premises, I mean everything. We roasted our own coffee, even made the chocolates and bonbons for the guests' gift boxes on such occasions as the opening of the opera or the horse show. We had tremendous refrigerators and cold rooms...."

All in all, the kitchens that were ruled by Louis Diat, the youngest chef ever to be given such a responsibility in a hotel comparable to the Ritz, occupied two floors of the hotel, and were unsurpassed anywhere.

Supplies were another matter, however, and it was some months before the new chef solved the problems he unexpectedly faced. There were no fresh truffles, as in France, so he used the canned. The thick cream required for certain dishes had to be sent down from Vermont. Fresh herbs, shallots, leeks, baby vegetables—none of these were available in the city's produce markets. But soon enough the word got around: the chef of the Ritz would pay a good price to get precisely what he wanted, and enterprising market gardeners were soon supplying his every need.

The name of the Ritz-Carlton Hotel was for forty years synonymous with excellent food, superbly prepared. For his " services in bringing to America the highest type of French culinary art, " Louis Diat was made an Officier du Mérite Agricole by the French Government. In the meantime, he was teaching his trade as well as practicing it. Chefs trained by him in the kitchens of the Ritz-Carlton carried their skills into fine restaurants and hotels throughout the country.

Monsieur Louis was convinced that anyone who was interested enough to read and study the philosophy and techniques of French cuisine and put them into practice in the kitchen could become a fine cook. But fluent as his English was for most purposes, he realized the difficulties of writing in an adopted tongue about a trade he had learned in his native tongue, so to speak, and sought a collaborator. It was my great good fortune that he chose me. I was a more-than-willing *apprentie*, sometimes learning in the Ritz kitchen, sometimes working under his guiding hand in my own kitchen, spending long hours at his desk in order to clarify and simplify every step he described.

Madame Diat turned over to me all Monsieur Louis' notebooks, his records, and his mementos. I have in my possession the thick, carefully indexed loose-leaf volumes in which he had his French secretary type his formulas for practically every dish in the classic cuisine. They are invaluable source books.

Unfortunately, Monsieur Louis did not live to see GOURMET's BASIC FRENCH COOKBOOK in print. But the people interested in its publication have honored his memory by their dedication to the task. Thanks are due to so many.

The inspiration and co-operation of GOURMET's publisher, Earle R. MacAusland, has never wavered during these many years. He once said, when we doubted the wisdom of including, in the Diat articles that appeared in GOURMET, material that might seem too elaborate by modern standards, " If it is interesting and in the classic tradition, include it; GOURMET is the place to record culinary history. "

9

Gourmet's BASIC FRENCH COOKBOOK

TECHNIQUES of FRENCH CUISINE

The Chef at Work

LE CHEF À L'OEUVRE

THERE IS A long-standing tradition in the kitchens of the great restaurants of France that when a chef reaches the top of the ladder that he has so painstakingly climbed, he must take on the responsibility of overseeing the *apprentis* who are always being trained in kitchens of any importance.

We French chefs take great pride in our *cuisine française*. We don't want it lost to posterity. Most certainly we don't want the great restaurants of the world ever to lack well-trained artisans. So passing along the *gros bonnet* has become a prideful duty and responsibility.

Some chefs go on to teach anyone interested in our art—prospective chefs or not—the ways of fine French cooking by becoming writing chefs. But readers sometimes say that writing chefs take too much for granted in the way of culinary background, knowledge, and skills. Neophytes have told me that in going through the many compilations of French recipes they seldom find simple, precise, step-by-step explanations, or the " whys " and " hows " of fine French cooking.

So when I assumed the role of a writing chef, the explaining of the techniques on which this famous cuisine is built became one of my major aims. Now it is the backbone of this book, and if fear and lack of confidence have been holding you back, I trust your uncertainty will disappear, little by little, until you are able to say, " This is how I have always wanted to cook. "

Teaching others, I find, makes you relive some of your own experiences—I remember well the period before my parents gave their permission for me to go into training to be a chef. My farmer *grand-père*, I recall, kept extolling the advantages of following in his footsteps. But I knew what I wanted. The kitchen was my lure, although not until years later did I realize that this wasn't purely accidental, but had been shaped almost unconsciously by my mother's concern for me.

I was born left-handed—unfortunate in days when schoolmasters would never let a child write or work with the left hand. The sharp edge of a ruler on your knuckles was a painful reminder you obeyed—and didn't run home and tattle about, either. This can do strange things to children. I, for instance, started walking in my sleep, rubbing my knuckles in a sad kind of way as I wandered. It always roused my mother, so my older brother told me years later, and she would lead me back to the bed I shared with him, saying gently, " *Vas dormir, mon petit.* " (Now go to sleep, child.) My waking hours were even more difficult; I was turning into a nervous, belligerent small boy.

Our town boasted no child psychologist. *Evidemment !* But a kind of sixth sense, or the simple realism of the French in trying situations, made up for this lack. *Mon père* asked the schoolmaster not to chastise me for something I couldn't help, and offered to work with me in encouraging me to use my right hand. For her part, *ma mère* coaxed me into helping her in the kitchen and gave me things to do with both my hands.

To quiet my nervousness she talked to me about cooking, about the different dishes *grand-mère* had taught her to make, about Emile Malley, the son of her best friend, who had gone to Paris to be a great chef (the same chef Malley, incidentally, who would one day get me started in Paris too). It proved to be a practical solution, and one that worked. And I learned much more than how to use my right hand. I learned to count as I got out the eggs or potatoes or onions for the cooking, and how to spell the words, too—and how to cook, *naturellement.*

There is a feeling that " chefs have secrets they won't give out. " Actually, a chef starting out on his day's work is probably thinking less of culinary secrets than he is of a race horse leaving the stable at Long-champs. But as soon as his *haute toque* is in place, and the *serviette* at his waist in its traditionally precise folds, and he turns his hand to a sauce or a garniture, his so-called secrets or tricks come into play. His response to the knife picked up, the spoon grasped, is so trigger-quick, so automatic, that he is quite unconscious of how dexterous he is. If asked for a recipe, he doesn't stop to think how few of his questioners have his dexterity. Add up the long days and many years the chef puts in at the preparation table and in front of the range, and you arrive at his tricks.

There are a few famous dishes that their originators have kept secret lest other restaurateurs take away the monopoly of hard-won laurels. But what appears secretiveness to a guest is more likely to be the inability of a French chef to write down a complicated recipe in any but his own language—the one in which he thinks and works. *Mettez-vous à sa place*—put yourself in his shoes. Also, there is the question of time. Picture the head chef of the kitchens of a large establishment. Hundreds of meals, thousands of dishes every noon and every evening must get from his noisy, fragrant confines to the diners beyond. Hot dishes, really hot; cold dishes, well chilled; and *mon Dieu,* never a curdled sauce or a fallen soufflé! Watch that tireless mechanism, the telautograph, that links the dining rooms to the kitchens and scribbles and scribbles the never-ending commands of impatient waiters. If, at the high point of the mealtime rush, the suave headwaiter makes his appearance, the chef is certain something has gone wrong. He drops whatever he is doing to rush over with a quick " What has happened ? "

A casual reply such as, " *Mais rien.* Madame Blanc simply wants your recipe for chicken hash, " invariably releases a Gallic temperament already tensed by too many split-second demands. Who wouldn't yell above the clatter, " *Nom d'un nom,* can't you see how busy I am ? Come back at two o'clock. "

The headwaiter merely shrugs his well-groomed shoulders. But Madame Blanc will believe that the chef would not part with his recipe.

At the outset it must be made clear that the French consider their cooking an art. And an artist is one who strives for perfection. But perfection, in turn, implies an ideal, a grand effect or perhaps exquisite workmanship, which is, *mes apprentis*, what you should seek.

That there aren't too many short cuts in any really fine cooking should also be made clear. The more you cook, of course, the more you learn about working quickly and avoiding clumsy, roundabout ways. But a fine *cuisinier* never sacrifices results to save minutes. As you progress you should become less dependent upon recipes, for you will have at your fingertips the techniques of French cooking. When you have acquired the " feel " of this famed art of the French, you are on your way to its mastery.

The dishes of the grand cuisine of fifty years ago did not lend themselves to short cuts—a reason why so many of them are gone. But modern kitchen equipment has made others easier. No chef today pounds raw meat by hand to make the fine, smooth paste required for *godiveau*, quenelles, and mousses. Good grinders have replaced strong muscles. No one blanches, dries, and then pounds and pounds almonds with sugar, when almond paste can be purchased so easily. No one uses a hand whip on a batch of forty or fifty egg whites to make spongecakes and ladyfingers.

Yet, the fine eating places of Paris still serve many dishes that give evidence of the painstaking cookery for which the French are famous. But their customs differ from American ways. The relaxed atmosphere is noticeable. Kitchens will not be hurried, and it does no good to be impatient. Guests are expected to show their appreciation by eating slowly, savoring each mouthful well.

Chef Saucier Wherever French chefs ply their trade, the *chef saucier*, or sauce chef, has no peer except, of course, the *chef des cuisines*, or head chef. And every head chef has at some time been a *saucier*. What chef can successfully direct a great kitchen unless he has mastered the art of sauces and can critically appraise the work of his *saucier?*

You may be interested in the workings of the kitchen of the famous Paris Ritz in those gay years before World War I, because it was a famous hotel, small and elegant, run almost like a gentleman's club, with exceedingly fastidious patrons. The staff of such an establishment knows all the little—and big—whims of its patrons, and it bends so much effort to satisfy them that the hotel becomes the patrons' second home. Hotels of this sort are gradually disappearing, but to them we owe the preservation of many traditions of fine cooking.

16

In that type of establishment, the head chef—called *le chef des cuisines* because he directed several kitchens—was the king of his kitchen domain, responsible for everything that had to do with the purchase and preparation of food. He bought it all, made the menus, established the prices. He also hired all the kitchen help and bought all the kitchen equipment. If the place were large enough, he had an assistant who was usually an ambitious *chef saucier* working his way up the ladder to the position of *chef des cuisines* in his own right in some comparable establishment. In a small place, the *chef saucier* simply doubled as assistant to the head chef and outranked all the other chefs in the kitchen. There were about twenty-five or thirty chefs at the Paris Ritz—an adequate number for our rather small but very exclusive hotel.

The *chef saucier* always had the support of two or three *commis*— that is, assistant chefs. Then we had a *chef poissonnier*, who was responsible for the fish cookery; a *chef potager*, who made the soups and the stocks for the sauces; a chef who was a combination *rôtisseur* and *grillardin*, which meant he handled both the roastings and broilings; and a *chef entremettier*, who cooked vegetables and eggs. Each of these chefs had one, two, or more *commis* to assist him.

The special posts of *chef garde-manger* and *chef pâtissier* were very important. The *garde-manger* was responsible for the storage rooms and iceboxes and for their contents. That takes good organization. But he was also the one in daily contact with the *marchand* who came in twice each day with the supplies of meats, poultry, and game. This *marchand*'s job included cleaning and trussing the birds to make them ready for the roasting pans, and the *garde-manger* had to make sure he didn't slip out before they were properly done. The *garde-manger* also made up the cold platters, and for these duties he required the assistance of three or more *commis*. The *chef pâtissier* was just as busy, because all the desserts came from his kitchen—elaborate pastries and *gâteaux*, ice creams and *bombes*, as well as routine soufflés, *oeufs à la neige*, tarts and compotes, and macédoines of fruit. So he, too, rated at least three *commis*.

And finally there was the *chef cafetier*, who prepared breakfast and afternoon tea and who also made the coffee and tea served at all meals. I might add, in passing, that in time most of these men became well-known chefs in hotels all over the world, and that many of them came eventually to the United States. Universal respect for the experience and training gained at the Ritz opened the kitchen door to any hotel.

In our dining rooms there were several specialists in serving. *Le*

Chef des Cuisines

Commis

Chef Potager Rôtisseur

Garde-Manger

Marchand

Chef Pâtissier

Chef Cafetier

Maître
de Chais

Trancheur

maître de chais opened and poured the wine, a job not to be confused with that of the *caviste*, who is custodian of the *cave*, or wine cellar, and is recognized by his traditional key and heavy chain. There was *le trancheur*, whose sole responsibility was carving meats and poultry and serving the *plat du jour*, and there was *le capitaine des salades et des fruits*, who made every salad and had charge of the fruit, too. Today the kitchen takes on most of these duties because the headwaiter, occasionally assisted by the maître d'hôtel, must handle all the special services of a busy dining room.

The Costume and Customs

Now a word or two about a chef's costume. The hat seems to intrigue most people, particularly men who make a hobby of cooking. Why this white cotton affair? And why so high? *Eh bien*, white is the symbol of cleanliness and cotton is washable. The height merely gives more air around the head in hot kitchens. It's as simple as that. Usually the *gros bonnet*, or very high hat, indicates the *chef des cuisines*; *sous-chefs* wear less stately ones.

Equally important are the apron and towel. Working quickly, handling foods that splash, would soon ruin one's clothes. So an apron is a must and a good cook changes it as soon as it becomes soiled. It's a kitchen maxim that a dirty apron is not the sign of a hard-working chef but of a careless one. Our aprons were made of heavy white cotton duck, about forty inches square, with strong tape sewn at the top corners. Such an apron is pulled up a bit higher than the waistline in front, the tapes crossed in back are brought around to the front at the waistline and tied at the side. This gives a band to tuck the towel under. And no chef could possibly work without the towel at his belt. He grabs hot handles of pans with it, carries hot dishes, and wipes off the drips on the sides of dishes. And he dries his hands, that endless washing and drying of hands that is so important, because cleanliness must always be the first rule with food. A busy chef will change his towel a dozen or more times a day.

There is a professional way of folding the towel: Grip one corner in your teeth and let the towel hang flat against you. Now take the corner near your right hand and fold it over about a third of the towel. Then with your left hand take the opposite corner and fold it over to meet the crease made by the first fold. This makes three layers. Next fold over the right side—about a third of the way—and the remaining left side over it. Smooth all the folds with your hands to flatten them. Finally, take the corner out of your teeth and tuck the towel under your apron string, the fold side out, with a four-or five-inch lap. It makes a thick holder for handling hot dishes, it opens easily to dry your hands, but it always falls back flat in place at your side.

Next, even though it may sound tiresome, I should not be doing my job if I didn't remind you that a good cook is a clean, tidy, well-organized worker. He arranges the equipment he is using—cutting board, knives, bowls, beaters, casseroles, kettles, and so forth—in an orderly fashion and stores them where he can put his hands on anything he may need at a minute's notice. He will never have time to search in cluttered drawers or cupboards for a tool or a utensil. Young apprentice chefs are taught to clean and scour all the things they use and keep the places where they work scrupulously clean and to respect their tools. Later they know from experience how much anyone delegated to clean up for them can be expected to do and how he should do it.

A good cook, like any other good worker, makes sure of what he is going to do before he begins. He sees that all ingredients and utensils needed are on hand. If written instructions (recipes) are used, they are read and reread to make certain every step is understood. Finally the time required for preparation and cooking—and chilling, if that is needed—is accurately estimated so that the dish will appear on the table at its peak of excellence, exactly on time.

Tools and Equipment

To cook skillfully and well, dependable equipment is a prime essential. Never be misled into buying anything unsuitable for its task or poorly made because it is cheap. That is poor economy.

Pans

Cutting Board

Knives

When buying new equipment, select good sturdy utensils of heavy metal. Food is less apt to scorch in heavy metal; a heavy pan will not dent and warp, and it holds the heat and distributes it better. The cutting board must be thick and heavy to resist warping even after hundreds of washings, because unless the board is absolutely flat the slicing knife misses making a thorough cut of the food on it. It also should be large enough to hold the food that falls away from the knife and perhaps scatters a bit. Knives are important; nothing can take the place of good steel that will hold a sharp edge. A chef has his knives regularly sharpened by a professional, and then keeps a steel handy to touch up the edge whenever he uses one. As you progress you will probably acquire knives of many sizes and shapes, but three really good knives—a small one for paring, one slightly larger for cutting vegetables and the like, and a big one for slicing meat and poultry—are better than a dozen poor knives that never hold a good cutting edge. Two sieves, one with a fine screen, the other coarser, will be needed, large enough to hold material poured through by the quart.

Sieves

The well-equipped kitchen needs 2 or 3 casseroles of different sizes. They are described in the section on braising and stews. Skillets are considered in the sections on sautéing and poaching.

Kettles and Bowls

In considering the most practical equipment, the size of kettles and bowls is more important than is apparent at first. A too-full kettle boils over the minute your back is turned, and mixtures that must be stirred splash onto the range. Mixing in bowls that are too small is equally untidy. And a quart measure saves filling a cup four times.

Spoons, Spatula, Whips, and Food Mill

Those interested in cooking usually have small equipment galore; those interested in French cooking should be sure to have wooden spoons in various sizes, a wooden spatula or two (these are like wooden spoons but with the bowl end flat), and a couple of French wire whips. A food mill for making purées of vegetables and fruits is also a standard item in a French kitchen.

New cast-iron pans are sometimes coated with a lacquer which must be removed by scrubbing with hot water and strong soap or a detergent before using them. To keep them, and also knives and other rust-prone equipment, free from rust, rub them very lightly with vegetable oil for storage.

The kind and number of mechanical devices you will require in your kitchen depend on how much cooking is done, and on what kind of cooking is done. Electric mixers are now considered basic equipment, but few home kitchens follow the practice of restaurants, which is to have an extra set of bowls and beaters available when the mixer must be used more than once during the preparation of a dish or a meal. Mechanical blenders can be a great aid, when a family-sized amount of food must be puréed for a fish mousse, cream soup, or for any recipe that calls for putting the ingredients through a fine sieve.

Mixers

Blenders

Some Tricks of the Chef

GOURMET cookery requires meticulous perfection even in small details. And the first detail every *chef apprenti* must learn is to cut up vegetables quickly and correctly, particularly the onions, potatoes, and carrots used every day. Everyone notices how evenly the vegetables are sliced and diced in first-class restaurants. Chances are that the chef who prepared them learned to do it when he was twelve or thirteen years old and has done it every day since. If you were to watch him, his hand would be quicker than your eye. Aside from the fact that a hodgepodge of uneven pieces is not attractive, uneven pieces cook unevenly. For example, small bits of onion cooking in butter will brown—may almost burn—before the larger pieces are soft, while tiny pieces of potato boil to a mush before the larger chunks are tender.

Cutting Up Vegetables

When a vegetable slips and rolls under the hand against the cutting board, it is only too easy to cut the fingers, too. But the curved side of the carrot, potato, or onion can be sliced off or the vegetable cut in half, so that it will rest flat and firm on the board. Also, a chef holds his hand on the vegetable in such a way that the ends of the fingers (his nails are always trimmed quite short) are curved a little away from the knife, and he angles the blade of the knife very slightly away from his fingers, and rests the back against his knuckles. He then can work with lightning speed without cutting himself.

Cut a thin slice from the top of the onion and peel the onion skin from top to bottom, tearing it away from the bottom. Trim the base a little, being careful to leave the layers of onion firmly attached to it.

Onions

To dice the onion, place it on its base and slash it in half from top

21

to bottom. Work with one half at a time. Lay the half onion cut side down on the board with the base end to the left. Hold the half onion with the left hand and cut it with the right, unless you too are left-handed! With the blade of the knife on the onion and its point about 1/2 inch away from the base, slash through the onion down to the board, making even, lengthwise slices from the base end and through the top end the thickness of the dice desired. The 1/2-inch butt keeps the slices attached to the base. Now hold the knife so that its flat side is parallel to the board and slice through the onion sidewise, starting at the top and again carrying the cuts to 1/2 inch from the base end, making horizontal slices the same thickness as the vertical ones. Hold this bundle of strips firmly with the left hand and cut across them, starting at the top end and working back toward the base. *Voilà !* Off fall the evenly diced pieces of onion. The tiny 1/2-inch bit left at the base can be cut separately

Shallots or used in the stock pot. Dice shallots the same way.

To slice an onion, cut a thin piece off one side of the peeled onion to make a firm flat surface to rest on the board. Lay the onion flat side down with the base of the onion at the left. Starting at the right and working toward the base, cut across the onion in even slices.

Carrots Peel or scrape the carrots, trim both ends, and cut them crosswise in halves or thirds. Work on one piece at a time. To dice the carrots, cut a thin slice from one side to make a flat surface and lay the carrot flat side down on a board. Slice it lengthwise to any desired thickness, discarding a thin slice from one side to make another flat surface. Turn over the pile of slices so that they rest on the last cut surface. Slice again lengthwise to the same thickness as the first slices, making square-ended strips. Grasp the bundle of strips with the left hand and slice across them to make square, uniform dice.

Julienne To make julienne—small thin square-ended strips—follow the procedure for dice, cutting the slices from 1/16 to 1/8 inch thick, then cut across the bundle of strips to make uniform pieces 1 to 1 1/2 inches long.

Bâtonnets To make *bâtonnets*, which are thicker julienne, follow the directions for julienne, but make the strips 1/4 inch thick and the pieces 1 inch long.

Paysanne To make *paysanne*, or thin discs, use small carrots 2 to 2 1/2 inches long or trim large carrots to this size. Cut a thin slice from one side to make a flat surface, lay the carrot flat side down on the board, and slice across the carrot as thinly as possible.

Potatoes Follow the directions for carrots, cutting the slices 1/2 inch thick, more or less, according to the requirements of the particular recipe. Keep peeled potatoes always covered with water to prevent darkening.

Follow the directions for carrots. For turnips *paysanne*, cut the turnips lengthwise into quarters and trim the quarters to the shape of carrots. Slice as for carrots *paysanne*.

Wash the celery and scrape off the strings. Cut the stalks in lengths of 1 or 1 1/2 inches as desired. To dice these lengths of stalks, cut them in strips about as wide as the stalk is thick and cut across the strips to make even dice. To make julienne, slice the stalks lengthwise, 1/16 to 1/8 inch thick. For *bâtonnets*, cut them 1/4 inch thick.

Cut off the coarse green tops and save them for the stock pot. Cut off the roots but leave the base intact. Lay the leek on a board and slice it lengthwise through the center, to within 1 1/2 inches of the base. Turn the leek and slice it again through the center, thus quartering the leek without separating it from the base. Clean the leek under running water.

To make dice, julienne, or *bâtonnets*, lay the leek on a board, cut it in 1- or 2-inch lengths, and proceed as for celery.

THE OBJECT of fileting a fish is to remove the skin and bones in such a way as to leave 2 filets ready for cooking. Only small firm-textured fish, such as sole and flounder, that weigh from 1 to 2 pounds are fileted. Lay the fish flat on a board. Holding the knife (fish dealers use a special filet knife that is very sharp) parallel to the board, cut in back of the head, and, working at an angle, slice close to the backbone and ribs, cutting the flesh away from the bones with one continuous cut down to the tail. This is one filet. Turn the fish over and repeat the cut on the other side to obtain the second filet. If there is a row of fine bones near the fins, trim them off with knife or scissors. To skin a filet, lay it skin side down and make a slit in the flesh about 3/4 inch from the tail end, being careful not to cut through the skin. Hold onto this end, insert the knife flat and close to the skin, and slide it along the filet to separate skin from flesh.

POULTRY is boned to make it easier to serve and to eat, as well as more attractive. All the bones may be removed, and the bird stuffed and re-shaped, or rolled for cooking. Or the bird may be only partially boned.

White Turnips

Celery

Leeks

To Filet Fish

To Bone Poultry

23

With the wing and leg bones retained, the bird can easily be stuffed, re-shaped, trussed, and roasted, and it is almost as simple to carve attractively as a completely boned bird. The method used for either kind of boning is the same up to the point where the leg and wing bones are actually withdrawn.

The only special equipment needed is a small, very sharp knife with a curved outer edge. There are special " boning " knives or paring knives that fit this description. A kitchen cleaver or scissors is also useful.

To Bone a Bird for Roasting
Lay the bird breast down on a board and make an incision down the backbone through the skin from the tail to the neck. Remove the tail, wing tips, and ends of leg. Using fingers and knife together, detach the flesh of the bird from the rib cage, pulling the flesh away from the bone with one hand and cutting with the other. With the knife, cut through the joints of the wing and the thigh, which are attached to the rib cage, and lift out the cage. Be careful not to allow the knife to go through the skin at any point. The skin serves as a casing for the stuffing.

To Bone a Bird for Galantine
Clasp the end of the wing bone nearest the carcass and use the knife to scrape away the flesh down the bone to the joint. Cut around the leg joint without severing the connecting tendon, scrape down further with the knife, and with a jerk pull the leg bone through toward the chicken, leaving the end of the skin inverted and skin surface rounded. The bone will pull through very easily. Handle the wing joint in the same way.

Lay the boned bird skin side down on a board and spread it with the stuffing to within an inch of the edge. Fold the halves together and sew or skewer the edges of the skin firmly to encase the stuffing.

If the leg and wing skin appendages revert to natural position, poke the skin back in with the finger so that a smooth roll may be achieved. If necessary, sew or skewer the holes in the skin where the leg bone and wing bones were. Tie the bird securely in a cloth before poaching.

To Bone Squab Chicken or Game Bird
Put one thumb on the thighbone, the other on the body, both close to the hip joint, and quickly snap the thighbone out of its socket. Fold back the skin at the neck, locate the wishbone, scrape the meat from it, and remove it. Push back skin and flesh, locate the wing bone joints, and cut the cartilage, to separate the bones from the carcass. Using fingers and knife, push and scrape the breast meat from the bones under it and, turning back skin and flesh, work around the ribs, scraping all the flesh from them. Free the thighbones by cutting the cords at the hip joints. Detach the carcass from the pope's nose, scrape back the flesh from the thighbones, and detach them at the leg bone joints. Pull out

the carcass, leaving the leg and wing bones intact and the bird turned inside out. Turn it right side out,·tucking in loose bits of flesh, cut off the wing tips, and sew up the opening at the tail.

FAT PORK, both fresh and salted, is used extensively in cooking in northern and central France. In this country, when we say fat salt pork we mean the wide slab that comes from the flank. This is sliced thin to line the baking dishes in which pâtés are cooked, cut into square strips for larding, and diced and sautéed in butter to add to the garniture of braised dishes. "Larding pork" means fat salt pork. (However, fat pork, unsalted, or fresh, from other parts of the animal, is what goes into the ground-meat combinations in pâtés.) Slices of fat salt pork are tied around or laid over the breasts of birds to be roasted, especially small game birds. The fat keeps the birds from becoming dry, and bits of the brown, crispy crackling are sometimes added to the garniture. If fat salt pork seems too salty or too stiff, parboil it for a minute or two and drain it.

To Use Fat Pork

To Bard

The fat around the pork kidney, the most delicate—called *la panne* in French—is used in preparing truffled birds.

SUCH cuts as rump, round, and filet of beef and rump of veal, as well as turkey breasts and the breasts of game birds, which lack a natural " marbling " or covering layer of fat, are pierced with strips of pork fat. This process is called " larding, " and the strips of fat are called *lardoons*. An experienced butcher will lard meat for you, but good cooks may like to be able to do it for themselves.

To Lard Meat

Place the fat on the board, rind down, and cut through it from top to rind at 1/4-inch intervals. Then make slices parallel to the rind, 1/4 inch thick, to make square strips. Cut the strips into 2-inch lengths. A special larding needle is necessary, a long one for larding large pieces of meat and a short one for small pieces. Push the pork strip into the needle. Working with the grain of the meat, not across it, insert the needle in the meat, force it about 1/3 to 1/2 inch under the surface, and bring it out again 3/4 to 1 inch from where it went in, pulling it through the meat until the two protruding ends of lard are the same length. Repeat the process down the length of the meat or poultry at intervals of 1 inch. You have now done 1 row of larding. Repeat as necessary.

Larding Needles

Large cuts of meat for braising are larded through and through.

For this kind of larding, the pork is cut into long strips and pushed through the meat, with the grain, by using a special *boeuf à la mode* larding needle. This needle, about 18 inches long, is a half-tube in shape and has a wooden handle. The strips of larding pork are set into the length of the open tube and the needle is pushed through the meat. When the needle is withdrawn, the strips remain in place.

Seasoning
and
Flavoring

THE French are never heavy-handed with seasonings, and it is therefore often difficult to identify what herbs or spices have been used to flavor a dish. Usually small amounts of several herbs and spices are combined, and whenever possible, fresh rather than dried herbs are used. Garlic is crushed to rid it of excessive pungency, and onions and shallots are gently cooked in butter, to make their flavor more subtle. In desserts,

Lemon and
Orange Zest

the vanilla bean and the zest of orange and lemon—the thin, top layer of skin without any of the white part underneath—are preferred to extracts or essences. The uses of these and other flavorings, such as wines, are explained at appropriate points throughout the book.

Faggot

Many recipes call for a faggot. To make a faggot, cut a stalk of celery in 2 pieces 3 or 4 inches long. In the curve of one piece, tuck a few sprigs of parsley, folding in the ends, lay on this a bay leaf, and sprinkle with a little thyme. If the recipe does not include carrots, a small piece of carrot is sometimes tucked in with the parsley. Place the other piece of celery on top very firmly and secure the faggot by winding a long piece of string closely around it. Unless you assemble a faggot firmly and bind it tightly with plenty of string, it is apt to roll apart during the cooking. Always discard the faggot before serving the dish it flavors.

Parisian
Spice

A seasoning widely used in France but not often heard of here is Parisian spice. It somewhat resembles American poultry seasoning; I often suggest poultry seasoning as an alternative. But anyone can make his own Parisian spice as follows: With a pestle in a small mortar, grind and pulverize separately 1 teaspoon each of bay leaf, thyme, mace, cloves, white peppercorns, rosemary, and basil. Blend these herbs and spices with 1 1/2 teaspoons ground cinnamon and 1/4 teaspoon red pimiento or a pinch of red pepper. Sift the mixture through a very fine sieve and store it in a dry place in a jar or box with a tight cover. This Parisian spice is used with salt to season marinades, stuffings, pâtés, terrines, braised meats, and forcemeat. The usual proportions are 3 tablespoons salt to 1/2 teaspoon Parisian spice.

POTAGES

Soups

Like most Frenchmen, I was raised on soup. In our country home in the *Bourbonnais*, we had soup for luncheon, soup for dinner, and always soup for breakfast. For us, a steaming bowl of thick hearty leek and potato soup was a far better way to begin the day than the porridge of the British or the American's strange meal of orange juice and ham and eggs. As it happened, the first dish I ever cooked on my own—at the age of eight—was a pot of leek and potato soup. This was the soup that twenty years later and three thousand miles away inspired me to create *crème vichyssoise glacée*, one of the first specialties of the old Ritz-Carlton. But more about that later.

If any one element of French cooking can be called important, basic, and essential, that element is soup. Soup stock is the base of many of the sauces that play so vital a role in French cuisine, and many an entrée would suffer badly if there were no soup stock to enrich it. As for soups themselves, they appear on home and restaurant menus in seemingly endless variety. One can choose, according to the occasion, from soups that run the gamut from simple, hearty *potages* and chowders through light broths and delicate consommés, rich creams and bisques, and shimmering jellied soups.

A hearty soup can be a meal in itself, the main course at luncheon or supper. A rich cream or bisque is the perfect supplement for a light entrée, but a long rich dinner should be introduced by an appetite-provoking consommé.

Canned Consommé   In many modern homes, the consommé may come from a can, and it will be very good. Soup manufacturers have not stinted on time, money, and skill in their attempt to produce a superior canned product. Indeed, many a good French chef has been hired away from the kitchen of a famous hotel to stir the soup kettle in a soup manufacturer's laboratory. The same canned consommés, of beef and chicken, are a particularly convenient substitute for stock, when time precludes the making of it.

The making of stock is a basic part of soup cookery, but it is a fairly complicated process. Therefore, instead of telling you first about stock, and the soups made with stocks, I will begin with the stockless soups and chowders that involve fewer steps in preparation and are far easier for the beginner to achieve.

Simple Soups and Chowders

VEGETABLES, fish, and shellfish, in various combinations, can be quickly cooked in water to make soups whose excellence depends upon the special affinity certain flavors have for each other. Neither poultry nor meat is necessary, although chicken stock is sometimes substituted for the water when there is no danger that its flavor will be overpoweringly dominant. Some of these soups are strained before they are served, most of them are not. Some are enriched with cream, egg yolks, or both. Some are thin and some naturally thickened by the potatoes, dried legumes, or corn they contain.

As you learn to master these easy soups, you will be practicing many cooking skills and techniques that are used in other, more complicated cooking methods. Ultimately, you will be pleased to discover that you can apply the same principles to whatever ingredients you have on hand and make delicious soups without having a precise recipe to follow. I should like you to make, as your first effort, the soup that was my first soup, *soupe bonne femme*. First, learn these rules:

If leeks are unavailable, use onions—a medium onion for 2 leeks—and the soup will be delicious even though the flavor is a little less perfect. When onions or leeks are cooked first in butter—and this is done to temper their sharpness—cook them very slowly and just to the point where they are soft and translucent, never brown.

Do not use a substitute for butter if you want a real French soup.

Cut vegetables for unstrained soups into convenient sizes for eating, never so large they must be broken with the spoon, never so small that they get mushy in cooking and lose their identity.

When the soup reaches the boiling point, turn down the heat to a simmer. Rapid boiling reduces the liquid too much and may break up or shred the solid ingredients unattractively.

Salt the soup only lightly at the beginning. Reduction of the liquid may make it too salty. Adjust the seasoning, if necessary, before the soup is served.

LEEK AND POTATO SOUP

Soupe Bonne Femme

REMOVE the green tops and roots from 4 leeks, clean them well, and cut them into 1/3-inch dice. There should be about 1 1/2 cups. (If there are no leeks available, use 2 onions.) Peel and dice 1 medium onion. There should be about 1/2 cup. Melt 1 tablespoon butter in a large soup kettle, add the leeks and onion, and cook them slowly, covered, for a few minutes, or until they are soft but not brown, stirring occasionally with a wooden spoon. Cut 4 or 5 peeled potatoes into 1/2-inch dice.

There should be about 3 cups. Add the potatoes, 4 cups hot water, and 2 teaspoons salt to the kettle, and simmer the soup, covered, for 30 or 40 minutes, or until the potatoes are soft. Add 2 cups hot milk and 1 tablespoon butter. Taste the soup and correct the seasoning with salt.

SPRING SOUP

Potage Printanier

REMOVE the green tops and roots from 2 or 3 leeks, clean them well, and cut them into small dice. There should be about 1 cup. Dice 1 small peeled onion. There should be about 1/4 cup. Melt 2 tablespoons butter in a large soup kettle, add the leeks and onion, and cook the vegetables slowly, covered, for a few minutes, or until they are soft but not brown, stirring occasionally with a wooden spoon. Cut 2 peeled potatoes into quarters and then into thin slices. There should be about 1 1/2 cups. Add the potatoes, 1 medium carrot, peeled and thinly sliced, 1 1/2 cups hot water, and 2 teaspoons salt to the kettle, and cook the soup slowly, covered, for 15 minutes. Add 1/4 cup rice and, if fresh asparagus is available, the top 3 inches of 10 stalks, cleaned and cut into small pieces. Cook the soup for 25 minutes longer and add 1/2 pound spinach, thoroughly washed and chopped. Cook the soup for 10 minutes longer, add 1 cup light cream, and bring it back to the boiling point. Taste it and, if necessary, correct the seasoning with salt.

BLACK OR WHITE BEAN SOUP

Soupe aux Haricots

WASH 2 cups dried black or white beans and soak for 2 hours in water to cover. Drain them and put them in a soup kettle with 1 1/2 quarts water and 1 tablespoon salt. Bring the water to a boil and skim it well. In a shallow saucepan, melt 1 tablespoon butter, add 2 leeks, 1 carrot, and 1 onion, all coarsely chopped, and cook them until they are golden brown. Add them to the kettle with 1/4 pound salt pork or a ham bone, a faggot made by tying together 1 or 2 stalks of celery, 3 or 4 sprigs of parsley, and 1/2 bay leaf, and a pinch of thyme. Simmer the soup, covered, for about 2 hours, or until the beans are very soft. Remove the pork and reserve it. Force the soup through a sieve or food mill, taste it and, if necessary, correct the seasoning with salt. Add a little pepper and if the soup is too thick thin it with milk. Bring it back to a boil.

If salt pork was used, dice it and add it. Soup made with white beans is improved by adding 1 cup cooked tomatoes. Serve sprinkled with croutons.

TOMATO BOUILLON

CHOP coarsely 8 large tomatoes, 3 or 4 carrots, 5 or 6 onions, 4 or 5 leeks, and 1 bunch of celery, and put the vegetables in a large soup kettle. Add 4 cups boiling water and 1 tablespoon salt and simmer the soup for 2 hours, adding water occasionally to replace that which is cooked away. In a small pan dissolve 1 tablespoon sugar in 1 tablespoon water and cook the mixture until the water evaporates and the sugar is caramelized. Strain the soup through a coarse sieve. Add some of the soup to the caramelized sugar, stir them to combine, and return the mixture to the soup. Correct the seasoning.

Chowders are not French, but I believe that they belong in a book for American cooks. After all, vegetable chowders are little different from our leek and potato soup, and New England clam chowder, made with milk, and Manhattan clam chowder, made with tomatoes and thyme, bear a family resemblance to our regional matelotes. Hard-shelled clams, which tend to be tough, should be chopped when they are used for chowder; the soft-shells are tender and may be left whole, but the necks and muscles should be discarded. For a richer chowder, use clam broth, made from extra clams, instead of water. Bouillabaisses and matelotes you will find in the section on poaching and boiling.

NEW ENGLAND CLAM CHOWDER

SCRUB 2 quarts soft-shelled clams, open them, remove the clams, and save the liquor. Cut out the soft bellies and reserve them. Add enough water to the liquor to make 2 1/2 cups and in it cook the necks and muscle parts of the clams for 15 minutes. Strain this broth. Cut 1/4 pound fat salt pork in small dice and brown them lightly in a soup kettle. Add 1 onion, chopped, and sauté it until it is soft but not brown. Remove the pork and onion and sauté 2 cups diced, peeled potatoes in the remaining fat. Add the strained clam broth and simmer it until the potatoes are soft. Stir 1 tablespoon cornstarch into 1/4 cup milk and add it to the kettle along with the rest of 1 quart milk. Bring the chowder to a boil and simmer it for 3 minutes. Add the soft bellies of the clams and cook the chowder for 3 minutes longer. Swirl in 2 tablespoons butter.

MANHATTAN CLAM CHOWDER

Manhattan Clam Chowder

IN A soup kettle over low heat brown 2 tablespoons diced salt pork. Add 1 onion and 2 leeks, chopped, and cook until golden. Add 3 potatoes, peeled and diced, 3 tomatoes, peeled, seeded, and chopped, 1 stalk of celery and 1 green pepper, with the pith and seeds removed, both chopped, 1/2 teaspoon each of thyme and marjoram, and a small bay leaf. Add 2 quarts clam broth or water and salt and pepper to taste. Simmer the chowder for 30 minutes, or until the potatoes are tender. Open 1 dozen large hard-shelled clams and reserve the juice. Chop the clams and add them, with the juice, to the simmering chowder. Cook it for 5 minutes longer.

CLAM BROTH

Clam Broth

SCRUB 36 large, hard-shelled clams and open them. Reserve the juice and chop the clams. Put the clams, juice, and 1 1/2 quarts water into a saucepan and add 2 stalks of celery. Cook the broth for 20 minutes, strain it through several thicknesses of cheesecloth, and add salt to taste.

OYSTER STEW À LA RITZ

Soupe aux Huîtres à la Ritz

DRAIN the juice from 2 or 3 dozen oysters. If the oysters are large, trim the hard edges. Put the oyster juice and enough water to make 2 cups liquid into a saucepan. Add the trimmings and cook them slowly for 10 minutes. Strain this hot liquor over the oysters in another sauce pan, cover the pan, and let the oysters stand in a warm place for a few minutes. They will cook sufficiently without heat. Bring 2 cups light cream to a boil and add it to the oysters and the liquor with 2 table-spoons butter. Correct the seasoning with salt, and if desired, a little nutmeg and freshly ground white pepper. Serve with oyster crackers.

AMERICAN FISH CHOWDER

American Fish Chowder

CUT 1/4 pound fat salt pork into small dice and brown it lightly in a soup kettle. Add 2 medium onions, 2 leeks, and 2 stalks of celery, all chopped, and sauté the vegetables, stirring, until they are soft but not brown. Add 2 quarts clam broth or water and 1 teaspoon salt, bring the liquid to a boil, and simmer it for 15 minutes. Add 1 1/2 pounds white-fleshed fish, such as sole, cod, or sea bass, cleaned, skinned, boned, and cut into 1-inch pieces, and 2 cups milk. Simmer the chowder for about 20 minutes longer. Add 1 cup cream. Taste the chowder and, if necessary, correct the seasoning with salt and add pepper.

Stocks and Stock-Based Soups

SOUP, in one form or another, is everywhere in French cuisine, and a big pot of soup stock simmers on the back of the stove in many French homes and in every French restaurant. In the restaurant kitchen, the soup station is usually the young chef's first job. *Eh bien*, how well I remember the endless parade of stock ingredients that passed through my hands on their way to the stock pot—bones, meat, fowl, carcasses of roasted birds, bits left from the carving of great roasts. And the vegetables—how many carrots I scraped, how many onions I peeled, how many leeks I anxiously washed and washed again, to flush out lurking grains of sand. And how proud I was to be guardian of that all-important station belowstairs at the Paris Ritz.

Stock is used not only for soups, but for sauces and entrées as well. **Stock in Quantity** Since it is as easy to make soup stock in large quantities as in small, many households will find it worthwhile to invest in a 6- or 8-quart kettle and to make a week's supply of 4 or more quarts of stock at a time. The surplus may be poured hot into scrupulously clean jars, cooled, and stored **Storing Stock**

33

in the refrigerator for about a week; as the stock cools, the fat will rise and form a protective seal. Or the stock may be cooled, freed of fat, and frozen for long storage in containers of various sizes especially designed for this purpose. If space in freezer or refrigerator is at a premium, reduce the stock by boiling it hard; the water that evaporates can be replaced when the soup is heated for serving. Clarified consommé contains no fat, but it forms a jelly that can be covered with a thin layer of Sherry or Cognac. To keep refrigerated stock longer than a week, boil it up again and repack it in clean jars. Before using it, remove the hardened fat on top. Strain vegetables out of any stock to be stored.

Names for Stock

Broth Bouillon

Before we begin to make our soup stock, let us talk for a minute about the terms used in discussing the subject. Stock may also be called "broth" or "bouillon;" whatever it is called, it is by definition the clear, flavorful liquid which remains after any of various combinations of meat and vegetables have been simmered in water for several hours, until their flavors are extracted, and then strained out of it. In usage, the term "broth," and the French word, "bouillon," usually refer to this liquid served as it comes from the pot, without further cooking, and simply garnished with rice, barley, or perhaps noodles. If the stock serves as the base for more elaborate soups, or is concentrated and used to make sauces, it is more likely to remain "stock." Stock made from beef is brown stock; chicken and veal make white stock; feathered or furred game, game stock. Consommé results when soup stock is further enriched with added meat or poultry, and clarified with egg white and sometimes chopped beef.

Stock

Consommé

So much for nomenclature. Now to make the stock.

Stock Ingredients

When meat or poultry is not available, bones and vegetables alone can make a very good stock. The bones are the most important ingredient in any stock; they contribute character, flavor, and substance. Browning the bones before adding them to the kettle emphasizes all these qualities, and adds handsome color as well. Calf's feet, chicken feet, and veal bones have high gelatin content, and help to produce a stock that jellies firmly when it is cold.

The ultimate strength of the stock depends upon the proportion of water to solid ingredients; the flavor of the stock is determined by the meats and vegetables used to make it. A good stock should taste of meat or poultry subtly seasoned with vegetables.

Of the stock vegetables—leeks, onions, carrots, celery, parsley, and tomatoes—I consider leeks the most important.

To Make Stock

Start the stock with cold water. If meat is plunged into hot water,

34

the pores on the surface are sealed and the meat tends to hold its flavor instead of releasing it into the stock. A little salt added at the beginning helps to extract flavors, but it should be used with discretion, because as the water cooks away the salt is concentrated. More salt can always be added at serving time, if it is needed.

As the water heats, certain insoluble substances that have been extracted from the meat and vegetables rise to the surface as scum. This scum is not harmful, but it is unattractive and will discolor and cloud the broth. Remove the scum as it rises, using a large, flat spoon. When the liquid begins to boil, stir it to encourage the last of the scum to rise to the top and remove it. Cover the kettle, reduce the heat, and simmer the stock for several hours without stirring it. The less you disturb the stock during the cooking, the clearer it will be.

At the end of the cooking time, ladle out as much as possible of the clear liquid without disturbing the solid ingredients—the bones and vegetables. Lift these out with a large perforated spoon and discard them. Add a cup of cold water to the kettle. In 10 to 15 minutes the liquid left will be clear, and can be ladled off the sediment at the bottom of the kettle. Line a large, fine-meshed sieve with several layers of cheesecloth and strain the bouillon into a large bowl. Set the bowl in cold water, uncovered, to hasten the cooling process. If the stock or soup is covered while it cools, it develops an off-flavor.

Stocks

BROWN STOCK OR BEEF BOUILLON

Fonds Brun ou Estouffade

HAVE the butcher cut into small pieces 3 to 4 pounds beef bones and 1 1/2 to 2 pounds veal bones. Spread the bones in a roasting pan and scatter over them 1 large carrot and 1 large onion, both cut into thick slices. Roast the bones and vegetables in a hot oven (400° F.) for 30 to 40 minutes, or until they are well browned. Transfer them to a large heavy soup kettle and add 5 quarts water. Discard the fat from the roasting pan and add to it 2 cups water. Bring the water to a boil over direct heat and deglaze the pan by stirring and scraping in all the brown bits that cling to the bottom and sides. Add this liquid to the soup kettle, along with any beef or veal trimmings, raw or cooked, or carcasses of roasted chickens you may have on hand. Add 1 tablespoon salt and 6 peppercorns and bring the mixture slowly to a boil. Skim off the scum as it comes to the surface. Add a handful of celery stalks and tops, several sprigs of parsley, 1 or 2 tomatoes, 2 leeks, 1 onion, and 1 carrot, all coarsely chopped, and 1 clove of garlic. Remove the last of the scum, cover the kettle, turn down the heat, and simmer the mixture for 4 to 5 hours, without stirring. Carefully ladle out as much of the stock as you can. Add 1 cup cold water to the kettle and let the small particles settle, and ladle out the remaining liquid. Strain the bouillon through fine cheesecloth and cool it, uncovered. There should be about 3 quarts.

If the stock is to be used at once, skim off all fat or chill the stock and remove the fat when it has hardened.

Fonds Blanc WHITE STOCK

IN a soup kettle, put 1 pound veal bones and 2 pounds chicken necks, backs, skinned feet, and bones. Cover these with water and parboil them until scum rises to the top. Drain them, return them to the kettle, and add 2 1/2 quarts water, 1 teaspoon salt, 1 carrot, 2 onions, and 2 leeks, all coarsely chopped, and a faggot made by tying together 1 stalk of celery, 3 sprigs of parsley, a small bay leaf, and a little thyme. Bring the water to a boil and skim it. Cover the kettle, turn down the heat, and simmer the mixture for 3 hours, without stirring. Carefully ladle out as much of the stock as you can without disturbing the bones and vegetables. Then, with a perforated spoon, remove and discard these. Add 1/2 cup cold water to the kettle and let the small particles settle for 10 to 15 minutes. Ladle out the remaining liquid. Strain the stock through a sieve lined with several thicknesses of fine cheesecloth and cool it, uncovered, as quickly as possible. There should be about 6 cups.

Pattes de Volaille pour les Fonds CHICKEN FEET FOR SOUP STOCK

CHICKEN feet add flavor to soup stock, but more important, they provide the gelatin needed for aspics or jellied soups. Prepare the feet as follows: Have the butcher chop off the nails. Wash the feet and put them in a kettle with salted water to cover. Bring the water to a boil and boil the feet for about 5 minutes, or until the scaly skin loosens. Plunge the feet into cold water and peel off and discard the skins. Add to the stock pot with other meats and bones.

The Great Soups

FOR MORE THAN ten centuries the popularity of one great dish of France has never wavered. The *pot-au-feu*, pot on the fire, is the traditional Sunday dinner in France. It has always been a dish for the peasant, tasty, hearty, and inexpensive, but it is also a dish for the *haut monde*. No one knows better than the gourmet Frenchman that an uninterrupted diet of rich foods is so surfeiting that soon nothing tastes good, nothing tempts the appetite. A weekly respite in the way of a simple soup and the boiled meat and vegetables that go with it is warmly welcomed.

If you ask the French chef of an important hotel to name his favorite meal, he may very well answer that he likes nothing better than to sit down to a good *pot-au-feu*. We chefs find it a soothing gustatory escape after days of working on elaborate menus and dishes that stint on neither skill nor money, and its simplicity helps our taste buds stay acute.

The soup kettle for *pot-au-feu* contains stock, beef, and vegetables, with bones added to give the broth more flavor. The broth is light-colored, but has a well-rounded flavor from the meat and bones cooked in combination with a faggot, some garlic, and a variety of root vegetables. Yet it is not quite so strong and rich as a concentrated consommé. *Maman* liked a soup to have a nice golden-brown color, so she always caramelized a little sugar and added it to the *pot-au-feu* at the end.

Some people like potatoes or cabbage with the *pot-au-feu*, but they are never cooked in the *marmite* with the other ingredients. Instead, the potatoes or cabbage are cooked separately in a little of the broth. There is always the necessity to keep the greater part of the stock pure for possible storage and later use.

The cut of beef my mother used was the plate, and I still like it best, because I find it juicier and more succulent than the leaner cuts. I must confess, however, that our plate beef was more meaty than the kind I buy now, perhaps because our beef creatures were larger, and not scientifically raised and fed. All the beef cuts were larger, and the meat between the layers of fat that are characteristic of the plate was thicker, if not so fine-grained and tender as that of American beef. We had to depend upon long cooking to achieve tenderness. The preferred cuts of beef for *pot-au-feu* in this country are rump or chuck, but shoulder or fresh brisket, preferably layered with fat, are also used.

Beef Cuts for Pot-au-Feu

In some parts of France other meats and poultry went into the *pot-au-feu*. In a region where beef was scarce and expensive, but where flocks of ducks waddled over every farm, less beef would go into the *marmite*, and a duck would serve to enrich the stock. At my house we used chicken. This gave us the *petite marmite Henri IV*, which that beloved king of France made famous when he said back in the eleventh century that every good Frenchman was entitled to a chicken in his Sunday pot. The chicken in every pot, then as now, was a symbol of well-being and security.

At home we always ate the soup of the *pot-au-feu* first, and then the meat, sliced, and the vegetables. Because the meat was mild in flavor from its long boiling, mustard, sour pickles, or a sharp sauce like horse-radish sauce was served with it. Some people, however, prefer to have broth, meat, and vegetables all together in the soup plate.

This recipe for *pot-au-feu* is generally followed all over France. (A French housewife's trick is to tie 2 or 3 hearts of celery with the leeks. As soon as they are cooked, they are removed, set aside to cool, and served with vinaigrette sauce for hors-d'oeuvre or for salad.)

Pot-au-Feu

POT-AU-FEU can be started in one of two ways. Cover a 4- to 4 1/2-pound piece of fresh plate or 3 1/2 pounds rump or chuck of beef and some beef or veal bones with cold water, bring to a boil, and parboil for 5 minutes. Take out the meat and bones, discard the water, and clean the kettle. Return the meat and bones to the kettle and add 4 1/2 to 5 quarts brown stock or water and 1 1/2 tablespoons salt. Bring the liquid slowly to a boil, skimming all the time until no more scum rises to the surface. Or, as an alternate method, cover the meat and bones with 4 to 4 1/2 quarts cold stock or water and bring slowly to a boil. When the liquid has reached a rolling boil, add 2 cups cold stock or water to bring the scum to the surface. Skim and continue to boil gently, skimming all the time until no more scum rises to the surface. The first method is a little more trouble, but it makes a clearer stock. It is important that all the scum is discarded either by changing the water or by careful skimming so that there will be none in the soup when the dish is done.

After the scum ceases to rise, turn down the heat, cover the kettle, and simmer the beef for 1 1/2 hours. Add 6 carrots, 4 small turnips, and 2 parsnips, all cut into pieces, 6 small onions, each studded with a clove, 6 or 8 leeks tied together, 1 clove of garlic, and a faggot made by tying together 2 stalks of celery, a few sprigs of parsley, a little thyme, and half a bay leaf. If a chicken is to be cooked in the pot, add it at this point. Cook for 2 hours longer. If the chicken is browned first in a hot oven, it will give the broth a richer color. Skim the fat from the finished soup or cool the soup until the fat hardens on the surface and remove it. Reheat the soup and correct the seasoning with salt. Ladle the soup off and strain it through a sieve lined with several thicknesses of cheesecloth. Serve the clear soup first. Slice the meat and serve it with the vegetables as a second course.

CHICKEN-IN-THE-POT   *Poule-au-Pot*

HAVE the butcher clean a fowl weighing at least 5 pounds. Tie the legs together and tie the wings close to the body. Put it in a large soup kettle, cover it with cold water, bring the water to a boil, and boil it for 4 or 5 minutes. Remove the fowl, pour out the water, and wash the kettle. Return the fowl to the kettle and add some cleaned chicken feet, if desired. Add 4 1/2 quarts white stock or water, or water and white stock combined, and 1 tablespoon salt. Bring the liquid to a boil and skim off the scum as it rises to the top. To hasten this process, stir the stock and add 1/2 cup cold water. Cover the kettle, turn down the heat, and simmer the fowl for 1 hour. Add 1 carrot, 2 leeks, 1 onion stuck with a clove, 3 stalks of celery, and 3 sprigs of parsley and simmer the stock for 1 hour longer. Remove the fowl and keep it hot. Strain the soup through a sieve lined with several thicknesses of cheesecloth. Discard the vegetables, clean the kettle, and return the stock to it. Add 3 or 4 carrots, 3 leeks, and 4 stalks of celery, all cleaned and cut in uniform pieces. Cook the vegetables until they are tender. Correct the seasoning with salt.

Carve the fowl into serving pieces and put a portion into each soup plate. The plates should be deep. Add a spoonful of cooked rice and some of the cooked vegetables and fill the plate with the soup. Or serve the clear soup as a first course and the chicken with *riz au beurre*, buttered rice, and vegetables as a second course. In this case, serve also cream sauce made with some of the chicken stock. The dish is then called *poule bouillie au riz*, boiled fowl with rice, and you will find directions for it in the section on boiling poultry.

CHICKEN BOUILLON OR STOCK

Fonds Blanc de Volaille

To make a chicken bouillon, follow the directions for *poule-au-pot*, adding to the kettle a veal knuckle or 1 pound veal bones.

As YOU might guess, the French make thrifty use of the meat and poultry left over from the *pot-au-feu* and *poule-au-pot*. They reappear within a day or two as hashes, salads, or in other succulent disguises. The piece of meat should always be large enough to allow for these leftovers.

The leftover bouillon has an even more important function; it is used to make other soups, among them the most famous soup in French cuisine, the triply rich *petite marmite*. Just as water is the liquid for brown stock and brown stock the liquid for the *pot-au-feu*, the *pot-au-feu* bouillon is the liquid for *petite marmite*. *Petite marmite* is thus much stronger and richer than *pot-au-feu*—one difference between the two soups, in many ways so similar. Another difference is that *petite marmite* is served only as a soup. It is usually further enriched with chicken, and the meat, chicken, and vegetables, cut into small enough pieces to be conveniently eaten, are served in it. Poached marrow bones often accompany the soup, the marrow to be scooped out and eaten with it.

PETITE MARMITE HENRY IV

Petite Marmite Henri IV

PARBOIL 1 pound lean beef brisket, 1 oxtail, and the legs of a chicken, all cut up, for 10 minutes, drain, and rinse in cold water. Turn the meat into a *marmite*, a deep clay casserole, or a soup kettle and add 2 to 3 quarts bouillon from *pot-au-feu* and 1 tablespoon salt. Bring the broth to a boil, skim, and cook gently for 2 hours, skimming as necessary.

Parboil 2 carrots, sliced, 1 white turnip, cut in small pieces, and 2 leeks and 2 stalks of celery, all cut in 1-inch pieces. Brown 2 small onions in butter, sprinkling them with a little sugar to give them color. Add the vegetables to the *marmite* and cook for 2 hours longer, skimming from time to time. Correct the seasoning with salt. Keep the soup hot, but not boiling, and remove all fat from the surface.

Marrow Bones

To prepare marrow bones, have a shin bone cut into slices 1/2-inch thick. Cover the slices with cold water and bring it to a boil. Take the pan from the heat, but keep the slices hot in the water until the soup is served. Serve them in the soup or separately. Serve grated Parmesan or Gruyère cheese separately, if desired, and small thin slices of crusty rolls.

Traditional oxtail soup has its own unique characteristics. The herbs that flavor it are never cooked in it. They are put on cheesecloth in a strainer and the hot bouillon poured over them. Finished with Sherry and usually thickened with a little cornstarch, the soup has a rich but delicate flavor and a smooth texture not unlike that of green turtle soup.

OXTAIL SOUP

Potage Queue de Boeuf à la Parisienne

IN a roasting pan, spread 1 1/2 pounds each of veal shin bones and beef shin bones and lay on them 1 large onion, cut in thick slices. Roast the bones in a hot oven (400° F.) for about 40 minutes, or until they are brown. Put an oxtail, cut into small pieces, in a kettle with enough water to cover, parboil it for 5 minutes, and drain it. Tie the pieces in a cheesecloth bag. Put the browned bones in a large soup kettle, add 4 quarts brown stock, or the bouillon from *pot-au-feu*, bring it to a boil, and skim it. Add the oxtails, 1 pound chopped lean beef, 1 large carrot, 3 leeks, 2 stalks of celery, 2 tomatoes, 1 clove of garlic, 1 bay leaf, 1/2 teaspoon thyme, 2 tablespoons salt, and 6 peppercorns. Bring the stock again to a boil and skim it. Cover the kettle and simmer the soup for 4 to 5 hours. Prepare 1 to 1 1/2 cups each of carrots and white turnips, cut in small balls, cook them separately in salted water until they are tender, and drain them. When the soup is done, remove the pieces of oxtail and reserve them, discarding the cheesecloth. Fit a piece of muslin into a large strainer and sprinkle over it 1/2 teaspoon each of rosemary, summer savory, sage, and basil. Strain the soup through the muslin into another kettle. Bring the strained soup back to a boil, taste it, and if necessary, correct the seasoning with salt. Add the oxtail pieces, carrots, turnips, and 1/2 cup dry Sherry.

For a slightly thickened soup, stir into the strained soup 1/2 cup cornstarch mixed with 1/4 cup of the Sherry. Cook the soup, stirring, just until it is clear and finish as above.

Croûte au Pot

REMOVE the carrots, turnips, and leeks that were cooked in a *pot-au-feu* and cut them into pieces about 1 inch long. Strain the bouillon and skim off most of the fat, leaving just enough to make a few tiny glistening beads over the surface. Remove the marrow from the bones that were cooked in the *pot-au-feu* and spread it on pieces of the crust of French bread. Reheat the bouillon and add the vegetables. Float the crusts on the soup or serve them separately.

Soupe à l'Oignon

IN a soup kettle, melt 1 tablespoon butter. Add 2 or 3 medium onions, thinly sliced, and sauté the rings very slowly until they are soft and golden. Add 1 teaspoon flour and cook, stirring, for a minute or two longer, then add 2 quarts brown stock or the bouillon from *pot-au-feu* and simmer the soup for 10 minutes. Correct the seasoning with salt and add a little pepper. If desired, 2 tomatoes, peeled, seeded, and chopped, may be added with the stock.

Soupe à l'Oignon Gratinée

POUR French onion soup into a large heatproof casserole or into individual soup crocks. Toast thick slices of French bread, sprinkle them with grated Parmesan cheese, and float them in the soup. Put the soup under the heat of the broiler until the cheese melts and browns.

Potage Paysanne

IN a soup kettle, melt 2 tablespoons butter, add 2 carrots, 1 white turnip, and 2 leeks, all cut into thin slices, 1/4 savoy cabbage, shredded, and 1/2 cup water. Cover the kettle and braise the vegetables over low heat until they are tender. Add 2 quarts chicken stock, bring it to a boil and skim it. Add 1/2 cup each of fresh peas and green beans and celery, cut in small pieces, and simmer the soup about 20 minutes, or until the vegetables are tender. Add 1/2 cup shredded lettuce and, if available,

1/2 cup shredded sorrel, bring the soup again to the boil, taste it, and if necessary, correct the seasoning with salt. If desired, a little cooked rice, barley, or vermicelli may be added.

Consommés

THERE are those who think that no soup is more perfect than a perfect consommé, and I sometimes agree with them. Fortunately, achieving such perfection is really not difficult. The consommé must begin with a good rich bouillon, as clear and as free of fat as possible. Then the bouillon is made crystal clear, and any remaining fat is removed, by the process called clarification. Beaten egg whites and lean chopped beef, or in the case of chicken bouillon, egg whites and sometimes chicken backs, are added to the simmering bouillon. As the egg whites and meat cook, they attract and hold the tiny particles of fat and other matter that cloud the soup. When this mass of solids is discarded, the resulting consommé is sparklingly clear, and if beef has been used, still richer in flavor.

Clarification

SIMPLE CONSOMMÉ

Consommé Simple

CHILL 3 quarts strained beef bouillon or brown stock. Remove the fat completely from the surface. Put the bouillon in a large soup kettle with 1 1/2 pounds coarsely chopped lean beef. Use inexpensive beef, entirely free of fat, from the neck or forequarter. Add a small carrot, 2 leeks, and 2 stalks of celery, all chopped, 6 cleaned and skinned chicken feet, and 2 egg whites lightly beaten with a fork. Bring the bouillon slowly to a boil, stirring constantly, but stop stirring just before the boil is reached. Cover the kettle and simmer the bouillon over low heat for 1 hour. Skim off any matter that might float on the top and discard it. Line a large strainer with several thicknesses of cheesecloth and ladle the consommé through it into another kettle.

*Consommé
de Volaille*

CHICKEN CONSOMMÉ

FOLLOW the recipe for simple consommé, using bouillon from *poule-au-pot* instead of beef bouillon and chicken backs instead of ground beef.

Consommés are so rich in flavor and so beautiful in appearance that they are often served just as they come from the pot. But even more often they are garnished with a spoonful of barley, rice, or pasta, cooked separately in order to preserve the clarity of the consommé, or with attractively cut vegetables, either cooked in salted water or braised in butter. The garnished consommé then takes its name from its garniture.

*Garnitures
Classiques*

TRADITIONAL GARNISHES

Julienne—VEGETABLE STRIPS. Cut vegetables—carrots, onion rings, leeks, celery, or turnips, in any combination—into thin strips about 1 inch long. In a small saucepan, melt 1 tablespoon butter for each cup of vegetables. Add the vegetables and 2 or 3 tablespoons consommé. Cover the vegetables with a round of buttered wax paper with a small hole in the center and cover the pan. Braise the vegetables slowly for about 20 minutes, or until they are tender. Drain them and add them to hot consommé just before serving.

Brunoise—DICED VEGETABLES. Follow the directions for julienne, but cut the vegetables into small dice.

Tomates—TOMATOES. Peel and seed ripe tomatoes and cut them into small dice or julienne. Poach them for a few minutes in consommé.

Pasta—PASTA. Cook vermicelli, noodles, spaghetti, or other pasta in salted water until it is just tender and drain it. Allow 3 tablespoons uncooked pasta for each quart of consommé. Add to hot consommé just before serving.

Chiffonade—SHREDDED GREENS. Parboil finely shredded tender sorrel or lettuce leaves in boiling salted water for 1 minute and drain them. Add to hot consommé just before serving.

Pluches—SHREDDED HERBS. Shred leaves of chervil, parsley, and tarragon and add them to hot consommé just before serving.

Royale—DICED CUSTARD. Beat together lightly 2 eggs and 2 egg yolks and add 1 cup chicken stock or milk that has been heated with a few sprigs of chervil, strained, and cooled. Strain the custard into a buttered straight-sided mold and set the mold in a shallow pan of hot water. Bake the custard in a moderately slow oven (325° F.) for about 30 minutes, or until it is set. Let it cool. Unmold the custard and cut it into dice. Add to hot consommé just before serving.

Windsor—EGG THREADS. Make egg *filés* as follows: With a fork, break up, but do not beat, 2 eggs and stir in 1/4 teaspoon flour. Bring 2 quarts consommé to a boil and strain the egg mixture into it through a fine sieve, stirring the consommé vigorously as the *filés* drop into it.

Célestine—HERBED PANCAKE STRIPS. Combine 2 tablespoons flour, 1 egg, 1/2 cup milk or chicken stock, and 1/2 teaspoon chopped parsley or chervil. Pour the batter by spoonfuls onto a buttered skillet, to make very small thin pancakes. Brown them lightly on both sides. Cut the baked pancakes into fine julienne or squares and add them to hot consommé just before serving.

Crêpes—PANCAKE STRIPS. Sift together 1 cup flour and 1/4 teaspoon salt. Beat in 2 beaten eggs and add 1 cup milk (or half milk and half broth). Follow the directions for making *célestine*, herbed pancakes, but make the pancakes larger. Cut them in fine julienne, 1/4 inch wide or less, or in small rounds or diamonds. Serve in consommé.

Petites Profiteroles—LITTLE PUFFS. Drop *pâte à chou*, cream-puff paste, onto a baking sheet in tiny mounds the size of peas and bake the puffs in a moderate oven (350° F.) until they are brown. Or make mounds as big as walnuts, slit the baked puffs, and fill them with chicken purée. Drop them into hot consommé just before serving or serve them separately.

Infante—PUFFS AND CUSTARD. Add diced *royale garniture* and *petites profiteroles* filled with chicken purée to consommé at servingtime.

Croûtes et Croûtons

BREAD GARNISHES FOR SOUP

PIECES of French bread, cut in various shapes and toasted or browned in butter, are frequently served with soup. *Croûtes* are larger slices and are floated on thick simple soups and chowders, or passed with the soup. To make *croûtes*, slice French bread thin and dry the slices in a slow oven. Or cut slices 1/2 inch thick and brown them on both sides in hot butter. Or butter the slices and brown them in the oven. Or cut the bread in inch-thick slices, cut the slices in half, and scrape out the soft part. Dry the crusts in a slow oven and pass a basket of these crisp curls with the soup.

Croutons, little crusts, are more usually served in cream soups and bisques. To make them, cut French bread into slices 1/4 inch thick, remove the crusts, and cut the bread into 1/4-inch cubes. Sauté the cubes in butter until they are golden on all sides or sprinkle them with melted butter and brown them in the oven.

Diablotins

CHEESE CROUTONS

To 1 beaten egg yolk add enough grated Parmesan cheese to make a thick paste. Season with salt and cayenne pepper to taste. Cut flutes, small round loaves of French bread, into slices 1/4 inch thick. Heap a little mound of the cheese mixture on each round and arrange the slices on a baking sheet. Brown the *diablotins* in a hot oven (450° F.) or under the broiler. Use to garnish rich beef or chicken consommé.

Consommés may be further flavored by a process of infusion; celery, for instance, is steeped in the hot broth, without actual cooking, until the consommé takes on the fine fresh taste of the vegetable. Consommés thus prepared add " au fumet " to their names.

CELERY CONSOMMÉ

*Consommé
au Fumet
de Céleri*

ADD a generous handful of celery, stalks and tops, to 2 quarts simple consommé. Bring the consommé slowly to a boil and keep it hot, over boiling water, for 30 minutes or more. Do not let it boil. Strain it. Just before serving, add a little cooked julienne of celery.

Cream Soups and Bisques

IN FRANCE, thick, velvety cream soups are made of all sorts of vegetables and of poultry, game, and shellfish, just as they are in America. However, we do not begin our cream soups with a white sauce, in the American fashion, but with a thick basic soup. The three most versatile basic soups are: cream of chicken, which is made by thickening chicken stock with a *roux* of butter and flour—rice or barley rather than wheat flour; *potage Parmentier*, puréed potato and leek soup that is thickened by the potatoes in it; and *potage Saint-Germain*, made of dried split peas, and also naturally thick. The additional vegetables are cooked in the base soup and the whole is forced through a fine sieve. A binder is necessary to prevent the soup from separating and the solids from settling; egg yolks and cream serve as a liaison and at the same time give the finished soup a texture indescribably smooth and rich.

Like all the basic soups, the *crème de volaille* is a delicious soup even without further embellishment.

CREAM OF CHICKEN BASE

*Fonds
de Crème
de Volaille*

IN A SOUP kettle, melt 4 tablespoons butter and gradually blend in 1/2 cup rice or barley flour—also called cream of rice or barley. Cook the

47

roux slowly, stirring, until it just starts to turn golden. Add 2 quarts hot chicken stock and, if available, some chicken bones. If no stock is available, add 3 quarts water and a fowl, cleaned but left whole and trussed. Add the white parts of 4 leeks or 2 onions, 2 stalks of celery, and 1 tablespoon salt. A veal knuckle, parboiled for a few minutes and washed in cold water before it is added, will improve the soup. Bring the soup to a boil, skim it, if necessary, and simmer it for 2 hours. Stir it occasionally to make sure the ingredients are not sticking. Remove the bones or fowl and force the soup through a fine sieve or food mill. Use to make *crème de volaille* and other soups.

Crème de Volaille   CREAM OF CHICKEN

MAKE cream of chicken base. Mix 2 egg yolks and 1 cup cream, stir in a little hot cream of chicken base, and return this mixture to the kettle. Heat the soup, stirring constantly, but do not let it boil. Add another cup of cream and correct the seasoning with salt. If the soup is too thick, add a little chicken stock or milk. To serve, add some cooked white chicken meat, finely diced.

Crème Favorite   CREAM OF GREEN BEAN

ADD 2 cups green beans, finely chopped, to 1 1/2 quarts cream of chicken base and cook until the beans are soft. Force the soup through a fine sieve. Mix 2 egg yolks with 1 cup cream, stir in a little of the hot soup, and combine this mixture with the soup. Heat the soup, stirring constantly, but do not let it boil. Add 1 cup cream and correct the seasoning with salt. Strain the soup once more through a fine sieve.

Crème Boston   CREAM OF CELERY

CLEAN and cut up enough celery to make 1 1/2 cups. Parboil the celery in salted water a few minutes, drain it, and add it to 1 1/2 quarts cream of chicken base. Simmer the soup until the celery is soft, force it through a fine sieve, and finish it with egg yolks and cream, as in *crème favorite*.

Crème Du Barry   CREAM OF CAULIFLOWER

PARBOIL a small cauliflower, separated into pieces, for a few minutes in salted water, and drain it. Add it to 1 1/2 quarts cream of chicken base and simmer the soup until the cauliflower is soft. Force the soup through a fine sieve. If it is too thick, add stock or milk and bring it back to a boil. Finish it with egg yolks and cream, as in *crème favorite*.

CREAM OF MUSHROOM   *Crème Forestière*

IN A saucepan, melt 1 tablespoon butter, add 1 onion, chopped, and sauté it until it is soft but not brown. Add 1/2 pound finely chopped mushrooms and cook them until most of the moisture is cooked away. Add 1 1/2 quarts cream of chicken base and simmer the soup for 1 hour. Force it through a fine sieve and finish it with egg yolks and cream, as in *crème favorite*.

CREAM OF MUSHROOM WITH CHICKEN   *Crème Béatrice*

To *crème forestière*, add 1/2 cup cooked white chicken meat, finely diced, just before serving.

Certain green, leafy vegetables, like spinach, water cress, and the lettuces, lose both flavor and color if they are cooked too long. So I wash the leaves, parboil them in a little water for 5 minutes or less, and plunge them into cold water to rinse and cool. This brief cooking makes the leaves tender without destroying the bright greenness or the natural fresh flavor. I drain the leaves, rub them through a fine sieve, and add the purée to the soup.

CREAM OF SPINACH   *Crème Florentine*

COOK 1 pound washed spinach in a little boiling salted water for about 5 minutes, dip it in cold water, and drain it well. Rub it through a fine sieve. Combine the purée with 1 1/2 quarts cream of chicken base and simmer the soup for a few minutes. Finish it with egg yolks and cream, as in *crème favorite*.

The second basic soup, potage Parmentier, has an affinity for sorrel and water cress. Use it as a foundation for these and other soups, to enlarge your soup repertoire.

*Potage
Parmentier*

PURÉE OF LEEK AND POTATO SOUP

FOLLOW the recipe for *soupe bonne femme* but use 3, instead of 4, cups of hot water. Cook the potatoes until they are very soft and force the mixture through a sieve or food mill. Bring the soup back to a boil, stirring constantly to prevent it from scorching, and add 3, instead of 2, cups hot milk and 1 tablespoon butter.

For a richer soup, beat 2 egg yolks lightly with 1/2 cup cream, gradually stir 1 cup of the hot soup into them, and return the mixture to the kettle, stirring briskly. Bring the soup just to the boiling point, stirring constantly, but do not allow it to boil.

*Crème
Santé*

CREAM OF SORREL

CLEAN and shred enough sorrel to make 1/2 cup, firmly packed. In a small saucepan, melt 1 tablespoon butter, add the sorrel, and cook it slowly until most of the moisture has cooked away, about 15 minutes. Add it to 1 1/2 quarts simple *potage Parmentier*, made without egg yolks and cream, and heat the soup. Mix 1 egg yolk with 1/2 cup heavy cream, stir in a little of the hot soup, and return this mixture to the kettle. Reheat the soup, stirring constantly, but do not let it boil.

*Crème
Cressonière*

CREAM OF WATER CRESS

WASH 2 bunches of water cress, cook the leaves for 3 to 4 minutes in boiling salted water, drain them, and force them through a sieve. Combine the purée with 1 1/2 quarts simple *potage Parmentier*, made without egg yolks and cream. Add 1 cup cream and bring the soup slowly back to the boiling point.

Purée of split peas, the third of our basic soups, and also purée of black beans, lentils, and tomato, may be made in double or triple quantities and stored in the refrigerator for quick and convenient later use. Follow the recipe for the given purée up to the point where milk, cream, and eggs should be added. Cool the purée in an open vessel—a lid or cover may produce off-flavors—and store it as you would stock, observing the same methods and precautions. To use the stored purées, heat 3 parts purée with 1 part cream, or milk and cream, and finish the soup as indicated.

CREAM OF PEA OR PURÉE OF SPLIT PEA SOUP

Potage Saint-Germain

COVER 2 cups split peas with water and soak them for 1 hour or more. Drain the peas and discard the water. Put the peas in a large saucepan with 1 quart fresh water and 1 teaspoon salt. Bring the water to a boil, skim it, cover the pan, and simmer the peas. In a soup kettle, melt 1 tablespoon butter, add 1/2 cup finely diced salt pork, and cook the dice until they start to turn brown. Add 1 onion, chopped, and sauté it until it is soft but not brown. Add 1 medium carrot, the green parts of 2 leeks, 1 cup spinach or green lettuce, all chopped, a small piece of bay leaf, and a pinch of thyme. Cook the mixture a few minutes longer, then add the partly cooked peas in their water. Cook the soup for about 1 hour, or until the peas are very soft. Rub the soup through a fine sieve, add 1 cup water or stock, and bring it back to a boil. Correct the seasoning with salt and add 1 teaspoon sugar, 1 tablespoon butter, and 1/2 cup heavy cream. If fresh peas are available, cook 1 cup in water until they are soft (include the pods, if the peas are very young), and rub them through a sieve into the soup.

CREAM OF PEA WITH VEGETABLES — *Crème Jubilé*

CUT enough carrots, celery, turnips, and leeks into *bâtonnets*, or squared strips, 1 inch long to make 1 1/2 cups. In a small saucepan, melt 1 tablespoon butter, add the vegetables and 1/2 cup chicken stock, and simmer them until they are tender. Add the cooked vegetables to 1 1/2 quarts *potage Saint-Germain* and reheat the soup.

MONGOLE SOUP — *Potage Mongole*

CUT enough carrots, celery, turnips, and leeks into fine julienne to make 1 1/2 cups. Cook them as for *crème jubilé*. Combine 3 cups each of *potage Saint-Germain* and cream of tomato and add the cooked vegetables.

Two other cream soups, popular in their own right—cream of tomato and cream of lentil—occasionally serve as bases for other soups.

CREAM OF TOMATO OR PURÉE OF TOMATO SOUP

Crème de Tomates

IN A soup kettle, melt 4 tablespoons butter, add 2 medium carrots and 2 medium onions, all chopped, and sauté the vegetables until they turn golden. Blend in 3/4 cup flour—wheat, barley, or rice—and cook the mixture a few minutes. Add gradually 2 quarts hot chicken stock and cook the mixture, stirring constantly, until it is thick and smooth. Water may be used instead of stock, but add also some chicken bones or a small fowl, cleaned and trussed, and, if available, a veal knuckle parboiled in salted water and drained. Add 1 quart canned Italian tomato purée, 3 leeks, 2 stalks of celery, 6 large tomatoes, 1 clove of garlic, 8 white peppercorns, 1 tablespoon sugar, and 1/2 tablespoon salt. Simmer the soup for 2 hours, skimming if necessary. Remove the bones or fowl and force the soup through a fine sieve.

Just before serving, bring the purée back to a boil and add 1 cup cream and 1 tablespoon butter. If the soup is too thick, add a little milk. Correct the seasoning with salt.

Crème Napolitaine　　　　CREAM OF TOMATO WITH SPAGHETTI

ADD 3/4 cup cooked spaghetti, cut into 1-inch pieces, to 1 1/2 quarts hot cream of tomato.

Crème Portugaise　　　　CREAM OF TOMATO WITH RICE

ADD 3/4 cup cooked rice to 1 1/2 quarts hot cream of tomato.

Crème Rose Marie　　　　CREAM OF TOMATO WITH SORREL

CLEAN and shred enough sorrel to make 1/2 cup, firmly packed. In a small saucepan, melt 1 tablespoon butter, add the sorrel, and cook it slowly until most of the moisture has cooked away, about 15 minutes. Add it to 1/2 quarts cream of tomato and reheat the soup.

CREAM OF LENTIL OR PURÉE OF LENTIL SOUP

Crème de Lentilles

SOAK 1 pound lentils in water to cover for a few hours and drain them. Cover them with fresh water, parboil them for 5 minutes, and drain them. Put them in a soup kettle and add 2 quarts water, 1 onion, studded with a clove, 1 carrot, 6 peppercorns, 1 teaspoon salt, and a faggot made by tying together 1 stalk of celery, 2 sprigs of parsley, 1 bay leaf, and a little thyme. Cook the lentils for about 1 hour, or until they are soft. In a small saucepan, melt 1 tablespoon butter, add 1/2 pound fat salt pork, cut in dice, and 1 onion, finely chopped. Cook the mixture until it is golden brown. Add 1 clove of garlic, crushed, and add the mixture to the lentils. Cook the soup for 15 minutes longer and force it through a sieve.

Just before serving, bring the purée back to a boil, and add 1 tablespoon butter and 1 cup cream. If the soup is too thick, add a little more water or milk. Correct the seasoning with salt.

CREAM OF GAME

Crème Saint-Hubert

IN A soup kettle, melt 2 tablespoons butter, and add the bones from a roasted game bird—partridge, pheasant, guinea hen, or other bird—and cook them until they take on a rich brown. Add 3 ounces dry Sherry or Madeira and 1 1/2 quarts simple cream of lentil soup, or purée, without cream or butter. Simmer the soup for 1 1/2 hours. Remove the bones. Add 1 cup cream and correct the seasoning with salt. Strain the soup through a fine sieve and add 1/2 cup cooked game, cut into fine julienne or dice. Cream of chicken base may be used instead of cream of lentil soup. Garnish with *petites profiteroles*, little puffs.

Nowadays we can buy cream of rice and cream of barley—very finely ground flours—and I prefer them to wheat flour for giving soups a light and delicate thickness. But some soups, like crème Crécy, *I thicken with whole grain rice, cooked in the soup until it is so soft that it can easily be forced through a sieve or food mill.*

CREAM OF CARROT

Crème Crécy

IN A soup kettle, melt 2 tablespoons butter, and add 4 medium carrots, thinly sliced, and 1 onion, diced. Cover the kettle and sauté the vegetables slowly for 15 minutes without letting them brown. Add 1 quart white stock, 1/2 cup rice, 1 tablespoon sugar, and 1 teaspoon salt. Simmer the soup for 45 minutes, or until the carrots are very soft. Force it through a fine sieve or food mill, return it to the kettle, and add 2 cups hot water. Bring the soup back to a boil and add 1 cup light cream and 1 tablespoon butter. Correct the seasoning with salt.

The making of shellfish bisques—fine, satin-smooth, full-flavored, and robust—requires a full measure of time, patience, and skill. Mais alors, they are surely worth the effort. One should know that the shells of crustaceans—lobster, shrimp, crayfish—contain a good deal of flavor. When I was a young chef, we pounded and ground the shells in a huge mortar whose great wooden pestle swung from the kitchen ceiling. What a backbreaking chore that was! I ask you only to put the tender shells through the food chopper and return them to the soup to simmer in it until the last bit of flavor has been extracted. Naturally, the shells must then be carefully strained out.

LOBSTER BISQUE

Bisque de Homard

SPLIT a live lobster down the back and remove the intestinal vein and the sac of gritty matter in the head. Using a heavy butcher's knife, cut the lobster crosswise into several pieces. Put the pieces in a soup kettle with 1/4 cup brandy and 2 quarts cream of chicken base, bring the liquid to a boil, and simmer the lobster for 20 to 25 minutes. Remove the meat from the lobster shells, and reserve it. Put the more tender shells through a food chopper and return them to the soup kettle. If the soup seems too thick, add a little water. Simmer it for 25 minutes and strain it through a fine sieve. Add 1 cup cream and correct the seasoning with salt. Strain the soup again through a double thickness of cheesecloth. Just before serving, bring the soup back to a boil and add 2 tablespoons Sherry and a few small dice of lobster meat. Use the remaining lobster meat for salads or other dishes.

SHRIMP BISQUE

Bisque de Crevettes

MAKE a mirepoix as follows: In a large saucepan, melt 2 tablespoons butter, add 1/2 carrot and 1/2 onion, both finely chopped, 2 sprigs of parsley, 1/2 bay leaf, and a little thyme, cover the pan, and cook the vegetables slowly until they are tender. Add 1 cup white wine and

24 well-washed fresh shrimp and poach them for 8 minutes. Remove the shrimp. Shell and devein 12 of them, reserving the shells. Cut the meat into dice and reserve it. Put the shells and the remaining 12 shrimp through the food chopper and add the chopped mixture to the kettle with the mirepoix and poaching wine. Add 2 quarts cream of chicken base, bring the soup to a boil, and simmer it for 20 minutes. Strain it through a fine sieve and, if it is too thick, add a little milk. Strain it again through a thickness of cheesecloth. Just before serving, bring the soup back to a boil and add 3 tablespoons cream and 2 tablespoons each of butter and brandy, Sherry, or Madeira. Garnish each serving with the reserved diced shrimp.

CRAYFISH BISQUE

*Bisque
d'Ecrevisses*

MAKE a mirepoix as for *bisque de crevettes*, shrimp bisque. Clean 30 crayfish and remove the intestinal vein at the tail. Lay the crayfish on the mirepoix and cook them, covered, until they are bright red. Add 2 tablespoons hot brandy and ignite it. When the flame burns out, add 1 cup white wine, 1/2 cup fish stock or water, 1/2 teaspoon salt, and a little pepper. Cover the pan and poach the crayfish for 10 to 12 minutes. Remove the meat from the bodies and tails and reserve it. Put the shells through the food chopper and return them to the kettle with the mirepoix and poaching liquid. Add 2 quarts cream of chicken base, bring the soup to a boil, and strain it through a fine sieve. If it seems too thick, add a little milk. Strain it again through a double thickness of cheesecloth. Just before serving, bring the soup back to a boil and add the reserved crayfish meat, cut in small pieces, 3 tablespoons cream and 2 tablespoons each of butter and brandy.

Clam and oyster bisques have a delicate flavor that is best pointed up not by cream of chicken base but by a velouté *based on fish stock.*

Velouté de Poisson

Fish Stock

FISH VELOUTÉ FOR SHELLFISH BISQUES

IN A large saucepan, put the bones and trimmings of 6 whitefish or other white-fleshed fish, add 2 quarts water, 1 cup white wine, 1 carrot and 1 onion, both sliced, 2 sprigs of parsley, 1/2 bay leaf, a little thyme, and 8 peppercorns. Bring the liquid to a boil and simmer it for 30 minutes, skimming as necessary. In another pan, melt 1/4 cup butter, blend in 3/4 cup flour—rice flour, preferably—and cook the *roux*, stirring, until it begins to turn golden. Strain the fish stock into the *roux*, stirring constantly, and cook the *velouté*, stirring, until it is thick and smooth. Cook it for 2 minutes longer, stirring occasionally and skimming as necessary, and strain it through a fine sieve.

Clam Bisque

CLAM BISQUE

SCRUB 3 dozen hard-shelled clams and open them. Reserve the juice and chop the clams. In a saucepan, melt 2 tablespoons butter, brown it lightly, and sauté the clams in it for 2 minutes. Add the clam juice, 1/2 cup white wine, and 2 quarts *velouté de poisson*, fish *velouté*. Cook the soup, stirring occasionally, for 20 minutes. Strain it through a fine sieve. Reheat it, but do not let it boil, and swirl in 4 tablespoons butter. Correct the seasoning with salt and add a little cayenne for color as well as flavor.

Bisque d'Huîtres

OYSTER BISQUE

OPEN 2 dozen oysters, reserving the liquid. Poach the oysters in it for 2 minutes, drain them, and mash them to make a purée. Strain the liquid. Combine the strained liquid and the oyster purée with 2 quarts *velouté de poisson*, fish *velouté*. Heat the soup, but do not let it boil. Press it through a fine sieve. Correct the seasoning with salt and add a little cayenne and 2 tablespoons each of butter and Madeira or Sherry. Do not allow the bisque to boil after the wine is added, or the fine aroma and flavor will be dissipated.

Cold Soups

Of the many specialties I created for the old Ritz-Carlton, none has gained the wide and lasting acclaim of crème vichyssoise glacée, *the chilled cream of leek and potato soup now served in restaurants everywhere. I suspect that some of the* fins becs *who order it would be much surprised to learn of its humble origins as my mother's simple leek and potato soup. Casting about one day for a new cold soup, I remembered how* maman *used to cool our breakfast soup, on a warm morning, by adding cold milk to it. A cup of cream, an extra straining, and a sprinkle of chives,* et voilà, *I had my new soup. I named my version of* maman's *soup after Vichy, the famous spa located not twenty miles from our Bourbonnais home, as a tribute to the fine cooking of the region.*

VICHYSSOISE

Crème Vichyssoise Glacée

FOLLOW the recipe for *soupe bonne femme,* leek and potato soup. When the potatoes are done, add 2 cups each of hot milk and light cream and bring the soup back to a boil, stirring it occasionally to prevent scorching. Strain the soup through a fine sieve, cool it, stirring occasionally to keep it smooth, and strain again. Stir in 1 cup heavy cream and chill the soup thoroughly. To serve, sprinkle each portion with finely chopped chives.

Crème Vichyssoise à la Ritz

VICHYSSOISE À LA RITZ

ADD 1 part tomato juice to 3 parts *crème vichyssoise* and chill the soup.

Consommé Froid

JELLIED CONSOMMÉ

A GOOD, rich consommé, made with enough bones, will jelly naturally when it is cold, but if necessary, it can be stiffened with unflavored gelatin. In order to judge the amount of gelatin necessary, chill the consommé thoroughly. If it does not thicken at all, the soup must be jellied by adding 1 tablespoon gelatin for each 2 cups liquid. Soften the gelatin in 1/4 cup of the soup, cool but liquid. Bring the remaining soup to a boil and dissolve the gelatin in it, off the heat. If the chilled consommé is thick and quivery in consistency, 1 to 2 teaspoons gelatin for each 2 cups is enough to produce a firm but tender jelly. Chill the consommé in the refrigerator for several hours or overnight—in the serving cups, if you like. Stir it with a fork before serving. Serve with a wedge of lemon.

Consommé à la Madrilène

JELLIED CONSOMMÉ MADRILÈNE

IN a large saucepan, combine 1 1/2 quarts chicken stock, 2 cups tomato juice, 1 tablespoon gelatin, 3 ripe tomatoes, chopped, and 2 egg whites, slightly beaten. Bring the mixture slowly to a boil, stirring constantly. Stop stirring as soon as it reaches a boil. Boil the consommé for 5 minutes, turn down the heat, and let it simmer for about 20 minutes. With a large perforated spoon, remove the solid material on top. Ladle off the soup and strain it through a double thickness of cheesecloth. Cool it and chill it. Serve with a wedge of lemon.

SAUCES

Sauces

WHEREVER you dine in France, you will see how French gourmets capture the last drops of sauce on their plates. And this is equally true in modest bistros and in world-famous restaurants that have been honored by the *Guide Michelin*'s three-star rating. The workingman may mop up his sauce with a thick slice of crusty bread, and the fastidious gourmet will impale a bit of bread on his fork, but the two have a common purpose, and in both cases not a vestige of sauce is wasted!

Sauce is the *sine qua non* of French cooking. That is why the *saucier*, the head sauce chef in a hotel or restaurant kitchen, stands second in rank only to the executive chef himself, and why every ambitious young *ap-*

prenti knows he must spend hours at the big copper pans, learning the art of the *saucier*.

In France, the word " sauce " encompasses salad dressings and brown gravies, as well as the white and brown sauces, butter sauces and butters, and various dessert sauces that Americans ordinarily speak of as " sauce. "

The number of sauces that must be mastered thus appears *formidable*, but fortunately for the amateur, most of these are variations on a few basic preparations. The combinations of ingredients seem endless, but the same basic methods are followed over and over again.

The sauce recipes presented in this chapter have been arranged to make this similarity clear. Read carefully the information that follows, as well as the instructions that introduce each new type of sauce. In order to save space, general information about procedures and techniques is not necessarily repeated each time it is applicable.

Utensils for Sauce Making Proper utensils are essential in making good sauces. The saucepan should be of heavy metal that holds and distributes the heat evenly. Sauces scorch readily in light-weight pans, despite constant stirring. If you have no heavy pan, put an asbestos pad between the source of heat and the saucepan. You will need a 2 1/2-quart saucepan to make 1 quart of sauce, and a 1-quart pan to make 1 or 2 cups of sauce. If the saucepan has a rounded bottom, thus eliminating sharp corners where the sauce can hide out of reach of the whisk, the possibility of catching and scorching is reduced. Use a wire sauce whisk of suitable size to stir the liquid into the *roux* and to stir the sauce as it thickens. During the long process of reduction, stir the sauce as necessary with a wooden spoon. In hotel kitchens, we use a wooden spatula for this purpose.

Quality of Ingredients As for ingredients, I cannot be too emphatic about the importance of quality. A good chef can produce a good sauce despite a poor range and inadequate utensils, but no amount of skillful manipulation can take the place of fresh, pure, high-quality ingredients. Inferior materials will make an inferior sauce. Most sauces require stock, preferably a good **Stock for Sauces** homemade stock of the sort described in the chapter on soups. A good canned consommé or dehydrated bouillon or meat extract makes an acceptable sustitute. A handful of vegetables and meat, poultry, or fish scraps simmered even briefly will make a small amount of useful stock.

Standards for a Good Sauce What is a good sauce? A good sauce complements and enhances by its flavor and texture the food it accompanies. It must neither overpower the food nor be overpowered by it.

When sauces which are thickened with flour or egg yolks are properly made, they are described in French as having *du corps*, body or consistency, or as being *à la nappe*, having the ability to cling to the food. You see and feel when a sauce has *du corps* as you stir it; you see that it is *nappe* when it coats the back of a spoon.

du Corps
à la Nappe

Long slow cooking blends the ingredients and produces fine flavor, and at the same time makes the sauce very smooth and light.

Most sauces begin with a *roux*, or thickening mixture of fat and flour. For each cup of sauce, melt 1 or 2 tablespoons butter. Only butter will give the proper flavor. The butter should be hot, but not sizzling. Add an equal amount of flour and cook the *roux* over low heat, stirring constantly. The flour must be thoroughly cooked, but high heat will shrivel the grains of starch in the flour and the texture of the finished sauce will suffer. For a white sauce, the *roux* should be cooked only until it barely begins to color.

Roux

Heat the liquid before adding it to the *roux*, to obtain a quicker and more thorough liaison. Add the hot liquid very slowly, stirring constantly with a wire whisk to keep the sauce smooth. As the sauce cooks, it begins to thicken. You will notice that sauce recipes call for what may seem like an inordinate amount of liquid to make a specified quantity of finished sauce, and that some recipes simply indicate that you use whatever liquid is on hand from the cooking of the fish or poultry with which the sauce is to be served, whether it happens to be 2 cups or 2 1/2 cups, or even 3 cups. The next step in sauce making, the reduction, reduces the amount of liquid and gives French sauces the special quality that distinguishes them from all others.

Liquid

To reduce a sauce, lower the heat and simmer the sauce very slowly until the liquid evaporates and is reduced by as much as 1/2, or even more. Stir brown sauces only often enough to keep them from sticking to the pan and scorching. White sauces improve in color and texture the more they are whipped. During this long, slow process, the flavors of the ingredients are extracted and blended, and the starch is thoroughly cooked, so that the sauce has a velvety texture obtainable in no other way.

Reduction

Straining the finished sauce gives an elegant smoothness characteristic of these sauces. Professional chefs pour the sauce into a muslin cloth, and two chefs, one at each end, twist the cloth to squeeze out the sauce. In your kitchen at home, a fine sieve will serve the purpose.

Straining

In restaurants and hotels the basic white and brown sauces are made up early in the day, and kept ready in a *bain-marie*, a kind of multiple

Bain-Marie

double boiler. Almost any sauce may be made ahead of time and reheated, but sauces containing milk, cream, or eggs should not be stored longer than one day. On the other hand, *velouté*, brown, and tomato sauces, all basic and useful for many purposes, can be stored in the refrigerator for several weeks. Pour the sauce into jars and cover them with a seal of melted fat, or float a little Sherry on the surface. If the sauce is not used within a week, boil it for a few minutes, pour it back into the freshly washed jars, and seal and store as before. Sauces stored in a home freezer will keep for several months and do not require the fat or wine.

Storing Sauces

The White Sauces

THE GENEALOGY of the "white sauces" — the white and yellow sauces that include milk, cream, stock, mushroom liquor, white wine, egg yolks, and cheese, in various combinations, variously seasoned with onion, shallot, lemon juice, herbs, and spices—is easy to remember. The basic white sauces are béchamel, made with a white *roux* and milk, and *velouté*, made with a white *roux* and white stock (of fish, poultry, or veal). To make cream sauce, add cream to the basic béchamel; to make *sauce Mornay*, add egg yolks and cheese to the cream sauce. Begin with *velouté* and add mushroom liquor and cream, and you have *sauce suprême*. Add egg yolks and more cream to the *sauce suprême*, and you have *sauce allemande*, the richest of all white sauces. Most white sauces fit into this family tree.

Adding Egg Yolks

When a sauce is to be thickened and enriched with egg yolk, break up the yolk with a whisk. A spoonful or two of cream may be added. Then warm the egg by mixing with it a little of the hot sauce and stir it into the pan. If cold egg is added to the hot sauce, it coagulates instead of blending in, and the sauce curdles. Stir the sauce constantly until it just reaches the boiling point, but do not allow it to boil. Remove the pan from the heat and continue to stir the sauce for a minute or two.

When cream is used as part of the liquid of a sauce, and will be reduced, use light cream. When cream is added at the last, to give the sauce more richness, use heavy cream. Cream

Salt a sauce only lightly at the beginning, since it concentrates as it reduces, and correct the seasoning just before serving. A little lemon juice or dry mustard will add piquancy to a bland sauce. Salt

When you make a cheese sauce such as Mornay, use a hard cheese like Parmesan or dry Swiss, in preference to the softer, richer Cheddar. Dry cheeses grate easily and blend thoroughly with the sauce without changing its texture and without adding excess fat. Cheese

Shallots, which have a flavor at once more intense and less sharp than that of onions, are frequently specified for sauces, but if necessary 1 tablespoon chopped onion may be substituted for each shallot. Shallots

The peelings and stems of mushrooms add fine flavor of their own to sauces, and seem to have the further quality of emphasizing and enhancing other flavors. They are strained out after the sauce is reduced. Mushroom Stems and Peelings

The best wine for white sauces is a dry white wine, which will neither discolor nor sweeten the sauce. If the wine is to be reduced in the very first step, as it is for *sauce Bercy*, it need be of only average quality. If it is to be used in the reduction, it should be better. Wines that are added at the last, and are not boiled, should have excellent flavor. A few drops of lemon juice may be added to the finished sauce, especially if the sauce is to be used with fish. Wine

Sauces are used to glaze food; that is, the sauce is spread over the food and the dish is put under the heat of the broiler or into the oven to brown. To obtain a high luster and an even brown, fold a tablespoon or two of whipped cream into 1/2 cup of the sauce for glazing. Glazing

A little fresh butter swirled into any sauce at the last minute will improve the flavor and thicken the sauce a little. Stirring prevents the thickening. Swirl the butter in by moving the pan in a circular motion and remove the sauce from the heat a moment before the butter is completely melted. Finishing with Butter

There is one more sauce ingredient that is typically French—*beurre manié*, kneaded butter. This is a mixture of 3 parts butter to 1 part flour, thoroughly creamed together. A generous tablespoon of this mixture will thicken 1 cup of the liquid in which fish has been poached or of very thin stew gravy. The *beurre manié* is added to the hot liquid and Beurre Manié or Kneaded Butter cooked for a few minutes, until the sauce thickens. You will find that classical formulas frequently call for the last-minute addition of a small amount of béchamel, cream, or *velouté* sauce to thicken a sauce. In such recipes, you may substitute *beurre manié*, plus a little heavy cream.

Sauce Béchamel

MELT 2 tablespoons butter and in it cook 1 tablespoon onion, finely chopped, until the onion is soft but not at all brown. Add 4 tablespoons flour, mix well, and cook the *roux* slowly, stirring constantly, until it just starts to turn golden. Add gradually 3 cups scalded milk, and cook, stirring vigorously with a wire whip, until the mixture is thick and smooth. Season the sauce with 1/4 teaspoon salt, 3 white peppercorns, a sprig of parsley, and, if desired, a tiny pinch of grated nutmeg. Cook the sauce slowly, stirring frequently, for about 30 minutes, or until it is reduced to 2/3 the original quantity. Strain the béchamel through a fine sieve. Makes about 2 cups.

Sauce Crème

CREAM SAUCE

REDUCE 2 cups béchamel sauce to about 1 1/2 cups and add 1/2 cup heavy cream. Correct the seasoning with salt. For fish, add a few drops of lemon juice.

Sauce Mornay

MORNAY SAUCE

MIX 3 slightly beaten egg yolks with a little cream, combine with 2 cups hot béchamel sauce and cook, stirring constantly, until the sauce just reaches the boiling point. Add 2 tablespoons each of butter and grated Parmesan or Swiss cheese. For fish, vegetables, poultry, poached eggs, noodle and macaroni mixtures, and other creamed foods.

Velouté

VELOUTÉ SAUCE

MELT 2 tablespoons butter in a saucepan, add 4 tablespoons flour, mix well, and cook the *roux* slowly, stirring, until it just starts to turn golden. Gradually add 3 cups boiling hot white stock, stirring vigorously with a wire whip. Add 3 white peppercorns, a little salt, and a sprig of parsley. Add 1/2 cup mushroom peelings and stems, if available. Simmer the sauce, stirring frequently, for about 1 hour, or until it is reduced to 2/3 the original quantity and is thick as heavy cream. Skim the sauce occasionally. Strain it through a fine sieve and correct the seasoning. If it is to be stored, stir it with the whip from time to time as it cools to keep the mixture smooth and to keep a scum from forming on the surface of the sauce.

For suprême sauce the heavier the cream the better. The country cream we used at the Paris Ritz, brought in each day from Normandy, was so thick we had to spoon it into the sauce.

SUPRÊME SAUCE
Sauce Suprême

COOK 2 cups chicken stock with 3 sliced mushrooms, or some mushroom stems and peelings, until the liquid is reduced to 1/3 its original quantity. Add 1 cup *velouté* sauce, bring the sauce to the boiling point, and simmer it until it is reduced to about 1 cup. Gradually stir in 1 cup heavy cream, correct the seasoning with salt and a little cayenne pepper, and strain the sauce through a fine sieve.

ALLEMANDE SAUCE
Sauce Allemande

MIX 2 lightly beaten egg yolks with a little cream and a little hot sauce and add them to 2 cups hot suprême sauce. Heat the sauce, stirring constantly, just to the boiling point. Finish it with 2 tablespoons heavy cream.

FISH VELOUTÉ
Velouté de Poisson

MELT 2 tablespoons butter in a saucepan, add 4 tablespoons flour, mix well, and cook slowly until the *roux* just starts to turn golden. Add, little by little, 3 cups hot fish stock, stirring vigorously with a whip. Cook for 15 to 20 minutes and strain through a fine sieve.

Or reduce the liquid in which fish is poached and thicken it by adding *beurre manié* made by creaming 1 tablespoon butter with 1 teaspoon flour for each cup of reduced fish liquor.

Less rich than the other foundation sauces, this white sauce is often used in-stead of hollandaise on vegetables like asparagus or on fish.

Sauce Blanche

MELT 1 tablespoon butter in a saucepan, add 1 tablespoon flour, and mix together without cooking. Add 1 cup boiling hot water, 1/2 tea-spoon salt, and a little pepper and mix all together well. Combine with 2 slightly beaten egg yolks and cook the sauce, stirring with a wire whip, until the boiling point is reached, but do not boil. Remove from the heat, and add 1 teaspoon lemon juice, and 2 tablespoons butter.

Sauce Aurore

AURORE SAUCE

ADD 3 tablespoons tomato purée or well-reduced tomato sauce to 2 cups béchamel or Mornay sauce. Add 1 tablespoon butter. For eggs.

Bercy sauce, or shallot sauce, may be made in several ways, depending upon which is more convenient. The sauce is spread over the cooked fish and glazed briefly under the broiler or in the oven.

Sauce Bercy I

SHALLOT SAUCE I

Cook 1 tablespoon chopped shallots in 3/4 cup white wine until the liq-uid is reduced to about 2 tablespoons. Add 1 1/2 cups fish *velouté* and cook slowly for 5 minutes. Remove the pan from the heat, add 1 teaspoon lemon juice, and swirl in 2 tablespoons butter.

Sauce Bercy II

SHALLOT SAUCE II

COOK 1 teaspoon finely chopped shallots in 1 tablespoon butter for a few minutes, but do not let the shallots brown. Add 1/2 cup dry white wine and simmer for a few minutes. Thicken with *beurre manié* made by creaming 1 tablespoon butter with 1 teaspoon flour. Simmer for a few minutes and add 1 teaspoon chopped parsley.

CAPER CREAM SAUCE   *Sauce Crème aux Câpres*

ADD 2 tablespoons capers and 2 teaspoons chopped parsley to 2 cups cream sauce. For fish or poultry.

CARDINAL SAUCE   *Sauce Cardinal*

ADD 2 to 3 tablespoons fish stock to 2 cups hot fish *velouté* or béchamel sauce. Add 3 tablespoons lobster butter and a little truffle juice, if available. For fish.

CHIVRY SAUCE   *Sauce Chivry*

COOK 1/2 cup white wine, 1 teaspoon each of chopped chervil, tarragon, and chives, and 1 tablespoon chopped water cress until the wine is reduced to about 1/3 the original quantity. Add 2 cups cream sauce and strain through a fine sieve. Cook 1 tablespoon chopped spinach with a little chopped tarragon and chervil and rub through a fine sieve. Add to the sauce to color it. For a richer sauce, add 2 tablespoons hollandaise sauce. For poached poultry.

CURRY SAUCE   *Sauce au Currie*

COOK 1 onion, finely chopped, in 1 tablespoon butter until it is soft but not brown. Add 1 small bay leaf, a little thyme, and 1 tablespoon curry powder and mix well. Add 1/4 cup chicken or fish stock and bring the sauce to the boil. Add 1 1/2 cups *velouté* sauce or fish *velouté*. Boil for another 10 or 15 minutes, strain through a fine sieve, and finish with 1/2 cup cream. For fish or poultry.

EGG SAUCE   *Sauce aux Oeufs*

ADD 2 hard-cooked eggs, chopped, and 1/2 teaspoon chopped parsley to 2 cups cream sauce. For a richer sauce, add 1 tablespoon hollandaise sauce. For steamed fish.

Sauce Hongroise   PAPRIKA SAUCE

COOK 1 onion, finely chopped, in 1 tablespoon butter until it is golden. Add 2 tablespoons paprika and mix well. Gradually add 1 cup cream, stirring constantly, and thicken the sauce with 6 tablespoons *velouté* or cream sauce. Correct the seasoning with salt. For fish, poultry, or veal.

Sauce Crème aux Champignons   MUSHROOM CREAM SAUCE

SAUTÉ 1/2 pound small mushrooms in 2 tablespoons butter until they are lightly browned. Add 1 cup cream and cook over low heat for 6 to 8 minutes. Stir in 1/4 cup *velouté* or cream sauce and season with salt and pepper to taste.

Sauce Moutarde Blanche   MUSTARD CREAM SAUCE

To 1 cup hot cream sauce add 1 teaspoon dry English mustard mixed to a paste with 1 tablespoon water.

Sauce Nantua   NANTUA SAUCE

ADD 1/2 cup cream to 2 cups béchamel and cook for 5 minutes. Add 3 to 4 tablespoons crayfish butter and mix it well with the hot béchamel sauce. Let the sauce cool and remove any butter that rises to the surface. If necessary add a little pink vegetable coloring to give the sauce its characteristic pink color. For fish or eggs.

Sauce Newburg   NEWBURG SAUCE

MAKE the sauce for lobster Newburg. This sauce may accompany any kind of fish or sea food.

Sauce Normande   NORMANDE SAUCE

MELT 2 tablespoons butter in a saucepan, add 1 teaspoon flour, and cook until the *roux* just starts to turn golden. Add 1 cup combined fish stock and mushroom liquor. (This is usually the cooking liquor from the fish, oysters, or mussels for which the sauce is being made and some of the cooking liquor from the mushrooms which will garnish the dish.)

Cook for about 10 minutes. Mix 2 lightly beaten egg yolks with 1/2 cup cream and combine with the sauce. Reheat the sauce and strain it.

MATELOTE SAUCE   *Sauce Matelote*

COOK 1 onion and 1 carrot, both finely chopped, in a saucepan with 1 tablespoon butter until golden. Add a little thyme, 1 bay leaf, 1 clove of garlic, some mushroom peelings, and some chopped fish heads and bones, preferably salmon or sole. Simmer for 10 minutes. Add 1 quart red wine, cover the pan, and cook until the sauce is reduced to 1/2 the original quantity. Strain through a fine sieve. Thicken with *beurre manié* made by creaming 1 tablespoon butter with 1 teaspoon flour. Bring to the boil again and finish with 1 tablespoon butter. For fish.

POULETTE SAUCE   *Sauce Poulette*

SAUTÉ 6 to 8 mushrooms, sliced, in 1 tablespoon butter until they just start to brown. Add 2 shallots, finely chopped, and 1/2 cup cream. Cook the cream until it is reduced to 1/2 the original quantity and add 1/2 cup béchamel or cream sauce. Bring the sauce to the boiling point, correct the seasoning with salt, and add 2 egg yolks mixed lightly with a little cream and a little of the hot sauce. Bring the sauce again to the boiling point, stirring constantly, but do not let it boil. Finish the sauce with the juice of 1/2 lemon and 1/2 teaspoon chopped parsley. For fish, calf's brains, and the like.

HOT RAVIGOTE SAUCE   *Sauce Ravigote Chaude*

COMBINE 1/3 cup each of dry white wine and vinegar, and 6 shallots, finely chopped, in a saucepan and cook until the liquid is reduced to 1/3 the original quantity. Add 2 cups cream sauce or white sauce and boil gently for 5 to 6 minutes. Remove from the heat, add 2 tablespoons butter and 1 teaspoon mixed chopped chervil, tarragon, and chives. For boiled poultry or fish.

ONION CREAM SAUCE   *Sauce Soubise*

PARBOIL 1 cup chopped onions for 3 to 4 minutes, and drain. Sauté the onions with 1 tablespoon butter until they are soft but not brown.

Add 2 cups béchamel sauce and cook for 15 minutes. Strain through a fine sieve, return to the heat, and add, little by little, 1 cup cream. Correct the seasoning with salt. For fish, lamb, veal, or sweetbreads.

Sauce Vin Blanc   WHITE WINE SAUCE

COMBINE 1/2 cup mushroom trimmings, 1/2 cup dry white wine, and 1/2 cup reduced fish stock. Cook the liquid until it is reduced to 1/3 its original quantity. Add 1 cup cream sauce or fish *velouté* and season to taste with salt and white pepper. Finish the sauce with 1/2 cup heavy cream or swirl in 2 tablespoons butter. Add a few drops of lemon juice and strain the sauce. Serve with poached fish. The liquid in which the fish was poached is usually reduced to make the stock for the sauce.

Sauce Livonienne   LIVONIENNE SAUCE

TO 2 cups white wine sauce add 2 tablespoons carrots, cut in julienne and cooked, and 1 tablespoon each of julienne of truffles, chopped green leaves of lettuce parboiled for 5 minutes, and chopped parsley. For fish.

The Brown Sauces

THERE IS a story that explains why the most important basic brown sauce in French cuisine is called *sauce espagnole*, or Spanish sauce. According to the story, the Spanish cooks of Louis XIII's bride, Anne, helped to prepare their wedding feast, and insisted upon improving the rich brown sauce of France with Spanish tomatoes. The new sauce was an instant success, and was gratefully named in honor of its creators.

Espagnole is one of the three basic brown sauces upon which numerous variations are built. The others are tomato sauce and *demi-glace* sauce, itself a variation of *sauce espagnole*.

Before you make your first brown sauce, reread the instructions at the beginning of this chapter, most of which apply to brown sauces as well as to white. However, there are certain differences that must be noted here.

Meat drippings sometimes replace butter in making brown sauce. They must be fine, fresh drippings, of course. Never use lamb fat or chicken fat for making brown sauces: their distinctive flavors do not blend well.

The *roux* for a brown sauce is cooked very slowly until it takes on a rich, hazelnut brown color. It must be stirred constantly to prevent scorching, which will make the sauce bitter. The sauce must also be stirred constantly while the liquid is being added and until the sauce thickens. During the reduction, however, stir the sauce only occasionally, or shake the pan, to prevent sticking and scorching. Too much stirring lightens the color of the sauce. More liquid is used in making brown sauce to permit longer reduction, to blend and concentrate the complex flavor. The reduction also causes fat and insoluble particles to rise to the surface, and the sauce should be skimmed as necessary.

Brown Roux

When a recipe calls for a little tomato sauce as a thickening agent, tomato purée and *beurre manié* may be used instead, but a brown *roux* must take the place of brown sauce suggested for thickening.

BROWN SAUCE

IN a heavy saucepan melt 1/2 cup fat—fresh, unsalted beef, veal, or pork drippings—or use clarified butter. In it cook 1 small carrot and 2 medium onions, coarsely chopped, until they just start to turn golden. Add 1/2 cup flour and cook, stirring frequently, until the *roux* takes on a good hazelnut brown color and the carrot and onions are brown. Bring to a boil. Add 3 cups hot brown stock, 1 clove of garlic, and a faggot made by tying together 1 stalk of celery, 3 sprigs of parsley, 1 small bay leaf, and a pinch of thyme. Cook, stirring frequently, until the mixture thickens and add 3 more cups hot stock. Cook the sauce very slowly over very low heat, stirring occasionally, for 1 to 1 1/2 hours, or until it is reduced to about 3 cups. As it cooks, skim off the excess fat. Add 1/4 cup tomato sauce or 1/2 cup tomato purée. Cook the sauce for a few minutes longer. Discard the faggot and strain the sauce through a fine sieve.

Sauce
Espagnole

Add 2 cups hot stock and cook the sauce slowly for about 1 hour more, or until it is reduced to about 4 cups, skimming it from time to time as needed. Cool it, stirring occasionally.

For a richer sauce, cook 1/2 cup diced fat salt pork with the carrot and onion and add before the final reduction 1/2 cup beef gravy or juice from roast beef.

Sauce Brune

SIMPLE BROWN SAUCE

IN 2 tablespoons fat brown 1 finely chopped onion very lightly. Add 2 tablespoons flour and cook, stirring, until the *roux* is brown. Add 2 cups stock and 3 tablespoons tomato purée and cook, stirring, until the sauce thickens, then cook until it is reduced to 1 cup. Season to taste.

Sauce Brune sans Graisse

BROWN SAUCE WITHOUT FAT

COOK 3/4 cup flour to a golden brown in the oven or under the broiler, stirring often. Brown 1 carrot and 1 onion, coarsely chopped, in the oven or under the broiler, shaking the pan occasionally. Put the flour in a heavy saucepan and gradually add 5 cups boiling hot brown stock, stirring until the sauce thickens. Add 1 cup tomato sauce or fresh to-matoes, the carrot and onion, 1 clove of garlic, 10 peppercorns, and a faggot made by tying together 2 stalks of celery, 3 sprigs of parsley, 1/2 bay leaf, and a pinch of thyme. Cook the sauce slowly for 1 1/2 to 2 hours. Strain it through a fine sieve and correct the seasoning.

The richest basic brown sauce, demi-glace, *accompanies dark meats and such delicacies as truffles and* foie gras.

Sauce Demi-Glace I

DEMI-GLACE SAUCE I

COOK 2 small carrots and 2 medium onions, both finely chopped, in 1 tablespoon butter until they are soft and golden brown. Add a few beef or veal bones that have been browned in the oven, the carcass of a roasted chicken, if possible, 3 sprigs of parsley, 1/2 cup mushroom stems and peelings, 3 cups brown sauce, and 2 cups brown stock. Cook the sauce slowly for 1 1/2 hours, skimming off the fat and foam frequently. Strain the *demi-glace* through a fine sieve, bring it to a boil again, and skim once more. At the last moment, add 1/3 cup Madeira or Sherry.

DEMI-GLACE SAUCE II

Sauce Demi-Glace II

COOK the chopped stems and peelings of a few mushrooms in 1/3 cup dry Sherry until the wine is reduced to about 1/2. Add 2 cups brown sauce and 1 tablespoon beef extract, or *glace de viande*. Simmer the sauce for 15 to 20 minutes and strain it.

TOMATO SAUCE

Sauce Tomate

TOMATO sauce must be watched especially carefully because the weight of the tomatoes encourages easy scorching. Stir it frequently.

Melt 3 tablespoons butter in a heavy saucepan. In it cook 1 small carrot and 1 small onion, coarsely chopped, until the onion is soft but not brown. Add 1/4 cup flour and cook, stirring, until the *roux* turns golden. Add 2 to 2 1/2 cups chopped fresh tomatoes or canned tomatoes, 1 1/2 cups brown stock or water, 2 cloves of garlic, crushed, a faggot made by tying together 2 stalks of celery, 3 sprigs of parsley, 1 small bay leaf, and a pinch of thyme, 1 teaspoon sugar, 1/2 teaspoon salt, and a little pepper. Cook the sauce slowly, stirring constantly, until it thickens. Continue to cook slowly, stirring occasionally and skimming the surface when necessary, for 1 to 1 1/2 hours, or until the sauce is reduced to about 2 cups. Discard the faggot and strain the sauce in a fine sieve, rubbing the pulp through. Bring the sauce again to a boil and cook for 4 or 5 minutes more, stirring constantly.

AMÉRICAINE SAUCE I

Sauce Américaine I

MAKE the sauce for lobster *à l'américaine*. This sauce may accompany any kind of fish or sea food.

Sauce Américane II   AMÉRICAINE SAUCE II

COOK 4 cups stewed tomatoes until most of the liquid has cooked away
and strain through a fine sieve. Heat 1 tablespoon olive oil and 2 tablespoons butter in a saucepan and add 2 shallots, finely chopped, 1 clove
of garlic, and 1 tablespoon each chopped parsley and chervil. Add the
tomato purée and simmer until the shallots are soft. Remove the clove
of garlic, add 2 tablespoons brandy, and cook for a few minutes without
letting the sauce boil.

Sauce Bordelaise   BORDELAISE SAUCE

COOK 2 shallots, finely chopped, in 1/2 cup red wine until it is reduced
to 1/4 the original quantity. Add 1 cup brown sauce and simmer the
sauce for 10 minutes. Cut the marrow from a split beef marrowbone
into small dice. Poach it in boiling salted water for a minute or two
and drain it. Just before serving the sauce, add 2 tablespoons diced
marrow and 1/2 teaspoon chopped parsley. For steak.

Sauce Chasseur   CHASSEUR SAUCE

PEEL and slice thinly the caps of 1 pound mushrooms. Melt 4 tablespoons butter, add the mushrooms with 1/2 teaspoon salt and pepper
to taste, and sauté them, shaking the pan frequently, until they are golden
brown. Add 2 shallots, chopped, and 1/2 cup dry white wine and cook
the sauce until the liquid is reduced to about 1/2 the original quantity.
Add 1 cup brown sauce, 2 tablespoons tomato sauce, and 1/2 teaspoon
each of parsley and tarragon, both chopped. For chicken or veal.

Sauce Château   CHÂTEAU SAUCE

COOK 3 shallots, finely chopped, in 1/3 cup dry white wine until the
wine is reduced to 1/2 its volume. Add 2 cups *demi-glace* sauce and cook
slowly for about 10 minutes. Remove the sauce to the side of the stove
and add 1/4 pound butter, stirring it in briskly with a whip to give the
sauce a light brown color. If the sauce gets too thick, whip in 1/2 teaspoon or more of water. Add 1 teaspoon chopped parsley. For delicately flavored meats like *escalope* of veal, *noisette* of lamb, breast of chicken,
or *escalope* of sweetbreads.

DEVIL SAUCE   *Sauce Diable*

ADD 3 shallots, chopped, and 8 peppercorns, crushed, to 1/3 cup dry
white wine or vinegar and cook until the mixture is reduced to a thick
paste. Add 1 cup brown sauce, 1 teaspoon Worcestershire sauce, and 1/2
teaspoon chopped parsley. For broiled foods.

GENEVOISE SAUCE   *Sauce Genevoise*

MAKE a *mirepoix bordelaise*: Cook slowly 1 carrot and 1 onion, cut in   Mirepoix
very fine dice, in 1 tablespoon butter with a little thyme, 1 small bay leaf,   Bordelaise
and 3 or 4 sprigs of parsley for 15 to 20 minutes, shaking the pan occasionally to prevent burning. Add the trimmings, bones, and chopped
head of a salmon and cook for 5 minutes longer. Add 2 cups red wine
and cook slowly until it is reduced to 3/4 the original quantity. Add 1
cup brown sauce and cook slowly for 1/2 hour. Lacking brown sauce,
add to the mixture before the wine 1 tablespoon flour creamed with 1
tablespoon butter, to thicken it. Strain the sauce and correct the seasoning. Finish with 2 tablespoons butter. The sauce can also be made
with the bones and trimmings of English sole. For salmon, or other fish.

HERB SAUCE   *Sauce aux Fines Herbes*

To 1/3 cup boiling dry white wine add 1 teaspoon chopped chives, 3
sprigs of chopped parsley, and the chopped stems of 3 sprigs each of
tarragon and chervil. Let this mixture infuse for about 10 minutes, off
the heat.

To 1 tablespoon melted butter in a saucepan add 1 teaspoon chopped
shallot and the strained herb infusion. Cook until the liquid is reduced to 1/2 its original quantity, add 1 cup brown sauce, and cook for
10 to 15 minutes longer. Swirl 1 tablespoon butter into the sauce and
add the juice of 1 lemon and the chopped leaves of 3 sprigs each of
chervil and tarragon.

ITALIAN SAUCE   *Sauce Italienne*

COOK 1 teaspoon chopped shallots and 2 tomatoes, peeled, seeded, and
chopped, in 3/4 cup Marsala wine until the tomatoes are soft and the
mixture has reduced about 1/2. Add either 1/2 cup brown sauce or 1/2

cup tomato sauce, and 2 tablespoons each of mushroom *duxelles* and chopped cooked ham. Boil for 5 minutes and add 1 teaspoon chopped parsley. For meat, fish, or poultry. Especially good for leftover cooked meat.

Sauce Madère   MADEIRA SAUCE

REDUCE 2 cups brown sauce to about 1 cup. Add 1/3 cup good Madeira and bring the sauce just to a boil, but do not let it boil. For beef, veal, ham, and poultry.

Sauce Madère aux Champignons   MADEIRA MUSHROOM SAUCE

CLEAN and dry the caps of 1 pound mushrooms and cut them in thick slices. Melt 4 tablespoons butter in a saucepan, add the mushrooms, 1/2 teaspoon salt, and a little pepper, and cook, shaking the pan frequently, until the mushrooms are golden brown. Add 1 shallot, finely chopped, 1/3 cup Madeira or dry Sherry, and 1 cup brown sauce. Simmer the sauce for 5 to 6 minutes. Add 1/2 teaspoon chopped parsley. For meat, especially filet mignon, or for poultry.

Sauce Moutarde Brune   MUSTARD SAUCE

To 1/2 cup devil sauce, add 1/4 teaspoon each of dry English mustard and salt, 1 teaspoon each of Worcestershire sauce and lemon juice, 2 tablespoons heavy cream, and a little pepper. Cook the sauce over low heat for 10 minutes, stirring frequently. For any meat or poultry, roasted or boiled.

Sauce Périgueux   PÉRIGUEUX SAUCE

To Madeira sauce add 1 tablespoon chopped truffles and a little of the truffle liquor. Swirl in 1 tablespoon butter. For croquettes, shirred eggs, eggs *en cocotte*, and chicken.

Sauce Périgourdine   PÉRIGOURDINE SAUCE

MAKE Périgueux sauce and add a generous quantity of truffles cut in 1/2-inch dice. For feathered game.

ROSSINI SAUCE   *Sauce Rossini*

MAKE Périgueux sauce, using sliced truffles. For tournedos of beef, breast
of chicken, sweetbreads, and *foie gras.*

PIQUANT SAUCE I   *Sauce Piquante I*

COOK 1 onion, finely chopped, in 1 tablespoon butter until it is lightly
browned. Add 2 tablespoons vinegar and cook until it is reduced to
almost nothing. Add 1 cup brown sauce and 1 tablespoon tomato sauce
or tomato purée and cook for 10 minutes. Add 3 tablespoons finely
chopped sour pickles and 1 teaspoon chopped parsley. Correct the seasoning. For fresh ox or veal tongue or any bland meat and for reheating
leftover cooked meat.

PIQUANT SAUCE II   *Sauce Piquante II*

COOK 1 onion, finely chopped, in 1/4 cup vinegar until reduced to almost
nothing. Add 1 1/2 cups strained canned tomatoes, 1/2 teaspoon salt,
and a little pepper and cook slowly for 10 minutes. Thicken with *beurre
manié* made by creaming 2 tablespoons butter with 1 tablespoon flour.
Add 3 tablespoons finely chopped sour pickles and 1 teaspoon chopped
parsley. For pork and other meats.

PORTUGUESE SAUCE   *Sauce Portugaise*

MELT 2 tablespoons butter in a saucepan and add 1 shallot, finely chopped,
and 1/4 cup red or white wine. Cook the sauce until it is reduced to 1/3
the original quantity. Add 2 tomatoes, peeled, seeded and chopped, and
cook them until they are soft. Add 1/2 cup each of brown sauce and tomato sauce, 1/2 teaspoon chopped parsley, 1/2 teaspoon salt and a little
pepper and bring to a boil. For any meat or poultry.

ROBERT SAUCE   *Sauce Robert*

COOK 2 onions, finely chopped, in 1 tablespoon butter until they are gold-
en brown. Add 1/3 cup dry white wine and 1 tablespoon vinegar
and cook until the liquid is reduced to about 3/4 the original quantity.
Add 1 cup brown sauce and 2 tablespoons tomato sauce and cook slowly

for 10 to 15 minutes. When ready to serve, add 1 tablespoon prepared mustard, 1 tablespoon finely chopped sour pickle and 1 teaspoon chopped parsley. For pork, and leftover meat.

Sauce Romaine
ROMAINE SAUCE

Cook 2 tablespoons sugar in a heavy saucepan until it has a light caramel color. Add 1/2 cup vinegar and let it reduce to almost nothing. Add 1 cup brown sauce, bring to a boil, and add 2 tablespoons raisins, Smyrna or Corinth. Cook 10 minutes. For veal, beef, tongue, and venison.

Sauce Tortue
TURTLE SAUCE

To 1/3 cup boiling Madeira or Sherry add 1 teaspoon *herbes à tortue*—mixed dried marjoram, rosemary, sage, bay leaf, thyme, and basil—and let the mixture infuse for about 10 minutes, off the heat. Strain it through cheesecloth and add to 2 cups hot brown sauce. For turtle and calf's head.

Pan Sauces and Meat Gravy

Pan sauces and brown meat gravy are described in the sections on sautéing and roasting, respectively, because each is an important step in the basic cooking procedure.

Glace de Viande

Anyone who has been in the kitchen of a large French restaurant or hotel knows the huge kettles in which gallons of stock are made for use in soups and sauces. When the stock has been strained off, there remain in the kettles bones and scraps of meat and vegetables from which one would think all goodness had been extracted. *Mais non*! We then take these odds and ends and coax from them the last vestige of succulence. The chef adds more water to the kettles and continues to simmer the bones and bits of meat and vegetables for a day and a night. Then the stock is strained and reduced by further cooking until it is thick and gelatinous, a paste dark brown in color and infinitely concentrated in flavor. This is *glace de viande*, meat glaze, or beef extract, as it is sometimes called.

Meat Glaze or Beef Extract

A little *glace de viande* goes a long way, and there was inevitably more of it than the kitchen needed. So it was customary in France for the head chef to permit the chef who made the *glace de viande*, usually the *saucier* who had charge of the stockpots, to sell the surplus and pocket the money. Luxury food stores were the prime purchasers, since they purveyed jars of the precious stuff to small restaurants and private homes. I was able to initiate this custom at the New York Ritz, where it held all during my forty-year tenure.

However, there is no reason for you not to make *glace de viande* for yourself, if you want to have it on hand and if there are no stores in your neighborhood that can supply you with it. The actual process, as you will see, is as simple as boiling water, and the extract keeps for months in the refrigerator, and may be sealed or frozen for longer storage. If mold should form on the surface, simply wash it off with hot water.

When *glace de viande* is very cold, it can be cut only with a good sharp knife, but it softens quickly at room temperature, and melts readily in hot liquid.

Most chefs consider *glace de viande* indispensable in *haute cuisine*. It is traditional with red meats, in brown sauces, and with poultry dishes, particularly those whose stuffing contains goose liver and truffles. A rosette of *glace de viande* may be used to garnish poached fish, or the *glace* may be mixed with an equal amount of Madeira and brushed on roasted or braised ham or filet of beef or other meats. The merest touch will brighten a lobster sauce—*glace de viande* should be used sparingly when a delicate flavor is wanted—and a generous spoonful can be added to brown sauces. Add *glace de viande* to taste to improve the color and flavor of pan gravies and of meat soups.

Glace de viande may also be used to make brown stock: 1 or 2 tablespoons to a cup of hot water makes a strong stock. For onion soup, in which most of the flavor should come from the onions, turn boiling water into a suitably light consommé with a tablespoon or so of *glace de viande*.

English beef extract, on sale at all food stores, may be used to substitute for *glace de viande*, if necessary. Beef extract is made from meat alone, so it does not have the richness and texture characteristic of *glace de viande*. Use the beef extract cautiously—it has a good but very strong flavor. Do not use as much of it as you would of the homemade extract.

Glace de Viande

MEAT GLAZE

HAVE enough beef and veal bones with some meat clinging to them and any leftover poultry carcasses that may be available to half fill a large, heavy kettle. For each 10 pounds of bones weigh out 2 pounds of mixed celery stalks and leaves, carrots, and onions. Brown the bones lightly with 1 carrot and 1 onion, each thickly sliced, in a roasting pan in a hot oven (450° F.), then put them in the kettle with the chopped vegetables. Fill the kettle with unsalted water and 2 cups canned tomatoes and simmer the bones and vegetables for 18 to 24 hours. Strain out the bones and vegetables, return the broth to the kettle, and cook until it is reduced to 1/2 or less the original quantity, skimming off the fat as it rises. Strain the broth again into a large saucepan, straining this time through a muslin or flannel cloth wrung out in cold water. Continue to cook the broth, stirring frequently, until it is very thick. Put into jars, cool, and store in the refrigerator or freezer.

Butter Sauces

GOOD BUTTER bears the same relationship to French sauces that good sauces bear to French cooking; one is inconceivable without the other. It is difficult to distinguish between cause and effect here, but the fact is that French butter is very good, and French sauces made with butter are therefore very good indeed!

White sauces use butter generously in their *roux*, and brown sauces are almost always finished with butter. Even if fish or meat is sautéed in another fat, the fat is poured off and butter is added to the pan to make the sauce. And, of course, there are the sauces of which butter is the main ingredient: the compound or flavored butters and hollandaise and its variations.

Compound Butters

I CONFESS that it was not until I came to this country that I learned to spread butter on my bread, something not at all usual in France, where one is more likely to find a pat of seasoned butter melting on grilled fish or meat. To make such *beurres composés*, or compound butters, the butter must be whipped to creamy consistency, but it must not be melted, or even softened to the point where it becomes oily. If the flavoring to be added includes lemon juice or another liquid, the liquid must be worked into the creamed butter very gradually, almost drop by drop. The finished butter must not be chilled in the refrigerator; excess chilling encourages the liquid to separate from the fat. Let the butter become firm in a cool place. If you like, the butter may be forced through a pastry tube to make an attractive garnish. Allow about 1 tablespoon compound butter for each portion of meat or fish. Compound butters are also used to enhance the flavor of bland sauces, and are spread on canapés as a base for other mixtures.

ALMOND BUTTER   *Beurre d'Amandes*

POUND 1/2 cup blanched almonds to a paste, adding a little water if necessary. Gradually add 1/4 pound butter. Rub through a fine sieve. Use in cream sauce for chicken sauté.

ANCHOVY BUTTER   *Beurre d'Anchois*

CREAM 6 tablespoons butter until it is very soft, and gradually add 2 teaspoons anchovy paste or 2 pounded filets. For broiled or sautéed fish.

Beurre Bercy BERCY BUTTER

COOK 4 shallots, finely chopped, in 3/4 cup dry white wine until the wine it reduced to 1/4 the original quantity. Cool the mixture. Cream 4 tablespoons butter with 2 teaspoons chopped parsley and season with a little salt and pepper. Add the shallots and liquid little by little. For broiled steak or chops.

Beurre Carlton CARLTON BUTTER

CREAM 6 tablespoons butter until it is very soft, and gradually add 2 teaspoons each of finely chopped chutney and chili sauce and 1 teaspoon Worcestershire sauce. For broiled or sautéed fish.

Beurre Colbert COLBERT BUTTER

TO 1/2 cup maître d'hôtel butter add 1/2 teaspoon each of melted beef extract, or *glace de viande*, and chopped tarragon. For broiled or sautéed fish.

Beurre d'Écrevisses CRAYFISH BUTTER

MAKE a *mirepoix*. Put 1 onion and 1 carrot, both finely diced, 1 small bay leaf, and a little thyme in a saucepan with 1 tablespoon butter and cook slowly for a few minutes. On this *mirepoix* put the finely chopped carcasses of 12 to 15 crayfish, cook all together slowly for about 30 minutes and let the mixture cool. Add 1/4 pound butter and pound all together until the butter becomes creamy. Rub through a fine sieve. The butter should have a good pink color. For finishing fish sauces.

Beurre Vert GREEN BUTTER

PARBOIL 6 to 8 spinach leaves, 2 chopped shallots, 1 tablespoon parsley, and 1 teaspoon each of chervil and tarragon leaves in water to cover for 5 minutes. Drain the greens and plunge them immediately into cold water. Drain them again and dry them on a towel. Pound the greens to a paste, add gradually 4 to 6 tablespoons butter, and cream the mixture until the butter is very soft. Rub it through a fine sieve. For broiled or sautéed fish and for finishing cream sauce for broiled poultry.

GARLIC BUTTER *Beurre d'Ail*

BOIL 6 cloves of garlic in water to cover for 5 to 6 minutes, and drain and crush them. Gradually add 6 tablespoons butter, cream it until soft, and rub through a fine sieve. Or, cream 6 tablespoons butter until it is very soft and gradually add 3 cloves puréed garlic. For fish or baked oysters.

LOBSTER BUTTER *Beurre de Homard*

POUND together about 1 pound cooked lobster shell plus any of the creamy part of the lobster that clings to it and the coral, if available, along with 1/4 pound butter. Melt the mixture slowly in the top of a double boiler, strain it through cheesecloth, and let it cool. Any small particles of shell that may have passed through the cloth will sink to the bottom of the pan. Spoon the butter off the top. For finishing fish sauces.

MARCHAND DE VINS BUTTER *Beurre Marchand de Vins*

COOK 4 shallots, finely chopped, in 3/4 cup good red wine until the wine is reduced to 1/4 the original quantity. Let the mixture cool. Cream 4 tablespoons butter with 1 teaspoon chopped parsley and season with a little salt and pepper. Add the shallots and liquid little by little. For broiled steak or chops.

MAÎTRE D'HÔTEL BUTTER *Beurre à la Maître d'Hôtel*

CREAM 1/4 pound butter with 1/2 teaspoon chopped parsley, the juice of 1/2 lemon, and a little salt and pepper. For broiled meat, poultry, fish.

MONTPELLIER BUTTER *Beurre Montpellier*

PARBOIL 1 cup spinach leaves and 1/4 cup each of the leaves of water cress, tarragon, parsley, and chervil in water to cover for 5 minutes. Drain the greens and plunge them immediately into cold water. Drain them again and dry them on a towel. Pound the greens to a paste.

Parboil 2 finely chopped shallots in water to cover for 5 minutes and drain them. Combine them with 1 sour pickle, finely chopped, 1 tablespoon capers, 1 anchovy filet, and 1 clove of garlic, chopped, and pound all to a paste. Combine this mixture with the pounded greens and add the mashed yolks of 2 hard-cooked eggs. Cream 1/2 pound butter and gradually add the prepared paste. When all is thoroughly blended, add 2 tablespoons salad oil and salt and pepper to taste, and rub through a fine sieve. For any hot fish.

Beurre de Paprika   PAPRIKA BUTTER

MELT 2 tablespoons butter in a saucepan, add 1/2 onion, chopped, and cook until light brown. Add 1 teaspoon paprika, mix well, and let cool. Add 4 tablespoons creamed butter and rub through a fine sieve. For broiled poultry or fish or to finish a paprika sauce.

Beurre d'Echalote   SHALLOT BUTTER

PARBOIL 4 teaspoons finely chopped shallots in a little water for 1 or 2 minutes. Drain and dry in a towel. Add the shallots to 6 tablespoons butter, cream the butter, crushing the shallots, and rub through a fine sieve. A little finely chopped chive may be added, if desired. For broiled meat, poultry, fish.

Beurre de Crevettes   SHRIMP BUTTER

POUND 12 to 15 cooked shrimp very fine with 1/4 pound butter, until the butter is soft and creamy. Rub through a fine sieve. For hot fish and to finish hot fish sauces.

Beurre de Tomates   TOMATO BUTTER

PEEL, seed, and chop 4 ripe tomatoes, and cook them until all the surplus moisture is cooked away. Let the mixture cool. Stir in 4 tablespoons creamed butter and rub through a fine sieve. For fish, meat, poultry.

Beurre d'Estragon   TARRAGON BUTTER

PARBOIL 6 tablespoons tarragon leaves in a little water for 2 or 3 minutes. Drain and dry on a towel. Gradually add 6 tablespoons butter, cream the mixture, crushing the leaves, and rub through a fine sieve. For broiled meat, poultry, fish.

WHITE BUTTER   *Beurre Blanc*

SIMMER 2 finely chopped shallots in 1/2 cup vinegar until the liquid is reduced to 2 tablespoons and cool it. Cream 6 tablespoons butter until it is very soft and gradually add the vinegar and shallot mixture, 1 teaspoon chopped parsley, and salt and pepper to taste. For poached freshwater fish.

These butter sauces are served hot.

BROWN BUTTER   *Beurre Noisette*

MELT butter—1 tablespoon for each serving—and cook slowly until it is hazelnut brown. For vegetables and fish.

BLACK BUTTER   *Beurre Noir*

COOK brown butter until it is very dark brown, almost black. Slow cooking will insure a more even browning and a better flavor. For calf's brains and vegetables.

MEUNIÈRE BUTTER   *Beurre à la Meunière*

ADD a little lemon juice and a little chopped parsley to brown butter. For broiled or sautéed fish. *Beurre meunière* is further described in the paragraphs on the sautéing of fish.

MUSTARD BUTTER   *Beurre de Moutarde*

ADD 2 teaspoons prepared mustard, little by little, to 6 tablespoons melted butter. For fish.

POLONAISE SAUCE   *Sauce Polonaise*

COOK 1/4 pound butter slowly to a light brown, adding 2 tablespoons fine fresh or dry white bread crumbs. Continue cooking until butter and crumbs are hazelnut brown. When the sauce is done, the butter stops bubbling and " falls down. " For vegetables such as cauliflower, broccoli, or asparagus. If desired, finely chopped hard-cooked eggs may also be sprinkled over the vegetable. Use polonaise sauce also for noodles and other pastas.

A GOOD hollandaise sauce has a rich yellow color, a tart flavor, and a fluffy texture somewhat resembling that of mayonnaise. Since it is essentially a mixture of cooked egg yolks, hollandaise has a tendency to curdle, but simple precautions can prevent this.

Whip the eggs in the top of a double boiler over hot water. Keep the water just below the boiling point; if it starts to bubble, cool it at *once* with a spoonful of cold water. Add the butter to the egg yolks in small portions and be sure that each bit is thoroughly incorporated before adding more. The sauce should be removed from the heat as soon as it is done. If necessary it may be kept warm in a warm place for no more than 30 minutes. Stir it from time to time as it waits. If all precautions fail and the hollandaise curdles, whip an egg yolk in another pan over hot water and gradually and thoroughly whip into it the curdled sauce.

Sauce Hollandaise

HOLLANDAISE SAUCE

HAVE 1/2 pound butter at room temperature. Combine 3 egg yolks and 1 tablespoon water in the top of a double boiler, over hot but not boiling water, and stir the mixture briskly with a wire whip until it is light and fluffy. Add some of the butter—not more than 1/3—and whip constantly until the mixture thickens slightly. Add the remainder of the butter in at least 2 parts, stirring briskly. Allow the mixture to thicken after each addition. Season to taste with salt and a little lemon juice. For a lighter sauce, thin with 1 tablespoon hot water. For poached fish and vegetables such as asparagus, artichokes, and cauliflower.

Sauce Maltaise

MALTAISE SAUCE

BLEND 3 tablespoons orange juice and 1/2 teaspoon grated orange rind into 1 cup hollandaise sauce, just before serving. Add a little red vegetable color for a pink color, if necessary. For asparagus and similar vegetables.

MOUSSELINE SAUCE

Sauce Mousseline

FOLD 2 tablespoons whipped cream into 1 cup hollandaise sauce, just before serving. Use instead of hollandaise for asparagus and other vegetables and for eggs and poached fish.

Béarnaise sauce is a first cousin of hollandaise. It has an added piquancy which comes from herbs, wine, and vinegar.

BÉARNAISE SAUCE

Sauce Béarnaise

HAVE 1/2 pound butter at room temperature. In the top of a double boiler, combine 3 sprigs each of tarragon and chervil and 2 shallots, all finely chopped, and 1/4 cup each of tarragon vinegar and white wine. Cook over direct heat until the mixture is reduced to a thick paste and let it cool slightly. Put the pan over hot but not boiling water, add 3 egg yolks and 1 tablespoon water and stir briskly with a wire whip until the mixture is light and fluffy. Add some of the butter—not more than 1/3—and whip constantly until the mixture thickens slightly. Add the remainder of the butter in at least 2 parts, stirring briskly. Allow the mixture to thicken after each addition. Season to taste with salt and a pinch of cayenne and strain through a fine sieve. Add 3 sprigs each of tarragon and chervil, both finely chopped. For broiled and sautéed meats and fish.

TOMATO BÉARNAISE SAUCE

Sauce Choron

ADD 1/4 cup hot tomato purée, or tomato sauce reduced until it is very thick, to 1 cup béarnaise sauce. For broiled meat, poultry, fish.

FOYON SAUCE

Sauce Foyon

ADD 1 teaspoon melted beef extract, or *glace de viande*, to 1 cup béarnaise sauce, for a light brown color. For eggs or broiled chicken.

Cold

Sauces

IN AMERICA we tend to think of mayonnaise and French dressing, or vinaigrette, primarily, if not exclusively, as salad dressings, which in fact they may be. But they are more than salad dressings; they are also the most important of the cold sauces that add piquancy and flavor to cold meats, poultry, fish, and vegetables. They serve to complement and garnish elaborate aspic preparations on the buffet, and to make last night's roast, served cold in thin slices, into a savory supper dish. They are indeed versatile. Cold sauces go with some hot foods as well: cold *sauce rémoulade* with sautéed fish, vinaigrette with asparagus or broccoli, horseradish-flavored *sauce Mona Lisa* with hot tongue. The cold sauces give distinction to the assortment of hors-d'oeuvre served regularly at luncheon even in modest French homes, which might consist largely of odds and ends of cooked vegetables, meat, and fish made savory and appetizing with well-seasoned cold sauces.

Vinaigrette and Its Variations

BEFORE YOU read this paragraph, refer to the section on vinaigrette in the chapter devoted to salads. The rules mentioned there for choosing ingredients should be heeded carefully, for off-flavor oil and too-acid vinegar can spoil any sauce. At home we used wine vinegar. When the

Wine
Vinegar

contents of the vinegar cruet became low, my mother would replenish it with the wine left in the bottle after we had finished our meal. Sometimes, or so my father teasingly said, *maman* did not wait until father had had his fill of wine before she slyly made off with the wine bottle. In any case, when the table wine was added to the mother of vinegar in the cruet, it made a fine, mild vinegar just right for *sauce vinaigrette*.

The names " vinaigrette " and " French dressing " are interchangeable, but in popular usage, the simple mixture of oil, vinegar, and seasonings used for tossed salads is called French dressing. Vinaigrette is either the simple mixture or it has chopped hard-cooked eggs, capers, and the like added to it.

VINAIGRETTE SAUCE OR FRENCH DRESSING

Sauce Vinaigrette

MIX thoroughly 1 tablespoon vinegar and 3 to 4 tablespoons olive oil, as desired and depending upon the strength of the vinegar. Add 1/2 teaspoon salt, a little pepper, and, if desired, 1/2 teaspoon dry or prepared mustard and mix well.

VINAIGRETTE WITH HERBS *Vinaigrette aux Fines Herbes*

MIX thoroughly 1 tablespoon vinegar and 3 to 4 tablespoons olive oil and add 1/4 teaspoon prepared mustard and 1 teaspoon mixed chopped parsley, tarragon, chervil, and chives.

VINAIGRETTE WITH MUSTARD *Vinaigrette à la Moutarde*

MIX thoroughly 1 teaspoon prepared mustard, a little salt, a little pepper, and either 1 teaspoon lemon juice or 1 tablespoon vinegar. Add gradually 4 tablespoons olive oil, stirring vigorously.

VINAIGRETTE FOR HORS-D'OEUVRE *Vinaigrette pour Hors-d'Oeuvre*

MIX thoroughly 2 tablespoons vinegar and 3 tablespoons olive oil. Add 1 teaspoon salt, a little pepper, 1 teaspoon each of capers, chopped parsley, tarragon, chives, and chervil, and 1 tablespoon chopped hard-cooked egg.

LORENZO DRESSING *Sauce Lorenzo*

MIX 1/2 cup chili sauce with 3/4 cup olive oil, 1/4 cup vinegar, 1 1/2 teaspoons salt, and 1/4 teaspoon pepper. Add some finely chopped water cress and combine well. For hors-d'oeuvre such as sliced tomatoes, and for green salads, and cold meat salads.

Sauce Ravigote RAVIGOTE SAUCE

MIX thoroughly 2 tablespoons vinegar and 5 tablespoons olive oil and add 1/2 onion, finely chopped, 1 tablespoon prepared mustard, 1 chopped hard-cooked egg, 1 teaspoon mixed chopped parsley, tarragon, chives, or chervil, and salt and pepper to taste. For cold cooked meat and fish.

Sauce Moutarde à la Crème CREAM MUSTARD DRESSING

MIX 1 teaspoon prepared mustard, a little salt, a little pepper, and a few drops lemon juice. Add 1/2 cup heavy cream, plain or whipped, little by little, stirring vigorously until the mixture is well combined. For cold cooked meat or fish.

Mayonnaise and Its Variations

DESERVEDLY or not, Cardinal Richelieu is credited with the discovery of mayonnaise, the delicately flavored, uniquely light and smooth mixture of oil, egg yolks, and lemon juice that is perhaps the most popular of the cold sauces. In any case, mayonnaise is made today in exactly the same way as it was made back in the seventeenth century, except that one may, using great care, combine the emulsion with an electric beater instead of a wire whip. Making mayonnaise presents only one problem; it may curdle or separate. For consistent success, have the egg yolks and the oil—a light, delicately flavored oil is best—at room temperature, and beat the oil into the egg yolks very gradually, drop by drop at first, and finally in a thin stream. Follow the directions precisely and you should have no trouble; if something does go wrong, and the mayonnaise separates, you can restore the emulsion. Wash the beater and in another bowl beat an egg yolk with 1/2 teaspoon water or vinegar. Gradually beat in the curdled mayonnaise, a teaspoon at a time at first, then more quickly. Store your mayonnaise in a cool place, but not in the refrigerator; excessive cold will cause it to separate.

MAYONNAISE

Sauce Mayonnaise

RINSE a mixing bowl with hot water and dry it well. Put in it 2 egg yolks, 1/2 teaspoon salt, a little white pepper, 1/2 teaspoon dry mustard and 1 teaspoon vinegar. Beat the mixture vigorously with a whisk or at low speed in an electric mixer and add 1 cup olive oil or a good salad oil drop by drop, until a little more than 1/4 cup oil has been added. Add 1/2 teaspoon vinegar, still beating, and then pour in the rest of the oil in a thin stream. Beat continually and stop adding the oil from time to time to make sure that the mixture is well blended. When all the oil has been added, finish with 1/2 teaspoon vinegar. Lemon or lime juice may replace the vinegar in the mayonnaise, and prepared mustard to taste may be substituted for the dry mustard.

Mayonnaise to be stored will stand up better if 1 tablespoon boiling water is mixed into it after the last of the oil has been added.

Every chef has a favorite mayonnaise variation, every cookbook offers others. These are classic.

MINT MAYONNAISE

Sauce Mayonnaise à la Menthe

BRING 1/2 cup vinegar to a boil and pour it over 1 tablespoon chopped mint leaves. Let the mixture infuse for a few minutes. Cool, strain, and use in place of plain vinegar in mayonnaise. Add a few chopped mint leaves to the finished mayonnaise. For cold vegetables such as broccoli or cold fish.

Sauce Mayonnaise à la Crème Fouettée   LIGHT MAYONNAISE

ADD the juice of 1/2 lemon to 1 cup mayonnaise and fold in 2 tablespoons whipped cream. For fruit salads.

Sauce Verte   GREEN SAUCE

WASH thoroughly 15 water cress leaves, 12 spinach leaves, and 8 sprigs of parsley stripped from the stems. Cover them with boiling salted water and let stand for 5 or 6 minutes. Drain the greens, plunge them in cold water, and drain again, pressing out all the surplus water. Rub the wilted leaves through a fine sieve and combine with 2 cups mayonnaise. For cold lobster, salmon, striped bass, or other fish and shellfish.

Sauce Vincent   VINCENT SAUCE

FOLLOW the recipe for green sauce, adding 15 sorrel leaves to the other greens. The finished sauce is sometimes seasoned with chopped tarragon and chives. For fried whitebait, oyster crabs, or soft-shell crabs, and for cold fish and shellfish.

Sauce Rémoulade   RÉMOULADE SAUCE

PRESS all the moisture from 1/2 cup finely chopped sour pickles and 2 tablespoons finely chopped capers and add to 2 cups mayonnaise with 1 tablespoon prepared mustard and 1 tablespoon mixed chopped parsley, tarragon, and chervil. For fried or cold poached fish and shellfish.

Sauce Tartare   TARTARE SAUCE

To 2 cups rémoulade sauce, add 6 ripe olives, finely chopped, and 1 teaspoon chopped chives. For fried fish and shellfish.

Sauce Niçoise   NIÇOISE SAUCE

COOK 1/2 cup tomato purée, stirring constantly, until most of the moisture evaporates and the purée is very thick. Chill the purée and add it to 2 cups mayonnaise. Add also 1 red or green pepper, chopped very fine, and 1 teaspoon mixed chopped tarragon and chives. For cold fish or shellfish.

AÏOLI SAUCE   *Sauce Aïoli*

CRUSH 4 small cloves of garlic very thoroughly and combine with 1/2 teaspoon salt and 2 egg yolks. Add 1 cup olive oil, a few drops at a time, until 5 or 6 drops have been added, then continue adding it in a thin stream as in making mayonnaise. If the mixture becomes too thick, add a little warm water. Some chefs add 1/2 cup mashed potato, cold or lukewarm, on the theory that it will prevent the sauce from separating. After all the oil is added, add the juice of 1/2 lemon. For hot or cold fish.

RUSSIAN DRESSING   *Sauce Russe*

ADD 3 tablespoons chili sauce and 1 teaspoon each of pimiento and chives, both finely chopped, to 1 cup mayonnaise. For cold eggs and vegetables, and for shellfish.

RUSSIAN DRESSING FOR SHELLFISH   *Sauce Russe pour Crustacés*

MIX the tomalley and coral of a cooked lobster with 1 tablespoon caviar and rub the mixture through a fine sieve. Add 1 teaspoon prepared mustard and combine with 1 to 1 1/2 cups mayonnaise. Add 1 teaspoon finely chopped chives and parsley and mix well. For cold shellfish.

MONA LISA DRESSING   *Sauce Mona Lisa*

ADD 1 teaspoon each of paprika, horseradish, and dry English mustard to 1 cup mayonnaise. Fold in 2 tablespoons very heavy cream, plain or whipped. For meat.

Sauce à la Ritz   RITZ SAUCE

ADD 1 tablespoon chili sauce, 1/4 teaspoon Worcestershire sauce, 1 fresh tomato, peeled, seeded, and finely chopped, and 1 teaspoon mixed finely chopped chives, chervil, and parsley to 1 cup mayonnaise and mix well. For sea-food cocktails.

Sauce Thousand Island   THOUSAND ISLAND DRESSING

IN the recipe for Ritz sauce, substitute 1/2 teaspoon each of chopped pimiento and chives for the mixed herbs. For eggs and vegetables.

Sauce Gribiche   GRIBICHE SAUCE

SAUCE *gribiche* has the richness of mayonnaise, but is not a mayonnaise.

Crush 3 hard-cooked egg yolks and rub them with a wooden spoon until they are very smooth. Add 1 teaspoon mustard, 1/2 teaspoon salt, and a little pepper. Beat in 1 1/2 cups olive oil, little by little, as in making mayonnaise, and add 1/2 cup vinegar, stirring constantly. Add 3 hard-cooked egg whites, chopped fine, 1/2 cup chopped sour pickles, from which all the moisture has been pressed, and 1 tablespoon mixed chopped parsley, chervil, tarragon, and chives. For chicken, fish, and shellfish, cold boiled beef, and calf's feet and brains.

MÉTHODES CULINAIRES

Methods of Cooking

T HERE is more than one way of learning how to prepare meats, poultry, and fish, and most cookbooks teach by giving separate instructions for each kind of food. However, that is not the way a French chef is trained. He does not learn how to cook beef in all possible ways, then lamb, then other meats and birds, *mais non*. He first learns the cookery methods that apply to all foods, and then concentrates on discovering the advantages and limitations of each method for specific foods. To me this system seems most logical. It has worked in the training of generations of chefs, *une grande recommandation, n'est-ce-pas?* And since the purpose of this book is to make every reader a skillful cook, that is the way I have approached the subject here.

If you have learned the techniques of roasting, for instance, you can apply them as readily to lamb as to beef; then if your butcher cannot supply you with the rib roast you had planned for dinner, or suggests that leg of lamb is a better buy at this time, it is a simple matter for you to alter your decision. This holds true for the various cuts of meat and the birds that are suitable for stewing and braising, and therefore more economical, and for various kinds and sizes of fish. If, for instance, you associate a tightly covered casserole and "*aromates*," such as carrots and onions, with braising, you are on your way to knowing how to braise anything at all.

The end result of learning the basic cookery methods and how they apply to various foods is that you develop versatility and flexibility obtainable in no other way. You come to understand recipes far more quickly and easily—the very reading of them can be a pleasure—and you become, also, less dependent on them. And this kind of assurance is, I believe, a test of a good cook.

Sautéing

IN FRANCE, where I was raised, fuel for cooking was always at a premium. Only the big hotels roasted lamb, beef, and poultry every day. Only the big brick oven of the *boulanger* baked loaves of crusty bread, which we youngsters were sent to buy each day, and the *pâtisserie* was the source of those irresistible sweet cakes, the *gâteaux*, *petits fours*, and *friandises*. But my mother and my grandmother knew ways of cooking that did not require great quantities of the carefully hoarded *fagots*. They could encourage the slowly rising bubbles in the big clay *marmite* with the merest handful of twigs, for instance. But many foods are so tender that they would fall to pieces in the *marmite*. Besides, they need outside crispness, a golden-brown crustiness, to contrast with their tenderness and seal in their special succulence. For foods like these, *maman* brought out the big black skillet. Just a few of the precious faggots could supply the heat for it.

To a French cook, there are only two permissible kinds of frying: deep frying, which requires a deep pan and fat deep enough to float the food as it cooks, and sautéing, cooking in a shallow skillet in just enough fat to keep the food from sticking. There is no word in French for the irregular, unclassified kind of frying that has given a bad name to the whole process. *Maman* would have been aghast to see delicate filets of fish or tender scallops of veal half submerged in fat possibly not quite fresh, and certainly not quite hot enough. When *maman* fried fish, or sautéed it, it was never dried out, never fat-soaked. I still abide by her rules, which I now pass on to you.

Only very tender foods are suitable for sautéing. Fish, young chicken, the loin and rib chops of lamb, pork, or veal, liver, hamburger patties, beef filets, onions, mushrooms, and the like can be cooked by this quick method. Thick slices of meat cannot be successfully sautéed. Very thin slices, or *escalopes*, of veal or beef can be cooked this way with far better results than can 2-inch steaks, for instance. Finally, the food should not be crowded in the pan and the pan should not be covered, because the steam thus held in will moisten and destroy the crispness of the surface.

About the pan itself. In France it is called either a *sauteuse* or *sautoir*, in America, frying pan or skillet. The sides, never deeper than 2 inches, may slant out or be straight. If the sides flare, the steam escapes more quickly and this helps to maintain a crisper surface. Different metals are used: there are old-fashioned skillets of cast-iron or tin-lined copper, the more modern aluminum, the copper-and-stainless-steel combinations, and the iron pans coated with colored enamels. All of them are excellent if—and this is very important—the metal is thick enough. Because sautéing is done over brisk heat, a very heavy metal pan that will diffuse the heat evenly is a necessity. Otherwise the food will not brown evenly and often will not be cooked through. Thin pans may overcook or even scorch the surface of the food before the inside is done. Also, when food is sautéed, the entire surface should touch the bottom of the pan at once; thin metal tends to warp with use, so that the food browns unevenly. The pan must be large enough to accommodate all the food easily, or it will steam and not be crisp. If necessary, use 2 pans.

When a French girl marries and leaves her mother's home for her

Pan for Sautéing

97

own, she always takes with her at least one *sauteuse*. My mother's *sauteuses* had sides that flared a little and very long handles, because they had been passed down in her family from the time when most cooking was done in open fireplaces, and long-handled pans were essential. The forks for turning food were long-handled, too. My little *grand-mère* dispensed with the fork. She was very skillful at turning food by tossing it up in the air, which is, incidentally, the way this kind of cooking got its name: *sauter* means to jump. Everyone treasured the old pans. Generations of use with fat and heat had seasoned them well, and seasoning is important to iron pans, which rust easily and do not cook so well when they are new.

To Season a New Iron Pan

An initial seasoning should be given an iron pan to get it off to a good start. Clean the pan thoroughly and dry it; put in half an inch or more of unsalted fat or oil and heat it very slowly on top of the stove or in a slow oven until the fat is very hot. Let the pan cool with the fat in it. Discard the fat and wipe out the pan with a paper towel.

Fat for Sautéing

The fat you choose for sautéing depends upon your personal preference and sometimes on your pocketbook. You may like a certain kind of fat because you have learned the "feel" of it, so that you can tell by its appearance or odor when it is hot enough.

In fine cooking and in preparing delicately flavored foods, butter is the favorite fat. Meat, poultry, or fish may be cooked in it. However, melted butter has a milky sediment that settles in the pan and scorches easily. Clarified butter is therefore used for sautéing. To clarify butter, heat it in a small pan until a froth rises. Spoon off the froth and pour the clear oil off the sediment.

Clarified Butter

Beef or Pork Drippings

In sautéing meat or poultry, you may use fresh beef or pork drippings from the roasting pan. Spoon the fat out of the pan as it accumulates. By the time the roast is cooked the drippings are usually overcooked and unsatisfactory for sautéing. Store the drippings in the refrigerator but don't keep them too long.

Goose Fat Salad Oil

Goose fat is excellent, second only to butter. You may also use a good salad oil.

Lamb fat, which has a strong flavor, is not recommended, and chicken fat, which has a very individual flavor, is not suitable for general use.

However, the rule is that if any fat other than butter is used for sautéing, it is discarded when the cooked food is removed (though the pan is not washed) and butter is added to make the pan sauce.

Some people like sautéed foods just as they come from the pan, without an accompaniment, some prefer only browned butter, and some want a sauce. Browned butter is simple to make: discard the fat the food was cooked in and brown some butter in the pan, about 1/2 to 1 tablespoon for each serving. If desired, a few drops of lemon juice and some finely chopped parsley can be sprinkled on the food, too.

Browned Butter

Pan Sauce for Sautéed Meat or Poultry

To make a simple pan sauce, discard the cooking fat (if it was not butter), add either stock or wine—about 2 tablespoons for each serving—and let it bubble up, stirring in all the brown particles that cling to the bottom and sides of the pan. This is called deglazing. Cook the liquid until it is reduced by half. Add salt to taste and if desired a little pepper. Swirl in 1 or 2 tablespoons butter for each 3/4 cup sauce, by moving the pan in a circular motion to distribute the butter as it melts. Don't let the butter cook. Remove the pan from the heat and pour the sauce over the food as soon as the butter melts. This gives the sauce just a little additional body and an attractive sheen.

Deglazing

A more elaborate pan sauce is made by adding butter to the pan after the fat is discarded and cooking a little finely chopped shallot or onion in it until the pieces are soft. Do not let them brown. Use 1 1/2 tablespoons butter and 2 teaspoons shallot or onion to serve 6. Add 2 tablespoons stock or wine for each serving, deglaze the pan, cook until the liquid is reduced by half, and swirl in a little butter. The combination of butter, shallots, and wine is a basic French flavor characteristic.

If you want more sauce or a slightly different texture and flavor, add a mere pinch of flour to the butter and shallots and, after the wine or stock has bubbled and reduced a little, add some canned tomatoes or tomato sauce. Finish by swirling in butter.

To make a mushroom pan sauce, add the butter, 1/2 pound cleaned, sliced mushrooms, and a tablespoon finely chopped shallot or onion. Cook until the mushrooms are soft. Add 1/4 to 1/2 cup stock or brown sauce and cook for a few minutes.

Mushroom Pan Sauce

Use brown or white stock, depending on the food cooked, and red or white wine. For veal or chicken, it is usual to use white wine.

In the recipes that follow you will find variations of these pan sauces. Many may be used equally well with steaks, chops, hamburger, or liver.

Sautéing Meat

Use any of the fats suggested. For pork chops or beef the best fat is its own, trimmed from the edges. Heat this suet or pork fat until the fat has cooked out and discard the brown cracklings that remain. This process is called "rendering" or "trying out."

Heat the fat very hot for sautéing meat, so that it will sear and seal the surface immediately. Then finish the cooking quickly, over brisk heat. Beef, lamb, or liver, or any meat that is to be cooked only to the rare stage will be done by the time both sides are browned, providing that it is not much more than a half inch thick. In cooking meats like pork and veal, which should be well done, brown the meat, turn down the heat, and cook it slowly until it is well done. To test sautéed meat for doneness, prick it with a sharp-tined kitchen fork. If the juice that comes out is clear, with no tinge of pink, the meat is well done; if the juice has a pink tinge, the meat is still rather rare. A good cook watches the food as it cooks and learns to recognize the various stages of browning and cooking and knows when to increase or decrease the heat.

To Test
Sautéed Meat

Tournedos
Sautés

SAUTÉED SLICED FILET

Tournedos are slices of filet of beef cut from a section near the end. Season 6 *tournedos*, cut less than 1 1/2 inches thick, with salt and pepper. Heat enough clarified butter in a skillet to cover the bottom of the pan well. Arrange the pieces of meat side by side and brown them over high heat for 2 to 5 minutes on each side, depending on the thickness of the meat and the degree of doneness desired. Remove the meat to a serving dish. Add 1/4 to 1/2 cup stock or red wine to the pan and cook, stirring in all the brown bits, until the liquid is reduced by half. Swirl in 1 tablespoon butter and pour the sauce over the meat.

SAUTÉED TOURNEDOS WITH GOOSE LIVER

Tournedos Rossini

CUT 6 slices of goose liver or *pâté de foie gras* about 1/4 inch thick, roll them in flour, and sauté them in hot butter or goose fat until they are golden brown on both sides. Sauté 6 *tournedos* in hot butter for 2 to 5 minutes on each side, or until they are medium rare. Arrange the *tournedos* side by side on a hot serving dish and place a slice of the cooked liver or pâté on each. Keep them warm. Discard the fat from the pan, add 2 tablespoons sweet butter, 4 to 6 chopped truffles, a little juice from the truffle can, and 1/4 cup Madeira or Sherry, and cook for 1 minute, stirring in all the brown bits. Add 1 cup brown sauce and 2 tablespoons *glace de viande*, or beef extract, and cook the mixture until it is reduced to 2/3 the original quantity. Correct the seasoning with salt, add a little pepper, and stir in another 2 tablespoons Madeira or Sherry. Pour the sauce over all. Accompany with potatoes *noisette*.

Madeira Pan Sauce

The pan sauce can be made without the truffles or truffle juice and is suitable for other sautéed meats and chicken.

HAMBURGER WITH RED WINE SAUCE

Bifteck au Vin Rouge

MIX 1 1/2 pounds chopped lean beef with a little salt and 3 tablespoons water or cream and shape the meat lightly into flat cakes about 3/4 inch thick. The moisture and light handling insure succulence. Heat enough suet or good fat in a skillet to cover the bottom generously. Cook the meat 3 to 4 minutes on each side, for hamburgers that are to be served rare. Remove the meat to a serving dish. Discard the fat from the pan, but do not wash the pan. Add 1 tablespoon butter and in it cook 1 teaspoon chopped shallot or onion until the onion is soft. Add 1/2 cup red wine and cook, stirring in all the brown bits, until the wine is reduced a little. Pour the sauce over the meat.

SAUTÉED VEAL SCALLOPS WITH BUTTER SAUCE

Escalopes de Veau Sautées au Beurre

FOR each serving allow about 1/3 pound veal cut from the leg in slices less than 1/2 inch thick. Have the butcher flatten each piece with a mallet. Season the scallops with salt and pepper and rub them with a little flour. For 6 servings, heat 3 tablespoons clarified butter in a large heavy skillet.

Sauté the pieces until they are golden brown on each side, about 7 minutes in all. Remove the scallops to a serving dish and pour the butter over them. Add 1/4 cup stock or white wine to the pan and cook, stirring in all the brown bits. Pour the sauce over the meat and sprinkle with finely chopped parsley.

SAUTÉED VEAL SCALLOPS HUNTER STYLE

Escalopes de Veau Sautées Chasseur

PREPARE veal scallops as in veal scallops with butter sauce, but after removing the meat to a serving dish, add to the butter in the pan 1/2 pound mushrooms, cleaned and sliced. Cook the mushrooms slowly until they are soft. Add 1 tablespoon finely chopped shallots or onion and about 1/2 cup white wine. Cook the wine until it is reduced to 1/2 the original quantity and add 1/4 cup tomato purée and 1 teaspoon beef extract. Cook the sauce for a few minutes and add 1 tablespoon chopped parsley and a little chopped tarragon. Pour the sauce over the meat.

SAUTÉED VEAL CHOPS WITH TARRAGON

Côtes de Veau à l'Estragon

To Blanch Tarragon

SEASON 6 veal chops, 1 inch thick, with salt and pepper and rub them with flour. Sauté the chops slowly in 3 tablespoons melted butter for about 12 to 15 minutes on each side and arrange them on a serving platter.

Parboil 30 of the choicest leaves from 6 sprigs of tarragon in a little boiling salted water for 1 minute, drain them, and plunge them into cold water. Chop the remaining tarragon sprigs and add them to the pan in which the chops have been cooked. Add 1/3 cup white wine and cook for a few minutes, stirring in all the brown bits. Add 3/4 cup veal stock and 1 teaspoon beef extract and bring the sauce to a boil. Decorate the veal chops with the parboiled tarragon leaves and strain the gravy over them.

GRANDMOTHER'S VEAL CHOPS

Côtes de Veau à la Grand-mère

SEASON 6 veal chops, 1 inch thick, with salt and pepper and rub them with flour. Melt 3 tablespoons butter, add 1/3 pound fat salt pork or bacon, diced, parboiled for 5 minutes, and drained, and cook until the dice are golden brown. Set the dice aside. Arrange the chops in the pan with 16 small parboiled onions and sauté over gentle heat 5 minutes. Add 3 large potatoes, diced, and continue to cook for about 25 minutes, turning the chops and moving the onions around to brown them evenly. Remove the chops and vegetables, add 3/4 cup stock or water to the pan, and cook for a few minutes, stirring in all the brown bits. Return the chops, vegetables, and pork dice to the pan and cook about 5 minutes longer to reheat them. Sautéed mushrooms may be added, if desired.

SAUTÉED LAMB CHOPS

Côtelettes d'Agneau Sautées

SEASON 6 lamb chops, cut about 1 inch thick, with salt and pepper. Heat enough clarified butter in a skillet to cover the bottom. Cook the chops for 3 to 5 minutes on each side, depending on the degree of doneness desired. Remove the chops to a warm platter. Add to the pan 1/2 tablespoon butter for each serving, cook the butter until it is hazelnut brown, and pour it over the chops.

KERNEL OF LAMB WITH GOOSE LIVER

Noisette d'Agneau Montpensier

CAREFULLY remove the meat from each side of a saddle of lamb, cutting it out in lengthwise pieces. Trim away any sinews. Cut each piece crosswise into 4 or 6 slices and sauté the slices in good fat for 3 to 5 minutes on each side. The meat should be a little pink when done *à point*. Place a slice of sautéed goose liver on each piece of meat and on the goose liver place a slice of truffle.

SAUTÉED PORK CHOPS

Côtelettes de Porc Sautées

TRIM the surplus fat from 6 pork chops, each about 3/4 inch thick, season the chops with salt and pepper, and rub them with flour. Put the trimmings of fat in a heavy skillet and cook them slowly to render the fat; there should be enough to cover the bottom of the pan. Discard the solid bits. Sauté the chops slowly about 12 to 15 minutes on each side. Prick the meat with a fork; if the juice shows no tinge of pink, the chops are done. Remove the chops to a serving dish, discard the excess fat, and add about 1/2 cup stock or red wine to the pan. Cook slowly, stirring in all the brown bits. Skim off the fat that rises to the surface. Cook the sauce until it is reduced to about 1/2 its original quantity, correct the seasoning, and pour it over the chops.

Côtelettes de Porc Charcutière

SAUTÉED PORK CHOPS CHARCUTIÈRE

SAUTÉ 6 pork chops and remove them to a serving dish. Pour off all fat from the pan except 1 tablespoon and add 1 tablespoon clarified butter. In this mixed fat, cook 2 tablespoons finely chopped onion until it is soft and golden. Add 1/3 cup white wine and 1 tablespoon vinegar and cook the liquid until it is reduced to 3/4 the original quantity. Add 1 cup tomato purée and 1 tablespoon beef extract and continue cooking the sauce slowly for 10 to 15 minutes. Correct the seasoning with salt and add 1 teaspoon prepared mustard, 4 or 5 slices sour pickle, and 1/2 tablespoon chopped parsley. Swirl in 1 tablespoon butter. Return the chops to the pan and heat the sauce, but do not let it boil. Boiling toughens the pickles and ruins their flavor. Arrange the chops on a serving dish and pour the sauce over them.

YOU will find recipes for sautéing variety meats in the chapter on these meats.

Sautéing Poultry

THERE are many dishes prepared in a *sauteuse*, or skillet, but the most important of them—and one which every good cook should be able to make—is *poulet sauté*.

Many a *poulet sauté* my mother and my grandmother used to cook, usually simply, *à la française*, and I learned much from them. But it was on my first job, at the Hôtel du Rhin in Paris, that I learned all the chef's tricks—how to fix the leg and second joint so that they lie flat in the pan and brown evenly, how important it is to cook the skin side first, and what dreadful fate befalls the sauces if the chicken or its juices are allowed to scorch even faintly.

M. Gaunard, the *chef saucier* at the Hôtel du Rhin, was my teacher, and a kind, if exacting, master. I remember my first *poulet sauté florentine*. I was so anxious for it to be perfect that I must have washed the spinach a hundred times, to make sure no sand lurked there.

What I learned from M. Gaunard I taught to hundreds of chefs during my years at the old Ritz-Carlton, and many a fine *poulet sauté* in this country owes its good flavor and succulence to lessons learned in that roomy old kitchen belowstairs at Madison Avenue at Forty-sixth Street.

Because it is relatively simple, *poulet sauté* can be done quickly. It is varied endlessly with different sauces and garnishes—*chasseur, portugaise, printanière* and so on. In a fine restaurant, the chickens are made ready for the pan early in the day, as are also the various garnishes listed on the menu. The chickens are not cooked until they are ordered in the dining room, because there is time to do it while the guests are having their appetizers and soup.

The smaller fryers, 2 1/2 to 3 pounds, are best for sautéing and when prepared for the pan as described below one will serve 3 or 4 people. **Fryers for Sautéing**

To Prepare Chicken for Sautéing

CLEAN and singe a young chicken. To singe the bird, rotate it over a flame to burn off any fine feathers. Lay the bird breast down on a board. With a sharp knife make 2 parallel cuts down alongside the backbone and neck. The backbone and neck can then be lifted out. Lay the bird flat, skin side down. With the fingers, break the rib cage bones away from the large breast bone, and pull out the breast bone. Divide the breast with a knife and cut off the first 2 joints of the wing. Leave the main wing bone attached. You may remove the small rib cage bones from the breast filets, but the large bone that runs the length of each filet should remain. (This is a *suprême*.) Divide the filets in half crosswise, so that **To Singe a Bird**

Suprême

105

each portion has a piece of the large bone in it. This keeps the breast meat from shrinking in cooking. Cut the legs from the body. With a cleaver or kitchen shears, separate the thighs from the legs just above the cartilage that joins them. Chop off the ends of the leg bones. Dry the chicken, season it with salt and pepper, and dredge it with flour. Shake off any excess, or the loose bits will scorch and spoil the appearance and flavor of the sauce.

The pan and the kind of fat are important, as you know from reading the first part of this chapter. Salad oil or fresh unsalted pork or beef drippings can be used and poured off before the sauce is made. But clarified butter is preferred and used whenever possible.

Chicken is never sautéed in smoking hot fat, as is customary in sautéing other foods. Very hot fat shrivels the skin and cooks the flesh near the skin so quickly that it dries before that near the bone is done. The fat needs only to be heated and the bird cooked over moderately low heat. Cook the skin side first. The skin side shows when the chicken is served so cook it to a beautiful golden brown. Then turn the chicken and cook it until it is tender. It won't matter if the underside is a little pale or **To Test** slightly overbrown. Test for doneness by piercing the pieces with a **Sautéed Chicken** kitchen fork or skewer. The juice that runs out should be clear, with no pink tinge. Test each piece and remove it when it is done. White breast meat is usually done 7 or 8 minutes before the darker leg and second joint, and wings need 3 or 4 minutes longer than the breasts.

You will notice that the chicken in the dishes that follow is not crisp. Its sauce is important and is served over it.

Poulet Sauté Bordelaise

SAUTÉED CHICKEN BORDELAISE

PREPARE a 2 1/2- to 3-pound chicken for sautéing. In a skillet melt 3 tablespoons butter and arrange the pieces of chicken skin side down on it. Cook the chicken over medium heat until the skin is golden brown. Turn the pieces and cook, partly covered, for 25 to 30 minutes. Remove the breast meat to a hot serving platter and cook the remaining pieces for 5 to 10 minutes longer, or until they are tender. Remove the remaining pieces to the platter. To the juices in the pan add 1 teaspoon flour, 1 tablespoon chopped shallots or onion, and a generous 1/3 cup red wine and cook until the sauce is slightly thickened. Return the chicken to the pan and simmer it for about 5 minutes. Arrange the chicken on a serving platter and garnish with French fried onion rings and parsley, artichoke bottoms sautéed in butter until tender, and potatoes *rissolées*. Correct the seasoning of the sauce and pour it over the chicken. Serves 4.

SAUTÉED CHICKEN BERCY

Poulet Sauté Bercy

PREPARE a 2 1/2- to 3-pound chicken as for *poulet sauté bordelaise*, sautéed chicken Bordelaise. To the juices in the pan add 1 tablespoon finely chopped shallots or onion and 1 teaspoon flour. Stir in 1/4 cup white wine, 1/4 cup chicken broth, and 3 tablespoons tomato sauce. Cook the sauce for a few minutes, stirring, until it is slightly thickened. Correct the seasoning. Return the chicken to the pan and simmer it for about 5 minutes. Arrange the chicken on the serving platter, strain the sauce around it, and sprinkle with chopped parsley. Serves 4.

SAUTÉED CHICKEN FLORENTINE

Poulet Sauté Florentine

PREPARE a *poulet sauté Bercy*. Sauté 1 1/2 pounds well-cleaned, cooked, and drained spinach in 2 tablespoons butter for 3 to 4 minutes. Make a bed of the spinach on a serving platter and arrange the chicken on it with cooked, sliced mushrooms or pieces of *foie gras* and slices of truffle on top. Pour the sauce over all. Serves 4.

SAUTÉED CHICKEN PRINTANIÈRE

Poulet Sauté Printanière

IN A saucepan combine 2 cups shelled peas, 8 small spring onions, 1/2 cup diced carrots, 5 or 6 leaves of lettuce, shredded, 1/4 cup water, 1/4 teaspoon salt, 1 tablespoon sugar, 3 tablespoons butter, and a faggot made by tying together 3 sprigs each of parsley and chervil. Cover closely and cook over medium heat for about 25 minutes, or until most of the water has cooked away. Discard the faggot. Prepare a *poulet sauté Bercy* and reserve half the sauce to serve separately. Add the vegetables to the chicken and simmer for 10 minutes. Arrange the chicken on a serving platter with the vegetables around it and strain the sauce over them. Sprinkle with 1 teaspoon chopped parsley. Serves 4.

*Poulet Sauté
aux Morilles*

SAUTÉED CHICKEN WITH MORELS

WASH 1 pound *morilles*, or morels, very thoroughly, making sure to wash every bit of sand from the crevices. Cook them in a saucepan with 2 tablespoons butter, 1 teaspoon lemon juice, a few spoonfuls of water, and a little salt for about 10 minutes, or until the moisture cooks away.

Prepare a 2 1/2- to 3-pound chicken for sautéing. In a skillet melt 3 tablespoons butter and arrange the pieces of chicken skin side down on it. Cook the chicken over medium heat until the skin is golden brown. Turn the pieces and cook, partly covered, for about 25 to 30 minutes. Remove the breast meat to a hot serving platter, cook the remaining pieces for 5 to 10 minutes longer, or until they are tender, and remove them to the platter. To the juices in the pan add 1 tablespoon chopped shallots or onion, 1 clove of garlic, crushed, and 1 teaspoon flour. Add the cooked *morilles*, 2 to 3 tablespoons chicken gravy, if available, and 1/4 cup tomato sauce. Stir well and cook for 5 minutes longer. Correct the seasoning with salt and add a little freshly ground pepper and 1 tablespoon chopped parsley. Return the chicken to the pan and simmer it for about 5 minutes. Arrange the chicken on the serving platter and pour over it the sauce and *morilles*. Serves 4.

*Poulet Sauté
Gloria
Swanson*

SAUTÉED CHICKEN GLORIA SWANSON

PREPARE a 2 1/2- to 3-pound chicken for sautéing. In a skillet melt 2 tablespoons butter and arrange the pieces of chicken skin side down on it. Cook over medium heat until the skin is golden brown. Turn the pieces and cook 5 to 6 minutes longer. Add 8 to 10 mushrooms and cook 5 minutes longer. Stir in 1 teaspoon chopped shallot or onion and 1 tablespoon flour and cook a few minutes longer. Add 1/4 cup white wine, 1/2 cup cream, a faggot made by tying together 3 sprigs of parsley, a bay leaf, and a little thyme, and salt. Cook slowly, partly covered, for about 25 to 30 minutes, or until the chicken is tender. Remove the chicken.

Discard the faggot. Stir into the sauce 2 egg yolks, lightly beaten with 1/2 cup warm cream. Shake the pan, off the heat, so the sauce will not curdle. Arrange the chicken on a serving platter and pour the sauce over it. Garnish the platter with 4 tomatoes, cut in half, sautéed in a little butter, and sprinkled with parsley, and with small molds of rice pilaff topped with slices of truffle. Serves 4.

SAUTÉED CHICKEN CHASSEUR

PREPARE a 2 1/2- to 3-pound chicken for sautéing. In a skillet heat 2 tablespoons salad oil and arrange the pieces of chicken skin side down in it. Cook the chicken until it is brown, turn the pieces, and cook until they are brown on the other side. Add 1/4 pound mushrooms, cleaned and sliced, and continue to cook until the mushrooms are tender. Remove the chicken and drain off the oil from the pan, but leave the mushrooms. Add 2 tablespoons butter, and when it is melted, add 1 tablespoon chopped shallots and 1 teaspoon flour and cook, stirring, until the flour is golden. Add 1/4 cup white wine and continue to cook until the wine is reduced to half. Stir in 3/4 cup cooked tomatoes and cook for about 5 minutes. Return the chicken to the sauce and simmer for 15 to 20 minutes longer, or until the chicken is done. Arrange the chicken on a serving dish. Correct the seasoning of the sauce with salt, add 1 teaspoon mixed, finely chopped tarragon, chervil, and parsley leaves and pour the sauce over the chicken. Serves 4.

Poulet Sauté Chasseur

SAUTÉED CHICKEN PORTUGUESE

PREPARE a 2 1/2- to 3-pound chicken for sautéing. In a skillet melt 2 tablespoons butter and arrange the pieces of chicken skin side down on it. Cook over medium heat until the skin is golden brown. Turn the pieces and cook, partly covered, until they are brown on the other side. Add 1 tablespoon chopped shallots or onion and continue to cook slowly for a few minutes. Add 1 teaspoon flour, 1 clove of garlic, crushed, 1/4 cup white wine, 1/2 cup stock and 1/2 cup cooked tomatoes, salt and pepper, and cook for 25 to 30 minutes. Remove the chicken to another pan and strain the sauce over it. Add 4 to 6 fresh tomatoes, peeled, seeded, and chopped, and cook 10 to 15 minutes longer. Arrange the chicken on a serving platter, pour the sauce over it, and sprinkle with 1 tablespoon chopped parsley. Serves 4.

Poulet Sauté Portugaise

SAUTÉED CHICKEN FRANÇAISE

PREPARE a 2 1/2- to 3-pound chicken for sautéing. Melt 3 tablespoons butter in a saucepan and arrange the pieces of chicken skin side down

Poulet Sauté Française

on it. Cook over medium heat until the skin is golden brown. Turn the pieces and continue to cook, partly covered, until they are light brown on the other side. Parboil 4 carrots and 4 onions, both thinly sliced, in a little water with 1 teaspoon sugar for 5 to 10 minutes. Drain the vegetables and add them to the chicken with 1 tablespoon coarsely chopped parsley. Add 1 cup cream and cook very slowly for 25 to 30 minutes. Remove the chicken to a serving dish and finish the sauce with 1 to 2 tablespoons cream or cream sauce and 1 tablespoon brandy. Season with salt and pepper to taste. Pour sauce and vegetables over the chicken.

Suprêmes de Volaille Elisabeth

BREAST OF CHICKEN WITH HAM AND CHEESE

REMOVE the breasts from 3 chickens, each weighing from 2 3/4 to 3 pounds, and trim off the skin. Separate the top filet section of each breast from the smaller one lying beneath. Flatten each filet a little with a small mallet or the broad side of a knife. The smaller filet, which is thicker, should be flattened until it spreads to the same size as the upper one. Cut 6 thin slices each of ham and Swiss cheese the same size as the filets. Put the filets together with 1 slice each of ham and cheese between. Moisten the edges of the filets with beaten egg to hold them together securely. Roll the breasts in flour, and shake off the excess.

Melt 3 tablespoons butter in a shallow pan large enough to hold the filets side by side. Sauté the filets for 10 to 12 minutes, or until golden brown on one side. Turn and continue to sauté for 5 to 6 minutes, or until the chicken breasts are done. Put them on a serving platter and keep warm.

To the butter in the pan in which the chicken was cooked, add 1/2 pound small mushrooms, 1 teaspoon chopped shallots, and 1/3 cup dry white wine, and cook until the liquid is reduced to 1/2. Peel 4 or 5 firm tomatoes, cut them in half, and squeeze gently to remove the seeds and juice. Chop the tomatoes coarsely and add them to the pan with the mushrooms. Cook briskly until most of the liquid is cooked away, but do not let the tomatoes become mushy. Add 1 cup sweet cream and continue to cook until the cream is reduced to 1/2. Add 1 cup cream sauce and correct the seasoning with salt. Pour the sauce over the chicken and sprinkle with finely chopped parsley. Garnish the platter with 6 small molds of rice and top each with a slice of truffle. Place water cress at each end of the platter.

SAUTÉED BREAST OF CHICKEN WITH APRICOTS

Suprêmes de Volaille aux Abricots

HEAT 3 tablespoons butter in a large skillet and in it sauté on the skin side 3 chicken breasts, cut in half and seasoned with salt. Turn the breasts and cook them over low heat for 15 to 18 minutes, until they are cooked through. Remove the chicken to another pan, and in the same butter sauté 6 rather thick slices of ham cut to fit the chicken breasts. Lay the chicken breasts on the slices of ham on a serving platter and keep them warm.

In the same pan heat 6 whole large apricots, cooked and pitted. Add 1/4 cup heated brandy and ignite it. When the flame burns out, stir in 1/2 cup apricot juice. Arrange the apricots at one end of the platter and put a bunch of water cress at the other end. Add a little chicken stock to the pan, swirl in 1 tablespoon butter, and pour the sauce around the chicken.

SAUTÉED TURKEY

Dindonneau Sauté

YOUNG turkeys are sautéed like chicken. It takes 30 to 40 minutes or longer to cook them, depending upon their size. They are split or cut up before cooking and served with gravy made from the juice in the pan and usually with a purée made of corn or mushrooms or other vegetables. One popular way of preparing young turkeys at the old Ritz was to cut them into pieces after they had been sautéed, coat the pieces of turkey with a vegetable purée and then with a light Mornay sauce, and brown the coating under the broiler.

The late spring and summer is the time to sauté squab—or what the French call pigeonneaux—*and also young guinea hens, called* pintadeaux. *In June* pintadeaux *are served with the cherries that ripen then. Squab and guinea hen are tiny and very tender, and must be cooked very quickly. Allow one of the little birds for each serving.*

SAUTÉED SQUAB OR BABY GUINEA HENS

Pigeonneaux ou Pintadeaux Sautés

SPLIT and clean 6 squab and season them with salt. Melt enough butter in a skillet to cover the bottom generously. Arrange the squab skin side down and sauté them until they are golden brown. Turn the squab and cook, partly covered, until they are done, about 20 to 25 minutes. Arrange the birds on a serving platter and pour over them a little melted butter. To the juices in the pan add 1/2 cup stock or water and cook until the liquid is reduced to 1/2, stirring in all the brown bits. Pour the sauce over the birds.

Pintadeaux aux Cerises

BABY GUINEA HENS WITH CHERRIES

PIT 4 cups black cherries and tie the pits in a cheesecloth bag. Put the cherries and the pits in a saucepan with 1/3 cup each of kirsch and water. Bring the liquid to a boil and simmer gently for several minutes until the cherries are tender.

Clean and split 6 young guinea hens and season them with salt and pepper. In a skillet melt 4 tablespoons butter and arrange the birds skin side down on it. Cook until the skin is golden brown. Turn them and cook them on the other side, partly covered, until they are done, about 20 to 25 minutes. Arrange the guinea hens on a serving platter. Discard the cherry pits and pour cherries and juice into the pan in which the birds were sautéed. Bring to a boil, stirring, and pour sauce and cherries over the birds. Sprinkle with 3 tablespoons warm Cognac and ignite.

Sautéing Fish

ACCORDING to a favorite story, the Emperor Napoleon stopped for luncheon one day at the little town of Royat, at an inn called La Belle Meunière because its proprietor was a miller and it was the miller's pretty wife who did the cooking. Napoleon asked for the specialty of the house, and *la belle meunière* served him a delectable *truite sautée*, dressed with butter cooked to a hazelnut brown. The Emperor was so pleased with his trout that he immediately christened it *truite à la belle meunière*, and to this day any fish sautéed and served in brown butter is called by the same name or simply *meunière*.

Fish for the skillet should be cleaned and the fins trimmed close to the body. The head may be left on. Small fish are frequently cooked and served with both heads and tails intact. If the fish has a heavy skin, remove it. If the skin is thin, slash the fish diagonally on both sides, every 2 inches or so. These tricks serve a double purpose: they keep the fish from curling up when the heat shrinks the skin, and the heat reaches the center of the flesh more easily. Fish steaks are often sautéed, but fish filets are usually thin and fragile and likely to dry out when they are cooked this way. I prefer to poach filets and serve them with a more elaborate sauce than the delicious but simple *meunière*.

To Prepare
Fish for
Sautéing

SAUTÉED FISH WITH BROWN BUTTER

*Poissons
Sautés
à la Meunière*

DIP the fish in milk, then in flour seasoned with salt. Shake off any surplus flour—hold the fish by the tail—so that no bits of flour will make unattractive burned specks in the skillet.

Sauté fish in the kind of heavy pan described previously, one large enough to hold the fish without crowding. Salad oil and clarified butter are preferred for cooking fish. Cover the bottom of the pan generously —the fat should be about 1/4 inch deep. And it should be very hot or the fish will stick. Cook the fish until it is golden brown on both sides, a matter of 12 to 15 minutes for small fish. For a 2- to 3-pound fish, reduce the heat and cook 15 to 20 minutes on each side. To test the fish, insert a small thin knife carefully into the side. If the flesh flakes easily from the bone, the fish is cooked.

To Test
Sautéed
Fish

Sautéed fish may be served just as it comes from the skillet or the bone may first be removed. To do this, detach the top filet, in two sections if it is large, and lay it on the side of the serving dish. Then remove and discard the backbone and the small bones along the edge, which come away easily in a well-cooked fish. Season the inside with a little salt and pepper and lay the top filet back in place.

To Remove
Fish Backbones

If oil has been used for the sautéing, pour it off. Do not wash the pan. Add 1 tablespoon butter for each serving. If butter has been used, add enough butter to make 1 tablespoon for each serving. Cook the butter until it is lightly browned. Add a few drops of lemon juice or sprinkle the fish with the lemon juice—as you like—and pour the butter over the fish, which should be kept hot on a hot platter. Season with salt and pepper and sprinkle with finely chopped parsley or parsley mixed with chives, and garnish the dish with slices of lemon dipped in chopped parsley.

Truite
de Rivière
Belle-
Meunière

TROUT WITH BROWN BUTTER

CLEAN 6 trout, each weighing 1/3 to 1/2 pound. Remove the fins and ends of the tails but leave on the heads. Cook the fish as described above. Place a slice of lemon on each fish and serve with the butter sizzling.

Truite Sautée
Amandine

SAUTÉED TROUT WITH ALMONDS

PREPARE and sauté trout as described above. Omit the lemon juice. Make the brown butter and add 1 tablespoon blanched, sliced, and toasted almonds for each serving, and brown them lightly. Pour butter and almonds over the fish.

Truite
Saumonée
à la Meunière

SALMON TROUT WITH BROWN BUTTER

PREPARE a 2- to 3-pound salmon trout for sautéing. Dip it in milk and seasoned flour. In a pan large enough and long enough to hold the whole fish, heat about 1/4 inch salad oil and in it sauté the salmon until it is golden brown on one side. Turn the fish and cook it on the other side until it is golden brown and done, basting it frequently after it has been turned with the hot oil in the pan. This basting will cook the side that is away from the heat and prevent it from drying out. Serve with browned butter, parsley, and lemon as described above. Serves 4.

Sautéing Kingfish, Bluefish, Sea Bass, Sole

KINGFISH, bluefish, sea bass and other fish are sautéed by following the directions for trout if the fish are small, and the directions for salmon trout if the fish weigh more than 2 pounds.

FILETS OF SOLE WITH SAUTÉED CUCUMBERS

*Filets de Sole
Réjane*

CUT some very small incisions in the top of each filet. Dip the filets in milk and then in flour seasoned with a little salt. Sauté the filets as described above. Make brown butter. Add a few drops of lemon juice and pour the butter over the fish. Sprinkle with finely chopped parsley and garnish with sautéed cucumbers.

FILETS OF SOLE WITH POTATOES AND ARTICHOKES

*Filets de Sole
Murat*

CUT 4 to 6 filets of sole *en goujon*, that is, in small strips about as big as your little finger (the size of the *goujons* found in French rivers). Dip the strips in milk, then in flour seasoned with a little salt. In a skillet heat 3 tablespoons butter and in it sauté the strips until they are golden brown all over, turning them as required. Sauté 1 cup potatoes, cut into very small julienne, in butter until they are well browned and tender and sauté 6 or 8 cooked artichoke bottoms, each cut into 6 or 7 pieces, in butter. Mix the vegetables with the fish and arrange on a serving platter. Or the fish can be put in the center of the dish and the potatoes and artichokes arranged alternately around it. Add 1 to 2 tablespoons butter to the pan, cook until it is hazelnut brown, and pour it over all. Sprinkle with a few drops of lemon juice and a little finely chopped parsley.

SAUTÉED SOLE WITH HERB BUTTER

*Sole Sautée
aux Fines
Herbes*

CLEAN 2 whole sole, each weighing from 1 1/4 to 1 1/2 pounds, and remove the heads, the tails, and the skin from both sides. Trim off the edges. Dip the fish in milk and seasoned flour. Heat oil or clarified butter in a skillet and in it sauté the fish for 15 to 18 minutes, or until they are golden brown on both sides. Remove the fish from the pan and remove the backbones as described above. Season the lower filets with a little salt, trim again to make the edges neat all around, and replace the top filets. Keep the fish warm on a serving dish.

Pour the oil from the pan, add 1 tablespoon butter for each serving, and cook the butter until it is hazelnut brown. Mix together 1 teaspoon each of chopped chives and parsley and 1/2 teaspoon each of chopped chervil and tarragon and sprinkle the herbs over the fish. Pour the butter over the fish, sprinkle with a few drops of lemon juice, and garnish with lemon slices sprinkled with chopped parsley.

Oeufs
d'Alose
Sautés

SAUTÉED SHAD ROE

ALLOW 1 shad roe for a serving. Dip the roe in milk, drain it, and sprinkle it with flour. Cover the bottom of a skillet with salad oil, heat it moderately hot, and add the roe. Half cover the skillet. Brown the roe slowly on one side, turn it, and sauté it on the other side until it is done, about 12 to 15 minutes. Make a small incision. If no pink tinge shows, the roe is done. Remove it, discard the oil, and add a generous piece of butter to the pan. Brown the butter and pour it over the roe. Garnish with lemon slices.

Oeufs
d'Alose
Sautés
Amandine

SAUTÉED SHAD ROE AMANDINE

FOLLOW the recipe for sautéed shad roe. To the brown butter in the pan add 1 tablespoon blanched slivered almonds for each roe. Brown the almonds and pour butter and almonds over the roe.

FOR tricks and recipes for sautéing shellfish, see the chapter on shellfish.

Sautéing Vegetables and Fruits

A PLATTER of sautéed fish or meat is attractively garnished with vegetables that have also been sautéed. Many vegetables, even some potatoes, can be sautéed without parboiling. It is a wise precaution however, to judge the tenderness of the vegetable before attempting to sauté it; large carrots, which have been a long time growing and developing cellulose, will surely require a preliminary cooking in water.

You will find recipes for sautéing various vegetables—cucumbers, eggplant, mushrooms, tomatoes, and so on—in the vegetable chapter. Some leftover cooked vegetables take well to reheating in butter, too.

Sautéed bananas and apples make different and delicious garnishes for meat. Sautéed apples are often more desirable than applesauce as a meat accompaniment because they are not so watery and not so sweet.

SAUTÉED BANANAS

Bananes Sautées

PEEL bananas and halve them lengthwise; if the bananas are very large cut them in quarters. Heat enough clarified butter in a heavy skillet to cover the bottom well and cook the pieces of banana until they are golden brown on both sides. Serve either as a garnish or in place of a vegetable.

SAUTÉED APPLES

Pommes Sautées

SELECT firm apples; Rome Beauty and Spitzenburg sauté well. Peel and cut them in small pieces, in balls, or in olive shapes, and roll the pieces in flour. Brown the apples in clarified butter on both sides, turning them often until they are just tender. Serve with pork.

Broiling

BROILING IS NOT a job that can be done with the left hand of a chef whose right hand is stirring a sauce or sautéing a fish. Broiling is an art which demands exclusive attention, great skill, and long experience. I have at least one friend, now a chef of considerable repute, who learned that fact the hard way! This chef, whom we shall call Leon, served his apprenticeship under me in the Ritz kitchens many years ago. We had also in training in the kitchen a young girl who worked in the home of one of the hotel's directors, and I am afraid that the young lady was something of a distraction to Leon. To put it bluntly, Leon was acting like a small boy riding his bicycle with no hands. He was showing off, and unfortunately for him he chose the wrong trick. He took half a shad and laid it on the broiling grill with all the flourishes of a master. But the grill was not quite hot enough, and the fish stuck to it so firmly that poor Leon had to call the grill chef to scrape it off for him. Then Leon had to watch, his face red from more than the heat of the broiler flame, while the chef marked the fish with a red-hot *pique-feu*, the poker which was also used to lift the round stove lids, to *quadriller* it with crossbars in imitation of the effect produced by proper broiling.

It is a captivating sight to see a talented grill chef expertly cooking fragile fish, with never a bit broken or a shred left sticking to the wires, each piece geometrically marked by the hot wires in an attractive pattern. And it is a sight that makes one appreciate the efforts of the *grillardin*.

The first *grillardin* I ever worked with, and certainly one of the best, was *père Auguste* of the Hôtel du Rhin in Paris. He was a huge man, and with a *gros bonnet blanc* perched on his massive head he made the other chefs look like people of another, and more diminutive, race. He was a skilled chef and a tireless worker, or Mr. Morlock, the manager, would never have put up with him, for *père Auguste* was seldom entirely sober. His own special and inviolable glass was, like himself, enormous. It could hold a whole bottle of wine. When he had drunk his own wine, we young *commis* gave him most of ours, and the *courrier*, in order to fuel his good humor, always brought him the wine the guests had left. So *père Auguste* was usually *très gai* and often so funny that we could barely keep our minds on our jobs. When the other chefs went off for their afternoon outing, and we *commis*, who never had any time off, were busy making the intricate garnishes for dinner—carving roses from beets and turnips, rolling out colored noodles to cut into fancy shapes, fashioning little lemon baskets for parsley and so on—*père Auguste* would settle himself in a large chair in the far corner of the kitchen and go to sleep.

Grunts and groans signalled *père Auguste's* awakening and were our cue to rush him a glassful of wine. After several false starts he would finally heave himself out of the chair and stagger to the range. But once at his broiler, *père Auguste* was all business, working furiously for hours on end, stopping occasionally, of course, for more wine. Every piece of meat or fish that came off his grill had the right shade of brown and a perfect *quadrillé*. It was always cooked *à point*, that is, to the exact degree of doneness. His hands may have been big and at times a little shaky, but, drunk or sober, when he tapped a *filet mignon* or a roast with his two big fingers, he knew at once whether it was done or needed more cooking, and he handled fragile pieces of delicate boned shad as casually as if he were frying eggs for a roadside diner. And his wine-blurred eyes saw even the smallest imperfection in one of the garnished platters waiting for the food from his grill.

Fifty or more years ago hotel kitchens used only charcoal or coke for broiling. Coke made a hotter fire and was preferred. It was hotter for the chef, too, and usually broiled him along with the meat. In the old Ritz in New York we had two charcoal broilers and one coke broiler, as well as several fueled by gas and electricity. Most modern establishments now use gas or electricity.

Broiling is a quick way to cook, but because it is a quick way it is an exacting one. In some instances even a minute or two of overcooking may spoil the results. Or the wrong temperature—not hot enough for a thick piece of beef, too hot for a thin fish filet—may cause disappointment. Practice helps you understand the intensity of the heat given off by your broiler, and practice teaches you how long to broil different foods, and at what distance from the heat. Generally speaking, thick cuts of meat and fish should be cooked at a greater distance from the heat than thinner cuts, and chicken should be broiled under moderate heat when it can be regulated, or sufficiently far from the source of heat so the chicken is cooked through by the time it is nicely browned.

Temperature in Broiling

Smoke, the inevitable accompaniment of fire and fat, can be minimized by trimming away the surplus fat; leave only the merest border to protect the edges of the meat. When you broil meat over charcoal, as you do outdoors and as is done in restaurant kitchens, the fat drips directly onto the coals, and there is danger of fire. The chef keeps a whiskbroom and a pan of water handy, and shakes enough water on the fire to quiet the flames without extinguishing the embers. You can do the same when you cook outdoors. In the oven broiler, where one uses a heavy rack to separate the fat that drips into the pan from the gas flame or electric unit above, a fat fire is less likely to blaze up. If the fat does catch fire, smother the flames with a large pot lid.

Smoke in Broiling

Broiling
à la Diable

There are two broiled specialties that intrigue amateur chefs. The first is *à la diable* or *diable*—or, in English, deviled. Favorite *à la diable* dishes are beef ribs and chicken, which first earned their reputation as supper dishes in English clubs. The *diable* mixture of butter, mustard, Worcestershire sauce, cayenne pepper, and bread crumbs is spread over the cooked meat, which is then browned under a broiler. Some like to add a little anchovy paste to the mixture, others a little curry powder. Leftover cooked meat is warmed just a little in the oven or broiler before it is spread with the seasoned bread-crumb coating. A somewhat similar dish is baby lamb *persillé*. In this case a young, tender lamb shoulder is broiled, then covered with bread crumbs mixed with chopped parsley, sprinkled with butter, and browned under the broiler again.

Planking Steak and Fish

The second broiling method that interests the amateur is planking. A new plank should be prepared as follows: scrub it well and dry it thoroughly. Then brush it generously with salad oil, put it in a cold oven, adjust the thermostat to 325° F., and let oven and plank heat at the same time. After about 25 minutes, remove the plank and let it cool, brushing it with more oil, which will be absorbed by the wood as it cools. This treatment helps to preserve the wood and will keep it from cracking and splitting under the hot broiler. In using the plank, prepare the garnishes first. Cook such vegetables as tiny green beans, lima beans, baby carrots and flowerettes of cauliflower or small, firm Brussels sprouts and keep them hot in a little butter and prepare potatoes *duchesse* for the border. Then broil the steak—or fish—on a grill or in a broiler pan in the usual way, turn it, and continue to broil until it is half done on the second side. While the meat is broiling, heat the plank in the oven. When you turn the steak, remove the hot plank from the oven and pipe the potatoes *duchesse* in a decorative border around the edge with a pastry bag and tube. When the steak is half cooked on the second side, transfer it to the plank and put the plank under the broiler to brown the potatoes and finish cooking the steak. Then arrange bouquets of vegetables between the potatoes and meat.

A plank used for fish will retain the fish taste and should not be used for any other purpose.

A final warning: Broiled foods, like soufflés, should be served the minute they leave the range. Broiled foods kept warm in a warming oven become dry and tough, and if put in covered dishes, they continue to cook in the steam and lose their crispness and tenderness. It's better to let guests wait than for broiled foods to wait.

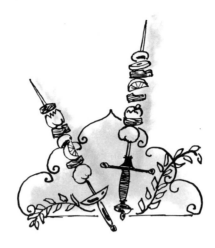

Broiling
Meat

THE dark meats are best suited, I believe, to broiling—beef, lamb, English mutton, and some of the big game. Have the broiler very hot, spread the meat with butter or good fat, and season it with a little salt. When it is done on one side, turn, spread the other side with butter or fat, season with salt, and finish broiling. Never pierce the flesh with a fork to turn it. Use a spatula or put the fork into the fat at the edge. **Best Meats
for Broiling**

Many people like red meats rare. If you look carefully, you will notice that when the meat reaches the medium rare stage, tiny drops of pink juice appear on the surface of the side being cooked. Touch the meat at this stage lightly with the first and second fingers: it is firm but still retains a noticeable springiness. If it feels soft it is not done, if it is quite firm, it is too well done. Always cook a piece of meat less than an inch thick very quickly, using high heat. For a thicker piece, turn down the heat a little so that the outside of the meat won't be unpleasantly scorched before the inside is cooked. A cut of meat more than 3 inches thick is best finished in the oven after it has been browned on both sides. **To Test
Broiled Meat**

White meats should be well done and should be cooked slowly, with moderate heat. Broiled spring chicken is very good, as is broiled baby lamb. But most people prefer veal and pork cooked in other ways.

Beef is the most popular meat for broiling. There are a number of suitable cuts and any of them can be sliced the thickness one prefers—or can afford to buy. The names of the various cuts vary depending upon where you buy your meat. Suppliers to French chefs in restaurants in large cities use one set of terms and housewives in the Middle West tell me that their butchers use terms quite different from those of butchers on the east coast. But the animal is the same. Thus, we have the short loin section which gives porterhouse and T-bone steaks, both of which have tenderloin or filet on one side of a T-shaped bone and, on the other side, what is variously called *contrefilet* or sirloin. But if the sirloin steak is cut after the whole *contrefilet* has been removed from the T-bone, it is often called a shell steak or *entrecôte*. If it is cut from the part of the loin near the forequarter, where there is no tenderloin, it is known as a club steak. The true sirloin steaks are larger pieces of meat cut nearer the hindquarters; they have an irregularly shaped bone. But whatever steak you buy, the preferred thickness for broiling is about 1 1/2 inches, although some people prefer thicker or thinner steaks.

The most expensive beef cuts for broiling are those from the tenderloin or filet, the long section lying in the lower or inner side of the T-bone area. The individual steaks vary in size because all tenderloins—or filets—taper off at one end. The narrow end, consequently, is usually sliced at an angle to make larger steaks. Slices of filet are named according to their thickness. A piece 1 inch thick is called a *tournedos*, 1 1/2 to 2 inches thick (or slightly thicker if it is cut from the narrow end) is a *filet mignon* and a piece 2 or 3 inches thick (preferably from the widest part of the tenderloin) is a *chateaubriand*. Because filets have very little fat a strip of bacon or pork fat is often tied around the edge of each piece.

Tournedos
Filet Mignon
Chateaubriand

Rib steak, as its name implies, is cut from the ribs. It is usually about 1 inch thick, and always includes the rib bone. Cook and serve rib steak as you would any steak of similar thickness.

Broiled beef really needs little in the way of sauce or gravy to enhance it but there are traditional sauce accompaniments such as maître d'hôtel butter, béarnaise, *bordelaise* or *bercy* sauces, and broiled filets are often garnished elaborately with such things as artichoke bottoms and mushrooms; then the dish takes its name from the sauce or garnishing.

*Chateau-
briand Grillé*

BROILED CHATEAUBRIAND

SPRINKLE both sides lightly with salt, spread with butter, and broil the meat in a preheated broiling oven for about 6 to 7 minutes on each side. Transfer the *chateaubriand* to a hot pan, spread it with 1 to 2 tablespoons butter, and continue to cook under medium heat for about 15 minutes for rare, or only a little longer for medium rare. Test by tapping the meat with the fingers. Serve with béarnaise sauce or maître d'hôtel butter and water cress and French fried or souffléed potatoes.

BROILED STEAK

HAVE the steak (porterhouse, sirloin, club or other) cut 1 1/2 inches or thicker. Sprinkle both sides lightly with salt and spread with butter. Preheat the broiler oven for 15 to 20 minutes. Broil a 1 1/2-inch-thick steak for 8 minutes on each side for rare, a 2-inch steak 10 minutes on each side. If steak at the medium stage is preferred, allow a few minutes more cooking time.

Bifteck Grillé

BROILED FILETS MIGNONS

SPRINKLE both sides lightly with salt, spread with butter, and broil the meat in a preheated broiling oven for about 3 to 4 minutes on each side for rare or a few minutes longer for medium-rare.

Filets Mignons Grillés

FILETS MIGNONS HENRY IV

BROIL the filets and serve them with béarnaise sauce and *pommes de terre pont-neuf*, French fried potatoes cut smaller than the conventional size.

Filets Mignons Henri IV

BROILED TOURNEDOS

SPRINKLE both sides lightly with salt, spread with butter, and broil the meat in a preheated broiling oven for about 2 to 3 minutes on each side for rare or a few minutes longer for medium-rare. Serve on pieces of toast sautéed in butter, with artichoke bottoms and a sauce such as Madeira, Madeira mushroom, *marchand de vins*, or béarnaise.

Tournedos Grillés

BROILED HAMBURGER

COMBINE 2 pounds chopped fresh lean beef with 3 tablespoons chopped beef marrow and 1/4 cup heavy cream or cold water. The liquid makes the meat more juicy. Season with salt and pepper, and, if desired, add 1/2 cup finely chopped onion cooked until soft in 2 tablespoons butter. Shape the mixture very loosely, brush with butter, and broil in a pre-

Hamburger Grillé

heated broiling oven for about 4 to 5 minutes on each side for medium or a little longer for well-done. Serve with *sauce portugaise*, Portuguese sauce.

*Boeuf
à la Diable*

DEVILED BEEF BONES

SOME restaurants serve portions of rib roast with the bone, but others carve the meat from the ribs, which then, deviled and broiled, appear on a luncheon or supper menu. The bones of a family-sized rib roast will serve 2, 3, or 4 persons, allowing one rib to a portion. Cut the bones apart. There should be meat on three sides of each rib. Put the bones in a roasting pan and bake them in a moderately slow oven (325° F.) for about 10 minutes, just long enough to warm them. Spread the bones with the *diable* mixture used for *poulet grillé à la diable* and broil them slowly, under moderate heat, until the crumbs are browned on all sides.

*Côtes de Veau
Grillées*

BROILED VEAL CHOPS

HAVE veal chops cut about 1/2 inch thick. Sprinkle them with a little salt and pepper, dust them with flour, and spread them with melted butter. This gives a golden color.

Broil in a preheated broiling oven for 7 to 8 minutes on each side. Transfer the chops to a hot pan, spread them with 2 tablespoons butter, and continue to cook under a medium flame for about 2 to 3 minutes longer on each side, basting often with the butter and juices in the pan. The veal should be well done with no pink juice showing when the meat is tested with a fork. Keep the heat moderate, so the meat will be juicy, even though it must be well done. Serve with the juices in the pan or with maître d'hôtel butter.

*Côtelettes
d'Agneau
Grillées*

BROILED LAMB CHOPS

LAMB chops for broiling should be cut thick, never less than 1 inch, usually 2 inches or more. Season the chops with salt and brush them with butter or melted fat. Broil them in a medium-hot broiler for 3 to 5 minutes on each side for rare, depending on the thickness of the chops, or a little longer for medium. The surface should be well browned, the inside pink or medium rare.

LAMB KEBAB

Kebab d'Agneau

CUT the tenderloin or any tender cut of lamb into small pieces about 1/2 inch thick. Thread the pieces on a metal skewer with small pieces of bay leaf and slices of onion between them. Sliced bacon, cut in small pieces, and mushrooms may also be put on the skewer, alternating with the pieces of lamb. Season with salt and pepper and marinate the kebabs in salad oil for an hour or more. Drain and broil the kebabs in a preheated broiler for 5 to 7 minutes, or until the meat is brown on all sides. Serve with tomato sauce and rice.

BROILED PARSLEYED MILK-FED LAMB

L'Agneau de Lait Grillé Persillé

USE the shoulder section of very young milk-fed lamb (the shoulder of older lamb will not be tender enough). Sprinkle the meat lightly with salt, spread it with butter and broil it several inches from the heat until it is hot but not brown, about 10 minutes on each side. Coat the meat with the following *persillade*: Mix together 1/4 cup butter, 1/4 cup chopped parsley, 1/2 teaspoon salt, a little white pepper, and 2 or 3 drops of lemon juice. Add 2 to 2 1/2 cups fine, fresh, white bread crumbs and toss all together lightly. Cover both sides of the meat with a thick, compact layer of this mixture. Return the shoulder to the broiler and brown the crust on both sides. Serve with a puréed vegetable.

BROILED MUTTON CHOPS

Côtelettes de Mouton Grillées

MUTTON chops are usually served rare or medium rare. They are cut thicker than lamb chops and have more fat on them. Broil thick mutton chops in a preheated broiler for 6 to 7 minutes on each side. Transfer them to a hot pan, spread with 1 tablespoon butter, and continue to cook under medium heat for about 10 minutes longer on each side for medium rare, basting often with the juices in the pan. If the chops include the kidney, cook for about 5 minutes longer.

Bacon
Grillé

BROILED BACON

BROIL sliced bacon on a rack in a broiling pan about 3 inches from the heat for 3 or 4 minutes or until it is crisp. Watch it carefully; it burns very easily.

Jambon
Grillé

BROILED HAM

BEFORE broiling, score the fatty edge to keep the slice from curling. Broil the ham 4 inches from the heat about 5 minutes on each side for a slice 1/4 inch thick and 8 to 10 minutes for a slice 1/2 inch thick or more. If the ham is precooked, broil it only until it is browned.

Broiling Poultry

Broilers

BROILERS, the smallest and youngest chickens, weigh from 1 1/4 to 2 1/2 pounds. Since they are too young to have put on much fat, they need to be brushed with butter before cooking and should be basted constantly during cooking. Split them in half lengthwise, or cut them into quarters. Broil the birds on a rack, 4 to 5 inches from the source of heat, skin side up, until the skin is a rich golden brown, about 15 minutes. Turn and finish the cooking, for 20 to 35 minutes, depending

To Test
Broiled
Poultry

upon the size and thickness of the pieces. Chicken must be well done, so that when a fork is inserted in the second joint the juices show no tinge of pink. On the other hand, overcooked chicken is dry and tasteless, and too hot a fire will scorch the surface. Here again, experience will be your best teacher.

BROILED CHICKEN

Poulet Grillé

SPLIT a broiler down the back, clean it, and dry it well. Spread the skin with butter and sprinkle it with salt. Cook the bird on a rack in a pre-heated broiling oven, skin side toward the heat, until the skin is golden brown. Turn the chicken, spread the underside with butter, and continue to cook until the bird is done, brushing often with melted butter.

The usual garnishes are broiled mushrooms, tomatoes, bacon, or ham or simply water cress. To make a sauce, add a little chicken stock or water to the butter and juices that drip into the pan under the broiler rack and cook on top of the range, scraping in all the brown bits that cling to the pan.

BROILED DEVILED CHICKEN

Poulet Grillé à la Diable

SPLIT a broiler down the back, clean it, and dry it well. Season the chicken with salt and brush it with butter. Cook in a moderately hot oven (400° F.) for 10 to 15 minutes, or just long enough to make the flesh firm and to give the skin a slight golden color. Make a *diable* mixture. Cream 2 or 3 tablespoons butter with 1 teaspoon English mustard, a little cayenne pepper and a few drops of Worcestershire sauce and mix it with 1 cup fine fresh bread crumbs. Remove the chicken from the oven and take out any bones that can be easily withdrawn. Spread the skin sides of the chicken with the *diable* mixture and broil the crumbed sides under medium heat for 20 to 25 minutes. Keep the broiling heat low enough so that the crumbs do not brown too much but have a nice golden color and turn carefully to keep the crust intact. Serve hot or allow to cool, but never chill in the refrigerator.

Diable Mixture

BROILED BABY TURKEY

Dindonneau Grillé

SPLIT a young turkey weighing 4 to 6 pounds, clean it, and dry it well. Season the turkey with salt and brush it with melted fat. Put it on a hot grill in a preheated broiling oven, with the skin side on the grill to mark it, and cook for about 15 to 20 minutes. Turn the halves skin side up, spread it with 3 to 4 tablespoons butter and continue to cook under medium heat for about an hour, or until it is done, basting often. After about 20 minutes of cooking, add 2 to 3 tablespoons water or stock to the pan to prevent scorching. When the turkey is tender, remove it to a serving platter. Add a little water or chicken stock and stir in the brown bits that cling to the pan. If desired, add a few spoonfuls of cream or cream sauce. Strain some of the sauce over the turkey and the rest into a heated sauceboat. Garnish with water cress.

Broiling Fish

BROILING is a quick and simple way of cooking fish that is particularly successful with bluefish, mackerel, salmon, shad, and similar fatty fish. The broiling oven and the broiling rack or pan should be very, very hot, and the grid should be rubbed with oil to prevent the fish from sticking to it. Fish should never be overcooked. Watch it carefully, and remove it from the heat when the flesh loses its translucency and flakes easily at the touch of a fork. Fish filets rarely need to be turned; the hot pan cooks the bottom sufficiently so that when the top is browned the filet is cooked through. Fairly thin whole fish, like flounder, will be nearly cooked through when the first side is browned, and must be turned promptly to prevent overcooking.

To Test Broiled Fish

Fatty fish are simply seasoned and brushed with butter or oil before broiling, but a light dusting of seasoned flour is sometimes used for less fatty fish. The flour forms a crust that helps to keep the fish moist, and makes it easier to lift from the rack or to turn it. Use 2 spatulas to turn or transfer fish without breaking it.

The sauce most often served with broiled fish is maître d'hôtel butter, but it is possible to achieve great variety by using other suitable sauces, and they should not be overlooked.

Most professional cooks prefer to broil whole fish with the head and tail intact, but this is a matter of personal taste.

BROILED FISH

CLEAN small fish but leave them whole. Cut a few diagonal slashes about 1 1/2 to 2 inches apart in the skin on each side to prevent the fish from curling when the skin shrinks during the cooking. Season the fish with salt and pepper and roll them in flour and in salad oil. Heat a large flat pan under the broiler, spread it with butter, and arrange the fish in it side by side. Turn down the heat and broil under medium heat about 8 to 10 minutes, or until the fish are golden brown. Turn the fish and broil them on the other side 8 to 10 minutes, until the flesh is opaque and flakes readily.

To broil fish filets, dry them thoroughly, brush them with oil or butter, and cook like whole fish, allowing 4 to 5 minutes to brown the first side. If the pan is very hot, it will not be necessary to turn the filets.

Fish steaks for broiling should be cut 3/4 to 1 inch thick and cooked for 10 to 12 minutes. Baste the steaks with butter once or twice during the cooking.

BROILED SMELTS

BUY smelts that are large enough to split and bone. Split each fish, lift out the backbone, reshape the fish, and cook as for broiled small fish. For smelts broiled *à l'anglaise*, roll the boned smelts in flour, then in a mixture of 1 egg beaten with 1/4 cup milk and 1 tablespoon salad oil, and finally, in fine fresh bread crumbs. Cook as for broiled small fish and sprinkle the smelts with a few drops of lemon juice and a little chopped parsley.

BROILED SHAD ROE

SPRINKLE shad roe lightly with flour and dip it in oil or melted butter. Place the roe on a hot pan and broil it for 10 to 15 minutes, turning it once.

Roasting

ON DEVIENT CUISINIER, *on naît rôtisseur.* One can learn to be a cook, but one must be born knowing how to roast, said Brillat-Savarin. And, indeed, of all the kitchen arts, roasting makes the greatest demands on the cook. The *rôtisseur* must exercise unerring judgment and make split-second decisions, and eternal vigilance is the price of his perfection. As soon as the roasts begin to cook, the watching begins. Down the line of ovens the chef goes, opening on schedule each oven door, pulling out the enormous pans, turning the meat in this one, the birds in that, and basting—forever and again pouring the pan liquids over the meat with his long-handled spoon. As the dinner hour approaches, the chef tests to see how well the meat is done by tapping it with his first two fingers, much as a doctor taps a patient's chest. He lifts the chickens to examine the color of the juices that run from them, or he may pierce the meat or poultry with a fork to watch the juices that are released. To the *rôtisseur* roasting means more than simply putting something into the oven, setting the temperature control, and leaving things to take care of themselves.

All roasting was once done on a spit before an open fire. In the kitchens of great private homes in France and England, roasting is still done on a revolving spit instead of in a closed oven, and many connoisseurs maintain that this is the only fit way to roast a fine piece of meat or a good bird. The introduction of electric spits, for the kitchen or the outdoor grill, has revived spit roasting in this country. The theory of spit roasting is that intense radiant heat, applied evenly to all the surfaces of the meat, browns the outside perfectly and lets the good flavor of the meat develop more fully than it can in the much more moist atmosphere of a closed oven. As the spit turns, the juices and fat drip over and into the meat, assuring succulence. The oven has replaced the spit in hotel and restaurant kitchens, but chefs have learned to manage ovens and roasting pans to achieve comparable results.

Spit Roasting

The rules that a *rôtisseur* follows are simple. He starts with a good hot oven, sometimes reducing the heat when the meat or bird begins to brown, but he keeps the heat high enough to discourage steaming. How much he lowers the temperature depends on the size of the piece being cooked. The smaller it is, the hotter the oven should be. A squab, for example, should be roasted at a temperature of 400° F. or more, a turkey at about 350° F. or less. Too hot an oven overbrowns large pieces before the heat penetrates to the center.

When the roast can be conveniently turned in the pan, it is turned frequently. Legs of lamb, rolled roasts, and most poultry are quite manageable, but heavy rib roasts of beef and large hams do not lend themselves to turning.

Turning Roasts

Of course, every roast is regularly and thoroughly basted. Chefs always liberally cover meat or poultry to be roasted with fat—beef or pork—if the piece lacks a generous layer of it. Slices of fat cut from the animal can be used, or the piece can be spread with fresh drippings. The meat is continually basted with this fat, and if it tends to scorch and smoke as it collects in the pan, a few tablespoons of water are added. But only the fat is skimmed up for basting, not the water underneath. Add the water a little at a time, as it cooks away. Never have so much that the meat steams. No water should be left when the roast is done. *Alors*, all this turning and basting may seem to be added work, but it is well worth the trouble if you are cooking for gourmets. A chef's finished roasts are well browned whether the interior meat is rare, medium, or well done, and each slice of meat has a characteristic flavor and succulence that indicate a fine job of roasting.

Basting Roasts

Fat for Roasts

Roasting Meat

Cuts for Roasting
DON'T try to roast anything but fine-grained tender meat. Tender cuts come from the parts of the animal that get the least exercise, and the animal must be properly raised and fattened. The cuts of beef suitable for roasting are the rib sections, the sirloin, the filet, and, in the finest beef, the rump. Suitable cuts of lamb are the rack, the saddle, and the legs or the whole hindquarter. Pork roasts include the loin and uncured or fresh ham. The loin, the rack, the rump, and often the breast of veal are roasted.

Roasting à Point
Meat should be roasted *à point*, to the appropriate degree of doneness for each kind of meat. For beef, *à point* is rare or medium rare. The degree of rareness depends on personal taste and on the animal; beef, for instance, is usually served a bit more rare than lamb. Veal and pork are roasted *à point* when they are well done. Like all very young animals, the very young milk-fed lamb—in France called the *pascal* lamb, here baby lamb—should be thoroughly cooked, as well done as veal or pork. Take care not to overcook even these meats, however, or they will be dry and without flavor. Older lamb is at its best pink, or medium rare. Be guided by the time and temperature given in recipes, but remember that every piece of meat varies according to the age of the animal, the shape of the cut, and the proportion of bone and fat to lean meat. I myself have never used a meat thermometer. This is, of course, a helpful device for some. If you use one, make sure that the end of it is deep in the thickest part of the meat and that it does not touch a bone. Chefs judge the approximate time from the weight of the piece, but depend on careful watching and frequent testing toward the end to tell them when to stop the cooking.

Roast beef can be tested with a sharp two-tined kitchen fork or

steel skewer. Pierce to the center at a thick place in the roast and with- To Test Roast Meat
draw the fork. Blood-red juice means that the meat is very rare, pink
means medium rare, and a clear liquid indicates that the meat is well
done. A better test, because it does not permit the juices to escape, is the
feel of the meat. Touch it gently but firmly with forefinger and second finger. It will feel soft if it is almost raw, springy if it is medium
rare, and firm when it is well done. (Chefs use the same test for
sautéed or broiled meat.)

Test veal, pork, and very young spring lamb, with a fork or skewer,
in the thickest part. The juices that run out should be perfectly clear
and colorless. A tinge of pink indicates that more cooking is needed.

To test a saddle or rack of lamb from an older animal, use a large
kitchen needle or skewer like a knitting needle and pierce the meat alongside the bone. Leave the needle there for about a minute and then put
the end immediately to your tongue. If the needle is comfortably hot,
the meat is rare and should cook more; if it is almost too hot to bear,
the meat is *à point*, or medium rare. There is a different trick for a
leg of lamb. Have the butcher remove the little piece of hip bone
that fits into the socket of the leg bone. Test the roasted meat by the
degree of heat in the hole left in the leg bone. If it feels comfortably
hot to your finger, the leg is still rare; if it is very hot, the meat is medium
rare and ready to come out of the oven.

In planning the meal it is wise to allow time for the meat to *reposer*, Reposer
or rest, in a warm place for about 20 minutes before you carve it. This
allows the juices to be reabsorbed by the tissues, giving the meat a succulent tenderness. Less juice escapes when it is carved, and the slices
tend to shrink less. The techniques of carving are discussed elsewhere.

*A simple brown meat gravy, a kind of pan sauce, neither fat nor thick
with flour, can be made for roast meat or poultry in the roasting pan. The
French describe meat served with this gravy as* au jus. *The juice and drippings in the pan, freed of fat and augmented with stock or water, are simply reduced to concentrate the flavor. Butter may be added at the last.*

PAN OR BROWN GRAVY

Pan or Brown Gravy

PUT a few slices of onion or carrot in the roasting pan with the meat or
poultry, if desired. Roast the meat in the usual manner and transfer it

to a heated platter. Carefully pour off the fat from the roasting pan and to the remaining juices add a little stock or water, enough to cover the bottom of the pan, about 1/2 to 1 cup. Cook the gravy over direct heat, stirring constantly to dissolve the brown crustiness on the bottom and sides of the pan. Let the liquid reduce until it has a good color and flavor. Correct the seasoning and swirl in 1 or 2 tablespoons butter. Add to this sauce any juices that escape when the meat is carved. Store any leftover gravy in the refrigerator, covered, for use in brown sauces.

A chef frequently puts a thick layer of coarse salt on the outside of a roast of beef, moistening it just enough so that it forms a crust that hardens in the oven and seals in all the juices. In the home kitchen the hot fat from a piece of suet tied around the roast seals the outside of the meat and prevents it from becoming dry.

ROAST PRIME RIBS OF BEEF

Côte de Boeuf Rôtie

RUB a rib roast of beef with salt and spread it generously with good fat. Put it in a roasting pan, curved side up, so that it rests on the bones. If it does not have a layer of fat, put a slice of beef suet on top. Brown the beef in a hot oven (450° F.) for about 20 minutes, reduce the heat to moderate (350° F.), and continue to roast, basting frequently, until it is done. Allow about 10 to 12 minutes per pound for rare, 15 minutes for medium, and 18 minutes for well-done roasts. Add a few tablespoons water to the pan to prevent the fat from burning, especially if the roast is large. Remove the meat to a warm serving platter and let it rest for about 20 minutes. Make pan gravy in the roasting pan. Serve the roast with Yorkshire pudding.

Yorkshire Pudding   YORKSHIRE PUDDING

SIFT together 1 1/2 cups flour, 1/2 teaspoon salt, 1/2 teaspoon baking powder, and a little grated nutmeg. Stir in 2 cups milk, 2 eggs, beaten, and 1/4 cup melted suet or 1 cup finely chopped suet taken from around the kidney. Put about 1/4 cup melted fat or drippings from the roast beef in a large shallow pan and put it in the oven to heat. Pour in the batter and bake in a moderately hot oven (375° F.) for 30 minutes or until the pudding is golden brown. Cut in pieces and serve immediately.

ROAST FILET OF BEEF

ALL the fat has to be removed from the outside of a tenderloin because beneath it are skin and sinews that must be cut away. Therefore, after the meat has been trimmed down to the tender center section, it is important to lard it with strips of larding pork or to have thin slices of larding pork or beef suet tied around it. Roast the filet in a hot oven (450° F.) for about 10 minutes per pound for very rare and 12 to 13 minutes for rare. The finished roast is often spread with *glace de viande*, for flavor and brilliance. It is usually served with a rich sauce, such as Madeira, and garnished elaborately with turned or stuffed mushrooms, artichoke bottoms, asparagus tips, and the like.

Filet de Boeuf Rôti

ROAST SIRLOIN OF BEEF

TIE slices of larding pork or beef suet around the sirloin, as you would around the filet or any solid cut of beef without bone, so that it is completely covered. Follow the directions for roast prime ribs of beef but allow only 10 minutes at 450° F. and then 10 minutes per pound at 350° F. for medium rare. Remove the suet or larding pork about 20 minutes before the meat should be done, so the meat will brown.

Contrefilet Rôti

ROAST RUMP OF BEEF

THE rump, too, lacks fat. Lard it with strips of larding pork, as you would filet of beef, and tie it with slices of larding pork or beef suet. Follow the directions for roast prime ribs of beef but allow only 10 minutes at 450° F. and then 10 minutes per pound at 350° F. for medium rare. This cut is also liked better done: add 5 minutes per pound.

Pièce de Boeuf Rôtie

ROAST LOIN OR RACK OF VEAL

SPRINKLE a loin or rack of veal with salt and spread it with fat. Roast the meat in a moderately hot oven (375° F.) for about 18 to 20 minutes per pound, until it is well done. Baste often and add water if the fat tends to scorch. Remove the meat and make pan gravy.

Longe de Veau ou Carré de Veau-Rôtis

The rump of veal is still another cut that has little fat. Since it must be well cooked, and may easily become dry, it is doubly important that it be larded. It may be braised rather than roasted, to preserve the moisture, and even then larding will improve it. The rump may be boned, rolled, and tied, or not, as you wish, but boning naturally makes it easier to slice. The breast is boned, stuffed, and rolled. Both cuts are roasted in almost the same way as chicken roasted en casserole—*that is, in fat, preferably butter, in a covered casserole just big enough to accommodate the meat.*

ROAST RUMP OF VEAL

Pièce de Veau Rôtie en Casserole

MELT 1/2 cup butter or fresh pork fat in a casserole not much larger than the piece of meat to be cooked. Add 1 carrot and 1 onion, both sliced, and cook them until they are heated through. Place a 3- to 4-pound rump of veal on the vegetables and cook in a moderate oven (350° F.), turning it every 5 minutes and basting it with the fat until it begins to brown all over. Cover the casserole and continue cooking the meat until it is done, allowing about 30 minutes per pound. Remove the cover about 15 minutes before the meat should be done, to give it a final browning. Remove the meat to a serving platter. Add 1/2 cup white stock or water to the pan and cook, stirring in all the brown bits that cling to the casserole. Add 2 teaspoons cornstarch mixed with 1/2 cup Sherry and continue cooking until the sauce thickens. Strain it and serve it separately.

ROAST BREAST OF VEAL

Poitrine de Veau Rôtie

SPREAD a boned breast of veal with any desired stuffing, roll it, and tie it in several places with soft string. Roast it *en casserole*, following the directions for roast rump of veal.

ROAST LOIN OF PORK

Longe de Porc Rôtie

SPRINKLE a loin of pork with salt and brown it in a hot oven (450° F.) for 15 minutes. Reduce the heat to moderate (350° F.) and continue to roast until the meat tests well done, basting often. Allow 20 to 25 minutes per pound. Remove the excess fat from the pan and add a little water if the fat tends to scorch. Remove the finished roast and make pan gravy.

ROAST LOIN OF PORK BOULANGÈRE

Longe de Porc Rôtie à la Boulangère

SEASON a 4- to 5-pound loin of pork with salt. Roast it in a large roasting pan in a hot oven (425° F.) for 1 hour, turning and basting it often. Remove the meat to a warm platter and make pan gravy. Pour the gravy into a small saucepan and reserve.

Put in the roasting pan 8 potatoes, peeled and sliced, 1 onion, chopped, 1 teaspoon chopped parsley, 1 teaspoon salt, and a little pepper. Spread 2 tablespoons soft butter over the vegetables and lay the half-roasted pork on them. Put enough hot water in the pan to come almost to the top of the potatoes, bring the liquid to a boil, and return the pan to the oven (400° F.). Cook for 1 1/2 hours longer, or until the meat tests done. The water should be almost completely cooked away and the potatoes brown on top. Reheat the gravy and serve it separately.

A leg of lamb may also be cooked in this manner. Spread the lamb with fat before roasting and cook it the second time, with the vegetables, for only about an hour.

ROAST FRESH HAM

Jambon de Porc Frais Rôti

THE skin of an uncured leg of pork, or fresh ham, can be removed or not, as you wish. If it is left on, score it every inch in 2 directions, to make a diamond pattern. Sprinkle the leg with salt a few hours before roasting it. Place it skin side up on a rack in a roasting pan and roast it in a moderate oven (350° F.) for 30 to 35 minutes per pound, or until it tests well done. Skim the fat from the pan and make pan gravy. Roast fresh ham is usually served with a purée of dried beans or lentils and with red or white cabbage and potatoes.

The leg of a small, very young lamb is usually cooked along with part of the loin. Or two legs are roasted with the whole saddle. This roast is called a baron. Or the rack and shoulder are cooked together. When the animal is larger, the legs, saddle, loins, and rack make separate roasts.

Baron d'Agneau de Lait Mireille

BARON OF LAMB WITH ARTICHOKES AND POTATOES

RUB the baron with salt. Young lamb, having little fat, should be spread generously with good fat, preferably beef drippings. Add 1/2 cup water to the roasting pan and roast the lamb in a hot oven (400° F.) for 1/2 hour, basting often. Reduce the heat to moderately hot (375° F.) and continue to roast, basting often. Add more water if the fat begins to scorch. For a baron, allow about 3 hours; for a demi-baron—a baron halved lengthwise—2 to 2 1/2 hours.

Peel small potatoes and cut them into slices about 1/8 inch thick. They should be the size and thickness of a silver dollar. Parboil the slices in water to cover for about 2 minutes and drain well. Heat 3 or 4 tablespoons butter in a skillet, add the potatoes, and cook in a hot oven (450° F.) or over moderate heat until they are golden brown, turning them from time to time. Season with salt and sprinkle with parsley.

Remove the meat to a hot serving platter and arrange around it alternately artichoke bottoms stuffed with tomato purée and the potatoes. Place water cress at the ends of the platter and between the legs of the baron. Make pan gravy and serve it separately. A saddle or leg of lamb can also be cooked this way but less roasting time is required.

Selle d'Agneau Rôtie

ROAST SADDLE OF LAMB

SPRINKLE a saddle of lamb with salt and spread it with fat. Add 1/2 cup water to the roasting pan and roast the saddle in a hot oven (425° F.), basting frequently. If too much fat cooks out of the lamb, skim it from the pan. Replenish the water as necessary. Allow about 15 minutes per pound. Remove the roasted lamb from the pan and make pan gravy.

Gigot d'Agneau Rôti

ROAST LEG OF LAMB

RUB a leg of lamb with garlic or insert a few thin slices into tiny slits cut in the flesh. Sprinkle the meat with salt and spread it with good fat. Roast it in a very hot oven (450° F.) for 15 minutes. Reduce the heat to moderately hot (375° F.) and continue roasting. Turn the lamb often and baste frequently. If the leg is from a very young lamb, allow about 18 minutes per pound, for well-done meat. For a larger leg weighing 6 to 7 pounds, allow about 12 to 15 minutes per pound, for medium rare. Remove the lamb and make pan gravy.

LEG OF LAMB WITH CÈPES AND POTATOES

Gigot d'Agneau à la Bûcheronne

SEASON a leg of lamb with garlic and roast it in the usual way. Remove the meat from the pan to a serving platter and make the pan gravy.

While the meat is roasting, prepare the following garnish: Drain 2 large cans of cèpes and sauté them in 1/2 cup very hot oil until they are golden brown. Drain the cèpes and transfer them to another pan containing 3 tablespoons butter. Season them with salt and pepper and add 1 tablespoon chopped shallots, 1 clove of garlic, crushed, 1 tablespoon chopped parsley, and 2 tablespoons fresh bread crumbs. Cook for a few minutes until the crumbs are brown, shaking the pan to combine the ingredients as they cook. Prepare sliced potatoes as for baron of lamb with artichokes and potatoes. Slice the lamb and arrange the slices on a warm serving platter. Arrange the potatoes and the cèpes alternately around the meat. Serve pan gravy separately.

LEG OF LAMB WITH ONION PURÉE

Gigot d'Agneau Maintenon

SEASON a leg of lamb with garlic and roast it in the usual way. Let it rest out of the oven for 1/2 hour. Carve the thick side of the leg and spread each slice of meat with *purée Soubise*, onion purée. Sprinkle with thinly sliced truffles. Reshape the leg on a heatproof platter and spread it with Mornay sauce. Sprinkle it with grated Parmesan. Set the dish in a pan of water and brown the topping in a hot oven (400° F.).

LEG OF LAMB WITH MUSHROOM PURÉE

Gigot d'Agneau Forestière

PREPARE as you would *gigot d'agneau Maintenon*, leg of lamb with onion purée, but use mushroom purée instead of the onion.

Roasting Poultry

ROASTING of poultry seems an unlikely subject for drama, but I remember a day when the lack of a few roasted chickens caused a crisis in the Ritz kitchen. A waiter came to me in panic, explaining that he had put an order for roast chicken for a small dinner party into his pocket and had forgotten to give it to the *rôtisseur*. The guests had arrived. He knew, and I knew, that his job was at stake, because at the old Ritz we could not break the rule that specially ordered birds had to be cooked just before servingtime. We could not reheat leftover birds.

"Tell the captain to keep the soup and fish courses on the table as long as he can," I said. "I'll have the chickens ready."

I snatched 4 small chickens, cleaned, trussed, and ready for the oven, from the cold room and hurried them into the huge kettle of deep fat that was always kept hot on the range. While they sizzled and cooked, the *rôtisseur* put a roasting pan with a quantity of butter in it into the oven. After 15 minutes in the fat the chickens were colored and partially cooked. We lifted them out, drained them well, sprinkled them with salt, and rolled them in the hot butter in the roasting pan. Ten or 12 minutes in the oven and they were done to a juicy turn, beautifully brown. The day was saved.

Roasting poultry is, of course, normally a more orderly procedure. Only young, tender birds should be roasted. A good roasting chicken, for example, is from 5 to 9 months old, weighs 4 to 6 pounds, and has a plump breast, smooth skin, and flexible breastbone and wing tips. Roasting chickens of this size are less widely available than they used to be, and have been replaced by capons or small turkeys or by 2 or

3 plump frying chickens, weighing about 3 to 3 1/2 pounds each, roasted together.

In the hotel kitchen, we cooked 10 to 30 birds at a time, spaced a few inches apart in a large pan. If you cook 2 or 3 birds at once in your oven, remember to keep the temperature somewhat higher than you would for a single bird. The high heat prevents the formation of steam that may make the birds taste more stewed than roasted.

Chicken or capon roasted in the French manner has an appetizingly brown, slightly crisp skin, and the flesh is juicy and succulent. Set your oven at a moderately hot temperature, around 375° F. Rub the bird with butter or fresh pork drippings and baste it and turn it frequently as it cooks, so that the juices go through the flesh somewhat as they do when the bird is roasted on a revolving spit. To prevent the juices in the pan from scorching, add a very little water, just enough to cover the bottom of the pan, and replace the water as it cooks away. If there is no danger of burning the drippings, a bird can be cooked at a higher temperature and more quickly, and will be less dry.

Stuff your bird or not, as you like. Fryers are rarely stuffed, but larger roasters, capons, and turkeys usually are. The chapter on stuffings will tell you how to do it. A stuffed bird takes longer to roast than an unstuffed bird, because the heat must penetrate the stuffing, slowing down the cooking of the meat itself. Allow 25 to 30 minutes longer for a stuffed 4-pound chicken, for instance, which would take about 1 1/2 hours unstuffed. If the bird browns too quickly at 375° F., turn the heat down or cover the breast with buttered paper or aluminum foil. Do not overcook a roasted bird and thus dry it out. Pierce the thickest part, the second joint of the leg, with a fork or skewer. If the juices that run out when the fork is removed are clear, with no tinge of pink, the bird is done. The juices of an unstuffed bird will run out at the tail when you lift the bird in the pan. They should be colorless. *To Test Roast Poultry*

Birds that are cooked whole, either in the oven or in a casserole, should be trussed. When the legs and wings are held close to the body, so the heat cannot force them out, the meat, especially the breast, remains moist. In addition, a trussed bird is easier to handle and to turn, and more attractive to serve. *To Truss Poultry*

To truss a bird, a chef uses a kitchen needle 8 inches long, threaded with soft white string. He pierces the second joint or thigh, cramped close to the body, and pushes the needle through the body and the other second joint; then he comes back and pierces the leg and pushes the needle through the body and the other leg, and ties the string ends. Using another string, he pierces the left wing, the body, and the right wing, then inserts the needle in the left wing tip and pushes it through the body and the right wing tip and ties the string ends. The tied string forms a cross on the back. Then the drumsticks are tied to the tail. Or you can wrap the center of a piece of string around the ends of the drumsticks, turn the bird on its breast, slip the wing tips over the wings, and bring each end of the string up the body and under each wing. Tie the two ends across the back.

You can also truss a chicken with skewers. Push a long sharp skewer through the cramped left joint, the body, and the right joint, and a second skewer through the left wing, the body, and the right wing. Put the bird on its breast, lay a string over the back and catch it around the ends of the wing skewer. Cross the string across the back, catch it around the ends of the leg skewer, and tie it across the back. A trussing string is never crossed or tied over the breast because it would leave noticeable marks.

Poulet Rôti

ROAST CHICKEN

TRUSS a young 3- to 4-pound chicken. Spread the bird with 2 tablespoons butter and sprinkle it with salt. Lay it on its side in the roasting pan and add 1/4 cup water to the pan. Roast the bird in a moderately hot oven (375° F.) for about 10 to 15 minutes, basting it frequently with the pan drippings. Turn the chicken on its other side and cook it for 10 to 15 minutes. Turn the chicken on its back and roast it until it is done, about 1 to 1 1/2 hours. Remove the bird to a warm serving platter.

Pan gravy for roast chicken is made as for roast meat, but if the fat used was butter, it is not discarded from the pan. Season the gravy with salt and a little white pepper and swirl in 1 tablespoon butter. Serve the pan gravy separately.

To Roast en Casserole

The French are also fond of chicken roasted in a partly covered casserole. The skin is not quite so crisp as it is when the chicken is roasted in an open pan, but the bird is cooked too quickly to seem braised.

Choose a young tender bird, nothing larger than a 4-pound roasting chicken. Stuffing is often used, and it is usually a rich one. Fill the cavity loosely, sew the vent or skewer it closed, and truss the bird. The casserole, of heavy enameled iron or earthenware, should be just large enough to hold the chicken and the vegetable garnish that usually accompanies it. (More information about casseroles is given elsewhere in the book.)

The chicken is slowly browned on sides, back, and breast in a generous quantity of fat, preferably butter. It is literally rolled in it. (Sometimes diced bacon or salt pork is first browned in the butter, to be removed and returned to the pot later.) Do not pierce the chicken with a fork, but use two wooden spoons to turn it. Baste it with the fat in the pan or with hot melted butter and add a few tablespoons of water or white wine to the pan juices if they tend to scorch, as they sometimes do if the heat cannot be kept low enough. Garnishes requiring longer cooking, such as onions and carrots, go in first; more quickly cooked vegetables, such as peas and mushrooms, are added later. The casserole is sometimes completely covered after the chicken is browned. Chefs prevent the resulting condensed steam from dripping on the bird by covering it with a piece of buttered paper or by spreading a double thickness of wax paper over the casserole before the lid is put in place.

This method of cooking—the verb in French is poêler *and the method* poêlage—*though it is* en casserole *and often over direct heat, should not be confused with braising or cooking* à l'étuvée. *In the latter two methods, the bird, which is often cut up, is cooked in liquid; here it is left whole and the cooking medium is always fat.*

If there are not enough juices in the pan to make a sauce, add a little chicken stock, and if the juices need thickening, use a roux *or a little* beurre manié *or* cornstarch. *A little Sherry or Cognac will improve the flavor of the sauce.*

Poêlage

ROAST CHICKEN IN CASSEROLE

Poulet Rôti en Casserole

SEASON a 3- to 3 1/2-pound chicken with salt inside and out and put a clove of garlic in the cavity. Truss the bird and place it on its side in a casserole. Add about 1/2 cup fat, preferably butter, and cook the chicken over low heat or in a moderate oven (350° F.) with the casserole partly covered until the bird is brown on one side. Turn it to brown the other side and continue to cook for about 30 minutes, turning and basting the chicken with the butter. If fat other than butter was used, pour it off and reserve it in a small skillet and add 2 tablespoons butter to the casserole. Put 12 small white onions around the bird and continue to cook until they are brown. Add 4 potatoes, peeled and cut into 24 pieces, and 2 more tablespoons butter, if needed, partly cover the casserole, and cook until the potatoes are brown. If desired, add 1/4 pound diced salt pork, blanched and sautéed until brown in the reserved fat or in butter. Add 1/4 pound mushrooms browned in the reserved fat or in butter and 1/2 cup chicken stock or water, if needed. Cook 20 to 30 minutes longer, or until the chicken tests done. Remove it, carve it, and arrange it on a warm serving platter. Place the vegetables around it and sprinkle with chopped parsley. Thicken the juices in the casserole with 1 teaspoon cornstarch mixed with 1/4 cup Sherry. Serve separately.

Poulet
en Cocotte

CHICKEN IN COCOTTE

TRUSS a 4-pound roasting chicken. Melt 1 tablespoon butter in a large cocotte or flameproof casserole and in it brown lightly 1/2 cup diced bacon or diced salt pork that has been parboiled for a few minutes and well drained. Skim out the bacon or pork dice and reserve them. Season the chicken with salt and lay it on its side in the hot fat in the casserole. Cook it over moderate heat for about 10 minutes until one side is brown. Brown the breast and the other side in the same way. Add to the cocotte 2/3 cup carrots, cut in large dice, and 6 small onions. Sprinkle the vegetables with 1/2 teaspoon sugar and cook them for 10 minutes, stirring occasionally until they begin to take on color. Add the reserved bacon or pork dice and 1/2 cup water, and cook for 20 minutes longer. If necessary, add a little more water. Add 1 cup fresh green peas. Turn the chicken on its back and cover it with a piece of buttered paper. Cover the cocotte tightly, and continue to cook for 20 minutes longer, until the peas are tender.

Peel and dice 3 potatoes and sauté the dice slowly in 3 tablespoons butter until they are tender and brown. Remove the chicken to a serving platter and carve it. Correct the seasoning of the vegetables and serve with the chicken. Serve the potatoes separately.

Poulet
en Cocotte
au Xérès

CHICKEN IN COCOTTE WITH SHERRY

PREPARE chicken in cocotte, but substitute 1/2 pound mushrooms, cleaned and cut in quarters, for the peas. Remove the chicken to a warm serving platter and surround it with the vegetables. In a small saucepan melt 1 tablespoon butter, add 1/2 teaspoon flour, and cook the *roux*, stirring, until it is golden. Add 1/2 cup hot chicken stock and 1 tablespoon tomato paste, mix well, and cook, stirring, for 5 minutes. Add this sauce to the liquid in the cocotte, correct the seasoning with salt, and finish with 3 tablespoons dry Sherry. Serve the sauce separately.

To roast guinea hens, follow the directions for roasting partridge, pheasant, and quail. If the breast only is served and is the main course of a meal, allow 1 hen for 2—that is, 1 breast for each serving. As a lesser course in a long menu, large birds will serve 4; each breast is enough for 2 people.

BREAST OF GUINEA HEN PERIGORD

Suprêmes de Pintade à la Périgourdine

CLEAN the birds, season them with salt, and spread them with good fat. Roast them in a hot oven (425° F.), basting often. Roasting time for birds weighing 1 3/4 to 2 pounds is about 40 to 45 minutes. Carve off the legs, then remove the breasts. Reserve the legs and carcass for making a *salmis* at another time.

Make *sauce périgourdine* in the roasting pan, as for *perdreau ou faisan truffé à la périgourdine*, truffled partridge or pheasant Perigord.

For each serving heat a slice of goose liver in a little butter. Skin the breasts and trim them neatly. Arrange the breasts on a warm serving dish, put a slice of goose liver on each, and pour the sauce over them.

GUINEA HEN STEW

Salmis de Pintade

ROAST guinea hens and prepare a sauce as for *salmis de perdreau ou faisan*, partridge or pheasant stew.

Slice the meat from the second joints of the legs and slice the breasts. Arrange the meat on a large *croûte*, a long slice of bread sautéed in butter, and pour the sauce over it. Garnish the meat with turned cooked mushrooms, with chicken quenelles decorated with slices of truffle, with triangular slices of *pâté de foie gras* heated in butter, and with pitted olives, parboiled for a minute or two and drained. Spread oval croutons with *rouennaise* and coat them with a little sauce. Arrange them around the meat alternately with servings of wild rice.

Thin slices of fat salt pork are usually arranged on the breasts of capons and turkeys, because these large birds require long cooking and tend to become dry. They can also be spread thickly with fresh pork drippings or butter, and it is especially important to baste them constantly. Large birds are usually stuffed, and the stuffing helps keep them moist on the inside as the fat does on the outside.

Dindonneau ou Chapon Rôti

ROAST TURKEY OR CAPON

STUFF the bird, if desired, truss it, and season it with salt. Lay the bird on its side in a roasting pan with slices of fat pork over the breast and spread it generously with good fat. Roast the bird in a hot oven (425° F.) for 15 minutes, turn it on its other side, and cook for 15 minutes longer. Reduce the heat to 350° F. and cook until the bird tests done, turning it from side to side and basting about every 20 minutes. Place the bird on its back for the last 15 minutes. Allow about 15 minutes per pound and an extra 5 minutes per pound if the bird is stuffed. If the fat in the pan tends to burn, add a little water.

Remove the bird to a warm serving platter. Pour off the fat in the pan and make pan gravy as for roast meat. A 12-pound turkey serves 10.

Chapon Souvarov

CAPON SOUVAROFF

FOLLOW the directions for partridge or pheasant Souvaroff. For a 9- to 10-pound bird make the stuffing with 1 to 1 1/2 cups goose liver, 6 to 8 truffles, 1/4 cup Cognac, and 1/3 cup Madeira. Spread the bird with good fat, tie around it thin slices of fat pork, and roast it on its side in a hot oven (425° F.) for 15 minutes. Turn it and roast it for 15 minutes longer. Reduce the heat to moderately hot (375° F.) and cook the bird for about 2 hours longer, turning it from side to side every 15 minutes and basting frequently.

Put the bird in a casserole, make the sauce as for partridge Souvaroff, seal the casserole, and finish cooking.

Roast only young ducks and geese. Geese over a year old are not worth cooking. Une vieille oye est nourriture de diable. *This archaic French means that an old goose is food only for the devil. Ducks of doubtful age can be braised or cooked in wine, like* coq au vin, *or made into terrines and pâtés. The great quantity of fat in the flesh of these birds, which presents its own roasting problems, does not guarantee tenderness, so be sure that the beak is soft and flexible enough to bend easily, a sign the bird is young. The words* canard *and* caneton *are used interchangeably on French menus, but* caneton, *or duckling, indicates specifically a younger bird.*

ROAST DUCK

Caneton Rôti

CLEAN a 5- to 6-pound duck and put an apple, cored and cut into quarters, and a few stalks of celery in the cavity. Truss the bird and lay it on its side on a rack in a roasting pan. Roast it in a moderate oven (350° F.) for about 1 3/4 hours, or until it tests well done, turning it from side to side and basting it every 15 minutes. Put it on its back for the last 30 minutes of cooking, to brown the breast. Pour the fat from the roasting pan and make pan gravy.

ROAST DUCK WITH WILD RICE STUFFING

Canard au Riz Sauvage

CLEAN a duck and fill the cavity with wild rice stuffing II. Sew up the vent with string and truss the bird. Put the duck in a roasting pan and sprinkle it with salt. Spread it with 1 tablespoon butter. Roast the duck in a hot oven (400° F.) for 25 minutes, or until it is well browned. Discard most of the fat. Add 1/2 cup water or white stock, 2 tablespoons tomato juice, 1 stalk celery, and a few slices onion and cover the pan. Reduce the heat to moderate (350° F.) and continue roasting, basting often, until the duck is very tender, about 1 hour. Transfer the duck to a platter, skim the fat from the pan juices, and strain them. Serve the gravy separately.

A goose has a quantity of surplus fat in the cavity. Pull it out and render it. Combine with fat from roasting. Prick the bird's skin in several places. Turn it frequently as it roasts so that the fat can drip out on all sides and pour off the fat as it collects. Never discard goose fat. It will keep indefinitely in jars in the refrigerator and is second only to butter as a fine fat for cooking.

L'Oie Rôtie

CLEAN a goose and fill the cavity with stuffing, preferably one containing fruit. Sew up the vent, truss the legs and wings close to the body, and rub the goose with a little salt. Lay it on its side in a roasting pan, add 1/2 cup hot water, and roast the bird in a hot oven (425° F.) for 1 hour. Turn the goose on its other side and continue to cook, turning it every 1/2 hour and basting frequently. As the water cooks away, add more and skim off the surplus fat that collects in the pan. Allow about 15 minutes per pound. Pierce the second joint to test the bird for doneness. Put the goose on its back for the last 15 minutes to brown the breast. Remove the goose to a warm serving platter, pour off the fat, and make pan gravy. A 12-pound goose serves 10.

Baking Fish

FISH cooked in a open pan, in dry heat, and basted with fat, is for some unknown reason, said to be baked, rather than roasted. Baking and braising are ordinarily reserved for large whole fish. The fatty fish such as shad, bluefish, and mackerel are usually baked, while less fatty fish, which are apt to become dry in baking, are better braised. The head and sometimes the tail are left on for baking, and so is the skin, so be sure to remove all scales. When a fish is baked whole, use a cooking dish handsome enough to bring to the table, so that you need not transfer the fish to a serving platter.

Poisson au Four

DIP the well-cleaned and carefully-scaled fish in flour seasoned with a little salt. Put a 1/4-inch layer of salad oil or freshly rendered pork fat in an ovenproof serving platter and put the dish in a hot oven (450° F.). When the fat is hot, lay the fish in it and bake for 10 to 20 minutes; the size and thickness of the fish determines the cooking time, and the fish is done when it flakes easily with a fork, loses its translucency, and can be cleanly lifted away from the bones. Baste frequently. Pour off the fat and serve with mustard sauce or with maître d'hôtel butter.

BAKED TROUT WITH CREAM

Truite Normande

CLEAN 6 brook trout. Butter an ovenproof serving platter generously and arrange the fish in it side by side. Add 1/4 cup water and the juice of 2 lemons. Season with salt and a little pepper and sprinkle over all 2 teaspoons chopped parsley and 3 tablespoons chopped chives. Bring to a boil over direct heat, with an asbestos mat under the platter, then put it in a moderately hot oven (375° F.). Bake for 12 to 15 minutes, or until the fish are done. Bring 2/3 cup heavy cream to a boil. Pour the cream over the trout, sprinkle the top with a few fresh bread crumbs, return to the oven or broiler, and let the crumbs brown.

BAKED WHITEFISH WITH PORTUGUESE SAUCE

Lavaret à la Portugaise

SCALE and clean a whitefish weighing about 3 pounds. The fish may be left whole or it may be split and the bones in the center removed. Dip the fish in milk and then in flour. Shake off the surplus flour and season the fish with salt and pepper. Put a 1/4-inch layer of salad oil in an ovenproof serving platter and heat the oil in a hot oven (425° F.). Put the fish in the baking dish and bake it for 20 to 25 minutes if the fish is split, and 10 minutes longer if the fish is whole, basting frequently with the oil. Drain off the oil and mask the fish with *sauce portugaise*.

FILET OF STRIPED BASS AU GRATIN

Bar Rayé de Mer au Gratin

REMOVE and set aside the stems from 8 medium mushrooms. Cook the caps for about 5 minutes in water to cover with 4 or 5 drops of lemon juice. Leave the mushroom caps in the cooking liquor.

Sauté 1 tablespoon chopped shallot or onion in 1 tablespoon butter until it is soft but not brown. Clean 6 medium or 12 small mushrooms, combine them with the reserved mushroom stems, and chop together until quite fine. Add the chopped mushrooms to the butter and shallots and cook slowly until almost all the moisture from the mushrooms is cooked away. Add 1 teaspoon chopped parsley and 1/2 cup brown sauce or good meat gravy or tomato sauce, and cook for a few minutes to combine the ingredients.

Spread the bottom of an ovenproof serving dish with about half the sauce and on it place the boned and skinned filets from 3 small striped bass. Sprinkle the filets with a little salt and pepper. Drain the mushroom caps, arrange them on the filets, and cover with the remaining sauce. Sprinkle with fine bread crumbs, 1 tablespoon melted butter, and about 1/3 cup white wine and bake in a hot oven (425° F.) for 12 to 15 minutes, or until the top is brown and the fish is cooked. Remove from the oven and sprinkle with a few drops of lemon juice and 1 teaspoon chopped parsley.

Poaching and Boiling

POACHING and boiling are perhaps the simplest of all cooking methods. Except when the word "boil" is qualified by a descriptive such as hard, vigorous, or rolling, both poaching and boiling are done in liquid that merely simmers, and the difference between the two methods is in the nature and amount of the liquid used. In boiling meat, poultry, or fish, the food is completely immersed in a large amount of seasoned liquid. In poaching, the food is barely covered with liquid. A large kettle is usually used for boiling, therefore, and a shallow pan for poaching. Tougher cuts of meat respond to gentle boiling, but this relatively vigorous treatment is not suited to most birds and fish. In many cases, the liquid is allowed to do no more than bubble almost imperceptibly, or is even kept below the boiling point.

A word of caution may be needed about salt in this kind of cookery. *Seasoning* One teaspoon salt for each quart of water is the rule when the cooking time is not much more than a half hour. Less salt must be used if the cooking time is long and the liquid will therefore be very much reduced, thus increasing the proportion of salt to water. More salt can always be added, but it can never be taken out.

Seasonings in the liquid give boiled or poached foods so much flavor that chefs never fail to add appropriate vegetables and herbs—onion, carrot, garlic, celery, parsley, bay leaves—depending upon whether they are cooking a whole fish or a piece of beef, or poaching a chicken.

Boiled foods lose some of their own flavor in the cooking liquor, *Sauces* so they are often served with piquant sauces. Sauces that include mustard, horseradish, capers, lemon, vinegar, sour pickles, and the like are best suited for boiled foods. On the other hand, the liquid from poaching is often reduced and used to make the sauce for the poached food. The reduction concentrates the flavors and these sauces are thickened with *beurre manié*, cream sauce, or egg yolk mixed with cream.

The poaching and boiling of meat, poultry, and fish are dealt with in this section. Other foods that are commonly poached, as for example eggs, fruits for compotes, and certain shellfish and variety meats, will be found under their respective headings.

Boiling, in the sense of cooking in violently agitated water, is so often frowned upon in this book that I feel obliged to point out that there are times when hard boiling is necessary; in bouillabaisse, for instance, in reducing certain liquids, where boiling hastens the rate of evaporation, or in cooking spaghetti, where the agitation helps to keep the strands of pasta separate, or in heating water for tea.

Poaching and Boiling Meat

THE BOILED meat dish best known in France is *pot-au-feu*, and no des- *Pot-au-Feu* cription of boiled food is complete without a mention of it. However since the famous *pot-au-feu* results not only in boiled beef, known as *boeuf bouilli*, but also in a soup, and since that soup is the basis for other

151

soups, in this volume the recipe appears in the section on soup. Still, the comments on *pot-au-feu* ought really to be read in conjunction with a discussion of boiled meat, and it would be good to do this now.

Few cuts from the younger, more tender animals are used for boiled or poached dishes. Why boil a delicate tender piece of veal or lamb that is perfect for roasting or broiling or braising? All its delicate flavor would be lost in boiling and the essence captured by the broth would never be strong enough to make a fine-flavored soup or sauce.

Many sauces served with boiled meat are made with some of the broth. And so we boil the tougher cuts of beef and the legs of mature lambs and mutton—the joy of every Englishman when served with caper sauce —and we give the shoulder meat of veal and lamb an initial poaching for *blanquette de veau* and Irish stew, but we cook few other cuts this way. Pork is such a fatty meat that except for the cured cuts—hams, butts, and shoulders—it demands cookery methods that brown the meat as the fat is drawn out.

You will find that boiled meat holds its shape better in the cooking and carves more easily if soft twine is tied around it every 2 inches or so. Scum will rise to the top when the liquid comes to a boil, and during the first half hour or so of cooking, and it should be skimmed off as long as it continues to rise. Then, if the boiling is gentle, the broth will be clear.

Gigot d'Agneau Bouilli

BOILED LEG OF LAMB

HAVE the butcher cut short the shank of a 5- to 5 1/2-pound leg of lamb and remove the irregular-shaped hipbone at the other end. Tie soft twine around the thick part of the meat at 2-inch intervals. Save the hipbone and beg another bone from the butcher for the broth. Put the lamb in a kettle, add water to cover and 1/2 teaspoon salt for each quart of water, and bring the water to a boil. Add the hipbone and any other bones, 4 medium carrots, and 3 white turnips, all cut in pieces, 2 onions, one studded with a clove, 3 leeks, and a faggot made by tying together 1 stalk of celery, 4 sprigs of parsley, half a bay leaf, and a little thyme. Skim the liquid until no more scum rises to the surface, then boil the meat gently, allowing 15 minutes for each pound of meat. When ready to serve, remove the leg of lamb from the broth, carve it, and serve with the boiled vegetables and with potatoes that have been boiled separately.

Make 1 cup béchamel sauce with equal amounts of milk and lamb stock and add 2 tablespoons coarsely chopped capers and 1 teaspoon each of lemon juice and chopped parsley. Serve with the lamb.

Caper Sauce

LAMB OR CHICKEN CURRY

Currie de Mouton ou Poulet

COOK 4 onions, chopped, in 2 tablespoons butter until they are lightly browned. Add 2 to 2 1/2 pounds diced uncooked lamb, seasoned with 1 tablespoon salt, from which the fat and sinews have been removed. Add 2 bay leaves, crushed, 1 clove of garlic, crushed, a little thyme, and 2 to 3 tablespoons curry powder. Mix well and add 4 cups stock or water and 2 tablespoons tomato sauce. Bring to a boil and cook slowly over low heat for about 2 hours, or until the meat is tender. When it is done, remove it to a serving dish.

To the sauce in the pan add 2 tablespoons grated coconut, 1 green apple, peeled and chopped, and 3 tablespoons chopped chutney. Thicken with 2 tablespoons arrowroot or cornstarch mixed with a little cold water. Bring the sauce to a boil, stirring constantly. Add 1/2 cup cream, correct the seasoning with salt, and pour the sauce over the lamb.

For chicken curry, substitute for the lamb a 3- to 3 1/2-pound chicken cut in 8 pieces and cook it for about 40 minutes, or until it is tender. Add a little more cream to the sauce because curry sauce for chicken should be lighter in color than for lamb.

HAMS may be either boiled or baked, but most hams are boiled before they are baked. Hams vary so greatly that it is almost impossible to give directions that will be correct for all of them. Very often, however, there are cooking directions attached to the ham you buy. A tenderized ham usually does not require precooking. For a Virginia-style ham that has had a long curing and aging or for a lightly smoked but not tenderized ham, you may follow these recipes, which were used at the old Ritz-Carlton. You want to finish the ham in the popular American way with brown sugar, molasses, or honey and cloves, or in the typical French fashion with Madeira. The French prefer this to the sweet coating.

For soaking and boiling, use a kettle large enough to permit the ham to be well covered with water. This quantity of water is essential for

Boiled Ham

extracting the surplus salt. The water should always simmer, never boil rapidly. It is almost impossible to time the cooking exactly—any specified time will always be approximate, depending on the shape of the ham, the proportion of fat, and so on. Ham is never pierced with a fork to see if it is tender. Piercing releases the juices. Instead, pull the small bone at the shank end that lies alongside the large one: when it is loose and slips out easily, the ham is done.

To Test Ham

Baked Virginia Style Ham

BAKED VIRGINIA STYLE HAM

COVER a long cured, aged Virginia style ham completely with cold water and soak it for 24 hours. Drain it and scrub it thoroughly in warm water. Place the ham skin side down in a large ham kettle, cover it with cold water, and add 2 cups cider vinegar. Bring the liquid slowly to a boil over moderate heat: this will take about 1 hour. Then let the ham boil slowly, adding hot water as needed to keep the ham constantly covered. Allow about 20 minutes cooking time per pound of ham, counting from the time the water boils. When the ham tests done, remove it from the water and place it fat side up in a roasting pan. Peel off the skin while the ham is hot, being careful not to tear the fat. If the layer of fat is very thick, trim away some of it.

Spread the ham with a little brown sugar, molasses, or honey, stud it with cloves, and bake it in a moderate oven (350° F.) until it is well browned.

Jambon Jubilé

JUBILEE HAM

FOR a tenderized ham of about 12 pounds prepare the following cooking liquor: Put in the ham kettle enough cold water to cover the ham when it is later added to the kettle (allowing for what will cook away in an hour) and add 1 quart dry white wine or cider, 2 or 3 carrots, sliced, 3 or 4 onions, cut in quarters, 4 or 5 stalks of celery, 4 or 5 sprigs of parsley, and a clove of garlic. Bring the liquid to a boil and simmer it for 1 hour. Then put in the ham, turn the heat down very low, and let the ham cook without boiling for about 2 hours, to heat it through. Remove the ham and put it in a roasting pan. Peel off the skin, being careful not to tear the fat. If the fat is very thick, trim away some of it to leave an

154

even layer. If desired, a little brown sugar, molasses, or honey may be spread over the ham. Stud it with a few cloves and pour over it 1 cup Madeira. Glaze the ham in a hot oven (425° F.) for 8 to 10 minutes, basting it several times. Serve Madeira sauce separately.

HAM WITH MADEIRA SAUCE

Jambon au Madère

SOAK and boil a thoroughly aged country ham as for baked Virginia style ham, omitting the cider vinegar. When the ham tests done, remove it from the water, place it in a roasting pan, peel off the skin, and trim the fat, if the layer is very thick. Pour over the ham 1 cup Madeira, cover the pan, and cook in a moderate oven (350° F.) for 30 minutes. Uncover the pan and pour over the ham 1 cup brown sauce. Return the ham to the oven and cook it, uncovered, basting often, until it is well browned. Allow about 5 minutes per pound. Serve with Madeira sauce or the sauce from the pan.

Poaching

and

Boiling

Poultry

THE boiled chicken dish best known in France is probably *poule-au-pot*. It is to boiled poultry what *pot-au-feu* is to boiled meat. Like *pot-au-feu*, this dish produces not only boiled fowl, but a soup that is the basis for other soups. You will see how this progression works if you will reread the section in the soup chapter in which the recipe for *poule-au-pot* appears. When the fowl in *poule-au-pot* is not served in the soup, but separately, it is called *poule bouillie*. For those who want or must have very simple, easily digested food, there is probably nothing better than *poule bouillie*, or *poulet poché*, with its broth and vegetables and a little rice. For a

Poule-au-Pot

richer dish, the chicken can be served with a sauce like *suprême* or *alle-mande* and for a more highly seasoned one, with a sauce like curry or paprika.

Birds for boiling, as for braising and stews, are usually the older heavier birds, weighing 5 or more pounds. They require a moist cooking method to give them succulence and long slow cooking to bring them to tenderness. Because they have more taste than younger birds, the resulting broth is rich in flavor. The bird is always left whole and trussed and is sometimes stuffed. Cooking times given are approximate, because the time it takes for a fowl to cook depends upon its age and original tenderness.

Tender young birds or capons may also be boiled or poached. A fowl must be cooked until tender; a young chicken should be cooked only until no pink juice follows a fork inserted in the second joint—as a sautéed, broiled, or roasted chicken is.

If boiled chicken is to be used in another dish—in a salad or in sauced mixtures for *vol-au-vent* or *bouchées*—it is cooled in the broth to prevent it from drying out.

Poule Bouillie au Riz   BOILED FOWL WITH RICE

PREPARE *poule-au-pot*, chicken in the pot. Half an hour before the fowl is done, prepare *riz au beurre*, buttered rice.

While the rice is cooking, prepare 1 1/2 cups *velouté* sauce, using stock in which the fowl is cooking. Mix 1 egg yolk with 1/4 cup cream and combine with the *velouté*. Add a few drops of lemon juice and bring the sauce to the boil but do not let it boil.

Make a bed of the rice on a serving platter, carve the fowl, and arrange it on the rice. Slice the carrots and arrange them around the bird. Pour half the sauce over the fowl and rice and serve the remaining sauce separately.

Poulet Poché au Riz   POACHED YOUNG CHICKEN WITH RICE

IN a kettle combine 2 quarts water, a few chicken bones, 2 carrots, 2 onions, 2 leeks, 2 teaspoons salt, and a faggot made by tying together 2 stalks of celery, 4 sprigs of parsley, 1/2 bay leaf, and a little thyme, and simmer the mixture for 1 hour. Truss the wings and legs of a young 2 1/2- to 3-pound chicken close to the body. Put it in the broth and simmer it for 30 to 35 minutes, or until it is done. To test, pierce the second joint with a kitchen fork or needle, and if no pink juice follows the fork, the chicken is done. Do not overcook it. Keep the chicken in the broth until ready to serve. Serve with rice and sauce as for *poule bouillie*, boiled fowl.

POACHED CAPON WITH CURRY SAUCE

Chapon Poché Edouard VII

STUFF a roasting chicken or capon weighing from 4 to 4 1/2 pounds with the following stuffing: Mix together lightly 3 cups cooked rice, 6 to 8 cubes of goose liver, sautéed quickly in butter, and 2 or 3 truffles, diced. Add 2 tablespoons *glace de viande*, or meat glaze, and 2 to 3 tablespoons *sauce suprême* or *velouté*. Sew up the vent. Poach the chicken in chicken stock to cover for 50 to 60 minutes, or until it is tender. Place the chicken on a warm serving dish and garnish with sautéed cucumbers. Add 1 tablespoon diced pimiento to 2 cups curry sauce and serve the sauce separately.

Poaching Fish

ANY kind of fish may be poached, but for the greatest success, choose firm-fleshed, fine-grained fish such as sole, sea bass, striped bass, pompano, and red snapper. Coarse fish break apart when they are poached. Smaller pieces of fish are easier to handle than large pieces, and filets take particularly well to poaching, especially filets of Dover and Channel sole because of their size and thickness. These come to us frozen from Europe. American gray sole and the flounder filets that sometimes pass for sole

Dover and Channel Sole

are soft fish that break easily after they are cooked, and should be rolled and skewered with wooden picks, or cut into small pieces that will fit on a spatula, so that they can be easily handled when they are cooked, with less risk of breaking.

Fish may be poached whole and fileted after cooking, but it is usually more convenient to do the boning before cooking. When you are dealing with large quantities of fish, this advance preparation is often essential, because of the time it takes.

Pan for Poaching Fish Since filets are flat, they do not require a deep pan, but the pan must be wide enough so that the filets can be arranged in it side by side. A large skillet is a good choice. Spread the pan with butter and sprinkle the butter with chopped shallots or onion. Any ingredients typical of the dish—mushrooms for *filets bonne femme* or chopped tomatoes for *filets dugléré*—that require some cooking are added, and the seasoned fish is arranged on these. Have as many of the ingredients as practical in the pan while the fish cooks. Sauce and fish alike will benefit from the savory blending of flavors produced. In *haute cuisine*, any large bones that have been removed in the fileting are laid on top of the fish in order to add flavor to the cooking liquor and to the resulting sauce. Some chefs believe that enough gelatin is extracted from the bones to improve the texture of the sauce at the same time. The bones should be discarded before the sauce is made.

Liquid for Poaching Fish Fish is usually poached in a mixture of white wine and water, but fish stock, tomato juice, lemon juice or mushroom liquor may be included. If the prescribed amount of liquid is very small, sprinkle it over the fish. In no case should the liquid more than barely reach the top of the fish. A piece of wax paper or buttered white paper, cut to fit the pan, is laid on the fish. A tiny hole in the paper permits a little steam to escape and prevents the paper from bouncing. The liquid is brought to a boil and the pan is then covered with a lid. As the liquid simmers, the savory steam helps to cook the fish and the filets are penetrated with **To Test Poached Fish** this sealed-in flavor. Be careful not to overcook fish. When the flesh loses its translucency and flakes readily at the touch of a fork, the fish is done. Small whole fish, weighing about 1/2 pound, should cook in 15 minutes or less; flat filets take even less time, 10 to 12 minutes.

The paper and bones are discarded and the cooked fish lifted to the serving dish with a broad, flexible spatula. The cooking liquid is then reduced, thickened, and enriched, and any ingredients that need only brief cooking, such as oysters, mussels, or grapes, are added last.

FILETS OF SOLE WITH MUSHROOMS

*Filets de Sole
Bonne Femme*

MELT 2 tablespoons butter in a large shallow pan and spread over it 2 shallots or 1 small onion, finely chopped, and 6 mushrooms, cleaned and thinly sliced. Season 6 filets of sole, or of other fish, with salt and pepper and arrange them side by side on the vegetables. Spread 6 more sliced mushrooms over the fish and sprinkle with a little parsley. Add 3/4 cup dry white wine. Cover the fish with a piece of wax paper the size of the pan, with a small hole in the center. Bring the liquid to a boil, cover the pan, and cook 10 to 12 minutes. Using a large broad spatula, remove the fish and the vegetables to a warm serving platter.

Make the sauce in one of the following ways: For a simple sauce, cook the liquid in the pan until it is reduced to about 1 cup and swirl in *beurre manié*, made by creaming together 1 tablespoon butter with 1 teaspoon flour. Correct the seasoning with salt, remove the sauce immediately from the heat, and pour it over the fish. For a rich sauce, cook the liquid in the pan until it is reduced to about 1/2 cup and thicken it by stirring in 1/2 cup cream sauce and 1 egg yolk beaten lightly with 1/4 cup cream. Bring the sauce just to the boiling point but do not allow it to boil. Correct the seasoning with salt and pour the sauce over the fish. Or you may make a *roux* by melting 2 tablespoons butter, adding 1 tablespoon flour, and cooking until it just starts to turn golden. As soon as the fish is cooked, remove it to a heated serving dish and stir the liquid in the pan into the *roux*. Bring the sauce to the boil, and stir it with a whip until it is perfectly smooth. Continue cooking until there is about 1 cup of sauce. Mix 2 egg yolks with 1/3 cup cream and combine this with the sauce. Bring the sauce to a boil but do not let it boil.

*Sauce for
Poached Fish*

FILETS OF SOLE WITH TOMATOES

*Filets de Sole
Dugléré*

SUBSTITUTE 4 tomatoes, peeled, seeded, and chopped, for the mushrooms in *filets de sole bonne femme*, and add 1/2 cup tomato juice and 1 clove of garlic. Thicken the sauce with *beurre manié*. Stir to blend the sauce and swirl in 1 tablespoon butter to finish.

Monsieur Malley, saucier *at the Paris Ritz and later* chef des cuisines *at the London Ritz, was my professional ideal. He was a gentleman to his fingertips, always immaculate, always perfectly groomed, whether he was in the kitchen or dressed to leave the hotel with cane and top hat. Monsieur Malley was especially expert in poaching and saucing fish. He taught me the importance of changing basic formulas to achieve variety and the tactical value of naming such newly created dishes in honor of special guests or occasions. Malley had a fertile mind, and many of the fish sauces served in good restaurants today were originated by him.*

Filets de sole Véronique, for instance, was a Malley invention. A special party was planned, and Malley decided to add tiny white grapes to the white wine sauce for the fish course. He gave instructions to a trusted underchef, and went out, as usual, for the afternoon. When he returned, he found the young man so excited that he could hardly work. Monsieur Malley discovered that the young man's wife had just presented him with a baby girl, their first child. Monsieur Malley asked what they would name the child. "Véronique," was the reply. "Alors," said the chef des cuisines, "we'll call the new dish filets de sole Véronique." And so it is called to this day.

Filets de Sole Véronique

FILETS OF SOLE WITH WHITE GRAPES

SPREAD 1 tablespoon butter in a shallow pan and sprinkle with 2 shallots or 1/2 small onion, finely chopped. Season 6 to 8 filets of sole with salt and pepper, roll and skewer them with wooden picks, and arrange in the pan. Sprinkle them with 1/2 cup each of white wine and water. Cover with a circle of buttered or wax paper cut the size of the pan with a small hole in the middle. Bring to a boil, cover the pan, and cook for 10 to 12 minutes. Remove the fish to a heatproof dish and remove the picks. Cook the liquid until it is reduced to about 1/2 cup and add 1/2 cup cream sauce mixed with 1 egg yolk and 2 tablespoons butter. Cook just until the butter is melted. Use drained canned grapes or simmer 1 cup small seedless white grapes in a little water for a few minutes, drain, and place them around the fish. Fold 2 tablespoons whipped cream into the sauce and pour it over the fish. Brown under a hot broiler flame.

Filets de Sole Reine Victoria

FILETS OF SOLE QUEEN VICTORIA

SPREAD 6 filets of English sole with a thin layer of fish mousse. Fold the filets in half lengthwise and press the edges together. Cut a shallow slit along the fold so the filets won't spring apart. Melt 2 tablespoons butter in a shallow pan and sprinkle with 1 teaspoon chopped shallots. Arrange the sole filets in the pan and pour over them enough dry white wine so that the liquid is about 1/2 inch deep in the pan. Cover the fish with a circle of buttered or wax paper with a small hole in the center. Bring the wine to a boil, cover the pan, and poach the fish for about 10 minutes, or until the flesh flakes easily.

Arrange the filets in a ring on a warm serving platter and cover them with Newburg sauce. Fill the center of the ring with 1 to 1 1/2 cups cooked, diced lobster meat and 12 to 18 poached oysters, both mixed with about 1 cup cream sauce. Decorate the top of the ring of filets with cooked shrimp and slices of truffles arranged alternately, and garnish the edge of the platter with croutons.

ENGLISH SOLE EDWARD VIII

Soles Edouard VIII

CLEAN 6 English soles, each weighing from 1 to 1 1/4 pounds. Poach the whole fish for 12 to 15 minutes as for *filets de sole reine Victoria*.

Place the fish on a flat board and trim off the fins. Cut away about 1/8 inch all around the edge of the fish, then cut down the center back to the depth of the backbone. Carefully lift off each half of the filet, discarding the backbone. Replace the halves and arrange the fish on a warm serving platter. Cook the liquid in the pan until it is reduced by 1/2, and stir in 1 teaspoon curry powder. Add gradually 1 cup cream sauce and 2 tablespoons heavy cream, mixing constantly with a wire whisk until the sauce reaches the boil. Correct the seasoning with salt and strain the sauce through a fine sieve. Meanwhile, prepare 12 tiny rice molds about the size of demitasse cups. Garnish each fish with a turned, or fluted, cooked mushroom, pour the sauce around the fish and mushrooms, and sprinkle the mushrooms with finely chopped parsley. Arrange the molds of rice around the fish, with a slice of truffle on each, and put cooked shrimp between the molds.

FILETS OF FISH WITH EGGPLANT

Filets de Poisson Persane

IN A SHALLOW pan melt 2 tablespoons butter and add 1 tablespoon chopped shallots or onions and 1 teaspoon crushed garlic. Arrange 6 filets on the vegetables, season with a little salt and pepper, and cover with 3 ripe tomatoes, peeled, seeded and coarsely chopped. Scatter over the tomatoes 6 mushrooms, sliced, and sprinkle with finely chopped parsley. Add 1 cup dry white wine and cover the fish with a circle of buttered or wax paper cut to fit the pan, with a small hole in the center. Bring the liquid to a boil, cover the pan, and cook on top of the stove or in a hot oven (450° F.) for 10 to 15 minutes, or until the fish flakes easily at the touch of a fork.

Remove the fish to a heatproof serving dish and continue to cook the liquid remaining in the pan until it is reduced by 1/3. Beat 2 egg yolks into 1 cup hot cream sauce and stir it into the sauce in the pan. Bring almost to a boil, stirring vigorously. Remove from the heat and swirl in 2 tablespoons butter. Fold in 2 tablespoons whipped cream.

Cut an eggplant into 6 pieces about 1/2 inch thick. Dip the pieces in milk, then in flour, and sauté them in very hot oil until browned on both sides. Arrange the eggplant on the fish, pour the sauce over the eggplant, and glaze under the broiler flame.

Perche Chez Soi   PERCH CHEZ SOI

SCALE and clean 6 perch, each weighing about 1/2 pound, and cut off the sharp fins. In a saucepan melt 2 tablespoons butter, add 1 cup each of chopped carrots and celery, 2 tablespoons chopped onion, and 6 or 8 sprigs of parsley, and cook gently for about 10 minutes, or until the vegetables are soft. Add 1 1/2 cups each of white wine and water and 1/2 teaspoon salt. Bring the liquid to a boil and simmer for 15 to 20 minutes. Arrange the perch in a buttered shallow pan and strain half the liquid over them. Bring to a boil and poach the fish for 12 to 15 minutes. Continue to simmer the vegetables in the remaining liquid in the saucepan.

Place the fish on a serving platter and remove the skins. Remove the vegetables and spread them over the fish. Combine the vegetable liquid with the liquid in which the fish was cooked, and boil until it is reduced to 1 1/2 cups. Stir in *beurre manié* made by creaming together 2 tablespoons butter and 1 tablespoon flour, and continue to stir until the sauce is smooth and thickened. Correct the seasoning and swirl in 2 tablespoons butter. Pour the sauce over the fish and sprinkle with chopped parsley.

Oranges go well with fish. I started using them during prohibition when wine sold for cooking contained salt to make it undrinkable. The salt also spoiled it for cooking. Orange juice was a good substitute in certain dishes. As soon as we were rid of prohibition I added wine as well, I must confess. Orange peel is used here somewhat as it is in duck à l'orange. *The trick in preparing the fine julienne of orange peel is to slice off a layer of rind, or zest, so thin that none of the white part is included. Then make sure that the flavor of the zest will not be overpowering by parboiling the julienne for a few minutes.*

Julienne of Orange Zest

FILETS OF POMPANO WITH ORANGES

REMOVE the zest from 2 oranges as described and cut it in fine julienne. Cover with water, parboil for a few minutes, and drain. Melt 2 tablespoons butter in a shallow pan and add 1 teaspoon finely chopped shallots or onion. Season 6 filets of pompano or other fish lightly with salt and arrange them in the pan. Add 1/2 cup fish stock or water and the juice of 1/2 lemon and 2 oranges. Spread the drained julienne of orange peel on top of the fish.

Cover the fish with a circle of buttered or wax paper cut the size of the pan, with a small hole in the center. Bring to a boil, cover the pan, and cook for 10 to 12 minutes. Remove the fish to a heated serving dish. Cook the liquid in the pan until it is reduced to 1/2 the original quantity and add 1 cup Newburg sauce. Bring back to the boil and add, if desired, 1/2 cup Sherry or Madeira. Strain the sauce over the fish, replacing the orange peel that falls off.

Filets de Pompano Florida

FILETS OF SEA BASS PERSHING

SPREAD 1 1/2 tablespoons butter in a shallow pan and sprinkle over it 3 shallots, finely chopped, and 1 teaspoon finely chopped parsley. Season 6 filets of sea bass with salt and a little white pepper and arrange them in the pan. Add about 1/3 cup white wine and 1 cup fish stock. Bring to a boil, cover the pan, and simmer slowly for 10 to 12 minutes. Add

Filets de Bars de Mer Pershing

12 oysters and cook for 2 or 3 minutes. Remove the filets and oysters to a heated serving dish and arrange with them 12 cooked shrimp and 12 cooked mushrooms. Surround with small cooked potato balls.

Cook the liquid remaining in the pan until it is reduced to about 1/2 its original quantity. Thicken it with 3 tablespoons cream sauce and add 1 1/2 tablespoons butter. When the butter is just melted, fold in 3 tablespoons cream, whipped. Correct the seasoning and pour the sauce over the fish and its garniture of oysters, shrimp, and mushrooms. Set under a hot broiler until golden brown.

Bars de Mer et Coquilles à la Poulette

SEA BASS AND SCALLOPS POULETTE

IN A shallow pan put 2 tablespoons butter and add 1 tablespoon chopped shallot and 1/2 pound of mushrooms, cleaned and sliced. On this arrange 6 filets of sea bass and season with salt and a little pepper. Add 2 cups scallops and 1/4 pound mushrooms, cleaned and sliced. Sprinkle with 1 tablespoon chopped parsley and add 1/3 cup dry white wine and 1/2 cup fish stock. Cover the fish with a circle of buttered or wax paper with a small hole in the center. Bring the liquid to a boil, cover the pan, and cook slowly for 10 to 12 minutes, or until the fish is done. Discard the paper and place the fish, scallops, and mushrooms in a serving dish. Cook the liquid remaining in the pan until it is reduced to about 1/3 its original quantity. Add 1 cup cream sauce and mix well. Beat 2 egg yolks with 2 to 3 tablespoons cream and a little of the hot sauce and stir into the sauce. Heat the sauce, stirring constantly, to the boiling point but do not let it boil. Correct the seasoning with salt, pour the sauce over the fish, and sprinkle with chopped chives.

Truite à la Bourbonnaise

BROOK TROUT BOURBONNAISE

CLEAN 6 brook trout, each weighing about 1/2 pound. Cut off the fins, split the fish and remove backbones. Prepare 1 1/2 cups fish mousse with 1/2 pound pike, 1 egg white, and 1 cup cream. Also prepare mushroom *duxelles* with 1 cup finely chopped mushrooms, 1 tablespoon butter, and 1 teaspoon chopped shallots or onion. Add 2 tablespoons tomato or brown sauce and 1 teaspoon chopped parsley and season with salt and pepper. Cool.

Combine the mushroom *duxelles* and the fish mousse and stuff the trout with the mixture. Season the fish with salt and pepper, roll each one in well-buttered paper, and tie with string. Arrange the fish in a deep saucepan side by side and add enough red wine barely to cover. Cover the pan, bring the wine to a boil, and poach the fish on top of the stove or in a hot oven (400° F.) for about 18 to 20 minutes. Remove the trout to a warm serving dish and continue to cook the liquid in the pan until it is reduced to 2/3. Add 1 1/2 cups heavy cream and continue to cook until the sauce is slightly thickened. Remove the sauce from the heat and stir in 3 egg yolks, beaten with a little of the hot sauce, and 3 tablespoons butter. Discard the strings and paper from the trout and remove the skins. Put a few small cooked mushrooms on the fish, correct the seasoning of the sauce with salt, and pour it over the fish.

SALMON TROUT ADMIRAL

Truite Saumonée à l'Amiral

CLEAN a salmon trout weighing from 3 to 4 pounds and trim off the fins. If the fish is too long for the serving dish, remove the head and tail; if not leave them. Peel 12 mushrooms. Turn 6 of them, and slice the rest. Simmer in 1/2 cup water with a little salt and the juice of 1/2 lemon for about 8 minutes.

Spread 1 tablespoon soft butter in a shallow pan. Sprinkle the butter with 1 tablespoon finely chopped shallots and place the fish on the shallots. Sprinkle the fish with salt and pepper and add the peelings and stems of the mushrooms, 1 cup white wine, and 1 cup fish stock. Cover the fish with a circle of buttered or wax paper cut the size of the pan, with a small hole in the center. Bring the liquid to a boil, cover the pan, and cook the fish slowly over low heat or in a hot oven (400° F.) for 35 to 40 minutes. If desired, the fish may be split and boned. In this case the bones should be put in the pan and the fish cooked for only 20 minutes.

Poach 12 to 18 shrimp, make 12 small fish quenelles, and bake 12 crescent-shaped croutons of puff paste or fry lozenge-shaped pieces of bread in butter until golden.

Remove the fish from the kettle, trim off the skin, and cut away the layer of dark flesh. Arrange the fish on a serving platter and keep warm.

Reduce the liquor remaining in the pan to half, or to about 1 cup.

In another pan melt 1 1/2 tablespoons butter, add 1 tablespoon flour, and cook, stirring, until the *roux* just starts to turn golden. Stir in the reduced cooking liquor and cook, stirring, until the sauce is smooth and well blended. Add 1 cup cream, bring to a boil, and correct the seasoning with salt. Add a few drops of lemon juice and strain the sauce through a very fine sieve.

Pour a little sauce around the fish on the platter. Serve the rest separately. Arrange the mushroom caps and sliced mushrooms on the fish and garnish the platter with the quenelles—each topped with a slice of truffle—the shrimp, the croutons, and parsley.

Oeufs d'Alose
Bonne Femme

SHAD ROE WITH MUSHROOMS

To 2 tablespoons butter in a shallow saucepan add 3 shallots and 1 tablespoon parsley, all finely chopped, 12 mushrooms, cleaned and sliced, 3 pairs of shad roe, arranged side by side, and a generous 1/2 cup white wine. Cover the roe with a circle of buttered or wax paper, cut to fit the pan, with a small hole in the center. Bring the liquid to a boil, cover the pan, and simmer for 10 minutes, or until the roe are tender. Remove the roe to a heatproof platter. Reduce the liquid in the pan to 1/2 its original quantity, blend in 1/4 cup cream sauce, and swirl in 1 tablespoon butter. Correct the seasoning with salt, pour the sauce over the roe, and brown them under the broiler. For a more even glaze, fold 2 tablespoons whipped cream into the sauce.

Boiling Fish

FISH are " boiled "—that is, gently simmered—in a flavored and seasoned liquid called a court bouillon, and, as in all boiling, are always deeply immersed in the liquid.

Boiling is a good way to cook large whole fish like salmon, halibut,

166

striped bass, and cod, or pieces of such fish large enough to weigh several pounds. Fish steaks are also boiled. To cook whole fish, the very best utensil is a fish boiler, called a *poissonière*. This long narrow pan has a rack on which the fish rests, and handles on the rack allow the fish to be lifted safely in one piece from the hot cooking liquid. The fish may be wrapped in cheesecloth for easier handling. There is a trick for keeping a large fish from curling in cooking—and a fish to be served whole on the cold buffet must lie straight and flat. Lay the uncooked fish on a thin wooden board and bind it lightly with strips of cheese-cloth, or wrap board and fish in cheesecloth.

Pan for Boiling Fish or Poissonière

In lieu of a fish boiler, you can use a roasting pan and lay the fish or fish steaks on the rack in the pan, then cover the pan closely with heavy foil. Slide the cooked fish from the rack to a plate. Or cut a large fish in half and cook the pieces side by side in an ordinary large shallow saucepan. Fish steaks can also be boiled this way. Remember, " boil " is a misnomer: the liquid is kept at a gentle simmer; a hard boil would break the fish.

There are 3 basic types of court bouillon. All use an acid of some sort with water. One includes lemon juice and milk, to keep such fish as halibut and cod white during cooking; another uses vinegar, and a third includes wine for the flavor it gives to delicate fish and shellfish. Most court bouillons also include aromatic vegetables like carrots or onions, and seasonings. The terms " court bouillon " and " fish stock " are often confused. Fish stock results from the cooking of fish in court bouillon or in another liquid, but court bouillon is not itself a fish stock since it gets none of its flavor from fish.

Court Bouillons

As in other fish cookery, it is important in boiling not to overcook the fish. The liquid in which the fish is placed should be cool; when fish is plunged into boiling liquid the seasonings in the liquid cannot penetrate the flesh. Fish steaks of the usual 1-inch thickness should cook in 12 to 15 minutes. Large whole fish such as salmon take about 8 minutes to the pound; fish weighing under 4 pounds require about 10 minutes to the pound. Always count the cooking time from the moment the court bouillon reaches the simmering point.

Leave the fish in the cooking liquor for a few minutes after turning off the heat, with the pan partly covered. This period allows the fish to become firm and makes serving and carving easier. If the fish is to be served cold, let it cool partly covered until the liquor has cooled a little, then uncover the kettle but leave the fish until it is cold.

Court Bouillon au Blanc — MILK COURT BOUILLON

COMBINE 2 quarts water, 1/2 cup milk, 1 tablespoon salt, and 3 slices of lemon.

Court Bouillon au Vinaigre — VINEGAR COURT BOUILLON

COMBINE 2 quarts water, 1/2 cup vinegar, 1 or 2 large onions, sliced, 1 or 2 carrots, 2 or 3 sprigs parsley, 2 stalks of celery, 2 bay leaves, 1/2 teaspoon thyme, 8 peppercorns, and 1 tablespoon salt. Bring the mixture to a boil, simmer it slowly for 45 minutes to 1 hour, let it cool, and strain it over the fish.

Court Bouillon au Vin — WHITE OR RED WINE COURT BOUILLON

COMBINE 1 quart water, 1 1/2 cups dry white or red wine, 1 onion, sliced, 3 sprigs of parsley, 1 bay leaf, a little thyme, 4 peppercorns, and 1 teaspoon salt. Bring the mixture to a boil, simmer it slowly for about 30 minutes, let it cool, and strain it over the fish.

Darnes de Poisson Bouillies — BOILED FISH STEAKS

ARRANGE haddock, salmon, cod, or halibut steaks, cut about 1 inch thick, side by side in a large shallow saucepan. Add white wine court bouillon or milk court bouillon to cover well, bring the liquid to a boil, cover the pan, and simmer gently for 10 to 15 minutes. Turn off the heat and let the fish stand in the liquid for a minute or two. With a broad spatula (or two, if the steaks are large) remove the fish to a serving dish, draining off all the liquid. Serve the steaks with cream sauce to which a little lemon juice has been added, caper cream or mustard sauce, hollandaise sauce, or any piquant fish sauce.

Poisson Bouilli — BOILED WHOLE FISH

WRAP A 5- to 6-pound fish in cheesecloth. Lay the fish on a rack in a fish kettle and add strained vinegar court bouillon to cover. Bring the court bouillon to a boil and simmer the fish for 40 to 50 minutes, or about 10 to 12 minutes per pound. The fish is done when a large kitchen needle easily detaches the meat from the backbone. The fish may be allowed to cool in the cooking liquid. In this case, the .cooking time should be shortened accordingly. To serve, carefully remove the cheesecloth and lay the fish on a napkin on a warm platter. The napkin will absorb any excess liquid. Carefully lift off the the top skin and cut away the layer of dark flesh. Serve hot with melted butter, hollandaise sauce, or any fish sauce, or chill and serve with mayonnaise.

Use this method for whole salmon, halibut, striped bass, cod, and similar large, meaty fish, but not for mackerel. The flesh of the mackerel is too dark and oily for this method.

Boiling is the most popular way of cooking salmon, and the most convenient, because boiled salmon can be served in either of 2 popular ways: hot with hollandaise sauce or cold with mayonnaise.

BOILED SALMON

Saumon Bouilli

USE vinegar court bouillon. The fish must be put into cold liquid and while the salmon is cooking it must just simmer. Salmon is extremely delicate and if the fish is dropped into boiling liquid or allowed to boil rapidly, it will break apart. Be sure to wrap the fish in cheesecloth and use a board, if possible. A 10- to 20-pound salmon cooks in about 1 to 1 1/2 hours. Remember, even if the salmon is to be served hot, cool it a little in the liquid, half covered. If it is to be served cold, cool it for 1/2 hour, covered, then uncover the kettle and let it cool completely. Drain the cool salmon well and remove the cheesecloth. Chill the fish in the refrigerator.

There is a special trick for telling when a salmon steak is done. After about 15 minutes of cooking, put the point of a small sharp knife in the middle of the round bone from which the smaller bones radiate. If you can lift the bone out without any of the flesh clinging to it, the fish is cooked.

Probably the most fascinating and unusual method of preparing fresh trout is au bleu. *But the method requires that the trout really be alive almost up to the minute of cooking—jumping, as it were, from the water of*

169

the brook into the water in the pan. And in a big city that's a trick. Yet in my early days in New York, many of our European guests expected it. So we installed a big marble trout tank that was filled twice a week with two or three hundred trout. For a while it was quite the smart thing for guests to come downstairs to the kitchen and see us catch with a little net the trout that they would soon be eating. Nowadays this treat is generally reserved for fishermen who can boil trout over a campfire. Still, there are restaurants whose fame rests, at least in part, on this famous dish.

BLUE TROUT

Truite au Bleu

PREPARE vinegar court bouillon, using 3 quarts of water, strain it into a shallow pan, and bring it back to a boil. Hit 6 live trout sharply on the head—*assommer*, in French—to kill them. Clean them quickly, sprinkle with vinegar, and plunge them into the boiling liquid. Turn down the heat and simmer them for 10 minutes. They will curl and take on a bluish color. Remove the trout from the liquid very carefully and drain well. To serve, arrange on a napkin and garnish with parsley. Serve hollandaise sauce or melted butter separately, and accompany with small boiled potato balls rolled in melted butter and then in finely chopped parsley.

RIVER TROUT IN WINE WITH TRUFFLE BUTTER

Truite au Montrachet au Beurre de Truffes

BRING to a boil 2 cups each of water and Montrachet wine with 1 carrot and 1 onion, both sliced, 1 teaspoon salt, 1 teaspoon peppercorns, and a small faggot made by tying together 1 stalk of celery, 4 sprigs of parsley, a little thyme, and a small bay leaf. Simmer this court bouillon for 15 minutes. Clean 6 fresh trout, each weighing about 1/2 pound, and put them in the bouillon. Bring the bouillon almost to a boil and simmer the trout for 10 to 15 minutes, or until done. To serve, remove the skin from the trout and arrange them on a warm serving plate. Pour over each trout 1 to 2 tablespoons of the bouillon and arrange decorative slices of the carrot and rings of onion on the fish. Garnish the platter with parsley and lemon slices dotted with paprika. Another dry white wine may be substituted for the Montrachet.

Truffle Butter

Add 1 tablespoon chopped truffles to 1/2 cup creamed butter, and season with salt and pepper. Serve this truffle butter with the trout.

Bouillabaisses
and
Matelotes

THAT Frenchmen love good food is no secret. What many people are not aware of is a Frenchman's loyalty not only to French cooking but to a particular kind of French cooking: that of his own small native section of France. When he says "*mon pays,*" he means Provence, the Midi, Brittany, Normandy, or wherever he comes from—but not "my country, all of France."

These regional culinary differences, and the passionate Gallic loyalties invoked by them, are particularly pronounced where fish is concerned. The fish found in the different parts of France are as varied as its many political parties. The catch from the bright blue Mediterranean differs from the catch taken from the turbulent, cold Atlantic. And neither at all resembles the fresh-water species.

There are two great regional specialties that involve boiled fish: bouillabaisses and matelotes.

Mediterranean fish are used in bouillabaisse. The popularity of this famous soup apparently began in the port of Marseille hundreds of years ago. In southern Provence bouillabaisse is eaten regularly by many a family and is not just a specialty in the restaurants. With beef scarce and expensive, bouillabaisse is the southern family's *pot-au-feu,* their Sunday dish, and enjoyed with the fondness and appreciation with which their northern cousins regard *pot-au-feu.*

Matelote is a dish of the interior, a stew made from fresh-water fish. Both dishes vary according to the section in which they are made, and usually only local fish go into the pot.

Some people, remembering the bouillabaisse turned out by famous French restaurants, claim that here in America we cannot make bouillabaisse as good, and that it never tastes quite as it does when it is eaten on the sunny shore of the Mediterranean between Marseille and Toulon and served by a swarthy, smiling Provençal waiter. I myself sometimes think that bouillabaisse is enhanced by the presence of the appetite-whetting mistral—the mad, wild wind that sweeps down from the Alps. But even though regional dishes cannot be exactly duplicated away from the little sections that made them famous, it is usually possible to substitute a different wine or cheese for the unavailable variety, a different vegetable or fish, and get excellent results. What if bouillabaisse in this country is not exactly the same as that in Marseille? Neither are the many different kinds served along the Mediterranean coast. Everyone from Cape Cerbère to Mentone claims the distinction of serving the best. Fine fish and shellfish are available in America, and I have made many a Frenchman homesick—and many a homesick Frenchman happy—with American bouillabaisse.

The bouillabaisse famous in Marseille is what it is not only because of the Mediterranean fish that go into it but because of the blended flavors of foods native to Provence—olive oil (never butter), garlic, tomatoes, onions, parsley, fennel, bay leaf, and the all-important saffron, fresh saffron. This undoubtedly contributes something special, because a fresh herb is always more aromatic and subtle than a dried one. And the bit of dried orange rind from native Provençal oranges adds a special bouquet recognized by connoisseurs of bouillabaisse.

Kinds of
Fish for
Bouillabaisse

Marseille bouillabaisse includes at least 5 or 6 kinds of fish, not counting shellfish. The local cooks use the *poissons de roches*, the fish that swim around the rocks, and the marine eel and either crawfish or lobster. Marseille bouillabaisse includes *crustacés*, such as lobster, but not *coquillages*, bivalves such as clams, mussels, and oysters. Parisian bouillabaisse does include mussels, and many chefs, I for one, think clams improve the dish. Use 6 to 10 pounds of fish and about 4 pounds of shellfish to make a bouillabaisse for 12 people. It is hardly practical to make much less than that amount.

The bulk of the fish must be firm-fleshed, a very important point. The soup must boil hard for at least 15 minutes, because it contains a considerable amount of olive oil which would separate out and float on top in a slow boil. In the hard fast boiling, the oil and stock seem to form a sort of emulsion, giving the bouillon the characteristic bouillabaisse consistency. Therefore, soft fish and mussels and clams must be added at the end, to prevent overcooking. I have never been able to find out the exact reason for the thickening effect of the fast boiling, but I have watched many a Marseille chef cook bouillabaisse and seen it work. It may be that gelatin extracted from the fish and its bones combines with the oil. The practice of thickening the soup with *beurre manié*, butter and flour creamed together, is frowned upon by purists.

The *croûte*, or bread, served with bouillabaisse has its ritual, with local variations. The *croûte* is part of the service, because bouillabaisse is a soup, not a stew, and should not be eaten with the ingredients all mixed together like a stew. Many do like it that way, however. The bouillon should be served first, with the *croûte*, and the fish served together on another plate, so that each kind can be easily identified and eaten separately. One of Marseille's best chefs recommends that the bread be untoasted and the bouillon poured over it so that it thickens the bouillon, something like a *panade*. A kind of homemade bread called *marette* is used in Marseille. Some want the bread toasted, rubbed with garlic, and floated on the soup, as the *croûte* is in onion soup. Some prefer a generous sprinkling of small croutons browned in oil or butter.

Here is a Marseille bouillabaisse made with American fish. You will need a large knife with a heavy blade and a heavy board on which to work.

One word more: the diners will appreciate a small plate onto which they can put the discarded bones.

Croûte

Marette

MARSEILLE BOUILLABAISSE

Bouillabaisse Marseillaise

Use 1 pound each of cleaned red snapper, perch, end tail of cod, and eel, 1 1/2 pounds either striped or sea bass, 2 1/2 pounds Spanish mackerel, and 2 live lobsters each weighing 1 1/2 to 1 3/4 pounds. Cut all into 1-inch slices, cutting the lobster through shell and flesh.

Into a large kettle put 3 large leeks, 2 medium onions, and 1 large carrot, all peeled and chopped. Add 1 pound fresh tomatoes, peeled, seeded, and chopped, 2 cloves of garlic, crushed, 2 tablespoons chopped parsley, 1 teaspoon saffron, 1 bay leaf, a little thyme, a pinch of chopped fresh fennel tips, if obtainable, and the dried rind of 1/2 orange. Add 1 tablespoon salt and a little pepper. Spread the cutup lobster on top of the vegetables and add all the fish except the perch and cod. Pour over 1/2 cup olive oil and enough water to cover the mixture well. Bring the liquid to the boil as quickly as possible and let it boil hard for 8 minutes. Add the perch and cod and cook for 8 minutes more. To serve, remove the fish and lobster to a serving dish. Slice French bread about 1/4 inch thick, place it in the bottom of a large soup tureen, and pour the bouillon over. Serve the soup and the fish separately. Serves 10 to 12.

Bouillabaisse
Américaine

USE 1 pound eel, 1 1/4 pounds each of striped and sea bass, 2 1/4 pounds of Spanish mackerel or red snapper or other firm-fleshed fish, and 2 live lobsters, each weighing 1 3/4 to 2 pounds. Cut all into 1-inch slices, cutting the lobster through shell and flesh. With a stiff brush, scrub thoroughly 2 dozen clams and 2 dozen mussels.

In a large kettle, heat 1/2 cup olive oil, add 2 large leeks, 2 onions and 1 large carrot, all chopped or cut into julienne, and cook slowly until the vegetables take on a light golden color. Add 1 pound fresh tomatoes, peeled, seeded, and coarsely chopped, or 1 can of tomatoes, 2 or 3 cloves of garlic, crushed, 2 tablespoons chopped parsley, 1 teaspoon saffron, 1 small bay leaf, a little thyme, a pinch of chopped fresh fennel tips if obtainable, 1 teaspoon salt and a little pepper. Spread the cutup lobster and eel on top of the vegetables and add 2 cups tomato juice and 2 quarts water. Bring the liquid to a boil and simmer for 15 minutes. Add the striped bass, sea bass, mackerel and red snapper and boil hard for 10 minutes longer. Add the clams and mussels and continue to cook until their shells open. Correct the seasoning with salt if necessary.

To serve, dish up the fish in deep bowls or individual casseroles, giving each person a piece or two of each kind, and pour some of the liquid over it. Remove the shells from the lobsters and place a couple of pieces on top of each serving. Remove the upper shells of the clams and mussels and place the lower shells with the clams and mussels around the lobster. Serve the soup in separate deep bowls with slices of crusty French bread in each to thicken the soup. Or rub the slices of bread with garlic, brown in olive oil and serve separately.

I WRITE about matelote with the most nostalgic of feelings because it is a favorite dish of *mon pays*, the *Bourbonnais*, an interior section of France. In my youth we depended on the local streams and lakes for our fish, and we ate the finest trout, carp, tench, gudgeon, pike, and eel. Every farm also had its own artificial fishpond, a low spot in the fields, perhaps an acre or more in size, dammed to hold water. From them, the farmers got most of the fish for their families in a practical and economical way. Every two or three years this pond had to be drained, to thin out the fish. Neighbors shared in the work—and in the fish. Only men and boys were allowed, and the gala occasions lasted all night, and sometimes through two nights, big fires lighting the bank where we sat eating and drinking wine and telling stories. At about sunrise—the farmers knew how to time the draining of the pond so that they could reach town with their wares early in the morning—the water was so shallow that fish formed an unbroken surface. The picnic ended, and we rushed back and forth filling our nets and emptying them into tubs on the bank, working fast to get out as many fish as possible before they were sucked into the mud. Following this exciting event came a delicious matelote.

The famous French gourmet, Brillat-Savarin, put matelote high in the scale of good fish dishes. He says that "Fish under skillful hands may become an inexhaustible resource of gustatory enjoyments. It is served up entire, sliced in pieces, done in water, in oil, in wine, hot or cold, and is always well received, but it never deserves a warmer welcome than when it is brought up *en matelote*... This stew, though of necessity a dish often eaten by the sailors on our rivers and made in perfection only by the innkeepers on the banks of such rivers, owes to them, nevertheless, a delicacy which is unsurpassed... It can be eaten in unlimited quantities without fear either of satiety or of indigestion."

In making matelote, as in making bouillabaisse, you should select firm fish and the kinds that are not full of tiny bones. In this country, carp, bass, and perch are a good selection, also lake—not brook—trout. Eels are always included. Since matelote is a stew, it does not require a great deal of liquid, but wine is the liquid that is always used—preferably a good dry white wine, although there are some who like a dry red better. The kind depends, as does the fish, upon the region where the matelote is made—the local fish is sauced with local wine.

Kinds of Fish for Matelote

In making any dish using fresh-water fish, it is best to discard the roe because the roe of fresh-water fish is not usually very good. If it seems to be especially good, it can be sautéed in butter and served as a garnish, but I would seldom advise doing it.

We used this matelote recipe in my family.

MATELOTE MARINIÈRE

Matelote Marinière

CLEAN well about 4 pounds fish—perch, carp, bass, and eels—cut in medium-sized pieces, put in a saucepan, and cover with white or red wine. Add 1 onion, minced, 2 cloves of garlic, minced, 1 teaspoon salt, and a faggot made by tying together a sprig of parsley, 1 bay leaf, and a little thyme. Bring to a boil and cook gently for 12 to 15 minutes. Cook separately 8 to 10 small white onions and 8 to 10 small mushrooms. Remove the fish to a serving dish and keep warm. Prepare *beurre manié* by creaming together 2 tablespoons butter and 1 tablespoon flour and add to the liquid in the pan. Bring to the boil and stir constantly until the sauce is thickened. Correct the seasoning with salt. Arrange the cooked onions and mushrooms over and around the fish and strain the sauce over it all. Garnish with slices of French bread toasted or browned in butter.

BOURBONNAIS MATELOTE

Matelote à la Bourbonnaise

SELECT 2 or 3 kinds of fresh-water fish, such as perch and carp, and 1 eel, having about 3 to 4 pounds of fish in all. Clean the fish thoroughly and cut it into 1-inch slices. Prepare 12 to 15 small white onions, 1/2 pound mushrooms, and 1/2 pound shrimp for garnishing. Put the fish and eel in a deep saucepan and cover with red wine. Add 1 onion, sliced, 3 sprigs of parsley, 1 stalk of celery, 1 small bay leaf, 2 cloves of garlic, and a little thyme. Add the stems and peelings of the mushrooms and 1 teaspoon salt. Bring the liquid to a boil, add 2 to 3 tablespoons warm Cognac, and ignite. When the flame burns out, cover the pan and simmer the stew 15 to 18 minutes.

Remove the fish to a serving dish, strain the liquid into another pan, and stir in bit by bit *beurre manié* made by creaming together 3 tablespoons butter and 2 1/2 tablespoons flour. Bring the liquid again to a boil, stirring constantly, and cook, stirring, until it is smooth and about as thick as cream. Correct the seasoning with salt and a little freshly ground pepper.

To serve, place the onions and mushrooms on the fish and pour the sauce over all. Garnish with the cooked shrimp and slices of French bread browned in butter.

NORMANDY MATELOTE

Matelote à la Normande

CLEAN 3 1/2 to 4 pounds fish—sole, striped bass, sea bass, and other firm fish—and cut in 2-inch pieces. Put in a saucepan 2 onions, finely chopped, 2 cloves of garlic, crushed, 2 tablespoons butter, and a faggot made by tying together 3 sprigs parsley, 1 bay leaf, and a little thyme. Add the fish seasoned with 1/2 teaspoon salt and a little pepper. Add 1 quart cider, bring to a boil, pour on 1 pony of Calvados, and ignite. When the flame burns out cover the pan, bring to a rapid boil, and simmer for 20 to 30 minutes or until the fish is done. Put the fish in a deep heatproof soup tureen or casserole. Add to the fish in the serving dish 1/2 pound cooked mushrooms, quartered if large, and 12 or more each cooked mussels, cooked oysters, and cooked shrimp. In another pan, melt 2 tablespoons butter, add 1 tablespoon flour, and cook until it just starts to turn golden. Combine with the cooking liquor of the fish and cook for 25 minutes. Finish the sauce with 3/4 cup heavy cream, bring to the boil, and correct the seasoning. Strain over the fish, mushrooms, and shellfish and garnish with French bread triangles browned in butter.

There is a famous matelote spécialité *called* la pochouse *that is made in Verdun sur-le-Doubs (not the Verdun of World War I fame). The Doubs is a good-sized stream, well stocked with fish, and the local hotels attract people from all over who come for a dish of* la pochouse.

VERDUN FISH STEW

La Pochouse de Verdun

CLEAN 4 pounds fish—pike, carp, perch, bass, eels—and cut in 2-inch pieces. Season with salt and pepper, put in a saucepan, and cover with dry white wine. In another saucepan parboil 1 cup diced salt pork for 5 minutes in water to cover. Drain the pork dice, brown them in a little melted butter, and add them to the fish in the stewpan, with 4 cloves of garlic, crushed, and a faggot made of 3 sprigs of parsley, 1 small bay leaf, and a little thyme. Bring to a boil and cook for 20 to 25 minutes. Add *beurre manié*, made by creaming together 3 tablespoons butter with 1 tablespoon flour, mixing it in a little at a time, moving and shaking the saucepan to blend it into the liquid. Do not stir with a spoon or a fork because this will break the fish. Cook slowly for 10 minutes longer or until the fish is done. Add 2 tablespoons butter, shaking and moving the pan to blend it. Brown slices of bread in butter, rub with a cut piece of garlic, and arrange in a serving dish. Place a piece of fish on each slice of toast. Discard the faggot from the sauce, then remove the pork dice and sprinkle them over the fish. Correct the seasoning of the sauce, strain it, and pour it over the fish.

Braising,
and
Making Stews

THE VERY SIGHT of an earthenware casserole reminds me of *mon pays*, of *maman's* kitchen, and of the wooden kitchen dresser where our casseroles used to stand, mellowed and stained with their years of faithful service. When the family gathered around the red-and-white cloth of the kitchen table, *maman* would fill our plates from the casserole that had simmered long on our big black stove.

Of course, the French family's meal *en casserole* resembles not at all American casserole dishes, which usually consist of a mixture of already cooked foods heated in a sauce, although these too are served in the " casserole " or baking dish. In France, the casserole is used to make braised meats like *boeuf à la mode* or the richly sauced *coq au vin*, or savory stews, or *ragoûts*. The meat or poultry is browned in fat, then cooked with just enough liquid to make the sauce. The rule of thumb is to select a casserole just large enough to hold the food, and add enough liquid to cover the food about halfway. If the piece of meat or poultry is in too big a pot, too much liquid is needed to cover it, and the food is therefore poached or boiled instead of braised or cooked liked a stew, and the savor of the sauce greatly diluted.

That *en casserole* cooking should be popular in France is natural. The French, with their great love of good food, are willing to go to any trouble to prepare a delectable dish and will do it in spite of limited quantities of fuel and the need to be thrifty. So the casserole proves a good friend; casserole dishes are usually cooked on top of the stove, and gentle simmering requires much less fuel than roasting or broiling. More important, long, slow cooking and the patient, gradual blending of flavors can work miracles with meat that is not naturally tender and chicken that is no longer young.

Meat Braising and Stews

SINCE braising is admittedly a fine way to cook many inexpensive cuts of meat, braised meats are associated with economy, and they do not carry the aura of sophistication that surrounds truffled birds and roasted filets of beef. But that is not to say that braised meats are scorned by the *haut monde*, or that they may be carelessly prepared. *Au contraire.* Braised meats were always served at the small, exclusive hotels in Paris at the turn of the century. Braised beef not unlike *boeuf à la mode* was the favorite dish of one famous munitions manufacturer who used to stop at the Bristol. When it was rumored that he might be arriving, the chef ordered a piece of beef put into a marinade every day, so that it would be ready to cook at a moment's notice. Similar dishes appeared regularly on the menu at the Ritz in New York, and because we devoted to them the necessary time and meticulous attention on which their success depended, their popularity never waned.

For the most part meat, poultry, or fish to be braised is not cut up, and the meat is often marinated and sometimes larded. A piece of meat that needs long cooking to make it tender is best braised, but even tender cuts lend themselves to braising. A leg of lamb that is to be served well done may be better braised than roasted, because if it lacks fat long roasting may make it dry. The same is true of pieces of veal.

Usually meat for braising is seasoned with salt and browned in fat on all sides in a skillet or in the casserole. Use fresh drippings, beef or pork, or an unsalted shortening for browning, but do not use butter, as it will burn at the necessary high temperature. Chicken fat has a distinctive flavor that is not universally popular, and lamb fat should be used only with lamb.

The bottom of the casserole or braising kettle, however, is spread with butter, then lined with sliced carrots and onions, on which a faggot is laid. The browned meat goes on this bed, described by the French as *aromatique* and characteristic of braising. Bones are added also, if possible, for the flavor they give the sauce and the thickening quality of the gelatin in them. Liquid for braising may be any combination of wine, stock, and water, and sometimes canned tomatoes—enough to cover or half cover the meat. The liquid should reduce in the cooking to about half the original quantity. Frequent basting keeps the top of the meat moist whether the long braising is done on top of the stove or in a moderate oven. A long-handled basting spoon will prevent burned fingers. Most braising requires that the cover be on the pan, but not all.

Vegetable garnishes that are cooked with the meat are quite simple, as a rule, usually carrots and onions glazed in butter, sometimes peas, beans, or mushrooms. Like the vegetables in stews, each is added at the appropriate time, to avoid overcooking.

Keep the cooking very slow, then the fat rises gradually to the surface of the liquid, and you can skim it off each time you baste. A fatty sauce results when too much flour or too rapid cooking holds the fat in the liquid. The sauce of braised food should be a rich extract of the flavors of the meat, liquid, and *aromates* and it should have body without being thick. Braising, although a simple method of cooking, produces fine sauces and succulent meat.

Some braised meats are as delicious cold as hot—*boeuf à la mode*, for instance. The sauce makes a jellied coating for meat and vegetables.

Utensils for Braising and for Stews

Use any utensil for braising and for stews providing it is heavy enough to prevent scorching during the long cooking and has a tightly fitting cover. A rather thin piece of meat, such as a veal cutlet, is best braised in a heavy iron skillet, closely covered. The fact is the word " casserole, " with which braising and stews are associated, has a much

Casseroles

wider meaning in French than in English. To the French chef any deep cooking utensil that can stand direct heat is a casserole. It may be a heavy metal saucepan or a kettle, or it may be a two-handled covered cooking dish. It is this last kind of utensil, made of clayware, tin-lined copper, or heavy enameled iron, that most people think of as the typical French casserole. French clayware can be protected against cracking by an asbestos mat placed between it and the heat, and the heat should be kept low. Most china and glass baking dishes, however, are not suitable for this kind of cooking.

The well-equipped kitchen needs two or three casseroles of different sizes. You'll find that even when you are serving the same number of people, the size of casserole you need will vary with the recipe. If, *par exemple*, the recipe includes several vegetables and also potatoes, the casserole will have to be larger than one used for a recipe that calls for just one or two vegetables with the meat. My advice is to add up roughly the cups of ingredients the recipe requires and then to use a casserole of suitable size.

A new clay casserole usually needs to be seasoned to remove the raw clay taste that it will otherwise impart to the food the first few times it is used. The process is explained in the section on garlic, an inportant element in the seasoning.

If you cook casserole dishes in the oven, remember to keep the heat low. Remember also that food cooked in the oven must be watched carefully and more liquid added as needed.

A second kind of casserole cooking is known as *cuire à l'étuvée*—to cook in an *étuvée* or a closely covered pot. Foods are cooked gently over low heat in a closed utensil with as little liquid as possible, or with none at all if the food itself can supply enough, as vegetables often can. Less liquid is used ordinarily than in braising and there is no basting. I would say it is a kind of stewing, except that stewing brings to my mind a picture of a kettle with the cover tap-tapping as the steam rises from the chicken or meat, apples or tomatoes bubbling inside. And that is not what the French mean when they say *cuire à l'étuvée*. They mean the slowest possible cooking in a very tightly closed or sealed pot.

For cooking *à l'étuvée*, the meat or poultry is usually cut up and enough liquid is added to barely cover it. It is essential that the pot be sealed so that none of the flavor can escape, and this sealing is accomplished in various ways: by closing the casserole with a very heavy, tightly fitting cover, by laying a sheet of wax or buttered paper, cut to fit the casserole, directly on top of the food before putting the cover on (this is sometimes done in braising, too), or by sealing the cover with a strip of flour and water dough. In the last method, the cover must have a small hole in it, or the pressure of steam will crack the seal. Meat and poultry cooked this way is always tender, always succulent, never stringy or tasteless, and the blending of flavors in the sauce is complete.

In my grandmother's big farm kitchen, there was a special stove for cooking in this way. The stone walls of her house were at least two feet thick, making wide sills for the casement windows. One of the sills in the kitchen was actually the top of a stove. It was made of colored tiles, with four openings. Under it, there was a recess in the wall lined with brick, a kind of oven without a door, with grates that held a few pieces of charcoal and pans underneath to catch the ashes. A pot was started on the kitchen stove, transferred to the window stove with its small charcoal fires, and allowed to simmer, or *mijoter*. If the contents of the casserole more than barely bubbled, the fire was considered too hot and a piece of the offending charcoal removed.

The word *mijoter*—to cook slowly and gently over very little heat, *faire cuire doucement*—applies to braising and the making of stews as

Cuire
à l'Etuvée

Mijoter

181

well as to cooking *à l'étuvée*. Its meaning includes the meanings of our three verbs " to fricassee, " " to simmer, " and " to stew. "

Stews

Many dishes cooked *à l'étuvée* result in what might be called in this country " stews ." But they are not stews, or *ragoûts*, in the French sense. The French show a persistent precision in culinary matters, and to them a stew is a very particular kind of dish of meat, poultry or fish cooked in liquid. The main ingredient is cut into uniform pieces, always.

Brown Stews
White Stews

The stew may be cooked *à brun*, that is, the meat browned, or *à blanc*, cooked without browning, and a vegetable garnish is optional. The prototype of brown stew is *ragoût de mouton*, called a *navarin*, and the prototype of a white stew is what we know as Irish stew.

Stews, no matter how simple, have their tricks. I might even say they have more need of tricks to bring them to gustatory perfection than other cookery, because they make use of the less tender cuts of meat, older fowl, and inexpensive vegetables. We must bring this kind of meat to tenderness without letting it become ragged and these vegetables only to firm succulence, not softness. The aroma must be fragrant enough to start the mouth watering before a bite is eaten, and finally, the all-important sauce must have a well-rounded flavor and perfect consistency.

Use stock of the same flavor as the main ingredient: lamb stock for lamb stew, beef for beef stew, chicken for chicken stew. Never let a stew cook too rapidly. The gentlest of simmering is essential during the long cooking, or the meat will fall apart and become stringy. Vegetables should be added with their cooking time in mind, so that none will be overcooked.

There are three ways to produce a brown stew with an appetizing rich brown color, and these also improve the flavor of the stew. The meat should be properly browned before the liquid is added. The onions and carrots should also be browned before they are added, and a little tomato sauce should be included.

To Brown
Meat

Wipe the pieces of meat dry and put them into very hot fat. Use the same fat as you would for browning meat to be braised. A heavy pan is essential, and it should be large enough to hold the meat without crowding. Brown a few pieces at a time. Too many pieces together will produce steam and the meat will develop a gray color instead of a rich brown. You will probably find it easier and more satisfactory to brown the meat in a skillet and then transfer it to the casserole. Meat always browns better in a utensil with shallow sides. All the rich brown bits in the skillet can be saved by adding a little of the liquid called for in the stew and deglazing the pan, that is, cooking the liquid a moment, stirring it, until all the crustiness dissolves. Then return the liquid to the stew.

Deglazing

Less heat is needed to brown vegetables than meat so butter can be used, which will add its flavor to the stew. Sprinkle a teaspoon or so of sugar over the carrots and onions and roll them in the hot butter until they are a light brown color. This adds color without an unwanted caramel flavor.

Glazing Vegetables for Stews

There should be just enough liquid in a brown stew to cover the solid ingredients. The liquid will cook down very little if the heat is low and the cover of the pan tight. Stews cooked *à blanc* generally start with a little more liquid and cook down more. Potatoes cut in pieces are sometimes included in the initial cooking and pressed through a sieve to thicken the sauce.

A true French stew does not have a thick sauce, but the sauce does have good body, the familiar *du corps*. Thicken the sauce if need be by adding a little *beurre manié* at the end of the cooking. If stirring is needed, do it gently with a wooden spatula or spoon, to avoid breaking and mashing the meat and vegetables.

BRAISED BEEF

Boeuf Braisé à la Mode

USE a 5-pound piece of boneless rump of beef, preferably top of rump. Lard the meat through the center with about 12 strips of larding pork and tie soft string around it every 2 inches. Season it with 1 tablespoon salt mixed with a little pepper. In a large bowl combine 1 large onion and 1 large carrot, both sliced, 2 cloves of garlic, 2 stalks of celery, 4 sprigs of parsley, 1 small bay leaf, a pinch of thyme, 2 cups red or white wine, and 1/4 cup Cognac. Let the meat marinate in this mixture in the refrigerator for 6 hours or more, turning it occasionally.

Remove the meat from the marinade, drain it, and dry the piece thoroughly. Melt 2 tablespoons fat in a skillet and when it is very hot add the meat and brown it on all sides. Transfer it to a large casserole and add a few beef and veal bones. Discard the fat from the skillet, melt in the skillet 2 tablespoons butter, sprinkle in 2 tablespoons flour, and cook the *roux*, stirring constantly, until it is browned. Gradually stir in the marinade and 4 cups water or stock. Bring the sauce to a boil, stirring constantly, and pour it over the meat. Add 1 cup canned tomatoes and 2 or 3 fresh tomatoes, chopped, if available. Parboil a split calf's foot for 10 minutes, drain it, and add to the casserole. Cover closely and braise on top of the stove or in a moderate oven (350° F.) for 2 hours.

Cut 5 or 6 carrots into pieces and parboil for 5 minutes. Glaze 24 small white onions in a little butter, sprinkling them with sugar. Clean 3 hearts of celery and parboil for 5 minutes.

Remove the meat and calf's foot from the casserole and remove and discard the beef and veal bones. Strain the sauce and skim all the fat from it. Wash the casserole, return the meat and calf's foot to it, add the vegetables, and pour the strained sauce over all. Cover closely and cook for another 1 1/2 or 2 hours, or until the meat is tender. Remove the vegetables and calf's foot, cut the meat from the calf's foot into small pieces, and combine with the vegetables. Remove the meat to a serving dish and arrange the vegetables around it. The sauce should be reduced to about 1/2 the original quantity. If it is not, reduce it more. Skim off any remaining fat and, if desired, add 1/4 cup Madeira or Sherry. Pass the sauce separately. To serve, slice the meat thinly across the grain, so that the larding will show.

Cold braised beef is called *boeuf à la mode en gelée*; you will find it in the section on dishes for the buffet.

Boeuf en Daube

BEEF STEW

Cut a 2 1/2-pound piece of rump of beef into 12 pieces. Season them with salt and pepper. Put them in a bowl with 1/2 cup red wine and 1 tablespoon chopped shallots or onion and let the meat marinate for 2 hours. Drain off and save the marinade. Dry each piece of meat well and brown the pieces, a few at a time, in 3 tablespoons beef fat.

Parboil 1/4 pound diced fat salt pork in water to cover for 3 to 4 minutes, drain the dice, and sauté them until they are golden brown. Spread a few beef or veal bones or both in a shallow pan, put the pan in a hot oven (450° F.), and lightly brown the bones. Put the bones in a casserole, add 1/2 the browned meat, 1 carrot, sliced, 1 onion, chopped, 2 cloves of garlic, crushed, 1/2 the sautéed pork dice and a faggot made by tying together 1 stalk of celery, a sprig of parsley, 1 bay leaf, and a little thyme. Add the remaining browned meat, another carrot, sliced, another onion, chopped, the remaining pork dice, the reserved marinade, and about 2 cups stock, or enough just to cover the meat. Lay 4 thin slices of fat salt pork on top.

Cover the casserole with a lid that has a small hole in it and seal the edges with a stiff paste made of flour and water. Bring to a boil and cook in a slow oven (325° F.) for 3 to 3 1/2 hours. Remove the cover, skim the fat from the juices in the casserole, and discard the faggot. Serve the stew from the casserole, sprinkled with 1 tablespoon chopped parsley.

Boeuf en daube may also be served cold. Directions are given in the section on dishes for the buffet.

BEEF STEW WITH VEGETABLES

Ragoût de Boeuf

CUT a 2 1/2-pound piece of rump into 12 pieces. Season them with salt and pepper and in a skillet lightly brown them on all sides in 3 tablespoons fat. Remove the meat to a casserole. Discard the fat from the skillet, melt 1 tablespoon butter in the skillet, sprinkle in 2 tablespoons flour, and cook the *roux*, stirring, until it is browned. Gradually add 2 cups stock or water and cook, stirring, until the mixture is smooth. Pour it over the meat in the casserole and add 1 clove of garlic, 1/2 cup tomato sauce, 2 or 3 tomatoes, peeled, seeded, and chopped, a faggot made by tying together 3 sprigs of parsley, 2 bay leaves, and a little thyme, and enough stock or water to cover the meat. Cook the meat slowly, covered, over low heat for about 1 1/2 hours.

Parboil for 5 minutes 4 carrots, cut in pieces, and glaze them in a little butter, sprinkling them with a little sugar. Glaze 12 small onions in a little butter, sprinkling them with sugar. Parboil for 5 minutes 2 hearts of celery, cut in pieces. Cut 6 large potatoes into even pieces.

Remove the meat from the casserole. Strain the sauce and skim the fat from it. Wash the casserole, return the meat to it, arrange the vegetables on top of the meat, and pour the sauce over all. Add chopped parsley, if desired, bring to a boil, cover, and cook slowly for another hour, or until the meat is well done.

Carbonnade de Boeuf Flamande

SLICED BEEF STEW

CUT a 2 1/2-pound piece of rump of beef into 12 slices and flatten each with a mallet. Heat 2 tablespoons beef or veal fat in a skillet and sauté the meat on both sides, a few pieces at a time; remove them to a plate as they are brown. When all have been cooked, pour off the fat in the pan, add 2 tablespoons vinegar, and stir in all the brown crustiness in the pan. Add 1 cup beer, 3 cups stock, and 1 teaspoon sugar, and simmer for a few minutes.

Chop 3 large onions and sauté in 2 tablespoons butter in a saucepan until they are soft and golden. Stir in 2 tablespoons flour. Put a layer of the sautéed onions in a casserole and add some of the sauce from the skillet and a layer of the browned meat slices. Continue to add onions, sauce, and meat until all the ingredients are used. Add a faggot made by tying together 1 stalk of celery, 3 sprigs of parsley, 1 bay leaf, and a little thyme. About 4 tablespoons tomato sauce may also be added. Strain the remaining sauce over all and add any juice that is left on the plate that held the browned meat. There should be just enough liquid to cover the contents. If not, add a little hot water. Cover the casserole with a lid that has a small hole in it and seal the edges with a stiff paste made of flour and water. Bring to a boil and cook in a slow oven (325° F.) for 2 to 2 1/2 hours. Serve from the casserole.

Paupiettes de Boeuf Braisées Bourbonnaise

BRAISED BEEF ROLLS

CUT a 2 1/2-pound piece of lean rump of beef into 12 or 15 slices and flatten each with a wooden mallet. Season the slices with salt and pepper.

Season 1 pound each of ground lean pork and ground fat pork with 1/2 teaspoon poultry seasoning mixed with a little salt. Add 3 ounces Madeira or Sherry and mix thoroughly. Spread the center of each slice of beef with some of this stuffing and roll them up. Wrap each roll with a thin slice of fat salt pork and tie with a string.

In a shallow casserole melt 1 tablespoon butter. Spread over the butter 1 onion and 1 carrot, both sliced, and place the rolls of beef side by side on the vegetables. Add 1 clove of garlic and a faggot made by tying together 1 stalk of celery, 4 sprigs of parsley, 1 bay leaf, and a pinch of thyme. Sprinkle a little melted butter over the beef rolls and cook them, uncovered, in a moderately hot oven (375° F.), until they take on a little color. Sprinkle 1 tablespoon flour over the vegetables around the meat and add 2 cups red or white wine. If the liquid does not just cover the rolls, add stock or water. Bring the liquid to a boil over direct heat, cover the casserole, and braise for 1 1/2 to 2 hours, basting from time to time. If the liquid reduces too much, add a little stock or water. One half hour before serving, add 1 pound mushrooms sautéed in butter and 18 small white onions browned and glazed in a pan with a little water, 1 tablespoon butter, and a sprinkling of sugar. If the larding pork on the beef rolls is not brown, uncover the pan, untie the rolls, and cook a few minutes longer. Remove the rolls to a warm serving dish with the piece of larding pork on each. Discard the faggot, correct the seasoning of the sauce, and pour sauce and vegetables around the rolls. Sprinkle with chopped parsley and serve with small cooked carrots or another vegetable.

BRAISED LOIN OF VEAL BOURGEOISE

Longe de Veau Braisée à la Bourgeoise

HAVE your butcher cut a 4-pound piece of veal from the loin or rack or the solid part of the leg. In a casserole put a few veal bones, 1 carrot and 1 onion, both sliced, and a faggot made by tying together 1 stalk of celery, 4 sprigs of parsley, a small bay leaf, and a sprig of thyme. Place the meat, seasoned with salt and pepper, on this and spread the top of it with 2 tablespoons butter. Cook, uncovered, in a hot oven (425° F.) for 25 to 30 minutes, or until the top is golden brown. Add 1 cup water or stock and continue to cook, basting often. When the liquid is reduced, add a little more water or stock to prevent scorching the meat and cover with a piece of buttered or wax paper cut to fit the casserole, with a small hole in the center to vent the steam. Cover the casserole, reduce the heat to moderately hot (375° F.) and cook for about 1 1/2 hours, basting occasionally.

While the meat is cooking, prepare the vegetables: Put 15 to 18 small white peeled onions in a shallow pan with 1 1/2 tablespoons butter and 1/2 tablespoon sugar, and cook slowly, moving them around in the pan until they are golden brown and glazed all over; pare enough small new carrots to make 2 1/2 cups either whole or cut in large dice; shell enough fresh peas to make 1/2 cup; chop enough parsley to make 1 tablespoon and also chop coarsely 2 large tomatoes. Remove the half-cooked meat from the casserole. There should be 1 1/2 to 2 cups liquid in the casserole; if not, add water or stock, and cook for 8 to 10 minutes, stirring all the brown crustiness that is around the sides of the pan into the liquid. Remove the bones and strain the sauce. Put the vegetables in the casserole, pour the sauce over them, and place the meat on top. Cover and cook on top of the range or in a hot oven (400° F.) for about 40 minutes, or until the vegetables are done.

Rouelle de Veau à l'Etuvée

CASSEROLE OF VEAL

CUT a slice of veal, 3/4 inch thick and weighing 2 1/2 to 3 pounds, into 12 pieces, season with salt and pepper, and roll in flour. Melt 2 tablespoons butter in a skillet and cook the meat in it, a few pieces at a time, until it is golden brown, removing the pieces to a casserole as they brown. Put 6 small onions and 6 small carrots in the fat in the pan, cover, and cook slowly until they start to turn golden, then transfer them to the casserole. Add to the fat 1 teaspoon chopped shallot or onion and 1 teaspoon flour and cook slowly, stirring constantly, until the flour is brown. Stir in gradually 1/2 cup red wine and cook the sauce until it is well blended. Add 2 cups water, bring the sauce to a boil, and pour it over the meat and vegetables. Add a faggot made by tying together 1 stalk of celery, 3 sprigs of parsley, 1 small bay leaf, and a little thyme. Cover the casserole closely and cook very slowly for about 1 1/2 hours, or until the meat is tender. Discard the faggot, correct the seasoning, and sprinkle with parsley.

Poitrine de Veau Farcie à la Dominicaine

STUFFED BREAST OF VEAL DOMINICAINE

CUT a pocket in a whole breast of veal. Toss lightly with a fork 3 cups cooked rice, 1/2 cup *pâté de foie gras*, cut in small dice, 2 tablespoons chopped truffle or 1/2 cup sliced sautéed mushrooms, 1 tablespoon beef extract, and 1/2 cup thick *velouté* or béchamel sauce. Fill the pocket of the veal with this stuffing and sew the edges of the pocket together.

Spread 2 tablespoons butter in the bottom of an oval-shaped casserole and add 1 or 2 carrots and 1 or 2 onions, both sliced. Put the veal on the vegetables, spread it with 2 tablespoons butter, and sprinkle with 1 teaspoon salt. Cook, uncovered, in a hot oven (400° F.) for 30 to 35 minutes until the carrots and onions turn golden and the meat begins to brown. Add 1 cup boiling stock or water and cover the meat with a piece of buttered or wax paper, cut to fit the casserole, with a small hole in the center to vent the steam. Cover the casserole, reduce the temperature to moderate (350° F.), and braise, basting often, for about 2 hours, or until the meat is tender. If the liquid cooks away, add stock or water.

Remove the veal to a serving platter. Add 1 cup sweet cream to the juices and cook until the sauce is reduced to 1/2 its original quantity. Strain the sauce into a saucepan, add 1 cup hot cream sauce, and correct the seasoning. To serve, cut veal and stuffing in slices and coat them with the sauce or serve the sauce separately.

In a blanquette, *a kind of* ragoût à blanc, *egg yolks and cream thicken the sauce.*

VEAL BLANQUETTE

Blanquette
de Veau

Cut 2 pounds veal from the shoulder into 1 1/2-inch pieces. Cover the meat with cold water and parboil for 5 minutes. Drain and rinse in fresh cold water. Cover again with 1 quart water, bring to a boil, and add 3 medium carrots, 12 to 15 small onions, 2 teaspoons salt, 1 clove of garlic, 1 leek, a few peppercorns, and a faggot made by tying together 1 stalk of celery, 3 sprigs of parsley, 1 bay leaf, and a little thyme. Boil the meat slowly for 1 to 1 1/2 hours, or until it is tender. Lift out meat, carrots, and onions and arrange in a serving dish. Reduce the cooking liquid to about 1/3 the original quantity and remove the faggot.

Clean 1 pound medium mushrooms, " turn " them, bring them just to a boil in 1/2 cup water with the juice of 1 lemon and 1/2 teaspoon salt, and let them stand in the liquid. In another pan melt 2 tablespoons butter, add 2 tablespoons flour, and cook until the *roux* starts to turn golden. Gradually add the cooking liquor from the meat and from the mushrooms and bring the sauce to a boil, stirring with a wire

189

whip. Cook it slowly 15 to 20 minutes. Mix 2 slightly beaten egg yolks with 1 cup cream, stir in some of the hot sauce, and combine this mixture with the hot sauce, stirring briskly. Bring the sauce to the boiling point, but do not let it boil. Correct the seasoning with salt and strain the sauce. Arrange the mushrooms on the meat and mask with the sauce. Serve with rice or boiled potatoes.

CURRIED VEAL BLANQUETTE

Blanquette de Veau à l'Indienne

PREPARE *blanquette de veau*, adding 2 tablespoons curry powder to the sauce. Serve with rice.

BRAISED VEAL CHOPS CHARTRES

Côtes de Veau Braisées à la Chartres

SEASON 6 veal chops 1 inch thick with salt and white pepper. Mix 2 cups fresh bread crumbs and 1 cup grated Parmesan and cover each chop with this mixture, pressing the crumbs and cheese together firmly to make a compact rounded topping. Melt 2 tablespoons butter in a shallow casserole and spread in it 2 tablespoons finely chopped onion. Place the chops side by side in the casserole and sprinkle with melted butter. Add 2/3 cup white wine to the casserole, cover it, and braise the chops in a hot oven (400° F.) for 1 to 1 1/2 hours, or until the meat separates easily from the bone. During the cooking add water, a little at a time, as the liquid is reduced and baste the chops to give them a golden brown color. If the topping cracks, press it together carefully but firmly.

Transfer the chops to a serving platter. Pour the gravy from the casserole into a saucepan, bring it to a boil, and thicken with 1 tablespoon arrowroot or cornstarch mixed with a little cold water or stock. Correct the seasoning, strain the sauce through a fine sieve, and pour it around the chops. Garnish the platter with parsley and piped mounds of carrot purée, spinach purée, or a purée of lettuce and chicory.

BRAISED LEG OF LAMB OR YOUNG MUTTON

Gigot d'Agneau Braisé

TRIM the skin and surplus fat from a 6- to 8-pound leg of lamb or young mutton and season the meat with salt. In the bottom of a large oval casserole spread 2 tablespoons butter and then 3 onions and 3 carrots, both sliced. Add a faggot made by tying together 2 stalks of celery, 4 sprigs of parsley, 1 bay leaf, and a little thyme. Sprinkle the vegetables with 1 tablespoon flour, cover them with cracked lamb bones, and put the leg of lamb on top. Cook the meat, uncovered, in a moderately hot oven (375° F.) until it is brown all over, turning it frequently. Add 1 1/2 to 2 cups water or stock and 2 or 3 tomatoes or 1 cup canned tomatoes. Cover the lamb with a piece of wax or buttered paper, cut to fit the casserole, with a small hole in the center to vent the steam. Cover the kettle, reduce the temperature to slow (325° F.), and braise for 3 to 3 1/2 hours, basting the meat from time to time. During the cooking add more water or stock if needed. Remove the lamb from the kettle, strain the gravy, and skim all the fat from the surface. Correct the seasoning with salt. If the gravy is too thin, cook it until it is reduced a little.

King Carlos of Portugal was a regular guest at the Paris Bristol, and his favorite dish was leg of lamb braised à la cuillère, *an unusually long and slow cooking process that resulted in meat so tender it could be served with a spoon, that is to say,* à la cuillère. *I had just begun my career in Paris when M. Tissier, the head chef, ordered me to cook the* gigot d'agneau *for the king. I was frightened, but M. Tissier reassured me and just reminded me to keep basting the meat all the time and to keep moisture in the pot by adding stock. The kitchen gods were with me, because I cooked that leg of lamb* à point. *It was so tender that the bone slipped out, away from the meat, and the surface was beautifully glazed by the rich stock. That was my first leg of lamb* braisé, *but not my last,* mais non! *During my years in Paris, London, and New York I must have prepared thousands of legs of lamb just that way and have taught hundreds of young chefs how to do it.*

BRAISED LEG OF LAMB WITH A SPOON

Gigot d'Agneau Braisé à la Cuillère

FOLLOW the recipe for *gigot d'agneau braisé*, braised leg of lamb or young mutton, omitting the flour sprinkled over the carrot and onion. Cook the meat 4 to 5 hours, or until it is so tender it can be served with a spoon. It must be basted often to keep it from becoming dry and stock must be added as the sauce reduces. As the meat cooks and is constantly basted, the rich sauce is absorbed and the meat becomes very succulent. The sauce should be reduced by half. Thicken it by adding 1 tablespoon arrowroot mixed with a little Sherry or Madeira, correct the seasoning, and strain it through a fine sieve.

STUFFED SHOULDER OF LAMB

Epaule d'Agneau Farcie

HAVE the butcher bone a shoulder of lamb and cut the bones into small pieces. Melt 1 tablespoon butter and in it cook 1 onion, finely chopped, until it is soft. Mix the onion with 1/2 pound sausage meat or finely chopped leftover meat, 1 cup fresh bread crumbs, 1/2 cup chopped cooked spinach, 1 tablespoon chopped parsley, 1 egg, 1/2 teaspoon salt, and a little pepper. Spread this stuffing over the boned lamb shoulder, roll up the meat, tie it securely with a string, and season with salt.

Melt 1 tablespoon fat in a casserole and spread over it 2 large onions and 2 large carrots, all sliced. Add a faggot made by tying together 1 stalk of celery, 4 sprigs of parsley, 1 bay leaf, and a little thyme. Scatter the pieces of lamb bone over the vegetables and lay the rolled lamb on top. Spread 1 tablespoon fat on the meat and cook, uncovered, in a hot oven (400° to 425° F.) for 30 to 40 minutes, until it is brown all over, turning it from time to time. Sprinkle 1 tablespoon flour over the vegetables and add 1 cup hot water or stock, 1/2 cup canned tomatoes, and 3 fresh tomatoes, chopped. Cover the lamb with a piece of buttered or wax paper, cut to fit the casserole, with a small hole in the center to vent the steam. Cover the pan, reduce the temperature to moderate (350° F.), and braise for 2 hours, basting often. If the liquid cooks away, add more water or stock. Transfer the meat, carrots, and onions to a serving dish. Strain the sauce, correct the seasoning, and skim off the fat. To serve, slice through lamb and stuffing and serve with sauce.

LAMB STEW WITH SPRING VEGETABLES

Navarin d'Agneau à la Parisienne

CUT 2 1/2 to 3 pounds shoulder of lamb into 12 pieces. Season the pieces with salt and pepper to taste. In 2 tablespoons melted beef or pork fat brown the pieces a few at a time, removing them as they are done to a casserole. Discard the fat from the skillet but do not wash the pan; in it melt 1 tablespoon butter over low heat and add 1 teaspoon finely chopped shallot or onion and 2 tablespoons flour. Cook slowly, stirring constantly, until the flour turns golden. Add 2 cups water, 1/2 cup canned tomatoes, and 2 tomatoes, peeled, seeded, and chopped. Bring to a boil, stirring constantly, cook 1 minute longer, until the sauce is smooth and thickened, and pour it over the meat. Deglaze the skillet with 1/2 cup red or white wine and add the wine to the casserole with 1 clove of garlic, crushed, and a faggot made by tying together 1 stalk of celery, 4 sprigs of parsley, a small bay leaf, and a little thyme. Bring to a boil, cover the casserole, and cook the stew 45 minutes.

Dice enough carrots to make 1 1/2 cups, or cut them in olive shapes, and enough white turnips to make 1 cup. Cover the vegetables with boiling water, parboil them for 3 minutes, and drain them. Sprinkle the vegetables with sugar and in a skillet in 1 tablespoon melted butter brown them lightly. Remove the vegetables and in the same skillet sauté 12 to 15 small white onions until golden, sprinkling with sugar.

Remove the meat to a dish, strain the cooking liquid into a bowl, and skim the fat. Wash the casserole, return the meat to it, and place  the vegetables on top. Cover the vegetables with a layer of 12 to 15 small potatoes and pour over all the strained cooking liquor. Bring to a boil again and simmer for 1/2 hour longer. Add 1 cup each of peas and green beans cut in 1/2-inch pieces. Cover the stew with a piece of buttered or wax paper cut to fit the casserole, with a tiny hole in the center. Cover the casserole and simmer the stew for 25 minutes longer, or until all the vegetables are tender. Discard the faggot. Sprinkle with finely chopped parsley and chives.

IRISH STEW RITZ-CARLTON

CUT 3 pounds lamb, preferably from the lower ribs or shoulder, into 12 pieces. Cover the pieces with water and parboil for 5 to 6 minutes. Discard the water, rinse the meat in fresh cold water, clean the pan, and return the meat to it. Add 2 quarts water, 3 onions, 3 or 4 potatoes, 4 leeks, and 4 stalks of celery, all chopped, 1 clove of garlic, 1 tablespoon salt, and 4 or 5 peppercorns. Bring the water to a boil and cook gently for 1 hour. Remove the meat to another pan.

Skim the fat from the broth and strain the broth, rubbing through the sieve as much of the vegetables as possible, and correct the seasoning. Meanwhile prepare 18 small white onions, 24 small potato balls, 18 small

Ragoût
Irlandais
Ritz-Carlton

white turnips, and 24 slices of carrot. Arrange all the vegetables on top of the meat. Sprinkle with 1 tablespoon chopped parsley and add the strained broth. Bring the broth to a boil and cook the stew for 45 minutes more, or until the meat is done. A few cooked green peas or string beans may be added just before serving. For a sharper flavor add 1 teaspoon Worcestershire sauce to the sauce.

Longe de Porc à la Boulangère

BRAISED LOIN OF PORK BOULANGÈRE

SEASON a 4- to 4 1/2-pound loin of pork with 1 teaspoon salt and put it in a deep roasting pan. Roast the meat in a moderately hot oven (375° F.) for 1 1/2 hours, or until brown, turning it several times. Remove the pork from the pan; pour off the fat. Make a pan gravy with stock or water and stir to dissolve all the browned juices in the pan. Thicken the gravy with a little *beurre manié* and pour it out of the pan.

Mix 8 potatoes, peeled and sliced, with 1/2 cup chopped onion, 1 tablespoon chopped parsley, 1 teaspoon salt, and a little pepper. Spread the seasoned potatoes in the roasting pan and sprinkle them with 2 tablespoons melted butter. Put the meat on top and spread it with 2 tablespoons of the gravy. Add about 1 cup hot water, or enough to come to the top of the potatoes. Cover the pan, bring the liquid to a boil, and braise in a moderate oven (350° F.) for about 1 1/2 hours, or until the bones separate easily from the meat and the potatoes are golden brown. Reheat the gravy and serve with the meat and potatoes. Serves 8 to 10.

Poultry Braising

and Stews

FOWL, older birds of 5 pounds or more, cook to tenderness if braised or made into stews, and the moisture insures succulence. The techniques are similar to those for braising meat or making meat stews. Young tender birds are also delicious cooked *en casserole*, but fowl are less expensive and more flavorful, and the long cooking required to make them tender results in sauces of inimitable flavor. The French delight in these simpler poultry dishes as much as they do in richer and more elaborate ones.

BRAISED CHICKEN

Poulet Braisé

CLEAN and truss a 4-pound chicken and season it with salt. Melt 1/4 cup butter in a casserole and in it cook the chicken quickly until it is brown all over, turning it from side to side. Remove it from the casserole. Put in the casserole 1 carrot and 1 onion, both sliced, and cook them until they start to turn golden. Return the chicken, breast up, and add 1 cup each of stock and white wine and enough water to make a depth of about 1 1/2 inches. Add a faggot made by tying together 1 stalk of celery, 2 sprigs of parsley, a bit of bay leaf, and a little thyme. If available, add some mushroom trimmings. Bring the liquid to a boil and cover the bird with a piece of buttered or wax paper, cut the size of the casserole, with a small hole in the center to vent the steam. Cover the casserole. Cook slowly on top of the stove or in a slow oven (325° F.) for 1 1/4 hours, or until the chicken tests done. If cooked in the oven uncover the casserole during the last 15 minutes and baste the bird frequently to glaze it. Remove the chicken to a serving dish. Thicken the liquid in the casserole with 2 teaspoons cornstarch mixed with 2 tablespoons Sherry and cook all together. Skim the fat from the surface, correct the seasoning with salt, strain the sauce and serve it with the chicken.

I wonder if my favorite Aunt Alexandrine remembers, as I do, the day she let the chickens cook too fast. It was her sister's wedding day. All the relatives had arrived at the farm—distant cousins, in-laws of all sorts, and dozens of the bride's new family. The wedding feast would last all afternoon.

Aunt Alexandrine was assigned to watch the coq au vin *on the window stove and to remove some of the charcoal if the fire got too hot. But I was her pet and easily enticed her away to toss a ball back and forth with me. The chicken was forgotten. Suddenly we heard* grand-mère's *angry voice.*

"Les poulets, les poulets, l'odeur est forte, ils cuisent trop vite." (*The chickens, the chickens. They are cooking too fast. I smell them.*)

Chez grand-mère *there were always special occasions for gala eating: reunions, weddings, christenings, and feast days. Quantities of food had to be prepared for these large gatherings. There was no room to broil or roast chickens for twenty or thirty people, but three large casseroles of* poulet au vin à l'étuvée, *or* coq au vin, *did the job very well—and without too much watching or last-minute attention.*

Such a food-loving family grand-mère *had to cook for; and how much good food passed through the kitchen door: vegetables and fruits, poultry and meat, milk and cream, all produced on the farm. And what a superb cook she was.*

Grand-mère's *skill, handed down through generations of good cooks, was passed along to each of her daughters with painstaking concern. The love for fine cooking aside, one simply did not waste good food by preparing it carelessly.*

Years after I had become a chef, I came back to tell her of the great kitchens where I had worked and she cooked for me her good poulet au vin. *And what a sauce it had. Any chef, no matter how famous, would have been proud of that dish.*

Coq au Vin   CHICKEN IN WINE

Cut a 4-pound spring chicken into 8 pieces: 2 legs, 2 second joints, 2 wings, and 2 breast pieces. Dry the chicken and season with salt and white pepper.

Melt 2 tablespoons butter in a casserole and in it brown lightly 1/2 cup diced bacon, or parboiled and drained fat salt pork. Skim off and reserve the dice, and in the hot fat brown the chicken pieces on both sides. To the casserole add 12 each of small mushrooms and small onions, adjust the cover, and continue to cook over low heat until the onions soften and begin to brown. Pour off about half the fat, add 2 finely chopped shallots or half an onion and 1 clove of garlic, crushed, and sprinkle the vegetables with 2 tablespoons flour. Cook, stirring, until the flour begins to brown, add 2 cups red wine and enough water to cover the chicken, and a faggot made by tying together 2 stalks of celery, 2 sprigs of parsley, half a bay leaf, and a sprig of thyme. Bring the liquid to a boil, add the reserved pork or bacon dice, cover the casserole closely, and simmer the chicken on top of the stove for about 40 minutes, until it is very tender. Skim off any fat that rises to the surface of the sauce, discard the faggot, and correct the seasoning with salt. Sprinkle with chopped parsley and serve the chicken from the casserole.

When the French braise a duck, they first cook it at a high temperature for a short time, turning it from side to side and back to breast until it is golden brown all over. This initial browning also releases quantities of surplus fat, which is discarded before the braising liquid is added to the pan. And the French almost always combine duck with a fruit or vegetable garnish.

DUCK WITH ORANGE SAUCE

Caneton à l'Orange

TRUSS a 5- to 6-pound duck and season it with salt. Place it on its side in a casserole or roasting pan and sear it in a hot oven (450° F.) for 15 to 20 minutes, or until it is golden brown, turning it. Remove the duck and discard all but 1 tablespoon of fat from the pan. Melt in the roasting pan 1 tablespoon butter, stir in 1 tablespoon flour, and cook over direct heat until the *roux* is brown, stirring. Gradually add 1 cup white stock or water and 1/2 cup dry white wine and cook the sauce, stirring constantly, until it is slightly thickened. Return the duckling to the pan and continue cooking it in a moderate oven (350° F.) for 1 to 1 1/2 hours.

Cut the zest from 2 oranges and cut it in very fine strips. Cover the strips with water, boil them for 3 minutes, and drain them. Pare away and discard all the pith remaining on the oranges and slice them. Transfer the duck to a warm platter and cook the sauce in the roasting pan until it is reduced to about 1 cup. In a small saucepan, cook together 2 tablespoons each of sugar and water until the syrup is a light caramel color and strain the reduced sauce into it. Cook all together, add the orange strips, the juice of 2 oranges and of half a lemon, and 2 tablespoons brandy, if desired. Correct the seasoning with salt. Carve the duckling and arrange the pieces on the platter. Surround the duckling with the orange slices and pour over the sauce.

DUCK WITH APRICOTS

Caneton aux Abricots

PREPARE *caneton à l'orange*, duck with orange sauce. To the finished sauce add the orange strips and 1/2 cup apricot juice instead of the juice of the oranges and lemon and the brandy. Garnish the duckling on the platter with 18 heated apricot halves alternately with orange slices.

During the time my brother Lucien was chef de cuisine *at the Plaza-Athénée in Paris, one of the specialties served at the hotel, famed for its good food, was* caneton aux olives.

Caneton aux Olives

TRUSS a 5- to 6-pound duck and season it with a little salt. Place it on its side in a casserole or roasting pan and cook it in a hot oven (425° F.) for 30 minutes, until it is golden brown, turning it. Remove the duck and pour off all but 1 tablespoon of fat from the pan. Melt 1 tablespoon butter in the pan, stir in 1 tablespoon flour, and cook over direct heat, stirring, until the *roux* is golden. Gradually add 1 cup stock or water and 1/2 cup dry white wine and cook, stirring constantly, until the sauce is slightly thickened. Season to taste with salt and pepper and add a faggot made by tying together 1 stalk of celery, 2 sprigs of parsley, a small piece of bay leaf, and a little thyme. Return the duck to the pan, cover it tightly, and braise in a moderate oven (350° F.) for about 1 hour, or until the duck is tender. Remove it to a hot serving platter.

Parboil about 2 dozen pitted green olives in water to cover, to free them of salt. Drain them. Discard the faggot and skim the surplus fat from the sauce. Pour some of the sauce around the duck and serve the rest separately. Garnish the duck with the olives and with water cress.

Caneton aux Navets

COOK a duck as for *caneton aux olives*, duck with olives, but braise it for only 25 minutes, then add vegetables prepared as follows:

Melt 2 tablespoons butter in a saucepan, add 12 small onions, sprinkle them with a little sugar, and cook until lightly brown. Remove the onions from the skillet. Add 2 to 3 cups white or yellow turnips, cut in pieces, to the pan, sprinkle them with a little sugar, and cook until brown. Add the glazed vegetables to the casserole with the duck and continue to braise for 40 to 45 minutes longer. Remove the duck, carve and arrange it on a serving platter, and surround it with the onions and turnips. Skim the fat from the gravy, correct the seasoning, and pour over all.

SQUAB CHICKENS WITH PEAS

Poussins aux Petits Pois

TRUSS 4 to 6 squab chickens to hold the legs close to the body. Sprinkle them with a little salt.

Parboil 1 cup diced fat salt pork in water to cover for 5 minutes and drain. In a heavy pan or casserole, melt 2 tablespoons butter and in it sauté the pork dice until golden. Remove the dice. To the fat remaining in the pan, add 18 small white onions and sauté them until golden brown all over, shaking the pan occasionally. Remove the onions. Sauté the chickens in the pan until they are evenly golden all over. Remove them.

Pour off all but 1 tablespoon fat from the pan, melt 2 tablespoons butter in it, add 1 tablespoon flour, and cook, stirring, until the *roux* turns golden. Stir in 1 cup chicken stock or water, add 1 cup finely shredded lettuce, 3 cups shelled fresh peas, and 1 tablespoon sugar, and bring to a boil, stirring constantly. Add the pork dice and onions and arrange the birds in the sauce. Add a faggot made by tying together 3 sprigs each of parsley and chervil and bring the sauce to a boil. Cover the casserole and cook over moderate heat for 40 to 50 minutes. Discard the faggot and correct the seasoning of the sauce with salt and a little freshly ground pepper. Arrange the birds on a serving dish, around a center of water cress, and arrange the peas and onions between them. Pour the sauce around all.

Fish Braising

BRAISING is ordinarily reserved for large whole fish. The head and the tail, left on for baking, are usually removed when the fish is to be braised.

Braising is especially good for lean fish, since it involves moist cooking in a closed utensil.

Sliced carrots and onions form a bed for fish to be braised as they do for meat and poultry, and the liquid—stock, wine, or water—after the cooking is completed, is thickened to make a sauce in much the same way that the liquid used in poaching is used to make the sauce.

Fish Stews   Fish stews, unlike meat and poultry stews, are poached or boiled, and not braised or cooked en casserole. You will find recipes for fish stews in the section devoted to poaching and boiling.

Poisson Braisé

BRAISED FISH

In a large pan or shallow casserole put 1 onion and 1 carrot, both sliced, some mushroom stems and peelings, if they are available, a sprig of parsley, a bay leaf, a pinch of thyme, 1 cup fish stock or water, and 1/2 cup red or white wine. Season a cleaned, carefully scaled fish with salt and pepper and lay it on the vegetables. Cover the pan and braise the fish in a moderately hot oven (375° F.) for 30 to 60 minutes, depending on its size. Transfer the fish to a heated serving platter and remove and discard the skin. Cook the liquid in the baking dish until it is reduced to one third the original quantity. If white wine was used, thicken the sauce with 1 cup cream sauce; if red wine was used, thicken the sauce with *beurre manié* made by creaming 2 tablespoons butter with 1 tablespoon flour. Strain the sauce over the fish.

Saumon Braisé

BRAISED SALMON

CLEAN and scale a baby salmon or a salmon trout weighing 4 to 5 pounds and season it with 1/2 teaspoon salt. Melt 1 tablespoon butter in a shallow casserole large enough to hold the fish, add 2 tablespoons chopped shallot or onion, some mushroom peelings, 2/3 cup white wine, and 1 cup fish stock or water. Bring the liquid to a boil and cover the fish with a piece of buttered or wax paper, cut to fit the casserole, with a small hole in the center to vent the steam. Cover the casserole and braise the salmon over a gentle heat for 45 to 50 minutes, basting often, until the flesh flakes easily. Remove the fish to a serving platter, take off the skin, and garnish the platter with mushrooms and shrimp.

Melt 2 tablespoons butter in a saucepan, add 1 teaspoon flour, and cook until the flour begins to turn golden. Stir in the liquid from the casserole in which the fish was braised and cook, stirring, until the sauce is well blended. Stir in 2 egg yolks mixed with 1/4 cup cream and bring to the boiling point but do not boil. Correct the seasoning, add a little freshly ground pepper and a few drops of lemon juice, and strain the sauce through a fine sieve over the hot fish and vegetables. Garnish with a few slices of truffle, and sprinkle with chopped parsley. Croutons of puff paste cut in fancy shapes may be added to the platter. Other large whole fish may be cooked this way and red wine may be substituted for white.

SHAD WITH SORREL

*Alose
à l'Oseille*

HAVE your fish dealer remove the scales, clean, and bone a 2 1/2- to 3-pound shad. Cut the fish into 6 pieces. Wash 1 pound sorrel, drain thoroughly, and cut it into julienne. Season the fish with salt and pepper and roll the pieces in flour. Melt enough olive oil or clarified butter in a pan to cover the bottom generously and heat until very hot. Sauté the fish in the hot oil for 5 to 6 minutes on each side, or until the pieces are brown on both sides. Butter a casserole and spread half the sorrel in the bottom, place the slices of fish on it, and cover with the remaining sorrel. Dot with 3 tablespoons butter, broken into small pieces, and add 1 cup dry white wine. Close the casserole and seal the edges of the cover with a roll of dough made by mixing flour and water. Bring the liquid to a boil over direct heat and cook in a moderate oven (375° F.) for 1 1/4 to 1 1/2 hours. Serve from the casserole.

Étuvée Variations: Meat, Poultry, Fish

MODIFICATIONS of cooking *à l'étuvée* are found in dishes prepared *en chemise*, rolled in a crust before baking; *en papillote*, French for cocoon, but in cooking, baked in a paper case; and in the various pâtés and meat and game pies. These do not always require very gentle heat and are usually baked in the oven, but they are always wrapped tightly so that the flavor is enhanced by the savory juices and steam that are trapped inside the wrappings.   These *entrées en chemise* can be very elaborate or quite simple, but they are usually made with fine meat and fish.

En Papillote

The four basic procedures in cooking en papillote *are making the sauce, preparing the pieces of meat, poultry, or fish for the cases, filling and closing the cases, and baking them.   For the paper cases, you will need a piece of thin strong paper—parchment paper or paper of about the quality of good typewriter paper—8 1/2 by 11 inches.   Round off the corners of each piece with scissors and trim away a bit in the center to make a modified heart shape.   Or fold the paper in half and cut out a more pronounced heart shape.*

Côtes de Veau en Papillotes

VEAL CHOPS IN PAPER CASES

SEASON 6 veal chops, 1/2 inch thick, with salt and pepper.   Sauté them gently in 3 tablespoons butter in a skillet for 20 to 25 minutes, or until they are golden brown on both sides.

Prepare a mushroom *duxelles* sauce as follows: Cook 1/2 pound mushrooms, minced, in a saucepan with 2 tablespoons butter, 1 teaspoon each of chopped shallot or onion and chopped parsley, and 1/2 teaspoon salt until all the moisture is cooked away.   Add 1 cup thick cream sauce.

Cut out 12 paper hearts.   Lay the hearts on a table and butter them. Put thin slices of cooked ham about the size of the chops on 6 of the papers and put a spoonful of mushroom *duxelles* sauce on the ham slices. Lay a cooked chop on this, pour the remaining sauce on the chops, and top with thin slices of cooked ham.   Cover with the other paper hearts, butter side down, and roll and pinch the edges together securely.

Bake the cases on a large baking sheet in a hot oven (400° F.) for 5 or 6 minutes, or until they start to brown.   With the point of a paring knife, cut 3/4 of the way around the top heart, just inside the folded edge, and roll the paper back to uncover the contents.   The chops, served on individual plates, are eaten from the paper cases—*en papillotes.*

One of the favorites at the London Ritz was jambon porte-maillot.   We used either a large York ham or the smaller Prague ham—for 6 to 10 people. The ham was baked at the end in bread dough, and the dough held in and concentrated the flavor of the ham juices and of the Madeira in which the ham had been cooked.   These, in turn, gave a delicious savor to the crust.

HAM IN CRUST

Soak an old-fashioned smoked ham in cold water to cover for at least 24 hours before cooking. Drain and scrub it thoroughly in fresh cold water. Put it, skin side down, in a large kettle with water to cover and bring the water slowly to a boil. This should take about 1 hour. Simmer the ham gently for 20 minutes per pound, or until it is done. Do not pierce it with a fork. To test for doneness, move the little bone in the shank end. It should be loose. Remove the ham from the kettle and cut off the skin and surplus fat, leaving a layer of fat about 1/2 inch thick. Put the ham in a roasting pan, sprinkle it with a generous 1/4 cup Sherry or Madeira and 1 1/2 cups Madeira sauce, and cook in a hot oven (400° F.) until it is brown, basting often.

Make a standard bread dough with 6 cups white flour or half white and half rye flour, let the dough rise once, and punch it down. Roll out about 1/3 of the dough in a sheet 1/2 inch thick and a little larger than the ham and place the ham in the center. Roll out the remaining dough and cover the ham. Press the edges together and seal. Make a hole in the dough on top to vent the steam and brush the dough with an egg beaten with a little milk. Bake the wrapped ham on a large baking sheet in a hot oven (400° F.) until the dough is well browned. To serve, cut off enough crust to permit carving and add a piece of the crust to each serving of ham. Pass Madeira sauce separately.

Chicken pies also take advantage of the principal of keeping flavor trapped inside a tasty crust. Different countries have their different ways of cooking them, however. The American spécialité—and very popular, as I so well know—puts precooked chicken in a seasoned white gravy. But at the London Ritz, and at the Ritz in New York, we made our chicken pies with raw chicken and a very thin gravy thickened with egg yolk and flavored with the acid of wine or a little vinegar. Quite a different flavor, but very delicious. We always ran out of them at Sunday lunch no matter how many we made.

ENGLISH CHICKEN PIE À LA RITZ

Cut a 3- to 3 1/2-pound chicken into 8 pieces: 2 legs, 2 second joints, 2 wings, and 2 breast pieces. Remove the bones from the legs and second joints. Clean and slice 8 to 12 mushrooms. Crush 4 hard-cooked egg yolks, force them through a fine sieve, and stir in gradually 1 cup chicken stock. Add 1 onion, finely chopped, 1 teaspoon finely chopped parsley, 1/2 teaspoon each of salt and Worcestershire sauce, a little pepper, and 1/4 cup white wine or 1 tablespoon vinegar. Add the chicken and toss until the pieces are well coated.

In each of 4 individual casseroles place 1 piece each of white and dark meat. Divide the mushrooms evenly among the casseroles. Lay 2 pieces of broiled bacon on top and add 1 cup chicken broth to each casserole. Roll out either puff paste or pie pastry about 1/4 inch thick and cut it into rounds to fit the casseroles. Cover the casseroles, fitting on the pastry securely. Brush the tops with an egg beaten with a little milk and prick them to allow the steam to escape. Bake in a moderately hot oven (375° F.) for 1 hour, or until the crust is brown and the chicken is cooked.

In France the famous chicken pie is a coq *en* pâte, *made with a whole chicken. Only the breastbone is removed so the bird can be rolled in the pie dough more easily. This is considered so elegant a dish that when a dandy is living up to the height of fashion people say, " Il vit comme un coq en pâte. " (He is living like a rooster in a pie.)*

Coq en Pâte

CHICKEN IN CRUST

USE a 4- to 4 1/2-pound young capon or roasting chicken. Carefully pull the skin back from the breast without tearing it, remove the breastbone, and replace the skin.

Cut 1/2 to 3/4 pound goose liver into large pieces, roll them in flour, and sauté for a few minutes in hot butter or goose fat. Or use sliced *pâté de foie gras* but do not sauté it. Put the goose liver in a bowl with 4 or 5 large pieces of truffle, sprinkle with 2 tablespoons Cognac, and mix with 1 cup chicken *mousseline*. Stuff the bird with this forcemeat, sew the opening neatly, and truss the bird. Rub the outside with a little salt. Melt 2 to 3 tablespoons butter or goose fat in a pan large enough to hold the capon or chicken and cook the bird in a moderate oven (350° F.) or over direct heat until it is well browned, turning it once or twice.

Make a mirepoix as follows: Melt 2 tablespoons butter in a small saucepan and in it cook 1 carrot, 1 onion, and 1 stalk of celery, all finely chopped, with a pinch of thyme, 1/2 bay leaf, finely crushed, and a little salt and pepper, until the vegetables are soft but not brown.

Pastry for
Entrée Pies

Make pie pastry using 4 cups flour, 1 cup lard or other shortening, 1/2 cup butter, 1 teaspoon salt, and about 6 tablespoons water. Roll a generous 1/3 of the pastry into an oval about 1/4 inch thick and about 2 inches larger than the bird. Lay the bird on the pastry and spread the mirepoix over the breast and legs. Arrange a few thin slices of raw ham on top and cover with thin slices of fresh larding pork. Roll out the remaining pastry and cover the bird. Moisten the edge of the lower piece of pastry, press top and bottom together, and pinch or flute attractively. Cut a small hole in the top to allow the steam to escape. Brush with an egg beaten with a little milk and bake in a hot oven (425° F.) until the crust starts to color, then reduce the heat to moderately hot (375° F.), and bake for 1 1/2 to 1 3/4 hours, or until the bird is tender. To serve, cut a slice from the top of the pastry to permit carving and give each guest a piece of pastry, a piece of chicken, a piece of ham, and some of the stuffing. Serve *sauce périgourdine* separately.

BUTTERFISH IN PAPER CASES

*Butterfish
en Papillotes*

CUT the heads and tails off 12 butterfish and brush the fish generously with butter. Broil them on a heated baking sheet for 5 to 6 minutes, or until they are golden brown. Prepare mushroom *duxelles* sauce as for *côtes de veau èn papillotes*, veal chops in paper cases. Cut 12 paper hearts as described and butter one surface of each. Put a generous spoonful of mushroom *duxelles* sauce on both halves of 6 of the paper hearts, place a broiled butterfish on each half, and pour the remaining sauce over the fish. Cover with the other paper hearts, butter side down, and roll and pinch the edges together securely. Bake the cases on a large baking sheet in a hot oven (400° F.) for 5 or 6 minutes, or until the cases start to brown. To serve, slit the top heart just inside the folded edge, 3/4 of the way around, and roll back the paper.

Fish filets can also be cooked this way and may be sautéed instead of broiled. Each heart should enclose a single serving of fish: one medium-large filet is a serving.

Deep Frying

L ONG ago, every city of any size in France had its roving vendors of
fried foods. These *frituriers ambulants* sold their hot, fragrant wares at
busy street corners, setting up business near one of the bridges that cross
the Seine or, on a feast day, not too far from a church. The peddler of
fritures was ingeniously equipped. Attached to a belt around his waist
was a large shallow basket, *un éventaire*, in which he carried a little stand.
Over his shoulder was slung another basket, *une hotte*, this one large and
deep, to hold the food and the fat. And in his hand he carried a third
basket that held the *réchaud*, the little stove, and the pan for the cooking.
When he found a likely spot, the *friturier* would unfold his stand, heat
the fat on the *réchaud*, and commence to hawk his wares—*pommes de
terre frites* and *fritures de charcuterie*, crisp fried potatoes and delectable
pork specialties.

When I was a young man in Paris, the *frituriers* were no longer
ambulants. They were housed in street stands, and could offer an assortment of fried foods. Fish was a standard item. The French love fish,
and since most of the great cities of France are located on or near rivers,
fish was easily come by. Even inexpensive, common fish are good when
they are freshly caught—as they were then a dozen times a day—and
plunged at once into hot fat. The French think fried-food stands inspired
the famous fish and chips shops of England.

We did not speak of the food we ate as being French fried because
in France there is only one sort of frying. The French sauté food in a
shallow pan with just enough fat to cover the bottom, or they fry it in
a deep pan filled with enough fat for the food to float. You will find this
explained more fully in the section on sautéing.

Deep fat frying is a French specialty for two reasons: France has
been fortunate in having a constant and excellent supply of frying fat
and oils—the olive oil of the South, the nut oils of other regions, and

the rendered beef and pork fats from areas where animal husbandry is the principal occupation. And, as we have often pointed out in this book, France has never had enough fuel. Top-of-the-stove cookery is less extravagant of fuel than oven cookery, and what thrifty Frenchman would be foolish enough to waste precious fuel to heat an oven when the same food can be cooked so quickly in a kettle of fat, and the fat, unlike the fuel, can be used again?

I think that deep fat frying is the quickest and simplest kind of cooking, if you know how.

First, there are tricks to learn about fat. There should be no problem about selecting a fat, because there are so many good kinds available. The canned shortenings made from vegetable oils are a good choice. Salad oils are good, although olive oil is not usually suggested, since at high temperatures it imparts its own flavor to the food cooked in it. Vegetable shortenings and salad oils are good for all deep frying, including frying of sweet *beignets* and other desserts. Rendered beef fat is a good choice for meats, fish, croquettes, and the less delicate foods, but it takes time to cook the fat from the suet fibers because the cooking must be done over very low heat, and the fat must be carefully watched to prevent scorching. Poultry fat and butter are not suitable for deep frying because they scorch at such a low temperature, to say nothing of the cost of a kettle of butter! There must be enough fat, enough so that the food can actually be submerged and be completely surrounded with hot fat during the brief cooking time.

Fat for
Deep Frying

Deep frying fat can be used over and over again, it is true, but fat used to fry fish cannot be used for any other food. At the Ritz we always had two pans of fat: one for the more delicate foods and the other for fish. After the cooking is finished, the fat should be boiled, strained through fine cheesecloth, and stored in a cold place. The fat is beyond use and ready to discard when it will no longer produce a fine golden crust.

Deep frying is a popular way of cooking fish and shellfish, especially in restaurants where the kettle of hot deep fat is always ready on the range. Meat is seldom cooked this way, but poultry and variety meats often are. Food to be deep fried may go into the kettle uncooked, as pieces of fish do, for example, or it may have been previously cooked, in which case it is usually chopped and forms part of a mixture, such as a croquette. This section will deal largely with fried fish and poultry, and with the croquette mixtures. Other deep-fried foods you will find included throughout the book, and fritters, or *beignet*s, have been given a special section of their own. The techniques discussed here will be generally applicable to all foods, however.

The famous *pommes de terre frites* are in the chapter on vegetables, along with other deep-fried vegetables. Sweet deep-fried foods—certain croquettes and *beignets*, for instance—have been included in the dessert chapter and in the section devoted to *beignets*.

When food to be fried is uncooked, the pieces should not be too large or too thick, or the heat cannot reach the center of the food before the outside becomes overbrown and hard. Temperature of fat cannot be lowered, as the temperature of an oven is, to allow time for the heat to reach and cook the center, because the fat must be kept very hot at all times or the food will absorb too much of it—the very thing you want to avoid. Always try to maintain the proper temperature of the fat. Cold food dropped into hot fat will lower the temperature 20 to 25 degrees, and the more quickly the temperature is raised again, the better the finished product will be.

Utensil for Deep Frying

It is helpful, if not absolutely necessary, to have a pan of very heavy metal for deep frying. The heavy metal helps to hold the fat at a fairly constant temperature. It is well to use a wire frying basket to lower the food slowly into the hot fat. Then, if the fat starts to bubble up and threatens to run over onto the stove, the basket can be lifted out for a moment until the bubbling dies down. The fried food can be removed from the fat easily and the surplus fat drains off readily if the food is in a basket.

Thermometer in Deep Frying

Cube-of-Bread Test in Deep Frying

A thermometer saves guesswork in judging the temperature of the fat, but a 1-inch cube of bread will serve almost as well. For uncooked foods, such as fish, chicken, fritters, and potatoes, the temperature of the fat should be about 370º F. At this temperature a 1-inch cube of bread will brown in 45 to 50 seconds. For cooked foods, such as croquettes, the fat should be about 390º F., and at this temperature a 1-inch cube of bread will brown in 25 to 30 seconds.

Electric Fryers

If you do a great deal of deep fat frying, you will probably enjoy an automatic electric fryer. This appliance is equipped with a thermostat that keeps the fat at the correct temperature and spares it the destructive processes of accidental overheating.

Properly fried foods come from the kettle golden brown, crisp, and tender. There are a few tricks that help to keep them that way. Remove the basket from the fat and shake off as much of the surplus fat as possible. Then spread the food—do not pile it up—on absorbent paper towels, which will absorb the remaining fat. Never put fried foods on a cold serving dish. A cold plate will work havoc with the crisp crust of the *fritures*. At the old Ritz-Carlton we always used a paper doily to protect the crispness, and of course the serving plates were heated, too. Never cover fried foods: steam forms under a cover and makes the food limp and soggy.

There are various ways of preparing food for the deep-fat kettle. Some foods can be fried without any sort of coating—potatoes, for example. Uncoated food should be dried as thoroughly as possible: a moist surface results in a less crisp product, because moisture reduces the temperature of the fat considerably, making for a tough crust instead of a tender crisp one.

Most foods, however, should be coated. The food may be simply dipped into milk and then into flour—this method is used for small fish and some vegetables, such as eggplant. Or the food may be coated a little more elaborately, with flour, egg, and bread crumbs—the familiar crusty surface on croquettes, fish filets, and so on. The French phrase for this operation is "*paner à l'anglaise.*" A third coating is a fritter batter made of flour, egg, a liquid—water, milk, or beer—and oil, used to coat foods such as pieces of fruit or to mix with chopped foods. This group called fritters or *beignets*, you will find in another section of the book. A fourth coating, much less used but delicious, is pastry, either puff pastry or flaky pie pastry. Finely chopped cooked foods mixed with rich sauces fill the pastry, and these delectable fried tidbits are called *rissoles*.

Most fried foods are sprinkled with salt or sugar after they have been drained. Neither can be absorbed by a fried surface, so be sure to use very fine salt or sugar that will give a pleasant sensation in the mouth, not a gritty one.

Coatings for Deep Frying

Simple Coating

TO COAT FRIED FOODS WITH FLOUR

Fariner

DRY thoroughly the food to be fried. Dip in milk and roll in flour. Shake to remove surplus flour. Only a thin, even coating of flour should remain. Use for smelts, whitebait, small fish filets, onion rings, eggplant cut into strips, and similar foods.

*For frying most fish the temperature of the fat should be about 370° F.
Larger pieces of fish require a slightly lower temperature so that the heat
can penetrate to the center before the surface browns, and smaller pieces a
correspondingly higher temperature. Fish rises to the surface when it is done.*

FRIED SMALL FISH

*Friture
de Petits
Poissons*

CLEAN and dry *goujons*, whitebait, or smelts well. Dip them in milk and
then in flour. Shake off the surplus flour and cook the fish in hot deep
fat (370° F.) 2 minutes for *goujons* or whitebait, 3 for smelts. Drain the
fish on absorbent paper and sprinkle them with fine salt. Serve with lemon slices and tartare mayonnaise or *sauce rémoulade.*

FRIED FISH STICKS

*Filets
de Poisson
à la Mode
de Goujons*

CUT filets of any good white-fleshed fish into pieces about the size of
the little finger, and dry them well. Coat, cook, and serve as described
for *friture de petits poissons,* fried small fish.

FRIED FISH FILETS

*Filets
de Poisson
Frits*

DRY the filets well, and if they are large, cut them into serving pieces.
Coat, cook, and serve as described for *friture de petits poissons,* fried
small fish.

À l'Anglaise Coating

TO COAT À L'ANGLAISE

*Paner
à l'Anglaise*

DRY thoroughly the food to be fried. Dip in flour and then into 1 egg
beaten with 4 tablespoons milk, 1 tablespoon salad oil, and 1/2 teaspoon
salt. Drain well and dip into fine bread crumbs. To make the crumbs,
trim the crusts from day-old white bread so there will be no brown specks
to darken during frying. Crumble the bread finely and rub the crumbs
through a coarse sieve to make uniformly fine crumbs. These fresh
crumbs are best for fried desserts and delicately flavored foods. For

fish, chicken, and less fragile foods, dry bread crumbs are better. These may be grated from hard dry bread, or the day-old crumbs may be allowed to dry. The *anglaise* coating is used for fish, chicken, croquettes, and vegetables, and for a great deal of deep frying.

For making croquettes and for covering some foods before coating them à l'an-glaise, *the chef uses what is called a Villeroy sauce, actually a very thick* velouté. *Use a pan of heavy metal, for the mixture tends to scorch as it cooks down in a light-weight utensil. And stir it often, to keep it smooth.*

VILLEROY SAUCE FOR COATING FRIED FOODS

Sauce Villeroi

Cook 3 cups *velouté* sauce until it is reduced to 2 cups, stirring. It should be very thick. Combine the sauce with 2 slightly beaten egg yolks and cook it until it reaches the boiling point, stirring constantly, but do not let it boil. Cool to lukewarm, stirring occasionally, before using.

FRIED CHICKEN

Poulet Frit

Cut a young, tender chicken into serving pieces, coat the pieces *à l'an-glaise*, and cook them in hot deep fat (370° F.) for about 6 to 8 minutes, or until they come to the surface of the fat and are a golden brown. Drain the chicken on absorbent paper and serve on a paper doily with fried parsley. Serve tomato sauce or cream sauce separately. The dish may be garnished with corn or apple *beignets*.

BREAST OF CHICKEN XENIA

Suprêmes de Volaille Xenia

Remove the breast from a chicken weighing about 3 to 3 1/2 pounds. Cut the breast away from the bone, splitting the meat in half, and discard the skin. Pound the filets into very thin slices. Season the slices with a little salt and pepper and spread the center with 1 teaspoon maître d'hôtel butter. Place a piece of *pâté de foie gras* containing a bit of truffle on the butter, fold the meat around the filling, and secure the rolls with toothpicks. Coat the filets *à l'anglaise* and store them in the refrigerator. When the filets are ready to serve, fry them in hot deep fat (370° F.) for about 4 minutes, or until they rise to the surface and are golden brown. Remove the toothpicks and serve immediately, so quickly, in fact, that when the rolls are cut with the fork, the butter and *foie gras* will not be melted, but just creamy. Garnish with slices of pineapple and peeled apple quarters sautéed in butter, sprinkled with powdered sugar, and glazed under the broiler. The garnish must be ready before the chicken is put in the fat to cook. Serve with *sauce suprême*. Serves 2.

Attereaux de Volaille

SKEWERED CHICKEN

CUT cooked chicken into large dice and cook as many medium-sized mushrooms as there are dice of chicken. Alternate on a small skewer a mushroom, a piece of chicken, and a piece of truffle until the skewer is filled. Roll the whole in thick, lukewarm Villeroy sauce, coat them *à l'anglaise*, and cook the skewers in hot deep fat (390° F.) until golden brown. Drain on absorbent paper and serve on a paper doily accompanied by *suprême* or tomato sauce and any desired vegetable.

Attereaux of meat, fish, shellfish, and poultry are served as light entrées and hors-d'oeuvre.

Attereaux de Ris de Veau

SKEWERED SWEETBREADS

FOLLOW the recipe for *attereaux de volaille*, skewered chicken, substituting cooked diced sweetbreads for the chicken and omitting the truffles. Serve with *suprême* or tomato sauce.

Poisson Frit à l'Anglaise

BREADED FRIED FISH

WHOLE small fish, pieces of fish, or fish filets may be cooked in this way. Wipe the fish dry and coat them *à l'anglaise*. Fry them in deep hot fat at 360° to 380° F., according to size and drain. Serve with tartare sauce.

FRIED FISH WITH MAÎTRE D'HÔTEL BUTTER

USE sole, whiting, or trout. Remove the skin from small whole sole, and make an incision that will permit removing the bone. Usually it is easiest to remove it in 3 sections. Leave the skin on trout. Open them down the back and remove the backbone and other bones. Dry the fish well, dip them in flour, and coat them *à l'anglaise*. Fry them in deep hot fat (370° F.) until they are golden brown. Drain on absorbent paper. Put maître d'hôtel butter in the slit where the bone was removed, arrange the fish on a platter, and serve maître d'hôtel butter on each fish. Garnish the platter with lemon slices and fried parsley.

Poisson Colbert

FILETS OF SOLE RICHELIEU

PREPARE sole as for *poisson Colbert*, fried fish with maître d'hôtel butter. Garnish the cooked fish down the back with slices of truffle.

Filets de Sole Richelieu

Croquettes are mixtures of finely diced or minced foods and very thick béchamel sauce—about 2 cups solid to 1 cup sauce—shaped into cylinders, balls, or cones that are then coated à l'anglaise *and fried in deep hot fat at 390° F. But there are variations such as fish balls that are made of mashed potatoes and dessert croquettes made of a rice-custard mixture.*

The softer the mixture inside its crusty anglaise *coating, the more delectable the croquette. But soft mixtures are difficult to handle, and for this reason, after putting together a croquette mixture, you must chill it well to make it firmer and easier to shape and coat. In the hot fat, the coating becomes brown and crusty and the filling soft and delectable.*

Very small croquettes are often served as hors-d'oeuvre.

BÉCHAMEL SAUCE FOR CROQUETTES

MELT 2 tablespoons butter in a small heavy saucepan, add 3 tablespoons flour, and cook until the *roux* starts to turn golden. Add gradually 1 cup boiling milk, stirring constantly with a whip or wooden spoon, and cook

Sauce Béchamel pour Croquettes

for about 12 to 15 minutes, or until the sauce is very thick, stirring to keep it smooth. Add 1/2 teaspoon salt and a little white pepper and stir in 2 eggs lightly beaten and mixed with a little of the hot sauce.

For a thicker sauce, especially for hors-d'oeuvre croquettes, use 4 table-spoons butter, 6 tablespoons flour, 1 1/2 cups milk, and 2 eggs yolks and 1 whole egg.

Croquettes de Volaille

CHICKEN CROQUETTES

To ABOUT 1 cup béchamel sauce for croquettes add 2 cups diced cooked chicken and 6 cooked mushrooms, diced, and cook, stirring constantly, until the mixture cleans the sides of the pan. Correct the seasoning with salt and spread the mixture on a flat buttered dish to cool. Shape the croquettes in cylinders, cones, or balls, coat them *à l'anglaise*, and cook in hot deep fat (390° F.) until they are golden brown. Serve with *suprême* or tomato sauce.

Croquettes de Ris de Veau et de Volaille

SWEETBREAD AND CHICKEN CROQUETTES

FOLLOW the recipe for chicken croquettes, substituting cooked, diced sweetbreads for half the chicken. Two tablespoons chopped cooked ham or smoked ox tongue may be added, and 2 to 3 tablespoons chopped truffles will give the croquettes a very special flavor.

Croquettes de Riz Sauvage

WILD RICE CROQUETTES

FOLLOW the recipe for chicken croquettes, substituting cooked wild rice for the diced chicken and using 1/2 cup cooked diced mushrooms.

Côtelettes de Dinde

TURKEY CUTLETS

To ABOUT 1 cup béchamel sauce for croquettes, add 2 cups diced cooked white meat of turkey and 6 mushrooms, cooked and finely diced. If desired, 2 or 3 tablespoons finely diced cooked ham may be added. Cook over low heat, stirring briskly, until the mixture leaves the sides of the pan. Correct the seasoning with salt and spread the mixture on a flat buttered dish to cool. Form it into cutlets and coat the cutlets *à l'an-glaise*. Fry the cutlets in hot deep fat (390º F.) or sauté them in butter until golden brown. Serve with tomato sauce or *sauce périgourdine*.

LOBSTER CROQUETTES

Croquettes de Homard

To ABOUT 1 cup béchamel sauce for croquettes, add 2 cups cooked lobster, 6 cooked mushrooms, both finely diced, and 1 tablespoon chopped truffles. Cook, stirring constantly, until the mixture cleans the sides of the pan. Correct the seasoning with salt and spread the mixture on a flat buttered dish to cool. Shape into croquettes, coat the croquettes *à l'an-glaise*, and cook them in hot deep fat (390º F.) until golden brown. Drain on absorbent paper and serve with white wine sauce.

FISH CROQUETTES

Croquettes de Poissons

FOLLOW the directions for lobster croquettes, substituting for the lobster cooked fileted haddock, sole, or cod.

OYSTER CROQUETTES NORMANDY

Croquettes d'Huîtres à la Normande

MELT 3 tablespoons butter in a saucepan, add 4 tablespoons flour, and cook, stirring, until the *roux* starts to turn golden. Add 1 1/2 cups hot milk and 1/2 cup strained oyster liquor. Cook this béchamel sauce until it thickens, stirring constantly, and cook it 25 minutes, stirring occasionally. Add 1/2 teaspoon salt and 4 egg yolks, lightly beaten and mixed with a little of the hot sauce. Heat just to the boiling point, remove the pan from the heat, and add 2 dozen large oysters, poached for 2 minutes, drained, and cut into dice, 1/2 cup mushrooms, cooked in acidulated water and chopped, and 2 tablespoons chopped truffles. Reheat the sauce without boiling it and correct the seasoning. Spread the mixture on a flat buttered dish to cool. Form croquettes of any shape and coat them *à l'anglaise*. Fry them in deep hot fat (375º F.) until they are brown. Drain on absorbent paper and serve with cream sauce enriched with 1 egg yolk.

Croquettes
de Gibier

GAME CROQUETTES

DICE finely enough cooked game to make 2 cups. Add 6 cooked mushrooms, finely chopped, and 2 to 3 tablespoons chopped truffles. Reduce 1 cup of Madeira sauce or brown sauce until it is very thick and mix it with the other ingredients. Cool. Shape the mixture into croquettes, coat the croquettes *à l'anglaise*, and cook them in hot deep fat (390° F.) until golden brown. Drain on absorbent paper and serve with any desired sauce.

Croquettes
de Pommes
de Terre

POTATO CROQUETTES

PREPARE *pommes de terre duchesse*, duchess potatoes, and let them cool. Shape the mixture into croquettes, coat the croquettes *à l'anglaise* and fry them in deep hot fat (370° F.) until they are golden brown. Drain on absorbent paper.

Fish Balls

FISH BALLS

COMBINE 1 cup each of freshly mashed potatoes and cooked flaked haddock, sole, or cod. Add 2 lightly beaten eggs and salt and pepper to taste, and cool the fish mixture. Shape it into small balls, coat the fish balls *à l'anglaise*, and fry them in deep hot fat (390° F.) until they are golden brown.

Fritter Batter Coating

PROBABLY one of the most delectable ways of preparing foods for frying is to coat them with fritter batter. Any solid food, or any mixture firm enough to hold its shape, cooked, or uncooked, may be treated in this fashion. Or cut-up food may be mixed with the batter. Since fritters, or *beignets*, play such an important role in French cuisine, they have a chapter to themselves, in which you will find the various fritter batters and further information about deep frying.

BATTER-FRIED FISH

Poissons Frits à Pâte à Frire

DIP the fish into thick fritter batter, drain off the surplus batter, and fry in hot deep fat at 360° F. to 380° F., depending upon the size of the fish. Drain thoroughly on paper toweling and serve with any desired sauce.

FILETS OF SOLE ORLY

Filets de Sole Orly

DRY small filets of sole well, dip them in flour, and then in fritter batter. Cook the fish in deep hot fat (370° F.) until they are golden brown and rise to the surface. Drain on absorbent paper, sprinkle with fine salt, and serve on a paper doily with fried parsley. Serve tomato sauce separately.

Pastry Covering

RISSOLES, as we have said, are pastry pockets, often crescent-shaped, like little *chaussons*. The usual fillings for *rissoles* (called *salpicons*) are very like croquette mixtures, and sometimes are identical—finely diced cooked food bound with a thick sauce, often béchamel enriched with eggs. A spoonful of filling is put in the center of a small square or round of puff pastry or flaky pie pastry, the pastry is folded over, and the edges rolled or pinched together to seal them. The pastries are usually fried, but they can also be brushed with a little milk and baked in a hot oven (450° F.) until they are brown.

Small *rissoles*, like small croquettes and *beignets*, are served as hors-d'oeuvre, and in the section on hot hors-d'oeuvre you will find more suggestions for *rissole* fillings.

CHICKEN RISSOLES FERMIÈRE

Rissoles de Volaille Fermière

COMBINE equal amounts of cooked chicken, ham or ox tongue, and mushrooms, all cooked and very finely diced, and add enough thick béchamel sauce for croquettes to bind the ingredients. Correct the seasoning with salt. Roll out puff paste or flaky pie pastry 1/8-inch thick and cut it in 2 1/2-inch squares. Put a little of the filling in the center of each square, fold the pastry to make a triangle, and roll the edges to seal them. Cook the *rissoles* in deep hot fat (360° F.) until they are golden brown. Drain them on absorbent paper and serve on a paper doily.

CRAB MEAT RISSOLES

Rissoles de Crabe

HEAT 1 cup crab meat in 1 tablespoon butter. Add 1/2 cup thick Mornay sauce and 3 tablespoons grated Parmesan or dry Swiss cheese. Season the filling with a little salt and pepper and fill and fry *rissoles* as for *rissoles de volaille fermière*, chicken *rissoles fermière*.

Leftovers

To a Frenchman thrift—care and wisdom in the management of one's resources—is a cardinal virtue.

No top-ranking chef is ever guilty of wastefulness. He may seem to be extravagant with heavy cream, good butter, truffles and *foie gras*, but actually he uses these always to best advantage, and there are households that could perhaps buy more cream and butter, and even sometimes truffles and *foie gras*, if waste in food preparation were cut down and nothing thrown away that could make another delicious meal.

The most important thing to remember about cooking leftovers is that the meat, poultry, or fish is already sufficiently cooked. The problem is to reheat it without further cooking. Meat, especially, should never be cooked twice. You cannot, for instance, put a roast back in the oven the next day, nor can you make a stew with cooked meat as you would with uncooked meat.

Anything more than the briefest possible heating overcooks meat, toughens the tissues, and dries out the juices. In combining leftover meat with a sauce, it is best to finish the sauce completely first. Have the meat at room temperature and the sauce very hot, then combine the two and heat them together for only a moment. Be sure there is plenty of sauce and that it is well-flavored with tomatoes, mustard, vinegar, onions, pickles, and the like. When meat or poultry is combined with other ingredients in a sauce and baked in a shallow casserole under a crust, the casserole and crust baffle the heat enough so that the food is just hot by the time the crust is brown.

The only exception to the rule on recooking is game. Leftover roast venison will make a good *civet*, or stew. So will the legs, second joints, and carcasses of roasted feathered game. At the old Ritz-Carlton there were many elaborate dinners at which breasts of guinea hen or of pheasant, but only the breasts, were served. We were left with the carcasses of 500 to 600 roast birds. Since these game birds were expensive, they represented a substantial investment. We made *salmis*, or stews, of the carcasses and had them on our menu almost daily during the season. They were one of our most popular entrées. Game stews of all kinds actually improve with time, because the meat marinates in the wine sauce and the reheated stew is delicious. *Leftover Game*

There are recipes that make use of leftovers throughout this book—soufflés, salads, shirred eggs, soups, and stuffed vegetables, for instance. Many hot and cold hors-d'oeuvre—canapé mixtures and croquettes, for instance—are based on leftovers. In this section, you will find a sampling of other recipes for cooked food.

Leftover Meat

MOST recipes for leftover meat can be used with equal success for beef, veal, lamb, and even pork, but chances are that most of your leftover meat will be beef, if only because beef cuts are larger.

The best possible source of leftover beef is the pot-au-feu, *which in the French household is deliberately made with a piece of beef large enough to provide leftovers for another meal or two. Dishes prepared with the beef from the* pot-au-feu *are a commonplace in French homes and in small French restaurants, especially in rural inns, but they are seldom seen on American tables. Roast beef can be used in the same way, but the meat is never as moist and tender as the boiled beef.*

COLD SLICED BEEF

*Boeuf Froid
à la
Parisienne*

SLICE 1 pound cold boiled beef and overlap the slices in an oblong serving dish. Garnish the sides of the dish with sliced cooked potatoes, sliced tomatoes, leftover cooked green beans, carrots cut in julienne, and sliced or quartered hard-cooked eggs. Arrange very thin slices of onion on top of the meat and sprinkle with chopped parsley. To 1/2 cup vinaigrette sauce add 1 teaspoon each of chopped chives and tarragon, and pour the sauce over the meat and vegetables.

VEAL PATTIES

*Fricadelles
de Veau*

CHOP finely 1 pound leftover cooked veal. Bake 3 large potatoes until tender, remove the pulp, press it through a sieve or food mill, and whip it smooth with a wooden spoon. Sauté 1/2 cup finely chopped onion in 2 tablespoons butter until the onion is golden. Add the meat and potato pulp, 1 egg, beaten, 1 tablespoon chopped parsley, and a little salt and pepper and mix thoroughly. Divide the mixture into portions the size of an egg, roll each in flour, and flatten it like a hamburger. Brown the cakes on both sides in 3 tablespoons hot beef or veal fat or butter. Place the pan in a moderately hot oven (375° F.) for 7 or 8 minutes to finish the cooking. Serve with tomato sauce or *sauce piquante.*

Fricadelles may also be made of leftover cooked beef.

A trick in using leftovers is to dramatize them. One dish capable of many dramatic variations, which can be depended upon to use up all leftovers, is, of course, hash. During the depression, we made a specialty of hashes at the Ritz. But what hashes—the most succulent and tasty we could devise. We combined many different sauces with the finely cut meat and poultry, bordered the dishes in all sorts of ways: with rice, duchesse potatoes, purée of peas and corn, and so on. On some hachis we spread Mornay sauce and glazed it. Some were sprinkled with bread crumbs and melted butter and browned, and on some we put a poached egg. We served the hachis on red-bordered plates, and called them Red Plate luncheons. Our normal supply of leftovers soon was not enough, so popular were the plates, and we had to cook meat and poultry especially for the Red Plate hashes.

LAMB HASH WITH POTATOES À LA RITZ

SAUTÉ lightly 2 tablespoons chopped onion in 1 tablespoon butter. Add 1 tablespoon flour and continue to cook until the mixture begins to turn golden. Add gradually 1 1/2 cups stock and 3 tablespoons tomato sauce or tomato purée and cook the sauce slowly for 20 to 25 minutes, stirring occasionally, and skimming as necessary. Add 1 tablespoon chopped parsley and about 1 pound leftover cooked lamb, finely diced. Mix all together lightly and bring the sauce just to the boil. Spread the mixture in a shallow heatproof serving dish.

Peel, quarter, and boil 3 or 4 large potatoes in salted water until they are done. Drain, dry them over low heat, shaking the pan, and force through a sieve or food mill. Add 1 to 2 tablespoons butter and beat with a wooden spoon. Add little by little about 1/2 cup boiling milk, or enough to make creamy mashed potatoes, and correct the seasoning with salt. Cover the meat mixture with the potatoes and sprinkle the potatoes with grated Parmesan or dry Swiss cheese, 1/2 tablespoon fine bread crumbs, and a little melted butter. Brown in a hot oven (450° F.) or under the broiler. This hash may also be made of leftover beef.

Hachis d'Agneau à la Ritz

Leftover Poultry

THE BEST leftover chicken is boiled chicken, such as comes from *poule-au-pot*. Roasted or sautéed chicken is drier and never so white. When chicken is cooked specifically for salad or pie, it is boiled or poached slowly and cooled in the stock.

White meat is preferred for creamed dishes and salads—with greens or molded in aspic—for chicken hash and sandwiches. Dark meat can be used in a creole or tomato sauce for spaghetti, in *rissoles*, or in croquettes. Dark and light meat are often combined, of course.

CHICKEN HASH À LA RITZ

Hachis de Volaille à la Ritz

REMOVE the white meat from boiled chicken (roasted chicken should not be used here) and chop enough to make 3 cups. Do not chop it too finely. Put the chicken in a saucepan with 1 cup light cream and cook until the cream is reduced to about 1/2 the original quantity.

Melt 2 tablespoons butter in a saucepan, add 2 tablespoons flour, and cook until the *roux* just starts to turn golden. Add 2 cups milk and cook, stirring constantly, until the sauce is reduced to about 1 cup. Stir in 1/2 cup cream. Add 1 cup of this cream sauce to the chicken mixture and season with a little salt and pepper. Place the hash in a heatproof serving dish. Combine the remaining cream sauce with 1 beaten egg and fold in 2 tablespoons whipped cream. Spread the sauce over the hash. Rub enough cooked green peas through a sieve to make 2 cups purée and stir over low heat until the surplus moisture is cooked away, then stir in 2 egg yolks, slightly beaten. Pipe a border of the purée around the dish with a pastry tube. Glaze in a hot oven (450° F.) or under the broiler. Serve at once.

CHICKEN CAPILOTADE

Capilotade de Volaille

SAUTÉ 2 tablespoons chopped onions in 2 tablespoons butter until they are golden. Add 1 tablespoon finely chopped shallots, 1 clove of garlic, crushed, and 1 cup sliced mushrooms. Cook slowly until the mushrooms are soft. Sprinkle the mushrooms with 1 tablespoon flour, mix well, and add 1/3 cup white or red wine, 1 cup stock or gravy or canned tomatoes, and 2 fresh tomatoes, peeled, seeded, and chopped. Cook, stirring constantly, until the sauce thickens and continue to cook for about 10 to 15 minutes. Add 2 cups diced leftover chicken and bring the sauce back to the boil, but do not let it boil. Correct the seasoning with salt and add a little pepper. Place the *capilotade* in a serving dish, sprinkle with chopped parsley, and garnish with croutons.

Here is a way to make a curry dish of turkey or chicken without making an authentic curry, which requires that the bird be cooked with the curry.

SLICED TURKEY WITH CURRY SAUCE

PREPARE about 3 cups *sauce au currie*, curry sauce. Heat 1 1/2 to 2 cups sliced leftover turkey in a little stock, pour the hot sauce over it, and bring just to the boil. Serve with boiled rice.

Dindonneau à l'Indienne

SLICED CHICKEN WITH PAPRIKA SAUCE

PREPARE about 3 cups paprika sauce. Heat 1 1/2 to 2 cups leftover sliced chicken in a little stock, pour the hot sauce over it, and bring just to the boil. Serve with boiled rice.

Poularde à la Hongroise

Leftover Fish

IN USING leftover fish one must be very careful to keep the fish in pieces large enough to pick up on a fork. Mixing and stirring fragile cooked fish into a sauce is sure to break and mash it. It is best to combine sauce and fish in layers: first some of the sauce, then a layer of fish, and then the remaining sauce, so the fish retains its identity. It is very important for a leftover fish dish to be served piping hot. This is not so simple as it may seem to achieve, since the fish must, for safety's sake, be kept refrigerated until the last moment. To warm the fish, put 2 tablespoons of water and 1 of butter in a shallow pan. Heat the fish very slowly in this until the water has cooked away. The steam will heat the fish without toughening it, and the butter will keep the flesh moist and juicy. Naturally, the skin and bones of cooked fish must be carefully removed and the meat taken from the shells of cooked shell-fish before these dishes can be prepared.

CREAMED FISH AU GRATIN

Poisson au Gratin

CUT 1 1/2 pounds leftover cooked fish into pieces and heat. Prepare 2 1/2 cups *duchesse* potatoes and 2 cups Mornay sauce. Make a border of the *duchesse* potatoes around a flat ovenproof serving dish, using a pastry bag. Spread 1 cup of the Mornay sauce in the center of the dish, put the reheated fish on the sauce, and cover the fish with the remaining sauce. Sprinkle the sauce with grated Parmesan cheese and a little melted butter. Brush the potatoes with melted butter and brown in a hot oven (450° F.) or under the broiler.

COLD FISH RAVIGOTE

Poisson Froid Ravigote

REMOVE the skin and bones from salmon, halibut, or any good white fish that has been cooked in one large piece. Place the fish on a serving dish in 1 or 2 pieces and garnish the edge of the dish with sliced peeled tomatoes and cucumbers and sliced or quartered hard-cooked eggs, arranged on lettuce leaves. Pour ravigote sauce over the fish or decorate it with mayonnaise and serve more sauce separately.

Shellfish

CRUSTACÉS
ET COQUILLES

SHELLFISH WERE NOT plentiful in my Bourbonnais countryside, but when I came to work at the Ritz in Paris, I saw my fill of them—baskets and baskets of squirming lobsters, pearly black mussels, scallops in their fluted shells, oysters and shrimp of all sizes. I was a *potager*, a soup chef, but my range was next to the fish station, and when I finished my own tasks, I watched Monsieur Cassagnac, who was probably the best fish chef in the world, at his work.

Almost every fine restaurant in Paris made a speciality of shellfish, and this was true also in New York. In the years before the first World War, the elegant restaurants for after-theater dining—nowadays they are called " night clubs "—were known as " lobster palaces. "

In France, and again in New York, our shellfish came to us no longer than 24 hours from the time it was hauled from the water, the lobsters and crabs still actively moving about, the mussels and oysters, and in America, the clams, with their shells firmly closed. The live bivalves sank to the bottom of the pan of water in which we washed them; the ones that floated had to be discarded.

Under Monsieur Cassagnac's tutelage, I learned that shellfish can be cooked by any of the basic methods, and that the tricks of sautéing, broiling, and the rest, apply to them as they do to other foods. You may wish to read over these sections before you begin to use the shellfish recipes that follow.

Lobster

French Langouste or South African Lobster Tails

THERE are two kinds of lobsters. One, called a spiny lobster, is not really a lobster at all, but a marine crayfish. The French call this crustacean *langouste*. The *langouste* is caught in sizable quantities off our west coast, off the south of France, and off South Africa. The meat lies in the tail and, since the advent of quick freezing, only the tail is shipped into this country. The cook need only thaw and cook these tails, broiling them about 4 inches from the broiler flame, first on one side for 3 to 5 minutes, and then on the other for about 10 minutes, until the meat is cooked through. These tails may also be boiled in a generous amount of water, for 25 to 50 minutes. I think the longer cooking makes the tails more tender.

Maine Lobster

Most of the lobsters sold in our markets come from Maine. This lobster, which the French call *le homard*, comes from the cold waters of the North Atlantic off Nova Scotia and off the northern European coast, as well as off the Maine coast and it is most plentiful in spring and summer. The *homard* has a dark green color; it turns red after cooking. The meat lies in the center body, in the tail, and in the claws. The intestinal tract and the small sac in the head where the intestinal tract begins are inedible and the spongy gray fringe of lungs is not eaten either, because it is very tough. The roe of the female, called the coral, which turns bright red in the cooking, is a great delicacy. The liver, or tomalley, which turns green when it is cooked, is another delicacy. Chefs usually set the uncooked liver aside to thicken the sauce.

Lobster Roe
Lobster Liver
or Tomalley

In all lobster cookery I advise starting with live lobster. Those unable to purchase fresh lobsters can, of course, use the frozen or canned products, but .the recipes must be adapted accordingly. As a rule, count on half a lobster per person. But if you are serving broiled baby lobster (1 to 1 1/4 pounds), many people will appreciate—and expect, in fact—a whole lobster. On the other hand, if you are making a dish which includes a rich sauce, two 1 3/4- to 2-pound lobsters will serve 6.

Pick up a live lobster by the body, so that your fingers are out of the way of its nipping claws. To split the lobster, proceed as follows:

Spread several layers of newspaper on a large cutting board and cover the papers with paper towels, which will absorb moisture. The papers can later be bundled up and discarded, leaving only the knife to clean. Lay the lobster, shell side up, on the board, and with a large, strong, sharp-pointed knife pierce through the shell at the head and cut down through shell and body to the end of the tail. Turn the halves flesh side up. Remove the intestinal vein, the sac near the head where the intestinal tract starts, and the lungs.

Splitting
Live Lobster

BROILED LOBSTER

Homard
Grillé

FOR each person, split a 1 1/4-pound live lobster. Arrange the lobster halves on a broiler pan, cut side up, season with a little salt and pepper, and spread generously with butter. Broil the lobster under moderate heat for 15 to 18 minutes, depending on the size, basting it from time to time with a little melted butter. Do not allow the top to brown until the end of the cooking time. If several lobsters are to be cooked at one time, cut off the claws and arrange the body sections and the claws compactly on the grill. Serve with lemon quarters and melted butter.

EVEN when lobster meat is to be served in a sauce, without the shell, the French chef cuts up the raw lobster and sautés the pieces, shell and

Cutting Up
Live Lobster

all, in butter or oil, usually with onion and shallots so that the flavor of the shell penetrates both meat and sauce. After this initial cooking the meat may be removed from the shell before the sauce is added, or shell and meat are served together.

Use a heavy knife to cut up a lobster. Cut off the claws and crack the large claws. Cut off the tail and slice it, if desired. Cut the body in half crosswise and divide the upper half in 2 parts lengthwise. Remove and discard the intestinal vein, the sac at the head, and the lungs.

Lobster Newburg may be prepared in two ways. Uncooked lobsters give a more distinctive flavor to the sauce. But if you use a chafing dish, you will probably prefer the second way, in which boiled lobster meat can be used, or defrosted frozen meat or canned meat. Canned lobster meat should not be first cooked in butter, but merely reheated in the finished sauce, just before serving.

*Homard
à la
Newburg I*

LOBSTER NEWBURG I

CUT up 2 or 3 live lobsters, 1 3/4 to 2 pounds each, as above. Season with 1/2 teaspoon salt and a little pepper. Sauté the lobster pieces in 3 tablespoons butter for about 5 minutes, or until the shells turn red. Add to the pan 1 tablespoon chopped shallot and 2 tablespoons chopped onion. Flame the lobsters with 3 tablespoons Cognac and when the flame burns out, add 1/2 cup dry Sherry, and 1 1/4 cups heavy cream. Bring the mixture to a boil, cover the pan, and cook over low heat for 20 to 25 minutes. Remove the pieces of lobster and keep them hot. Cook the liquid until it is reduced to 1/3 its original quantity and add 1 cup cream sauce. Correct the seasoning with salt, add 1/4 cup cream, rub the sauce through a fine sieve and add 1/4 cup Sherry. Remove the lobster meat from the shells, cut it in thick slices, and combine it with the sauce. Serve with boiled rice.

*Homard
à la
Newburg II*

LOBSTER NEWBURG II

MELT 2 tablespoons butter in a saucepan, add 2 cups cooked lobster meat cut in thick slices and heat the lobster well. Stir in 1 tablespoon flour and gradually add 1 cup cream. Cook the sauce, stirring carefully, until it is smooth and thick. Be careful not to mash the pieces of lobster. Add a generous 1/3 cup dry Sherry and cook the sauce for 5 minutes longer. Mix 2 egg yolks with 1/4 cup cream and combine with the lobster and sauce. Reheat the sauce, stirring constantly, but do not let it boil. Correct the seasoning with salt. If a chafing dish is used, turn the sauce into the upper pan and sprinkle with Cognac or Sherry. Do not let the water in the lower pan become too hot, to avoid curdling.

LOBSTER AMÉRICAINE

Homard Américaine

CUT up 2 or 3 live lobsters, 1 3/4 to 2 pounds each, as above. Cut the tail crosswise in 3 or 4 slices. Remove the tomalley, the liver, and set it aside. Season the lobster with salt and sauté in 1/4 cup very hot olive oil. Make a *mirepoix bordelaise* as follows: Put 1 tablespoon butter in a saucepan, add 1 carrot, finely chopped, and 1 small onion, finely chopped, and cook until lightly browned. Add a little thyme, a bay leaf, and a sprig of parsley. When the lobsters start to turn red (5 to 7 minutes), add them to the *mirepoix*. Add 1 tablespoon butter, 2 shallots, chopped (or a little chopped onion), and 1/2 cup dry white wine. Sprinkle 1/4 cup warm brandy into the pan and ignite it. When the flame has died down, add 1/2 cup tomato sauce or tomato purée, 1/2 cup fish stock or white wine, 1 clove of garlic, crushed, and 3 tomatoes, peeled, seeded, and chopped. Cover tightly and cook for 20 to 25 minutes. Remove the lobster and take the meat from the shells. Strain the sauce and thicken it as follows: Crush the tomalley and cream it with 2 tablespoons butter and 2/3 teaspoon flour. Add a little crushed garlic, and, if available, some finely chopped chervil and tarragon. Combine lobster and sauce and reheat, but do not boil. Add salt and pepper to taste and serve very hot, with boiled rice.

Mirepoix Bordelaise

FISH MOUSSE WITH LOBSTER AMÉRICAINE

Mousse de Poisson au Homard Américaine

MAKE fish *mousseline* forcemeat with 1 pound of fish, as described in the chapter on garnishing. When all the cream has been added, slip a small ball of the *mousseline* forcemeat into a little warm water and bring the water slowly to a boil. Turn the ball to poach it on the other side. The ball should become firm. If it does not, work the *mousseline* forcemeat more over ice.

Butter a ring mold and fill it full with the forcemeat. Knock the mold against a table once or twice to remove any large air pockets. Place the mold in a pan of hot water, cover it with a piece of buttered wax paper, and bake the mousse in a moderate oven (375° F.) for 12 to 18 minutes, or until a skewer inserted in the center comes out clean. Let the mousse stand a few minutes and invert it on a serving dish. Fill the center with lobster *à l'américaine.*

Many lobster devotees like a simple boiled lobster, served hot with melted butter, or cold with mayonnaise. This is the easiest way of preparing them. Plain, salted water may be used or a court bouillon.

Homard au Court Bouillon

BOILED LOBSTER

MAKE a vinegar court bouillon with 3 quarts water. (Increase the other ingredients proportionately.) If the lobsters are to be served hot, plunge them into the court bouillon and cook them for 20 to 25 minutes. Remove them from the kettle, split the bodies and discard the sac at head, the intestinal vein and the lungs and crack the large claws. Arrange the lobsters, cut side up, on a serving dish and serve with melted butter and lemon. If the lobsters are to be served cold, cook them for only 15 minutes and let them cool in the liquid. Split the bodies, discard the inedible parts, chill, crack the claws, and serve with mayonnaise and lemon.

Removing Boiled Lobster Meat

Lobster Shells

FOLLOW the directions for boiled lobster to be served cold. As soon as the lobsters are cool enough to handle, crack the claws and remove the meat from the larger ones. Save the small claws to garnish the dish. Take out the body and tail meat. If you want to serve a lobster mixture in the shell, you must keep the shell intact. First remove the claws, then put the lobster on the board, shell side down, and with a sharp knife or scissors cut through the thin under shell. Remove the tail meat, lay it with the red-skinned side down, on the board, and with a small knife cut down the center, expose the intestinal vein, and remove it. You can then slip your fingers or a two-tined kitchen fork under the body meat and lift it out. Discard the sac and the lungs. Wash the shells, drain them, and dry them thoroughly.

DEVILED LOBSTER

REMOVE the meat from 3 or 4 boiled lobsters, as above, keeping the shells intact. Cut the lobster meat in small pieces and keep it hot in a saucepan with 2 tablespoons butter. Prepare 2 1/2 cups Mornay sauce and add 1 teaspoon English mustard mixed to a paste with water. Add the lobster meat to 2 cups sauce, bring to a boil, season with 1/2 teaspoon salt and a little pepper, and fill the shells. Mix the remaining 1/2 cup sauce with 2 tablespoons whipped cream and spread over the tops. Sprinkle with a little grated Parmesan cheese and brown in a broiler.

Homard à la Diable

LOBSTER ALBERT

USE 3 live lobsters, 1 3/4 to 2 pounds each. Remove and crack the claws and split the lobsters. Season them with salt and pepper. Melt 3 tablespoons butter in a saucepan, add the lobsters, and sauté 3 or 4 minutes. Sprinkle them with 1/4 cup Cognac and ignite. Add 2 shallots, chopped, 1/2 cup each of dry white wine and fish stock or water, and 6 mushrooms, sliced. Simmer, closely covered, for 20 to 25 minutes. Remove the meat. Wash the shells and turn them upside down to dry. Reduce the cooking liquor to 1/3 its original quantity; add 1/2 cup *sauce américaine*, 2 tablespoons cream sauce or *velouté* sauce, and a little chopped parsley. Add 1 tablespoon butter and correct the seasoning. Dice the lobster meat, combine it with 2/3 of the sauce, and fill the shells. Mask with sauce mixed with 1 tablespoon whipped cream and brown.

Homard Albert

LOBSTER FRENCH STYLE

USE 3 live lobsters, 1 3/4 to 2 pounds each. Remove and crack the claws and split the lobsters in half. Season with salt.

Slice 3 carrots and 4 small onions very thinly, parboil them for 5 or 6 minutes and drain. Melt 2 tablespoons butter in a large, shallow pan, add half the carrots and onions and 1 tablespoon chopped shallots. Place the lobster halves side by side in the pan and add the remaining carrot and onion and 2 tablespoons chopped parsley. Arrange the lobster claws on top. Add 3/4 cup dry white wine and 1/2 cup fish stock or water, bring the liquid to a boil and cover the lobster with a circle of buttered

Homard à la Française

paper cut to fit the pan. Pierce a hole in the center to vent the steam. Cover the pan and cook in a hot oven (400° F.) or over low heat on top of the stove for 20 to 25 minutes, or until the lobster meat detaches easily from the shell. Remove the lobsters from the pan, detach the meat from the shells, then replace it and arrange the shells on a serving platter. Remove the meat from the claws and arrange it at the head. Keep the lobster warm. Return the pan to the heat and reduce the sauce to 1/3 its original quantity. Add 1 cup cream sauce and finish by swirling in 2 tablespoons butter. Remove the pan from the heat as soon as the butter melts. The sauce should be light and not too thick. Correct the seasoning with salt and add a little freshly ground pepper, 2 tablespoons Cognac, and 1 teaspoon chopped chives. Pour the sauce and vegetables over the lobster in the shells.

Homard Thermidor

LOBSTER THERMIDOR

SPLIT 3 live lobsters, 1 3/4 to 2 pounds each. Season them with 1/2 teaspoon salt. Put 1/4 inch salad oil in a large pan, arrange the lobsters in the pan, and bake them in a hot oven (400° F.) for 20 minutes, basting from time to time with the oil. Melt 2 tablespoons butter in a saucepan, add 1 tablespoon chopped shallot and 1/2 cup dry white wine, and cook until it is reduced to 1/4 its original quantity. Add 2 cups Mornay sauce, 1 tablespoon chopped parsley, and 1 teaspoon English mustard and cook, stirring, until the sauce is smooth. Correct the seasoning with salt and add more mustard if desired. Remove the lobster meat from the shells and dice it. Wash and dry the shells. Arrange the shells on a heatproof platter and put a little sauce in each. Distribute the lobster meat among the shells. Add 1 tablespoon whipped cream to the remaining sauce and spread this over the lobster meat. Sprinkle with grated Parmesan or dry Swiss cheese and brown the topping under the broiler or in a very hot oven (450° F.).

Crayfish

FRESH-WATER crayfish are particularly popular in sections of France where lobster is not available. Some people consider them better than lobster, sweeter and more succulent. For each size there is a suitable method of preparation. The small crayfish are best in bisque; the medium size do well as garnish, and the large ones generally go into main dishes. In America, we often begin a meal with shrimp cocktail. In France, it is common to start dinner with *écrevisses en buisson* (literally, crayfish in a bush), whole boiled red crayfish supported on a three-tiered serving dish and generously garnished with fluffy green parsley.

Crayfish are served in the shell, except when they are used for bisque, and only the tail and claw are eaten. Remove the end of the intestinal tract under the tail before cooking the crayfish. To bring out their best flavor, white wine is almost essential. Lemon juice may be used with water as a substitute, but the result is not the same.

Cleaning Crayfish

CRAYFISH IN WHITE WINE SAUCE

WASH 4 dozen crayfish well and remove the end of the intestinal tracts under the tails. Melt 2 tablespoons butter in a saucepan and add 1 carrot and 1 onion, both finely diced, 1 tablespoon chopped shallots or onion, 2 sprigs of parsley, 1 clove of garlic, crushed, a little thyme, and 1 small bay leaf, crumbled. Cook very slowly for about 15 minutes, or until the vegetables are soft. Add 4 tomatoes, peeled, seeded, and chopped, 1/2 teaspoon salt, and the crayfish, and cook over high heat, shaking the pan constantly, until the crayfish turn red. Add 4 tablespoons warm Cognac

Ecrevisses à la Bordelaise

and ignite. Add 2 cups white wine and continue to cook over high heat for 12 minutes longer. Remove the crayfish to a deep serving dish. Cook the liquid until it is reduced to half and thicken it by swirling in *beurre manié* made by creaming 3 tablespoons butter with 1 teaspoon flour. Correct the seasoning with salt and add a little freshly ground pepper. Pour the sauce over the crayfish and sprinkle with parsley.

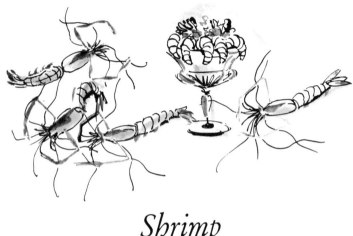

Shrimp

SHRIMP vary in color and in size but all have much the same flavor. The larger the shrimp, the more they cost. They are in good supply all year round, and are so well liked that they have become a traditional appetizer in this country, with a spicy tomato sauce.

Opinions differ about whether it is easier to remove the shells before or after cooking. But some gourmets insist that the meat tastes better **Shelling Shrimp** if it is cooked in the shell. Either way, you can shell shrimp with just two motions: Hold the tail end in the left hand and slip the thumb under the shell between the feelers. Lift off two or three of the shell segments in one motion, then, still holding firmly to the tail, pull the shrimp itself out from the remaining shell and tail.

Boiling Shrimp In cooking shrimp the important thing to remember is not to overcook them—2 to 5 minutes' cooking time will do the job. The water in which they cook should be well salted—1 tablespoon salt in 1 quart water is about right for each pound of shrimp. Bring the water to a boil and add the shrimp. When the water returns to the boil, turn down the heat and simmer until the shrimp are done. Or the shrimp may be cooked in vinegar court bouillon. Remove the black vein that runs along the top, using a small sharp knife or a " deveiner. "

To sauté shrimp, shell and devein the raw shrimp and cook them in butter until they are pink. Season them with salt and white pepper. A pinch of curry adds an interesting flavor.

Sautéing Shrimp

SHRIMP WITH CURRY SAUCE

Crevettes à l'Indienne

MAKE *sauce au currie*, curry sauce, with 1 1/2 cups *velouté* sauce. Add 1 pound cooked shelled shrimp and reheat the sauce to the boiling point. Serve with boiled rice.

SHRIMP CREOLE

Crevettes à la Créole

SAUTÉ 1/4 cup chopped onions in 1/4 cup butter until they are soft. Add 2 pounds cooked and shelled shrimp. Sauté the shrimp quickly and add 1/2 cup Madeira or Sherry. In another pan melt 2 tablespoons butter and in it sauté lightly 16 sliced mushrooms. Add 2 small green peppers and 2 pimientos, all diced, 6 tomatoes, peeled, seeded, and chopped, and 1 cup tomato sauce. Cook the vegetable mixture for a few minutes, then combine it with the shrimp and heat well. Serve with boiled rice.

SHRIMP BORDELAISE

Crevettes à la Bordelaise

SHELL and devein 2 pounds of shrimp. Melt 2 tablespoons butter in a saucepan, add 1 carrot and 1 onion, each finely chopped, 2 shallots finely chopped, 1 sprig of parsley, 1 clove of garlic, crushed, a pinch of thyme, and a small bay leaf. Cook slowly until the vegetables are soft, about 15 minutes. Add the shrimp, 1 teaspoon salt, 1/4 cup Cognac and 1/2 cup white wine. Cook quickly for about 5 or 6 minutes, or until the shrimp are pink, shaking the pan constantly. Remove the shrimp to a serving dish. Discard the bay leaf. Cook the liquid in the pan until it is reduced to 1/2 the original quantity, then add *beurre manié* made by creaming together 1 teaspoon flour and 1 tablespoon butter. Cook the sauce for a minute or two and pour it over the shrimp. Sprinkle with chopped parsley.

Crabs

RESTAURANTS serve two kinds of crabs: Alaskan crabs, with very long legs and claws in which most of the meat lies, and small East Coast crabs, called blue crabs because of the bright blue on their claws before they are cooked. From the body section come solid chunks of tender succulent flesh called "lump-back" crab meat. Bits of fine shell-like fiber must be picked out of the claw meat, and it is not so choice.

Because the extremely perishable Eastern blue crabs require immediate cooking, they are not generally sold live, in the shell. The cooked meat is packed in containers and shipped to market under refrigeration. It is this crab meat that fine restaurants use for cocktails, canapés, salads, and hot dishes, and that I have always used in these recipes.

Soft-shell crabs, one of the great shellfish delicacies, are young blue crabs that have shed their old shells, like a child outgrowing its coat, and have only a soft covering. They are cooked whole, either sautéed or deep-fried. Soft-shell crabs are sold fresh or frozen. The fish dealer will clean fresh soft-shells for you.

Finally, there are the tiny oyster crabs that live within an oyster's shell, and are available during the East Coast oyster season. They are choice morsels, what the French call *recherché*, and only the finest restaurants serve them. They are served with minnowlike whitebait, the crabs and fish sautéed in butter or deep-fried in hot oil for only a minute or two and accompanied with tartare sauce.

Crabe à la Diable

DEVILED CRAB MEAT

MELT 3 tablespoons butter in a saucepan and add about 2 cups fresh crab meat. Heat it over very low heat. Add 2 teaspoons English mustard mixed to a thin paste with water. Make 1 1/2 cups Mornay sauce and sea-son it well with 1/4 teaspoon salt, and a little freshly ground pepper. Combine 1 cup sauce and the crab and fill 6 individual baking shells or a deep heatproof platter with the mixture. Add 2 tablespoons whipped cream to the remaining 1/2 cup Mornay sauce and spread the filled shells with it. Sprinkle with a little grated Parmesan cheese and brown under the broiler or in a hot oven.

CRAB MEAT RAVIGOTE

Crabe Ravigote

To 1 1/2 cups mayonnaise add 1 teaspoon each of prepared mustard and chopped chives, 1/2 teaspoon Worcestershire sauce, and 1 teaspoon each of chopped parsley, tarragon, and chervil, and capers. Mix 1 cup of this sauce with 2 1/2 cups fresh crab meat, correct the seasoning with salt, and pile the crab in individual dishes. Coat the crab meat with the re-maining sauce and garnish the dish with a border of mimosa—chopped hard-cooked egg and chopped parsley. Serve with lemon slices.

CRAB MEAT CREOLE

Crabe à la Créole

FOLLOW the directions for *crevettes à la créole*, shrimp creole, substituting crab meat for shrimp. Do not, however, sauté the crab meat.

FRENCH FRIED SOFT-SHELL CRABS

Crabes Mous Frits

DIP cleaned crabs in flour, then in egg beaten with a little milk and in bread crumbs. Fry them in deep hot fat (360° F.) until they are well browned, about 5 minutes. Drain them thoroughly on absorbent paper, sprinkle with salt, and serve with lemon wedges and tartare sauce.

SOFT-SHELL CRABS WITH BROWN BUTTER

Crabes Mous Meunière

DIP cleaned crabs in milk, then in flour. Melt enough butter in a skillet to cover the bottom generously and when it is very hot add the crabs. Brown them on one side, turn, and brown the other side. Remove to a serving dish. Add to the pan 1/2 tablespoon butter for each crab and cook the butter until it is hazelnut brown. Pour it over the crabs and sprinkle them with lemon juice.

Oysters

ONE need not have *la bonne bouche*—that is, a gourmet's fine sense of taste—in order to enjoy oysters. But if you *are* a gourmet, oysters are undoubtedly one of your favorite foods. And history will tell you that gourmets through the ages have felt the same way about this odd little shellfish. The evidence is everywhere: in the kitchen middens remaining from prehistoric times in Western Europe, in the records left by the ancient Greeks and Romans, in the heaps of shells that the first white men found along our own Maine coast.

Travel the world over and eat oysters of many kinds, but nowhere will you find more care, effort, money, and research devoted to the production of fine oysters than in the United States. As every chef knows, no food, not even milk, is more carefully protected against contamination, largely because so many oysters are eaten raw.

R Rule for Oysters   We buy oysters only in the R months. Why? Tradition inherited from Europe is largely responsible, and it is hard to put down. European oysters, for example, are susceptible to a summer disease that doesn't occur in oysters in the United States coastal beds. Also, Old World oysters are gritty in summer when they are breeding. Ours are not, but the memory of Europe's summertime ban persists. Finally, until fairly recently, transporting such perishable food in warm weather was not practical.

There still remains one valid reason for the R rule: oysters are not in their prime in summer, the breeding season. After spawning, they lose weight and become watery and less flavorful. They fatten again after a resting period, and this cycle carries them close to cold weather.

Raw oysters, which are served as hors-d'oeuvre, you will find in the hors-d'oeuvre chapter.

There is only one rule that is important in cooking oysters and that is not to overcook them. They require hardly any heat at all. They are never boiled, at the most merely simmered, and then only for about 2 minutes. If they boil, they shrink and toughen. To poach oysters, remove them from their shells, put them in a pan with their own juices, bring the liquid to a boil, remove the pan from the heat, and let the oysters stand for a few minutes. Drain them thoroughly on paper towels. Reserve the liquor. Strained and reduced it may be used as part of the liquid in the sauce.

Poaching Oysters

If oysters are to be fried or broiled, poach them very briefly first in their own juices. Poaching removes the slippery viscous coating.

Poached oysters, coated *à l'anglaise*, as described in the section on deep frying, are cooked in deep hot fat (375° F.) for 2 or 3 minutes, drained, and served with parsley, a lemon wedge, and tartare sauce. Or the poached oysters may be drained, dipped in seasoned beaten egg and in fine bread crumbs and simply browned in butter. Turn them once.

Fried Breaded Oysters

For batter-fried oysters, drain the poached oysters, sprinkle them with lemon juice and finely chopped parsley, and coat them with fritter batter. Cook until golden brown in deep hot fat (375° F.), about 3 minutes. Drain and serve with fried parsley and tartare sauce.

Batter-Fried Oysters

You will find oyster *beignets* and oyster croquettes elsewhere in the book.

ANGELS ON HORSEBACK OR SKEWERED OYSTERS

Anges à Cheval

POACH 6 oysters for each skewer. Drain the oysters on paper towels, roll each in a thin slice of bacon, and thread them on the skewer, not too close together. Sprinkle with a little melted butter and broil lightly. Serve the oysters on toast with maître d'hôtel butter, a sprig of parsley, and a piece of lemon.

Or skewer the oysters with partly cooked squares of bacon, beginning and ending with a piece of bacon. Roll the filled skewer in melted butter and broil. Sprinkle with fresh bread crumbs when the bacon is almost done. Serve with maître d'hôtel butter, a sprig of parsley, and a piece of lemon.

CREAMED OYSTERS

Huîtres à la Crème

POACH 3 dozen freshly opened oysters in their own juices and transfer them to a bowl with just enough liquid to keep them moist. Reduce the rest of the oyster liquor to 1/2 its original quantity by boiling it rapidly. Combine it with 2 cups béchamel sauce. Add the poached oysters to the hot sauce and thin the sauce, if desired, with a little cream. Reheat all together, but do not allow the mixture to boil.

Oysters Cooked in Shells

When preparing dishes in which the oysters are cooked in their own shells, remember to reserve the deep shell, not the shallow one, for this. Also, have a supply of rock salt on hand to spread in the tray or pan in which they will be cooked. This is a trick to keep the shells level and prevent the juice or sauce from spilling. If the oysters are very large, trim off a little of the edge, which sometimes becomes tough in cooking. Allow 5 or 6 oysters per person.

OYSTERS WITH GARLIC BUTTER

Huîtres à la Bourguignonne

ARRANGE oysters in their deep shells on a tray of coarse salt and bake them in a hot oven (400° F.) for 2 minutes. Mix 2 cloves of garlic, crushed, and 1 teaspoon finely chopped shallots with 1 cup butter. Add 1 teaspoon each of chopped chives, tarragon, and parsley. Season with salt and a little freshly ground pepper. Spread each oyster with 1 teaspoon of this butter. Sprinkle with fine crumbs and bake in a hot oven (400° F.) or under the broiler until the crumbs are lightly browned. Serve with a wedge of lemon.

OYSTERS PORTIA

Huîtres Portia

POACH 6 freshly opened oysters for each serving and drain them well. Prepare 1 cup Mornay sauce and add to it 2 tablespoons purée of spinach, 1 teaspoon finely chopped chives, and 1 tablespoon finely chopped mixed parsley, tarragon, and chervil. Put a little of this sauce in each deep shell, and add the oyster. Spread the remaining sauce over the oysters. Sprinkle with a little grated Parmesan and brown under a hot broiler. Garnish with parsley and a wedge of lemon.

OYSTERS CASINO

Huîtres Casino

OPEN 6 oysters for each serving and leave them in the deep shells. Cover each with a square of sliced bacon and bake in a hot oven (450º F.) or under the broiler about 5 minutes, or until the bacon is crisp. Add to each a little maître d'hôtel butter. Serve the oysters hot, with lemon wedges.

Scallops

THE French name for scallops is actually *pétoncle*, but few people, Frenchmen or others, ever use it. *Coquilles Saint-Jacques* is the name scallops go by in France.

The shells themselves have a most attractive appearance. The outside is marked with radial ribbing in various shades of brown, and the smooth white hollow interior holds about as much as a small sauce dish. They make practical dishes for browning and serving any sauced fish mixture. In the early days in New England, any creamed dish baked in the oven was called "scalloped."

Scallop Shells

You can certainly work more easily with the scallops you buy in this country than those in my native France. Here you buy them ready for cooking. There is absolutely no waste—no need for even a little trimming.

In France they come to you in their shells, just as they were taken from the water. You must open them and discard all the insides except the edible little white muscle. But the French scallops have one advantage. By opening them yourself you can take out the coral—the orange-colored roe—which I never have seen here. We consider it a great delicacy, and, if you ever eat *coquilles Saint-Jacques* in France, you will probably find some of the coral in the mixture. I add diced shrimp, where appropriate.

Buying Scallops   The scallop season comes in the fall. In this country, there are two types. Sea scallops, the larger and more plentiful, are either iced and shipped to nearby markets or quick-frozen in packages to be sold all during the winter. Few scallops can be had in summer except for an occasional batch that may come in from northern waters. They run 12 to 15, sometimes more, to the pound. The large ones are often cut in quarters or slices before being cooked, especially when they are combined with a sauce and baked in the shell. Bay scallops are the special delight of gourmets. These small dainty scallops, as many as 40 to the pound, are very tender and have a more delicate flavor than sea scallops. They come to market in late September and last only as long as good weather holds. The first winter storms end the season for bay scallops.

Always remember that scallops, as one of the more perishable shellfish, must be cooked as soon as possible after purchasing—or after defrosting if they are bought frozen.

Most people seem to prefer scallops fried, sautéed, or broiled and served with tartare sauce. They are ready for the table in a matter of minutes. Scallops may also be combined with a sauce, arranged in their shells, and browned quickly in the oven or under the broiler. A pound of scallops sautéed or deep fried will serve 3 or 4 persons, but when mushrooms and a sauce are combined with the scallops the pound will make 6 servings.

I cannot emphasize too strongly one very important rule in cooking scallops: do not overcook them. With even an extra minute or two of heat, their fine tender flesh will shrink and become tough and chewy.

When frying or sautéing scallops or when broiling them, allow about 3 minutes, never more than 5. Always dry scallops thoroughly when they are to be sautéed, fried, or broiled. Use oil in sautéing instead of butter; it must be very hot so that the scallops brown before any of their moisture cooks out. The brown crusty surface protects their inner succulence. Fry or sauté scallops a few at a time. Overcrowding reduces the heat of the fat and prevents them from browning quickly. If you cook scallops in white wine or in court bouillon, allow about 6 minutes. Never boil scallops; lower the heat as soon as the liquid reaches the boiling point so that they will merely simmer.

Never cook scallops ahead of time and keep them hot for later serving. They must be served immediately.

SCALLOPS WITH BROWN BUTTER

WASH 2 pounds scallops and dry them thoroughly. Dip them in milk and in flour and shake off the surplus flour. Sauté the scallops quickly in very hot oil until they are a golden brown all over. Turn the scallops into a serving dish, season them with salt and freshly ground pepper, and sprinkle them with a little lemon juice. Pour off the oil in the pan, add 1/2 tablespoon butter for each serving, and cook the butter until it is hazelnut brown. Pour the browned butter over the scallops, sprinkle with finely chopped parsley, and garnish with slices of peeled lemon. Lemon juice, and the parsley, also, may be added to the butter before it is poured over the scallops.

*Coquilles
Saint-Jacques
Meunière*

FRIED SCALLOPS

WASH 2 pounds scallops and dry them thoroughly. Dip them in milk, roll them in flour, and shake off the surplus flour. Brown them in deep hot fat or oil (370° F.) for 2 to 3 minutes. Drain on paper towels and season with a little salt. Serve very hot with fried parsley, a wedge of lemon for each serving, and tartare sauce.

*Coquilles
Saint-Jacques
Frites*

SCALLOPS WITH SPAGHETTI

MIX 2 1/2 cups cooked spaghetti, cut in 1 1/2 inch lengths, with 1/4 cup each of cooked ham and cooked ox tongue cut in small julienne. Heat all together well in melted butter. Add 1 tablespoon julienne of truffle. Prepare 1 pound *coquilles Saint-Jacques meunière*, scallops with brown butter. Put a mound of the spaghetti mixture at each end of a serving platter and arrange the scallops in the center. Pour the brown butter over the scallops and sprinkle them with chopped parsley.

*Coquilles
Saint-Jacques
Carlier*

SCALLOPS WITH CURRY SAUCE

Coquilles Saint-Jacques à l'Indienne

MAKE *sauce au currie*, curry sauce, with 1 1/2 cups cream sauce. Poach 1 pound scallops in white wine and drain them well. Combine sauce and scallops and reheat the sauce just to the boiling point. Serve with rice pilaff.

SCALLOPS MARINIÈRE

Coquilles Saint-Jacques Marinière

WASH 1 1/2 pounds scallops and put them in a saucepan with 2 tablespoons butter, 1 tablespoon finely chopped shallot, 1/2 teaspoon salt, a little white pepper, and 1 cup dry white wine. Bring the liquid to a boil and simmer the scallops for 6 minutes. Remove the scallops to a heated serving platter. Boil the liquid to reduce it to 1/3 its original quantity, add 1 cup cream sauce, and bring it to a boil. Mix 2 beaten egg yolks with 1/2 cup cream and a little of the hot sauce and return the mixture to the pan. Bring the sauce gradually to the boiling point, stirring it constantly, but do not allow it to boil. Add 1 tablespoon chopped parsley and any scallop juice which may have drained into the bottom of the serving dish, correct the seasoning with salt, and pour the sauce over the scallops.

SCALLOPS WITH MORNAY SAUCE

Coquilles Saint-Jacques Mornay

MELT 2 tablespoons butter in a saucepan and add 1 tablespoon chopped shallot, 6 to 8 mushrooms, cleaned and sliced, 1/2 cup dry white wine and 1 pound scallops. Bring the liquid to a boil and simmer the scallops for about 6 minutes. Add 12 cooked diced shrimp and heat all together for 2 minutes. Remove scallops, shrimp, and mushrooms and reduce the liquid to about 2 or 3 tablespoons. Prepare 2 cups Mornay sauce, and strain the sauce through a fine sieve. Combine 1 1/3 cups of the sauce with the scallops, shrimp, and mushrooms, add 1 tablespoon chopped parsley, and correct the seasoning with salt. Pour the mixture into 6 scallop shells. Add 2 tablespoons whipped cream to the remaining Mornay sauce and spread the sauce over the filled shells. Sprinkle with a little grated Parmesan or grated Swiss cheese and brown the *coquilles* under the broiler or in a very hot oven (450° F.).

SCALLOPS AU GRATIN

CLEAN 1 pound mushrooms and slice enough of the best ones to make 1 cup. Sauté the sliced mushrooms in a little butter. Chop the remaining mushrooms very fine and cook them with 1 tablespoon butter and 1 tablespoon chopped shallot or onion until all moisture is cooked away. Add 1/2 cup tomato sauce, 1/2 cup brown sauce, and 1 tablespoon chopped parsley. Continue to cook for 10 minutes, correct the seasoning with salt, and add a little pepper. Wash 1 pound scallops. Cover them with white wine court bouillon, bring the liquid to a boil, and simmer them for about 6 minutes. Drain them and cut them in thick slices. Put 1 tablespoon of the mushroom sauce in each of 6 scallop shells and divide the sliced scallops and mushrooms among the shells. Cover with the sauce and sprinkle the *coquilles* with bread crumbs and a little melted butter. Brown them under the broiler. Sprinkle with lemon and parsley.

Coquilles Saint-Jacques au Gratin

SCALLOPS WITH SPINACH

WASH 2 to 3 pounds spinach and cook it for 5 or 6 minutes in the water that clings to the leaves. Drain the leaves well. Heat 2 tablespoons butter in a saucepan, add the spinach, and cook it until it is as dry as possible. Season the spinach with salt and pepper and spread it in a shallow heatproof serving dish. Poach 1 pound scallops in 1/2 cup white wine for 6 minutes, drain them well, and lay them on the spinach. Cover all with 1 1/2 to 2 cups Mornay sauce and sprinkle with grated Parmesan. Brown the topping under the broiler or in a very hot oven (450° F.).

Coquilles Saint-Jacques Florentine

Clams

CLAMS do not enjoy the popularity in Europe that they do in many sections of this country, where they are a favorite shellfish. Clams can be subsituted for oysters or mussels in most recipes, though clams are not poached before other cooking, as oysters are. Like oysters, they should be cooked only slightly or they will toughen.

Hard-Shelled Clams

The hard-shelled kind, the quahog, known also as littleneck and cherrystone, is most often served raw, on the half shell, embedded in ice and garnished with lemon wedges. They can also be dipped in fritter batter and deep-fried, or broiled on skewers.

Soft Clams

Soft clams are usually simply steamed, but they can be minced, raw, and made into *beignets*.

Clams, unlike oysters, are easy to open. Press a knife between the shells and cut the muscle that holds them together.

Clams à la Ritz

CLAMS À LA RITZ

SCRUB 6 dozen soft clams and open them, reserving the liquor. Strain it through cheesecloth. Remove the clams and rinse them to dislodge all traces of sand. Clean 72 half shells. Discard the necks of the clams. Trim off and chop very fine the bands around the edges.

Sauté 1 onion, chopped very fine, in 2 tablespoons butter until it is soft but not brown. Add the chopped clam trimmings and the liquor and cook for 1 minute. Add 1 cup very thick *sauce suprême* and cook until the mixture is well blended. Put a spoonful in 36 shells and set the shells in a large flat pan covered with coarse salt. Put 2 trimmed clams in each shell, sprinkle with a few drops of white wine, and add a little maître d'hôtel butter. Lay a small piece of thinly sliced bacon on each shell and cook the clams in a hot oven (400° F.) or under the broiler until the bacon is brown. Warm the other 36 half shells in the oven. Arrange the cooked clams on 6 serving plates, and cover each with a warm shell.

Mussels

NATURE is generous when it comes to mussels. Wherever mussels are found, on the coastlines of this country and Europe, they appear in great quantities. They attach themselves to every rock, to any pole in the water, and cover mud flats when the tides go out, clinging tenaciously to any available support. Their plentitude and the fact that they are so popular with the French make supplying *moules*—as they are called—to restaurants an important industry in France. Any good French restaurant within a day's distance from the coast will have *moules* on the menu.

Whether you gather mussels yourself or buy them in the market, the rule for them is the same as for other shellfish: they must be alive when they are cooked. Live mussels hold their shells together so tightly that it is difficult to pry them apart. Discard any with open shells. A French shopper is also suspicious of mussels that are overly heavy, because this sometimes indicates that a dirty stone or other foreign material has gotten inside the shell and will be released when the shells open, spoiling the sauce.

The basic rules about the preparation of mussels are simple, and there are just three of them. Mussels must be thoroughly scrubbed, one by one, to remove all the mud, dirt, and bits of seaweed that cling to them. Use plenty of water, changing it often, and a good stiff brush. Next, trim off the " beard " or fringe of vegetation around the edges. And last, don't cook the mussels too long. When the shells open they are ready to eat. Longer cooking will toughen them.

Cleaning Mussels

You'll notice that in most recipes a little white wine is used in the kettle along with the seasonings and that the cooked mussels are served on the half shell with a sauce made from the cooking liquor poured over them. The true devotee eats the mussels with a small fish fork and drinks the sauce from the shell, and usually he spoons up what is left in the dish or mops it up with his bread.

STEAMED MUSSELS

Moules Marinière

SCRUB 24 to 36 mussels well and wash them in running water. Put them in a saucepan with 2 tablespoons finely chopped shallots and 1 cup white wine. Cover the pan and cook the mussels for 6 to 8 minutes or until they open. Remove one shell from each mussel, leaving the meat attached to the other shell. Put the mussels in a serving dish. Reduce the liquor in the pan to 1/2 its original quantity and thicken it with *beurre manié* made by creaming together 2 tablespoons butter and 1/2 teaspoon flour. Roll the pan to swirl in the butter. Add 1 more tablespoon butter, 1 tablespoon chopped parsley, and if desired 1/2 teaspoon finely chopped chives. Correct the seasoning with salt, add a little freshly ground pepper, and pour the sauce over the mussels. Serves 3 or 4.

If a richer sauce is preferred, thicken the sauce with 1/4 cup cream.

Or, if a very plain sauce is preferred, cook the liquor until it is reduced to 1/2 the original quantity and finish it with 2 or 3 tablespoons butter.

FRIED MUSSELS

Moules
Frites   STEAM mussels open as for *moules marinière*, using 1/4 cup white wine. At servingtime, dip the meat in fritter batter and fry in deep hot fat (375° F.). Drain and serve with fried parsley and tomato or cream sauce.

Or the opened mussels may be coated *à l'anglaise* (described in the section on deep-fat frying), to be fried in deep fat or sautéed in butter.

MUSSELS POULETTE

Moules
à la Poulette   SCRUB 24 to 36 mussels well and wash them in running water. Put them in a saucepan with 2 tablespoons finely chopped shallots, 6 mushrooms, thinly sliced, and 1 cup white wine. Cover the pan and cook for about 6 to 8 minutes, or until the shells open. Remove one shell from each mussel, leaving the meat attached to the other shell, and arrange them in a serving dish. Reduce the liquor in the pan to 1/2 its original quantity and add 1/2 cup cream sauce. Bring the sauce to a boil and add 1 egg yolk beaten with 1/4 cup cream and a little of the sauce. Cook slowly, stirring briskly, until the sauce is well blended and slightly thickened, but do not allow it to boil. Correct the seasoning with salt, add a little freshly ground pepper and 1 tablespoon chopped parsley, and pour the sauce over the mussels. Serves 3 or 4.

MUSSELS WITH CELERY

Moules
au Céleri   FOLLOW the recipe for *moules poulette*, mussels *poulette*, adding to the pan with the mussels 1/2 cup celery, cut in fine julienne, parboiled for 10 minutes and drained.

248

Variety Meats   ABATS

I WAS CHAGRINED to learn in my first months at the New York Ritz that the average American did not appreciate *les abats*, the meat specialties. But I soon became reconciled to the fact that Americans had enjoyed little opportunity to develop a taste for these variety meats, since they were seldom served here, and usually indifferently prepared. I think that the situation has altered over the years, and that it is now generally acknowledged that liver, kidneys, and the rest are not only highly nutritious foods, but delicious as well.

European connoisseurs have always been partial to variety meats. I am reminded of an incident that demonstrates this partiality. Two of our English guests, in New York to supervise the final details at the British Pavilion of the 1939 World's Fair, learned that I had once worked at the London Ritz, and one day came to me with a special

249

request. They were homesick for a real English steak and kidney pie. I took no chances but went into the kitchen myself and made steak and kidney pie exactly as I had been taught to by an English cook. Apparently I had not forgotten my lesson, because, after they had enjoyed the pie, the gentlemen asked me to prepare identical pies for a dinner for the Pavilion's board of directors on opening day.

When the pies were ready and carefully wrapped, I waited for a messenger to pick them up. But no, these two distinguished gentlemen, not trusting anyone else to handle them with sufficient care, came themselves to take their pies to the Fair. And the two carried off the boxes as if they held the British crown jewels.

Sweetbreads

THE FIRST of the variety meats, for the gourmet, is *ris de veau*, sweetbreads. My memories of them go back forty years and more—memories of Europe's kings and queens and a way of life that the world will probably never see again. Look at old menus of the royal banquets served in Europe during the early days of this century, and more often than not you'll find that sweetbreads are truly a dish of kings. *Ris de veau Eugénie, vol-au-vent de ris de veau toulousaine, ris de veau parisienne, ris de veau à la régence*—the list goes on and on, the sauces rich, the garnishings elegant. What long hours we worked in hot kitchens on these fine dishes and, *mon Dieu*, what exacting masters trained us. You must know how to prepare sweetbreads to get the most in good eating from them. They can be dull and unappetizing when they are poorly prepared.

Sweetbreads, the thymus glands that lie in the throat of the young calf, are largest at birth and gradually become smaller. They disappear in a fully grown animal. They come in pairs joined by an inedible tough sort of tube called in French *la gorge*, the throat, that looks something like the gullet of a turkey and is always cut off and discarded. Of the two sweetbreads that make up the pair, each one has two parts. There's a round center section called either the " kernel " or the " heart sweetbread "—*la noix*—and a more elongated portion that lies nearest the throat and therefore is called the " throat sweetbread. " It's the round heart sweetbread that is the most delectable because the throat sweetbread, although as good in flavor, has bits of connective tissue hidden in it. Particular cooks cut up this section for creaming or for croquettes.

Butchers sell sweetbreads in various ways. Some sell the whole structure—the heart and throat sections and the connective throat, too. Some remove the throat, which you would have to remove, anyway; some sell the trimmed pairs, and others also trim off the throat sweetbreads and sell you only the heart sections. The heart sections are sold individually (one, two, three, or more) instead of in pairs and are more expensive because there's no waste and you are getting only the most desirable part. Plan 1 sweetbread to a serving. But creamed or combined with chicken or mushrooms in a sauce, they will naturally go farther. One important warning is that sweetbreads are very perishable. They must be absolutely fresh when purchased and then soaked and precooked—or blanched—as soon as possible after you get them home. Frozen sweetbreads must be kept firmly frozen until they are soaked and blanched. No matter how you plan to prepare and serve sweetbreads, they will require this preliminary blanching. The final fine cooking is not done until just before they are served.

Blanching is very simple. Cover the sweetbreads well with very cold water and let them soak for several hours. Then drain them, cover with fresh cold salted water, bring it slowly to a boil and boil them gently for 5 minutes. Drain them again and plunge them into fresh cold water. When they are cold, remove them from the water and cut away and discard the " throat " and sinews, if that has not already been done. Spread them on a flat dish, place a heavy plate on top of them, and store them in the refrigerator until they are to be cooked. This little trick makes them easier to handle when they are cooked whole and more attractive when they are served.

There are endless ways of cooking sweetbreads. They may be simply sautéed or broiled or made into the very elaborate and famous

Heart
Sweetbread

Throat
Sweetbread

Blanching
Sweetbreads

dishes of classic French cuisine. A second cooking does not toughen them as it does most meats. Rather, they become more fragile during the second cooking. Actually sweetbreads should be cooked three times. For a really delectable dish, the blanched sweetbreads need the overtones of flavor that come from cooking them in a vegetable broth before you sauté or broil them or from braising them before they are combined with the sauces and garnishes of more elaborate dishes. Omitting this step may simplify the preparation, but the results are not as savory.

Ris de Veau Etuvés

SWEETBREADS COOKED IN VEGETABLE BROTH

To make the broth, add 1 small carrot and 1 small onion, 1 sprig of parsley, 3 peppercorns, and 1/2 teaspoon salt to 3 cups water and cook until the liquid is reduced to about 2 cups. Add the blanched sweetbreads and simmer them for 20 minutes. (This is the method of cooking that the French call " *étuver*, " to cook gently in just enough liquid to cover.) Drain the sweetbreads and dry them well. Split each in two, and they are ready for the final cooking.

Ris de Veau Sautés

SAUTÉED SWEETBREADS

BLANCH sweetbreads and cook them in vegetable broth. Roll the prepared sweetbreads in bread crumbs, then in egg, and then in more bread crumbs—or, as we say, coat them *à l'anglaise*—and sauté for about 5 minutes on each side. Serve with tomato or Madeira sauce.

Ris de Veau Grillés

BROILED SWEETBREADS

BLANCH sweetbreads and cook them in vegetable broth. Season the prepared sweetbreads with salt and pepper, dredge them with flour, and roll them in salad oil. Broil about 3 inches from the heat for about 6 minutes on each side. Serve with melted butter to which a little lemon juice and chopped parsley have been added. Serve them on a slice of broiled ham, garnished with broiled mushrooms or broiled tomatoes.

SWEETBREADS WITH SPINACH

BLANCH sweetbreads and cook them in vegetable broth. Cut them in slices about 1/2 inch thick. Season the slices with salt and pepper, sprinkle them with flour, and sauté them in butter for 5 to 6 minutes on each side. Arrange on a heatproof platter cooked spinach that has been sautéed in butter or creamed. Arrange the sautéed sliced sweetbreads on the spinach, cover with Mornay sauce, and sprinkle the dish with a little grated Parmesan and melted butter. Brown it in a hot oven or under the broiler.

Braised sweetbreads gain flavor from the vegetables and seasonings with which they are cooked, as sweetbreads cooked in vegetable broth do. But braising is not just foundation cooking, a first step in more sophisticated recipes. It is also a very good and simple way of preparing them to serve in their own sauce. Sweetbreads are braised à brun *or* à blanc—*browned or unbrowned—depending on how they are to be used.*

BRAISED SWEETBREADS

MELT 3 tablespoons butter in a casserole and in it cook over direct heat 1 medium onion and 1 large carrot, both sliced, with 1 bay leaf, 1/2 teaspoon thyme, and 3 sprigs of parsley until the vegetables start to turn golden. Sprinkle about 1 teaspoon flour around the edge, on the vegetables. Season 3 pairs of blanched sweetbreads with salt and pepper and arrange them on the vegetables. Add 1/2 cup dry white wine and 1 cup veal or chicken stock. Bring the liquid to a boil, put the casserole in a moderately hot oven (375° F.), and braise the sweetbreads, basting often, for 45 minutes to 1 hour. To braise sweetbreads *à brun*, leave off the cover so that they brown as they cook. If the casserole is covered, the sweetbreads remain light colored and are braised *à blanc*. When they seem to be breaking apart slightly—look at the edges, to judge this—or if they start to break when touched lightly with a fork, they are done.

Remove the braised sweetbreads to a serving dish. Strain the sauce through a sieve, correct the seasoning with salt, and for a richer flavor, add 2 tablespoons dry Sherry or Madeira. Pour the sauce over the sweetbreads. They are often served on toast, sometimes with a slice of ham.

Ris de Veau Florentine

Ris de Veau Braisés

à Brun

à Blanc

Sweetbreads that are creamed and served in a vol-au-vent *or in patty shells are usually combined with white meat of chicken and mushrooms. The mushroom caps are first peeled and cooked for 3 to 5 minutes in 1 cup water— for each pound of mushrooms—with 1 tablespoon butter and the juice of 1 lemon.*

CREAMED SWEETBREADS

Ris de Veau à la Crème

BLANCH 3 pairs of sweetbreads, and either cook them in vegetable broth or braise them *à blanc*. Cut them in large dice. Melt 2 tablespoons butter in a saucepan, add 2 tablespoons flour, and cook the *roux* for a few minutes, but do not allow it to brown. Add 1 3/4 cups hot milk and cook, stirring constantly, until the mixture thickens. Then cook gently for about 30 minutes, stirring often to prevent scorching. Add 1/4 cup cream and correct the seasoning with salt. For a richer sauce, add another 1/4 cup cream mixed with 1 egg yolk. Add the diced sweetbreads, 1 cup diced cooked chicken, 1/2 cup sliced cooked mushrooms, and 2 tablespoons dry Sherry or Madeira. Mix very carefully with a fork, taking care not to break up the fragile sweetbreads. Serve in a *vol-au-vent* or in patty shells, or lacking them, on toast or with rice.

Larding and Studding Sweetbreads

In very fine cookery, sweetbreads, after they are blanched and flattened, are enriched with strips of fat pork or with strips of truffle or of ox tongue, singly or in combination. The method is the same as larding a beef filet or other meat except that the needle used is about half as long and the end just big enough to hold a 1/8-inch julienne strip. When fat pork is used, the expression is " to lard, " or piguer, *but when truffles or ox tongue are used, it is " to stud, " or* clouter.

The recipes that follow are typical of those popular with the haut monde *at the turn of the century. These recipes may seem unusual to you and some of the ingredients may be unobtainable. Cockscombs, for instance, may not be sold in the markets where you shop. But you can modify the recipes and include only the ingredients you can purchase. You will still have a fine dish, if thought and care go into the preparation. And you may create a new recipe on the basis of a classic one.*

In classic cuisine, sweetbreads often appear in vol-au-vent *or* timbales, *and you might read the section on these pastry shells before going on with the recipes. For a simpler dish, rice can usually be substituted for the pastry. The garnishes indicated can be found elsewhere in the book.*

VOL-AU-VENT OF SWEETBREADS TOULOUSAINE

Vol-au-Vent de Ris de Veau Toulousaine

BLANCH 3 pairs of sweetbreads. If they are very large, cut them at an angle into 2 or 3 thick slices. Braise them *à blanc*.

Combine in a saucepan 12 quenelles of chicken, 12 cooked cockscombs, 12 mushroom caps, cooked until tender in just enough water barely to cover, and 1/2 cup dry Sherry. Heat gently and keep the mixture hot.

For the sauce, reduce to 1/2 cup the liquid in which the mushrooms were cooked, adding the chopped stems of the mushrooms and a little juice of truffles, if obtainable. Add 4 cups *velouté* or béchamel sauce, cook until well combined and reduced a little, and add 2 1/2 cups heavy cream, little by little. The sauce should be thick enough to coat the back of the spoon. Correct the seasoning with salt and strain the sauce through a muslin cloth. Combine half the sauce with the quenelles, cockscombs, and mushrooms. Have the sweetbreads very hot and arrange them in a ring in a *vol-au-vent* shell, fill the center with the mixture, and cover all with sauce. Any sauce left over should be served in a sauceboat. Garnish the top with truffles cut into julienne strips. Place the cover of the *vol-au-vent* on top, leaving it half off to show the truffles.

Ris de veau Eugénie were named for the Empress Eugénie, wife of Napoleon III, last of the Napoleons. I often saw her when I worked in Paris because she lived until 1920, to the ripe old age of ninety-four. Not exiled from France, she spent her last years mostly in Paris, living in the Continental Hotel where she could enjoy a view of the Tuileries.

SWEETBREADS EUGENIA

Ris de Veau Eugénie

BLANCH 3 pairs of sweetbreads. Cook them in a vegetable broth or braise them *à blanc*. If they are large, cut them at an angle into 2 or 3 thick slices.

Ham Mousse

Prepare a ham mousse: Chop as finely as possible 1/2 pound each of cooked ham and breast of raw chicken or good white veal, free of sinews. Force the chopped meat through a sieve or food mill. Add a little pepper and salt, unless the ham is salty. Put the meat mixture in a bowl set in ice, stir in 4 egg whites, little by little, then 2 1/2 cups heavy cream, also very gradually, working the mixture to smoothness with a wooden spatula. Add a few drops of vegetable color to give a pink ham color. Turn the mixture into a buttered ring mold, cover the mold with buttered paper, and set it in a pan of water. Bake the mousse in a slow oven (300° F.) for 20 to 30 minutes, or until it is firm. Loosen the edges and unmold the mousse on a serving dish. Put the sweetbreads in the center and cover them with creamed mushrooms.

Ris de veau parisienne *was a favorite dish of King Alphonse of Spain, which I prepared for him and his lovely bride when they stopped at the London Ritz on their wedding trip.*

Ris de Veau à la Parisienne

SWEETBREADS PARISIAN

BLANCH 3 pairs of sweetbreads, lard them with strips of fat pork, and braise them *à brun*. Arrange them in a ring and in the ring arrange cooked artichoke bottoms, filled with cooked asparagus tips, alternately with tiny glazed spring carrots and *rissole* potatoes. Sprinkle with chopped parsley.

Brains

BRAINS, which Continental gourmets have always relished, are considered great delicacies in America, too—an exception to the general indifference to variety meats. Calf's and lamb's brains are considered the best, beef brains slightly less desirable. At the Ritz, we served 40 or 50 portions of calf's brains every day, and as the years went by, the demand increased. Many people who eat brains in restaurants, however, feel they lack the special skill to prepare them at home. Brains, like sweet-breads, require a soaking and precooking, or blanching, but they must be left in the cooking liquor. The thorough soaking and the vinegar in the cooking liquor make them attractively white—the only trick in pre-paring them. One brain is ample for 2 or 3 portions.

Wash the brains in cold water. Remove the membrane which covers them, and any blood. Soak the brains in cold water for several hours, changing the water frequently. Put them in a saucepan, cover them with cold water and add 2 tablespoons vinegar, 1 teaspoon salt, 5 peppercorns, 1/2 onion, sliced, 1 small carrot, sliced, 4 sprigs of parsley, a little thyme, and 1 bay leaf. Bring the liquid to a boil, cover the pan and simmer the brains for 25 to 30 minutes. Let the brains cool in the cooking liquor. Take them out only when they are drained for final cooking.

Blanching Brains

SAUTÉED BRAINS

BLANCH 2 or 3 brains and cut each one into 6 slices. Drain and dry the slices and dip them in flour and sauté them in butter until they are nut-brown on both sides. Arrange the brains on a heated serving dish and keep them hot. In a saucepan cook 4 tablespoons butter until it is brown. Pour over the brains and garnish with parsley and lemon slices.

Cervelles Sautées

BRAINS WITH VINAIGRETTE SAUCE

BLANCH 2 or 3 brains and cut each one into 6 slices. Arrange the slices on a serving dish and pour over them *sauce vinaigrette* to which a chopped hard-cooked egg has been added. Sprinkle the slices with finely chopped chives, tarragon, and chervil. Serve either hot or cold.

Cervelles Vinaigrette

BRAINS WITH BLACK BUTTER

BLANCH 2 or 3 brains, cut each one into 6 slices, and reheat the slices in 2 tablespoons of the cooking liquor. Arrange the slices on a hot serv-

Cervelles au Beurre Noir

ing dish, season them with salt and pepper and sprinkle with chopped parsley, 1 tablespoon vinegar and about 12 capers. In a small pan cook 3 tablespoons butter until it is almost black. Pour the black butter over the brains and serve them very hot.

Calf's Head

I N EUROPE, *tête de veau*, calf's head, is a highly regarded delicacy, and every good housewife knows how to cook it. But she doesn't attempt to do the trimming herself. When you order a calf's head, ask the butcher to skin it and remove the bones. Soak the head in a generous quantity of water. This draws out the blood and gives the meat a good white color. Texture and color are also improved by adding flour and vinegar to the court bouillon in which the head is cooked.

Tête de Veau
Vinaigrette

CALF'S HEAD WITH VINAIGRETTE SAUCE

SOAK a skinned, boned calf's head in a large quantity of water for 3 to 4 hours, or until all the blood has been drained out. Parboil the head for 5 minutes in enough water to cover, drain, and cool it in fresh cold water. Cut off the tongue, remove and reserve the brains, and cut the rest of the meat in pieces for serving.

In another pan mix 2 tablespoons flour with 3 tablespoons vinegar or the juice of 1 lemon. Add 2 quarts water and 1 tablespoon salt. Add the meat and tongue, bring to a boil, and cook for about 1 to 1 1/2 hours, or until the meat is tender. Slice the tongue and arrange meat and tongue on a platter. Garnish generously with parsley. Its flavor is particularly good with calf's head. Serve with vinaigrette sauce.

Leftover calf's head may be cut in julienne and mixed with cold cooked vegetables. May also be used for hors-d'oeuvre.

VINAIGRETTE SAUCE FOR CALF'S HEAD *Vinaigrette pour Tête de Veau*
COMBINE 1/3 cup vinegar, 2/3 cup oil, 1/2 teaspoon each of salt and dry mustard and a little pepper. To this basic vinaigrette add 1 sour pickle, chopped, a generous amount of chopped parsley, a few capers, 1/2 teaspoon chopped onion, and 1/2 calf's brain that has been blanched, drained, and crushed. The brain thickens the sauce.

Hearts

O F ALL the edible animal hearts, only the heart of the calf, the veal heart, deserves special preparation and serving. Lamb and mutton hearts go into a kind of stew with meats like liver and kidneys. In a French *charcuterie*, or pork store, pork hearts are ground with other parts of the pig to make sausage and pâté mixtures. As for beef hearts, their coarse texture, strong flavor, and toughness makes them unpopular. But veal hearts are truly delicious.

Veal hearts are usually prepared *en casserole*, but they are tender enough to be sliced thin and sautéed. Before cooking veal hearts, cut out the arteries and wash out any coagulated blood.

SAUTÉED VEAL HEART

Coeur de Veau Sauté

CUT 2 veal hearts in thin slices, remove the arteries, and wash out the blood. Drain and dry the slices and season them with salt and pepper. Heat 4 or 5 tablespoons good fat very hot in a large skillet and brown the veal slices in it quickly on both sides. Remove them and keep them warm. Pour off the fat from the pan but do not wash it and add 3 to 4 tablespoons butter, 10 mushrooms, cleaned and sliced, and 1 onion, finely chopped, and cook until the vegetables are golden brown. Stir in 2 shallots, finely chopped, and 3 tablespoons flour, and cook until the shallots begin to brown. Add 1 cup canned tomatoes and cook the mixture, stirring occasionally, until it is slightly thickened. Finish the sauce with 1/2 cup Sherry and 1 tablespoon chopped parsley and add the sautéed heart slices. Reheat the sauce just to the boiling point, but do not let it boil. Serve the sautéed veal in a ring of rice pilaff.

Hachis de Coeur de Veau

PEPPERS STUFFED WITH VEAL HEART HASH

CUT 2 veal hearts into small pieces, remove the arteries, and wash out the blood. Drain and dry the pieces. In a skillet, heat 1/4 cup salad oil very hot and in it quickly sauté the pieces of heart until they are lightly browned on all sides. Remove them, drain off all the fat, and chop them very fine. In a skillet heat 3 tablespoons beef or veal fat and in it cook 1 large onion, finely chopped, until it is golden. Add 1 cup canned tomatoes, 1 tablespoon chopped parsley, 2 cloves of garlic, crushed, and salt and pepper. Simmer the mixture for about 30 minutes and combine it with 2 cups cooked rice and the chopped veal hearts.

Cut the tops from 6 green peppers and remove the seeds. Parboil the shells for about 5 minutes and drain them. Fill them with the veal heart mixture, arrange them in a baking dish, pour in thin gravy or tomato sauce, and bake in a moderately hot oven (375° F.) for 20 minutes.

Liver

SINCE the discovery of its extraordinarily high nutritional value, liver, once seldom seen on American dinner tables, now appears regularly, and is served in the best restaurants too. In fine cooking, calf's liver is the first choice, and beef liver, with its stronger flavor, is less used. Pork liver, less expensive than calf's and less strong than beef liver, makes an excellent pâté and can also be sautéed. Lamb liver has a distinctive flavor best complimented by a savory sauce, and chicken livers, like calf's liver, can be simply sautéed or broiled, or served with a sauce.

Liver should not be overcooked. Long top-of-the-stove cooking will toughen liver as it toughens kidneys. The exact cooking time depends on the thickness of the slice and on whether it is to be rare, medium, or well done. Liver that is sautéed, and cooked only to the rare stage, should be done by the time both sides are browned, so watch it carefully as it cooks.

SAUTÉED CALF'S LIVER

Foie de Veau Sauté

IN A skillet sauté 2 slices of bacon for each portion of calf's liver. Cook the bacon until it is crisp, drain it on paper towels and set it aside to keep hot. Season thin slices of calf's liver with a little salt and sprinkle them with flour. Brown them quickly on both sides in the hot bacon fat. Arrange the liver on a serving dish and keep it warm. Discard the fat from the pan in which the liver was cooked but do not wash the pan. Add 2 tablespoons butter to the pan and cook it until it is brown. Sprinkle the liver with a few drops lemon juice, pour the browned butter over it and sprinkle it with chopped parsley. Garnish the platter with the crisp bacon.

SAUTÉED CALF'S LIVER WITH WINE SAUCE

Foie de Veau au Vin Rouge

Pan Sauce for Liver

COOK 12 slices of bacon and 6 slices of liver as for sautéed calf's liver. Pour the fat from the pan and add 2 tablespoons butter and 1 teaspoon finely chopped shallots or onion, and cook until the shallots are soft but not brown. Add 1/2 cup red wine or Sherry and cook for a few minutes, stirring in the brown bits from the bottom of the pan. Correct the seasoning with salt and swirl 1 tablespoon butter into the sauce until it is just melted. Pour the sauce over the liver and serve garnished with parsley.

Foie de Veau
Grillé

DIP thin slices of calf's liver in seasoned flour and arrange them on a baking sheet. Brush the meat with melted butter. Broil the slices for 4 minutes about 5 inches from the heat, turn them, and broil for 4 minutes on the other side. Serve with crisp bacon.

The French find it practical and simple to prepare liver for a large family by braising the whole liver in red wine. Any leftover cold liver is used for sandwiches or served with a salad.

Foie de Veau
Braisé

HAVE the butcher lard a whole calf's liver with strips of fat salt pork. In a deep pan just large enough to hold the liver put 1 tablespoon butter. Add 2 medium onions and 2 carrots, all sliced, 1 clove of garlic, and a faggot made by tying together 1 stalk of celery, 4 sprigs of parsley, 1 small bay leaf and a little thyme. In another pan heat 2 tablespoons butter or suet, and in it brown the liver on all sides. Put the liver on the vegetables and cook them together over low heat until the onions and carrots start to brown.

Meanwhile, add 2 tablespoons flour to the fat in the pan in which the liver was browned and cook the *roux* for a few minutes, stirring it constantly. Add 2 cups red wine and 1 cup water or stock, and cook, stirring, until the sauce is smooth. Strain the sauce over the liver. If necessary, add water to cover the liver well. Cover the pan and braise the liver in a moderately hot oven (375° F.) for 2 to 2 1/2 hours, turning it occasionally. Remove the liver to a serving dish. If the liquid has not already cooked down to about 1/2 the original quantity, reduce it further. Strain the sauce and skim off the fat. Serve with the liver.

A soaking in milk improves the flavor of pork liver. Soak the liver for an hour or two and drain it. Dry the slices thoroughly before flouring them, or they will steam in the moisture and lose crispness.

SAUTÉED PORK LIVER WITH ONIONS

ALLOW 2 teaspoons butter, 1/2 onion, and 2 thin slices of pork liver for each serving. Melt clarified butter in a skillet, add the onions, sliced, and cook them until they are golden. Season well-dried slices of pork liver that have been soaked in milk with salt and pepper, dust them with flour, and shake off any surplus. Heat some pork fat in another skillet, enough to cover the bottom of the pan generously, and in it sauté the liver over high heat until it is brown, about 2 minutes on each side. Remove the liver to a serving dish.

Discard the fat from the pan and add the cooked onions and 2 teaspoons vinegar for each serving. Bring this mixture to a boil and pour it over the liver.

Foie de Porc aux Oignons

SAUTÉED LAMB LIVER

COOK 1/4 pound fat salt pork, cut in small dice, in 1 1/2 tablespoons fat until the dice are golden brown and remove them. Cut 1 1/2 pounds lamb liver into small pieces and season them with salt and pepper. Heat the fat remaining in the pan very hot and in it sauté the lamb liver very quickly for about 2 or 3 minutes, or until it is brown. Remove the liver from the pan, drain all the fat from it, and keep it warm. Cook 3 thinly sliced onions in the hot fat in the pan for a few minutes, stirring. Add 1 1/2 tablespoons flour and 1 clove of garlic, crushed, and cook a few minutes, mixing all together. Add 1/2 cup red wine and 3/4 cup stock or water, mix well, add the browned salt pork dice, and cook the mixture slowly for 15 to 20 minutes, stirring occasionally. Add the cooked liver and reheat the mixture but do not allow the sauce to boil. Remove liver and sauce to a serving dish and sprinkle with chopped parsley.

Foie d'Agneau Sauté

SAUTÉED CHICKEN LIVERS

CUT 2 to 3 cups chicken livers in pieces or leave them whole and season them with salt and pepper. Heat 3 to 4 tablespoons butter very hot in a skillet, and in it sauté the livers quickly for 3 or 4 minutes, or until they are brown. Serve plain or with crisp bacon slices. Sautéed chicken livers may be used to fill an omelet.

Foies de Volaille Sautés

263

Foies
de Volaille
Sautés
au Madère

SAUTÉED CHICKEN LIVERS WITH MADEIRA SAUCE

SAUTÉ chicken livers and remove them from the pan. Do not wash the pan but add to the butter remaining in it 1/2 cup Madeira or dry Sherry. Cook the liquid, stirring in all the brown bits that cling to the pan, until it is slightly reduced and stir in 1/2 cup brown sauce. Add the chicken livers and reheat them, but do not let the sauce boil. Serve with rice pilaff.

Foies
de Volaille
à la Grecque

CHICKEN LIVERS GREEK STYLE

PREPARE chicken livers with Madeira sauce. Peel, seed, and chop coarsely 3 tomatoes and sauté them quickly in a little butter. Prepare 5 cups rice pilaff. Put 1/2 the rice in a serving dish, arrange the sauced livers and the cooked tomatoes in the center, and shape the rest of the rice into a dome on top. Garnish with slices of eggplant sautéed in oil and seasoned with salt and pepper. Serve tomato sauce separately.

Kidneys

KIDNEYS vary considerably in size and tenderness. The beef kidney is, of course, the largest, but also the least delicate. It will serve 2 or 3 people. Veal kidneys are smaller, and 1 makes a portion, but 2 lamb or mutton kidneys are needed to serve 1 person. The kidney is surrounded by fat, and the suet from the beef kidney is considered one of the best animal fats for cooking. In England, kidney suet is an indispensable part of Christmas puddings and dumplings. A thin layer of fat is left on veal and beef kidneys, but the fat of lamb and mutton kidneys is always discarded, because its very strong flavor is not acceptable. Lamb

**Beef Kidney
Suet**

and mutton kidneys have a thin skin under the fat, and this too is pulled off and discarded.

Kidneys are broiled or sautéed or cooked whole *en casserole*. In the broiler or on top of the stove, they are usually cooked at high heat for a short time. Long cooking there toughens them. In the oven, they can safely cook longer at moderate temperature.

BROILED VEAL AND LAMB KIDNEYS

Rognons de Veau et d'Agneau Grillés

TRIM the surplus fat from 6 veal kidneys, split them, season with salt and pepper and put them on skewers to keep them flat. Brush the kidneys with melted butter. Broil them in a preheated broiler about 5 inches from the heat for about 8 minutes on each side, with the flat sides toward the heat. Serve the kidneys at once, with broiled bacon or ham and broiled mushrooms or tomatoes, and with maître d'hôtel butter or *sauce diable*. To broil lamb kidneys, remove fat and membrane and prepare as veal kidneys. Broil nearer heat, 5 minutes on each side.

SAUTÉED VEAL KIDNEYS

Rognons de Veau Sautés

TRIM the surplus fat from 6 veal kidneys. Split the kidneys in half, but don't cut them all the way through, and open them so that they lie flat. Season the kidneys with salt and pepper and rub them with flour. In a skillet melt 6 tablespoons butter and in it cook the kidneys, over moderate heat, partly covered, for about 10 to 12 minutes on each side, or until they are golden brown and tender. Arrange the kidneys on a serving platter and pour over them some of the butter from the pan. Add 2/3 cup veal gravy or chicken stock to the pan and cook, stirring in all the brown crustiness. Pour the pan gravy over the kidneys.

To assure tenderness and delicacy of flavor when kidneys are to be served in a sauce, sauté the diced kidneys quickly in very hot fat, tossing them so that they cook on all sides, and drain off the cooking fat immediately. Make the sauce while the kidneys are draining. Add them and bring the sauce just to the boiling point, to reheat the kidneys without further cooking, which would toughen them.

Rognons
de Veau
Sautés aux
Champignons

SAUTÉED VEAL KIDNEYS WITH MUSHROOMS

TRIM the surplus fat from 6 veal kidneys, cut them into small pieces, and season with salt and pepper. In a skillet heat the fat removed from the kidneys. Cook the kidneys in it for about 5 minutes and turn them into a colander to drain. Discard the fat but do not wash the pan. Add 3 tablespoons butter and 1 large onion, chopped, and cook the onion until it is golden. Add 3/4 pound mushrooms, cleaned and sliced, and cook the mushrooms until they are tender. Stir in 1 1/2 tablespoons flour, 1/2 cup white or red wine, 1 cup cooked tomatoes, and 1 1/2 tablespoons parsley. Cook the sauce, stirring, until it thickens. Add the kidneys and reheat them without letting the sauce boil.

Steak and
Kidney Pie

STEAK AND KIDNEY PIE

CUT in small dice 1 pound tender beef and 4 veal kidneys. Combine the meats and add 2 hard-cooked eggs, finely chopped, 8 mushrooms, peeled and sliced, 1 onion, finely chopped, 1 teaspoon chopped parsley, 1/2 teaspoon salt, a dash of pepper, 1/4 cup dry Sherry or Madeira, 1 teaspoon Worcestershire sauce, and 1 cup simple brown sauce or meat gravy. Turn the mixture into a casserole and cover it with puff paste or pie pastry. (The pie pastry often includes some kidney suet with the shortening.) Decorate with simple pastry cutouts, if desired. Bake the pie in a moderate oven (350° F.) for about 1 hour, or until the top is browned.

A chef tests a whole kidney by piercing it with a kitchen fork. After the fork has been in the kidney for a minute or two, he touches it to his tongue. If the fork is very hot, the kidney is done. If the fork is barely warm, the kidney needs longer cooking.

Rognons
de Veau
en Casserole

VEAL KIDNEY CASSEROLE

PUT 1 carrot and 1 large onion, both sliced, in a casserole and add 2 sprigs of parsley, 1/2 teaspoon salt, and a little pepper. Trim the surplus fat from 6 veal kidneys, leaving a layer about 1/4 to 1/2 inch thick. Arrange them on top of the vegetables and bake uncovered in a moderate oven (350° F.) for about 20 minutes, or until they are brown. Cover the casserole and continue baking for about 30 to 35 minutes, or until the kidneys are done when tested with a fork. Remove them.

Drain off as much fat as possible from the casserole and add 1/2 cup dry white wine and 1 cup meat gravy, stock, or water. Cream together 2 teaspoons flour and 2 tablespoons butter and stir this *beurre manié* into the mixture in the casserole. Return it to the oven and cook for a few minutes longer. Strain the thickened sauce. Replace the kidneys in the casserole, pour the strained sauce over them, and add a garnish of cooked, diced hot potatoes, sautéed mushrooms, small cooked onions, and chopped parsley.

Tripe

TRIPE is one of the great and popular dishes of France and a regular specialty of Parisian restaurants. Americans usually prefer tripe *bordelaise* or *lyonnaise*, but the French love it best prepared *à la mode de Caen*.

Authentic *tripes à la mode de Caen* is made with beef tripe—plain, not honeycomb—and an ox foot. Devotees of the dish can even discern the substitution of a calf's foot. The quantity of fat used forms a thick protective layer that keeps the tripe white as it cooks. The French make the dish in a special earthenware casserole with sides that curve inward leaving rather a small opening. *Tripes à la mode de Caen* cooks for as long as 10 hours, and the cover is sealed with dough to hold in the flavor and aroma. All tripe takes at least 3 or 4 hours to cook.

Tripe must be absolutely fresh to be good, so it is wise to order it specially. You must be careful about the amount of salt you use in preparing it, because tripe is sold already parboiled, and the amount of salt in the water varies.

TRIPE À LA MODE DE CAEN

Tripes à la Mode de Caen

CUT 4 onions and 4 carrots in small pieces and spread them in an earthenware casserole. Lay a split ox foot· or calf's foot on the vegetables. Cut 4 pounds parboiled plain tripe into 2-inch squares and add it to the casserole with 4 leeks, tied together, and a faggot made by tying together 2 stalks of celery, 4 sprigs of parsley, 2 bay leaves, and a little thyme. Add 4 cloves of garlic, 1 teaspoon salt, a little pepper, a pinch of Parisian spice or poultry seasoning, 1/2 pound beef suet, 1/2 cup hard cider, 1/4 cup Calvados or applejack and enough water to just cover the ingredients. Cover the casserole and seal it with a roll of dough made by mixing 2 cups flour with enough water to make a stiff paste. Bring the liquid to a boil, put the casserole in a slow oven (325° F.), and cook the tripe for 8 to 10 hours. Uncover the casserole and skim all the fat from the mixture. Remove the tripe to another casserole. Take out the ox foot, cut away the meat, discard the bone, and cut the meat in pieces. Add it to the tripe. Strain the liquid, discard the vegetables, and skim off any fat remaining on the liquid. Pour it over the tripe and bring it just to a boil. Serve the tripe very hot, from the casserole, accompanied with baked potatoes. Serves 8 to 10 people.

TRIPE BORDELAISE

Tripes à la Bordelaise

CUT 1 1/2 pounds parboiled tripe into large julienne. Cook 2 onions, chopped, in 2 tablespoons butter until they are golden brown. Add 1 clove of garlic, 3 tomatoes, peeled, seeded, and chopped, 1/2 cup tomato sauce or 1 cup canned tomatoes, 1 cup chicken or veal stock or water, 1/2 teaspoon salt, a little pepper, and a faggot made by tying together 2 stalks of celery, 3 sprigs of parsley, 1 bay leaf, and 1/2 teaspoon thyme. Bring the liquid to a boil and cook the tripe over very low heat or in a moderate oven (350° F.) for 3 to 4 hours, or until it is tender. Remove the faggot, skim off the fat, and add a little water if the sauce is too thick. Correct the seasoning with salt and add 1 teaspoon chopped parsley. Serve with baked or boiled potatoes.

TRIPE LYONNAISE

Cook 1 1/2 pounds parboiled tripe in water to cover for 3 to 4 hours, or until it is tender. Cut the tripe into small pieces and drain them well. Cook the tripe in 2 tablespoons butter, turning the pieces often, until they are golden brown. In another pan melt 2 tablespoons butter and in it cook 2 onions, thinly sliced, until they are golden. Add 3 tablespoons vinegar, a little salt and pepper, 1 tablespoon chopped parsley, and the tripe and heat the mixture. Serve with baked, boiled, or sautéed potatoes.

Tripes à la Lyonnaise

Ox Tongue and Oxtails

SMOKED *ox tongue should be soaked in a generous amount of water for several hours or overnight before it is cooked. The soaking time depends upon how salty the meat is, but 3 to 4 hours should be enough for the average tongue.*

BOILED OX TONGUE

Soak a smoked ox tongue and drain it. Put it in a large kettle, and cover it generously with cold water, and bring the water to a boil. If the water tastes very salty, pour it off and begin with fresh. Cook the tongue slowly for 2 1/2 to 3 hours, or until it is very tender when tested with a fork. Turn off the heat and leave the tongue in the water for

Langue de Boeuf Bouillie

269

about 1/2 hour. Cut off the tough muscular end with the bones, and peel the skin. Slice diagonally and serve with Madeira or piquant sauce.

Tongue to be served cold should stand in the cooking water until it is completely cool before it is trimmed and skinned.

Oxtails are rich in fat, which must be cooked out to make them digestible. If this ragout is cooked a day ahead and allowed to cool overnight, the fat will rise and harden so that it can be lifted off.

Queue de Boeuf à la Parisienne

OXTAILS PARISIAN

HAVE the butcher cut into pieces at the joints 2 oxtails weighing about 4 pounds. Wipe the meat with a damp cloth and put it in a deep bowl. Add 1 carrot and 2 onions, all coarsely chopped, 10 peppercorns, 1 teaspoon salt, a pinch of Parisian spice or poultry seasoning, a faggot made by tying together a stalk of celery, 3 sprigs of parsley, a small bay leaf, and a little thyme, and 2 cups red wine. Marinate the meat overnight in the refrigerator. Remove the oxtails and drain them. Reserve the marinade.

Dry the oxtails well and brown the pieces in a skillet, a few at a time, in 4 tablespoons hot beef fat. Remove the meat to a casserole. In the skillet brown the carrots and onions from the marinade and add them to the casserole. Skim most of the fat from the skillet. To what remains add 4 tablespoons flour and cook, stirring, until the flour turns golden. Add the reserved marinade, 1 cup tomato purée or canned tomatoes, and 1 cup beef stock. Bring the mixture to a boil, stirring, and pour it over the oxtails. Add the faggot from the marinade, 1 clove of garlic, crushed, and enough water to cover. Bring the liquid to a boil, cover the casserole, and cook over low heat for about 3 hours, or until the oxtails are tender. Remove them to a bowl and strain the sauce over them. Cool and store in the refrigerator overnight, or until the fat rises to the surface and hardens. Remove the layer of fat.

About 40 minutes before servingtime, return the oxtails and sauce to the casserole. Cook 12 to 15 small white onions and 12 to 15 large carrot dice in a little hot butter until they are glazed. Bring the sauce to a boil, add the vegetables, and cook them until they are tender. Add 12 small boiled potatoes, correct the seasoning with salt, and sprinkle with chopped parsley.

GIBIER

Game

In the Bourbonnais, where I grew up, local sportsmen waited for their farmer friends before they went hunting. But after the crops were harvested, hunting boots appeared and the men inspected and oiled their guns. The dogs quivered with excitement at the intoxicating smells. To meet the demand from the hunters for tasty meat pies to take along for lunch, the local pastry shops—and every town had a good *pâtisserie*—made quantities of pâtés. The men ate them in the open, under a bright fall sky, with local white wine and newly ripened peaches, plums, pears, and grapes.

My grandfather was a famous hunter, as was my uncle. As for me, I confess that my own interest in game, even in those days, was more in the kitchen than in the field. *Grand-mère* let me help prepare the marinade for the hare in my uncle's bag, and taught me how to wrap quail for roasting in sheets of larding pork and grape leaves. Later, as a young apprentice in Moulins, I was often sent into the kitchens of the neighboring great châteaux to prepare the venison, boar, and game birds that our local *chasseurs* brought back from their strenuous days of hunting.

A hunter inevitably takes special interest in the fate of game he himself has bagged, so we always took extra pains in its preparation and serving. At the Ritz Hotel in Paris, and also in London, we chefs were regularly asked to cook grouse and pheasant and other game, furred as well as feathered, brought to us by Europe's kings and sporting nobility, international diplomats and financiers. And in the New York Ritz, in the days when the practice was permitted, our guests brought their game for us to cook for private dinner parties. Those were truly proud hosts!

Millions of hunting licenses are issued in this country each year. When you multiply this figure by the bag limits permitted in the various states, it is obvious that the amount of game shot annually is *formidable*. I sometimes wonder, however, how much of this game is properly cooked for full enjoyment. Actually game cookery is not mysterious; one need only to master the recommended procedures to make cooking a game bird as simple as roasting a barnyard fowl.

Civet
Salmis

Game makes an excellent stew, called *civet* if the game is furred, *salmis* if the game is feathered. Because most game is dry, and may also be tough, stewing or braising, which tenderize the meat and provide quantities of sauce, are favorite methods of cooking it. Roast game is delicious, but only tender young birds and animals can be roasted. Game pâtés and terrines—highly seasoned game mixtures cooked until tender in pastry or in earthenware molds—have the advantage of being able to be served cold.

But successful game cookery begins long before one is faced with the necessity of deciding between roast and stew; it begins with the hunter. The hunter must learn how to treat his bag, and follow the rules conscientiously, or no amount of good cooking will make it fit to eat.

Feathered Game

THE HUNTER'S first responsibility is his choice of shell. Too large a shell will tear a bird to pieces, and a bird full of shot is equally undesirable. The birds should be tied by the feet and hung separately in such a way that air can circulate freely around them. Birds put into a bag immediately after they are killed will sweat and even mold.

Plucking and drawing may wait until the hunter reaches home, but no longer. Birds should be plucked dry. Dipping them in hot water makes the feathers come out easily, but it also loosens the skin so that it may slip off, and a skinned bird cannot be properly cooked. Pull the feathers out in the direction in which they grew, to keep the tender, easily torn skin intact. When the bird is clean and drawn, put a few pieces of celery in the cavity and store the bird in the refrigerator. Large game birds like geese and turkey will hold for 2 weeks in the refrigerator; small birds like grouse, quail, and woodcock should be cooked within 2 to 4 days.

Young and tender birds, 5 or 6 months old, can be roasted. Older birds are made into *salmis* or terrines. One way to tell whether a bird is tender is to look at its feet. If the spur on the inside of the foot is very pointed and sharp, the bird is an old one and probably tough. In a young bird, the end of the spur is rounded and dull—and the breastbone is flexible and easily broken. It is safest to assume that a bird of unknown age and habitat is tough and not to risk roasting it.

The flesh of game birds, except that of ducks and sometimes geese, is normally dry, and requires generous applications of fat in cooking. The breasts of large birds may be covered with large, thin slices of pork

Larding
Feathered
Game

273

fat or larded with strips of the fat. Larding pork is usually salted, rather than fresh. A short larding needle works best for game birds. Push the needle only part way into the flesh, insert the end of the strip of larding pork in it, and push the needle through and out, about an inch from the point at which it was inserted, as though you were taking a stitch. Gently pull the larding strip through the flesh and out. The ends of the strip should protrude evenly on either side of this " stitch. " Usually 10 to 12 strips are required for the breast of a large bird. Larding takes practice because pork fat is fragile and breaks easily. Manipulate the needle slowly and carefully, and avoid jerky movements that might tear the strip. Larding is also described in the chapter on the chef at work.

Truss game birds as you do domestic birds, and for the same reasons: they look better and are less likely to dry out during cooking. If the bird is to be larded with sheets of pork fat, put the fat on and secure it with a crisscross string after the bird is trussed.

Duck Press

Connoisseurs prefer wild ducks shot by hunters to the domesticated wild ducks raised on game farms, because they have a better flavor, their breasts are larger and plumper, and they have more blood, an important ingredient in the sauce. Wild duck should be cooked rare for maximum flavor and tenderness. Only the breasts are served. The legs and carcass are pressed in a device called a duck press, which extracts the blood for making the sauce au sang, *traditional accompaniment to wild duck. In carving the breasts every drop of blood should be saved, too. Restaurants that serve game usually have a duck press, but you can accomplish almost the same thing by cutting up the carcass and running it through the food chopper, using the coarsest blade. The juice extracted thus may be strained through a fine sieve or cheesecloth. In fine restaurants, the duck is cooked in the kitchen, then the headwaiter or* trancheur *carves it, operates the duck press, and finishes the sauce beside the table—an operation gourmets love to watch. Choose a heavy-bladed knife to cut the carcass up, and a thin, flexible, razor-sharp knife for carving the breast meat.*

Canard Sauvage Rôti

ROAST WILD DUCK

CLEAN the bird and truss the legs close to the body. Put a roasting pan in the oven and heat the oven to hot (475° F.). Put the duck in the hot pan and roast it for 8 to 12 minutes, depending on the weight. Let the duck stand for about 10 minutes, remove the breasts, and put them where they will keep warm but not cook. Usually the legs are too tough to eat, but if the duck is a very tender one, the legs may be cut off at this point, broiled, and sliced. They require more cooking than the breast. Make *sauce au sang*. Cut the breasts into thin slices and arrange the slices on a serving dish. Garnish with triangular croutons spread with *rouennaise*. Serve with currant jelly and fried hominy or wild rice. Serve the sauce separately or pour it over the breast meat.

BLOOD SAUCE   *Sauce au Sang*

COMBINE 1/2 cup red wine, 5 peppercorns, crushed, 1 small bay leaf, 1/2 teaspoon thyme, and 2 shallots, chopped, in a saucepan and cook until the liquid is reduced to 1/3 the original quantity. Add 2 tablespoons brown sauce and rub the mixture through a fine sieve. If brown sauce is not available, use *beurre manié* made by creaming 1 tablespoon butter with 1/2 teaspoon flour. As soon as the duck is cooked to the rare stage and the breasts have been removed, crush the legs and the carcass in a duck press or put them through a food chopper, extracting all the juices possible. Combine this juice with the blood saved when the breast is carved and very gradually add the blood to the sauce, stirring it vigorously near—but not over—the heat until it thickens. Do not let it boil.

WILD DUCK IN BRANDY SAUCE

*Canard
Sauvage
à la Fine
Champagne*

ROAST 2 or 3 wild ducks as for roast wild duck and press the juice and blood from the carcasses.

Prepare the following sauce: Sauté 2 duck livers, chopped, in hot fat or butter for 2 to 3 minutes, turning them as they cook. They should be rare. Sprinkle them with salt and pepper. In another pan put 1 tablespoon chopped shallot, 1 small bay leaf, a little thyme, 5 peppercorns, and 6 tablespoons red wine and cook slowly until the wine is reduced to 2/3 the original quantity. Stir in 2 tablespoons brown sauce or good gravy and bring again to a boil. Add the cooked livers, mix well, and rub through a fine sieve. Return the sauce to the pan and add the blood as for *sauce au sang*. Add 2 tablespoons Cognac. Slice the breasts, arrange the slices on a serving dish, and pour the sauce over them. Garnish with crescent-shaped croutons.

*Canard
à la
Rouennaise*

CLEAN a wild duck, stuff with *rouennaise*, and roast it in a hot oven (450°
F.) for about 18 minutes, depending on the size of the duck. If it is a
tender duck, cut off the legs and broil them for a few minutes. Remove
the *rouennaise* stuffing and place it in the center of a chafing dish. On
opposite sides place the legs, cut in two pieces, and on the other two sides
the breasts, thinly sliced.

Chop up the carcass finely (and also the legs if they were too tough
to broil), add 1/4 cup Cognac and a few drops of lemon juice, and press
all together in a duck press. Have a separate heater, a *réchaud*, ready
near the chafing dish and put on it a small pan containing about 1/2 cup
sauce rouennaise. Add to this the Cognac-flavored juice pressed out of
the duck carcass. Correct the seasoning with salt.

The duck in the chafing dish should be very hot. Be sure that the
water in the lower pan of the chafing dish is kept hot but never boiling,
or the delicately cooked meat of the bird will toughen. Sprinkle it
with a little Cognac and then pour a little of the *sauce rouennaise* over it.
Put the remaining sauce in a separate serving dish. Serve each person
with some of the duck and *rouennaise* stuffing and pass the sauce.

*Wild goose and wild turkey usually come from one of the southern states.
These birds are very apt to be tough; if possible, hang them for a week or
two in the refrigerator to make them more tender. Cook them unstuffed or
with English stuffing—a bread-crumb, onion, and herb mixture. They can
be roasted but unless you are sure that the bird is young enough to be tender,
braising is a wiser choice.*

*Oie Sauvage
Braisée
ou Dindon
Sauvage
Braisé*

CLEAN the bird and, if desired, stuff it. Truss it and tie slices of fat salt
pork around it. Roast it in a hot oven (400° to 425° F.) until it is well
browned all over, turning it from side to side. Remove the fat from the
pan and add 1 carrot and 1 onion, both sliced, 3 sprigs of parsley, 1 stalk
of celery, 1 bay leaf, a pinch of thyme, and 1 quart chicken or veal stock.
Braise the bird, covered, in a moderate oven (350° F.), basting frequently,
for 2 to 3 hours, or until it is tender. Remove the bird to a hot platter.
Strain the liquid into a saucepan, skim off the fat, and reduce it to 1 or
1 1/2 cups. Add 1 tablespoon potato flour or cornstarch mixed with 2 ta-

blespoons cold water and cook the sauce until it thickens slightly. Serve the sauce separately. Accompany with cranberry or applesauce and wild rice, fried hominy, or corn fritters.

Connoisseurs wait eagerly for the first game of the season, the Scotch grouse, which makes its appearance in this country during the second week of August. Until the outbreak of World War II, the first shipment of grouse to leave Great Britain after the opening of the season was always consigned to New York's old Ritz, and its arrival was cause for celebration.

Grouse are small birds, about the size of partridge but with a much more gamy flavor. Usually only their plump breasts are eaten; the tiny legs have almost no meat on them. Allow 1 grouse per person. They are traditionally served rare, on toast spread with rouennaise, *with bread sauce served separately, but towards the end of the season, when the birds are older, it is sometimes prudent to serve them masked with a* suédoise *or* danoise *cream sauce, to give them greater succulence.*

ROAST SCOTCH GROUSE ON TOAST

Grouse d'Ecosse Rôti sur Canapé

CLEAN the birds, truss the legs close to the bodies, and using soft string tie a slice of fresh fat pork around each. Season with a little salt. Preheat a roasting pan in a very hot oven (450° to 475° F.), put the birds in the pan, and roast them for 12 minutes. Remove the fat pork, which should be golden brown and crisp, and reserve it. Place the birds on a serving platter. Discard the fat from the pan but do not wash it. Put 1 teaspoon butter and 2 tablespoons chicken stock or water in the pan for each bird and reduce the liquid a little, stirring. Serve each bird on a piece of toast spread with *rouennaise* and garnish with a piece of the browned fat pork. Serve the pan sauce separately, and bread sauce, if desired.

Partridge is a small bird, smaller than pheasant, although one is occasionally large enough to make 2 portions. My uncle used to collect partridge eggs from their nests in the fields around the farm, and my aunt would persuade her hens to hatch them. In the fall, she could sell them all to the town restaurants for a very good price—so good, indeed, that while I saw many partridge readied for market, I never tasted one until I began my training as a chef.

Recipes for partridge and pheasant can in almost all cases be used for either bird and for other game birds. The legs of pheasant are seldom tender enough to eat, but even so, a pheasant usually serves 2. Quail is so small that even a large quail makes only a single serving.

Perdreau, Faisan, ou Caille—Rôtir

ROAST YOUNG PARTRIDGE, PHEASANT, OR QUAIL

CLEAN the bird and with soft string truss the legs (and the wings of a pheasant) close to the body. Cover the bird with thin slices of fat salt pork and tie them on securely. Partridge and quail are often first wrapped in grape leaves, under the fat and next to the skin. Very particular cooks lard the breasts, especially those of pheasant, with strips of fat pork.

Roast the bird in a very hot oven (450° F.). Place it on its side in the pan, turn it on the other side when it is golden brown, and finish cooking it on its back. Baste frequently. As soon as the salt pork is brown and crisp, remove it and reserve it to garnish the bird. Roasting time depends on the type of bird and its size. For partridge and pheasant, allow 10 to 15 minutes on each side, and 10 to 15 minutes on its back. For quail, preheat a roasting pan in an oven that is a little hotter—475° F. Put the quail in the hot pan and roast it about 5 to 7 minutes on each side and 5 minutes on its back. The quail is such a tiny bird that by the time it is browned to a rich golden color on all sides in a hot oven, it is also cooked to the proper degree of doneness.

To test for doneness, lift the bird up. If the juice that runs out is clear, with no pink tinge, the bird is done. Remove it to a heated platter.

To make a pan sauce, skim the fat from the liquid in the roasting pan and add butter and water, 1 to 2 teaspoons butter and 2 tablespoons water for each bird. Reduce the mixture to the desired concentration over direct heat, stirring in all the brown crustiness that clings to the pan. Strain the sauce.

ROAST YOUNG PARTRIDGE ON TOAST

ROAST the birds. Serve a whole or half bird, according to size, on toast spread with *rouennaise* and garnish with the pieces of browned fat pork or bacon. Pass the pan sauce separately.

Perdreau Rôti sur Canapé

PARTRIDGE SWEDISH STYLE

SPRINKLE tender, young partridge with salt and pepper to taste and rub them well with butter. Wrap a thin sheet of larding pork around each one and tie it with string. Roast the birds.

Remove them and in the pan make *sauce suédoise*, Swedish sauce, omitting the vinegar and finishing with the juice of 1/2 lemon. Serve the sauce separately.

Perdreau Suédoise

PARTRIDGE DANISH STYLE

FOLLOW the directions for partridge Swedish style, but in the roasting pan make *sauce danoise*, Danish sauce.

Perdreau Danoise

TRUFFLED PARTRIDGE OR PHEASANT PÉRIGORD

STUFF the birds with any truffle stuffing and arrange slices of truffle over the breasts as described in the section on truffle stuffing.

Put the birds on their sides in the roasting pan in a hot oven (425° F.) and cook them for 15 minutes, basting often. Turn them to the other side and cook for 15 minutes longer. Reduce the heat to 400° F. and roast the birds for 1 to 1 1/2 hours, or until the juices that follow the fork when the second joint is pierced are clear, with no pink tinge. Turn and baste the birds from time to time.

Remove the roasted birds from the pan and skim the fat from the pan juices. For a simple pan sauce, add 1/3 cup Madeira or Sherry and 1/2 cup stock or water to the pan and cook, stirring in all the brown bits that cling to the pan, until the liquid is reduced to 1/2 the original quantity. Or make *sauce périgourdine* in the roasting pan in this way: Add to the pan juices 1/3 cup Sherry, 1 to 2 tablespoons juice from a can of truffles,

Perdreau ou Faisan Truffé à la Périgourdine

Sauce Périgourdine

1 tablespoon *glace de viande*, or meat extract, if available, and 1 cup brown sauce. Cook the sauce slowly for 10 minutes, stirring in the brown bits in the pan, and strain it. Add 2 to 4 tablespoons diced truffles and 2 tablespoons Sherry or Madeira. Correct the seasoning and reheat the sauce. Serve the sauce separately.

Perdreau ou Faisan Souvarov

PARTRIDGE OR PHEASANT SOUVAROFF

SAUTÉ in butter 1/2 pound fresh goose liver or canned natural *foie gras*, cut in pieces. Add an equal quantity of whole small truffles or larger ones cut into pieces and combine with 2 tablespoons beef extract or *glace de viande* mixed with 4 tablespoons Madeira or Sherry.

Clean the bird, stuff it with the mixture, and sew up the opening. Truss the legs and wings close to the body. Lard the breast with thin strips of fat salt pork and cover with more salt pork, securing the slices with string. Put the bird in a roasting pan, and spread with good fat. Roast it in a hot oven (425° F.) for about 15 minutes, turn, and roast it for 15 minutes on the other side, basting frequently. Remove the string and slices of pork and put the bird on its back in a casserole.

Skim the fat from the roasting pan and to the drippings in the pan add 1/3 cup Madeira or Sherry, 2 or 3 tablespoons truffle juice, 2 truffles, diced, and 1/2 cup Madeira sauce or brown sauce. Cook the sauce for a few minutes and pour it around the pheasant in the casserole. Put 1 tablespoon butter on the breast. Cover the casserole with a lid that has a small hole to vent the steam and seal the edges with a stiff paste made with flour and water. Bake in a hot oven (425° F.) for about 30 minutes. Bring the casserole to the table right from the oven. When the seal is broken, and the cover removed, the diners will get the full aroma of the truffle sauce. Remove the bird to a hot platter and carve it.

This recipe may be used for any poultry.

Chartreuse de Perdreau ou Faisan

PARTRIDGE OR PHEASANT WITH CABBAGE

FOR older, less tender birds. Clean the bird, truss it and roast it in a very hot oven (450° F.) for about 20 minutes, turning it from one side to the other and last on its back. Parboil 1 large cabbage, quartered, for 5 minutes. Drain the cabbage, rinse it in cold water and drain it again. Put

4 slices salt pork or bacon in a deep casserole and add a layer of 1/3 of the cabbage leaves. Lay the bird on the cabbage leaves and add 1 carrot, 1 onion studded with a clove and a faggot made of 2 stalks of celery, 3 sprigs of parsley, 1/2 bay leaf and a pinch of thyme. Add the second 1/3 of the cabbage leaves and 1 large piece of uncooked garlic sausage or Italian sausage.

Parboil 1/2 pound fat salt pork for 5 minutes. Drain it and add it. Cover the pork with the remaining cabbage and add 1 quart stock. Cover the cabbage with a round of buttered paper with a tiny hole in the center to vent the steam. Cover the casserole and braise the bird in a moderate oven (375° F.) for 35 to 40 minutes, or until the sausage and fat pork are done. Remove and reserve the sausage and fat pork and continue to cook the *chartreuse* until the legs of the bird fall away from its body, about 45 minutes longer. Remove the bird and the carrot and discard the faggot. Slice the meat of the bird.

Line a buttered, round-bottomed timbale with the sausage, sliced, slices of carrots and small rectangles of the cooked salt pork in a neat pattern. Cover the inside of the mold with a thick layer of cabbage and sliced meat and fill the timbale with the cabbage and meat. Finish with a final layer of cabbage leaves. Press firmly with a fork, tilting the timbale to drain off the liquid fat. Then unmold the timbale onto a hot platter.

The timbale need not be used and the partridge meat may simply be served on a bed of the cooked cabbage, garnished with the sausage, carrot and salt pork.

PARTRIDGE OR PHEASANT STEW

Salmis de Perdreau ou Faisan

ROAST the birds. Remove the breasts and set the legs and the carcasses aside. Put the breasts on a warm plate and spread them with butter or with fat from the roasting pan to prevent drying.

Make a sauce as follows: In 2 tablespoons salad or vegetable oil, sauté 1 onion, chopped, until it is golden brown. Add 1 tablespoon chopped shallot, 1 clove of garlic, crushed, and 1 1/2 tablespoons flour and cook 2 minutes longer. Add 3/4 cup red or white dry wine and cook the mixture, stirring constantly, until it thickens. Add 1 cup each of stock and strained tomatoes, 1/2 teaspoon salt, 4 peppercorns, crushed, a pinch of thyme and a faggot made by tying together 2 stalks of celery, 3 sprigs of parsley and 1 small bay leaf. Add the reserved legs and the carcass, chopped fine, and simmer slowly for 1 hour, until the leg meat is tender. Strain the sauce and if it is too thick add more stock. Just before serving add 2 tablespoons Cognac.

Slice the leg meat from the bones and arrange it with the sliced breast meat on a serving dish. Meanwhile, simmer 12 mushroom caps in 1/2 cup water with 1 teaspoon butter and the juice of 1 lemon. Drain the mushrooms and garnish the meat. Pour the sauce over the mushrooms and meat. Garnish the platter with triangular croutons spread with *rouennaise*.

Cailles Rôties sur Canapé

ROAST QUAIL ON TOAST

ROAST the birds. Serve each bird on a piece of toast spread with *rouennaise* and garnish with pieces of the browned fat pork. Make the pan sauce and serve it separately, and, if desired, serve bread sauce and currant jelly. Small white grapes or canned pitted cherries, drained of juice, may be added to the pan sauce.

Cailles sous la Cendre

CHARCOAL ROASTED QUAIL

CLEAN 6 quail and stuff with truffle stuffing Diat. One-third of the recipe will make sufficient stuffing for 6 quail. When stuffing the birds, put one whole truffle in each. Sew up the vent well. Wrap each bird in grape leaves and then in a large, thin slice of fat pork. Wrap in two thicknesses of buttered or wax paper. Put the birds on a bed of hot ashes of a charcoal broiler or a wood fire. Cover them with hot ashes. Cook for 35 to 40 minutes, depending upon the size of the birds, changing the ashes as they cool so that the birds will always be surrounded with hot ashes. Remove from the ashes, take off the paper, and serve immediately with *sauce périgueux*.

Cailles Chaudes Richelieu

HOT QUAIL RICHELIEU

ROAST 6 quail. Remove the birds to a heatproof casserole and add a little water to the juices in the roasting pan, cooking and stirring in the brown crustiness. Meanwhile, parboil 3/4 cup carrots, celery and onion, cut in very fine uniform pieces, for 2 or 3 minutes. Drain the vegetables and cook them until tender in 3/4 cup veal or chicken stock. Stir in a *beurre manié* made by creaming 2 teaspoons butter with 1 teaspoon flour. Combine this with the quail juices and heat it well. Pour the sauce over the birds and simmer all together for 4 or 5 minutes longer.

The woodcock is the smallest bird commonly eaten in this country. It should be roasted à point, that is, not well done, not too rare, but just to the point when the flesh begins to lose its pink color.

ROAST WOODCOCK

PREPARE and roast woodcock like grouse, cooking it for about 8 to 10 minutes and basting with butter. Serve it on toast with pan sauce made by reducing the juice in the pan with a little butter and water.

Bécasse Rôtie

The famous hotels in Europe had certain specialties as well as details of service that are rarely duplicated in this country. In Paris, small game birds were served in the chafing dish with great ceremony. I can still see in my mind's eye that most famous of all maîtres d'hôtel, Olivier of the Paris Ritz, unobtrusively watching a waiter flamber a bécasse au fumet with fine Cognac, casually walking by the table to make sure that the sauce was just right and would not boil and curdle. Thousands of bécasses were served in the dining room of that hotel on the place Vendôme!

WOODCOCK FLAMED IN BRANDY

BÉCASSES are not always cleaned like other birds but are sometimes cooked with the intestines intact. Season the birds with salt and spread them generously with butter. Roast in a hot oven (450° F.) for about 10 minutes. Remove the legs and breasts and arrange them in a chafing dish, the legs at the bottom. Spread the breasts with a little melted butter and cover the pan. The water in the lower pan should be hot but not boiling. Chop up the carcasses finely, replace in the roasting pan, and pour over them 1/4 cup warm Cognac. Flame the spirit. Mix well and rub through a fine sieve.

Add 2 tablespoons of the strained pan juices to enough *rouennaise*

Bécasse au Fumet

to spread small triangles of toast. To the remaining pan juices add an equal quantity of game or poultry gravy and a few drops of lemon juice to make a sauce.

Sprinkle the legs and breasts with Cognac and ignite. Pour over them the sauce made from the carcasses and arrange the toast triangles around the dish. The woodcock may be prepared in the kitchen and served on a platter.

Furred Game

M Y EXPERIENCE with furred game has included the 85-pound deer of France and the 200 pounders common here, the giant hare of Europe and the little American rabbits, and out of that experience I must emphasize again the hunter's responsibility for his bag. Furred game must be cleaned and cooled as quickly as possible after it is brought down. A guide, an experienced hunter, or your butcher can tell you how to clean and draw the animal. As soon as game is cleaned, cover it loosely with cheesecloth and hang it in a shady place. If the weather should turn suddenly warm, head for home and refrigeration at once. Keep the meat cool and well aired on the way, but do not allow it to get dusty or wind-dried.

In general the same rules apply to furred game as to domestic meats, but the rules must be modified because wild game does not carry a birth certificate, and one cannot control its feeding and exercise. One can only gamble on whether a deer will be young and tender or tough and stringy. The meat of wild animals has a distinctive gamy taste that intrigues gourmets but it must be seasoned accordingly and served with suitably rich or piquant sauces.

Furred game is always marinated before cooking. There are two kinds of marinade, cooked and uncooked. They may be used interchangeably, but when the marinade is to be used in the sauce, uncooked marinade is chosen because the cooked is too pungent and highly flavored for that purpose. Less tender meat, which is usually braised or stewed, and always sauced, is therefore marinated in the uncooked marinade, and only roasts and other tender cuts in the cooked. Marinade, a highly seasoned pickling mixture made with wine or vinegar and water, helps to make the meat tender and adds flavor to it and to the sauce.

To marinate, put the meat in a deep bowl, add the marinade, cover the bowl, and let the meat stand overnight, or for as long as 48 hours, in the refrigerator. Turn the meat from time to time so that the marinade can penetrate it evenly. Drain the meat and carefully wipe it dry before cooking or roasts will be steamy and stews not properly braised.

UNCOOKED MARINADE I — *Marinade Crue I*

IN A bowl combine 2 onions and 2 carrots, thinly sliced, 2 shallots, minced, 1 clove of garlic, 1 stalk of celery, 2 bay leaves, 12 peppercorns, 2 cloves, a little thyme, 2 cups red or white wine, and 1/2 cup salad oil.

UNCOOKED MARINADE II — *Marinade Crue II*

IN A bowl combine 2 onions and 2 carrots, thinly sliced, 3 sprigs of parsley, 2 bay leaves, 12 peppercorns, a little thyme, 2 teaspoons salt, 1 1/2 cups white wine and 2 tablespoons salad oil. Half this amount should be enough for rabbit or hare.

COOKED MARINADE — *Marinade Cuite*

IN A saucepan combine 1 quart water, 1 1/2 cups vinegar, 2 onions, chopped, 1 carrot, sliced, 1 clove of garlic, 1 teaspoon thyme, 2 bay leaves, 4 sprigs of parsley, 12 peppercorns and 1 tablespoon salt. Bring the mixture to a boil and simmer it for 1 hour. Cool the marinade thoroughly.

BEAR — *Ours*

BEAR may be cooked like venison, but it is very fat and the fat that collects in the pan must be discarded. The sauce for bear is traditionally flavored with rosemary. Only very young bear is suitable for roasting.

Sanglier   WILD BOAR

WILD boar is not very common in this country, and the season lasts only a short time. Even at the elegant old Ritz we prepared boar for private parties, but we never put it on the regular menu. Only small young boar that are sure to be tender are cooked. They can be roasted whole, after they are marinated, and must be cooked thoroughly because they are a species of wild pig. Serve boar with wild rice, *velouté* of celery, and currant jelly. Any leftover meat can be served cold with Cumberland sauce.

Hare and rabbit are cooked in the same ways, although hare is a wilder, gamier, and larger animal. Both are at their best at the age of 7 or 8 months, when they have reached their full weight but are still young, plump, and tender. The animal's ears indicate its age: a young one has ears that are soft and tear easily; the ears of an old hare are thick and tough.

Râble de Lièvre à la Crème Aigre   LOIN OF HARE WITH SOUR CREAM SAUCE

SKIN, draw, and clean a rabbit and place the saddle or loin in a deep dish. Marinate the meat in uncooked marinade II in the refrigerator for about 24 hours. Drain and dry the meat thoroughly and wrap it in thin slices of fat salt pork. Season with salt and pepper. Put enough salad oil in a roasting pan to cover the bottom of the pan generously and put the pan in a hot oven. When the oil is smoking hot lay the meat in it and roast in a very hot oven (450° F.) for about 18 minutes. The meat should be medium rare. Remove the roasted meat to a hot serving platter.

Pour off the fat from the roasting pan. To the pan add 1 teaspoon chopped shallot or onion and 2 tablespoons vinegar and cook until it is reduced to almost nothing. Add 3 tablespoons *poivrade* sauce and reduce to about 2 tablespoons. Add 1/2 cup heated heavy cream. If desired, the meat may be sliced and arranged on the platter, and the sauce poured over it. Or the sauce may be passed separately. Or instead of the *poi-*

vrade sauce add a few drops of lemon juice and 1 tablespoon beef extract or good gravy after adding the cream. This will give the sauce an ivory color.

WILD RABBIT NORMANDY

CUT a 3-pound dressed rabbit into about 12 uniform pieces and marinate the pieces in the refrigerator overnight in uncooked marinade II. Drain and dry the rabbit pieces and sauté them in 3 tablespoons butter without permitting them to take on color. Season the meat with salt and a little pepper, sprinkle it with 1 teaspoon flour, and remove it from the skillet. Then add to the skillet 2 green apples, peeled, cored and sliced, and 3 medium onions, sliced. Lay the rabbit on top of this mixture and add 1 1/2 to 2 cups cream, barely to cover the meat. Cover the pan and cook the rabbit slowly for 1 to 1 1/2 hours, until it is tender. Transfer the meat to a serving dish and keep it hot. Force the sauce through a fine sieve, or purée it in an electric blender, reheat it, correct the seasoning with salt and pepper and finish with the juice of 1/2 lemon. Pour the hot sauce over the meat and serve.

Deer should be hung for several days, or at least 24 hours. They are butch- ered like beef, the venison cuts being comparable to those of the beef animal. The hindquarters, saddle, and loin are the choice cuts. The venison cut which corresponds to the tenderloin of beef is very small and makes only 2 servings. The sirloin of venison, a tender cut about the size of a beef filet, is sometimes called the noisette, *sometimes the* suprême *of venison. It is usually sliced 1 1/4 to 1 1/2 inches thick, marinated, drained and dried, and quickly sautéed in very hot oil.*

The forequarters, neck, and breast are less tender and are usually made into stew, or civet.

In preparing a deer for cooking, both the hairy outer skin and the tough second skin next to the flesh must be removed. The tough sinews of less tender cuts should be cut out and the bones discarded before the meat goes into the marinade. Venison has much less fat than beef and lacks the tenderness of prime beef. Therefore it must be marinated and a generous amount of fat must be used in its cooking. Venison should marinate for at least 2 or 3 days; some cooks continue the process for almost a week.

Larding
Venison

There are three ways of compensating for the lack of natural fat in venison. One is to lard the pieces with strips of fat salt pork, using a large larding needle and long strips of larding pork cut 1/4 inch wide. Insert the needle into the meat, running it through the center, then put the pork strip in the pronged end and very carefully pull it through. This takes patience and practice. If your butcher knows how to lard a piece of meat, ask him to let you watch him do it. A second method is to wrap slices of fat salt pork around the piece of venison. This will not take the place of larding, but it is easier to do and is better than nothing. And always use a generous amount of fat in the roasting pan and sauté the tender steaks in a generous quantity of oil.

*Selle
de Chevreuil
Rôtie*

ROAST SADDLE OF VENISON

REMOVE the sinews from a saddle of venison. Marinate the meat for 24 to 48 hours in the refrigerator. Use an uncooked marinade if there is to be a sauce, cooked marinade, if not. Drain the meat and dry it well. Lard the saddle with strips of fat salt pork, cover it with slices of fat salt pork, and season it with salt to taste. Roast the saddle in a very hot oven (450° F.) with a generous amount of fat or oil in the pan, basting it often. Saddle of venison should be cooked only to the rare stage, and a saddle weighing 5 to 6 pounds should cook in 45 minutes to 1 hour. Remove and discard the slices of fat pork and brush the roast with *glace de viande* or beef extract.

Serve with *poivrade* sauce, if desired, currant jelly, chestnut purée, and wild rice.

*Civet
de Chevreuil*

VENISON STEW

REMOVE and discard skin, bones and sinews from about 3 pounds of shoulder or neck of venison. Cut the meat into cubes and marinate it in the refrigerator for a day or two in uncooked marinade I, made with red wine. Drain and dry the meat thoroughly and reserve the marinade.

Parboil 1 cup fat salt pork, cut in small dice, in water to cover, then drain it. Heat 1/2 cup salad oil in a heavy skillet and in it brown the salt pork dice. Remove the dice and set them aside. In the hot fat in the pan brown lightly 12 to 15 small white onions. Add 1/2 cup carrots, cut in pieces and lightly sugared, and cook for about 5 minutes, until both onions and carrots are a golden brown. Remove the vegetables from the fat with a skimmer and set them aside with the pork dice. Sauté 1/2 pound cleaned mushrooms (if large, cut in two) in the skillet until they are soft and the moisture is cooked out of them. Skim off the mushrooms and put them with the pork and vegetables. Heat the fat well and in it brown the drained and dried venison, a few pieces at a time.

Put the browned meat in a saucepan, sprinkle it with 2 tablespoons flour and cook it in the oven or on top of the stove until the flour is browned. Add 1 clove garlic, crushed, 1 tablespoon finely chopped shallot or onion, 3/4 cup red wine, the strained marinade and a faggot made by tying together 2 stalks of celery, 4 sprigs of parsley, 1/2 bay leaf and a pinch of thyme. If necessary add enough water barely to cover the meat. Bring the liquid to a boil and simmer the meat for 1 1/2 hours. Add the brown pork dice and vegetables and continue to cook for 40 minutes longer, or until the meat is tender. Discard the faggot and correct the seasoning with salt. Serve sprinkled with finely chopped parsley.

Two or 3 dozen chestnuts, shelled and skinned, may be added to the stew with the vegetables.

GRENADIN OF VENISON ST. HUBERT

Grenadin de Chevreuil Saint-Hubert

HAVE the loin of venison cut away from the bone and sliced 1 1/2 inches thick. Marinate the meat in the refrigerator for 24 to 48 hours in uncooked marinade II. Drain and dry the slices well and brown them for about 3 minutes on each side in a generous amount of salad oil. Serve with *poivrade* sauce and chestnut purée.

VENISON CUTLETS DIANE

Côtelettes de Chevreuil Diane

HAVE slices cut about 3/4 inch thick from the leg or loin of venison. Marinate the meat for 24 to 48 hours in uncooked marinade II, drain and dry the slices well, and brown them for about 3 minutes on each side in a generous quantity of hot oil. Transfer the meat to a heated serving dish. Discard the oil and add to the pan 3 tablespoons red wine and 1 cup *poivrade* sauce. Cook for 2 minutes, stirring. Add 1/4 cup truffles cut in fine julienne, cook a minute, and fold in 3 tablespoons whipped cream and 1 chopped hard-cooked egg. Pour the sauce over the cutlets.

Game Sauces

IN FINE game cookery, the sauce must make up for something game often lacks—the richness and succulence that prime domestic meats have as a result of planned scientific feeding. Game sauces serve still another special purpose: their piquancy tempers and at the same time enhances " gaminess, " the characteristically pungent flavor of game.

Sauces of this quality can never be made by thickening the juices in the roasting pan with a little flour. They depend upon the subtle blending of many flavors—wine, spices, herbs, vegetables, stock, butter, sour cream. Frequently they include something sweet—currant jelly, Port wine, or raisins. For the connoisseur, the perfect harmony between game and sauce is achieved when the sauce is also flavored by the game. This may be accomplished by various means. The marinade in which furred game is seasoned and tenderized may become part of the sauce. Sauces for feathered game are always made in the roasting pan and begin with the bird's own juices. And lastly, the blood of game, when it is available, gives the sauce special savor and color, and thickens it as well.

Blood of Game The blood of rabbits and hare is easier to obtain than that of other game, and it can be saved. Add 1 tablespoon vinegar to 1/2 cup blood. The vinegar will keep the blood from coagulating, and permit it to be stored in the refrigerator for a few days.

The blood of game birds is not used except in making sauce for wild duck, as indicated in the recipe.

Always add blood to a sauce at the last minute, with the pan off the heat. If the sauce is allowed to boil after the blood is added, it will curdle.

If the recipe requires blood and none is available, thicken the sauce with arrowroot or cornstarch mixed with red wine.

Sauce poivrade, *the classic brown sauce traditional for venison, is the base for many other game sauces.*

POIVRADE SAUCE I   *Sauce Poivrade I*

BROWN lightly 1 carrot and 1 onion, cut in small pieces, in 5 tablespoons salad oil. Add 3 or 4 sprigs of parsley, 1 bay leaf, a little thyme and 1/4 cup each of vinegar and liquor from uncooked marinade. Cook the liquid until it is reduced to 1/3 the original quantity and add 3 cups brown sauce. If any bones from the game are available, brown them well in the oven and add them to the mixture. Bring the sauce to a boil and cook it slowly for 1 hour. Add 5 or 6 peppercorns and cook for a very few minutes more. If peppercorns are cooked too long in a sauce, they give it a bitter taste. Strain the sauce into another pan and add another 1/2 cup strained liquor from the marinade. Bring to a boil and cook slowly for 30 minutes, skimming off the fat as it rises. Add 1/2 cup red wine. This recipe makes 3 cups sauce, for use with large furred game, with roast saddle of hare, and with marinated leg of lamb or mutton.

POIVRADE SAUCE II   *Sauce Poivrade II*

IF NO brown sauce is available, *poivrade* sauce may be made as follows: Brown 1 carrot and 1 onion, both diced, in 6 tablespoons salad oil. Add 1/2 cup flour, stir well, and cook until the flour is browned. Add 3 cups brown stock or double-strength beef consommé and 1 cup tomato purée and mix well with a whip. Cook, stirring constantly, until the sauce is well blended. Add 3 or 4 sprigs of parsley, 1 bay leaf and a little thyme. If any bones from the game are available, brown them well in the oven and add them. Cook the sauce for 1 1/2 hours, stirring it occasionally and skimming as necessary. Cook 1/2 cup each of vinegar and liquor from uncooked marinade and 6 peppercorns, crushed, until the liquid is reduced to 1/3 the original quantity. Strain the sauce into this reduced liquid and cook it for about 30 minutes longer, skimming off the fat as it rises. Add 1/2 cup red wine. Use as you would *poivrade* sauce I.

CHEVREUIL SAUCE   *Sauce Chevreuil*

BRING 1 1/2 cups *poivrade* sauce to a boil and add 1/2 cup each of red wine and liquor from uncooked marinade. Cook the sauce for 30 or 40 minutes, skimming it as necessary. Add 1 teaspoon sugar and continue to cook the sauce until it is reduced to about 1 1/4 cups. Swirl in 2 tablespoons butter, off the heat, and strain the sauce. For venison or marinated leg of lamb or mutton.

Sauce Grand Veneur   GRAND VENEUR SAUCE

BRING to a boil 2 cups *poivrade* sauce and add 2 tablespoons truffles cut in fine julienne or fine dice. If the blood of a hare or rabbit is available, thicken the sauce with it, adding it slowly to the sauce and moving the pan in a circular motion to swirl it into the mixture. Do not cook the sauce after the blood has been added. For large furred game.

Sauce Romarin   ROSEMARY SAUCE

MAKE an infusion of 1 teaspoon dry rosemary in 1/4 cup boiling red wine. Let this stand for a few minutes and strain the wine into 2 cups boiling Grand Veneur sauce. For large furred game, especially for that with a heavy game flavor like boar or bear.

Sauce Suédoise   SWEDISH SAUCE

AFTER a game bird has been roasted, hold it up to let the juice from inside run into the pan. Skim the fat from the pan juices. Follow the recipe for cream sauce for venison, but omit the *poivrade* sauce. This is a cream sauce for all game birds.

Sauce Danoise   DANISH SAUCE

AFTER a game bird has been roasted, make *sauce suédoise*, Swedish sauce, in the roasting pan, but omit the vinegar or lemon juice. To the finished sauce add 1 tablespoon red currant jelly and 2 tablespoons cooked ham cut in fine julienne or dice. This is a cream sauce for all game birds.

Sauce à la Crème pour Venaison   CREAM SAUCE FOR VENISON

AFTER venison has been roasted or sautéed, remove it from the pan. Discard the fat from the pan, but do not wash the pan. Add 1 tablespoon vinegar and 1 cup heavy cream. Cook the sauce for a few minutes, or until it is reduced to about 2/3 the original quantity. Add 2 tablespoons *poivrade* sauce and 2 tablespoons cream sauce or *velouté* sauce. Correct the seasoning with salt and strain the sauce through a fine sieve. If the flavor of lemon juice is preferred, omit the vinegar and add 1 teaspoon juice to the finished sauce. For roasted venison or hare.

CUMBERLAND SAUCE   *Sauce Cumberland*

CHOP 3 shallots very fine and parboil them for 1 or 2 minutes in a little water. Drain them well. Peel the thin surface skin, or zest, of 1 orange and 1 lemon, cut the zest in very fine julienne, and parboil the julienne in water to cover for 5 minutes. Drain them well. Combine shallots and zest with the juice of the orange and of 1/2 the lemon. Add a pinch each of powdered ginger and cayenne and 6 tablespoons melted red currant jelly mixed with 5 tablespoons Port and mix well. If a sharper sauce is desired, add 1/2 teaspoon prepared mustard. For cold furred game and other cold meats such as beef, veal, lamb, or mutton.

ROUENNAISE SAUCE   *Sauce Rouennaise*

COMBINE 1/2 cup red wine, 5 peppercorns, 1 small bay leaf, 1/2 teaspoon thyme, and 2 shallots, chopped. Bring the mixture to a boil and cook until it is reduced to 1/3 the original quantity. Add 2 tablespoons brown sauce or 1 tablespoon butter creamed with 1 teaspoon flour. Bring the sauce again to the boil, remove it from the heat, and keep it hot, without boiling. Add 2 or 3 very finely chopped duck or chicken livers, mix all together well, and rub through a fine sieve. If there is any blood from a duck available, stir this slowly into the sauce. Finish with 2 tablespoons Cognac. For wild or domestic duck.

Rouennaise, *a rich paste of poultry liver and seasonings, is spread on toast or croutons used to garnish game dishes.*

POULTRY LIVER PASTE   *Rouennaise*

HEAT 2 tablespoons rendered salt pork fat until it is very hot. Add 1 cup chicken or duck livers, 1 bay leaf, a pinch of thyme, 1 teaspoon salt and a little pepper. Cook for 3 to 4 minutes over high heat. Add 3 tablespoons Cognac or Sherry. Mix well crushing the livers, and rub the mixture through a fine sieve.

Sauce au Pain   BREAD SAUCE

STUD 1 onion with 2 cloves, put it in a saucepan with 2 cups milk, and add a little cayenne and a little salt. Bring the mixture to a boil, cook it for about 5 minutes, and strain. Add about 1 cup fresh bread crumbs or enough to thicken the milk. Correct the seasoning with salt. For a richer sauce, finish with butter or cream. For birds, especially grouse.

When time is at a premium, a pan sauce for game can be quickly made. The first of these sauces includes marinade; the second can be made with marinade or without it.

Sauce Simple pour Gibier I   PAN SAUCE FOR GAME I

THIS pan sauce is for furred game that has been marinated in red wine and then roasted or sautéed.

Remove the cooked game. Discard the fat, but do not wash the pan. Put in 2 teaspoons finely chopped shallot or onion, 2 tablespoons butter, and 2 teaspoons flour, mix well, and cook for about 2 minutes. Add 2/3 cup red wine, stirring. Then add about 1 1/3 cups of the strained liquor from uncooked marinade, stirring it in slowly, and cook the sauce until it thickens. Add 2 teaspoons currant jelly and correct the seasoning.

Sauce Simple pour Gibier II   PAN SAUCE FOR GAME II

THIS pan sauce, a cream sauce, is for roasted or sautéed game.

Remove the cooked game from the pan. Discard the fat, but do not wash the pan. Put in 2 teaspoons finely chopped shallots, 2 tablespoons butter, and 1 1/2 teaspoons flour, mix well, and cook for about 2 minutes. If uncooked marinade liquor is available, stir in 1/2 cup, strained. Add 1 1/2 cups heavy cream, stirring it in slowly, and cook the sauce until it thickens. If the sauce is for feathered game and no marinade is available, add the cream to the flour and butter mixture and finish the sauce with about 1 teaspoon lemon juice. Two teaspoons red currant jelly may be added. Correct the seasoning with salt.

FARCES

Stuffings

LOOKING BACK over my career—more than fifty years of working with food and with other chefs—it seems to me that there must be as many different recipes for stuffings as there are cooks. Each cook will decide that a little more of this or less of that, or perhaps a *soupçon* of something else, will improve the flavor. Though they vary, most stuffing recipes are easy to follow. And in spite of individual differences, there is a similarity among these recipes, regionally and nationally.

And let us remember that stuffings are not limited to use in birds, but may also enhance the interest of fish and meats, particularly lamb and veal. Many vegetables and even some fruits also become more appealing with a savory filling, and you will find some of these elsewhere in this volume.

Stuffings for Poultry

As a child, I loved to watch *grand-mère* in the kitchen. With no mechanical food chopper to help her, she made the traditional French poultry stuffing, chopping and chopping with her biggest knife until the mixture was fine and smooth enough to meet her strict standards. I once asked her why she didn't just cook the turkey without all that *farce* inside—it would have been so much easier. Her reply was practical and definitive: "There will be sixteen for dinner tomorrow, *mon petit*, and with the *farce*, everyone will have enough. Besides, some of them like my stuffing better than they like the bird!"

And indeed, in French cooking, *la farce* that goes inside any bird must be rich and elegant. If possible, it should have *le parfum des truffes*. We believe that the mixture must have an irresistible succulence or it is pointless to stuff the bird. Generally, a French stuffing uses equal amounts of fresh lean and fat pork, to which are added such things as chestnuts, truffles, mushrooms, and sometimes bread crumbs. Often the cook adds an egg or two and always flavorful ingredients like onions and herbs and spices.

Bread Crumbs for Stuffing

In English cooking, a poultry stuffing consists mostly of bread crumbs. But don't underrate it. The crumbs are usually rich with butter and highly seasoned. Bread crumbs for stuffing may be very dry and fine or they may be soft, from day-old bread. The dry crumbs usually go in with the other ingredients as they are. The soft crumbs are either lightly browned in hot butter or soaked in milk, water, or consommé, squeezed out, and tossed to separate them.

In the United States, there are scores of regional stuffings, unusual and delicious. Like the English bread crumb mixtures, most have a starch base—corn bread or sweet potatoes, rice or wild rice, and so on, depending on the tradition in the region. (I will make no attempt to cover these, which can readily be found elsewhere.)

A stuffing in a bird serves more than one purpose. It tends to make the flesh of lean birds more juicy and succulent. And as my grandmother knew, it also is a delectable addition to a meal and extends the number of servings. Still, stuffing is a matter of personal taste. Large birds such as turkeys, geese, capons, and large chickens are usually stuffed. Smaller ones are as often as not cooked without stuffing.

Preparing a Bird for Stuffing

When you prepare a bird for stuffing, remember these few important rules: Wash out the bird thoroughly, pulling away any bits of lung that cling to the frame, then dry it carefully with cheesecloth or paper towels. Some people sprinkle a little salt in the cavity, but the advisability of doing that depends, I believe, upon the saltiness of the stuffing. A good French cook never uses too much salt or seasoning.

The stuffing should always be cold. In a large bird, a little stuffing usually goes into the neck aperture and the remainder into the body cavity. Stuffing should not be crowded into the cavity. It swells in cooking and, even when very loosely packed, will become quite firm for serving. The vent may be sewed with a large needle, such as a darning needle, or one side may be drawn over the other and held firmly in place with small skewers. The bird is then trussed, as described in the section on roasting. Allow a maximum of a scant 1 cup stuffing for each pound the bird weighs when it is dressed and ready for the oven, and fill both cavities loosely.

Amount of Stuffing

Most stuffings may be used for any bird, but some of them are particularly good with certain birds, as noted in the recipes.

CHICKEN LIVER STUFFING

Farce à la Carlton

SOAK 1 cup chicken livers in milk to cover for 1 hour or more, drain them well, and chop them fine. Sauté the livers in 1 tablespoon butter with 1 onion, finely chopped, and 2 bay leaves, until they are golden brown. Add a scant 1/2 cup Sherry or Madeira, 1 teaspoon salt, and a little pepper and continue cooking, stirring, until all is well blended. Discard the bay leaves. Add enough milk to 1 cup day-old bread crumbs to moisten them well, squeeze out the milk, and add the crumbs to the liver mixture. Remove the stuffing from the heat and mix in 1 teaspoon chopped parsley.

APPLE STUFFING

Farce aux Pommes

SAUTÉ 2 medium onions, finely chopped, in 1/4 cup butter until they are soft and golden, add 2 cups white bread crumbs, 1 teaspoon chopped parsley, a pinch of powdered thyme, and a little salt and pepper and cool the mixture. Peel, quarter, and core 5 green apples. Sauté them in butter until they are soft and add them to the bread-crumb mixture. Particularly for duck.

Farce aux Pommes et aux Pruneaux

LIGHTLY brown 1 small onion, finely chopped, in 2 tablespoons butter. Combine with 1 1/2 cups bread crumbs, 1 cup each of chopped celery, diced cooked prunes, and chopped tart apples, and 1/4 teaspoon salt. Blend thoroughly. Particularly for goose or duck.

Farce aux Huîtres

MELT 1 cup butter in a saucepan, and brown very lightly 1 cup chopped onions. Add 2 cups day-old bread crumbs, firmly packed, 1 tablespoon chopped parsley, 1/2 teaspoon thyme, a little rosemary, and salt and pepper to taste. Cool the mixture and add 2 stalks of celery, cut in small pieces and simmered until tender in water. Open 3 or 4 oysters for each serving, about 2 dozen for a 10-pound turkey. Moisten the crumb mixture with a little of the oyster liquor. Dry the oysters, roll them in flour, in beaten egg mixed with a little salad oil, and in cracker crumbs. Sauté the oysters in hot butter for 1 minute on each side, until they are golden brown but still juicy. Fill the bird alternately with the crumb mixture and the oysters. Particularly for turkey.

Farce aux Abricots

COOK 1/2 cup wild rice or 3/4 cup white rice in boiling salted water for about 30 minutes and drain. This will give about 1 1/2 cups cooked rice. Heat 2 tablespoons butter in a saucepan and add the rice. Mix well and season with salt and pepper. In another pan, sauté 2 tablespoons raisins in a little butter until they become puffy and stir them lightly into the rice. Slice about 12 apricot halves, using canned apricots or dried ones soaked and cooked until soft. Add the apricots to the rice with 2 or 3 tablespoons beef gravy or beef extract and 3 tablespoons chicken *velouté*.

ENGLISH BREAD STUFFING

In a shallow pan, in 1/2 cup butter, sauté gently 2 medium onions, finely chopped, until they are soft but not brown. Crumble a 1-pound loaf of bread, without crust, and add 1/2 tablespoon chopped parsley, 1/2 teaspoon salt, a little pepper, and 1/4 teaspoon powdered thyme. Stir all together over the heat until the mixture is well combined and the crumbs are thoroughly mixed with the butter.

Farce à l'Anglaise

RICE AND GOOSE LIVER STUFFING

Mix together 4 cups cooked rice, 1 cup goose liver or goose liver pâté cut in large dice, and 4 or 5 whole truffles (cut in two, if large). Add 1/2 cup thick chicken *velouté* or béchamel and 1 to 2 tablespoons beef extract. Correct the seasoning with salt and pepper.

Farce à la Derby

RICE AND TRUFFLE STUFFING

Mix together 4 cups cooked rice and 1/2 cup finely chopped peelings of truffle or chopped truffles that have been sautéed in a little butter. Add 1/2 cup thick chicken *velouté* or béchamel. Add 1 tablespoon beef extract and correct the seasoning. An appropriate sauce for the stuffed bird may be made in the roasting pan, using some of the truffle juice.

Farce à la Piémontaise

WILD RICE STUFFING I

Combine 2 to 3 cups cooked wild rice with 1/2 cup chicken livers sautéed in butter. Add 1/4 cup meat gravy or *velouté* to hold the mixture together.

Farce au Riz Sauvage I

WILD RICE STUFFING II

Sauté 3 tablespoons finely chopped onion in 3 tablespoons butter until it is soft but not brown. Add 1/2 cup thinly sliced mushrooms, and continue cooking until the mushrooms are soft. Toss with 3 cups cooked wild rice and add salt and pepper to taste. Particularly for duckling.

Farce au Riz Sauvage II

Farce aux
Marrons I

CUT into pieces 1 pound each of fresh lean pork and fresh fat pork and run them twice through the finest blade of the food chopper. Combine the ground pork and 1 pound shelled and cooked chestnuts and add 1 cup fresh bread crumbs, 1 teaspoon salt, 1/4 teaspoon Parisian spice or poultry seasoning, and 1/4 cup Cognac, Madeira, or Sherry.

Farce aux
Marrons II

HERE is my mother's stuffing for the Christmas goose.

Melt 3 tablespoons goose fat in a saucepan, add 2 tablespoons chopped onions, and cook until the onions are golden. Add the chopped goose liver, mix it well with the hot fat and onions, but do not cook it. Season with salt and pepper. Put 1/2 pound each of fresh lean pork and fresh fat pork through the food chopper or use 1 pound very lightly seasoned fresh sausage meat. Season the meat with 1/2 teaspoon salt mixed with a tiny pinch of poultry seasoning. Add either 3 tablespoons brandy or 1/2 cup Madeira or Sherry. Add the onion and liver mixture, 1 well-beaten egg, 2 to 3 dozen shelled and cooked chestnuts, depending on the size of the bird, and 1 teaspoon chopped parsley. Mix all together well.

Truffle Stuffings

IN FRANCE, during the months of *les grands dîners*—that is, " the season, " November, December, and January—nature brings to maturity some of her most succulent treasures. Three of them—birds, *foie gras*, and truffles—when properly combined produce the culinary masterpieces of the holidays, truffled birds.

Like the thought of many elegant dishes—now seen infrequently because they take so much time and skill to prepare—the mention of truffled birds carries me back to Paris. I was only sixteen and starting my first job at the Hôtel Bristol. I thought my rugged apprenticeship in Moulins had taught me every basic culinary skill, but I did not know how to use fresh truffles or how to prepare truffled birds. It was from

Monsieur Jules Tissier of the Bristol, a great chef, that I first learned these secrets. By the time I took over the kitchens of the Ritz-Carlton in New York, I was well versed in this art. During the holiday season, I followed the practice of the best Parisian restaurants. Just inside the entrance to the Oval Room a large buffet table was set up where the birds on which so much time and care had been lavished were displayed. There were the usual turkey and capon and game birds such as pheasant and partridge. Each had its traditional stuffing, and Madeira-steeped slices of truffle were tucked between the breast meat and the covering skin. The birds—uncooked, of course—were arranged on silver platters, each on its own tray of finely cracked ice. Guests who had spent holiday seasons in Paris were accustomed to this type of buffet and looked forward to selecting the bird they wished cooked. At the hour set, it would be served piping hot, to send forth at the first stroke of the carving knife the exciting aroma which is the great joy of every truffle-loving epicure.

The traditional truffle stuffing is made with fresh truffles, *foie gras*, the large white goose livers of France, special seasonings, brandy or Madeira or both, and pork fat. Butter is not used. But the pork fat must be that fine, delicate, sweet-flavored fat that surrounds the kidney of the hog. In France it is called *la panne*, but the American term by which it should be ordered is, I find, "the best pork leaf fat." There are certain possible modifications in this formula, of course. We can, for example, use canned truffles when the fresh ones are unobtainable, and *pâté de foie gras*, the fine goose liver paste that comes in crocks or tins, instead of fresh goose livers. Sherry may be substituted for Madeira. As the bird is turned in the roasting, it is laved inside by the fat, which at the same time carries the *parfum* of the truffles. The stuffing is really the truffles and goose liver, not the fat. A bird that is to be stuffed with truffles must be prepared in a special way.

Panne or Pork Leaf Fat

REMOVE all the pin feathers, taking care not to break the skin. When the head is cut off, the bird should have as much neck skin as possible left on. Slit the neck skin on the back of the bird far enough to cut out the neck and remove both neck and crop. Now, with a small sharp knife carefully take out the wishbone. Use this aperture to clean out the bird. Cut as small an opening as possible at the tail end to detach the intestinal

To Prepare Poultry for Truffle Stuffing

tract, and draw the whole insides out through the neck aperture. Make sure the bird is thoroughly drawn and then wipe the inside of it with damp cheesecloth.

Put the cold stuffing in the cavity, reserving about 2 cups for the crop. Carefully loosen the skin from the breast and slide in some of the sliced truffles that have been soaked in Madeira, arranging about 6 slices on each breast. Stuff the crop and slip in the remaining slices of truffles next to the skin and that stuffing. Bring the neck skin over the top of the bird to the back and sew it in place.

To Roast Truffled Birds

SPRINKLE the stuffed bird with a very, very little flour and cover the breast with thin slices of fat pork. Wrap in buttered or wax paper and tie up securely. Store the bird in the refrigerator for 24 hours, to allow the *parfum* of the truffles to permeate it. Remove from the refrigerator 1 or 2 hours before roasting and take off the paper. Place the bird on its side in a deep roasting pan, season with a little salt, and brush it with some good fat such as fresh goose, beef, or pork drippings. Sear the bird quickly on all sides in a hot oven (400° F.) and roast it for 1 hour, turning it from one side to the other every 15 minutes and basting frequently with the fat. Reduce the heat to moderately hot (375° F.) and continue roasting until the bird is done, turning it every 15 minutes and basting it. Allow 18 to 20 minutes per pound, weighing the bird after stuffing. Put the bird on its back for the last 15 minutes, so it will be golden brown. Remove the bird to a warm serving dish, skim the fat from the pan juices, add 1/2 cup water, and cook, stirring in all the brown crustiness clinging to the pan. Serve the pan juices with the bird, or serve *sauce périgourdine*, to which they have been added.

Farce Truffée I   FRESH TRUFFLE STUFFING

To Prepare Fresh Truffles

CLEAN truffles very thoroughly by brushing them well in water, changing the water several times until there is no soil left in the crevices of the skin. Peel the truffles very carefully, removing the rough skin by cutting it away in as thin a layer as possible. Reserve the peelings.

Remove the skin and membranes from 2 pounds best pork leaf fat. Add 1/2 pound goose liver or goose liver pâté. Add the truffle peelings and pound all together well or run through the finest blade of the food chopper. Season with 1/8 teaspoon Parisian spice or poultry seasoning mixed with 1 teaspoon salt. Rub the mixture through a fine sieve.

Put half of it into a heavy saucepan and let it melt very slowly over gentle heat. As soon as it is melted, add 6 whole truffles (cut in half, if large). Add a pinch of thyme and 1/2 bay leaf, finely crushed. Continue cooking the pork fat very gently so that it is kept white; it must not be allowed to turn yellow. Cook for 10 to 12 minutes and let cool. When it is cold, add the other half of the mixture. Add 1/4 cup good brandy and 1/2 cup good Madeira. Store the stuffing in the refrigerator or other very cold place for 24 hours; it must not be allowed to freeze, however. Slice 3 truffles thinly and sprinkle the slices with Madeira or Sherry. They will be used on the breast of the bird. Particularly for chicken, turkey, and game birds.

CANNED TRUFFLE STUFFING   *Farce Truffée II*

CANNED truffles come peeled and unpeeled. If they are unpeeled, peel them very carefully, removing the rough skin by cutting away as thin a peel as possible.

To Prepare
Canned Truffles

Follow the recipe for fresh truffle stuffing through the point at which the mixture is rubbed through a fine sieve. Do not divide or heat the mixture, but add 6 whole truffles (cut in half, if large), 1 pinch thyme and 1/2 bay leaf, finely crushed. Add the juice from the can of truffles, about 1/2 cup, and 1/4 cup each of good brandy and Madeira or Sherry. Store the stuffing in the refrigerator or other very cold place for 24 hours; it must not be allowed to freeze, however. Slice 3 truffles thinly and sprinkle the slices with Madeira or Sherry and a little truffle juice from the can. They will be used on the breast of the bird. Particularly for chicken, turkey, and game birds.

For those who prefer a stuffing less rich but with the same exquisite flavor as the traditional recipes, here is my own combination.

TRUFFLE STUFFING DIAT   *Farce Truffée à la Diat*

THIS will be sufficient for a 10- to 12-pound bird.

Remove the skin and membranes from 1 1/2 pounds best pork leaf fat. Add 1/4 pound each of lean veal, lean pork, and goose liver or pâté, and 1/4 cup finely chopped peelings from canned truffles. Put all together through the finest blade of the food chopper. Add 1/8 teaspoon Parisian spice or poultry seasoning, mixed with 1 teaspoon salt, a pinch of thyme, 1/2 bay leaf, finely crushed, 1/4 cup good brandy, 1/3 cup Madeira or Sherry, and 1/2 cup truffle juice from the can. Mix all together well and add 2 small eggs, slightly beaten. Mix together until well combined and add 6 whole truffles (cut in half, if large). Store the stuffing in the refrigerator or other very cold place for 24 hours; it must not be allowed to freeze, however. Slice 3 truffles thinly and sprinkle the slices with Madeira or Sherry and a little truffle juice from the can. They will be used on the breast of the bird. Particularly for chicken, turkey, and game birds.

Many people hate the bother of a dish that requires a day or two to mellow, as the conventional truffle stuffing does. Here is one which can be used right away, what we call a " warm " stuffing.

Farce Truffée III

WARM TRUFFLE STUFFING

REMOVE the skin and membranes from 2 pounds best pork leaf fat, chop it, and melt it carefully, but do not allow to cook. Then run it through a fine sieve. Peel 8 or 9 canned truffles, cutting off as thin a skin as possible. Chop the peelings very fine and add to the strained fat. Let it cool. Season with 1/8 teaspoon Parisian spice or poultry seasoning mixed with 1 teaspoon salt. Add 1/2 pound goose liver or goose liver pâté. Add 6 whole truffles (cut in half, if large), 1/4 cup each of brandy and Madeira or Sherry, and a little of the truffle juice from the can.

Chapon Truffé

ROAST TRUFFLED CAPON

PUT twice through the finest blade of the food chopper 3/4 pound each of fresh lean pork and fresh fat pork. Add 1 1/2 teaspoons salt mixed with 1/4 teaspoon Parisian spice or poultry seasoning, 2 truffles, finely chopped, 1/3 cup each of Cognac and Sherry, 3 tablespoons juice from the truffle can, and 2 beaten eggs.

Clean a tender 9- to 10-pound capon and loosely stuff the neck aperture with this truffle mixture. Carefully loosen the skin from the breast meat and the drumsticks, taking care not to break it. Slip a thin truffle slice under the skin on top of each drumstick, and arrange 12 truffle slices in 2 parallel rows down the breastbone. Fill the body cavity of the bird with the remaining stuffing, sew the vent, and truss the bird in the usual way. Tie a thin slice of fat pork over the breast, rub the exposed skin of the bird with goose or pork fat, and roast according to the directions for roasting truffled birds.

Stuffings

for

Meat

I N MY opinion, the two best stuffed-meat dishes are stuffed shoulder of lamb and *paupiettes* of veal. Traditional French favorites, both are braised and thrifty to serve because the meat goes much further when cooked this way. In preparing either one, be sure to use soft string to tie the meat and fasten the meat securely enough so that the stuffing will remain in place as it cooks. Stuffed shoulder of lamb has been included in the section on braising.

VEAL BIRDS WITH FORCEMEAT STUFFING

MIX together 2/3 cup boiling water and 2 tablespoons butter, add 1/4 cup flour and cook the mixture, stirring constantly, until it is smooth and rolls away from sides of pan. Remove the pan from the heat and beat in 2 small eggs, one at a time. Spread the *pâte à chou* on a buttered plate to cool. Remove the sinews from 1/2 pound lean veal, run the meat

Paupiettes
de Veau
Bourbonnaise

twice through the finest blade of the food chopper, and add 1/2 teaspoon salt, a little white pepper, and a few grains of nutmeg. Combine the veal with the *pâte à chou* and add 1/2 cup soft butter, 1 egg, and 2 egg yolks. Clean and chop very fine 1/4 pound mushrooms, add 1 tablespoon finely chopped shallot or onion, and sauté the mixture slowly in 1 tablespoon butter until all moisture is cooked away. Add 1/4 teaspoon salt and 1 teaspoon chopped parsley. Let the mushrooms cool and add them to the forcemeat.

Have the butcher flatten eight 1/4-inch-thick slices rump of veal, each weighing about 1/4 pound. Spread each slice with forcemeat stuffing, keeping it well within the edges. Roll up each slice, wrap around each roll a thin slice of fresh fat pork, and tie the rolls with string, winding the string from end to end. Spread 1 tablespoon butter in a casserole, add 1 carrot and 1 onion, both sliced, and place the rolls side by side on top of the vegetables. Add 3/4 cup white wine and a faggot made by tying together 1 stalk of celery, 3 sprigs of parsley, 1/2 bay leaf, and a little thyme, and cook the veal until the liquid is reduced to almost nothing. Add 3 cups white stock and bring it to a boil. Cover the rolls with a circle of buttered paper with a small hole in the center to vent the steam. Cover the casserole. Braise the veal in a moderately hot oven (375° F.) for 1 1/2 hours, basting occasionally. Remove the strings and pork from the rolls and continue cooking them until they are well browned. Transfer the rolls to a serving dish, reduce the sauce to about 1 cup, and strain it over them.

Poitrine de Veau Farcie à la Florentine

BREAST OF VEAL STUFFED WITH SPINACH

HAVE the butcher cut a pocket in a breast of veal.

Clean 2 pounds spinach, parboil it in salted water for 10 minutes, drain it well, and chop it coarsely. Sauté 1 medium onion, finely chopped, in 2 tablespoons butter until it is soft but not brown. Add the spinach, season with salt and pepper, and cook, stirring, until the water is cooked out of the spinach. Measure the spinach and combine with an equal quantity of fresh bread crumbs. Stuff the pocket of the veal and sew the edges of the pocket together. Cover the bottom of a casserole with chopped carrots and onions mixed with 1 tablespoon butter. Put the veal on the vegetables and cook in a moderate oven (350° F.) about 2 hours, or until the meat is tender. Add a little hot water to the casserole occasionally to prevent scorching and baste the meat frequently. Remove the veal to a warm serving dish. Add to the juices 2 teaspoons cornstarch mixed with 2 tablespoons Sherry and cook until the liquid has thickened a little. Strain the gravy over the meat. To serve, cut veal and stuffing in slices.

Stuffings for Fish

I HAVE found stuffed fish to be less common in France than in England and America, possibly because stuffed fish are usually baked and the French often avoid baking to conserve fuel. This frugality in cooking applies especially to foods like fish that lend themselves so well to poaching or braising. Large fish are usually selected, and they are stuffed with the English type of bread-crumb mixture, seasoned with onions and parsley rather than poultry seasoning. After the fish has been cleaned, cut it back toward the tail far enough and deep enough to make a pocket for the stuffing. If desired, you may open the fish wide enough to remove the bone, cutting it away from the flesh with a small sharp knife. In the recipe for trout *bourbonnaise*, in the section on poaching fish, fish mousse is combined with mushroom *duxelles* for a stuffing. It may also be combined with artichoke purée and such a stuffing can be spread on fish filets, which are then rolled and poached.

TROUT STUFFED WITH DUXELLES

Truite à la Mellecey

FOR each serving, allow a 3/4-pound trout. Clean the trout and cut back from the opening just far enough to make a small slit. Using the forefinger, work in and around the backbone, loosening it completely from the flesh, and pull it out in one piece. Fill the cavity with mushroom *duxelles* made with 1/2 pound mushrooms. In a shallow pan, melt 2 tablespoons butter, add 2 tablespoons chopped shallots or onion, and arrange the trout side by side in the pan. Add white wine and water in equal amounts to just cover the fish. Bring the liquid to a boil, cover the pan, and simmer the trout for 18 minutes, or until they are done. Transfer the trout to a platter, remove the skin, and cut away the tails. Keep the trout warm. Reduce the cooking liquid to about 1 cup, add 1/4 cup heavy cream, and correct the seasoning with salt. Bring the sauce back to the boil and thicken it with *beurre manié* made by creaming 1 tablespoon butter with 1/2 tablespoon flour, and pour it over the trout.

CARP STUFFED WITH BREAD CRUMBS AND ROE

Carpe Farcie à la Charolaise

SCALE and clean 2 carp, each weighing from 2 to 2 1/4 pounds, reserving the roe.

Soak 2 cups fresh bread crumbs in a little milk, then press out most of the liquid. Sauté 1 teaspoon finely chopped shallots in 1 tablespoon butter until the shallots are soft but not brown. Press the roe through a fine sieve. Combine the bread crumbs, the shallots and the butter in which they were cooked, and the roe. Add 1 teaspoon each of chopped chives and parsley. Mix thoroughly and stir in 1 tablespoon melted butter, 1 egg and 1 egg yolk, beaten with 1/2 teaspoon salt, a little pepper, and a dash of freshly grated nutmeg. Stuff the fish and sew up the openings.

In the bottom of a deep oval fish pan, place 1 onion and 1 carrot, both sliced, 2 or 3 sprigs of parsley, 1 small bay leaf, a little thyme, and 1 clove of garlic. Season the fish with salt and pepper, put them in the pan, and pour over them 2 cups red wine. Bring the wine to a boil, cover the fish with a piece of buttered paper, cut to fit the pan, with a small hole in the center and cover the pan. Cook the fish over very low heat or in a hot oven (425° F.) for 25 to 30 minutes, or until they are done. Place the fish on a warm serving platter and remove the skin. Garnish the platter with sautéed mushrooms, crisp bacon, and small glazed onions. Strain the liquid from the fish pan, bring it to a boil, and thicken it with *beurre manié* made by creaming together 2 tablespoons butter and 1 tablespoon flour. Correct the seasoning with salt and pour the sauce over the fish and garnishing.

LE BON TRANCHEUR

Carving: Meat, Poultry, Fish

EVERY HOME should have its *trancheur*, some member of the family who takes a real interest and pride in carving. And as it is traditionally a man's job, I think that the education of young men in the home should be considered incomplete if it does not include this fine and ancient art. Boys should be taught by the father to handle the carving tools as soon as they are old enough to be interested, and the earlier the better.

When I was a boy at home I was eager to learn to carve, especially after I decided I wanted to train to be a chef. But, because I was left-handed, I was not permitted to handle the knives. In France there was a kind of old-wives' tale that a left-handed carver always cuts himself. Of course, it isn't true, and we left-handers could say the same about right-handed people. As a matter of fact, I became ambidextrous, to get around the problem.

One of my uncles was sympathetic to my interest, and he gave me my first lessons. He helped *grand-père* run the farm and he was an excellent carver, perhaps because he knew the anatomy of birds and animals, but more likely because he took such great pride in his skill. I always asked to sit next to him at our big family dinners, because as I watched him officiate he would explain what he was doing and why.

In any great hotel of prewar Europe the post of *trancheur* was an important one in the dining room. As a matter of fact every thoroughly trained hotel manager who had any professional stature at all was always a good *trancheur*. He could on occasion, when the dinner hour was very busy or when very, very distinguished guests were dining, pick up the right knife, lift the huge silver cover of the *tortue*, and do a perfect job of carving and slicing—and do it so quickly and with such skill that the eyes of an admiring audience would follow his movements. It saddens me to think that tableside carving is becoming an almost lost art. It seems to me that it was a true part of gracious dining. Watching a skillful carver is both pleasant and provoking to the appetite. In the early days of the old New York Ritz all the carving was done in the dining room in front of the guests. Sometimes one of them would even ask to take over the knife.

In some homes the carving is done in the kitchen and the food arranged on a platter to be brought to the table. The only advantage in this —except for saving embarrassment if the carver is awkward—is that you can have a big board to work on. But the advantages of carving in the dining room are many. In the first place, your *pièce de résistance* looks so much more important when it appears whole before your guests. Then the food itself is served with the heat of the oven still in it, each piece obviously juicy and succulent. Finally, the host gets a chance to show off his skill and has the pleasure of being rewarded by the compliments of his guests. And remember, good carving gives more servings, the servings look better and therefore taste better. Things to be considered, *n'est-ce pas?* Now, to be proficient in carving you must have good

Carving Tools

tools: the best knives obtainable, a good hard steel for whetting them, and a strong two-tined fork with a finger guard. A single carving set is not enough. You need more than one knife; you should, in fact, have two or more, in different lengths, and a round-ended slicer. For fish, most experts like a silver knife and fork, believing that steel used on fish is apt to impair the delicate flavor, and furthermore the sharp edge of a steel knife is not needed to cut fish.

For a really fine job of slicing roast beef and *boeuf à la mode*, or for ham or even the breasts of very large turkeys, the correct knife is called professionally a *tranche-lard*, a long, thin, flexible knife with a rounded or pointed end. It cuts easily through meat and makes possible slices of even thickness, as thin or as thick as you like. The *tranche-lard* is named for the flexible blade used in cutting narrow strips of fat pork for larding beef cuts and game. In French *tranche* means a slice, *lard* means pork fat; together the words mean pork-fat slicer. In restaurants these knives often have blades as long as 14 inches, but for the home this is neither necessary nor practical. I'd say even 12 inches is too long for easy handling and storing. Ten and a half inches, which, with the handle, makes a knife about 15 inches long, is a good size for home use. This isn't a wide-bladed knife; in fact it is only about 1 1/4 inches wide. There is another good slicer that is shorter and wider. The whole knife, including the handle, is 12 1/2 inches long and the blade 1 1/2 inches wide. These flexible slicers are to be used when you want to curve the cut surface gradually as you work along the bone of a ham or a leg of lamb, to make all the slices the same generous size. Flexible Knife or Tranche-Lard

For carving birds (except for slicing the breasts of large ones) and for smaller pieces of meat such as loin of pork and rack of lamb, firmer and shorter knives than the *tranche-lard* are used. They have strong 4- to 5-inch handles and similarly shaped blades of different lengths. The backs and the cutting edges of the blades curve slightly to a V-shaped point. With these firm knives and their sharp, pointed blades, you can work easily in places near bones. In short, the general rule of expert carvers is to use long flexible knives for slicing and shorter ones with firmer blades for such things as cutting off the legs and wings of chickens, separating the chops of loins of pork, roasts of lamb, and crown roasts, and for carving steaks. Firm Knives

Three sizes in the firm-knife group will take care of most needs. A large one with a blade never less than 8 1/2 inches long and 1 3/4 inches wide, called a butcher's knife, does heavy work such as cutting through a lobster or the bones of a large uncooked fish, like salmon, to make steaks. Sometimes the blade is placed where the cut is to be made and a wooden mallet used to drive it through the shell or bone. Large

One of medium size with a blade about 5 1/2 inches long and 1 1/2 inches wide, called a French chef's knife, is a better size for cutting up Medium chickens, small game birds, and carving a porterhouse steak.

Small A smaller size with a blade about 4 1/2 inches long, called a trimming knife, is used for cutting off untidy looking edges and fatty portions and for shaping pieces of meat and fish into suitable serving pieces, for doing, in fact, what the name says—trimming.

Those who carve well enough to be *les bons trancheurs* often prefer to use these kitchen knives when carving at the dining table. However, the fine carving sets of matching knife, fork, and sharpening steel are more often seen in the dining room. These sets can be bought in various sizes, with knives designed for many purposes.

"A good workman is known by his tools." I learned that also from my uncle in my early years. Whether it was the scythe he used in the fields or the knives to carve a holiday goose, he gave them the same loving care. A good workman really loves his tools. He loves to run his fingers carefully over the edge of a cutting tool, feeling the smooth, firm line of the edge, searching for any small roughness that may have been left after the final run-over of the whetting stone or steel.

Care of Knives So if you are to be the *trancheur* in your home, look to your tools. In selecting knives your first consideration must be to get good steel that will sharpen well and hold its edge. This is more important than any other thing about a knife. Once you have invested in good knives, take good care of them. Have them sharpened fairly regularly by a professional knife sharpener—how often depends upon how much you use them. In addition to this, you must keep after them constantly with your own sharpening steel. No chef or butcher could manage without this round, poker-like tool. Always the blade is passed over it before the first cut. The expression is "to whet your knife," *aiguiser le couteau*. Remember, you can never have a knife too sharp. The sharper the blade the better the job, and there's less chance of cutting yourself because you won't have to force the knife and perhaps have it slip and cut you. You should be able to cut exactly where you want to, and stop exactly where you want to.

Storing Knives When storing knives, clean them thoroughly, of course, and then dry them well. If they are not used often, it is wise to rub the blades with a little salad oil. Keep them in a dry place, propped in a drawer with the sharp edges of the blades down for safety, or hanging on a special board.

Boards and Platters A word or two should be said about boards and platters. There is a saying that a good carver never scratches the platter. But this is pretty difficult when cutting through a rack of lamb or carving a small bird. Of course the best surface is a flat board with no edge to get in the way; if you do your carving in the kitchen, I advise using a board. Transfer the slices or pieces of meat to a hot platter and garnish the platter with greens or vegetables. At table, you will probably always use a platter. For meats that are to be sliced in a horizontal direction, like roast beef, use either china or silver. With roast pork loins and steaks, a silver platter is soon badly scratched. The platter must be large enough so the bird or meat can be moved around as you work, and it should have no garnish to get in your way.

Always warm the platter on which the food is to be placed and the plates on which it is to be served. Time roasting to allow 15 to 20 minutes for the meat to stand after it is out of the oven and before it is carved. This allows it to *reposer*, or rest, during which time the juices settle back into the tissues. You will find that the slices of meat will be more succulent, especially if the meat has been roasted to the rare stage, because less juice will run out on the platter when the meat is cut. Always spoon some of the juice from the platter onto the slices.

Letting Roast Meat Rest or Reposer

Common sense will tell you how to carve or slice many kinds of meat, poultry, and fish. The directions below describe the more difficult carving jobs, or the most basic.

Carving Meat

SET the roast on the platter with a flat, meaty side on the dish: Do not allow it to rest on the bone ends as it did in the oven. The bony side should be on the left and toward you, the rounded, meaty side toward

Carving Rib Roast of Beef

the right. The carving fork with its finger guard should be inserted at an angle in the roast about 1 inch below the top, where you will be slicing. The guard—a prong about 1 1/2 inches long—will then rest on the top of the meat and really "guard" the hand holding the fork. Using a long flexible knife, or *tranche-lard*, slice horizontally across the top from the outside edge toward the bone. Cut with long even strokes to give slices of meat as wide as the roast, curving the knife upwards to cut the slice away from the bone. The thickness of the slice depends upon individual preference. Some people, the English for example, prefer two thin slices to one thick one, slices that are sometimes no thicker than 1/8 inch. Americans are apt to ask for one good thick slice. Those who prefer well-done beef are served the first slices. As soon as enough slices have been removed to expose it, cut away the first bone, lay it on the side of the platter, and start slicing against the next bone.

Carving Boeuf à la Mode or Pot Roast

Boeuf à la mode, or pot roast, is usually sliced on a board in the kitchen. Even the best carver finds it hard to slice this cut after it has been put on the platter with the garnishing vegetables around it. Place the largest side down on the board and cut vertically with a flexible knife from top to bottom—as many slices as needed, as thick or thin as desired. Arrange the slices, with or without the uncut portion, on the serving platter and place carrots, onions, potatoes, and parsley garniture around the meat.

Carving Whole Filet of Beef

Place the filet on a board and, using a medium-sized, firm knife, cut vertically against the grain in slices 1/4 to 1/2 inch thick. Serve 2 slices to each person.

It is possible to carve a steak into neat, attractive slices and leave hardly a scrap of meat on the bones.

For a steak 2 1/2 to 3 inches thick, using a medium-sized, firm knife, cut diagonally across the grain, slanting the knife to make a larger surface on each slice. Cut the slices 1/2 to 3/4 inch thick.

Carving Sirloin Steak

Using the point of a medium-sized, firm knife, detach the meat from the bone to release both the sirloin section and the tenderloin section. Cut each section into pieces about 1 inch wide, or more. Serve a piece of each section to each person.

Carving Porterhouse Steak

This piece, often served as London broil, is not more than 1 1/2 inches thick, so place it flat on the board. Using a flexible knife, cut diagonally across the grain, slanting the knife to make a larger surface on each slice. Cut the slices rather thin, because this is not the most tender cut of beef. Overlap the slices on the platter, allowing several for each serving.

Carving Flank Steak

If the steak is 1 to 1 1/2 inches thick and has been broiled or sautéed, with a firm knife cut across the steak to make pieces about 2 inches wide. If the steak is 2 or more inches thick and has been braised, cut diagonally across the grain, slanting the knife to make a larger surface on each slice. Make the slices 3/4 to 1 inch thick.

Carving Round Steak

Place the roast on the platter thick side up. Using a long carving knife or *tranche-lard*, start cutting at the shank end. Make the first cut about 1 1/2 inches from where the meat starts on the bone and cut out a tiny, curved chunk. Slice the meat parallel to this cut, using a curving stroke and working up the leg to make increasingly large slices that are thin and rounded. When the thick side is sliced, turn the leg over and slice the meat of the other side parallel to the bone.

Carving Roast Leg of Lamb or Venison

Place the meat on the platter so that the cross piece of the T-bone rests horizontally on the dish and the stem of the T points up vertically. Using the point of a firm knife, make a long cut from the top of the saddle down its entire length, loosening the meat from the bone. Then, using a long, flexible knife, or *tranche-lard*, cut 10 or 12 very thin slices with the grain

Carving Saddle of Lamb or Venison

of the meat the entire length of the saddle on one side, parallel to the backbone. Use one long stroke for each slice. Cut the first slice at the edge of the saddle and move inward toward the bone. Turn the platter and repeat on the other side of the backbone. Serve 2 or 3 slices to each person. The saddle should never be sliced against the grain.

Carving Rack of Lamb or Veal

PLACE the rack on the platter with the ends of the rib bones standing up. Using a large, firm knife, cut down vertically between the bones, carving the rack into pieces either one or two chops thick.

Carving Crown Roast of Lamb or Pork

IF THE center of the roast is filled with vegetables that will roll—onions, carrots, potato balls, peas—the carver should have a vegetable dish at hand to remove them to. Stuffings or mashed vegetables will not hamper the carver. Using a firm knife cut down vertically between the ribs and remove the chops one at a time.

Carving Shoulder of Lamb or Pork

THE best meat lies between the shoulder bone and the flat bone adjoining it. Using a firm knife cut diagonally from the top to the V made by the bony structure. When this section has been sliced, grasp the bone with a napkin and turn over the shoulder. Cut slices horizontally from the bottom part.

Carving Loin of Pork

HAVE the butcher detach the backbone by sawing it parallel to the base across the length of the ribs, but leave it tied in place during roasting. To carve, remove strings and backbone and place the roast on a board or platter with the rib ends up, the concave rib side toward the carver, the meaty side toward the guests at the table. Using a firm knife cut down vertically between the ribs, working from right to left. If thin pieces are desired cut one with a rib bone in it, the next without a bone.

Carving Smoked Ox Tongue

IN THE kitchen remove the skin from the tongue and cut away the root, which is tough and has a number of tiny bones in it. Then, using a medium-sized firm knife, start at the tip end of the tongue and cut it diagonally into thin slices 1/8 to 1/4 inch thick.

316

Carving
Ham

Lay the ham on a platter or carving board, thick side up. Ham is slippery, and a pronged base to keep it steady is a great help. With a short firm knife, trim off the surplus fat and any remaining skin. Save the fat to spread over the exposed surface of the ham and keep the meat from drying out after the carving.

Holding the shank bone in your left hand and using a long flexible knife, or *tranche-lard*, cut into the meat about 4 inches from the spot where the skin ends on the shank. Remove a 3-inch piece of meat, curving it out to within 1 inch of where the skin ends on the shank. The piece that comes out should be curved on the cut side, leaving a concave surface where it is removed. Following this curve, slice off thin pieces and work up the ham evenly and neatly. The meat becomes wider as you continue up the ham and the slices will, therefore, be larger. They will have a curved appearance as you cut them, but will flatten out as you lay them on the plate. Two or three thin slices are more desirable than one thick one. The underside can be carved parallel to the bone, like a leg of lamb. The remainder of the meat and the chunk cut away at the beginning should be used for julienne of ham for salads or for any dish in which chopped ham is used.

Carving Poultry

To really show off your skill as a *trancheur* there is nothing, I suppose, that quite does the trick like carving a bird, especially a big one with a large breast from which you can slice off slim, well-shaped pieces and establish your prowess. You will find your carving of birds will be easier and better if you study their anatomy. A really skillful carver can locate the joints instantly and never needs to fumble or hack at the bird to find where the bones come together in order to slip in his knife to cut the connecting cartilage.

Carving
Roast Chicken

USING a small firm knife, remove the wishbone by inserting the knife point at the center of the breast and, following the edges of the bones, cut toward the two ends, then pull the wishbone out. (This is usually done in the kitchen.) To carve use a medium-sized firm knife. First turn the bird on its left side and remove the right leg along with the second joint. Next cut off the wing, cutting along with the wing about one-half of the breast lying next to it. Then cut the remainder of the breast from the breastbone. Place the cut pieces on the platter or another plate. Now turn the chicken over to rest on the side that has been cut away and repeat the same procedure on the left side. Cut through the joints between the legs and second joints to separate them. There will be: 4 pieces of dark meat (2 legs and 2 second joints), 4 pieces of white meat (2 wings with part of the breast on each one and 2 pieces of breast). Serve each person a piece of dark meat and a piece of white unless someone prefers just one kind. The breast of a very large chicken may be cut parallel to the skin into 2 or 3 slices, or crosswise against the grain of the meat. The legs and second joints of a large chicken may be cut parallel to the skin into 2 to 4 pieces.

Carving Small
Roast Chicken
for Two

CUT OFF both legs with their second joints, then cut off each wing and the breast next to it, also in one piece. This will serve 2 people, giving each one 2 sections—a leg with a second joint, and a wing and half a breast. Or you can cut through the chicken lengthwise and serve one-half to each person. The first method, however, makes it easier for the guest to eat the chicken and presents a more handsome serving.

Carving Turkey
or Capon

TURN the bird onto its left side so that it rests on the left leg, which forms a natural support and makes your work easier. Using a medium-sized firm knife, remove the right leg with its second joint and lay it on the side of the platter or on another plate. Remove the wing, but just the end of it, however. The section nearest the breast is left on to be sliced with the breast. Using the point of the knife, make an opening where the second joint was removed that is large enough to put in a spoon to get out the stuffing. Now change to the long flexible knife, or *tranche-lard*, and start slicing the breast, cutting parallel to the skin in large, thin slices. With the firm knife cut off what remains of the wing. Cutting parallel to the skin, cut meat from the leg into 2 to 4 pieces and from the second joint into 4 to 6 pieces, depending upon the size of the bird. Turn the bird over and repeat on the other side. Serve some white and some dark meat and stuffing to each person. Cut only as much as you need, as the meat not served is less dry if left on the bones.

FOLLOWING the directions for roast chicken, remove the wishbone with a small firm knife. Change to a medium-sized firm knife and cut off the 2 legs along with the second joints. Make an incision, cutting in vertically, along the middle of the breastbone and detaching the meat from it. Then slice the 2 breast sections parallel to the skin. Cut into the meat of the wing at the same time to make long, thin slices which the French call *aiguillettes*. You may cut from the breastbone out, or cut toward the breastbone, making the first slice hardly more than an inch wide. Cut the leg and second joint apart to make 2 pieces or cut the second joint in 2 pieces, which with the leg makes 3 pieces in all. (In this case the bone can be removed.) — Carving Roast Duck

GOOSE may be carved in two ways: After removing the leg and second joint, carve it like a duck or like a turkey. The second way is usually followed for a large, very tender bird. Then slice the meat on the leg and second joint, removing the bones. Slices of breast, leg, and second joint—and also a piece of the crispy skin—are served to each person. The goose is all dark meat. — Carving Roast Goose

BECAUSE the legs of these birds are apt to be tough, they are not usually served. Cut them off and put aside for making *salmis*, a kind of stew or fricassee. Detach the wings, cutting half the breast with each wing as in carving a chicken. Cut the remainder of each breast in 2 slices unless the bird is small, in which case cut the remainder of each breast in one slice. Serves 1 or 2 people, depending on the size of the bird. — Carving Roast Guinea Hen or Pheasant

Serving Fish

Boning Small Sautéed or Poached Fish

SPLIT small whole fish down the back, sliding the knife along the upper side of the backbone. Turn back the flesh, remove the bone, and replace the flesh. Usually, this task is left to the guest. In restaurants, the waiter does it.

Serving Medium-Sized Baked or Poached Fish

BEFORE bringing the fish to the table, place it on a serving platter and remove the upper skin. Cut across the fish every 2 1/2 to 3 inches, as deep as the top of the backbone. Lift off a piece for each serving. Remove the backbone and place on the side of the platter. Then cut across the lower half every 2 1/2 to 3 inches. Never try to slice through the bone.

Serving Very Large Baked or Boiled Fish

THE FISH is usually salmon. It may be hot or cold. If you attempt to slice straight down through fish and bone, as you do when slicing uncooked fish, the fish will break apart unattractively. Place the drained fish on a large fish platter and carefully remove the skin and the dark flesh that lies under the skin. (This flesh is edible, but rich and oily, and usually indigestible.) Dip a thin sharp knife into warm water. Cut down the center from head to tail as deep as the backbone. Then, holding the knife parallel to the platter, slit the fish from edge to center just above the bones, to detach the flesh from them. Turn the platter around and repeat. The flesh thus loosened should lie in place and not be the least disarranged. On each side of the center cut, cut through the top half of the fish just down to the bone, making pieces about 2 1/2 inches wide. Lift off each piece as you cut it onto the plate that you are serving. When the whole top part has been served, lift off and set aside the bones. Cut and serve the bottom section the same way, but slip the knife between the skin and flesh as each piece is removed. Other very large fish may be served in this way.

LÉGUMES

Vegetables

No FRENCHMAN ever looks on vegetables with scorn—not on any
kind, whether simple carrots and spinach or the more elegant
mushrooms and artichokes. Believing that his countrymen grow the
best vegetables in the world, he treats them with due respect and, except
for potatoes, serves them on a separate plate as a separate course. Why?
Because this way, one gets the full enjoyment of the vegetable and of the
good cooking. Even vegetables cooked in a stew get special attention.
They are never all dropped in at once. *Mais non.* Those requiring the
longest cooking go in before those requiring less.

I remember how horrified I was, in my early days at the Ritz-Carlton in New York, to see the hodgepodge of peas—some small, some

grown tough and coarse—that I was expected to serve as *petits pois*. We quickly found a solution to that problem: we simply shook the peas through a coarse sieve, and the big ones were screened out for use in soups and purées. And we solved other vegetable problems as well; the cooks separated the tender young *haricots verts* from large pods in which the beans had already formed, and they sculptured uniform plump little carrots from those of various sizes and shapes that were delivered to us.

Eventually I found market gardeners who could supply us with young and tender vegetables, fresh herbs even in winter, early tomatoes, and hothouse melons. Most of these accommodating suppliers were retired chefs who understood a colleague's difficulties in those days before airplane transportation made out-of-season delicacies a commonplace.

The French use vegetables in many ways: in salads and aspics, as hors-d'oeuvre, as garnish, but the most important way—and the first I wish to discuss—is as a hot dish. You will notice that the vegetable recipes that follow are not arranged in the usual alphabetical order, but rather in the order in which I learned to cook them, and in which I taught hundreds of apprentice chefs to cook them, either according to type—all the root vegetables being treated together, for instance—or according to season or method of preparation.

It is not easy to give exact cooking times for vegetables because so many factors enter in: freshness, size, age, variety, season, and so on. You will learn to judge approximate times by experience. When vegetables can be easily pierced with a sharp knife or fork, they are tender and done.

Potatoes

IN THE toast, "*Vive la France et les pommes de terre frites*" the world recognizes the love my countrymen have for this, their favorite vegetable.

Deep-fried they really are, *pommes frites* the French call them, but else-where French fried is the name they go by—and the word " French " is never omitted.

The French cuisine without potatoes is unthinkable. Yet until the late 1700's, the government labeled them " dangerous to eat ." Parmentier, an eighteenth-century Parisian chemist who lived in a German prison camp on little but potatoes for five long years first realized that they could very well solve France's recurring famine problem, when crop failures made grain for bread almost unobtainable. He introduced the plants at the French court—not for food, *mais non*, but as an attractive vine for gardens and table decorations. Then he grew potatoes in Paris, where everyone could see them, and believing that forbidden fruit is the most desirable, he had them carefully guarded by the *gardes-françaises* by day but unwatched by night. The fence-jumpers were numerous. His subsequent well-publicized experiments in cooking and eating this new food started a trend. France pays tribute to Parmentier by calling dishes characterized by potatoes " Parmentier ."

In my youth the first potatoes of the year were dug on St. John's day and called *pommes de terre Saint-Jean*. They were about the size of pigeon eggs, and so thin-skinned that we had only to shake them in a burlap bag with crude salt to rub the skins off. Then we washed them, dried them, and cooked them in butter until they were crusty brown and tender. Finally we sprinkled them with plenty of chopped parsley. For stews, however, we preferred small potatoes with yellowish skins that held their shape in cooking, and there were still other types for frying, baking, and other uses. In this country, I have used the pinkish early Bermudas and Floridas in season, then California, Virginia, and Long Island varieties as they came to market. In winter, I have found that potatoes from Maine and Canada keep best, and I prefer Idaho potatoes for baking.

BAKED POTATOES

Pommes de Terre au Four

SCRUB uniform potatoes well, so that the skin may be enjoyed, and bake them in a hot oven (400-425° F.) for about 1 hour, depending upon their size. Pierce the potatoes with a fork to test them for doneness, remove them from the oven, and pierce them again. Cut a small cross in the top. This procedure prevents steam from condensing inside the skin and making the potato moist and soggy instead of dry and mealy. Press gently to open the cut and put a pat of butter into the opening.

Baked potatoes have other uses in the French kitchen. The pulp can be removed from the skin, mashed, seasoned, and returned to the skin to heat and brown in the oven. Potatoes prepared in this way make a vegetable course or even a main course at luncheon or dinner.

Pommes de Terre Suzette

POTATOES WITH PARMESAN

BAKE 1 large potato for each serving. When the potatoes are done cut an opening in the top of each large enough so that the pulp can be removed with a spoon. Rub all the pulp through a sieve or food mill or crush it with a fork. For each potato, add 2 tablespoons cream and 1 egg yolk to the pulp, and season with salt. Replace the potato pulp in the shells. Sprinkle the tops with grated Parmesan cheese and brown in a hot oven (400° F.) or under the broiler.

Pommes de Terre Nouvelles

NEW POTATOES

RUB the skin off 2 pounds or about 18 tiny new potatoes and parboil them in salted water to cover for 2 or 3 minutes. Drain them well. For each cup of potatoes melt 2 tablespoons good fat (preferably goose or beef, not chicken) in a pan. When it is quite hot, add the potatoes, and cook them until they are tender and golden brown all over. Drain them and pour off the fat from the pan. Return the potatoes, add 1 tablespoon butter for each cup of potatoes, and cook them, rolling them in the butter as it melts until they are completely coated. Season with a little salt and sprinkle with finely chopped parsley. Butter may be used for cooking instead of goose or beef fat, but it must be clarified or the potatoes will stick to the pan and break.

Pommes de Terre Macaire

BAKED POTATO MOLD

BAKE 6 potatoes. Remove the pulp, mash it with 2 tablespoons butter, and season it with a little salt and pepper. Butter the bottom and sides of a round mold generously and pack the potatoes in it. Spread butter on the top and bake the potatoes in a hot oven (400° F.) until they are golden brown. Unmold on the serving dish.

GLAZED BAKED POTATO MOLD

PREPARE *pommes de terre Macaire*. Unmold them on a heatproof serving dish, spread 2 to 3 tablespoons whipped cream over the top, and glaze in a hot broiler.

Pommes de Terre Byron

BOILED POTATOES

BOIL potatoes in their skins or peeled, as preferred, in salted water to cover. The time depends upon the size of the potatoes. Test them with a fork to ascertain doneness. Drain the potatoes at once and shake the pan over low heat for a few minutes, or put it in a moderate oven (350° F.), until all the surplus moisture has evaporated and the potatoes are quite dry.

Pommes de Terre Bouillies

BAKED POTATO CROQUETTES

CUT 2 pounds or 6 to 8 medium potatoes, peeled, into pieces and boil them in salted water to cover until they are soft. Drain them and shake the pan over low heat for a few minutes to dry them. Force them through a sieve into a hot saucepan and work the mixture with a wooden spoon until it is smooth. Add 2 tablespoons butter, 1/2 teaspoon salt, and a little white pepper. Mix together and shape the mixture into rolls or oblongs like croquettes. Roll them in a little flour. Melt 2 or 3 tablespoons butter in a shallow baking pan, arrange the croquettes in it, and bake them in a hot oven (425° F.) until they are browned on both sides, turning them once.

Pommes de Terre Fondantes

POTATOES HASHED IN CREAM

BOIL 2 pounds or 6 to 8 medium potatoes in their skins in salted water until they are just tender. Drain them and cool. Peel them and cut into 1/4-inch slices or 1/2-inch dice. Put them in a saucepan with just

Pommes de Terre à la Crème

enough hot rich milk or light cream barely to cover. Add 1/4 teaspoon salt, a little white pepper, and a little nutmeg. Simmer the potatoes until the milk or cream is reduced to about 1/2 the original quantity, shaking the pan frequently to keep them from sticking. Add 2 tablespoons butter, swirling it in as it melts to combine it with the milk to make a sauce. If desired, a little heavy cream may be added to make the sauce richer. Correct the seasoning with salt. Avoid stirring the potatoes with a spoon; it tends to mash them.

Pommes de Terre Lyonnaise

SAUTÉED POTATOES AND ONIONS

PEEL and slice enough boiled potatoes to make 3 cups and sauté the slices slowly in 6 tablespoons butter until they are golden brown on both sides. Remove them from the pan. Sauté 1 small onion, thinly sliced, in the butter in the pan, until it is golden brown. Return the potatoes to the pan and cook all together, shaking the pan, until the potatoes are hot. Sprinkle with finely chopped parsley.

Many people cook potatoes that are to be mashed too long, thinking the potatoes will be creamy. Overcooking actually makes the potatoes water-soaked and flavorless. They should break under the pressure of a fork, but not be mushy. Half an onion, cooked in the pot with each pound of potatoes, gives an interesting flavor.

Purée de Pommes de Terre

MASHED POTATOES

BOIL peeled potatoes, with half an onion, if desired, in salted water to cover until they are tender and break when they are pierced with a fork. Allow 1 good-sized potato for each portion. Drain the potatoes and shake the pan over low heat for a few minutes, or put it in a moderate oven (350° F.), until all the surplus moisture has evaporated and the potatoes are quite dry. Put them through a food mill or sieve. Return the pan to the stove and over low heat work the potatoes with a wooden spoon until they are very smooth. For 6 medium potatoes, add 2 tablespoons butter and work in gradually from 1/2 to 1 cup hot milk to reach the desired consistency. Tastes vary, and the mashed potatoes may be made fairly firm or quite soft. Adjust the seasoning with salt and white pepper.

Duchess potatoes are mashed potatoes, but egg takes the place of milk in them so that they will hold their shape when they are piped through a pastry tube and browned in the oven or under the broiler as a garnish for meat and fish platters.

DUCHESS POTATOES

Pommes de Terre Duchesse

CUT 2 pounds or 6 to 8 medium potatoes, peeled, into pieces and boil them in salted water to cover until they are soft. Drain them and shake the pan over low heat for a few minutes to dry them. Force them through a sieve into a hot saucepan and work the mixture with a wooden spoon until it is smooth. Add 2 tablespoons butter, 1 teaspoon salt, a little white pepper, a little nutmeg, and 2 whole eggs and 2 yolks, slightly beaten. Mix together very thoroughly. Makes 4 to 5 cups. If the potatoes are made ahead of time brush the top with a little butter to prevent a crust from forming. When ready to use reheat them over very low heat, stirring constantly. Pipe the mixture through a pastry tube to make a border around heatproof platters, and brown under the broiler. Or shape roses or mounds on a buttered baking sheet and brown in a hot oven to use as a vegetable accompaniment, or to garnish serving platters on which various cooked foods are arranged.

POTATOES LORETTE

Pommes de Terre Lorette

MAKE cream puff paste: Bring 1/2 cup water or milk or equal parts of each to a boil with 2 tablespoons butter and 1/4 teaspoon salt. Add 1/2 cup flour and cook, stirring constantly to combine the mixture thoroughly, and continue until the mixture rolls away from the sides of the pan. Remove it from the heat, let it cool for a minute, and add 2 eggs, one at a time, beating in the first one completely before adding the second. Add an equal amount of duchess potatoes. Slip the mixture from a tablespoon into deep hot fat (350° F.) and cook until the potatoes are puffed and brown. Drain them on paper towels.

POTATOES DAUPHINE　　　　　*Pommes de Terre Dauphine*

FOR *pommes Dauphine* slip the mixture into the hot fat from a teaspoon instead of a tablespoon.

Small whole potatoes, or large potatoes cut into uniform small balls, dice, or oval shapes appear on French menus under various names that indicate small differences in their preparation. The professional cook makes every piece exactly the same size and shape, and takes great care not to mash or crush the potatoes as they cook. He turns or stirs them very gently with a fork or spatula, or simply shakes them in the pan to achieve even cooking.

Pommes de Terre Parmentier

POTATOES PARMENTIER

CUT 2 pounds or 6 to 8 medium potatoes, peeled, into small dice, parboil them for 3 to 4 minutes, and drain them. Heat 4 tablespoons butter in a shallow pan, add the potatoes and cook them on top of the stove or in a hot oven (400° F.) until they are golden brown, stirring occasionally with a spatula without crushing them. Season with salt and pepper and sprinkle with finely chopped parsley.

Pommes de Terre Parisienne

POTATOES PARISIAN

FOLLOW the recipe for potatoes Parmentier, but cut the potatoes into small balls instead of dice.

Pommes de Terre Parisienne au Persil

PARISIAN PARSLEYED POTATOES

CUT potatoes into small balls and boil them in salted water until they are tender. Drain them and roll them in a mixture of 3 tablespoons each of melted butter and hot chicken stock and 1 tablespoon finely chopped parsley until they are coated all over.

Pommes de Terre Rissolées

POTATOES RISSOLÉ

USE the small Bermuda or Florida potatoes that come to market in the early spring. If larger potatoes are used, cut them in halves or quarters and trim them to make them round. Peel 2 pounds potatoes, parboil about 8 minutes and drain them. Heat 4 tablespoons butter in a shallow pan and sauté the potatoes until they are tender and lightly browned. Season with salt and pepper and sprinkle with finely chopped parsley.

CHÂTEAU POTATOES

FOLLOW directions for potatoes *rissolé*, but cut the potatoes into large olive shapes instead of balls. Use as a garnish for meat and poultry entrées.

Pommes de Terre Château

NOISETTE POTATOES

CUT 2 pounds potatoes into little round balls. Heat 4 tablespoons butter in a shallow pan and sauté the potatoes, occasionally shaking the pan, until they are golden brown all over. Season with salt. Use as a garnish for meat, poultry, or fish entrées.

Pommes de Terre Noisette

French fried potatoes—the beloved pommes frites *of France—are easy to make if none of the details of preparation are neglected.*

Only firm, dry potatoes will become soft and mealy inside and brown and crisp on the outside in the short cooking time that is essential. And they must be well dried on a towel before going into the fat. Poor potatoes or poorly dried ones must cook longer and so come out grease-soaked.

FRIED POTATOES

CUT the potatoes into uniform sticks, strips, or very thin slices, for chips. Use a kettle large enough so that the pieces float in the fat, but it should not be too full, or the fat may bubble over and catch on fire. A heavy metal pan will help to keep the fat at a fairly constant temperature. Use rendered beef suet, vegetable oil, or canned shortening, but not olive oil, which in deep-frying tends to impart its flavor to foods, nor poultry fat, which has a low scorching point. Heat the fat to 375° F., the temperature at which a 1-inch cube of bread browns in 45 seconds. Put the potatoes in a wire basket, a generous handful at a time, and lower the basket into the fat. Too many cold potatoes lower the temperature of the fat too quickly. Lift out the basket and drain and shake off the surplus fat. Spread the fried potatoes on absorbent paper to drain further and serve them promptly, on heated plates. Or, for extra crispness, cook the potatoes only until they barely begin to brown, drain them, reheat the fat to 400° F.—the temperature at which a bread cube will brown in 25 seconds—

Pommes de Terre Frites

and finish the frying. Never cover fried potatoes, even with a napkin, or they will lose their crispness.

The fat used for frying can be strained through cheesecloth, stored in a cool place, and used over and over again until it loses its fresh flavor and does not brown the food well. We then say it is " fried out ," and it must be discarded.

FRENCH FRIED POTATOES

Pommes de Terre Frites à la Française

CUT 2 pounds or 6 to 8 medium potatoes, peeled, into small uniform sticks about as thick and as long as a man's little finger. Wash them in cold water and dry them thoroughly in a towel. Cook the potatoes in deep hot fat (375° F.) for 7 or 8 minutes, until they are soft and begin to turn brown. Remove them from the fat and drain them well on absorbent paper. Heat the fat to 390° to 400° F. and cook the potatoes again for 1 or 2 minutes, until they are golden brown. Remove them from the fat and drain on absorbent paper. Sprinkle with salt and serve immediately.

SHOESTRING POTATOES

Pommes de Terre en Julienne

CUT 2 pounds or 6 to 8 medium potatoes, peeled, into thin matchlike strips. Wash them in cold water and dry them thoroughly in a towel. Fry them in deep hot fat (375° F.) until they are golden brown, about 4 or 5 minutes. Remove them from the fat and drain them well on absorbent paper. Sprinkle with salt and serve immediately.

The discovery of the crisp, hollow, puffed potatoes, like little balloons, that are called pommes soufflées *has been credited to many chefs on many occasions. All the stories differ a little, but are essentially the same. The tale says that a chef had already begun to prepare* pommes frites *when he was informed that his guests would be delayed. He quickly removed the potatoes from the fat. When the guests finally arrived, he put the potatoes back into the fat, which had in the meantime become very hot—et voilà,* pommes soufflées! *Use firm oval baking potatoes. The slices must be uniform in size, shape, and thickness: ovals 1/8 inch thick are recommended. And the temperature of the fat in both kettles must be exactly as specified.*

SOUFFLÉED POTATOES

TRIM 2 pounds peeled potatoes of the Idaho type into oval shapes about 2 1/4 inches long and cut them lengthwise into uniform slices about the thickness of a half dollar, or a scant 1/8 inch. Do not use the uneven end slices. Chill the slices in a bowl of ice water for about 15 minutes, drain them and dry them thoroughly on a towel. Heat a kettle of fresh fat to 275° F., put the potatoes in a frying basket, and cook them for 4 or 5

minutes, turning them at least once. Lift them out of the fat and drain them on absorbent paper. Let them cool for about 5 minutes. (They may be kept in the refrigerator until the final frying or cooked immediately after cooling.) For the second frying, heat the fat to 400° to 425° F., until it starts to smoke. Lower the cool potatoes in the frying basket into the hot fat, a few at a time. The extreme heat causes instantaneous expansion.

As soon as the potatoes are puffed and brown, remove them quickly or they will burn. Drain them on absorbent paper. Salt them lightly and serve at once.

When I was a lad in the Bourbonnais, one of my mother's dishes was a potato pie. I don't know whether we enjoyed it more served hot, with cold cuts, or cold, the following day, with salad. Many a homesick countryman, stopping at the Ritz-Carlton, has confessed to me that he had never eaten a potato pie outside his own home—except the one I prepared for him, according to my mother's recipe.

POTATO PIE

SLICE very thin 2 pounds or 6 to 8 medium potatoes, peeled, and 2 medium onions. Sprinkle them with 1 1/2 teaspoons salt, a little pepper, and 1 tablespoon chopped parsley. Let the mixture stand while you prepare enough pie pastry to make a 10-inch, 2-crust pie. (Or use leftover puff paste.) Roll out half the pastry and line the bottom and sides of a 10-inch pie plate. Drain off the juice that has been drawn out of the potatoes and onions and spread them lightly in the pastry shell. Spread 3 tablespoons butter over the potatoes and onions. Roll out the remaining pastry and fit it over the top. Turn the lower edge over the upper and press them together, to seal. Prick the top to allow steam to escape. The top may be brushed with a mixture of beaten egg and milk to give a golden color. Bake the pie in a moderately hot oven (375° to 400° F.) for about 1 hour, or until potatoes seem tender when pierced with a skewer or a small sharp, pointed knife. Remove from the oven and cut a round piece out of the center of the top about as big as a half dollar and pour into the pie very carefully 1 to 1 1/2 cups heavy cream. The exact amount depends upon the potatoes; some varieties will absorb more then others. Replace the cutout piece and let the pie stand about 10 or 15 minutes before serving, while the cream is absorbed.

POTATOES WITH ONIONS

Pommes de Terre Boulangère

CUT 2 pounds or 6 to 8 medium potatoes, peeled, into slices about 1/4 inch thick and slice 2 onions very thin. Sprinkle them with 1/2 teaspoon salt, a little pepper, and 1 teaspoon chopped parsley. Spread the potatoes and onions in a heatproof platter, about 1/2 inch deep, spread 3 table-spoons soft butter over them and add 1 cup boiling water. Cook in a hot oven (425° F.) for 30 to 40 minutes, or until the potatoes are tender, the water has cooked away, and the top is brown and crusty.

MOLDED POTATOES

Pommes de Terre Anna

PEEL and slice as thin as possible enough potatoes to make 6 cups. Drain them and dry well on a towel. Season them with 1/2 teaspoon salt and a little pepper. Butter a round mold or small baking dish and lay in it 1/3 of the potatoes, overlapping the slices in a neat pattern and packing them in tightly. Spread them with 1 tablespoon butter. Add another layer of 1/3 the potatoes and spread them with 1 tablespoon butter. Finish with the remaining potatoes and 1 more tablespoon butter. Cover the baking dish and bake the potatoes in a hot oven (425° F.) for 40 to 50 minutes, or until they seem tender when pierced with a small sharp pointed knife. Tilt the mold to drain out the butter before inverting the potatoes on a serving dish. Slip them carefully out in molded form. (Reserve the butter to use in sautéing.)

INDIVIDUAL POTATO MOLDS   *Pommes de Terre Annette*

PREPARE individual molds and bake them as for *pommes de terre Anna*, molded potatoes.

POTATOES AND TRUFFLES   *Pommes de Terre Sarladaise*

PREPARE *pommes de terre Anna*, molded potatoes, but add alternate layers of sliced truffles.

POTATOES AND CARROTS   *Pommes de Terre Crécy*

PREPARE *pommes de terre Anna*, molded potatoes, but add alternate layers of thinly sliced carrots sautéed *à la Vichy*—cooked in butter and a little water until the water cooks away.

MOLDED JULIENNE POTATOES   *Pommes de Terre Champs-Elysées*

FOLLOW the directions for *pommes de terre Anna*, molded potatoes, but cut the potatoes in julienne—not too fine—instead of in thin slices. When the potatoes are done, tilt the mold and press out the butter before inverting the mold on a serving dish.

Mushrooms

MUSHROOMS are as essential to French cuisine as potatoes. Imagine French gourmets trying to get along without them. They go with practically everything from robust broiled beef and full-flavored brown sauce to delicately sauced sweetbreads and subtle wine sauces with fine fish filets. They do for sauces what leeks do for soups and lemons for fruit: their flavor brings out, enhances, and blends other flavors. They appear all through this book. Scores of meat, poultry, and fish recipes include them, and they are delectable in themselves—as a side dish, hors-d'oeuvre, or main course.

The fresher mushrooms are, the better. When they have started to turn brown and the underside of the cap is black, they are not worth buying. Don't plan to keep them on hand long. If you have more than you can use, wash them and cook them for about 5 minutes in a little water with a few drops of lemon juice and a little salt and store them in a jar in the refrigerator. The lemon juice prevents darkening. If fresh mushrooms are not available, use canned ones, which are available whole, sliced, or in pieces.

Preparing
Mushrooms
for Cooking

Use mushrooms of uniform size. To prepare them for cooking, remove the stems and wash and drain the caps. Whether they should be peeled or not depends, I think, on the mushroom. If the skin is thick and apt to be tough, it should come off. If it is fine and thin, it can be left on. Cook the skins, which are full of flavor, and the stems, chopped, in a little water and use this liquor with stock in sauces.

Champignons Sautés

SAUTÉED MUSHROOMS

MUSHROOMS are watery. When they are sautéed, the fat should be very hot and the mushrooms cooked quickly. Shake the pan all the time to dry them out and cook them evenly.

Prepare 1 pound mushrooms for cooking as above and season the caps with salt and a little pepper. Heat 4 tablespoons clarified butter in a saucepan and sauté the mushrooms in it until they are golden brown. Serve them on toast or as an accompaniment to any sautéed meat. Pour over them the butter from the pan and sprinkle with finely chopped parsley.

Champignons Sautés à la Provençale

SAUTÉED MUSHROOMS WITH SHALLOTS AND GARLIC

COOK 1 pound mushrooms as for sautéed mushrooms. Remove them and to the butter in the pan add 1 teaspoon chopped shallots or onion and 1 crushed clove of garlic. Sauté the shallots and garlic for 2 minutes, return the mushrooms to the pan, and cook a few minutes longer to reheat them, shaking the pan constantly. Sprinkle with chopped parsley.

BROILED MUSHROOMS

PREPARE 1 pound large mushrooms for cooking as above and season the caps with salt and pepper. Arrange them, cup up, in a shallow pan spread with hot butter or oil. Broil them for 8 to 10 minutes. Serve on buttered toast, on broiled ham on toast, or as a garnish for broiled meat.

*Champignons
Grillés*

CREAMED MUSHROOMS

COOK 1 pound medium mushrooms as for sautéed mushrooms. When they are golden brown add 1 tablespoon flour and mix it in thoroughly. Add 1 cup light cream and bring to a boil, stirring constantly. Cover the pan and cook slowly for 10 minutes. Remove the mushrooms to a serving dish. Cook the sauce, stirring, until it is thick and smooth, correct the seasoning with salt, and add 1/2 teaspoon lemon juice. Pour the sauce over the mushrooms. Serve on toast or in *bouchées*, patty shells.

*Champignons
à la Crème*

MUSHROOMS IN CROÛTES

MAKE *croûtes* from 6 slices of bread as described in the garnish chapter.
Melt 3 tablespoons butter in a saucepan, add 2 tablespoons flour, and cook the *roux* until it starts to turn golden. Stir in 1 1/2 cups white stock and add a faggot, 1/4 teaspoon salt, a little pepper, and a little nutmeg, and cook, stirring constantly, until the sauce is thickened. Wash 1 pound mushrooms, peel, and add the peelings to the sauce. Continue cooking the sauce slowly about 20 minutes. Cook the mushrooms in 1/2 cup salted water with the juice of 1/2 lemon for 5 minutes. Mix 1 egg yolk with 2 tablespoons cream and combine with the sauce. Bring it back to the boil, stirring constantly, but do not allow it to boil. If necessary, thin the sauce with a little mushroom liquor. Drain the mushrooms and divide them among the browned *croûtes*. Strain the sauce over them.

*Croûtes aux
Champignons
Ménagère*

STUFFED MUSHROOMS

PREPARE mushroom *duxelles* and add 1 tablespoon tomato sauce or good meat gravy and 3 tablespoons fine fresh bread crumbs. Remove the stems

*Champignons
Farcis*

335

from 12 very large mushrooms. Wash and drain the caps and season them with salt and pepper. Brush them with a little salad oil and arrange them, cup up, in a shallow pan. Bake in a hot oven (425° F.) for 5 minutes. Fill the caps with the *duxelles* mixture, sprinkle them with bread crumbs and a little melted butter, and brown them in a hot oven or under the broiler.

Purée de
Champignons

MUSHROOM PURÉE

WASH, drain, and chop very fine enough mushrooms to make 1 1/2 cups. Squeeze out all surplus moisture. Melt 3 tablespoons butter in a saucepan, add the mushrooms and cook them, stirring constantly, until the liquid has evaporated. Make a very thick béchamel sauce with 1/4 cup each of butter and flour and 2 cups milk. Add it to the cooked mushrooms and cook the mixture, stirring, until it is thoroughly combined.

Morels—in French, morilles *—sometimes called spring mushrooms because they appear in May, are a rare delicacy. In Alsace, where the greatest number are found, and the best, farmers, youngsters, and farm hands are all out during the short season, poking among the leaves and brambles under hedgerows to uncover the precious wild fungus. Each day baskets are sent off by train to Paris to eager chefs of the great restaurants. A good chef buys only as many as he can immediately use. Stale* morilles *are worse than none at all. There are some morels in this country, but only a few, and they are as highly prized as they are in Europe.*

Morels have a cone-shaped cap covered with tiny pockets, like a honeycomb. There are two kinds—the dark brown ones, which have a fuller flavor, and the light tan. The tiny pockets collect sand as the morels push up through the soil and to flush it out requires more than ordinary washing. The bulbous stem is cut off and discarded primarily because the sand lodging there can seldom be removed. Shake out as much water as possible and dry the morels on towels. They are moist anyway and added moisture is a nuisance.

Dried Morels
To dry morels, discard the bulbous stems. Do not wash the morels but with a large kitchen needle thread them on a soft white string. Hang them in the sun for several days and finish drying them indoors in a warm place or in a very slow oven. To use dried morels, soak them in lukewarm

water for a few hours, wash them, and use as you would fresh ones. Both fresh and dried morels may be cooked in all the ways you would cook ordinary mushrooms.

MORELS WITH HAM

Morilles Séville

PREPARE 1 pound morels as above. Leave them whole or, if large, halve or quarter them. Heat 1/4 cup salad oil and in it sauté 1 1/2 cups diced cooked ham until it is golden brown. Remove it, draining all the oil back into the pan. Add the morels and 1/4 cup finely chopped onion and cook until the onion is golden. Drain off as much oil as possible and return the ham to the pan. Add 1/2 cup Sherry and cook all together until the wine is reduced to about 1/4 cup. Add 1/2 cup veal or chicken gravy or Madeira sauce, 1 or 2 red pimientos cut in julienne, a little salt, and freshly ground white pepper, and cook slowly for 20 to 25 minutes. Serve the morels in a large *croustade* or *vol-au-vent*, in patty shells or on toast.

CREAMED MORELS

Morilles à la Crème

PREPARE 1 pound morels as above. Leave them whole or, if large, halve or quarter them. Heat 3 tablespoons butter and sauté the morels for about 8 minutes, or until they are golden brown. Add either 1 tablespoon flour or 1/4 cup thick cream sauce and mix well. Add 1 cup hot light cream, bring to a boil, stirring, and simmer the morels, covered, about 10 minutes. Season with salt and a little ground white pepper. Serve on hot toast.

Cèpes—or esculent boletus—are a type of wild mushroom that grows in the woods, under oak trees. They have their own special flavor, are very soft and tender, and are the joy of gourmets. French cèpes are canned and shipped all over the world.

FRENCH WILD MUSHROOMS WITH SHALLOT AND GARLIC

Cèpes à la Bordelaise

LEAVE small *cèpes* whole, but halve or quarter large ones. For 1 can of *cèpes* heat 3 or 4 tablespoons salad oil in a shallow pan until it is very hot, and sauté the *cèpes* quickly until they are golden brown. Remove from the pan, drain in a strainer, and season with salt and pepper. Pour the oil from the pan and in it melt 2 tablespoons butter. Add the *cèpes*, 1 shallot, chopped, or 1 tablespoon finely chopped onion, a small piece of garlic, crushed, some chopped parsley, and 1 tablespoon fine bread crumbs. Cook all together a few minutes, shaking the pan to combine the ingredients.

Root Vegetables

CARROTS, beets, parsnips, turnips, celery knob, and oyster plant—known collectively as root vegetables—keep well and are most welcome in winter, when other fresh vegetables are not so easily come by. I realize that in America the root vegetables, with the exception of carrots and possibly beets, are not generally liked, perhaps because they are indifferently cooked and seasoned, or perhaps because too often they are allowed to grow to overmaturity, so that they are characterized by a strong taste and a woody, fibrous texture. The exact cooking time for any of these vegetables will depend, of course, on their age and size. If you would enjoy root vegetables, I counsel you to choose them cautiously and to prepare them as carefully as you would new asparagus, for instance.

Young carrots may be scraped and cooked whole, often in very little water and a little butter, in a tightly closed pan that permits them to steam until they are just tender. A little sugar—more for winter carrots than for the sweet summer variety—brings out the natural sweetness of the carrot. The length of cooking depends upon the age of the carrots.

Larger carrots may be sliced or cut into balls, dice, julienne or bâtonnets—*small square-ended sticks 1 to 2 inches long and 1/4 to 1/2 inch thick.*

These pieces must always be of even size for uniform cooking. Large carrots may also be trimmed down to the size and shape of small carrots for decorative purposes.

Carrots and onions combine naturally, and together go into many stews and braised meat and poultry dishes and, glazed, are used for garnish for both hot and cold dishes.

GLAZED CARROTS

Carottes Glacées

SCRAPE and cut into balls with a vegetable cutter enough carrots to make 2 to 2 1/2 cups. Or cut them into olive shapes or cut little carrots from large ones. Combine them with 1 cup lightly salted chicken stock, 1 tablespoon butter, and 1/2 tablespoon sugar. Simmer the carrots, covered, over very low heat until all the liquid has cooked away. Uncover the pan and continue to cook the carrots, shaking the pan constantly, until they are lightly glazed by the butter and sugar in the pan.

GLAZED PARSLEYED CARROTS

Carottes Vichy

SCRAPE and slice very thin enough carrots to make 2 to 2 1/2 cups. Combine them with 1/2 cup water, 2 tablespoons butter, 1 tablespoon sugar, and, if desired, a very little salt. Cook and glaze the carrots as for *carottes glacées*, glazed carrots. Sprinkle them generously with chopped parsley.

CARROT PURÉE

Purée de Carottes

PUT 2 cups scraped, chopped carrots, 1/4 cup rice, 2 cups water, 1 tablespoon sugar, and 1/2 teaspoon salt, in a heavy saucepan, cover closely, and cook for 30 to 35 minutes, or until most of the water is cooked away. Rub the carrots through a sieve into a saucepan, add 1 tablespoon butter and 1/4 cup cream and reheat, stirring to combine the ingredients thoroughly.

Beets should be cooked whole, whether they are the tiny beets of spring and summer or the larger varieties of fall and winter. Trim off all but 1/2 inch of the beet top (the greens of fresh young beets are an excellent vegetable, also), but do not peel the root, or cut it in any way, or the rich color will bleed into the cooking water. Drop the cooked beets into cold water for a moment ; the skins will easily slip off, and the beets may then be sliced or diced, and seasoned with sugar, if desired. Again, cooking time depends upon the age and size of the vegetable.

Betteraves au Beurre

BUTTERED BEETS

WASH and trim 24 young beets as above. Cook them in unsalted water to cover from 30 to 50 minutes, or until they are tender and can be easily pierced with a fork. Drop them in cold water for a moment and slip off the skins. If they are very small, leave them whole; if large, slice or dice them. Melt 2 or 3 tablespoons butter in a saucepan and reheat the beets in it over low heat, shaking the pan. Season the beets with salt and freshly ground pepper.

Betteraves à la Crème

CREAMED BEETS

FOLLOW the directions for *betteraves au beurre,* but leave the beets whole. Add 1 cup cream sauce and shake them over low heat until they are well coated.

Betteraves à la Poitevine

BEETS IN SAUCE

FOLLOW the directions for *betteraves au beurre,* but cut the beets into slices about 1/4 inch thick. Make *lyonnaise sauce*: Sauté 2 onions, finely chopped in 2 tablespoons butter until they are golden brown. Add a generous 1/3 cup white wine and cook until the sauce is reduced to 1/2 the original quantity. Add 1 cup brown sauce and cook slowly for 15 minutes. Add 1 teaspoon chopped parsley and 1 tablespoon vinegar. Combine with the beets and shake all together over low heat until the slices are well coated.

In France, parsnips are inevitably part of the pot-au-feu, *to which they lend an inimitable flavor that would be sorely missed. When they are plentiful and cheap in the markets, thrifty housewives serve them as a vegetable,*

*creamed or cooked, coated with batter, and deep-fried to make a delicious
fritter. Young parsnips take about half an hour to cook, but parsnips that
have been stored for winter use may require 45 minutes or longer.*

FRIED PARSNIPS

Cut peeled parsnips into small uniform sticks about as thick and as long
as a man's little finger. There should be 2 to 3 cups. Cook the parsnips
in salted water to cover for 30 to 40 minutes, or until they are just tender
and drain them well.

Combine 1/2 cup flour, 2 teaspoons salad oil, 6 tablespoons lukewarm
water and a little salt, and blend the mixture until it is smooth. Fold in
1 egg white, stiffly beaten. Dip the parsnips in this fritter batter and fry
them in deep hot fat or oil (375° F.) until they are golden brown, about
4 minutes. Drain the fritters on absorbent paper and sprinkle them with
salt. Serve with fried parsley.

*In France, we prefer the white turnip to the yellow variety that in America
is peeled, boiled, mashed, and seasoned like potatoes. The white turnip is
more delicate in flavor and will cook to tenderness in half an hour. It can
be browned and served whole.*

BUTTERED WHITE TURNIPS

Peel 6 to 8 young, tender white turnips and cut them into slices or large
dice. Cook them in salted water to cover for 30 minutes, or until they
are just tender. Drain them well. Melt 2 to 3 tablespoons butter and
sauté the turnips lightly. Season with salt and white pepper and sprinkle
with finely chopped parsley.

STUFFED WHITE TURNIPS

Peel round, young white turnips and cut out the centers, leaving a shell
and base about 1/2 inch thick. Parboil the shells for 8 to 10 minutes and
drain them. Fill with a well-seasoned meat hash, as for stuffed cabbage,
and sprinkle with fine crumbs and melted butter. Arrange the turnips
in a shallow casserole and add enough stock to come halfway up them.

Bake in a hot oven (375° F.) for about 25 minutes, or until the tops are brown. Serve with the liquid from the casserole.

TURNIP PURÉE

Purée de Navets

CUT peeled turnips into pieces and cook them in boiling salted water to cover for 30 minutes, or until they are quite soft. Drain them well and force through a fine sieve. Return the purée to the heat and cook out all the surplus moisture, stirring constantly to avoid scorching. Add enough butter and cream to give the purée the consistency of mashed potatoes and season with salt and pepper.

Céleri-rave—in English, celery root or celery knob—has a flavor like stalk celery but an entirely different texture. Select small young roots. It is tender when young, but grows large, knobby, and woody when older. Cook celery knob carefully. It becomes tender quickly and can easily be overcooked. Cut in julienne or bâtonnets, *cooked for only a couple of minutes, to preserve the crispness, and pointed up with a sharp vinaigrette dressing, celery knob makes an excellent hors-d'oeuvre. Diced and cooked, it can be combined with cream sauce.*

CELERY KNOB PURÉE

Purée de Céleri-Rave

PEEL and cut in quarters enough celery knob to make 1 1/2 cups and cook it in boiling salted water for about 20 minutes, or until it is tender. Peel and cut in quarters enough potatoes to make 1/2 cup and cook in boiling salted water until tender. Drain the celery knob and potatoes separately and dry them over low heat. Combine them and force them through a fine sieve. Add 1 tablespoon butter and 1/4 cup hot heavy cream, stirring the mixture over the heat until it is smooth and creamy. Season with salt and a little white pepper.

CELERY KNOB COUNTRY STYLE

Céleri-Rave Fermière

PARBOIL 1/2 cup diced fat salt pork for 5 minutes in water to cover and drain it. Melt 2 tablespoons butter in a saucepan, add the pork dice and

1 onion, chopped, and sauté them over high heat until they are golden. Add the white parts of 2 leeks, cleaned and sliced, and 1 tablespoon flour and cook for a few minutes, stirring. Stir in gradually 1 cup water or stock and add 3 stalks of celery, cleaned and sliced, a faggot made by tying together 2 sprigs of parsley and a small bay leaf, a pinch of thyme, and 3 or 4 celery knobs, peeled and cut in large dice. Simmer the mixture, covered, for 50 minutes, or until the celery knob is tender. Discard the faggot. Sprinkle the vegetables with finely chopped parsley.

Oyster plant, also known as salsify and thought to resemble oysters in flavor, is an old-fashioned vegetable that deserves to be revived. It is first boiled until it is tender, then prepared in various ways.

Cut off the tops of 5 to 7 oyster plants or salsify and scrape them. Cut up large plants so that all the pieces are about 3 to 4 inches long. Oyster plant darkens quickly when it is peeled, and must be immediately dropped into water acidulated with vinegar or lemon juice. Use about 2 tablespoons vinegar for each quart of water. Stir 1 tablespoon flour to a thin paste with a little water in a saucepan, add 1 quart water, 1 tablespoon vinegar, and 1/2 teaspoon salt. Bring the mixture to a boil, add the oyster plant, and cook it 1 to 1 1/2 hours, or until it is tender.

Cooked oyster plant may be reheated in chicken or veal gravy.

SAUTÉED OYSTER PLANT

Salsifis Sautés

MELT 2 or 3 tablespoons butter in a skillet and in it sauté 5 to 7 cooked oyster plants until they are golden brown. Sprinkle with finely chopped parsley.

OYSTER PLANT FRITTERS

Beignets de Salsifis

ROLL pieces of 5 to 7 cooked oyster plants in chopped parsley, put them in a bowl, and sprinkle them with a marinade made of 6 tablespoons salad oil and 3 tablespoons lemon juice. Let the oyster plant stand for 15 minutes. Drain it.

Fritter Batter

Combine 3 tablespoons flour, 1/3 cup lukewarm water, a little salt, and 1 teaspoon salad oil and blend the mixture until it is smooth. Fold in 1 egg white, stiffly beaten. Dip each piece of oyster plant in this fritter batter and fry the pieces in deep hot fat or oil (375° F.) until they are golden brown, about 4 minutes. Drain the fritters on absorbent paper and sprinkle them with salt.

Artichokes are generally considered one of our most elegant and naturally delectable vegetables, and are usually prepared simply. But in good French cooking, " simply " does not mean carelessly or indifferently. The artichoke that is selected at the peak of its fresh ripeness, freshened by an hour's rest in a bowl of cold water—stem down, like a flower—and cooked to tender perfection needs only the simplest of sauces to point up its delicate flavor: melted butter or hollandaise, if the artichoke is served hot; a simple vinaigrette sauce, if it is served cold.

Artichauts ARTICHOKES

BREAK the stems of the artichokes (this pulls out the stringy fibers) and trim the bases with a knife. Rub the cut surface with a piece of lemon to keep it from discoloring. To remove the spines, lay the artichoke on its side on a cutting board and slice off about 1/2 inch from the top. With scissors, trim about 1/4 inch from the outside leaves. Bring a large amount of water to a boil and add a little vinegar, about 1 tablespoon for each quart. Boil the artichokes for about 45 minutes, or until a leaf can be readily slipped out. Turn the artichokes upside down to drain and squeeze them very gently to rid them of water. Spread the leaves apart gently and pull out the fine prickly leaves in the center of the vegetable. Use a small spoon to scrape out the hairy choke that covers the center of the artichoke bottom. Be sure to remove all of it. Press the leaves back into shape again.

Serve individual dishes of whatever sauce you choose. Each guest

344

detaches one leaf at a time, dips the fleshy end into the sauce, and scrapes the pulp off between his teeth. When all the leaves have been scraped and discarded, he uses a fork to cut the choice artichoke *fond*—the bottom or heart—into pieces and dip it in the sauce.

ARTICHOKE BOTTOMS WITH MUSHROOMS

Fonds d'Artichauts à la Sarah Bernhardt

COOK and drain 6 artichoke bottoms, as described in the hors-d'oeuvre chapter. Peel 1/2 pound small mushroom caps and season them with salt and pepper. Sauté the mushrooms in 2 tablespoons butter until they are golden brown, shaking the pan. Add 1/2 cup cream and cook the mushrooms very gently, covered, for about 10 minutes. Arrange 2 to 3 mushrooms in the center of each artichoke. Continue to cook the sauce until it thickens a little and add 1 egg yolk beaten with a little of the hot sauce. Correct the seasoning with salt, add 2 or 3 drops of lemon juice, and fold in 1 tablespoon whipped cream. Cover the mushrooms with the sauce and brown under the broiler.

Put the glazed artichokes on a serving dish and around each arrange 3 to 4 cooked asparagus tips and a few small carrot balls, cooked and glazed to a golden brown with a little butter and sugar.

STUFFED ARTICHOKES

Artichauts Farcis

COOK 2 finely chopped shallots or 2 tablespoons finely chopped onions in 1/4 cup butter until they are soft but not brown. Add 1/2 cup finely chopped mushrooms and cook until the moisture has cooked away. Add 1/4 cup chopped cooked ham, 2 teaspoons chopped parsley, 1/2 teaspoon salt, a little pepper, and 1/4 cup tomato sauce or tomato purée.

Fill 6 artichokes prepared as above but cooked only 15 to 20 minutes. Tie a piece of fat salt pork around each with soft string. Put 1 sliced carrot and 1 sliced onion, 2 sprigs of parsley, 1 small bay leaf, and a pinch of thyme in a casserole and add 1/2 cup white wine or water with lemon juice. Arrange the artichokes side by side. Bring the liquid to a boil on the top of the stove, and bake the artichokes, covered, in a moderate oven (350° F.) for 1 hour. About 15 minutes before they are done, remove the cover to let the slices of fat pork brown. Remove the artichokes to a serving dish and cut away the strings. Strain the liquid from the casserole into a saucepan, skim off the fat, and cook it until it is reduced to 1/2 the original quantity. Pass this sauce separately.

In Europe vegetables like celery, fennel, endive, and cardoons are often braised: that is, they are cooked until tender in a covered pan, on top of the stove or in the oven, in a very small amount of liquid. Americans who know the first three only as salad vegetables are generally quickly converted to the European method of serving them.

Céleris Braisés — BRAISED CELERY

WHEN celery is to be braised, the individual stalks are not separated from the head. In order to wash the sand out of the head without breaking it, cut off the top leaves, discard the tough outer stalks, and split the head lengthwise. Parboil the heads for 5 minutes and plunge them into cold water. The parboiling makes the stalks so pliable that they can be gently spread apart without breaking, and any dirt lodging inside can be rinsed out under running water.

Place a few slices of onion and carrot in a heatproof casserole and arrange on them 4 or 5 heads of celery, all lying in one direction, and add enough stock or water to cover it, a little salt, and 1 tablespoon butter. Cover with a piece of wax paper cut the size of the casserole and having a tiny hole in the center. Bring the liquid to a boil, cover the casserole, and braise the celery in a hot oven (375° to 400° F.) about 1 hour, or until the celery is tender. Remove the celery to a serving dish and cook the liquid until it is reduced to about 1/2 cup. Thicken it with *beurre manié* made by creaming 1 tablespoon butter with 1/2 tablespoon flour. Strain the sauce over the celery.

Céleri à la Crème — CREAMED CELERY

CLEAN, scrape away the stringy fibers, and cut in 2-inch pieces enough celery stalks to make 1 quart. Braise them, as for braised celery. Drain well, reserving the liquid. Skim the fat from it and strain it. Melt 2 tablespoons butter in a saucepan, add 1 tablespoon flour, and cook the *roux* until it starts to turn golden. Gradually add the celery water and cook the sauce, stirring constantly, until it is thick and reduced to about

1/2 cup. Add 1/4 cup heavy cream and bring back to a boil. Correct the seasoning with salt and combine with the celery, shaking the pan over the heat until all the pieces are coated.

FENNEL

Fenouil

FENNEL, not very common in this country, is served like celery, either raw as an hors-d'oeuvre or braised like celery as a vegetable. It is also cooked in soup with other vegetables, especially in borsch.

BRAISED ENDIVE FLAMANDE

Endives Braisées à la Flamande

WASH 1 to 1 1/2 pounds endive and drain it. Arrange the heads in one direction in a single layer in a heatproof casserole. Add 1/2 cup water, the juice of 1/2 lemon, 2 tablespoons butter, 1 tablespoon sugar, and 1/2 teaspoon salt. Cover the endive with a piece of wax paper cut the size of the casserole and having a tiny hole in the center. Bring the liquid to a boil, cover the casserole, and braise in a moderate oven (350° F.) or on top of the stove over very low heat for 40 to 45 minutes. Remove the endive to a serving dish and cook the liquid until it is reduced to about 1/2 cup. Add 1 tablespoon butter and pour the sauce over the endive.

CARDOONS

Cardons

DISCARD the outside tough stalks of the cardoons. Separate the other stalks from the heart and clean them, scraping off the strings. Cut these stalks in 3- or 4-inch pieces but leave the heart whole. Add to 2 quarts boiling water 1 tablespoon flour blended with the juice of 1/2 lemon and add the cardoons. Cook them, covered, for about 2 hours. Drain the cardoons and serve them with cream sauce, Mornay sauce, or *sauce bordelaise*. Cut the heart in 1/2-inch pieces and garnish the dish. Garnish also with pieces of marrow poached for 5 minutes in simmering water.

Eggplant is one vegetable that grows better in America, where it is comparatively seldom on the table, than it does in France, where it is so pop-

ular. The flavor of eggplant goes very well with onions, garlic, tomatoes, mushrooms, and other vegetables, and with cheese—and it has a satisfying quality that makes it an excellent choice for a main dish of a light meal or a hearty accompaniment to a light entrée.

Eggplant is a watery vegetable ; if it is cut into thick slices, salted, and let stand under a weight, some of this excess water will drain away. This method may be followed in preparing the vegetable for French fried or sautéed eggplant, which should be cooked in very hot oil, to discourage absorption and consequent sogginess. Never cover fried or sautéed eggplant and thus destroy its characteristic crisp surface, but salt and serve it at once, as you would French fried potatoes. In France, fried eggplant is often served on paper doilies, as other fried foods are.

SAUTÉED EGGPLANT

Aubergine Sauté

CUT peeled eggplant in 1/3 to 1/2 inch slices and season with a little salt. Dip in milk, then in flour, and sauté in very hot oil for 2 or 3 minutes, or until golden brown on both sides. Have enough oil to almost cover the eggplant. Drain the slices on paper towels. Arrange them, overlapping, on the serving dish and sprinkle them with butter cooked to a hazelnut brown and with chopped parsley. If desired, 1 or 2 crushed cloves of garlic may be added to the brown butter.

FRIED EGGPLANT

Aubergine Frite

CUT peeled eggplant into small uniform sticks about as thick and as long as a man's little finger. Dip the sticks in milk, drain them, and dip in flour. Shake off the surplus flour and fry them in deep hot fat or oil (390° F.) for a minute, until they are brown. Drain the sticks on paper towels and sprinkle with salt. Serve at once on a hot plate covered with a paper doily.

FRIED EGGPLANT À L'ANGLAISE

Aubergine à l'Anglaise

CUT a peeled eggplant in 1/3 to 1/2 inch slices. Coat *à l'anglaise* as follows: dip in flour, then in a mixture of 1 beaten egg, 2 or 3 tablespoons milk, 1 tablespoon salad oil, and 1/4 teaspoon salt. Drain the slices and dip in fine dry bread crumbs, completely covering each slice. Fry in deep hot fat or oil (390° F.) for 2 or 3 minutes, or until the slices are golden brown. Drain on paper towels and sprinkle with salt. Serve at once on a hot plate covered with a paper doily.

EGGPLANT AU GRATIN

Aubergine au Gratin

CUT an eggplant in quarters lengthwise and score the inside with cuts about 1/2 inch deep. Fry the quarters in deep hot fat (390° F.) for 5 to 6 minutes and drain them on paper towels. Scrape the pulp from the skin, chop it fine, and mix with half its volume of mushroom *duxelles*. Season with salt and a little pepper and fill the skins with the mixture. Sprinkle the stuffed eggplant with fine bread crumbs and a little melted butter and brown in a hot oven or under the broiler. Serve plain or with gravy.

EGGPLANT ALGERIAN

Aubergine à l'Algérienne

CLEAN, drain, and peel 8 mushrooms and sauté them in 1 tablespoon very hot butter for a few minutes. Stir in 1 shallot or 1/2 onion, finely chopped, and 1 teaspoon flour. Add 1/2 cup cream and cook, stirring, until the sauce is thickened and reduced to about 1/3 cup.

Cut a peeled eggplant into slices 1/2 inch thick. Season the slices with salt and pepper, dip in milk, then in flour, and fry in deep hot fat or oil (390° F.) until they are golden brown or sauté them in oil. Drain on paper towels. Dip 8 thick slices of tomato in flour and sauté them in hot oil. Prepare 1 cup rice pilaff and spread in a serving dish. Arrange the eggplant and tomato slices on the rice, overlapping them alternately, and pour over them the creamed mushroom mixture.

EGGPLANT HOUSEWIFE'S STYLE

Aubergine Ménagère

CUT a peeled eggplant in large dice and sprinkle them with flour. Sauté the dice very quickly in 1/3 cup very hot salad oil. Add 2 tablespoons chopped onion, 2 cloves of garlic, crushed, 3 ripe tomatoes, peeled, seeded, and chopped, 1/2 teaspoon salt, a little pepper, and a faggot made by tying together 1 stalk of celery, 3 sprigs of parsley, 1/2 bay leaf, and a little thyme. Simmer the mixture for 20 minutes, or until the tomatoes cook down to a thick sauce. Discard the faggot and sprinkle with 1 tablespoon chopped parsley.

Aubergine aux Tomates

EGGPLANT WITH TOMATOES

SAUTÉ 1/2 onion, finely chopped, in 1 tablespoon butter until it is golden. Stir in 1 clove of garlic, crushed, and 1 teaspoon flour, and add 4 large tomatoes, peeled, seeded, and chopped. Cook the mixture, stirring, until the tomatoes cook down to a thick sauce. Cut a peeled eggplant in 12 slices about 1/2 inch thick. Season the slices with salt and pepper, dip in milk, then in flour, and fry in deep hot fat or oil (390° F.) until they are golden brown or sauté them in hot oil. Drain them on paper towels. Arrange the slices, overlapping, on a heatproof serving dish, pour over the tomato sauce, and warm over very low heat for about 5 minutes. Sprinkle with chopped parsley.

Aubergine à l'Orientale

EGGPLANT ORIENTAL

COOK 1 finely chopped shallot or 1 tablespoon chopped onion in 1 tablespoon butter until it is soft. Add 4 tomatoes, peeled, seeded, and chopped, and cook, stirring occasionally, until the mixture is reduced to 1/3 the original quantity. Add 1 cup cream sauce and 1 teaspoon chopped parsley and season with salt and pepper. Remove from the heat and combine with 2 beaten egg yolks. Stir in 2 tablespoons butter. Cut a peeled eggplant in 1/2 inch slices. Dip each slice in milk and then in flour and fry the slices in deep hot fat or oil (390° F.) until they are golden brown or sauté them in hot oil. Drain on paper towels and season with salt. Arrange the slices, overlapping, on a heatproof serving dish and spread some of the sauce on each slice. Add 2 tablespoons whipped cream to the remaining sauce and mask the dish with it. Sprinkle with a little grated Parmesan cheese and brown under the broiler.

There are several varieties of chestnuts, but the two sold most widely are the marrons *and the* châtaignes. *Marrons* are the large nuts grown in *southern France and in Italy and used primarily in desserts, and for making* marrons glacés. Châtaignes, *which are grown farther north, in the center of France, are used for poultry stuffing and garnishing, and for making the chestnut flour prescribed for many Italian pastries.*

The easiest way to shell a chestnut is the method devised by the street-corner hot-chestnut vendors. They cut a cross in the flat or concave side of the nut shell, using a very sharp pointed knife. Then they roast the nuts over a charcoal fire until the shell and skin are detached from the nut and the meat is tender. You can roast chestnuts in this manner in your oven and they make delightful nibbling, but for other purposes, it is wise to roast the nuts only until the shells and skins can be easily removed, and to finish the cooking by simmering them in stock. Test the nuts for tenderness by piercing them with a skewer.

BOILED CHESTNUTS

Châtaignes

Shelling
Chestnuts

WITH a sharp pointed knife cut a small cross in the flat side of each shell. Spread the nuts in a shallow pan, brush them with fat or oil, and cook them in a very hot oven (450° to 500° F.) for 5 to 6 minutes, or until the shells open and are loosened from the nut meat. Remove the shells and skin underneath.

Put the shelled nuts in a saucepan with enough water or white stock to cover them, add 2 or 3 stalks of celery, bring the liquid to a boil, and simmer for 25 to 30 minutes. Let the nuts cool in the liquid until they are to be used. Serve as a vegetable or use in stuffing or to make chestnut purée.

Cooking
Chestnuts

For pastries and desserts, simmer the nuts in milk, or water.

BRAISED CHESTNUTS

*Châtaignes
Braisées*

SHELL 18 to 24 chestnuts as above. Butter a skillet and arrange the chestnuts in it side by side. Do not heap them. Add enough strong veal stock to just cover them and cook them slowly, moving them around carefully to keep them from sticking without breaking them. As the stock reduces, roll the chestnuts carefully in it to glaze them. The chestnuts should be done and have a bright coating by the time the stock is cooked away. Braised chestnuts are sometimes combined with buttered Brussels sprouts and are used for garnishing poultry.

Purée de Châtaignes

SHELL and cook chestnuts as above. Rub the boiled chestnuts through a fine sieve, add enough hot milk and a little butter to give them the consistency of mashed potatoes, and reheat the purée over low heat, being careful that it does not scorch.

Chestnut purée may also be made from packaged chestnut flour. Use 2 cups milk for each cup of flour. Bring the milk to a boil and gradually sprinkle in the flour, stirring briskly all the time, but cook the mixture only until it is completely combined. If the purée is thin, add a little more flour. Finish with 1 tablespoon or more of butter.

The indispensable onion, they call it, and with good reason. What would any good cook do without the onion as a flavoring for meat, fish, sauces, soups, stews, for almost everything except sweets? The onion is the vegetable backbone, so to speak, of many stews and braised dishes, and a favorite accompaniment to broiled and sautéed meats. Fortunately onions keep well; they can be stored in string bags, which allow for circulation of air, in a cool, dry place during the winter months when fresh green vegetables are scarce and expensive in some localities. A French salad basket makes a good storage container and holds about 5 pounds. White onions are more perishable than the everyday large yellow varieties, and should be purchased in smaller quantities. The small white onions are used for garnishing and serving whole. Large onions of uniform size may be stuffed and baked, or sliced for deep-frying or sautéing (sautéed onions are also called " smothered "). Yellow onions of varying sizes may be sliced or chopped and used to flavor soups or other dishes.

But however the onions are to be cooked, they should be cut into even slices or chopped into even bits. This trick insures that all the onion will be uniformly cooked.

Oignons Glacés

PEEL enough small uniform white onions to make 2 cups. Put them in a saucepan with 1/2 cup each of lightly salted chicken stock and water, 1 tablespoon butter, and 1/2 tablespoon sugar. Simmer the onions until the liquid has cooked away. Continue cooking, shaking the pan constantly, until the onions take on a golden glaze.

SAUTÉED ONIONS

Oignons Sautés

HEAT enough clarified butter in a skillet to cover the bottom generously. Add peeled, sliced onions and cook them over moderate heat until they are richly golden and soft, stirring and turning them frequently to insure even cooking.

FRIED ONIONS

Oignons Frits

PEEL 4 to 6 large onions, slice them 1/4 inch thick, and separate the rings. Dip the rings in milk, then in flour, and fry them in deep hot fat or oil (375° F.) until they are golden brown. Drain on absorbent paper and sprinkle with salt. Serve at once.

BRAISED SPANISH ONIONS

Oignons d'Espagne Braisés

SPANISH onions are usually the ones selected for braising because they are large and sweet. Slice 1 small yellow onion and spread the slices in a saucepan or casserole with 4 thin slices of fat salt pork. Place on this 6 peeled Spanish onions. Add 1 cup meat gravy or stock, bring the liquid to a boil, and cover the pan closely. Put it in a moderate oven (350° F.) and braise the onions 30 to 40 minutes, or until they are tender. Remove the pork slices and continue cooking, uncovered, basting with the juice in the pan until they are golden brown. Remove the onions to a warm serving dish and add 1/3 cup Sherry to the pan. Heat the liquid and strain it over the onions.

STUFFED ONIONS

Oignons Farcis

PARBOIL 6 large onions about 10 minutes and drain well. Cut out the centers, leaving a shell about 3/4 to 1 inch thick and a base about 1/2 inch thick. Chop the part that was removed and combine with chopped leftover meat or cooked rice or mushroom *duxelles* or a mixture of any of them. Season with salt and pepper. Fill the shells with the mixture and sprinkle the tops with fine bread crumbs and a little melted butter. Arrange in a shallow casserole and add enough stock or strained canned tomatoes to come about halfway up the onions. Cook in a very hot oven (450° F.) for 20 to 25 minutes, or until the tops are brown. Remove each onion to an individual serving dish and pour around it a little of the cooking liquid.

Purée
Soubise

MELT 1/4 cup butter in a large saucepan, add 8 large onions, chopped, and cook slowly, stirring, until they are soft but not brown. Add 1/2 cup rice, 1 cup boiling water, and 1/2 teaspoon salt. Cover the pan closely and cook the onions over very low heat for 35 to 40 minutes, or until the water is entirely cooked away. Make a very thick béchamel sauce with 1/4 cup each of butter and flour and 2 cups milk. Cook, stirring briskly, until the sauce is thick and smooth. Continue to cook slowly, stirring occasionally, until it becomes very thick and is reduced to about 1 cup. Rub the cooked onion and rice mixture through a fine sieve and return it to the heat to cook away all the surplus moisture, stirring constantly to avoid scorching. Combine it with the béchamel and continue cooking and stirring until the purée is smooth and blended.

The Cabbages

THERE are two schools of thought about preparing cabbage, and most Americans prefer to cook or steam the leaves only until they are translucent and flexible, but still crisp. As for me, I like to season cabbage with onion, carrot, and herbs, and to cook it for 1 1/2 hours or more.

Perhaps some of the vitamins are lost in this long cooking, but I think one can make up the loss by eating fresh fruits and salads. I have also discovered that cabbage becomes entirely digestible, even for people who have not been able to enjoy it, if it is parboiled for 5 minutes in a generous quantity of boiling water, then plunged into cold water, before further cooking.

BRAISED CABBAGE

Chou Braisé

CUT 1 large or 2 small cabbages in quarters and remove the hard cores. Put the pieces in a large kettle of water, bring the water to a boil, and parboil for 5 minutes. Drain and rinse in a generous amount of cold water. Drain the cabbage again, squeezing out as much water as possible. Cut 1/2 pound sliced bacon in pieces and cook it in the kettle until it starts to brown. Add the cabbage, 1 carrot, 1 onion stuck with a clove, 1 or 2 leeks, 1 clove of garlic, 6 peppercorns, and a faggot made by tying together 2 stalks of celery, 2 sprigs of parsley, 1 bay leaf, and a small pinch of thyme. Add enough water or water and stock to just cover the cabbage and 1 teaspoon salt. Simmer the cabbage, covered, over low heat for 1 1/2 to 2 hours. Remove the cabbage, letting the surplus liquid drain back into the kettle.

Discard the faggot, onion, carrot, and garlic, and reserve the liquid. Combine it with stock and vegetables to make a good cabbage soup.

STUFFED CABBAGE

Chou Farci I

WASH a firm cabbage, put it in a kettle of boiling water, and parboil it 10 minutes. Drain it and plunge it into cold water. When it is cool, drain it thoroughly in a colander, top down. For the stuffing cook 1 finely chopped medium onion in 1 tablespoon butter until it is soft. Combine it with 1/4 pound pork sausage meat, 1/4 pound leftover cooked meat, finely chopped or ground, 2 tablespoons fresh bread crumbs, 1 cup cooked rice, 1 clove garlic, crushed, 1/2 teaspoon salt, a little pepper, and 1 beaten egg. Mix all together well.

Place the well-drained cabbage, right side up, in a bowl and carefully cut out the core to within 1 inch of the bottom. Sprinkle a little salt and pepper through the leaves. Fill the cavity with some of the stuffing and distribute the remainder as evenly as possible between the leaves all around. Wrap 2 or 3 slices of fat pork, salt or fresh, around the cabbage and tie them securely. Put in a casserole 1 carrot and 1 onion, both sliced, and add the cabbage and enough boiling stewed tomatoes to reach about 1/3 of the way up the cabbage. Cook the cabbage, covered, in a moderate oven (350° F.) for about 2 hours, basting it from time to time. Remove the cabbage to a serving dish and take off the fat pork. Strain the liquid into a saucepan, skim off the fat, and cook until reduced to about 1 cup. If leftover meat gravy is on hand, add it. Correct the sasoning with salt and pour the sauce around the cabbage.

Chou Farci II   STUFFED CABBAGE LEAVES

PARBOIL and drain a cabbage as for stuffed cabbage and prepare the stuffing. Cut the leaves from the core of the cabbage, lay 2 or 3 of them together, and spread them flat. Cover with a few spoonfuls of stuffing, roll up the leaves, and tie the roll with a string. Repeat, until all the stuffing is used. Arrange the rolls in a shallow casserole and add enough boiling stewed tomatoes to reach halfway up the rolls. Cook the rolls in a moderate oven (350° F.) for 45 minutes to 1 hour. Remove them to a serving dish and take off the strings. Strain the liquid into a saucepan, skim off the fat, and cook until reduced to about 1/2 the original quantity. Correct the seasoning with salt and pour the sauce around the rolls. Cold cabbage rolls are often served with vinaigrette sauce as an hors-d'oeuvre.

Red cabbage is always cut in small pieces and cooked with wine, vinegar, or fruit to help it retain its color. I add a little fat in cooking it, always butter or goose fat.

Chou Rouge   RED CABBAGE WITH WINE
au Vin

CUT 1 large or 2 small red cabbages in quarters and clean them well. Remove the hard cores and cut the cabbage in fine julienne. Parboil the cabbage in boiling water for 10 minutes. Remove it to cold water and when it is cool, drain it well. Season with 1 teaspoon salt, a little pepper, and a few grains of nutmeg. Cook 1 finely chopped onion in 2 tablespoons butter or goose fat until it is soft and add 1 tablespoon vinegar, 2 cups each of white or red wine and water, and the drained cabbage. Simmer it for 30 minutes. Add 2 or 3 green apples, peeled, cored, and chopped, and cook for 25 to 30 minutes longer, adding more water if necessary to prevent scorching.

Lettuce may be stuffed, as cabbage is.

STUFFED LETTUCE

Laitues Farcies

CAREFULLY remove the center leaves of 2 heads of lettuce. Use them for salad. Leave a shell of outside leaves about an inch thick attached to the core, left intact and about an inch thick. Wash the shells under running water and parboil them for 2 or 3 minutes in boiling salted water. Drain thoroughly, upside down, in a colander. Place each lettuce shell right side up in a bowl and fill the center with the stuffing for stuffed cabbage. Tie each head with soft string. Put 1 carrot and 1 onion, both sliced, in a casserole, place the stuffed lettuce heads on them, and add enough boiling stock or canned tomatoes, or both, to reach about 2 inches up the lettuce heads. Put a strip of bacon or fat salt pork over each head. Bring the liquid to a boil on top of the stove and cook, covered, in a moderate oven (350° F.) for 45 minutes to 1 hour. Remove the lettuce to serving dish. Strain the liquid, skim off the fat, and cook it until it is reduced to about 1 cup. If leftover meat gravy is on hand, add it. Correct the seasoning with salt and pour the sauce around the lettuce. Serve as a luncheon or supper dish.

Brussels sprouts, which look like tiny cabbages, should be washed in a generous amount of cold water with a little vinegar in it to draw out any insects that may be hiding in the leaves. It is important not to overcook sprouts: after an initial parboiling, 20 minutes simmering in salted water is usually enough to make them tender. To prepare sprouts, trim the stems, discard any yellow leaves, and cut a small cross in the bottom of each little core. Cover them with cold water and parboil for 5 minutes. Drain the sprouts, rinse in cold water, and drain again. Then proceed with the cooking in any way you choose.

Choux
de Bruxelles
Ménagère

BRUSSELS SPROUTS WITH BACON OR FAT PORK

PREPARE 1 quart Brussels sprouts as above. Cook them in boiling salted water to cover for about 20 minutes, or until they are tender. Drain thoroughly. Sauté 2 or 3 slices of bacon or fat salt pork cut into fine dice and 1 teaspoon finely chopped onion in 1 tablespoon butter or goose fat until the pieces are golden brown. Add the well-drained sprouts and toss all together until the sprouts are hot. Season with salt and pepper and sprinkle with chopped parsley.

Choux
de Bruxelles
au Gratin

BRUSSELS SPROUTS AU GRATIN

PREPARE 1 quart Brussels sprouts as above. Cook them in boiling salted water to cover for about 20 minutes, or until they are tender. Drain the sprouts and sauté them quickly in a little butter, shaking the pan to dry out the sprouts and glaze them slightly. Season them with salt and pepper. Prepare duchess potatoes or sliced boiled potatoes and make a ring on a heatproof serving dish. Spread a little Mornay sauce in the ring and arrange the sprouts on top of it. Cover them with more Mornay sauce. Combine equal amounts of fine dry bread crumbs and grated Parmesan cheese and sprinkle over the potatoes, sprouts, and sauce. Sprinkle melted butter over all. Put the dish in a very hot oven (450° F.) or under the broiler and cook until the top is golden brown.

Choux
de Bruxelles
Châtelaine

BRUSSELS SPROUTS WITH SWEET POTATO AND LENTIL PURÉE

COMBINE 1 1/2 cups each of cooked, mashed sweet potato and purée of lentils with 1 tablespoon butter and mix all together well. Using a pastry bag or a spoon and a spatula, form a ring of the mixture on a heatproof platter. Brush the ring with melted butter and brown it in a hot oven (425° F.). Fill the ring with Brussels sprouts that have been cooked, drained, and sautéed lightly in a little butter.

Prime cauliflower is snowy white and very firm. Soaking in cold salted water will help to clean the head and rid it of any insects hiding there. The stem and the green leaves are discarded. The head may be broken into flowerets or cooked whole. In either case, parboil the cauliflower for 5 minutes and plunge it into cold water before proceeding with the cooking. Be careful not to overcook cauliflower; it tastes best when it is barely tender to the fork, simmered in salted water to reach this point. Drain the cauliflower thoroughly on absorbent paper before serving it with melted butter or sauce. If necessary, the cauliflower may be tied in cheesecloth and reheated in a sieve over boiling water.

SAUTÉED CAULIFLOWER

Chou-Fleur Sauté

BREAK cauliflower into flowerets and prepare it for cooking as above. Simmer it in salted water until it is barely tender. Drain it well on absorbent paper. Cook 2 tablespoons butter until it is hazelnut brown, add the well-drained cauliflower, and sauté it quickly on all sides, shaking the pan and taking care not to mash the flowerets in turning them. Season with salt and a little white pepper. Sprinkle the cooked cauliflower with finely chopped parsley.

CAULIFLOWER WITH SAUCE POLONAISE

Chou-Fleur à la Polonaise

PREPARE cauliflower for cooking as above and simmer it in salted water until it is barely tender. Drain it well on absorbent paper. Arrange the whole head, or the flowerets, on a serving dish and cover generously with *sauce polonaise.*

CAULIFLOWER AU GRATIN

Chou-Fleur au Gratin

BREAK cauliflower into flowerets and prepare it for cooking as above. Simmer it in salted water until it is tender. Drain it well on absorbent paper. Spread 1 cup Mornay sauce in a shallow heatproof dish and re-form the well-drained flowerets into a head, as nearly as possible. Cover with 1 cup Mornay sauce. Sprinkle with grated cheese, a few fine bread crumbs, and a little melted butter and cook in a very hot oven (450° F.) or under the broiler until the top is brown.

Chou Brocoli

FRESH broccoli is a rich green color; never buy a bunch in which tiny flowers have started to yellow. More than any other member of the cabbage family, broccoli has a tendency to harbor small insects, and should be soaked, head down, in a large amount of cold water with vinegar in it. Cut off the tough stem ends and peel the lower part of the stalks. If the heads are large, they may be split lengthwise through flower and stalk. Simmer the broccoli in a large amount of salted water until the stems can be readily pierced with a sharp fork. Broccoli usually sinks to the bottom of the kettle when it is tender. Remove the cooked broccoli carefully to absorbent paper to drain, or use a hot cloth towel, and serve it hot with melted butter, hollandaise, or *sauce polonaise* or cold with *sauce vinaigrette*. Or substitute broccoli for cauliflower in the recipe for cauliflower au gratin.

Spring and Summer Vegetables

ASPARAGUS are prepared simply, but most carefully. They must be carefully washed and are refreshed by standing stem down in cold water. It is important not to overcook asparagus; the stalks should be tender but not limp, and the flowers firm. Asparagus should be very well drained before they are sauced. The usual sauces are hollandaise, *maltaise*, or *mousseline*, or simply hot melted butter. Asparagus are also served cold, or, better, at room temperature, as hors-d'oeuvre or salad, with *sauce vinaigrette* to which a little chopped hard-cooked egg and chopped parsley is added, or with mayonnaise.

The lower ends of asparagus stalks are too tough to eat, and fit only for the stock pot. Bend the stalk and it will snap off at the point where it becomes tender. The thicker stalks are considered prime, and in France we scrape or peel the lower three inches or so of the butt. Tie the stalks in bunches of 8 or 10 so that they may easily be removed from the pan. Lower the bundles into simmering salted water and cook gently for 12 to 20 minutes, depending upon the age and natural tenderness of the asparagus. Test the butt ends with a sharp-tined fork and remove the asparagus to drain on a towel as soon as the ends are tender.. An American way to cook asparagus is to stand the stalks upright in the bottom of a double boiler and cover the pan with the top of the boiler so that the tips cook in steam. There are also asparagus cookers that work on the same principle.

ASPARAGUS AU GRATIN

Asperges au Gratin

PREPARE, cook and drain well 1 bunch of asparagus. Align the stalks in the same direction in a shallow heatproof serving dish. Spread 1 cup Mornay sauce over them and sprinkle with a little grated Parmesan or dry Swiss cheese and a little melted butter. Brown under the broiler.

ASPARAGUS WITH BROWN BUTTER AND CRUMBS

Asperges Polonaise

PREPARE, cook, and drain well 1 bunch of asparagus. Arrange on a serving dish and sprinkle with 1 chopped, hard-cooked egg, 2 tablespoons chopped parsley, and the juice of 1/2 lemon. Melt 6 tablespoons butter and cook it until it is lightly browned. Add 3 tablespoons fine, white bread crumbs and cook, shaking the pan to cook the crumbs evenly, until they are lightly browned. Pour butter and crumbs over the asparagus.

Browning
Bread
Crumbs

Spinach has such a long growing season nowadays that it can be considered a year-round vegetable, but the first pickings of spring, so young and tender that they can be eaten raw in a salad, are still a special treat. Spinach is one of the most versatile of vegetables. Not only is it made into soups, soufflés and molded rings, but it is combined with fish, eggs, meat, and poultry to make a number of main-course dishes, all of which are called Florentine. Spinach should never be stored in the tightly packed plastic bags in which it is usually purchased; it spoils very quickly if the leaves are not given plenty of air. There is less sand in spinach now than there used to be, but it is still necessary to swish the leaves through cold water to clean them. Lift the leaves out of the bowl of cold water, and repeat the washing until no sand falls to the bottom of the bowl. Spinach may be cooked in the water that clings to the leaves after washing or, like cabbage, it may be cooked in a large amount of boiling water. In either case, it takes only a few minutes to wilt the leaves, and they should then be thoroughly drained.

BOILED SPINACH

Epinards en Branche

WASH thoroughly 3 pounds young, tender spinach and boil it rapidly in 1 quart boiling water with 1/2 teaspoon salt for 6 to 8 minutes. Drain in a colander, pressing out as much water as possible. Return the spinach to the stove and shake the pan over moderate heat until the greens are as dry as possible. Serve with melted butter.

SPINACH IN CREAM

Epinards à la Crème

COOK 3 pounds spinach as for *épinards en branche*, boiled spinach. Chop the drained spinach very fine or force it through a coarse sieve. Melt 2 tablespoons butter in a saucepan, stir in 2 teaspoons flour, and cook the *roux*, stirring, until it begins to turn golden. Stir in the spinach and cook it for a few minutes, or until it is quite dry. Season with 1/2 teaspoon salt and, if desired, a grating of nutmeg. Stir in 1/2 cup rich milk or cream, bring the mixture to a boil, and cook it for a few minutes longer. Garnish the spinach with small triangular croutons or with quarters of hard-cooked egg.

The tart, acid flavor of sorrel is highly prized by Europeans, who make it into soup, and particularly by French gourmets, who braise sorrel and serve it with meats. Sorrel with shad is a seasonal delicacy avidly awaited by knowing gourmets.

SORREL PURÉE

Purée d'Oseille

WASH thoroughly 3 pounds sorrel, drain it, and cook in the water that clings to the leaves over high heat about 15 or 20 minutes, or until it is very soft. This is called " melted " sorrel. Drain, pressing out as much water as possible. Rub through a sieve. Makes 2 cups purée. To serve, add melted butter to taste and correct the seasoning with salt.

BRAISED SORREL

Oseille Braisée

USE 5 pounds sorrel to make 3 cups purée. Melt 3 tablespoons butter in a saucepan, add 2 tablespoons flour, and cook the *roux* until it starts to turn golden. Add the sorrel purée, mix well, and add 1/2 teaspoon salt, 1 tablespoon sugar, and 1/2 cup stock. Mix all together and bring to the boiling point. Cover with a piece of buttered wax paper, cover the pan, and cook the sorrel in a moderate oven (350° to 375° F.) for about 1 hour. Remove it from the oven, add 2 beaten eggs, and mix well. Bring it back to the boiling point but do not allow it to boil. Remove the sorrel from the heat, correct the seasoning with salt, and add either 1 tablespoon butter, 2 tablespoons cream, or 3 tablespoons gravy from the meat with which it is to be served.

Although they are available all the year round, at least in communities of any size, beans, peas, corn, cucumbers, and tomatoes remain for most of us summer vegetables. The fact remains that locally grown vegetables, in the height of their abundance, have an unmatched delicacy and freshness. If you have a vegetable garden, you can enjoy the further luxury of vegetables that are truly young: of tiny peas so tender that they cook in a few minutes, of corn kernels whose sweetness will later turn to starch, of green beans whose seeds are so tiny that they are hardly noticeable in the slender, flexible pods. As for cucumbers and tomatoes, no one who has eaten out of hand a warty, crisp-skinned cucumber or a sun-warmed, sun-ripened tomato freshly plucked from the vine, needs to be told how important is is for these to be young, fresh, and unblemished.

It is a good idea to wash green beans and let them stand in cold water for a short time before cooking. Tiny beans may be cooked whole; simply trim the ends. Larger beans may be cut into even lengths, or slit down the middle, or " Frenched," slit and then sliced on the diagonal. Be careful not to overcook the beans; they should be crisp to the teeth.

Haricots Verts au Beurre

BUTTERED GREEN BEANS

WASH, trim, and slice as desired 1 1/2 pounds green beans. Bring 1 quart water to a boil with 1 teaspoon salt. Add the green beans gradually, so that the water continues to boil. Cook the beans 18 to 20 minutes, until they are tender but still crisp. Drain off the water and shake the pan over low heat for a minute or two to dry the beans thoroughly. Add 2 to 3 tablespoons butter, bit by bit, and continue shaking the pan over the heat until the butter melts.

Haricots Verts à la Lyonnaise

GREEN BEANS WITH ONION

COOK 1 1/2 pounds green beans. Melt 3 tablespoons butter and in it cook until golden 1 onion, finely chopped. Add the beans, thoroughly drained, and shake the pan over the heat to mix the beans, butter, and onion. Adjust the seasoning and sprinkle with chopped parsley.

Haricots Verts Paysanne

GREEN BEANS COUNTRY STYLE

PREPARE and cook 1 1/2 pounds young green beans. Parboil 1/2 cup diced salt pork or bacon in water to cover for 5 minutes and drain it. Brown the pork dice lightly in 2 tablespoons butter and remove the dice. In the fat in the pan brown lightly 2 onions, finely chopped. Add 4 tomatoes, peeled, seeded, and chopped, 2 peeled potatoes, cut in large dice, 3/4 teaspoon salt, a little pepper, the pork dice, and beans. Cover with 1/2 cup water, bring the liquid to a boil, and simmer the mixture, covered, about 30 minutes, or until the vegetables are tender.

Haricots Flageolets

FLAGEOLETS

SOAK 2 cups small dried kidney beans, green or white, for 2 hours and drain them. Put them in 2 quarts salted water, bring the water to a boil, and cook them for 1 to 2 hours, or until they are tender. Drain them. Sauté 1/4 cup chopped onions in butter until they are soft and add them to the beans. Dress the beans with melted butter and sprinkle them with chopped parsley.

The time for cooking green peas can vary greatly, depending upon the size, age, and freshness of the peas. Overcooked peas disintegrate, so it is very important to test them frequently as they cook and to remove them from the heat at the critical moment.

GREEN PEAS COUNTRY STYLE

Petits Pois Paysanne

CUT enough fat salt pork into fine dice to make 1/2 cup, cover the dice with water, and parboil them for 5 minutes. Drain off the water. Melt 1 tablespoon butter in a saucepan, add the pork dice, 1/2 cup carrots, scraped and diced, and 10 tiny white onions. Cook the vegetables, shaking the pan occasionally, until they are all lightly browned. Remove the vegetables.

In the fat in the pan lightly brown 1 teaspoon flour. Gradually add 3/4 cup chicken stock or water, bring the liquid to a boil, and add the browned carrots, onions, and pork dice, 2 cups shelled peas, 4 shredded lettuce leaves, and 4 sprigs each of parsley and chervil tied in a faggot. Add 1 tablespoon sugar, bring the liquid to a boil, and simmer the vegetables, covered, for 30 minutes, or until they are tender. Discard the faggot. Reduce the liquid, if necessary, to 1/2 cup. Correct the seasoning with salt.

GREEN PEAS FRENCH STYLE

Petits Pois à la Française

MELT 2 tablespoons butter in a saucepan, add 6 tiny white onions, 5 or 6 shredded leaves of lettuce, 1 tablespoon sugar, 1/2 teaspoon salt, and 3 sprigs each of parsley and chervil tied in a faggot. Add 2 to 3 cups freshly shelled tiny peas, mix all together, and add 1/2 cup water. Bring the liquid to a boil and simmer the peas, closely covered, for about 25 minutes, or until they are just tender. Only about 2 or 3 tablespoons water should remain in the pan. Remove the faggot, take the pan from the heat, and add a little *beurre manié* made by creaming 1 tablespoon butter with 1/2 teaspoon flour. Reheat, shaking the pan to combine the peas with the butter and flour mixture, until the liquid boils again.

Corn is another vegetable in which freshness is of prime importance. There have been many jokes about corn-lovers putting the pot of water on to boil before they go out to the garden to pick the corn, and husking the ears as they sprint back to the kitchen. In my opinion, this is hardly an exaggeration of the ideal way to cook corn on the cob. Older ears of corn, still sweet but possibly tough-skinned, need special treatment. Boil the corn for the designated time, usually no longer than 8 minutes. Cool it in cold water and with a sharp knife or a sharp-tined kitchen fork, rip down the center of the kernels, exposing the pulp. Press the pulp out with the side of the knife or fork; the tough skins may then be discarded with the cobs.

Purée de Maïs

CORN PURÉE

Cook corn and press out the pulp as above. To 2 cups of pulp, add 2 tablespoons melted butter and salt and pepper to taste and reheat the purée. If desired, add a little cream.

Cucumbers are usually eaten raw, but they make an excellent addition to the usual assortment of cooked vegetables. The more mature cucumbers are likely to be seedy; cut out the seedy parts and cook the rest very briefly, so that the watery flesh does not disintegrate. Raw cucumber cases, freed of seeds and with the rinds scored, are filled with cold salad mixtures or purée of foie gras *as garnish for cold entrées.*

Concombres Sautés

SAUTÉED CUCUMBERS

Cut 3 or 4 large peeled cucumbers in half lengthwise. Remove the seeds and cut the halves into pieces about 1 inch long. Cook the cucumbers in boiling salted water for 5 to 6 minutes and drain them. Sauté the pieces in enough very hot butter to cover the bottom of a skillet until they are light golden color, sprinkling them with a little sugar as they cook. Season with salt and sprinkle with chopped parsley. If desired, add 2 tablespoons good meat gravy at the end of the cooking.

During my years of supervising the kitchens of a great hotel, tons of tomatoes have gone through my hands: fresh, canned, whole, juiced, puréed—more tomatoes, surely, than any other vegetable. Tomatoes are used in an endless number of ways, for every course on the menu except perhaps dessert—and I say only perhaps—and with every course on the menu, as well.

If this versatile vegetable has a fault, it is that it contains an unusually large proportion of water. To rid the tomato of this excess liquid, cut the tomato in half, and holding it gently in the palm of the hand, carefully squeeze out the seeds and most of the water. The flesh should not be broken or bruised, and the tomato will quickly regain its shape. If the tomato is to be peeled, dip it whole into boiling water for an instant, and then into cold water; the skin will slip off readily. Tomatoes for cooking should be firm and heavy for their size, so they will hold their shape in spite of the heat.

Ridding
Tomatoes
of Water

SAUTÉED TOMATOES

CUT firm tomatoes in thick slices, season the slices with salt, and roll them in flour. Heat oil or clarified butter in a heavy skillet and sauté the tomato slices on both sides.

*Tomates
Sautées*

FRENCH FRIED TOMATOES

BEAT 2 eggs, add 1/2 cup milk, 2 tablespoons salad oil, and 1 teaspoon salt, and combine thoroughly. Cut firm tomatoes in thick slices and dip each slice in flour and then in the milk and egg mixture, covering it completely. Cover the slices with fine dry crumbs and brown both sides in butter.

*Tomates
Frites*

TOMATOES LYONNAISE

HALVE 6 tomatoes and squeeze out seeds and water as above. Sauté them in 3 tablespoons hot salad oil or butter until they are golden brown. Remove them to a serving dish. Add a little butter to the pan and sauté 2 finely chopped onions until they are golden. Divide them among the tomato halves and sprinkle with finely chopped parsley.

*Tomates à la
Lyonnaise*

TOMATOES PORTUGAISE

PEEL and halve 6 or 8 tomatoes and squeeze out seeds and water as above. Cut each piece in half again. Sauté the pieces in 3 tablespoons hot olive oil until they are browned and a little soft. Add 2 shallots, finely chopped,

*Tomates
Portugaise*

or 1 tablespoon chopped onion and 1 clove of garlic, crushed. Season to taste with salt and pepper and sprinkle with finely chopped parsley.

TOMATOES PROVENÇALE

Tomates à la Provençale

HALVE 6 or 8 tomatoes and squeeze out seeds and water as above. Season with salt and pepper. Mix 1 cup fine fresh bread crumbs with 2 teaspoons finely chopped parsley and 1 clove of garlic, chopped and crushed. Spread the tomato halves with this mixture and sprinkle with melted butter or salad oil. Arrange on a shallow heatproof serving dish and cook in a very hot oven (450° F.) or under the broiler for 10 to 15 minutes, or until the tomatoes are soft and the tops browned.

TOMATOES STUFFED WITH MUSHROOMS

Tomates Farcies à la Parisienne

PREPARE mushroom *duxelles*, using 1/2 pound mushrooms. Add to the *duxelles* 2 tablespoons tomato purée or meat gravy. Remove just the center of the tops of 6 tomatoes and squeeze out seeds and water as above. Fill the tomatoes with the *duxelles* mixture. Arrange them in a shallow, buttered heatproof dish and sprinkle the tops with fine fresh bread crumbs and a little melted butter. Bake in a hot oven (400° F.) for 20 minutes.

TOMATOES STUFFED WITH CHICKEN

Tomates Farcies Elisabeth

MIX together 1 1/2 cups thick béchamel sauce or chicken *velouté*, 1 cup coarsely chopped cooked chicken, 1/2 cup chopped and cooked mushrooms and, if available, some diced truffle. Stuff and cook 6 tomatoes as for *tomates farcies à la parisienne*, tomatoes stuffed with mushrooms.

SALADES

Salads

WHEN SPRING turned the hedgerows of our *Bourbonnais* countryside white and sweet smelling with blossoming hawthorn, we children knew the time had come for us to gather the season's first wild field salad sprouting in lush profusion in the nearby meadows. And no one had to tell us that the farmers guiding their plows through the fields were uncovering in the furrowed soil tiny, tender dandelion shoots, hardly more than an inch of curled white leaf tipped with green. We knew, too, how our gift of salad greens endeared us to *grand-mère* waiting in the farmhouse kitchen to make the first salad of the season, her favorite of all salads, the greens of early spring tossed with bits of browned bacon or salt pork and hard-cooked eggs dressed with vinegar. Later, of course, we had the different lettuces and salad greens, and the salad herbs—parsley, chives, chervil, and tarragon—and our favorite *salade aux fines herbes* would be tossed every day in our mother's big white china *saladier*.

Market gardeners overlooked nothing that might hasten the growth of our beloved salad greens, including asking aid from on high. Our man in Montmaurault, for instance, sowed his seeds on January 17, *la fête de Saint-Antoine*, and his lettuce was always the first to reach our table. The fact that he tended his seedlings as carefully as he would a new baby had nothing to do with his success. It was his pact with St. Anthony that brought *la bonne chance*.

Simple Green Salads

THE MAKING of a good tossed salad has nothing at all to do with *la bonne chance*. It has everything to do with fine oil, the right kind and quantity of acid juice or vinegar, and a variety of different crisp, fresh salad greens and delicate herbs.

Choose Boston, iceberg, Bibb lettuce, romaine, escarole, endive, chicory, and water cress, and field salad and dandelion greens when you can find them, in the market or in the fields. If you can grow some greens in your own kitchen garden, your salad will be a constant delight. The more kinds of greens you toss together, the better the salad. Allow 3/4 cup greens for each serving.

Salad Greens   Firm, compact heads of lettuce, romaine, and escarole have the greatest proportion of tender, light-colored leaves. Greens must be very fresh and unwilted. Don't buy or pick any more than you can use in a day or two. If necessary, discard any brown or dry outer leaves. Don't wash or break up the heads before storing them in the refrigerator; separate the leaves and wash them as you require them. Salad greens need very careful washing, in quantities of cold water, especially Boston lettuce and romaine; sand hides in their crevices. It is very important to dry the greens thoroughly. Salad dressing slips off wet leaves and forms a watery pool in the bottom of the bowl, instead of clinging to make every leaf shiny and full of flavor. At home we put the washed greens in a special wire basket, a *panier à salade*. It was my chore to carry the basket out into the garden and swirl it around until all the water was gone. I used to welcome this task, particularly when I could steal up behind my little sister and sprinkle her with showers of cold water. Sometimes we used a kitchen towel instead of the wire basket, and you, lacking a garden and a little sister to tease, may find it more convenient to tie the wet leaves in a towel and shake them gently over the sink. When the leaves are clean and dry, break them up (use a silver knife if you wish to shred the leaves, because steel darkens the edges), wrap them in a dry towel, and return them to the refrigerator until time to make the salad. Knowing cooks chill the salad bowl and the salad plates, as well.

Many people use wooden salad bowls and wipe them out with absorbent paper instead of washing them, so that flavorful vinaigrette sauce can season the bowl. I could not approve of this custom in the hotel because in our hot kitchens the oil absorbed by the wood spoiled too easily and could impart an off-flavor to later salads. In fact, I prefer a china or glass bowl, trusting the dressing to take care of the seasoning. **Salad Bowls**

Tossed salads are traditionally dressed with this vinaigrette sauce, the mixture of oil, acid, and seasonings that Americans call French dressing. And what better name for something so typically French? The salad expert is truly put to the test in making the dressing. His hand is light with salt and vinegar; if a sharper dressing is desired, he adds a little mustard, not more vinegar.

The oil most generally used for salad is olive oil—I prefer a light olive oil—but any good, fresh oil will do. Buy only as much oil as you can use in a reasonably short time, because oil begins to deteriorate as soon as the container is opened, and may become rancid. Keep oil in a cool place—the refrigerator, if necessary. **Oil**

The acid of vinaigrette sauce may be vinegar or lemon juice, or a combination of the two. Any vinegar, cider, malt, or wine, may be flavored with herbs. To make tarragon vinegar, for example, put a large handful of tarragon, on the stalks, in a bottle of vinegar, and let the vinegar stand in a warm place for about two months. **Acid**

Garlic A soupçon of garlic is, for many, an indispensable part of the good salad. You can achieve this *goût* of garlic in several ways. Cut a piece of garlic from the clove, put it in the salad bowl with salt and pepper, and crush it with the back of a spoon. Then add the vinegar and oil to finish the dressing. Or rub the inside of the bowl with a cut clove of garlic.

Chapons Or rub small pieces of French bread crust with garlic and toss them with the greens. These *chapons* are not served with the salad, but make a tasty morsel for the cook or cook's assistant who has a fondness for bits of bread drenched in garlicky dressing.

Fines Herbes The *fines herbes* that give an elusive herbal flavor to the tossed salad are traditionally a mixture of equal parts of chopped parsley, chives, tarragon, and chervil, but they can be used in any combination.

Pepper and Salt If you have never tasted pepper freshly ground in a mill or pounded in a mortar at the moment of using, you cannot know how pepper really tastes and smells. As for salt, add only a little, and allow the diners to adjust the amount to suit themselves.

TOSSED GREEN SALAD

Salade
à la Française PREPARE 4 cups salad greens, as described above. Pile them in a chilled salad bowl and add 1/2 cup vinaigrette sauce. Toss the greens over and over with a wooden fork and spoon until they are well coated and no dressing remains in the bottom of the bowl. If desired, flavor the salad with garlic, as described above.

Sauce Vinaigrette VINAIGRETTE SAUCE OR FRENCH DRESSING

MIX together 1 teaspoon salt, a little freshly ground pepper, and 2 tablespoons vinegar. Add 6 tablespoons salad oil and mix well. For a sharper dressing, add a little dry mustard or prepared mustard. Enough for 6 servings of salad. Variations are in the sauce chapter.

GREEN SALAD WITH HERBS

FOLLOW the recipe for *salade à la française*. To each 4 cups of greens add 1 teaspoon each of finely chopped parsley, chives, tarragon, and chervil. If garlic flavor is desired, add *chapons*.

Salade aux Fines Herbes

FIELD SALAD

WASH thoroughly 1 pound of the young field salad that comes into markets in the early spring. Drain the greens and dry them, handling them carefully. They are very fragile and bruise easily. Just before serving, add vinaigrette sauce and toss the greens until all the leaves are coated.

Salade de Doucette

DANDELION SALAD

USE only very young dandelions for salad. Those just starting to sprout are best because they are tender and delicate in flavor. Tear apart 4 cups of the plant, wash well, drain, dry, and chill. Just before serving, toss the greens with vinaigrette sauce. If desired, field salad or other salad greens may be combined with the dandelions.

Salade de Pissenlit

CHIFFONADE SALAD

WASH, drain, and dry equal amounts of romaine, lettuce and chicory. Break up the greens and combine them in a salad bowl. Add celery cut in julienne, peeled and quartered tomatoes, chopped hard-cooked eggs, water cress, and chopped cooked beets, as desired. Mix well with vinaigrette sauce, allowing about 1 tablespoon for each serving, and sprinkle lightly with a little finely chopped chives.

Salade Chiffonnade

I doubt that any two chefs ever made a chef's salad in precisely the same way or, indeed, that any chef ever made his version in precisely the same way twice. However, all chefs' salads begin with a bed of fresh salad greens, shredded or in larger pieces, according to preference, but in any case cut up smaller than for other green salads. Then the ingenuity of the salad maker and the contents of the refrigerator dictate whether the salad shall be topped with julienne of chicken, cheese, ham, tongue, or other meats, plus quartered hard-cooked eggs, tomatoes, and perhaps other vegetables. The julienne should be arranged in an attractive pattern on the greens and the salad dressed and tossed at the table. Chef's salad is light, but still hearty enough to make a satisfying luncheon or supper.

Chef's Salad
CHEF'S SALAD

WASH, drain, and dry salad greens, cut or shred them coarsely, and pile them in a salad bowl. About 4 to 6 cups serve 6. On the greens arrange equal amounts of cold boiled chicken, smoked ox tongue, smoked ham, and Swiss cheese, all cut in julienne. Use 1 to 2 cups in all of these ingredients. Add 1/2 hard-cooked egg for each portion and put a spray of water cress in the center. At servingtime, sprinkle 1/2 cup vinaigrette sauce over the salad and toss with a fork and spoon. The guests should be allowed to admire the arrangement before the salad is mixed.

Salade Paysanne
COUNTRY SALAD

SAUTÉ 1/2 cup finely diced fat salt pork or bacon in a little fresh pork fat until it is golden brown. Wash, drain, and dry 1 pound field salad or other greens and put the greens in the salad bowl. Sprinkle the pork or bacon dice over them and add 1 or 2 hard-cooked eggs, chopped. Season with salt and pepper to taste, add 1/2 teaspoon *fines herbes* and 3/4 tablespoon vinegar, and mix all together.

Salade Maison
SALAD OF THE HOUSE

PUT in a salad bowl 1 cup each of cooked cauliflower, string beans, and chicken, cut in pieces, and 2 tomatoes, peeled, seeded, and chopped. Cut the whites of 2 hard-cooked eggs in julienne and add them. Crush the yolks of the eggs to a smooth paste, season with 1/2 teaspoon each of dry mustard and salt and a little pepper, and add 3/4 tablespoon vinegar. Gradually add 6 tablespoons olive oil. Toss the salad with this dressing until all the ingredients are coated. Sprinkle with 1 teaspoon *fines herbes*.

Main-Course
and Buffet Salads

THE HEARTIER salads use greens only as garnish. There are endless combinations of fish, meat, poultry, and vegetables for these salads. The following recipes only suggest the repertoire you can develop. Dress these salads with mayonnaise or with vinaigrette sauce or with another cold sauce and garnish with mayonnaise or pass it separately. Just remember that mayonnaise is rich and use it with restraint. A little goes a long way.

Recipes for mayonnaise and other salad dressings are included in the sauce chapter.

If you order a potato salad in France, it will be served to you at room temperature, never chilled and clammy cold. I think that once you have tasted potato salad French style, you will prefer it, too. In any case, you must season and dress the potatoes while they are still hot and can absorb the dressing readily. Use small, firm-fleshed potatoes for salad, rather than the large, mealy baking potatoes, which tend to break more easily. Spread the slices on a flat dish, cover them with the dressing, and turn them carefully in it to insure even seasoning. The potatoes will absorb most of the liquid.

POTATO SALAD

BOIL 5 to 6 medium potatoes, unpeeled, in salted water to cover until they are tender. Drain, peel, and cut them into thin slices. While the potatoes are still hot, season them with 1 teaspoon salt and a little pepper and sprinkle them with 2 or 3 tablespoons vinegar and 6 to 7 table-

Salade de Pommes de Terre

375

spoons olive oil. Add 4 tablespoons stock or hot water and chopped parsley, chives, chervil, and tarragon to taste. Chopped spring onions may also be added. Let the salad stand at room temperature until most of the liquid is absorbed. Serve it without chilling.

Salade d'Oeufs

EGG SALAD

ARRANGE 2 cooled, sliced or quartered hard-cooked eggs in lettuce nests on 6 individual serving plates. Blend thoroughly 1 cup mayonnaise, 1/4 cup cream, and 1 teaspoon each of Worcestershire sauce and salt. Pour the sauce over the eggs and sprinkle with paprika.

Salade d'Asperges

ASPARAGUS SALAD

SNAP the tough ends from 36 asparagus stalks. Wash them well, flushing water through the tips to dislodge all sand. Cook the asparagus in boiling salted water until it is just tender, plunge it into cold water to chill it quickly, and drain on a towel. Chop 2 chilled hard-cooked eggs and add 1 tablespoon chopped parsley. Arrange the asparagus on lettuce on individual plates and sprinkle it with the egg and parsley. Sprinkle each serving with 1 tablespoon vinaigrette sauce.

Salade de Betteraves

BEET SALAD

WASH 6 medium beets and bake them in a moderately hot oven (375° F.) for about 40 minutes, or until they are tender. Cool, peel, and cut them into julienne. Combine the beets with 1/2 cup chopped scallions and 1/2 cup vinaigrette sauce or cream mustard dressing. Mix very carefully to avoid breaking the beets.

Salade de Céleri-Rave et Betteraves

CELERY KNOB AND BEET SALAD

THE CELERY knob for this winter salad may be raw, partly cooked, or well cooked, depending upon the crispness preferred.

    Raw: Peel 6 medium celery knobs and cut them into julienne. Spread them on a platter, sprinkle generously with salt, and let stand 1/2 hour. Drain the julienne and press out the moisture with a towel.

Partly cooked: Peel 6 medium celery knobs, cut them into julienne, cover with boiling water, and cook 1 minute. Drain the julienne, rinse with fresh, cold water, drain again, and dry on a towel.

Cooked: Peel 6 medium celery knobs and boil them in salted water to cover for 30 minutes, or until they are tender but not too soft. Drain them, rinse with cold water, drain again, and cool. Slice them or cut into dice.

Wash 6 beets and bake them in a moderately hot oven (375° F.) for about 40 minutes, or until they are tender. Peel, cool, and cut them as the celery knobs are cut, into slices, julienne, or dice. Combine the prepared celery knob and beets and add 1/4 cup chopped scallions or 1 tablespoon chopped chives or an onion that has been boiled for 15 minutes, drained, cooled, and diced. Add enough vinaigrette sauce or cream mustard dressing to moisten generously.

SPRING SALAD

Salade à la Printanière

In a salad bowl, mix together 1/2 teaspoon each of salt and dry mustard, a little pepper, 2 tablespoons vinegar, and 6 tablespoons olive oil. Add 1/2 cup each of cooked asparagus stalks, cut in pieces, cooked peas, and sliced radishes, 2 artichoke bottoms, cooked and sliced, 2 chopped hard-cooked eggs, and 1 teaspoon *fines herbes*. Toss the salad gently and let it marinate for 1/2 to 1 hour. Just before serving add 1/4 cup mayonnaise, mixing it in carefully with a fork to prevent crushing the vegetables.

VEGETABLE SALAD

Salade à la Parisienne

Mix vegetables such as cooked carrots, cooked green beans, tender celery stalks, or parboiled celery knob, all coarsely chopped, with cooked meats such as ham, beef, veal, ox tongue, chicken, and duck, cut in julienne. There should be 4 to 5 cups of salad. Add 3 quartered hard-cooked eggs and 1/2 cup mayonnaise and mix the salad gently. Pile the salad in a large bowl lined with lettuce and sprinkle it with capers.

ENDIVE AND BEET SALAD

Salade Élisabeth

FOR each serving, clean 2 or 3 Belgian endives and cut the stalks in half lengthwise. Arrange them on an individual salad plate and sprinkle with 2 tablespoons cooked beets cut in small julienne or use a few thin beet slices. Moisten with vinaigrette sauce. Sprinkle the beets with a mixture of equal parts of finely chopped chervil, tarragon, and chives.

Salads made with chicken, fish, or shellfish taste best when they are not composed of too many other ingredients, and when mayonnaise, if that is the moistening sauce, is used sparingly. A little celery, approximately 1/2 cup for each cup of chicken, for example, lends interesting texture contrast, but other vegetables, eggs, and tomatoes should be used as a garnish, not mixed into the salad itself.

CHICKEN SALAD

Salade de Volaille

COMBINE 4 cups cooked white meat of chicken, cut into small pieces, with 1 cup each of diced celery and shredded lettuce. Add 1 cup vinaigrette sauce and mix carefully. Turn the salad into a salad bowl lined with lettuce leaves and sprinkle with chopped parsley and chives. Garnish with sliced tomatoes and quartered hard-cooked eggs.

CHICKEN MAYONNAISE

Mayonnaise de Volaille

COMBINE 1 cup each of diced celery and shredded lettuce and 1/4 cup mayonnaise and spread the mixture in the bottom of a salad bowl. Mix 4 cups cooked white meat of chicken, cut in large dice, and 1 cup mayonnaise and season with salt. Pile the mixture on top of the celery and lettuce. Sprinkle the salad with 1 tablespoon capers and garnish the bowl with lettuce leaves and quartered tomatoes and hard-cooked eggs.

LOBSTER MAYONNAISE

Mayonnaise de Homard

COMBINE 2 cups boiled lobster, cut in pieces, and 1 cup chopped celery. Add enough mayonnaise to moisten the mixture well. Serve on lettuce leaves arranged in a bowl or deep platter.

To prepare lobster for salad, follow the directions for boiled lobster. As soon as the lobsters are cold, split them and carefully crack the claws. Open them and remove the meat from body and claws. Save the ends of the claw meat to garnish the salad and cut up the rest of the meat.

Lobster for Salad

Fish flakes break and mash very easily, making a heavy, unattractive salad. To avoid this, mix in mayonnaise or vinaigrette sauce with a fork, very gently lifting and tossing the fish to distribute the sauce.

FISH SALAD

Salade de Poisson

CUT into pieces 1 pound cooked fish such as salmon, halibut, tuna, or striped bass and mix it with about 2 1/2 to 3 cups cooked vegetables, using any combination of beans, lima beans, peas, and diced carrots. Add 1 cup mayonnaise and mix the salad gently with a fork, taking care not to mash the fish. Put it in a salad bowl lined with lettuce leaves and arrange slices of peeled tomato and cucumber alternately around the edge. Garnish with quartered hard-cooked eggs.

AVOCADO PASADENA

Avocat Pasadena

To 2 1/2 cups fresh crab meat add 2 ripe tomatoes, peeled, seeded and chopped, 1 tablespoon tarragon vinegar, 1 teaspoon chopped chives, 1 tablespoon mixed chopped parsley, tarragon and chervil, 1 1/2 cups mayonnaise, 2 tablespoons chili sauce, and 1 teaspoon Worcestershire sauce. Mix all together and correct the seasoning with salt. Peel 3 avocados, halve them, and remove the pits. Fill the avocado halves with the crab meat mixture. Garnish each with half a ripe olive.

379

Tomates
Farcies

STUFFED TOMATOES

To prepare a tomato for stuffing, plunge it for a moment into boiling water, then into cold. The skin will slip off. Cut a slice from the top, spoon out some of the pulp, and holding the tomato in the palm of the hand, squeeze it gently, upside down, to remove seeds and surplus juice. Drain the tomato shell for about an hour and chill it. Fill it with chicken, fish, or shellfish salad and garnish with finely chopped parsley, cutouts of pimiento, olive, or hard-cooked eggs, rosettes of mayonnaise, or sprays of water cress.

Tomates
Bombay

TOMATOES STUFFED WITH RICE AND RAISINS

COMBINE 2 cups cooked rice, 1/2 cup raisins that have been cooked in a little butter for a few minutes, 1/2 green pepper, diced, and 1/2 pimiento, diced. Make a dressing with 3 tablespoons olive oil, the juice of 1 lemon, 1/2 teaspoon each of salt and curry powder, a little pepper, and 1 tablespoon chutney sauce. Mix the dressing and rice mixture gently. Prepare 6 firm tomatoes for stuffing, as above. Fill them with the rice mixture and re-place the tops. Chill. Serve on lettuce leaves or garnish with water cress.

Tomates
Farcies de
Salade de
Concombres

TOMATOES STUFFED WITH CUCUMBER SALAD

PEEL, cut in half lengthwise, and remove the seeds of 2 or 3 fresh, crisp cucumbers. Slice the cucumbers very thinly, put the slices in a bowl, and sprinkle a little salt over them. Let them stand for 1 to 2 hours to draw out the water. Drain, spread the slices on a towel, squeeze out the water, and return them to the bowl. Add 2 or 3 tablespoons vinaigrette sauce and 1 teaspoon each of chopped parsley and chives. Chill the salad. Prepare small, bright red tomatoes for stuffing and fill them.

Tomates
Washington

TOMATOES WASHINGTON

COMBINE 1 1/2 cups cooked fish, cut in pieces, 1/2 to 3/4 cup cooked lobster and shrimp, if available, 1 1/2 cups chopped celery, 1 cup mayon-naise, 1 tablespoon finely chopped mixed chives, parsley, and tarragon, and a little Worcestershire sauce. Toss all together gently with a fork without crushing the fish. Prepare 6 firm medium tomatoes for stuffing, as above. Fill them with the fish mixture and replace the tops. Place them on lettuce leaves and decorate the top with mimosa, made by mixing together chopped hard-cooked egg and parsley.

BEEF SALAD COUNTRY STYLE

Salade de Boeuf Fermière

SAUTÉ 1/2 cup diced salt pork until it is golden brown. Drain it and let it cool. In a salad bowl combine 1/2 cup each of vinaigrette sauce and lukewarm chicken stock, 1 tablespoon mixed finely chopped parsley, chervil, and tarragon, 1 teaspoon salt, and a little freshly ground pepper. Cut about 1 pound cooked beef that is still a little warm into small dice or into small thin slices. Combine the warm beef, 1 cup freshly cooked rice, and the sautéed salt pork dice in the salad bowl and toss gently. Garnish with sliced tomatoes and hard-cooked eggs.

Aspic Salads

THERE are few foods more beautiful than a molded salad—the many-colored meats and vegetables covered (and effectively protected against drying out, even overnight) with transparent, sparkling aspic. The aspic used for salads is usually based on beef or chicken consommé; either is used for vegetables, but chicken-flavored aspic is preferred for chicken salads and also for fish. Jellied salads must be very firm if they are to stand up. You will find instructions for making and using aspic in the section on aspic dishes.

Salade en Gelée

ASPIC SALAD

POUR cool but still liquid aspic about 1/2 inch deep into a mold or oblong loaf pan and chill it until it is set.

Combine 1 1/2 cups mixed cooked vegetables such as sliced or diced carrots, green beans cut in small pieces and lima beans, and 1/2 cup thinly sliced celery with 1/4 cup vinaigrette sauce. Turn this vegetable mixture into the mold and fill the mold with cool but still liquid aspic. If desired, arrange thin slices of cooked breast of chicken or boiled beef in the mold before adding the vegetables. Chill in the refrigerator.

Unmold the salad onto a chilled serving platter and garnish it with lettuce or water cress and hard-cooked eggs and tomatoes.

Salade Parisienne en Gelée

JELLIED VEGETABLE SALAD WITH LOBSTER

CHILL a charlotte or other mold thoroughly and line it with cool but still liquid chicken aspic. Chill until the aspic is set. Decorate the sides with slices of lobster and sliced truffles dipped in aspic. Chill the mold until they adhere firmly. Fill the center with a mixture of small cubes or julienne of cooked carrots, lima beans, peas, and green beans well mixed with mayonnaise *chaud-froid*, using one part *chaud-froid* to three parts vegetable mixture. Add aspic to fill the mold. Chill the mold in the refrigerator until it is firm. Unmold on a serving dish and garnish.

Turban de Tomates en Gelée

TOMATO RING MOLD

COMBINE 5 cups tomato juice, 3 or 4 very ripe fresh tomatoes, cut in pieces, 1/2 teaspoon sugar, 1 clove, 1/2 bay leaf, and 1/2 teaspoon salt, and simmer the mixture for 10 minutes. Stir in, off the heat, 2 1/2 tablespoons gelatin softened in 1/2 cup cold water. Add the juice of 1/2 lemon and strain the mixture through a fine sieve. Fill a ring mold and chill the jelly in the refrigerator until it is set. Unmold the jelly onto a serving dish and fill the center with a vegetable salad.

SOUFFLÉS

Soufflés

To my knowledge, no other country has developed in its cuisine a dish put together and cooked quite like a soufflé. Any French chef, whatever his department—sauce or soup, fish or pastry—also knows how to create from simple ingredients a light succulent soufflé. And the *cuisinière* in a fine French home, with leftover chicken to use for luncheon, reaches for the eggs, to make a *soufflé de volaille à la reine*.

Most of the renowned dishes of French cuisine have come, I think, not from sudden bursts of inventiveness but from imaginative use of ingredients regularly in good supply. Eggs have always been abundant in France, except in crises, and so have milk, butter, and flour. Put them together with French skill, and *voilà*, a soufflé. A soufflé combines many characteristics that the French like, for instance, a fine-grained soothing smoothness and a blending of flavors—a predominate one like cheese, fish, or chocolate enhanced by the more subtle ones of milk, butter, and eggs. The versatility of soufflés also appeals to Frenchmen, who like adding flavorful native foodstuffs to basic formulas such as soufflés, cream soups, and so on, to achieve variety. Finally, *la dextérité* required in making and serving a perfect soufflé gives its preparation a touch of artistry.

I remember my friend Bordeaux's stories of dealing with soufflés in the kitchen of the Baron Alfred Rothschild, famous London financier and gourmet in the early 1900's. The baron had quite a passion for them, and if a business conference lasted too long, or guests lingered over a course at dinner, Bordeaux, who was head chef, kept everyone on the staff on the *qui vive*, watching anxiously as the soufflés in the oven started to puff up. He had 3 sets of soufflés cooked in relays, 5 to 10 minutes apart, timed according to the butler's reports on the progress of the meal. And if a mishap occurred and a soufflé did collapse when it reached the dining room, Bordeaux always went himself to the baron later, in fresh apron and *bonnet*, to apologize profusely and convey the impression that he was gallantly protecting his incompetent underchefs. The baron was really a tolerant man, so the whole thing was a kind of ritual, ending with a 2-pound *pourboire* for Bordeaux.

I made my first soufflé in the kitchen of the Hôtel du Rhin, on the Place Vendôme. Very exclusive old hotels like the du Rhin had no public restaurants; the guests' suites had private dining rooms and the kitchens were often as far from them as possible. Food sometimes had even to be carried across a court, but I learned, after many tries, exactly when to put a soufflé into the oven so that it would arrive at table, protected by a hot covered tray, at exactly the right moment. A hostess who wants to serve guests a superb soufflé would do well to practice a few times on the family.

At the Ritz-Carlton, in New York, soufflés were one of our specialties. They offer so many problems in a busy kitchen, few restaurants will bother with them, but we were proud of our skill and, like Bordeaux, we made 2 soufflés for each order, the second ready to come out of the oven if the first waited too long. And for 40 years, the popularity of our soufflés continued.

Soufflés have for so long been associated with *haute cuisine* that many people, unfortunately, never attempt to make them. Expensive, they say, and difficult to make. *Quel dommage!* It's a pity—because neither fact **Basic Soufflé** is true. You can make an entrée soufflé that will serve 4 or 5 people **Formula** with 4 or 5 eggs and 1 cup of thick béchamel sauce (the butter-flour-milk mixture) and 1 cup of purée, always something particularly flavorful. The purée can be made from leftovers, from a single foodstuff, or from a combination of two. The result—delectable elegance hardly more costly than the cereal, milk, and eggs that make an ordinary breakfast. This is French artistry, a culinary achievement evolved from a skillful use of eggs. Furthermore, when you have made several soufflés, have acquired the " feel " of this mixture and know how to make your oven respond to your needs, the technique becomes second nature.

I can't repeat too often that the first rule for the soufflé cook concerns the serving. Remember, guests must wait for the soufflé, never the other way round, because all the skill put into making a soufflé is wasted unless it is brought directly from oven to table.

For the soufflé base, a good thick béchamel sauce is required. Its **Entrée Soufflé** basic proportions are: 3 tablespoons butter, 3 tablespoons flour, and 1 1/4 cups milk. The sauce is cooked until it is reduced to 1 cup or a little less. **Base**

The egg yolks, beaten just enough to mix them thoroughly, are added **Egg Yolks** after the sauce is removed from the heat. Then the mixture is returned to the heat and stirred vigorously for a minute or two to produce the liaison, or binding action. Whether the purée, cheese, or any other ingredient is added before or after the egg yolks depends upon how much cooking is needed to disperse it through the sauce. Remove the mixture again from the heat and stir it a few minutes to cool it a bit. It should be warm, not hot, when the beaten egg whites are added.

The way the whites are beaten and added plays an important role. **Egg Whites** They should be beaten stiff but not dry. Stop whipping them when they form glistening, moist-looking peaks. Fold the stiff egg whites in, never stir them in. Folding is a matter of cutting through the mixture—a spatula is a good tool—lifting the batter up, over, and under the whites in such a way that the egg whites become part of the mass without losing the air so carefully beaten into them. Stirring crushes the delicate network of beaten egg white and releases the air. I find that I get best results if I add about a fourth of the whites first and combine them very thoroughly. Then I fold in the remainder, incorporating them thoroughly, but even more carefully and very lightly.

The purée may be made in different ways. Moist foods, like toma- **Purée** toes, may be cooked to make a paste. Spinach and similar vegetables should be forced through a sieve. Chicken and mushrooms are chopped very, very fine, and may be forced through a sieve for a smoother result. There is one exception to the rule that entrée soufflés are made with a purée. You cannot make a light and delicate soufflé by mixing coarse particles of food into the soufflé batter, but sometimes better flavor and a delightful contrast of texture results if the food is cut into small, thin slices, as the lobster is in a *soufflé de homard*. Or the larger bits of food, combined with a thick sauce, may be poured first into the dish, and the soufflé batter poured over the mixture.

Soufflé Dish The best baking dish for a soufflé is a round one with perfectly straight sides. The traditional French soufflé mold is a white heatproof china dish with vertical lines on the outside. The molds come in several sizes. Unfortunately, it is impossible to serve a large group with one soufflé. The texture will never be right if there is too much in the baking dish. The puffing requires that the heat go quickly and evenly right through to the center of the mixture. So soufflé recipes cannot usually be depended upon to take care of more than 4 generous or 5 medium servings and the baking dish is usually a 1 1/2-quart size. You can, however, make smaller soufflés. For example, increase the ingredients by half, bake the mixture in 2 dishes, and thus serve 6 or 7. Or you can use individual casseroles or ramekins.

Paper Collar To get greater height on a soufflé, use a smaller dish than usual and tie a paper collar around it. Tear off a length of wax paper long enough to go around the dish and slightly overlap. Fold the paper in half lengthwise and butter it well on one side. Wrap it around the dish, butter side inside, so that it stands above the rim about 4 inches and secure it with string. The soufflé will climb the paper collar as it cooks. Remove the collar from the baked soufflé, which will be puffed attractively above the rim of the dish.

Preparing the Dish For an entrée soufflé, butter the mold with sweet butter. For some soufflés, like cheese, you may sprinkle it with fine bread crumbs, also, or if the purée has made the mixture quite thin, butter and flour the mold. For a dessert soufflé, butter the mold and sprinkle it with sugar; this forms a thin sweet crust, and the soufflé slips out of the mold more easily. Pour in the batter lightly, smooth it with a spatula, and run your forefinger to a depth of about half an inch around the inside of the mold to separate the mixture from the mold. There is a rim in French soufflé molds to guide you. This makes the soufflé rise evenly, without spilling.

Baking Soufflés The proper baking of a soufflé is very important because on it depends not only the puffiness but also the crust and the texture of the interior. The ideal soufflé puffs up high and light, has a golden-brown, delicate crust on the bottom and sides as well as on the top, and a center that is very creamy but yet cooked throughout.

Dessert soufflés bake 18 to 20 minutes in a moderately hot to hot **Dessert** oven (375° to 400° F.). The top crust should not form before the mixture has reached its maximum volume and a crust has formed on the bottom of the dish. This is not always easy in the short time that it takes to brown the top. Our Ritz chefs heated the oven to hot (400° F.) and put the soufflé on the floor of the oven, as close to the source of the heat as possible. After the soufflé had baked for 8 or 9 minutes, they moved it to a rack set on the bottom of the oven. Some chefs preferred to put a heavy flat pan in the top of the oven to heat during those first 8 or 9 minutes, and instead of moving the soufflé to a rack, they would slip the pan under the soufflé dish for the remainder of the baking time. Either method baffled the heat just enough. We never had an underdone bottom crust; always a perfectly puffed soufflé. When the soufflé was removed from the oven, the dish was placed on a hot plate, brought to the table for the guests to view, and then spooned out. Each serving should include some of the top, side, and bottom crusts, and the center.

Entrée soufflés bake in a moderate to moderately hot oven (350° to **Entrée** 375° F.). They take more time to bake than sweet soufflés—from 25 to 35 minutes—because the batter is denser. Bake an entrée soufflé, also, on the bottom of the oven for the first 8 or 9 minutes, then slip a rack under it or move the dish up to a rack for the balance of the cooking time. But you will want to experiment with your oven, so that you can be certain of the time and temperature requirements that apply.

Entrée Soufflés

IN THE CLASSIC cuisine, entrée soufflés appear on the menu in several roles. They make a much-favored main course for a light luncheon or supper. At the old Ritz in New York, many guests who lived in Carlton House and ordered their meals from the Ritz kitchen made a habit of lunching at least once a week on a fish, mushroom, or cheese soufflé. A clear soup of some kind would start the meal and fruit dessert end it; these made a combination hard to surpass as well as one superbly satisfying, yet light and refreshing. In a long dinner menu, on the other hand, the same soufflés serve as a first course or as a *petite entrée*. At an elaborate dinner, the *soufflé de homard*, for instance, can be fish course and *petite entrée* at one and the same time, coming to the table between the soup and the meat.

An entrée soufflé has the advantage of being very easily digested because simple, wholesome ingredients are carefully combined and just as carefully cooked. It is wonderful for those recovering from an illness and not up to their regular meals. The *haut monde* turns to soufflés for a simple dish, the devout for a perfect dish for Lent.

Cheese Soufflés

Cheese soufflé is probably the most popular of all the entrée soufflés and the best one to learn to make in starting off your soufflé repertoire.

Cheese that is too rich in fat never makes a perfect soufflé; that requires a Parmesan or a dry Swiss. Cheddar, sometimes called store cheese, however, can be used so long as it is a natural cheese.

*Soufflé
au Fromage*

CHEESE SOUFFLÉ

MELT 3 tablespoons butter in a saucepan, add 3 tablespoons flour, and cook slowly until the flour just begins to turn golden. Add 1 1/4 cups hot milk and cook for about 5 minutes, stirring constantly with a wire whip or slotted spoon until the mixture reduces to 1 scant cup thick sauce. Add 1/2 teaspoon salt, a little cayenne, and a little grated nutmeg. Beat 4 egg yolks until light, turn a little of the hot sauce into them to heat them up, then turn this back into the hot sauce and mix all together. Add 3/4 cup finely grated cheese, Parmesan, dry Swiss, or Cheddar. Cool the mixture. Beat 5 egg whites stiff but not dry and fold them carefully into the mixture. Pour it into a buttered soufflé dish and bake in a moderately hot oven (375° F.) for about 30 minutes, or until the soufflé is well puffed and delicately browned.

If desired, cut very, very thin slices of Swiss cheese in a diamond pattern and arrange them around the top in a circle just before the soufflé is put into the oven.   Serves 4.

Cheese soufflés are sometimes thickened with bread crumbs, which should be light and fresh so that they combine with the milk to make a smooth, creamy panade. *The kind of wet, sticky bread that refuses to crumble will not do for this purpose.   These soufflés baked in small ramekins make an excellent first course.*

SMALL CHEESE SOUFFLÉS

Petits Soufflés au Fromage

BRING 1 cup milk to the boil and add to it 2 cups fresh soft bread crumbs, mixing together well to obtain a thick *panade*.   If not good and thick, add a few more crumbs.   Beat in 5 egg yolks, 1 at a time, combining each thoroughly before adding the next.   Add 1 cup grated cheese, Parmesan or dry Swiss, and 1 tablespoon butter.   Cool the mixture.   Beat 5 egg whites stiff but not dry and fold them in.   Fill 6 to 8 individual buttered molds 2/3 full and sprinkle with a little grated cheese.   Set the molds in a pan of boiling water and bake in a moderately hot oven (375° to 400° F.) for 12 to 15 minutes, or until the soufflés are well puffed and delicately browned.

Cheese soufflés made with semolina or farina are a trifle heartier than those made with a flour-thickened base.

SEMOLINA SOUFFLÉ WITH CHEESE

Soufflé de Semoule au Fromage

BRING 1 quart milk to the boil, add 3 tablespoons butter and 1 teaspoon salt, and then add gradually 1 cup farina, stirring all the time with a whip. Cook slowly over low heat for 30 minutes, stirring occasionally.   Remove from the heat and add 1 cup grated cheese, Parmesan or dry Swiss.   Beat 6 egg yolks and add them and 1 more tablespoon butter.   Cool the mixture. Beat 6 egg whites stiff but not dry and fold them in.   Fill 6 to 8 buttered individual molds 3/4 full and sprinkle a little cheese on top.   Place in a pan of boiling water and bake in a hot oven (425° to 450° F.) for 10 to 15 minutes.

Still another way of making cheese soufflé is to use more egg yolks than whites and bake them in tomatoes. This is a very attractive dish and, since the recipe serves twelve to fourteen, is nice for a party entrée.

*Petits Soufflés
au Fromage
en Tomates*

SMALL CHEESE SOUFFLÉS IN TOMATOES

CUT a hole in the tops of 12 to 14 large tomatoes and carefully scoop out the seeds and liquid, leaving the shells firm. Drain them upside down.

Combine 6 tablespoons cream in a saucepan with 2 tablespoons flour and mix well with a whip. Add 3 egg yolks, 2 tablespoons melted butter, 1/2 teaspoon salt, and a little cayenne. Mix together well and cook over low heat, stirring briskly until the mixture is creamy. Remove from the heat and add 1 cup grated dry cheese and 3 more egg yolks. Mix together well and let the mixture cool. Beat 4 egg whites stiff but not dry and fold them in. Fill the tomatoes about 3/4 full and bake on an ovenproof platter in a moderate oven (375° F.) for about 20 to 25 minutes.

Sea-Food, Meat, Poultry Soufflés

Fish and shellfish make very good soufflés and are, of course, particularly appropriate for Lenten dishes. Either fresh raw fish may be used or canned fish or leftover fish. If fish is to be purchased especially for a soufflé, I suggest a white fish: cod, haddock, halibut, or filet of flounder. Cold boiled leftover salmon or canned salmon are good. In fish soufflés, a very thick Mornay sauce, substituted for the béchamel sauce (the butter-flour-milk mixture), makes a pleasant, cheese-flavored variation.

*Soufflé
au Poisson*

FISH SOUFFLÉ

MELT 1 tablespoon butter in a saucepan, add 1 shallot, chopped, or 1 teaspoon chopped onion. Place a 1/2-pound piece of fish without skin and bones on top and sprinkle with salt and a little pepper. Pour over 1/4 cup dry white wine. Cover and cook for about 15 minutes, or until the fish is done and the liquid cooked away. Force the fish through a fine sieve or food mill. Or heat 1 1/2 cups leftover fish in 1 tablespoon butter and force it through a sieve.

In another saucepan, melt 2 tablespoons butter, add 3 tablespoons flour, and cook until the flour just starts to turn golden. Add 1 1/4 cups hot milk and cook, stirring constantly with a wire whip or slotted spoon, for 5 to 10 minutes, or until the sauce is reduced to 1 scant cup. Add the fish, correct the seasoning, and remove from the heat. Beat 3 egg yolks lightly, put a little of the sauce-and-fish mixture into them to heat them, then turn them back into the sauce-and-fish mixture. Allow it to cool. Beat 4 egg whites stiff but not dry and fold them in. Fill a buttered soufflé dish 3/4 full and bake in a moderately hot oven (375° F.) for about 30 minutes, or until the soufflé is well puffed and delicately browned.

Lobster soufflé can be cooked, of course, in a deep baking dish just like other soufflés, but in many restaurants in France it is baked in the lobster shell itself, a very attractive way of serving it. The process of cleaning the shell is described in the chapter on shellfish.

LOBSTER SOUFFLÉ

Soufflé de Homard

PLUNGE a 1 3/4- to 2-pound lobster in a boiling vinegar court bouillon and cook for 20 minutes. Remove and, when cool enough to handle, cut in half lengthwise. Remove the lobster meat and chop it very finely. Season with a little salt and pepper. Melt 3 tablespoons butter in a saucepan, add 3 tablespoons flour, and cook until the flour just starts to turn golden. Add 1 1/4 cups hot milk and cook, stirring constantly with a wire whip or slotted spoon, for about 5 minutes, or until the sauce is reduced to 1 scant cup. Combine with the lobster and force through a sieve or food mill. Add 3 egg yolks, one at a time, return to the heat, and bring just to the boil, stirring briskly all the time, but do not allow to boil. Cool slightly. Beat 3 egg whites stiff but not dry and fold them in. Fill the two lobster shells 3/4 full, sprinkle each soufflé with a little grated cheese, and bake in a moderately hot oven (375° F.) for 20 minutes, or bake in a buttered soufflé dish about 30 minutes, until the soufflé is well puffed and delicately browned. If desired, a few slices of truffles may be added to the mixture, and Newburg or white wine sauce may be passed separately. Serves 2 or 3.

When I went back to France in the early 1950's, I spent some happy hours reminiscing with my brother Lucien, long the chef des cuisines *of that top-*

ranking Paris hotel, the Plaza-Athénée. I wanted to give a dinner party at the hotel for the American friends who accompanied me to Paris, so I asked Lucien to suggest for the menu one of his own well-known spécialités. He promptly replied, " Soufflé de homard." Soufflé de homard, I thought to myself with a smile. Certainly no New York chef would be likely to make that suggestion!

I must digress for a moment to tell you about the Plaza-Athénée. Have you ever been in Paris in April, when the horse-chestnut trees are in their final, vulnerable full bloom and each whisper of the spring breeze sends the petals drifting lazily to the ground? To me, after so many years of New York's hustle and bustle, the gentle fluttering of those petals was symbolic of the relaxed, unharried air of dinnertime in France. In the main dining room of the Plaza-Athénée the same mood prevails. The décor breathes leisure and elegance. High ceilings and heavy rugs discourage noise; three magnificent gold-and-crystal chandeliers light the gold damask hangings that cover the window wall; perfectly appointed tables are gay with flowers and gleaming with silver and crystal. As I stood in the doorway of this charming salon, I was convinced again that this is one of the loveliest dining rooms in all Paris. Mais, revenons à nos soufflés. *I still have my copy of the menu we decided on, which the Plaza-Athénée printed for us as a souvenir:*

Germiny en Tasse

Paillettes Diable

Soufflé de Homard Plaza-Athénée

Baron de Pauillac Princesse

Salade de Chicorée aux Fines Herbes

Coeur de Jeannette

Mignardises

And here is the soufflé recipe.

Soufflé de Homard Plaza-Athénée

PLAZA-ATHÉNÉE LOBSTER SOUFFLÉ

REMOVE the claws and tails from 3 lobsters, each weighing 1 3/4 to 2 pounds, and with a large heavy knife divide each of the body sections into three or four pieces. In a large saucepan make the following vegetable mirepoix: Melt 2 tablespoons butter, add 1 medium carrot cut in fine dice, 2 tablespoons finely chopped onion, and 1 tablespoon chopped chives. Cook the mirepoix over very low heat until the vegetables are soft but not brown. Add 1 tablespoon chopped parsley and remove the pan from the heat.

Sprinkle the cut up lobsters with salt and pepper. In a large shallow pan, cook them in 1/2 cup very hot salad oil, turning them to cook all sides evenly. Put the lobster pieces—they will be red—on top of the mirepoix and sprinkle them with 1 teaspoon paprika. Mix all together and add 2 tablespoons Cognac, 1/2 cup dry white wine, and 1 cup heavy cream. Bring the sauce to a boil and cook the lobsters for 18 to 20 minutes. Remove the lobsters from the pan, carefully separate the meat from the shells, and cut the meat into slices 1/4 inch thick. Over high heat reduce the liquid remaining in the pan to about 1/2 the original quantity. Add 1 cup cream sauce and 3 tablespoons each of heavy cream and dry Sherry. Strain the sauce, making sure that no fine bits of shell get through the sieve, and combine half of it with the lobster meat. Butter a pair of 1-quart soufflé dishes and divide the lobster mixture between them. Keep the rest of the sauce warm.

Prepare a cheese soufflé mixture as follows: Melt 2 tablespoons butter in a saucepan, add 1/4 cup flour, and cook the *roux* until it starts to turn golden. Stir in 3/4 cup hot milk and cook for about 5 minutes, or until the sauce is very thick, stirring constantly. Add 1/2 teaspoon salt and a little cayenne pepper. Beat 5 egg yolks, combine them with the first mixture, and heat all together just to the boiling point, stirring briskly. Do not allow the sauce to boil. Add 3/4 cup grated Parmesan or dry Swiss cheese. Fold in 5 egg whites beaten stiff but not dry.

Spoon the cheese soufflé mixture over the lobster-and-sauce mixture in the molds. Bake the soufflés in a moderate oven (350° F.) for 18 to 20 minutes, or until they are well puffed and delicately browned. To serve, put some of the top of the soufflé on one side of each plate and some of the lobster mixture from the bottom on the other side. Pass the reserved lobster sauce separately.

OYSTER SOUFFLÉ

Soufflé d'Huîtres

BRING to a boil in their own liquor 2 dozen large or 3 dozen medium-sized shelled oysters. Drain and cut the large ones in two. Melt 3 tablespoons butter in a saucepan, add 3 tablespoons flour, and cook until the flour just starts to turn golden. Add 3/4 cup hot oyster liquor and 3/4 cup hot milk and cook, stirring constantly with a wire whip or slotted spoon, for 10 to 12 minutes, or until the sauce is reduced to 1 cup. Add 1/2 teaspoon salt, a little pepper, and 1 tablespoon butter. Beat 4 egg yolks, put a little of the hot sauce in with the yolks, and then turn this into the remaining sauce. Return to the boiling point but do not allow to boil. Add the oysters. Fold in 5 egg whites beaten stiff but not dry. Fill a buttered soufflé dish 3/4 full and bake in a moderately hot oven (375° F.) for about 30 minutes, or until the soufflé is well puffed and delicately browned. Serves 4.

CLAM SOUFFLÉ

*Soufflé
de Clams* FOLLOW the recipe for oyster soufflé, using the soft part, the belly, of the clams.

CHICKEN SOUFFLÉ

*Soufflé
de Volaille
à la Reine* CHOP very finely 1 1/2 to 2 cups cooked chicken, using all white meat, or a mixture of white meat and the more tender parts of the dark meat. The meat may be rubbed through a sieve; it should be as fine as a purée. Prepare a thick béchamel as follows: Melt 2 tablespoons butter in a saucepan, add 3 tablespoons flour, and cook the *roux* until it starts to turn golden. Stir in 1 cup hot milk, combining it with a whip. Return the pan to the heat and cook the sauce for about 5 minutes, or until it is very thick, stirring it constantly with the whip. Season the sauce with grated nutmeg. Add the chicken and 4 lightly beaten egg yolks. Correct the seasoning with salt. Fold in 4 egg whites beaten stiff but not dry. Pour the batter into a buttered soufflé dish and bake the soufflé in a moderate oven (350° F.) for about 30 minutes. Serves 4 or 5.

CHICKEN SOUFFLÉ VIRGINIA — *Soufflé de Volaille Virginie*

FOLLOW the recipe for chicken soufflé, but use 1 1/4 cups very finely chopped chicken and 1/2 cup very finely chopped Virginia ham.

HAM SOUFFLÉ — *Soufflé de Jambon*

IN a saucepan melt 1 tablespoon butter, add 2 cups leftover cooked ham, very, very finely chopped, and cook over low heat for 6 to 7 minutes to heat the ham. Add 3/4 to 1 cup thick, hot béchamel sauce and mix well. Stir in 3 large or 4 small egg yolks, lightly beaten, mix well, and bring almost to the boil, stirring constantly. Correct the seasoning with salt and add a little white pepper. Whip 5 egg whites stiff and fold 1/2 in carefully but thoroughly. Fold in the remaining egg whites lightly. Bake in a buttered soufflé dish in a moderate oven (350° F.) for 30 minutes.

Vegetable Soufflés

Vegetable soufflés can be made from dozens of different vegetables, using the basic formula of sauce, purée, and eggs. To make the purée, strain the cooked vegetable through a fine sieve and, if necessary, cook it down until it is thick. It should not be watery. Cook watery purée, such as spinach, in 1 tablespoon melted butter, stirring, until the moisture evaporates. For thin purée, such as tomato, reduce the béchamel mixture to 2/3 cup.

TOMATO SOUFFLÉ — *Soufflé aux Tomates*

MAKE 1 cup tomato purée as follows: Chop enough tomatoes to make about 3 cups and drain them in a colander. Put the drained pulp in a saucepan and cook it until it is reduced. Strain through a fine sieve to remove skins and seeds and cook the purée until it is reduced to 1 cup. Melt 3 tablespoons butter in a saucepan, add 3 tablespoons flour, and cook until the flour just begins to turn golden. Add 1 1/4 cups hot milk and cook for about 10 minutes, stirring constantly with a wire whip or slotted spoon until the sauce is reduced to about 2/3 cup. Add 1/2 teaspoon salt and a little cayenne. Remove from the heat, add the tomato purée, and, if desired, 2 tablespoons grated Parmesan or dry Swiss cheese. Add 4 beaten egg yolks, a little at a time, beating well after each addition. Cool the mixture. Fold in 4 egg whites beaten stiff but not dry. Fill a buttered soufflé dish about 3/4 full and bake the soufflé in a moderately hot oven (375° F.) for about 30 minutes, or until it is well puffed and delicately browned. Serves 4.

Soufflé aux Champignons I

CLEAN 1/2 pound mushrooms, caps and stems, and chop very finely. Put 1 tablespoon butter in a saucepan, add 1 shallot, chopped, or 1 teaspoon chopped onion, and cook until the onion is soft but not brown. Add the chopped mushrooms and slowly cook all the moisture out of them. In another saucepan melt 2 tablespoons butter, add 3 tablespoons flour, and cook until the flour just starts to turn golden. Add 1 1/4 cups hot milk and cook, stirring constantly with a wire whip or slotted spoon, for about 5 minutes or until the sauce is reduced to 1 scant cup. Season with 1 teaspoon salt, a little cayenne, and a little grated nutmeg. Add the mushrooms, bring to the boil, and remove from the heat. Beat 4 egg yolks lightly, put a little of the hot sauce into them to heat them, and turn this back into the remaining sauce mixture. Cool slightly. Beat 5 egg whites stiff but not dry and fold them in. Fill a buttered soufflé dish about 3/4 full and bake in a moderately hot oven (375° F.) for about 30 minutes, or until the soufflé is well puffed and delicately browned on top. Serves 4.

Soufflé aux Champignons II

CLEAN 1/2 pound fresh mushrooms, drain them thoroughly and dry them on a towel. Chop the mushrooms very finely—they should be almost a purée. Put them in a saucepan with 1 cup milk, bring the milk to a boil, and cook the mixture slowly for 10 to 15 minutes.

In another saucepan, melt 2 tablespoons butter, add 3 tablespoons flour, and cook the *roux* until it starts to turn golden. Stir in the hot milk-and-mushroom mixture. Return the pan to the heat and cook the sauce, stirring constantly, for about 5 minutes. Season the sauce with 1/2 teaspoon salt, a little pepper, and a little grated nutmeg. Beat 5 egg yolks lightly and add them to the mushroom mixture. Heat the mixture to the boiling point, but do not let it boil. Remove the pan from the heat and stir the sauce for a few minutes as it cools. Fold in 5 egg whites beaten stiff but not dry. Pour the batter into a buttered soufflé dish and bake the soufflé in a moderate oven (350° F.) for about 30 minutes, or until the soufflé is well puffed and delicately browned. Serves 4.

MUSHROOM SOUFFLÉ WITH CHEESE — *Soufflé aux Champignons et Fromage*

FOLLOW the recipe for mushroom soufflé I, adding 2/3 cup grated dry cheese to the sauce-mushroom-purée combination.

SPINACH SOUFFLÉ — *Soufflé d'Épinards*

MELT 1 tablespoon butter in a saucepan and add 1 cup well-drained purée of spinach or very finely chopped cooked spinach and 1 teaspoon salt. Cook over low heat to remove any remaining moisture.

Melt 2 tablespoons butter in another saucepan, add 3 tablespoons flour, and cook until the flour just starts to turn golden. Add 1 1/4 cups hot milk and cook, stirring constantly with a wire whip or slotted spoon, for about 10 minutes, or until it is reduced to 1 scant cup. Remove from the heat. Beat 5 egg yolks, turn a little of the hot sauce into them, then turn this back into the hot sauce. Mix well and add the spinach purée. Cool the mixture. Beat 5 egg whites stiff but not dry and fold them in. Fill a buttered soufflé dish about 3/4 full and bake in a moderately hot oven (375° F.) for about 30 minutes, or until the soufflé is well puffed and delicately browned. Serves 4.

Spinach soufflé lends itself to several variations which are popular in France. For example, 2 tablespoons grated cheese can be added to the mixture, or perhaps 2 tablespoons cheese along with 3 or 4 anchovy filets cut in dice.

SPINACH SOUFFLÉ WITH POACHED EGGS — *Soufflé d'Épinards aux Oeufs*

ANOTHER delectable variation of spinach soufflé includes poached eggs. Spread about half the soufflé mixture in the dish, arrange 4 well-drained poached eggs on it, cover with the remaining mixture, and bake as usual. The eggs heat up to the proper degree, but they don't become overcooked.   To serve, cut down through the soufflé with a spoon so that an egg is included in each serving.

Soufflé aux Pommes de Terre

ADD 1/2 cup cream to 2 cups thick mashed potatoes and season with 1 teaspoon salt and a little nutmeg.   Stir the mixture over low heat, to avoid scorching, until it is very hot.   Remove it from the heat and add 2 tablespoons grated Parmesan or dry Swiss cheese.   Add 3 beaten egg yolks, a little at a time, beating well after each addition.   Cool the mixture and then fold in 4 egg whites beaten stiff but not dry.   Fill a buttered soufflé dish about 3/4 full and bake in a moderately hot oven (375° F.) for about 30 minutes, or until the soufflé is well puffed and delicately browned. Serves 4.

Soufflé de Maïs

BOIL corn on the cob for about 8 minutes, cool it, and with a sharp knife cut down the center of the kernels.   Press the pulp out with the side of the knife.   Cook 1 cup of this corn pulp with 1 tablespoons butter over low heat until the juice is reduced to almost nothing.

In another saucepan melt 2 tablespoons butter, add 2 tablespoons flour, and cook the *roux*, stirring, until it starts to turn golden.   Add gradually 1 cup hot milk and cook, stirring constantly, until the sauce thickens. Continue cooking the sauce very slowly for about 15 minutes, stirring with a wire whip.   Combine the sauce with the corn and mix well.   Beat 4 egg yolks, combine them with the sauce and corn mixture, and reheat the mixture, but do not let it boil.   Season with salt and white pepper. Fold in 5 egg whites beaten stiff but not dry.   Fill a buttered soufflé dish about 3/4 full and bake in a moderately hot oven (375° F.) for about 30 minutes, or until the soufflé is well puffed and delicately browned.

Dessert Soufflés

SWEET soufflés, like entrée soufflés, are made of a butter-flour-milk combination bound with egg yolks and lightened with egg whites. Naturally, they contain sugar, also, and a flavoring of some kind. One method combines the butter, flour, and milk in a sauce similar to the sauce used in entrée soufflés. In a second method, the flour cooks in the milk and the butter is added after the mixture thickens. (This method requires less butter.) A third method employs *crème pâtissière*, a thickened pastry cream with a milk base, and is frequently used in restaurant kitchens, which always have pastry cream on hand.

There are two soufflé variations that are popular in French homes: a pudding soufflé with the base made in the same way as *pâte à chou* (cream puff paste), a unique soufflé in that it can be reheated if it has to wait before being served; and an omelet soufflé, which is like a puffy omelet baked in an oven.

Beat the egg yolks for dessert soufflés until they are very light and foamy; the egg whites are beaten stiff but not dry. To prevent them from becoming too dry, add a little sugar during the last few minutes of beating—1/2 to 1 tablespoon to each 4 to 6 egg whites—sprinkling it in when the whites glisten. Turn back to the general instructions for making soufflés for the basic procedure and special tricks.

You can prepare endlessly varied dessert soufflés. The most popular are chocolate, coffee, the fruit flavors like lemon, orange, and strawberry and the various liqueurs. To make these, follow any of the vanilla soufflé recipes and substitute the desired flavor for vanilla. However, in making liqueur-flavored soufflés, ladyfingers or macaroons are moistened with the liqueur and placed in the center, between two layers of the soufflé, and a little of the liqueur is sprinkled on the bottom of the mold. This way as the heat evaporates the liqueur the *parfum* rises through the whole mixture.

Whether a sauce is served with a dessert soufflé is a matter of taste. If the soufflé is made well and has the creamy center it should have, a sauce is not actually necessary, but it does give the dessert added elegance. For vanilla, chocolate, and coffee soufflés, the best sauce is made by adding to a custard base whipped cream and a flavoring that complements the flavoring of the soufflé. Sauces flavored with a liqueur such as Grand Marnier are very popular. With berry soufflés, however, a fruit sauce made with the same kind of fruit used in the soufflé should be chosen. A little liqueur may be added to the fruit sauce.

VANILLA SOUFFLÉ I

Soufflé à la Vanille I

MELT 2 tablespoons butter, add 1 1/2 tablespoons flour and cook, stirring, until the *roux* just starts to turn golden. Add 1/2 cup scalded milk and a 1-inch piece of vanilla bean (or add 1/4 teaspoon vanilla extract after the mixture has cooked). Cook the sauce, stirring constantly until it thickens, and then continue cooking, stirring constantly for 5 minutes longer. Remove the vanilla bean or add the extract. Beat 5 egg yolks well with 3 tablespoons sugar and combine them with the batter. Beat 6 egg whites stiff, adding 1 tablespoon sugar during the last minutes of beating. Fold them in. Pour the batter into a buttered and lightly sugared soufflé dish and bake the soufflé in a moderately hot oven (375° to 400° F.) for 18 to 20 minutes, until it is well puffed and delicately browned.

VANILLA SOUFFLÉ II

Soufflé à la Vanille II

SCALD 1/2 cup milk with a 1-inch piece of vanilla bean. If extract is used, it must be added later. Stir 1 tablespoon flour and 1/4 cup sugar to a paste with 3 tablespoons cold milk. Add this paste to the hot milk and cook the mixture, stirring constantly until it thickens. Remove the vanilla bean, or add 1/4 teaspoon vanilla extract, and add 1 tablespoon butter. Remove the pan from the heat. Beat 4 egg yolks until they are light and foamy and combine them with the batter. Beat 5 egg whites stiff, adding 1 tablespoon powdered sugar during the last few minutes of beating. Fold them in. Pour the batter into a buttered and lightly sugared soufflé dish and bake the soufflé in a moderately hot oven (375° to 400° F.) for 18 to 20 minutes, until it is well puffed and delicately browned.

VANILLA SOUFFLÉ III

Soufflé à la Vanille III

BEAT 4 egg yolks well with 1/2 tablespoon sugar and add 1/3 cup *crème pâtissière*. Add the pulp scraped from a 1-inch piece of vanilla bean, or add 1/4 teaspoon vanilla extract. Beat 5 egg whites stiff, adding 1 tablespoon sugar during the last few minutes of beating. Fold them in. Pour the batter into a buttered and sugared soufflé dish and smooth off the top with a spatula. Bake the soufflé in a moderately hot oven (375° to 400° F.) for 18 to 20 minutes, until it is well puffed and delicately browned.

CHOCOLATE SOUFFLÉ

Soufflé au Chocolat

FOLLOW the recipe for vanilla soufflé I or II. In the hot milk, melt 1 1/2 squares or ounces of grated chocolate. If unsweetened chocolate is used, add to the milk and chocolate mixture 2 more tablespoons sugar; if sweetened chocolate is used add 1 more tablespoon sugar, or a little more if a sweeter flavor is preferred.

COFFEE SOUFFLÉ

Soufflé au Café

FOLLOW any one of the recipes for vanilla soufflé. Add to the thickened base 2 tablespoons double-strength coffee.

LEMON SOUFFLÉ

Soufflé au Citron

FOLLOW any one of the recipes for vanilla soufflé. Omit the vanilla and add to the mixture just before folding in the egg whites the finely grated rind of 1 lemon and juice of 1/2 lemon.

ORANGE SOUFFLÉ

Soufflé à l'Orange

FOLLOW any one of the recipes for vanilla soufflé. Omit the vanilla and add to the mixture just before folding in the egg whites the finely grated rind of 1 small orange and 2 tablespoons orange juice or 1 tablespoon Cointreau.

Soufflé aux Fraises

STRAWBERRY SOUFFLÉ

FLAVOR 1 cup crushed strawberries with 1 tablespoon kirsch and 2 table-spoons sugar. Follow any one of the vanilla soufflé recipes, and add the berries to the thickened base. Serve with a sauce made by mixing 1 cup crushed or coarsely chopped strawberries, 2 tablespoons melted currant jelly, and 1 tablespoon kirsch.

Soufflé aux Pommes

APPLE SOUFFLÉ

REDUCE 3 cups sweetened thick applesauce to 2 cups to thicken it even more. Beat 4 egg yolks and add them to the applesauce. Beat 4 egg whites until they are stiff but not dry and fold them in lightly but completely, raising and folding the mixture over and over. Fill a buttered and sugared soufflé dish about 3/4 full with the mixture and bake the soufflé in a moderately hot oven (375° to 400° F.) for about 20 minutes, or until it is well puffed and delicately browned.

Soufflé Jeannette

SOUFFLÉ JEANNETTE

FOLLOW the recipe for vanilla soufflé I or II and pour 2/3 of the batter into a buttered and sugared mold. Make a shallow depression in the batter. Carefully fold into the rest of the batter 2 tablespoons melted chocolate. Pour the chocolate batter into the center of the vanilla batter, leaving a rim of vanilla. Smooth the soufflé with a spatula and run a finger around the edge of the mold, inside. Bake as usual. The chocolate and vanilla mixtures will remain separate.

Soufflé Rothschild

SOUFFLÉ ROTHSCHILD

FOLLOW any one of the recipes for vanilla soufflé. Mix 2 or 3 tablespoons finely chopped candied fruits with 2 tablespoons Cognac. Spread this on a layer of half of the soufflé batter in the mold and fill with the remaining soufflé batter. Garnish the finished soufflé with halves of cherries or strawberries.

GRAND MARNIER SOUFFLÉ

Soufflé au Grand Marnier

MOISTEN 6 or 8 ladyfingers in Grand Marnier. Melt 2 tablespoons butter in a saucepan, add 1 tablespoon flour, and cook slowly until the *roux* begins to turn golden. Stir in 1/2 cup hot milk and a 1-inch piece of vanilla bean (if vanilla extract is used it must be added later) and cook slowly for 5 minutes, stirring constantly with a sauce whip. Remove the vanilla bean or add 1/2 teaspoon vanilla extract. Beat 5 egg yolks with 4 tablespoons sugar and add the eggs to the sauce. Beat 6 egg whites stiff, adding 1 tablespoon sugar during the last few minutes of beating. Fold the beaten egg whites thoroughly and carefully into the mixture, cutting them in lightly but completely by raising and folding the mixture over and over. Pour 1/2 the mixture into a buttered and sugared soufflé mold or straight-sided baking dish. Cover it with the ladyfingers and fill the dish with the rest of the soufflé mixture. Smooth off the top with a spatula. Bake the soufflé in a moderately hot oven (375° to 400° F.) for 18 to 20 minutes or until it is well puffed and delicately browned. A minute or two before removing the soufflé from the oven, sprinkle it with a little powdered sugar to glaze the top. Serve at once with Grand Marnier sauce. If desired, the soufflé may be baked in a soufflé dish around which a paper collar has been tied, so that the soufflé can puff above the dish. Remove the paper collar and put the baked soufflé, in its baking dish, inside a larger silver or copper serving dish.

PUDDING SOUFFLÉ

Pouding Soufflé

CREAM 3 tablespoons butter with 6 tablespoons flour until the mixture is light and fluffy. Scald 3/4 cup milk with a 1-inch piece of vanilla bean. If extract is used it must be added later. Add the butter and flour mixture to the milk, and cook the mixture, stirring constantly until it rolls away from the sides of the pan. Remove the pan from the heat. Remove the vanilla bean or add 1/2 teaspoon vanilla extract. Add 4 egg yolks, well beaten with 3 tablespoons sugar and a pinch of salt, and mix all together well. Beat 4 egg whites stiff, adding 1/2 tablespoon sugar during the last few minutes of beating. Fold the egg whites lightly but completely into the first mixture, raising and folding the mixture over and over. Pour the batter into a buttered and sugared mold with a tube in the center. The mold should be only 3/4 full. Set the mold in a pan of hot water and bake the soufflé in a moderate oven (350° F.) for 40 to 50 minutes. If the soufflé browns too quickly, cover it with a piece of buttered paper. Remove the mold from the oven and let the pudding settle for a minute. To serve, invert the mold on a serving dish and cover it with custard or sabayon sauce. If the pudding drops from standing too long, put the mold in a pan of hot water and reheat the pudding in the oven until it puffs again.

Omelette Soufflé

OMELET SOUFFLÉ

Add 5 tablespoons sugar and the pulp scraped from a 1-inch piece of vanilla bean to 4 egg yolks, and beat the mixture until it is very light. Beat 4 egg whites stiff, adding 1/2 tablespoon sugar during the last few minutes of beating, and fold them lightly but completely into the first mixture. Heap this mixture in an oval-shaped mound about 4 inches high on a well-buttered heatproof serving platter. Smooth the mixture with a spatula, then draw the spatula lengthwise across the top to make a furrow about 2 inches deep (like the crease in the top of a man's felt hat). Bake in a moderately hot oven (375° to 400° F.) for 18 to 20 minutes, until the soufflé is well puffed and browned. A few minutes before taking the soufflé from the oven, glaze the top by sprinkling it with a little sugar. Serve the soufflé at once.

CRÊPES ET BEIGNETS

Pancakes and Fritters

CARNAVAL—the period between January 6th, Epiphany, and Ash Wednesday—is the season in France for eating crêpes and *beignets* (pancakes and fritters). By the time February comes to country towns in France, the drifting smell of the *friture*—the oil for frying fritters— fills the air and announces that Lent is not far away. Country folk have their gay parties between supper and bedtime, and in February, when the days are still short, and the farm work therefore light, *les veillées* are happily long. The weeks before Lent are traditionally festive, and crêpes and *beignets* have become the traditional food for these gay evening parties. Why pancakes and fritters? Possibly because long ago fresh foods were very scarce during the winter, and party menus had to be based on the always-obtainable flour, milk, and eggs. Of course, we had *beignets* and crêpes all year round but never so frequently or in such quantity as at *Carnaval* season. Making crêpes over the open fire was part of the fun at the party honoring the unmarried girls—a party always held on the second Thursday preceding Ash Wednesday. Each girl had to make a crêpe and toss it successfully to brown the other side—not an easy thing to do without practice. But according to the superstition, unless a girl could pass the test, she would never get a husband. After all, what man would be so foolish as to marry a girl who couldn't make perfect crêpes?

Crêpes

I SHOULD POINT OUT that French crêpes are quite different from American pancakes. The batter contains less flour and more eggs in proportion to the amount of milk. This mixture makes possible very thin cakes that are not at all fluffy, but delicately light in texture, and almost as fine-grained and smooth to the tongue as custard. They don't become soggy when a *confiture* is rolled into them or a sauce is poured over them, and will roll up or fold without cracking or breaking.

I know that in America pancakes are a favorite breakfast dish: actually, breakfast is the only meal at which we French do not eat crêpes even during *Carnaval!* But we do have them for dessert and for hors-d'oeuvre and as an entrée, and sliced into slivers, as a soup garnish. You will notice that the batters for the crêpes other than those used for dessert are not at all sweet, and contain no liqueur flavoring.

Whatever the recipe you use, I caution you not to beat the batter too eagerly; overbeating results in toughness. After the batter is mixed, let it stand for a couple of hours. This trick seems to improve both texture and flavor.

I know now that it takes practice to make good crêpes, but I assure you that once you master the technique you will not find it at all difficult. Here are a few practical hints: First, be sure to use a skillet with a bottom heavy enough to hold the heat well and distribute it evenly. A lightweight pan, or a pan that is warped and uneven, will not do. Use a pan just the size of the crêpe you wish to make.

Pan for Crêpes

Butter the hot pan lightly; brush melted butter on the pan with a pastry brush, or if you like, run the end of a stick of butter over the pan. The amount of batter determines the thickness of the crêpe; a little experimentation will soon show you the best amount to use. To ensure crêpes of uniform size, use a measuring spoon or a ladle. Generally, 1 1/2 tablespoons of batter will be enough for a 5-inch crêpe. When the butter is very hot, pour in the batter all at once and quickly lift the pan from the heat and tilt it with a circular motion so that the batter coats the pan evenly and forms a perfect round crêpe. This is the critical moment; the batter should spread before it begins to set. The crêpe browns quickly; the top side will begin to look dry in less than 2 minutes. Lift the edge of the crêpe with a spatula to make sure that the bottom is browned, and quickly flip it over. Never turn the crêpe more than once.

If crêpes are to be filled and reheated for serving, they may be made in advance, as long as a day before they are to be served.

SWEET PANCAKES I

Crêpes I

SIFT together 2/3 cup flour, 1 tablespoon sugar, and a pinch of salt. Beat together 2 whole eggs and 2 egg yolks and add them to the dry ingredients. Add 1 3/4 cups milk and stir the mixture until it is smooth. Add 2 tablespoons melted butter and 1 tablespoon rum or Cognac. Let the batter stand for 2 hours before using.

To cook the crêpes, melt just enough butter in a hot pan to coat it thinly. Pour in a thin layer of crêpe batter. The crêpe should set and become brown in about 1 minute. Turn it over to brown the other side.

For a mixture that is not quite so delicate but which is easier to handle, use 1 1/2 cups milk and 3 eggs and 3 egg yolks to the amounts of other ingredients given in the recipe.

Crêpes II

SWEET PANCAKES II

SIFT together 2 cups flour, 6 tablespoons sugar, and a little salt. Add 6 eggs and mix well with a wire whip. Add 1 cup each of milk and cream. When everything is well combined, flavor with orange, vanilla, or rum. Cook according to the directions above.

Crêpes III

SWEET PANCAKES III

SIFT together 2 cups flour, 6 tablespoons sugar, and a little salt. Add 2 whole eggs and 3 egg yolks and mix well with a wire whip. Add 2 cups milk and when all is well combined, fold in 3 stiffly beaten egg whites. Flavor with vanilla, orange, or rum. Cook according to the directions above.

Crêpes Ménagère

COUNTRY STYLE PANCAKES

SIFT together 1 cup flour, 2 tablespoons sugar, and 1/4 teaspoon salt. Beat in gradually with a wire whip 3 beaten eggs. Add 1 1/4 cups milk and a little vanilla, rum, or brandy. Mix the batter until it is smooth, strain it through a fine sieve, and let it stand for 2 hours. Brown the crêpes on both sides, arrange them on a hot serving dish, and sprinkle them with powdered sugar, or serve them with maple syrup or honey or spread them with jelly or marmalade and roll them.

When it comes to making crêpes Suzette, *there seem to be about as many recipes as there are people who make them. But certain characteristics common to them all are that the batter is made quite thin and the cakes themselves are never very large, about 5 to 5 1/2 inches across; the sauce is always rich with butter and flavored with orange; and flaming brandy is the final flourish. You can buy special equipment for making* crêpes Suzette *at the table; it's a kind of chafing-dish with an alcohol burner under a flat pan on which the* crêpes *can be cooked and which is then used in making the sauce. More often the* crêpes *are cooked in the kitchen and only the sauce done at the table. Or everything can be prepared in the kitchen and the finished dish brought flaming to the table. In most restaurants, the headwaiter cooks the sauce on a side table set close to where the guests are eating so that they can watch him. He reheats cooked* crêpes *brought to him from the kitchen and usually makes quite a ceremony of it. In homes where* crêpes Suzette *are served, many hosts like to do it this way, too.*

CRÊPES SUZETTE

PREPARE 18 crêpes, each about 5 inches in diameter, and keep them warm. Rub 4 lumps loaf sugar on the skin of an orange. Mash the lumps of sugar on a plate with 3 tablespoons sweet butter. Put in a skillet or the blazer of a chafing dish 2 or 3 tablespoons butter, the juice of 1 orange, a few drops of lemon juice, and 1/2 cup curaçao, Cointreau, Bénédictine, or Grand Marnier or a mixture of them. Bring the mixture to a boil, and stir in the butter and sugar mixture. Lay the crêpes in the sauce and spoon the sauce over them. Add 1 or 2 more tablespoons butter if desired. Fold the crêpes in quarters, sprinkle them with 1/2 cup warm brandy, and ignite it.

*Crêpes
Suzette*

PANCAKES STRASBOURGEOISE

PREPARE 18 small crêpes and spread them with sweet butter creamed with a little powdered sugar and flavored with kirsch. Roll up the crêpes, arrange them on a heatproof serving dish, sprinkle them with a little sugar, and glaze them quickly under the broiler. Finely grated chocolate may be used for flavoring in place of the kirsch.

*Crêpes
Strasbour-
geoise*

PANCAKES WITH APRICOT JAM

PREPARE 18 small crêpes. When each crêpe is done, spread it with apricot jam and roll it up. Place them side by side on a platter and sprinkle with powdered sugar. Brown them, if desired, under the broiler flame or in a very hot oven.

*Crêpes aux
Abricots*

409

Crêpes aux
Pommes

PANCAKES WITH APPLES

PEEL 1 or 2 apples, remove the cores, and chop the fruit. Sauté quickly in a little butter. Make a crêpe batter and put a very thin layer in a buttered skillet. When it is set and brown on the underside, spread it with a layer of the minced apple. Pour another very thin layer of crêpe batter over this, turn over the whole cake, and cook until brown on the other side. Arrange on a hot dish and sprinkle with powdered sugar.

Crêpes aux
Cerises
Hélène

PANCAKES WITH CHERRIES HELEN

PREPARE crêpe batter and make small crêpes. Roll them up with a few cherries drained from cherry compote inside of each one. Arrange side by side in a shallow baking dish. Prick the tops a little with a fork. Cover with vanilla sauce, sprinkle with crushed macaroons, dot with a little butter, and brown the top in a hot oven.

Crêpes
à la
Bourbonnaise

PANCAKES WITH PASTRY CREAM

PREPARE 18 small crêpes and place each on a warm platter as it is done. Put a generous tablespoon *crème pâtissière* on each and roll it up so that the filling is enrobed in the crêpe. Place side by side in a shallow baking dish or chafing dish. When ready to serve pour a hot, rather thin apricot sauce over them and sprinkle with warm kirsch or rum. Ignite the liquor and serve the crêpes flaming.

Savory Crêpes

I am quite sure that the first time crêpes were filled with a sauced mixture of fish, poultry, or vegetables, the cook's inspiration was necessity. What more economical way of stretching a few spoonfuls of leftover food to make another delicious meal? Yet today crêpes of this sort are found on the most elaborate menus, as hors-d'oeuvre and as the main course for luncheons. An endless variety of fillings can be devised, once the basic principles of filled crêpes are established. Some suggestions are given here; you will find others in the section on hot hors-d'oeuvre, under the general heading of " salpicons. "

The instructions for making and cooking entrée crêpes are exactly like those for dessert crêpes.

LUNCHEON PANCAKES

Crêpes pour Déjeuner

SIFT together 1 cup flour, 1/2 teaspoon salt, and 1 teaspoon sugar and add gradually 2 eggs and 2 egg yolks beaten together. Add 1 3/4 cups milk and stir to make a very smooth batter. Let it stand 2 hours.

PANCAKES WITH SPINACH

Crêpes aux Épinards

MAKE luncheon crêpes and spread them with creamed spinach. Roll the crêpes and serve them hot, with *sauce Mornay*, if desired.

PANCAKES WITH CHICKEN

Crêpes à la Reine

SIMMER 2 cups chopped cooked chicken meat in 1 cup cream until the liquid is reduced to 1/2 its original quantity. Add 1/2 cup cream sauce, salt to taste, and a little white pepper.

Spread luncheon crêpes with this chicken hash mixture, roll them, and serve them hot, with *sauce Mornay*, if desired.

PANCAKES WITH SHELLFISH

Crêpes aux Crustacés

MAKE luncheon crêpes and spread them with finely diced lobster or shrimp or crab meat mixed with enough béchamel sauce to bind the fish. Flavor with a little dry Sherry. Roll the crêpes and serve them very hot.

POTATO PANCAKES

Crêpes de Pommes de Terre

PEEL and soak in cold water for several hours 2 large potatoes. Grate and drain them and put in a bowl with 1 medium-sized onion, grated, 1/2 teaspoon chopped parsley, 2 tablespoons flour, 1/2 teaspoon salt, a little pepper, and a little nutmeg. Mix all together well and add 2 egg yolks, slightly beaten. When well combined, fold in the 2 egg whites, beaten stiff. Heat a little butter in a skillet and spread 2 tablespoons of the mixture in the pan for each cake. Cook them over medium heat until golden brown on each side, turning the cakes only once.

Crêpes au Fromage

MAKE crêpes as for soup garnish, about 3 inches in diameter. Cut Swiss cheese into small sticks the thickness of a pencil and 2 or 3 inches long. Roll the cheese sticks in the crêpes, dip the crêpes in egg beaten with 1 teaspoon cold water and then in fine, fresh bread crumbs. Fry the rolls in deep hot fat. The cheese will melt to a creamy mass.

Beignets

IN FRANCE, the name "*beignet*" is given to several different kinds of fried foods that in this country we might call French crullers, jelly doughnuts, or fritters. The first two, and the fruit fritters, were *Carnaval* specialties.

All *beignets* are fried in deep hot fat. I suggest that you read the instructions on this kind of cooking elsewhere in this book before you proceed.

Much of the success of *beignets* depends upon their cooking; the temperature of the fat is of great importance. It must be hot enough to keep the cakes from becoming fat soaked, and yet not so hot that the *beignets* brown on the outside before the inside cooks. Until you learn from experience what the proper temperature is and how to maintain it, a thermometer is your best guide; 370 ° F. to 375° F. is the right temperature for *beignets*.

Have the oil several inches deep in the pan, deep enough to float the *beignets*, but use a pan that allows 2 or more inches between the surface of the oil and the top of the pan to allow for sputtering.

As it browns on the bottom, the *beignet* turns itself over in the fat. If you prefer a more richly browned *beignet*, you may turn it several times to· brown it evenly to the degree you prefer. Unlike crêpes, *beignets* do not suffer from this treatment. It is very important to drain as much of the fat from the surface of the cooked *beignet* as possible. Lift the browned *beignet* from the fat with a slotted spoon and let the excess fat drain off. Then transfer the *beignets* to a plate covered with crumpled paper towels. When the paper is crumpled, it touches more of the surface of the *beignets* and absorbs more of the fat.

Beignets *of the cruller and doughnut type taste best while they are still warm. They can be sprinkled with sugar and eaten in the hand or served with a dessert sauce such as apricot sauce or* sauce vanille.

Sweet Beignets

FRIED TWISTS

DISSOLVE 1/2 cake or envelope yeast in 3 tablespoons lukewarm water. Dry granulated yeast requires slightly warmer water. Sift 4 cups flour onto a board or into a bowl and make a well in the center. Put the dissolved yeast in the well and add 1/2 cup soft butter, 1/3 cup sugar, a pinch of salt, 4 eggs, 2 tablespoons rum, a little vanilla extract, and the grated rind of 1 lemon. Mix all together well with the hands or with a heavy wooden spoon, gradually pulling the flour into the center. Knead the dough until it is smooth and elastic. Cover it and let it stand in a cool place for a few hours or overnight. Roll the dough into a very thin sheet and cut it into strips about 2/3-inch wide and 8-inches long. Tie each strip in a loose knot and let the knots rest for 20 minutes. Fry the *beignets* in deep hot fat (375° F.) to a golden brown. Drain them on paper towels, sprinkle them with sugar, and serve immediately.

Beignets de Carnaval

FRITTERS SUZETTE

HEAT 2 cups milk with a piece of vanilla bean and gradually add 1/2 cup farina, stirring briskly to prevent lumps. Cook, stirring occasionally, for about 10 to 15 minutes, or until the mixture is very thick. Remove the vanilla bean. Add 1/2 cup sugar, 1 tablespoon sweet butter, and 2 slightly beaten egg yolks, and mix all together well. Return the pan to the heat and cook for 2 minutes longer, stirring constantly. Spread the mixture about 3/4-inch thick on a buttered shallow pan or baking sheet, and chill it. Invert the pan on a floured pastry board. Cut the dough with

Beignets Suzette

413

a doughnut cutter. Dip the *beignets* in flour, then in beaten egg, and finally in fine white bread crumbs, and sauté them in hot butter to a golden brown on both sides. Arrange the fritters in a ring and put a candied cherry in the center of each. Sprinkle with confectioners' sugar and serve hot, with a fruit sauce.

Beignets d'Orléans

JELLY DOUGHNUTS

DISSOLVE 1/2 cake or envelope yeast in 3 tablespoons lukewarm water. Dry granulated yeast requires slightly warmer water. Add 1/4 cup lukewarm milk and then 1 cup flour, and beat all together well. Cover the sponge with a towel and put it in a warm place to rise until it is light and bubbly. Sift 3 cups flour into a bowl, make a well in the center, and in the well put 2 tablespoons sugar, 1/2 teaspoon salt, 3/4 cup soft butter, 3 eggs, and the grated rind of 1 lemon. Gradually pull the flour into the center with the hands or a heavy wooden spoon and add 1 cup warm milk little by little to make a soft dough. Add the yeast mixture and work the dough until it is smooth and elastic. Cut off small pieces of the dough, flatten them in the hands, and put 1 teaspoon jam in the center of each. Form the dough into balls around the jam. Let the *beignets* rise in a warm place until they double in bulk and fry them to a golden brown in deep hot fat (375° F.). Drain them on absorbent paper and sprinkle with confectioners' sugar.

When pâte à chou, *or cream puff paste, for* beignets soufflés *is forced through a pastry tube into a ring shape, the fried* beignet *is iced with confectioners' sugar and becomes a " French cruller. " The* pâte à chou *puffs up in the fat just as it does when it is baked to make cream puffs.*

Beignets Soufflés

SOUFFLÉ FRITTERS

PUT 1 cup water or half milk and half water, 1/2 cup butter, a pinch of salt, and 1 teaspoon sugar in a saucepan and bring the mixture to a boil. When the butter is melted add 1 cup flour all at once. Mix

Pâte à Chou quickly with a wooden spoon and cook, stirring briskly, until the mixture rolls away from the sides of the pan without sticking. Remove the pan from the heat and add 4 eggs, one at a time, beating the batter thoroughly after each addition. Add 1 teaspoon vanilla extract.

Fill a tablespoon with the mixture and slip half of it off into a pan of deep hot fat (375° F.). Then slip off the other half, making 2 *beignets* from each tablespoon. Let them brown on both sides. Remove, drain well, and sprinkle with confectioners' sugar or serve plain with *sauce vanille*. Or cut a little opening in each drained *beignet* and fill them with well-drained cooked or canned cherries.

Of course a fritter can be made of anything, and in thrifty French households many leftover bits of fish, meat, fowl, and vegetables are coated for the friture *as savory* beignets *for hors-d'oeuvre or for a luncheon or supper entrée. But at* Carnaval *time, it is the fruit fritters that are universally enjoyed.*

Any fruit, canned or freshly cooked or fresh, can be used to make fruit fritters. It is important that the surface of the fruit be completely dry or the fritter batter will not adhere to it. Be careful to mix fritter batter only until it is smooth; overmixing will result in a tough, elastic crust instead of a tender, crisp one. Dip larger pieces of fruit into the batter one by one, making sure that each piece is thoroughly covered. Drain off the excess batter and drop the fritter into deep hot fat. It usually takes about 5 minutes to fry fruit fritters. Small pieces of fruit or berries should be mixed into the batter, and the mixture dropped by spoonfuls into the hot fat. Arrange the fritters in a shallow pan, sprinkle them with sugar, and glaze the sugar quickly under the broiler flame. Or sprinkle them with powdered sugar. Fruit fritters are usually served hot with fruit sauce, sabayon, or sauce vanille.

FRITTER BATTER FOR FRUIT FRITTERS

Pâte à Frire pour Beignets de Fruits

Sɪꜰᴛ together 1/2 cup flour and 1/4 teaspoon salt. Add 1 tablespoon melted butter beaten with 1 egg. Add 1/2 cup flat beer gradually, stirring only until the mixture is smooth. Do not overmix. Put the batter in a warm place for 1 to 2 hours, until it is light and foamy. Just before using, fold in 1 stiffly beaten egg white.

APPLE FRITTERS

Beignets de Pommes

Pᴇᴇʟ and core 1 large apple for 2 servings. Cut and slice them into rings 1/4 inch thick. Sprinkle with sugar and a few drops of rum, brandy, or kirsch and, if desired, a few drops of lemon juice. Marinate the apple rings for about 1 hour, turning the pieces so that they absorb the marinade evenly. Dry the slices a little, dip them in fritter batter for fruits and fry in deep hot fat (370° F.) until they are golden brown, on both sides. Drain the fritters on paper towels, arrange them in a hot serving dish, sprinkle with powdered sugar, and glaze under the broiler.

Beignets d'Ananas

PINEAPPLE FRITTERS

CUT slices of canned pineapple in half and drain well. Sprinkle them with a little rum, brandy, or kirsch and, if desired, a few drops of lemon juice, and let them marinate for 20 minutes. Dry the slices, dip them in fritter batter for fruits and fry them in deep hot fat (370° F.) until they are golden brown on both sides. Arrange the fritters on a shallow pan, sprinkle them with powdered sugar and put under broiler to glaze them. Serve them in overlapping rings on a hot dish.

Beignets de Cerises

CHERRY FRITTERS

PIT about 1 quart large sweet cherries and sprinkle with sugar and a little kirsch or maraschino liqueur. Mix the fruit with fritter batter for fruits and drop from a tablespoon into deep hot fat (370° F.). Fry the fritters until they are puffed and browned. Drain well on paper toweling and sprinkle with confectioners' sugar.

Savory Beignets

Fritter batter is used to coat pieces of cooked fish, meat, and poultry for frying—these beignets *are also called* fritots. Croquettes, *which are mixtures of cooked food bound with* sauce béchamel, *are also sometimes coated with fritter batter for frying, rather than* à l'anglaise, *with egg and bread crumbs.*

416

If the food to be coated is moist and likely to ooze, a thicker batter should be used than is required for very dry foods. As always, the surface should be dry so that the batter will adhere to it.

FRITTER BATTER

SIFT into a warm bowl 1 cup flour and pinch of salt. Make a well in the center and add 1 tablespoon salad oil, 3/4 cup lukewarm water, and 1 egg yolk. Mix all together lightly, quickly, and thoroughly; be careful not to overmix or the coating will be tough. The mixture should be quite thick. Cover it and set in a warm place for 3 to 4 hours. When ready to use, fold in 1 egg white, beaten stiff.

For thinner batter, use 3/4 cup flour, 2 tablespoons salad oil, 3/4 cup water, and 1 egg yolk. Fold in 1 egg white, beaten stiff.

BRAIN FRITTERS

CLEAN a pair of brains and remove the membranes. Prepare a court bouillon made by simmering a mixture of 2 tablespoons salt, a few peppercorns, a little thyme, and a small bay leaf with 1 quart cold water. Add the brains and simmer them for 20 to 25 minutes. Cool the brains in the court bouillon, drain them, and cut them in pieces. Sprinkle the pieces with a little salad oil and lemon juice and some finely chopped parsley. Marinate the brains for 15 to 20 minutes. Dry the pieces and dip them into fritter batter, 2 or 3 pieces to a fritter. Fry in deep hot fat (375° F.), drain on paper towels and serve immediately.

SWEETBREAD FRITTERS

CUT cooked sweetbreads in pieces and sprinkle with a little oil and lemon juice and finely chopped parsley. Let them marinate for 15 to 20 minutes. When ready to serve, dry the sweetbreads' surfaces and dip them into fritter batter, 2 or 3 small pieces to each fritter. Fry in deep hot fat (370° F.) to a golden brown. Drain on paper towels and serve immediately.

Fritters may be made in this way with other foods. Substitute for the sweetbreads small slices of cooked chicken, pieces of cooked fish, uncooked tomatoes, cut in quarters, or cooked artichoke bottoms, cut in quarters, for instance.

Beignets de Champignons

MUSHROOM FRITTERS

COMBINE 1 cup cooked mushrooms cut in dice with 1 cup cooked ham cut in dice. Add 1/2 cup thick béchamel sauce. Cool the mixture. Roll heaping tablespoons of it into balls or egg shapes. Cover with thick fritter batter and fry in deep hot fat (370° F.) to a golden brown. Drain on paper towels and serve immediately.

The pâte à chou *for* beignets soufflés, *without the sugar and flavoring, is used for entrée* beignets.

Beignets d' Huîtres

OYSTER FRITTERS

POACH 2 dozen large oysters, drain them, and cut them in dice. Add to the batter for *beignets soufflés*, without sugar or flavoring. Drop by spoonfuls into deep hot fat (375° F.) and fry the *beignets* until they are brown on both sides; they will turn in the fat as they cook. Drain on paper towels and serve very hot, with cocktail sauce à la Ritz or Mornay sauce.

Beignets Soufflés de Maïs

CORN FRITTERS

MAKE 1/2 the recipe for *beignets soufflés* omitting the sugar and flavoring. Add 1/2 cup whole kernel canned corn or fresh corn, cooked and cut from the cob. Fry according to the directions for *beignets soufflés* and drain well on absorbent paper.

Beignets Soufflés d'Oignons

ONION FRITTERS

MAKE 1/2 the recipe for *beignets soufflés* omitting sugar and flavoring. Add 1/4 cup finely chopped onions and a little paprika. Fry by teaspoons, according to the directions for *beignets soufflés*, and drain well on absorbent paper.

OEUFS, FROMAGE, ET RIZ

Eggs, Cheese, and Rice

Too few visitors to the small towns of France ever see beyond the formal fronts of the houses into the charming little rear yards, although railroad travelers may catch a fleeting view of the long narrow gardens that are the pride of every French household. Neat rows of carrots, onions, beets, and lettuce stretch away from the house. Flowers edge the parallel walks, interspersed with strawberry plants, clumps of fragrant herbs, and carefully trimmed berry bushes. Apple, peach, pear, and apricot trees are espaliered against the fences in the space-saving French fashion. And at the very end of the garden, partly hidden by shrubs, partly shaded by a plum tree, a busy clucking announces the presence of the *poulailler*, the chicken coop.

Chicken is an important part of the family diet, of course, but eggs are even more important, and many of the fuzzy little chicks that overrun the chicken yard in the spring will be kept to supply eggs during the winter. Eggs are absolutely essential in French cuisine. As a cooking ingredient, the egg is used to give a lighter texture to a mixture, as for soufflés or cakes, or to thicken it, as for sauces, or simply to enrich it. And there is no more popular entrée for luncheon or supper in France than an omelet or another egg dish.

When I think of eggs, I remember only too well my first Easter Saturday at the Maison Calondre, where I served my apprenticeship. Hundreds of pounds of brioche dough, rich with eggs, had to be prepared for the weekend, and it was my task to break the eggs—four or five hundred of them. I had been taught the technique, and if practice does indeed make perfect, I surely had the opportunity to become perfect that day.

Breaking Eggs The classic method of handling eggs is this: Crack the shell on the edge of the bowl and, with half a shell in each hand, empty the contents into the bowl. Run the right thumb around the inside of the half-shell in the left hand to completely clear it of egg white. Fit the other half-shell into this one, and clean it in the same way. Then put aside the tightly wedged shells. To separate eggs, hold the two halves over a bowl and slide the yolk from half to half until all the white has fallen out except the stringy portion attached to the yolk. Remove this by running the thumb against the edge of the shell. Empty the yolk into another bowl and clean both half-shells with the thumb.

We were never permitted to break eggs directly into the large container that held the dozens or hundreds of eggs being readied for the day's cooking. Instead, we broke 3 or 4 at a time into a small bowl, and made sure each one was sweet and fresh.

Eggs have a characteristic delicacy which is easily spoiled. An egg may have a fishy or other extraneous flavor if the hen has supplemented her diet with strongly flavored morsels. This foreign taint may also develop if the egg is stored in the proximity of malodorous foods. This has its advantages as well as disadvantages. If eggs are stored with fresh truffles, for instance, they make an exquisitely truffle-flavored omelet, even though truffles are not used in the omelet. But a tainted or spoiled egg can ruin an entire batch of freshly broken eggs, and it is wise to sniff each egg as you break it.

Eggs should be stored in the refrigerator, but it is a good trick to

EGGS, CHEESE, AND RICE

keep at room temperature the eggs that will be required during the day. Eggs at room temperature are less likely to break in hot water than refrigerated eggs, the yolks and whites mix together more readily, and the whites can be beaten to greater volume.

Eggs are one of the quickest things in the world to cook, and in one way, one of the easiest. On the other hand, there are many pitfalls in egg cookery, as anyone knows who has broken the yolk of a poached egg in lifting it from the water, or been embarrassed by a separated hollandaise or a curdled custard. Eggs are sensitive to high heat and to overcooking, both of which toughen the whites, darken the yolks, and cause separation or curdling of custards and sauces.

Even in so-called " boiling, " eggs are actually cooked slowly, and at moderate temperature. The water should never be allowed to boil.

The most popular breakfast egg is probably the soft-cooked egg, or *oeuf à la coque*. It has a jellied, opaque white and a soft, runny yolk. For the same results every time, time the cooking carefully and use enough simmering water to cover the eggs completely.

SOFT-COOKED EGGS

Oeufs à la Coque

LOWER the eggs gently into simmering water and cook them for 3 minutes. Or cook the eggs for 1 minute, remove the pan from the heat, and allow the eggs to remain in the water for 3 minutes.

Coddled eggs are characterized by a firm white and a soft yolk. They may be shelled whole and used whenever poached eggs are specified.

CODDLED EGGS

Oeufs Mollets

LOWER the eggs gently into boiling water, lower the heat at once, and simmer for 5 to 6 minutes. Plunge the eggs into cold water to stop the cooking. Remove the shells. If these eggs are not to be served at once, they may be briefly reheated in warm salted water.

When we speak of a fried egg in America, we mean a sautéed egg, an egg cooked gently in enough hot fat to keep it from sticking to the pan. Most people like these eggs not at all brown, with firm whites and soft yolks, but if you prefer them lightly browned on the bottom and crisp around the edges, simply cook them a little longer. A fried egg in France is deep-fried.

FRIED EGGS

Oeufs Sautés

MELT enough butter or rendered bacon fat in a skillet to cover the bottom well. Heat the fat until it bubbles. Break the eggs into a saucer, one at a time, slide them into the pan, and cook over low to moderate heat to the desired stage of doneness. Season with salt and pepper and serve at once.

FRIED EGGS FRENCH STYLE

Oeufs Frits

IN A pan melt fat or oil, of a depth of about 3 inches, and heat it very hot. Break each egg into a small dish and slide it into the hot fat. Move the egg with a wooden spoon as it cooks to help it keep its shape, being very careful not to break the yolk. Fry the egg until it is golden brown. This takes less than a minute. Remove it from the fat, drain it, and season with salt. Serve with rice or vegetables as a main dish, or with tomato sauce and fried parsley, as a garnish.

Hard-Cooked Eggs

As A small boy, I spent almost all the holidays at *grand-père's* farm. At Eastertime, *grand-mère* would take time from her myriad duties to decorate a basketful of hard-cooked eggs for each of us children. On Easter Monday, as soon as breakfast was over, we ran to the meadows for the egg-rolling, a symbol of Easter joy after the stern weeks of Lent. When we tired of the game, we put the eggs back into the baskets and rushed off past hedgerows suddenly turned white and sweet-smelling with blossoming hawthorn, across fields sprinkled with purple violets—to watch my grandfather and uncle plowing and uncovering tiny pale shoots of dandelions that had lain dormant all winter, fresh, young growths not yet exposed to the sun, and not yet green. In the salad that *grand-mère* made—a traditional post-Lenten dish in our home—they were combined with fresh spring greens which we picked in the meadow and with wedges of our hard-cooked Easter eggs. And of course, our thrifty French grandmother saw to it that none of our hard-cooked eggs was wasted. Eventually all of them found their way into one dish or another.

Although we had our own eggs on the farm, and knew that nothing tastes quite so good as the unsurpassed delicacy of a new-laid egg, very fresh eggs were not used for hard-cooked eggs, or for eggs *mollet*, which had to be removed from the shells whole. For these, *grand-mère* used eggs that she had stored in a cool place for two days or even longer, to allow a little space to develop between the egg and the shell. Otherwise the shells would not peel smoothly from the cooked egg. She took a further precaution: when the eggs were cooked, she transferred them immediately to a bowl of cold water. This prevented a dark ring from forming around the yolk and allowed moisture to condense between egg and shell, separating the two, so that the shell could easily be slipped off without marring the smooth perfection of the white.

HARD-COOKED EGGS

COOK fresh but not new-laid eggs for 10 minutes in simmering water to cover. Plunge the eggs at once into cold water, and if convenient, shell them as soon as they are cool enough to handle.

Oeufs Durs

CREAMED EGGS AND ONIONS

Oeufs à la Tripe

MELT 2 tablespoons butter in a saucepan, add 1/2 cup chopped parboiled onions, and sauté slowly until they are soft but not brown. Add 2 tablespoons flour and blend well. Add gradually 2 cups hot milk, salt and pepper to taste, and cook, stirring constantly, until the sauce thickens. Simmer it until it is reduced by 1/3, fold in 6 hard-cooked eggs, sliced into strips, and serve in heated cocottes.

When stuffed eggs are served as hors-d'oeuvre, allow 1 for each person; as an entrée, allow 2 eggs for each serving.

Oeufs Farcis à la Chimay   STUFFED EGGS CHIMAY

CUT in half lengthwise 6 hard-cooked eggs. Rub the yolks through a sieve and mix with an equal amount of finely chopped, cooked mushrooms, 1 1/2 tablespoons soft butter, 2 tablespoons Mornay sauce, 1/2 teaspoon salt, and a little pepper. Fill the whites with the mixture, heaping it up. Spread a layer of Mornay sauce in a shallow baking dish, arrange the stuffed eggs in the dish, and cover with enough Mornay sauce to coat each egg well. Sprinkle with grated Parmesan and brown under the broiler or in a very hot oven (450° F.).

Oeufs Farcis à la Diable   HOT DEVILED EGGS

CUT in half lengthwise 6 hard-cooked eggs. Mash the yolks with 1 teaspoon prepared mustard, 4 tablespoons béchamel sauce, and 1/2 teaspoon salt. Stuff the egg whites and press the halves together. Put one stuffed egg into each of 6 individual buttered casseroles and add Mornay sauce to cover, using 2 cups in all. Sprinkle with grated Parmesan and brown under the broiler or in a very hot oven (450° F.). Sprinkle with paprika and serve very hot.

Poached Eggs

EGGS for poaching, unlike eggs for hard-cooking, must be very fresh. The whites of very fresh eggs will coagulate quickly and surround the yolks with a protective coating at once. If you cannot be sure that the eggs are very fresh, add a little vinegar to the water. The acid helps to coagulate the white and hold the egg in shape.

The easiest way to poach eggs—that is, to cook them without their shells in water—is to slip them, one at a time, from a small saucer into simmering water deep enough to float them. It helps to produce shapely ovals if you stir the water so that it forms a whirlpool, and slip the egg directly into the center of the swirling water. Then continue to move the spoon around the edge of the pan so that the swirling water shapes the egg. An experienced chef can poach several eggs at a time in a wide, shallow pan, by using the spoon to turn the eggs as they cook. Cook poached eggs for 3 to 3 1/2 minutes, until the white is firm. Remove them from the pan with a perforated spoon, trim off any ragged edges, and drain thoroughly. If the eggs are not to be served at once, cover them with cool water. Just before serving, reheat them, without allowing them to cook further, in hot salted water. Two poached eggs is the usual entrée serving; for hors-d'oeuvre, serve 1 to each guest.

POACHED EGGS

Oeufs Pochés

BRING to a boil 1 quart water with 1 tablespoon vinegar and 1 teaspoon salt. Reduce the heat so that the water simmers gently. Break an egg into a saucer and slip it gently onto the surface of the water. Simmer gently until the whites are firm, basting with water. Remove the eggs with a perforated spoon, trim them, and dry thoroughly before serving.

POACHED EGGS BENEDICT   *Oeufs Pochés Bénédictine*

PLACE a slice of broiled ham on half a toasted English muffin. Put a hot poached egg on the ham and cover it with hollandaise sauce. Garnish with a slice of truffle.

POACHED EGGS BEATRICE   *Oeufs Pochés Béatrice*

PLACE hot poached eggs on rounds of toast, cover them with Mornay sauce to which sliced cooked mushrooms have been added, sprinkle with grated Parmesan cheese, and brown under the broiler. Garnish with asparagus tips and tomato sauce.

POACHED EGGS WITH SPINACH   *Oeufs Pochés à la Florentine*

PLACE hot poached eggs on a bed of cooked, drained and buttered spinach or purée of spinach. Cover with Mornay sauce, sprinkle with Parmesan cheese, and glaze lightly under the broiler. Serve with toast points.

POACHED EGGS IN RED WINE   *Oeufs Pochés à la Bourguignonne*

IN A shallow pan bring to a boil 3 cups dry red wine and 1 cup water with 1 small bay leaf, 1 tablespoon chopped shallots, 2 sprigs of parsley, 1 clove of garlic, 1 teaspoon salt, and a pinch of pepper. Poach 12 eggs in this liquid and transfer them to a basin of salted lukewarm water.

Reduce the cooking liquid to 1/3 its original quantity and, stirring vigor-ously, add gradually *beurre manié* made by creaming 1 1/2 tablespoons butter with 1 1/2 tablespoons flour. Correct the seasoning of the liquid with salt and add 2 tablespoons butter. Serve the eggs on rounds of toast and strain the sauce over them.

Oeufs Pochés à la Portugaise   POACHED EGGS PORTUGUESE

PLACE hot poached eggs on rounds of toast. Cover with *sauce portugaise* combined with an equal quantity of Mornay sauce.

Cold poached eggs are usually covered with aspic. They often are garnished with spring vegetables and sliced tomatoes, and accompany cold meats such as ham and tongue.

Oeufs Pochés Froids   COLD POACHED EGGS

POACH eggs as described above and remove them at once from the sim-mering water to a pan of cold water to cool. Trim neatly and prepare as indicated in the recipes.

Oeufs Pochés en Gelée   POACHED EGGS IN ASPIC

Egg-White Flowers

COAT 6 small molds with clear aspic and chill the aspic until it is set. Decorate the center of each mold with a lily-of-the-valley, made by cutting hard-cooked egg white into flower shapes with a truffle cutter, or a sharp knife, and arranging blanched tarragon leaves for the leaves and stem. Decorate the sides of the molds with slices of truffle and hard-cooked egg whites, ham and ox tongue, both cut in julienne, and blanched tar-ragon leaves. Place a cold, trimmed poached egg in each mold, cover it with aspic, and chill for 45 minutes, or until the aspic is set. Fill the molds almost to the top with cooked peas, and green beans, carrots, and white turnips, all diced. Cover the vegetables with a layer of aspic and chill it for 45 minutes, or until the aspic is set. Unmold on individual plates and garnish with chopped aspic and parsley.

COLD EGGS PRINTANIÈRE *Oeufs à la Printanière*

FOR each serving, coat a small mold with aspic and chill the aspic until it is set. Combine equal parts of green beans, carrots, and turnips, all cooked and cut in 1-inch strips or small dice, and cooked green peas, and add just enough mayonnaise to bind the vegetables. Place a layer of the vegetable mixture in each mold, arrange a cold poached egg or *oeuf mollet* on top, and fill the mold with aspic. Chill the aspic for 45 minutes, or until it is set.

Or pour a layer of aspic on a platter and chill it. On the aspic arrange 6 cold poached eggs or *oeufs mollets*, and top them with the vegetable-mayonnaise mixture. Cover the platter with the aspic and chill it for 45 minutes, or until it is set.

COLD EGGS WITH PEPPERS *Oeufs Pochés Louisiane*

SLICE off the tops of 2 large or 3 medium green peppers and remove the pith and seeds. Mash the yolks of 5 hard-cooked eggs and add to them 1/2 cup chopped red pimentos and 1/2 cup mayonnaise *chaud-froid*. Pack this mixture into the peppers and chill them. With a sharp knife, cut the stuffed peppers into 1/2-inch slices and arrange a cold poached egg on each slice. Finish with a coating of clear aspic.

COLD EGGS WITH PÂTÉ DE FOIE GRAS *Oeufs à la Strasbourgeoise*

PLACE cold poached eggs or *oeufs mollets* on slices of *pâté de foie gras*. Coat the eggs with *chaud-froid blanc*, jellied white sauce, and chill for 30 minutes, or until the sauce sets. Decorate the tops of the eggs with slices of truffle, cut in fancy shapes, cover with aspic and chill.

Scrambled Eggs

EGGS may be scrambled properly in one of two ways—over very low direct heat in a skillet or in the top of a double boiler. The top of a double boiler or a chafing dish is ideal for scrambling eggs because these maintain a constant low temperature which assures smoothness and delicacy. They may be served plain or with bacon, sausages, mushrooms, asparagus tips, tomato sauce, or another garnish.

Oeufs Brouillés

SCRAMBLED EGGS

BREAK eggs into a bowl and beat them until they are well mixed but not fluffy. For 6 eggs, melt and heat 1 1/2 tablespoons butter in a skillet or in the top of a double boiler. Add the eggs and cook, stirring constantly, over low heat or hot water. When the eggs begin to set, add 1 tablespoon butter, 2 tablespoons cream, and salt to taste.

Oeufs Brouillés Magda

SCRAMBLED EGGS MAGDA

GARNISH scrambled eggs with tomato sauce and sprinkle them with finely chopped parsley and grated Parmesan cheese.

Oeufs Brouillés Princesse

SCRAMBLED EGGS PRINCESS

GARNISH scrambled eggs with asparagus tips and slices of truffle.

Oeufs Brouillés à la Reine

SCRAMBLED EGGS À LA REINE

FILL a heated patty shell with a layer of scrambled eggs, a layer of creamed chicken, and a final layer of eggs. Garnish with a slice of truffle.

Shirred Eggs

EGGS that are baked or broiled in shallow ramekins are called shirred eggs.

Oeufs sur le Plat

SHIRRED EGGS

HEAT ramekins and melt a little butter in them before the eggs are put in. Then the eggs are baked in a moderate oven (350° F.) or grilled 4 inches from medium broiler heat for 10 to 12 minutes, or until the whites are set. When shirred eggs are broiled, bits of butter on the yolks help to keep them moist.

SHIRRED EGGS WITH SPINACH *Oeufs sur le Plat à la Florentine*

PLACE a layer of cooked, drained, and seasoned spinach leaves in a buttered ramekin, and sprinkle the spinach with grated Parmesan. Break 2 eggs over the spinach and bake them in a moderate oven (350° F.) for 10 to 12 minutes, or until the whites are set. Garnish with sautéed mushrooms.

SHIRRED EGGS OPERA STYLE *Oeufs sur le Plat Opéra*

GARNISH one side of a ramekin containing shirred eggs with sautéed chicken livers in Madeira sauce, the other side with cooked asparagus tips.

SHIRRED EGGS AMERICAN *Oeufs sur le Plat à l'Américaine*

GARNISH shirred eggs with a broiled sausage link, a sautéed chicken liver, a strip of broiled bacon, and a broiled tomato half.

SHIRRED EGGS BIBESCO *Oeufs sur le Plat Bibesco*

ARRANGE 3 thin slices of ox tongue in a buttered ramekin. Break 2 eggs into the ramekin and bake in a moderate oven (350° F.) for 10 to 12 minutes, or until the whites are set. Garnish each egg with a ring of *sauce périgueux*.

SHIRRED EGGS WITH TARRAGON *Oeufs sur le Plat à l'Estragon*

GARNISH the yolks of shirred eggs with a cross of tarragon leaves that have been parboiled for 1 or 2 minutes and surround the eggs with a ribbon of tarragon-flavored chicken or veal gravy.

SHIRRED EGGS IN BLACK BUTTER *Oeufs sur le Plat au Beurre Noir*

BREAK 2 eggs into a shallow ramekin and bake in a moderate oven (350° F.). Take the eggs from the oven before the whites are set and pour over them 1 tablespoon butter that has been seasoned with a dash of vinegar and cooked until dark brown. The hot butter will finish cooking the eggs. Garnish with 1/2 teaspoon capers.

Eggs en cocotte *resemble shirred eggs in the way they are served, but they are more delicate in texture. The cocottes, small straight-sided baking dishes, are placed in a pan of hot water and covered, so that direct heat never touches the eggs and they cook without hardening.*

Oeufs en Cocotte EGGS IN COCOTTE

BRUSH a cocotte with melted butter, break an egg into it, and add 1 tablespoon sweet cream. Place the cocotte in a shallow pan of boiling water, cover it, and cook either on top of the stove or in a moderate oven (350° F.) for 10 to 12 minutes, or until the white is set. Garnish with asparagus tips, tomato, truffles, or sautéed chicken livers. Or break eggs into a cocotte in which has been spread a layer of chicken hash, asparagus tips or peeled, seeded and chopped tomato. If desired, coat the eggs with a light Mornay sauce, sprinkle with grated Parmesan cheese, and glaze under the broiler.

When I was a young chef in Paris, an egg dish created to honor the Queen of Portugal became a favorite of royalty. I have never seen this recipe in print, for reasons which will be apparent to you, and I set it down here as a matter of history. To make oeufs Reine Amélie, *egg-shaped ovals of butter were coated twice* à l'anglaise—*with flour, egg, and crumbs. A cutter removed a small plug in the end of each butter-egg, and the eggs were thoroughly chilled. Then they were deep fried. The butter melted and could be emptied out of the hole in the end of the egg, and the shells were filled with*

eggs scrambled to delicate creaminess with chopped truffles. Nests for these eggs were made by lining the bottom and sides of a wire frying basket with shoestring potatoes and setting a smaller frying basket to hold the potatoes in place until they fried. When the baskets were separated, the crisp nest slipped out. It was a tasty dish, and an amusing one, but you will understand why it does not appear on many menus.

Omelets

THERE are 3 rules for preparing omelets.

One, the omelet pan should be used exclusively for the making of omelets. It should never be washed but should be cleaned after use with coarse salt and with paper towels. If other foods are cooked in the omelet pan or if it is rinsed with water, the next omelet will stick. *Omelet Pan*

Two, never make an omelet with more than 5 or 6 eggs. An omelet made with 4 eggs is easier to handle.

Three, never beat eggs for an omelet. Stir them only until the whites and yolks are combined. Too much beating and stirring will result in an omelet that is heavy and watery. My mother made two kinds of omelets, the rolled omelets that are familiar to Americans and a flat kind that is less often seen here but that is more common than the rolled in many sections of France. A flat omelet, when the bottom has set, is flipped over like a pancake, but it can be made just as creamy inside and tender as the rolled variety. Our favorite omelet was the hearty *omelette paysanne*, a flat one that combines salt pork or ham, potatoes, and herbs with the eggs. We also liked those made with tomatoes and onions, and in September, when the fields were covered with mushrooms, they went into every omelet. You may also make omelets with grated cheese, sliced artichoke bottoms, diced or sliced truffles, croutons, or asparagus tips or, indeed, any savory or sweet filling that is appetizing. Sprinkle a cooked omelet with parsley or paprika, if you like.

PLAIN OMELET

FOR 2 servings, mix 3 or 4 eggs lightly with a fork and add 1/2 teaspoon salt. Melt 1 tablespoon butter in an omelet pan and cook until it is light *Omelette Nature*

431

brown. Pour in the eggs and stir them briskly with a fork. Quickly, with the fork, pull the edges of the egg mass toward the center as it thickens. The liquid part will immediately fill the vacant spaces. Repeat this until there is no more liquid but the eggs are still very soft. Gently press down the handle of the pan so that the omelet will slide toward it. When a third of the flat omelet has slid up the edge of the pan, fold this toward the center with the help of a spatula. Then lift the handle of the pan so that the omelet slides in the opposite direction. When that third has slid up the edge across from the handle, hold a heated oval dish under it. As the rim of the omelet touches the dish, lift the handle up higher and higher until the pan is turned upside down and the omelet slips onto the dish. The entire cooking process should not take more than 2 or 3 minutes, and the result should be an oval-shaped, lightly browned omelet.

Omelette à la Florentine   SPINACH OMELET

FILL an omelet with 3 tablespoons freshly cooked, well-drained and seasoned spinach just before folding it. Or fill the center of the omelet with 3 tablespoons creamed spinach purée.

Omelette aux Champignons   MUSHROOM OMELET

MIX 1/2 cup chopped or sliced sautéed mushrooms with the eggs before cooking the omelet.

Omelette à la Reine   CHICKEN OMELET

FILL an omelet with 3 tablespoons creamed chicken just before folding it. Surround the omelet with a ribbon of béchamel sauce and garnish it with parsley.

Omelette aux Tomates   TOMATO OMELET

PEEL 3 ripe tomatoes, squeeze out the seeds, and chop the pulp rather coarsely. Cook the pulp in 3 tablespoons oil with 2 slices onion, finely chopped. Add salt and pepper to taste and 1 tablespoon finely chopped parsley. Spoon the seasoned tomato purée into the center of a 4-egg omelet and fold the omelet.

OMELET PEASANT STYLE _Omelette Paysanne_

PARBOIL 1/3 cup diced salt pork, bacon or ham for a few minutes and drain. Melt 1 tablespoon butter in an omelet pan, add the meat and sauté it until it is brown. Remove the meat and reserve it. Sauté 3/4 cup potatoes, finely diced, in the same pan until they are cooked and golden brown. Return the meat to the pan. Add 6 lightly beaten eggs combined with 1 cup cooked sorrel, drained, 1 teaspoon each finely chopped parsley and chervil, and 1/2 teaspoon salt.

Stir the eggs with a fork, at the same time moving the pan in a circular motion. When the omelet begins to set around the edges, lift it and slip 1 tablespoon butter under it. When the first faint odor of browning is evident, turn the omelet as you would a pancake and brown it lightly on the other side. Slide it carefully onto a hot serving platter and serve at once.

JELLY OMELET _Omelette à la Confiture_

SPREAD an omelet with jam or marmalade and roll it. Turn the omelet onto a hot serving dish and sprinkle it with sugar.

In really cold weather, we occasionally ended a light supper with a sweet omelette au rhum, _as a special treat._

RUM OMELET _Omelette au Rhum_

POUR about 1/4 cup rum, warmed in the omelet pan, over an _omelette à la confiture_, jelly omelet. Light the rum and spoon the flaming spirit over the omelet until the flame dies out. Serve immediately.

APRICOT OMELET _Omelette à la Confiture d'Abricots Flambée_

PREPARE a plain omelet and when it is half cooked, put 1 or 2 tablespoons apricot jam in the center. Roll the omelet, finish the cooking, and sprinkle the top with powdered sugar. Pour over it 1/4 cup warmed rum or kirsch and light the spirit. Or score the top by drawing a piece of red-hot iron or large skewer at intervals across the omelet, sprinkle with liqueur, and light. Serve the omelet while the spirit is flaming.

433

Cheese

I SHALL never forget the cellar under the big farmhouse where *grand-mère* performed her cheese-making ritual each summer. How refreshing it was to come from the fields, where the hot sun beat down on the ripening wheat, and take refuge in the cellar, with its claylike soil floor and thick stone walls that gave an even, predictable coolness. And what wonderful smells—fragrance of grapes and the *vin du pays* in wooden casks, and best of all, the soothing aroma of the cheese making: the sweet moisture of fresh milk and the hint of faintly acid curd.

Grandmother started the job in the cowshed, milking the cows rhythmically. Indeed, Grandmother did everything in a rhythmic, orderly manner. She was petite, and her small hands belied their strength just as her quiet manner belied her efficiency. Her farmhouse was spotless, her meals succulent and bountiful. It was part of her nature to find time for everything, and yet never seem hurried. Twice a week, without fail, she churned the fresh sweet butter, and each day she went through the chores connected with cheese making. Nor did she ever miss her weekly trips to the village, to mass on Sunday and to market on Wednesday with her freshly churned butter and firm rounds of good *fromage du pays*, her contribution to the farm income.

Grand-mère made cheese in the typical country manner of her day. She used the big straight-sided earthenware jars that country people everywhere like for making pickles and sauerkraut, and putting up fruit in brandy. Each jar held 10 quarts of milk. There were always 18 jars lined up on the cellar floor. Grandmother scalded 6 of them freshly each day and filled them with the results of the day's milking. In another 6 jars, the yellow cream had risen to the surface of yesterday's milkings to be skimmed off for the butter churn. It was Grandmother's custom to take a little of the slightly sour milk from these jars, after skimming off the cream, and add it to the fresh milk as a " starter, " although some people used rennet for this purpose. In the remaining 6 jars the milk had been curdling long enough for the big snowy curds to become so firm that they separated from the cloudy whey. Grandmother lined with cheesecloth round wicker baskets or round metal molds pierced like a colander, and poured the curds into them to drain for a day or two.

When the curds formed into a compact mass, we had *fromage blanc*, something like American cottage cheese. We usually took some of this upstairs for our own use. Grandmother added a little fresh cream to this cheese to make the local *spécialités* like cheese and potato pie or cheese fondue in the country style. In summer, she added chopped chives and fresh tarragon to it and we ate this fresh-tasting mixture with crusty French bread.

Fromage Blanc

But we took only a very small part of our cheese to use as *fromage blanc*. We put most of the compact rounds outdoors to cure in a shelved contraption with wire sides that looked like an enormous cage. It was built on stilts, away from the dampness of the ground. In about a week each cheese was turned from its mold, unwrapped, and covered thickly with layer upon layer of fresh grape leaves. Then we returned the rounds to the cellar to ripen, or *maturer*, between thick layers of straw. A week or ten days later, the outside of the cheeses would be firm and fairly dry, while the inside would be soft and creamy, just right for the market. Our cheese resembled Camembert, but it had its own distinctive flavor and we made our wheels about twice the size of the familiar Camembert.

My family's devotion to cheese was in no way unusual. In most French families, cheese plays an important role in everyday meals. *Le fromage*, in its many forms, is as basic and universal as bread. Each section of France has its own favorite cheeses, and nearly every Frenchman eats cheese once a day. My father expressed the general sentiment when he said, as he often did, that he would willingly forego meat, providing he could have cheese.

Of course, cheese is widely used in cookery, and each country has its own preferences. In America, Cheddar cheese seems very popular, but French cooks believe that Cheddar has too strong a flavor and, along with some other cheeses, too high a fat content to be suitable for anything except Welsh rabbits. In France, we favor Parmesan and Swiss cheeses for cooking, and use them almost interchangeably, to melt in sauces, or sprinkle on a dish to be browned. Their flavor blends with other ingredients rather than overpowering them. Parmesan always grates easily; when Swiss is too moist to grate, it may be shredded or cut into fine

435

dice. A cheese soufflé made with Swiss or Parmesan is lighter and more delicate than one made with any other cheese. It has been my experience that cottage cheese, Parmesan, and Swiss are the most dependable cheeses for cooking. They can be purchased almost anywhere, and their flavor and fat content are predictable, so that they can be used confidently when other cheeses, because of their variability, might fail you. You will find only a few cheese recipes in this section, because cheese is an important part of so many other kinds of cookery that it is dealt with often elsewhere in this book, in the chapters on hors-d'oeuvre and soufflés, for instance.

The recipes that follow are suggested for luncheon or supper, but most of them make excellent appetizers as well, in small portions.

Cheese for Cooking (margin note)

Neufchâtel Fondue (margin note)

FONDUE NEUFCHÂTEL

RUB an earthenware casserole with a cut clove of garlic and put in it 1 1/2 pounds grated Swiss cheese and 1 1/2 cups dry white wine. Cook the wine and cheese over low heat, on an asbestos pad, stirring with a wooden spoon until the mixture is creamy. Stir in 1 tablespoon potato starch mixed with a little cold water, and season the fondue with salt and pepper to taste.

When ready to serve, add 1/4 cup kirsch and place the casserole on a *réchaud*, or table heater, to keep it hot. Serve with large cubes of bread. These are pierced with forks and dipped in the simmering fondue. No liquor should be served with this dish, but after it is eaten, hot coffee or tea is served, with a little kirsch.

Ramequin de Fromage (margin note)

CHEESE RAMEKIN

BUTTER a rather shallow round earthenware casserole. Remove the crusts from 6 slices of bread and cut each slice in half. Cut Swiss cheese into 12 thin slices the size of the bread. Arrange the bread and cheese in a ring in the bottom of the dish, overlapping each by about an inch. In a bowl beat 2 eggs, stir in 2 cups milk, a little salt, and grated nutmeg and pour the mixture over the bread and cheese. Place the casserole in a pan containing 1 inch of hot water and bake in a moderately hot oven (375° F.) for about 30 minutes, or until the top is golden brown.

CHEESE TOAST VAUDOISE

*Croûte
Vaudoise*

IN A saucepan put 1/2 pound grated Swiss cheese and 1/4 cup white wine and cook over gentle heat, stirring, until the cheese melts and the mixture is the consistency of a thick paste. Add 1 egg, beaten, and a little salt and pepper. Spread freshly toasted bread with the cheese mixture and brown in a hot oven (450° F.) or under the broiler.

TOMATO AND CHEESE CASSEROLE

*Tomates
en Casserole*

MELT 1/2 cup butter in a saucepan, add 1 tablespoon chopped onion and cook slowly until soft. Stir in 1/2 cup flour, and add gradually 2 1/2 cups hot milk, stirring constantly until the sauce is thick and smooth. Cook, stirring frequently, for 10 to 20 minutes. Season the sauce with 1/2 teaspoon salt and a little pepper and paprika.

Beat 2 egg yolks with 1/4 cup cream and gradually stir in the hot thick sauce. Cook over very low heat, stirring constantly, until the sauce almost reaches a boil and add 3/4 to 1 cup grated dry Swiss or Parmesan cheese.

Cut the tops from 6 firm tomatoes. Squeeze them very gently to remove seeds and excess liquid. Arrange them in a shallow baking dish and pour over them the sauce. Bake the tomatoes in a hot oven (425° F.) for about 15 minutes, or until the tomatoes are soft and the sauce is browned.

POTATO AND CHEESE PIE

*Tarte
aux Pommes
de Terre
et au Fromage*

BEAT 2 cups cottage cheese with a wire whip until it is smooth and rub it through a fine sieve or food mill. Whisk in 1/2 cup sour cream. Peel and boil enough potatoes to make 2 1/2 cups after they are run through a food mill or ricer. While they are still warm, add them to the cheese mixture and season with 1/2 teaspoon salt. Make pastry for a 9-inch pie and line the bottom and sides of the pie plate with it, shaping the edge to form a border. Fill with the cheese and potato mixture, brush the top with milk, and dot with small pieces of butter. Bake in a moderate oven (350° F.) for about 45 minutes, or until the top is brown.

Cheese for Dessert *Probably the dessert most frequently served in France is cheese—with bread or crackers and often a bowl of fresh fruit. The French gourmet is likely to save a glass of wine to sip with it, as well. Traditionally an assortment of cheeses is offered, rather than a single variety. A typical combination on a cheese tray in this country might include a full-flavored blue such as Roquefort, Stilton, or Danish blue, a pungent Camembert or Liederkranz, a mellow Port du Salut, or one of the Dutch cheeses, and a wedge of sharp American Cheddar. Soft fresh cheese like Neufchâtel or our American cream cheese are also served for dessert, with tart* confitures *of currants or quince, and sometimes cheeses like the* fromage blanc *of my grandmère are sprinkled with sugar and cinnamon and laved with heavy cream to make a sweet ending for a meal.*

Rice

RICE HAS all the virtues for which the French value a food. It is economical in price, easy to prepare, and because it is so bland, goes well with many other foods and flavors. In addition to all this, rice keeps well, and may be kept on hand for long periods without danger of spoiling. For these reasons you will find rice used for every course on the menu, from soup to dessert.

In the days when rice was sold in bulk from great burlap sacks, it required repeated washing. The rice was put into a sieve, and the sieve lowered into a basin of cold water. Then it was lifted by handfuls and swished through the water to rinse it. As many changes of water were used as were necessary to remove any impurities, as well as the loose starch that coated the grains. Nowadays, packaged rice is of such high quality that it rarely requires even brief rinsing.

In the Ritz kitchens, we used long-grain varieties such as Patna or Carolina rice for pilaff, risottos and other entrées, and one of the short grained types for puddings and sweet dishes. Of course, there are many kinds of rice to choose from today. Precooked or converted rice should be cooked according to the directions on the package. I must warn you, however, that converted rice cannot be reduced to a cream by cooking, and should not be used for desserts.

Varieties
of Rice

No matter what kind of rice is used, the ideal that everyone strives for is to have every grain separate, tender but not soft, so that when the grains are tossed with melted butter or a sauce, they tumble over each other and every grain is coated. Properly cooked rice is never mushy, never gummy.

To achieve these results consistently with rice is not so difficult as it must sometimes seem to disappointed cooks. Actually, my favorite method is very simple, and requires no stirring, no draining, no rinsing. Furthermore, the rice will not scorch. The pan should be one that can be used on top of the stove and in the oven, and it should have a tight cover to hold in the steam. First toss the rice in a little melted butter so that every grain is coated. Add twice as much boiling liquid as rice and bring the liquid back to a boil. Then put the pan, covered, in the oven or over very low heat on top of the stove, and cook until the liquid is absorbed and the rice is tender. The step that follows after the cooking is of great importance. Invert the pan over a hot platter and turn out the rice without touching it with a spoon or fork that might mash or crush the grains. As the steam evaporates, toss the rice with a little melted butter, just a little, not enough to make the rice greasy. Use a long-tined kitchen fork for this operation. Transfer the rice to a hot serving dish. And the dish, let me emphasize, must be hot. A cold dish may give even well-cooked rice an objectionable gummy texture.

Buttered
Rice

RICE PILAFF

Riz Pilaf

SELECT a pan that can be covered very tightly to keep in the steam. Melt 1 tablespoon butter in the pan and in it cook 1 teaspoon finely chopped onion until it is soft but not brown. Add 1 cup rice and mix well. Add 2 cups boiling water or chicken stock. If water is used, add 1 teaspoon salt. Cover tightly and cook in a moderate oven (350° F.) or over low heat on top of the stove for 18 to 20 minutes, or until the liquid is cooked away. Turn the rice into a hot serving dish, separate the grains with a fork, and sprinkle with 1 tablespoon melted butter. Keep the pilaff in a warm place until ready to serve.

Riz à la Grecque

RICE GREEK STYLE

MELT 2 tablespoons butter in an ovenproof casserole that has a tight cover, add 1 onion, finely chopped, and cook until it is soft but not brown. Add 1/2 clove of garlic, crushed, 4 green leaves of lettuce, shredded, 4 mushrooms, sliced, 4 tomatoes, peeled, seeded, and chopped, or 1 cup canned tomatoes, and 3 fresh sausages, peeled and crushed. Add 1 1/2 cups rice and mix all together well. Add 3 cups boiling water or chicken stock, 1 1/2 teaspoons salt, and a little pepper. Cover the casserole tightly and cook in a hot oven (400° F.) for 20 to 25 minutes. Invert the casserole on a hot platter. Toss the rice with a long-tined kitchen fork, meanwhile adding 1 tablespoon melted butter, 3/4 cup cooked peas, 1 pimiento, diced, and 3 tablespoons dried raisins sautéed in a little butter. Serve as an entrée or with meat or poultry, or use for poultry stuffing.

Riz au Fromage

RICE WITH CHEESE

PREPARE rice pilaff with 2 tablespoons butter, 1 medium onion, finely chopped, 1 cup rice, and 2 cups chicken stock. Add to the cooked pilaff 1/2 cup grated Parmesan and toss with fork to mix. Turn the rice into a hot serving dish, spread it with 2 tablespoons hot meat gravy or *jus* from a roast, and sprinkle with more grated Parmesan.

Riz à la Milanaise

RICE WITH SAFFRON

IN a saucepan cook 1 onion, finely chopped, in 2 tablespoons butter until the onion starts to turn golden. Add 2 cups rice and mix well. Add gradually 4 cups boiling chicken stock, stirring constantly. Add 1/2 teaspoon powdered saffron, cover the pan, and cook the rice over very low heat for about 16 to 18 minutes, or until the stock has been absorbed and the rice is tender. If very soft rice is preferred, use an extra 1/2 cup stock and cook a few minutes longer. Add 1 tablespoon butter and 1 or 2 tablespoons grated Parmesan and mix carefully with a fork. The rice should not be mushy, but the mixture should be creamy. Correct the seasoning and serve immediately.

RICE WITH TOMATOES

Riz à la Turque

PREPARE rice pilaff and toss with 1/2 teaspoon powdered saffron, 2 tomatoes, peeled, seeded and chopped, and 2 tablespoons tomato sauce.

RICE INDIAN STYLE

Riz à l'Indienne

BRING a large amount of salted water to a boil in a kettle. Sprinkle in the rice slowly and boil it rapidly for 16 minutes. The grains should be just cooked through. Drain the rice in a colander and rinse it thoroughly in running cold water. Spread a napkin on a tray, spread the rice on it, and set the tray in a warm place for 20 to 30 minutes. This rice is served with curry.

I confess that I had never seen wild rice before I came to the United States. As a matter of fact, it is my impression that until comparatively recent times, very few people outside the lake region in Minnesota where the rice grows knew it. There are hardly any recipes for preparing wild rice in cookbooks of thirty-five years ago. As everyone knows now, wild rice is not a rice at all—although it resembles brown rice in appearance and flavor—but a wild grass. In recent years it has replaced hominy as the popular American accompaniment to game, but it is definitely something of a luxury.

Wild rice is apt to be dusty, and requires thorough soaking and washing to assure cleanliness. It cooks for a longer time than ordinary rice, and in a larger amount of water. You will notice that it triples in bulk in cooking. The nutty flavor of wild rice makes it a fine poultry stuffing—it is particularly good with chicken livers and mushrooms—but the recipes in the stuffing chapter may also be used when the rice is planned as an accompaniment.

Riz Sauvage

WILD RICE

CLEAN 1 cup wild rice in several waters, soaking it for 15 to 20 minutes if it is very dusty. Bring 2 quarts water with 2 teaspoons salt to a boil, add the rice, and cook slowly for 40 to 45 minutes, or until the rice is soft. Drain. Serve at once with butter or gravy. If the rice is not used immediately, reheat it as follows. Melt 3 tablespoons butter in a pan and let it become hazelnut brown. Add the rice and shake the pan over the fire until the grains are coated with butter and the rice is hot. Season with salt and a little freshly ground pepper.

Riz Sauvage aux Champignons

WILD RICE AND MUSHROOMS

CLEAN 6 to 8 mushrooms and slice or cut in dice. Sauté them in 1 tablespoon butter and combine with 2 cups cooked wild rice. Shake the pan over the heat until the mushrooms and rice are well combined and are heated through.

Polenta

POLENTA

BRING to a boil 3 cups salted water. Stir in 1/2 pound polenta, or yellow corn meal, and continue to stir until all the lumps have disappeared. Cook the polenta until it is thick and smooth, about 15 to 20 minutes, stirring occasionally. Stir in 2 tablespoons butter and 1/4 cup grated Parmesan and spread the polenta in a shallow buttered baking dish to cool. Turn the cooled polenta out onto a board and cut it into diamond shapes. Spread a layer of tomato sauce in a serving platter and arrange the pieces of polenta in it. Arrange around the polenta small broiled sausages. Polenta is often served just after the butter and Parmesan have been stirred in, without being cooled and cut up. It may be served with meat gravy, and it sometimes accompanies small game birds such as quail.

GARNITURE

Garnishes

I T IS no secret that people who dine in good French restaurants expect everything to be exceptionally well prepared. But during forty years in the business of catering to gourmets, I have learned that they expect more: they expect every dish to look particularly appetizing as well. Every chef must understand garnishing, for in France garnishes are more than mere decoration; they are an indispensable part of the dish.

Some foods are naturally decorative: cutouts and slices of truffle, bouquets of asparagus tips, tiny glazed carrots, artichoke bottoms, and tomato shells. But the chef considers as garniture even the vegetables that go into the stew, the vermicelli and other *pasta* that go into the soup. So the instruction "*préparer la garniture*" as often means the cutting and shaping and cooking of the turnips, onions, carrots, and potatoes for an oxtail ragout as it does the notched orange slices for *caneton à l'orange*.

Indeed, the chef begins to consider the appearance of the finished dish as he neatly trusses a bird for roasting, trims the ragged edges of a fish filet, or cuts vegetables into uniform dice or olive shapes. He considers the artistic effect of the whole presentation when he selects the platter on which it is to be served: the platter must always be large enough to hold food and garnish within a frame of shining bare silver or china. He plans his accompanying garnish for suitability and convenience as well as for flavor: stuffed mushrooms are most appropriate and attractive on a platter of sliced meat or chops, but they are likely to get in the way of the carving knife and slip off the platter if they are used to garnish a standing rib roast. If a sauce is served with the meat, only a little goes on the platter and the rest is served separately. Garnishes are arranged in orderly fashion alongside the meat. Simplicity and understatement are always the keynote.

In the language of the chef, there are two kinds of garnish: the **Garnitures Simples** *garnitures simples*, a category that embraces such things as mushrooms, browned potatoes, broiled tomatoes, croutons of sautéed bread or puff pastry, shrimp or mussels, and parsley and water cress, and the more **Garnitures Composées** elaborate *garnitures composées*, such as stuffed artichoke bottoms or tomatoes, sauced quenelles, *barquettes*, and other pastry shells filled with mushroom *duxelles*, and mélanges of vegetables like that for *garniture Montpensier*, a mixture of artichoke bottoms sautéed and mixed with julienne of truffles, asparagus tips, and *rissolé* potatoes. As you can readily see, garnishes are very important in *haute cuisine*, so important, indeed, that the name of a dish often comes from its garnish. The word " *Véronique* " in a recipe title indicates the presence of green grapes in the sauce; " *florentine* " involves spinach; an entrée described as " *à la Soubise* " is garnished with onion purée; meat or poultry " *strasbourgeoise* " is served with goose liver and truffles, both of which come from Strasbourg.

Tools for Garnishing IN preparing garnishings, sharp knives and a cutting board are indispensable for the slicing, dicing, and chopping involved. Small cutters, usually called truffle cutters, in fancy shapes, vegetable cutters for making balls and olive shapes, slotted vegetable peelers for butter or chocolate curls, graters, sieves, and pastry bags and tubes of various sizes and shapes are very useful, as are various molds.

VEGETABLE purée, potatoes *duchesse*, mayonnaise, softened pâté mixtures and finely chopped aspic are forced through a pastry bag to shape rosettes **Pastry Bag** and borders and to fill small cups, tartlets, artichoke bottoms, and so on. Insert a large pastry tube into a canvas pastry bag and fold the top down into a broad cuff. Spoon in the filling, being sure you start packing it in just above the tube, to avoid leaving air in the bag. As it fills, shorten the cuff. Do not fill the bag completely; the end must be pleated together and then twisted, to hold in the filling. It is of the utmost importance to eliminate air pockets in the packing and closing of the bag, to insure an even flow of filling as you shape rosettes and borders.

Put your thumb around the twisted end of the pastry bag and grasp the bag at the top. Apply pressure only from here, never in the middle of the bag. Squeeze the bag with one hand and guide the tip with the other. As the bag empties, twist the canvas down on the filling.

BECAUSE parsley is not only the easiest garnish to obtain, but the quickest **Parsley** and simplest to use, it has become the most used of green garnishes. Parsley keeps in a jar in the refrigerator for 2 weeks or more.

Wash the parsley, drain it thoroughly, and discard wilted leaves and broken bits. To make a parsley bouquet, hold the flowers in a bunch and trim the stems off evenly. To chop parsley, first dry it thoroughly on a towel. Moist leaves stick to the knife during the chopping, and cling and clump together instead of scattering evenly when you try to sprinkle them. Hold the sprays with the stem ends together and cut across the leaves, using even strokes of a sharp knife. Discard the stems, which are bitter. To chop the parsley more finely, hold the point of the knife on the board and rock the blade up and down until the bits are as fine as desired. Chopped parsley is sprinkled on many dishes as a final touch, and it is used lavishly in decorating canapés and other hors d'oeuvre.

A favorite garnish for deep-fried foods—as much because the deep-frying kettle is already on hand as for the crisp, delicious flavor and attractive appearance—is deep-fried parsley. Wash and trim parsley sprigs and dry them thoroughly. Drop them in very hot deep fat or oil **Fried Parsley** (390° F.) and cook them for a minute or two, or until the parsley rises to the surface and is crisp. Drain on paper towels and sprinkle with salt.

Water Cress   SPRAYS and bouquets of water cress are used to garnish both hot and cold entrées as well as hors-d'oeuvre and salads. Water cress is more fragile than parsley; its leaves bruise and tear easily, and the leaves yellow quickly when they are exposed to air. Buy water cress only as you need it; wrap the remains of a bunch loosely in foil or waxed paper and store it in the refrigerator. To make bouquets, wash and dry the cress on a towel, discard bruised leaves, and trim the stems evenly.

Lemons   LEMON is one of the most frequently used of garnishes, and because of its value as a flavoring, one of the most useful. For maximum efficiency, the lemons should be cut into wedges, to be squeezed, and they are most often served this way with fish and shellfish. However, lemons are more decorative when they are cut into thin slices and notched or scalloped or otherwise shaped according to the fancy of the chef, and perhaps sprinkled with chopped parsley or paprika for color contrast. Chefs make lemon baskets, which may be left whole or scooped out and filled with a cold sauce.

Truffles   ALL the vivid black designs, mosaics, and patterned embellishments of *haute cuisine* are achieved with the help of truffles, which are both tender and firm, so that they can be easily sliced or cut into fancy shapes and yet handled without danger of breaking. Since they are expensive, they are cut into very thin slices, but their unique *parfum* is nevertheless imparted to whatever food they come into contact with.

Olives   PITTED green olives are used to garnish cold entrées, hors-d'oeuvre, and salads, often with radishes. Pimiento-stuffed olives are sliced to make red-centered green circles, a flavorful and colorful decoration. In southern France, particularly in Provence where olives grow, olives are often included in sauces: *caneton aux olives*, duck with olives, is a classic example. Ripe olives, which are black rather than green, are also used for decoration, and are often sliced or cut into fancy shapes to use instead of truffles.

Radishes   THE radish rose is a familiar garnish for cold dishes. Trim off the large outside stems, but leave 2 or 3 tiny center stems. With a small sharp

knife, cut petal-shaped strips of peel from the center of the radish tip to
1/4 inch from the base, without detaching the peel. A second layer of
petals may be cut under the first, if desired. Put the cut radishes in ice
water and the " roses " will open and bloom.

THE bright red color and fine flavor of the pimiento makes it a popular **Pimiento**
garnish for many uses. The peppers come packed in oil and should
be thoroughly dried on paper towels before they are used. They can be
cut into dice, julienne, or any desired shape with a knife or small cutters.

HARD-COOKED eggs are much used for garnishing, and for good reason. **Eggs**
They have their lovely colors—pure white and clear yellow—to recommend them, plus excellent texture and a bland flavor that nearly everyone
likes and that goes with almost everything. They are always available,
too, and quite inexpensive. Even a single egg goes a long way in garnishing and decorating.

The secret of turning out perfect hard-cooked eggs—and this simple
procedure does seem difficult to some people—is explained in the section
on eggs elsewhere in this volume. Read it so that you will have smooth-
surfaced eggs and precisely centered yolks to work with.

Cut in eighths or quarters, hard-cooked eggs traditionally garnish hearty
salads. The whites are sometimes chopped for garnishing, but the yolk is
always forced through a sieve. In elaborate preparations, the egg white
is cut into fancy shapes with truffle cutters and used to make flower petals
and the like. Deviled or stuffed eggs are another popular salad garnish.

Finally, there is the classic French mixture named " mimosa, " after
the flower whose appearance it repeats. Mimosa garnish is not much
used in this country, and I wonder why, because it is simple to make,
delicious, and beautiful. Mix together equal parts of chopped hard- **Mimosa**
cooked egg white and parsley and sieved hard-cooked egg yolk. Use to
garnish salads, canapés, and hors-d'oeuvre.

TOMATOES brighten every food they appear with, they are inexpensive, **Tomatoes**
readily available, come to market in various sizes, and are equally good
cooked or raw. They can be used whole, sliced, and cut in wedges or
cubes; can be grilled, baked, stewed and puréed; can be stuffed for serv-

ing cold or hot; and their flavor complements meat, poultry, fish, vege-tables, salads, cheese—in fact, almost everything except desserts. Fur-thermore, almost everybody likes them.

Tomatoes are always peeled in fine cookery, except that when they are to be baked, the skin is left on to keep the tomato from losing its shape. For baking, the tomatoes are pricked with a fork in the hope that this will provide a release for the steam and save the tomato from splitting. It sometimes works, but not always. To peel a tomato, plunge it into boiling water and then into ice-cold water. The skin will then slip off easily.

Directions for preparing tomatoes for stuffing, as well as various salad mixtures with which to fill them, are given in the salad chapter. Small tomatoes make the most attractive garnish; if they are too small to cut in half, simply cut a slice from the top. Any salad mixture may be used for stuffing. One of the most popular is made of cooked vege-tables bound with mayonnaise *chaud-froid*. One of the simplest is cucumber salad.

Tomatoes are also sliced for garnishing, thickly or thinly depend-ing upon the nature of the food they accompany. Peel the tomatoes and slice them an hour or so before servingtime. Salt them lightly and lay them on a perforated pie plate to drain. When the tomatoes are to be sautéed, broiled, or fried, they should be cut into very thick slices or they will not hold their shape. I prefer to drain these as I do the slices that are to be served raw, although this is not done by all chefs.

For salads and other cold dishes, cut peeled tomatoes in eighths and make fan shapes with hard-cooked eggs that have been cut in quarters or sixths. Or place slices of hard-cooked egg on tomato slices and center each with a slice of ripe or stuffed green olive. Or overlap very thin to-mato slices around a dish and sprinkle them with a band of finely chopped parsley. The variations on this theme are endless. Whole stuffed to-matoes show up best on nests of small lettuce leaves; slices look best with a few sprigs of parsley or water cress tucked sparingly around them.

My favorite tomato garnish for sautéed fish, meat, or poultry is this simple preparation.

Hot Tomato Garnish — Peel, seed, and chop coarsely enough firm ripe tomatoes to make 3 cups pulp. Drain in a strainer for 1 hour. Heat 2 tablespoons butter, add the tomatoes, and cook them, stirring gently, until they are hot. Season with salt and pepper, pile lightly around sautéed food on the platter, and sprinkle with finely chopped parsley.

Artichokes

ARTICHOKES play a distinguished role as garniture in *haute cuisine*. Except when the very small artichokes are available, only the bottoms are used. You will learn how to cook them in the chapters on vegetables and on hors-d'oeuvre. To prepare the cooked artichoke for garniture, trim away the leaves and cut out the hairy choke. Quarter the bottoms and sauté them lightly in butter. They may be used alone or in combination with sautéed potatoes and other vegetables or the bottoms may be left whole, appropriately stuffed, and baked or browned under the broiler.

The artichoke garnish below is an example of the sophisticated treatment accorded this delicate vegetable. This version is for beef and lamb; for poultry, the artichoke bottoms might be filled with a creamed ham mixture and the tops glazed under the broiler before serving.

ARTICHOKE BOTTOMS STUFFED WITH TOMATO PURÉE

*Artichauts
Garnis
de Fondue
de Tomates*

PEEL and halve 6 medium tomatoes and squeeze out the seeds. Chop the flesh coarsely and cook in 1 tablespoon butter until most of the moisture cooks away. Season with salt and 1 teaspoon sugar. Fill 12 hot cooked artichoke bottoms and sprinkle with julienne of truffles.

SINCE cooked vegetables are the natural choice to accompany cooked dishes, it is only natural that vegetable garnishes, including potatoes in many forms, should be among the most usual and best-liked.

Glazed
Vegetables

Cut vegetables into desired uniform shapes. Small onions and beets may be left whole. Cook the vegetables separately, covered, in a little salted water, with a tablespoon of butter until they are barely tender and most of the liquid has been absorbed. Add a little butter to prevent them from sticking to the pan, sprinkle them lightly with sugar, and cook for a few minutes, shaking the pan constantly, until the vegetables are brown and shiny. Arrange the glazed vegetables in portion-sized mounds or bundles around the entrée.

Bouquet des
Légumes

The combination of vegetables called *bouquetière* on menus is composed of carrots, lima beans, peas, turnips, and green beans, in any combination. To prepare the vegetables, cut the carrots and turnips into balls the size of the lima beans, and use tiny green beans or larger beans cut into 2-inch lengths. Cook and glaze the vegetables as for glazed vegetables, mix them, and arrange them in small piles around the entrée, interspersing the bouquets with sprays of water cress. The vegetables may be sprinkled with chopped parsley. Or simply cook the vegetables in water and dress the bouquets with melted butter, omitting the glazing. Flowerets of cauliflower are sometimes added to the bouquet.

The secret of the excellent flavor of these bouquets is separate cooking. Every vegetable thus retains its individuality.

Vegetable Purées PURÉED vegetables—carrots, spinach, sorrel, chestnuts, potatoes, artichokes, asparagus, mushrooms, and onions (called *Soubise*)—frequently accompany and garnish hot entrées. A border of purée of peas was the distinguishing garnish of the chicken hash à la Ritz that was one of the most popular entrées, day in and day out, at the old Ritz-Carlton in New York. Since the purées are most attractive when they are piped through a pastry tube, they should be thick enough to hold their shape. If the purée is too thin, heat a little butter in a saucepan, add the purée, and stir it over moderate heat until most of the moisture evaporates. The purées may also be shaped with a spatula on the platter, to make a bed on which the entrée can be arranged. Some purées are described in the chapter on vegetables; the same general method applies to other vegetables as well.

Vegetables in Aspic MIX finely cut cooked vegetables—carrots, peas, beets, French-cut green beans, white onions, Jerusalem artichokes, and so on—with mayonnaise *chaud-froid*, using 1/3 as much sauce as vegetables. Line small cylindrical molds with aspic and chill. Add the vegetables and fill the molds with aspic. Chill until the aspic is set. Unmold and use to garnish cold dishes.

Mushrooms MANY of the mushroom preparations given in the chapter dealing with vegetables are used for garnishing, particularly stuffed broiled mushrooms.

Nothing proclaims the experience and skill of a chef so surely as a beautifully " turned " mushroom, blooming like a flower on top of a beef filet or a baked fish. Turning mushrooms is a tricky job to learn, but because it carries such prestige, I would like to explain it.

Turned Mushrooms Choose very white, very fresh and firm mushrooms of uniform size. Soak them in cold water, with a little lemon juice to keep them white, for 15 minutes. Slice off the stem even with the base of the cup. Hold the mushroom rounded side up with the left hand. Press a short, narrow-bladed knife almost flat against the mushroom and push the mushroom against the knife to make a fairly deep cut swirling from the center to the edge of the cap. Dip the knife into the lemon water before each cut. Repeat this cut at 1/8-inch intervals around the mushroom cap. The trick is in forcing the mushroom into the knife, instead of forcing the knife into the mushroom. The slivered peelings drop off, and the " petals " are revealed. Cook the mushrooms for 5 minutes in a little water with lemon juice and leave them in the cooking liquid until it is time to use them. The stock can be used to flavor soups and sauces, and the stems and peelings are used to make *duxelles*, a stuffing with many uses.

MUSHROOM DUXELLES   *Duxelles*

WASH, drain, and chop very fine 1/2 pound mushrooms or mushroom stems and peelings. Melt 4 tablespoons butter, add the mushrooms and 2 finely chopped shallots or 2 tablespoons chopped onion, and cook, stirring, until the moisture has evaporated. Add 1/2 teaspoon salt and 2 teaspoons finely chopped parsley. Use for stuffings or for sauces, or to fill tomato shells or artichoke bottoms for *garnitures composées*, elaborate garnishes.

THE French have many uses for bread as an adjunct in serving foods or as a garnish. The words " *croûte* " and " crouton, " which mean " crust " and " little crust, " are generally applied to such adjuncts. *Croûtes* and croutons for garnishing soup and the garlic-flavored bread garnishes for salad called *chapons* are described elsewhere in the book.
<!-- margin note --> *Bread Garnish*

Another kind of *croûte* is often used instead of toast as a base for eggs and creamed mixtures. Such a *croûte* is made this way: Cut a slice of bread about 3/4 inch thick. Lay the point of a small sharp-pointed knife at the center of the slice and, rotating the bread, hollow out the center a little, to make a saucerlike shell. Brush the *croûte* with melted butter and brown on a baking sheet in a hot oven.
<!-- margin note --> *Croûtes as Bases*

Small whole game birds and squab chickens, and the breasts of larger birds, are usually served on *croûtes*. To make this kind of *croûte*, a loaf of bread is cut lengthwise into slices about 1 inch thick, 4 inches wide and 5 inches long. The edge of the *croûte* is scalloped with a sharp knife and the bread is then buttered and browned under the broiler.

The small *croûtes* or croutons that often garnish fish, meat and poultry are made by cutting thin slices of bread into decorative ovals, diamonds, or crescents, and browning these shapes on both sides in clarified butter. These are arranged around the edge of the platter alternately with other garnishes, such as mushrooms or artichokes, or whatever is appropriate. One or two are prepared for each serving. When these *croûtes* are served with game, they are spread with *rouennaise*.

Similar croutons, called *fleurons*, are made by shaping and baking puff paste.

Croustade Remove all the crusts from a loaf of bread. With a sharp knife, cut down from the top 3/4 inch from the edges of the 4 sides to within 3/4 inch of the bottom. Remove the center part, leaving a 3/4-inch base. Brush this shell all over inside and out with melted butter and brown it in a hot oven (400° F.).

Bread Crumbs Another important use for bread is bread crumbs. For fresh bread crumbs, trim the crusts from French or Italian bread at least a day or two old, because really fresh bread refuses to crumble and rolls up into doughy balls. Cut up or slice day-old bread, let it dry a little, and crumble it between the palms of the hands. To make fine fresh bread crumbs, rub these crumbs through a sieve. Dry bread crumbs are best made from very stale bread; to make dry crumbs from fresh bread, break the bread up and spread the pieces on a flat pan. Put the pan in a warm oven until the bread is very dry, but not brown. Crush the bread with a rolling pin and sift the crumbs to assure uniformity.

Rice Molds BIND cooked rice with a little béchamel sauce and pack it into small well-buttered molds or demitasse cups. Keep the molds warm until ready to serve.

Cockscombs FRESH cockscombs are not so easily available nowadays as they were before most poultry came to market ready to cook. In classic cuisine, they were used mainly for the contrast in texture they provided. They are available, cooked, in cans.

Quenelles, Mousselines, and Godiveau SMALL balls and egg-shapes of *mousseline* forcemeat, resembling feather-light dumplings, are a classic garnish. The forcemeat may be made of poultry, fish, or meat, depending upon the use to which the quenelles, *mousselines*, and *godiveau* are to be put. The forcemeats have other uses as well, in stuffings and in making steamed mousses.

An electric blender can take the place of the old-fashioned mortar and pestle and of the fine sieve as well. Blend the egg whites with the chopped or cubed chicken or fish, add the seasonings, and very gradually add the heavy cream, until all the ingredients are combined into a very smooth, light paste, about the consistency of stiffly-whipped cream, which should leave the spoon clean.

To test the consistency, put a small nut of forcemeat in a shallow pan, carefully add a little water, and poach the ball gently. The small quenelles will be cooked in 2 minutes. If the mixture is too soft, a little more egg white may be worked into it; if it is too firm, add a little cream and test it again by poaching a small ball.

Chicken Mousseline Forcemeat or Mousse

GRIND finely 1 pound raw chicken flesh, place it in a mortar with 1 teaspoon salt, 1/2 teaspoon pepper, and 1/4 teaspoon nutmeg, and pound it to a paste. Add gradually the whites of 2 eggs, working the paste vigorously with a wooden spoon. Rub the forcemeat through a fine sieve, place it in a saucepan over cracked ice, and gradually work in about 2 cups heavy cream.

Chicken Quenelles

Shape ovals of chicken *mousseline* forcemeat between 2 tablespoons as follows: Dip the spoons in boiling water. Heap the mixture in one and round it off with the bowl of the second spoon. Dip the second spoon again into hot water, slip it under the shape, and slide the quenelle into a buttered pan. Add carefully enough hot salted water or chicken stock to float the quenelles, bring the liquid to the simmering point, and poach the quenelles over low heat for 10 to 15 minutes, until they are firm. Do not allow the water to boil, or the quenelles will split. Remove the quenelles from the pan with a perforated spoon and dry them on paper towels.

Mousselines *Mousselines* are made of the *mousseline* forcemeat used for quenelles, but they are poached in small oval molds or in cutlet molds. Butter the molds, pack the *mousseline* forcemeat into the mold firmly, smooth the top with a spatula, and put the molds in a pan and add enough simmering salted water to cover them. When the *mousselines* are cooked, they will float to the top of the pan and may be lifted off with a perforated skimmer and dried. Molded *mousselines* have a rounded surface and a flat bottom, very convenient for garnishing.

Fish Mousseline Forcemeat or Mousse Pound 1 pound fresh pike, cod, sea bass, or sole, free of skin and bones, on a board, using the dull edge of a large knife or a wooden potato masher, or run it through a food grinder using the finest blade. Season the fish with 1/2 teaspoon salt and a little pepper and add very gradually 3 egg whites, pounding constantly until the mixture is very smooth. Force the mixture through a fine sieve and put it in a saucepan set in a basin of cracked ice. Work the mixture vigorously with a wooden spoon, adding very gradually 2 to 2 1/2 cups heavy cream.

Fish Quenelles Fish quenelles are shaped and cooked like chicken quenelles. They are used as garnish or as an entrée, in which case they are served with *sauce américaine* or another fish sauce and garnished with shrimp.

Panade Make a *panade* as follows: Bring to a boil 2/3 cup water, a pinch salt, and 1 tablespoon butter. Add 1/4 cup flour and stir with a wooden spoon over the heat until the mixture is smooth and does not cling to the side of the pan. Remove from the heat, stir in 1 egg, and set aside.

Godiveau Grind 1/4 pound of lean veal, sinews removed, and 1/3 pound of beef kidney suet, free of membranes, through the finest blade of the food chopper. Add 1 teaspoon salt, a little pepper, and a grating of nutmeg. Add the *panade*, mix well, and spread on a flat plate. Cover the *godiveau* with wax paper and chill for 3 to 4 hours.

Veal Quenelles Divide the forcemeat into small pieces to roll into fingers about the size and shape of tiny sausages. Bake them on a flat baking dish in a slow oven (300° F.) for 10 to 15 minutes, or until the quenelles are firm but not crusty or brown.

Shrimp Mussels COOKED shrimp and mussels are used to garnish cold and hot fish dishes. They may be glazed with aspic for the former, and coated with melted butter for the latter. Use boiled shrimp and steamed mussels.

In using shrimp to decorate the top of a fish entrée, split them in half so that they lie flat.

Hors-d'Oeuvre

HORS-D'OEUVRE

WHEN I WRITE of hors-d'oeuvre, I think nostalgically of the château country of France, where I served my apprenticeship. At Monsieur Calondre's catering establishment in Moulins, there were always 5 or 6 apprentices in training, and each afternoon one of us went with the delivery man on his round of the châteaux to unpack huge hampers of hors-d'oeuvre and other delicacies, and to garnish these foods.

The people we served all had a fine, almost exquisite, feeling for food that was shared by all who prepared and supplied it: chefs, *cuisiniers*, and *charcutiers*. We apprentices took turns on the deliveries during the week, but on Sundays and holidays, all of us were needed. Though we loved the work, and knew our fathers were paying good round sums for our training, we enjoyed the chance to get out of the hot kitchen. We made deliveries in a maroon-colored vehicle that had glass windows and a door on each side. I used to love to perch beside the driver on the front seat, which was level with the roof, and jog along behind the two fine horses down country roads lined with trees, evenly spaced and trimmed to a matching tidiness. And it was not unpleasant to wait in the big kitchens with the cooks and servants, after we had arranged the first course, until the time came to serve our sauced *vol-au-vent* or elegantly garnished ice creams.

In most countries in Europe, not alone in France, it is the custom to start luncheon or dinner with hors-d'oeuvre, savory foodstuffs that are literally " outside the work ," and not a regular course of the meal. In America, where cocktail parties are so much the mode, hors-d'oeuvre are less often served in the dining room but are eaten out-of-hand at cocktail parties. *Ma foi*, if Frenchmen ate hors-d'oeuvre only at cocktail parties, they would eat them very seldom.

Every family in France serves *les hors-d'oeuvre variés* almost every day, not just when guests have been invited to dinner. Housewives like my mother, proverbially thrifty—and truly so—have never thrown away good food, not even small amounts. Instead, leftover cooked vegetables brightened with a vinaigrette sauce or cooked fish with a spicy marinade and cold meat neatly sliced would be supplemented with deviled eggs and perhaps *saucissons* or a pâté. With fresh crusty bread and a light dry *vin blanc* these hors-d'oeuvre made a delightful luncheon in the warm weather. The French also serve hot hors-d'oeuvre as the main course of light luncheons. These are then sometimes preceded by cold hors-d'oeuvre and followed by fresh fruit.

This French custom I helped introduce to New York at the old Ritz-Carlton, and a luncheon of hors-d'oeuvre became so popular there that we offered a different selection each day, which were called " *les petites entrées* ." Eventually we had to hire a *charcutier* to make the various pork dishes such as head cheese, pâtés and *saucissons*, and an Italian chef to make the antipasto specialties of his country.

In France, hors-d'oeuvre that introduce a luncheon or dinner are eaten at the table as a first course, and with the exception of the pâtés, which some people like to spread on bread, they are eaten with a fork. I think Americans, particularly men, find this a most acceptable change from the American practice of serving canapés in the living room before the guests are seated for dinner.

Remember that hors-d'oeuvre should whet the appetite, not satiate it, and therefore should be small in size, piquant rather than rich, and tastefully sauced and seasoned.

456

In both France and this country everyone who serves hors-d'oeuvre takes advantage of the excellent fish, meat, and pâté products that are sold in cans and jars. Foods packed in shallow containers or in glasses or crocks—such delicacies as caviar, *pâté de foie gras*, and so on—are placed on the serving dishes in their own containers after the covers have been removed. Strange as it may seem, this is the conventional way.

Packaged
Hors-d'Oeuvre

In choosing hors-d'oeuvre to begin a luncheon or dinner consider the courses that follow. A generous assortment will be most welcome before an omelet, but at *un repas grand et élégant*, the soup can be preceded by a single elegant selection: *pâté de fois gras*, oysters, or caviar, for example. At a less formal affair, either the soup or hors-d'oeuvre may be omitted. For home meals, if the hors-d'oeuvre is either expensive or its preparation lengthy—as is the case with pâté, *quiche lorraine*, or tiny hot croquettes, for instance—you should serve only one kind.

Be sure not to include among the hors-d'ocuvre flavors or foods that will be repeated in the meal. Omit fish if fish is the main dish, and do not introduce a main course using chicken livers with an hors-d'oeuvre of liver pâté. Vegetables served with the dinner or in the salad, and garnishes used during the meal, should not appear among the hors-d'oeuvre.

There are hundreds of hors-d'oeuvre recipes. Some, like those for marinated vegetables, are simple; others, like *quiche* or tiny *beignets* or croquettes, are more complex. When you know how to make some of the marinated foods, a piquant salad or two, a pâté, and a few hot dishes, you will be able to start experimenting with your own new combinations.

Cold

Hors-d'Oeuvre

THE cold hors-d'oeuvre most frequently served at cocktail parties are canapés. Canapés are essentially open-faced sandwiches based on toast spread with savory butters and cut into fancy shapes. You will find these compound butters—anchovy, shallot, tarragon, and so on—in the sauce chapter. Use them without further embellishment or build up the canapé with other toppings appropriate to the flavor of the butter combination.

It is possible to make canapés on crackers, rather than on bread, but toasted bread is more desirable because it retains its crispness.

To make canapés, cut slices 1/4 inch thick the length of the loaf, toast them or brown them in butter, and cut them into small rounds, diamonds, crescents, or oblongs. The entire loaf may be spread with the basic canapé spread before the shapes are cut out and garnished. Canapés served before dinner are likely to consist very simply of caviar, smoked salmon, or smoked sturgeon, but the canapés for a cocktail party are usually more elaborate. They may include sardines, shrimp, anchovies, cheese, mixtures of finely chopped sea food bound with mayonnaise, and pâté mixtures, either homemade or canned, and are decorated with pimiento, parsley, chopped hard-cooked egg, slices of green or black olives, and other colorful accents. A most popular garnish is mimosa. The edges of finished canapés are dipped into the gold, green, and white mixture to make an attractive border.

Canapés may be brushed with clear aspic, which sets and serves to hold the garnishings in place while it makes them shine attractively.

Here are cocktail party canapés, all of them based on toast.

Canapés Seville   CANAPÉS SEVILLE

SPREAD toast with anchovy paste and cover it with alternating strips of pimiento and anchovy filets. Garnish with slices of green olive.

Canapés Olga   CANAPÉS OLGA

COVER half the toast with thinly sliced smoked sturgeon and top with caviar, cover the other half with smoked salmon and top with anchovy paste. Decorate the edges of the canapé with mimosa.

Canapés Moscovite   CANAPÉS MOSCOVITE

COVER toast with a slice of smoked salmon, spread it with caviar, and cross 2 anchovies in the center. Decorate the edges with mimosa.

CANAPÉS DIPLOMAT   *Canapés Diplomat*

COVER toast with a slice of Westphalian ham, decorate it with a cross of anchovy filets, and put slices of stuffed green olive between the filets. Decorate the edges with mimosa.

CANAPÉS CARDINAL   *Canapés Cardinal*

PLACE a thin slice of tomato on toast, spread it with mayonnaise mixed with a little chili sauce and finely chopped chives, parsley, and tarragon, and decorate with a split cooked shrimp.

CANAPÉS AMIRAL   *Canapés Amiral*

COVER 1/3 of the toast with a slice of smoked sturgeon, 1/3 with a slice of smoked salmon, and the remaining 1/3 with caviar. Decorate the edges with mimosa.

CANAPÉS ASTRAKAN   *Canapés Astrakan*

COVER toast with a slice of smoked sturgeon and spread caviar over the sturgeon. Decorate the edges with mimosa.

CANAPÉS CAPE COD   *Canapés Cape Cod*

POACH oysters in their own juices for 2 minutes. Drain them on absorbent paper and cool them. Cover the corners of toast with caviar and place an oyster in the center. Put a few drops of chili sauce carefully on top of the oyster; it should not run into the caviar. Decorate the edges with mimosa.

CANAPÉS FAVORITE   *Canapés Favorite*

COVER toast with a slice of Swiss cheese and a slice of ox tongue and decorate the edge with finely chopped sour pickle.

CANAPÉS DU MAINE   *Canapés Du Maine*

MIX together 2 cups chopped, cooked lobster meat or 1 2/3 cups lobster

459

and 1/3 cup cooked crab meat, 1/2 cup mayonnaise, 1 tablespoon chili sauce, 1 teaspoon finely chopped chives, a little chopped tarragon, and salt and pepper to taste.   Spread on toast, put a slice of lobster claw meat in the center, and decorate the edge with mimosa.

Canapés Portuguese   CANAPÉS PORTUGAISE

ALTERNATE skinless and boneless sardines with slices of spring onions on a piece of toast and decorate with pimiento.

Canapés Bellevue   CANAPÉS BELLEVUE

COVER 1/4 of the toast with a slice of smoked salmon, 1/4 with smoked sturgeon, 1/4 with caviar, and the remaining 1/4 with egg yolk forced through a fine sieve.   Place a slice of ripe olive in the center and decorate the edge with mimosa.

Canapés Béatrice   CANAPÉS BEATRICE

MIX 1 cup chopped hard-cooked egg, 1/2 cup fine julienne of ham, 1/2 cup fine julienne of tongue, and 2 tablespoons julienne of truffles with 1/2 cup mayonnaise.   Spread on toast and decorate the edge with mimosa.

Hors-d'Oeuvre Variés

Raviers

TRADITIONALLY, *hors-d'oeuvre variés* are served in *raviers*, shallow dishes of porcelain, china, or glass, oblong or 4 to 6 inches square, with edges 1/2 to 1 inch high.   You can buy these simple uniform dishes with a tray into which they fit, or a number of them can be lined up on a rolling teacart or server—a convenience because the dishes take up a great deal of space on the table.

The appearance of hors-d'oeuvre is very important.   The sliced vegetables and meats should be thinly and evenly cut and overlapped neatly in the dish.   Cut salad ingredients into small even pieces, cabbage into thin shreds.   The dishes may be garnished with parsley or other herbs—chervil, chives, tarragon—used singly or in combination, or with the parsley and hard-cooked egg mixture that is called mimosa.   Chop any of these finely and evenly, not hit or miss, and sprinkle them in a narrow strip down the center of the dish or in a neat border around the edge, or scatter them lightly over the surface, but do not toss them in clumps on the food. For a touch of bright red, use diagonal strips of pimiento or arrange tomato wedges around the dish. Quarters or slices of hard-cooked egg will brighten a dish, as will strips of green pepper and tiny bouquets of parsley or water cress. You will find more ideas and techniques in the chapter on garnishing.

The sauce should not form a pool in the dish. Use only enough to moisten the food and to highlight its flavor. The use of separate dishes, or compartments of a divided dish, keeps the different sauces from mingling or from moistening unsauced food.

Hors-d'oeuvre variés are simple. We are not concerned here with pâtés or *mousse de foie gras* or with any of the hot hors-d'oeuvre. A selection may consist of 2 or 20 different foods—the latter number usual only in restaurants. For home meals, 3 to 6 hors-d'oeuvre provide a varied combination and a practical number to prepare. You will not need large quantities, because only a very little is served. Of course, for a buffet supper, you may serve some of these foods as part of the main course and so will need to increase the quantities, but as appetizers, only a slice or two of meat, a piece or two of fish, a few spoonfuls of salad are needed. The fewer hors-d'oeuvre you offer, of course, the more you will need to serve of each.

Here are some suggestions for *hors-d'oeuvre variés* to augment the recipes that follow: sliced tomatoes, sliced cooked beets or tiny whole ones, and cooked asparagus tips, each dressed with vinaigrette sauce, then sprinkled with finely chopped herbs; sliced hard-cooked eggs, pieces of raw cauliflower in Russian dressing; cooked shrimps, crab meat, or lobster with an appropriate mayonnaise dressing; hearty salads (found in the salad chapter); various kinds of *saucissons*; and sardines, anchovies, pimientos, and pickled onions.

Cold Vegetables

ARTICHOKES come in various sizes, the very small ones being used whole for hors-d'oeuvre, the large ones cut up.

Artichauts à la Vinaigrette

ARTICHOKES VINAIGRETTE

USE very tiny artichokes, about 1 to 1 1/2 inches in diameter. Discard the coarse outer leaves, cut away the thorny tips, and trim the stems. If the artichokes are large, break off the stem, trim the base, and rub the cut surface well with a piece of lemon. Cut down the whole artichoke and trim the leaves so that there is no more than 1/2 inch above the bottom. Then cut the artichoke in quarters or sixths and carefully cut away all the prickly choke from the center parts. Mix 1 tablespoon flour with enough cold water barely to cover the artichokes and add the juice of 1 or 2 lemons or 2 tablespoons vinegar. Bring the liquid to a boil, add the artichokes, and cook for 30 to 40 minutes, or until the artichokes test done. A leaf should slip out easily when pulled. Drain the vegetable well. Combine the cooled artichokes with vinaigrette sauce.

Petits Artichauts à la Grecque

LITTLE ARTICHOKES GREEK STYLE

USE very tiny artichokes, about 1 to 1 1/2 inches in diameter. Discard the coarse outer leaves, cut away the thorny tips, trim the stems, and rub the cut surface with lemon. Bring to a boil 3 cups water with the juice of 1 or 2 lemons or 2 tablespoons vinegar, 1/2 cup olive oil, 1/2 teaspoon salt, 2 stalks of fennel, sliced (if available), 2 or 3 stalks of celery, sliced, a few coriander seeds, and 8 peppercorns. Add the artichokes and cook for 20 minutes, or until they are done. Test by pulling out a leaf, which should slip out easily. Cool them in the cooking liquid.

Céleri-Rave à la Vinaigrette

CELERY KNOB VINAIGRETTE

PREPARE celery knob in any of the ways described in *salade de céleri-rave et betteraves*, celery knob and beet salad. Combine the raw or cooked ju-

462

lienne, slices, or dice with vinaigrette sauce mixed with finely chopped parsley and, if available, a little chopped tarragon and chervil.

This is a very simple dish but be sure the cabbage stands long enough in the salt.

MARINATED RED CABBAGE

Chou Rouge Mariné

CLEAN a red cabbage, cut it in quarters, and remove the hard core. Cut in very fine julienne and put in a bowl with 1 tablespoon salt. Leave it in a cold place for 24 hours, turning it over from time to time. Squeeze out all the water. Add 1 clove of garlic, 1 bay leaf, 8 peppercorns, and 2 tablespoons vinegar and let the cabbage stand for a few hours to pickle.

MARINATED CUCUMBERS

Concombres Marinés

PARE very small cucumbers and slice them very thin or pare and halve lengthwise larger cucumbers, remove the seeds, and finely chop the pulp. Spread the cucumbers on a plate, sprinkle them with salt, and let them stand for about 1 hour. Drain them, press them in a towel to remove surplus moisture, and combine them with enough vinaigrette sauce to flavor them well.

FIDDLEHEADS GREEK STYLE

Fougères à la Grecque

TRIM and discard the stems from 2 quarts fiddleheads and wash the ferns well. Bring to a boil in a saucepan 3 cups water combined with the juice of 1 lemon, 3 tablespoons salt, a stalk of fennel, if available, 2 stalks of celery, chopped, 5 coriander seeds, and a few peppercorns. Add the fiddleheads and cook them 15 to 25 minutes, or until they are tender. Let them cool.

MARINATED CARROTS

Carottes Marinées

SCRAPE 10 or 12 young carrots and quarter them. Make a marinade by combining in a saucepan 1 cup water, 1/2 cup white wine, 5 tablespoons salad oil, 1 clove of garlic, crushed, 1 tablespoon sugar, 1/2 teaspoon salt, and a faggot made by tying together 2 sprigs of parsley, 1 stalk of celery, 1 bay leaf, and a little thyme. Bring the mixture to a boil and simmer it for 5 minutes. Add the carrots, cook them until they are just tender but still quite firm, and cool them in the marinade. Arrange the carrots in a serving dish, pour over them enough cool marinade to moisten them well, and sprinkle them with finely chopped parsley.

Poireaux Marinés   MARINATED LEEKS

TRIM the green tops from leeks, halve or quarter the leeks lengthwise, and wash them thoroughly, making sure all the sand is removed from inside the leaves. Simmer the leeks in salted water for 45 minutes to 1 hour, or until they are tender. Drain and cool them. Cover them with vinaigrette sauce mixed with finely chopped parsley, tarragon, and chives, or other herbs.

Champignons Marinés   MARINATED MUSHROOMS

USE small button mushrooms, if possible. Wash them and remove the stems. If large mushrooms must be used, cut them into large dice. For each pound of mushrooms put in a saucepan 2 tablespoons lemon juice, 1 tablespoon each of chopped shallots and onion, and 3 tablespoons olive oil. Add the mushrooms, cover the saucepan, and stew the mushrooms for 10 to 12 minutes. Cool, turn the mushrooms into a *ravier* with some of the cooking liquid, and sprinkle them with chopped parsley. The liquid may be thickened with a little mayonnaise or cream mustard.

Salade de Riz   RICE SALAD

PUT in a bowl 2/3 cup cooked rice, 1/3 cup leftover cooked meat, poultry or fish, chopped rather small, 1 tablespoon minced green pepper, and 1 small onion, finely chopped. Add enough vinaigrette sauce to moisten the mixture well and carefully toss all together, using a fork to avoid crushing the rice grains. Turn the mixture into a serving dish and sprinkle with chopped parsley.

MELON WITH PORT

SELECT 1 or 2 large melons, depending on the number of people to be served. With a sharp knife carefully cut a round opening 1 1/2 to 2 inches in diameter in the stem end. Remove this circular plug, and set it aside. With a long-handled spoon empty out the seeds and fibre. If the melon is not too sweet, sprinkle in 2 tablespoons powdered sugar, but for a very sweet melon omit the sugar. Pour in 1 cup Port and replace the plug. Set the melon in a bowl, surround it with cracked ice, and put in the refrigerator for a few hours.

Melons prepared this way are not cut in slices. To serve, cut an opening in the top large enough to permit spooning out the meat. Serve in small deep dishes with some of the wine.

Cold Stuffed Eggs

STUFFED EGGS

HALVE lengthwise hard-cooked eggs and remove the yolks. Press the yolks through a fine sieve and mix them with half their volume of mayonnaise, some finely chopped chives and parsley, and salt to taste. Fill the egg whites with the yolk mixture, using a pastry tube, and arrange them in a serving dish. Garnish the eggs with mayonnaise and sprinkle with paprika, or coat them with aspic and sprinkle with tarragon.

EGGS STUFFED WITH CAVIAR

HALVE lengthwise hard-cooked eggs, remove the yolks, and fill the whites with caviar. Force the yolks through a sieve, mix them with a little finely chopped parsley, and sprinkle them around the edges of the egg whites. Arrange the eggs on a serving dish and garnish them with parsley.

EGGS STUFFED WITH FISH

HALVE lengthwise hard-cooked eggs and remove the yolks. Force the yolks through a fine sieve and combine them with cooked fish or shellfish, chopped very fine. Add mayonnaise, salt, and finely chopped parsley to taste. Fill the whites with this mixture, arrange the eggs on a serving dish, and garnish them with parsley or water cress. If desired, the eggs may be coated with clear aspic.

Cold Fish and Shellfish

*Anguilles
Marinés
au Paprika*

SKIN, clean, and cut eels into pieces 1 1/2 inches long. Sauté 1 small onion, chopped, in 1 tablespoon oil until the onion begins to turn golden. Add the eels, 1 tablespoon paprika, 2 cups white wine, or enough to cover the fish, 1 tablespoon chopped shallot or onion, a little thyme, 1 bay leaf, 1 stalk of celery, minced, 3 sprigs of parsley, a little salt, and 6 to 8 peppercorns. Bring to a boil, cover the pan and simmer for 15 to 18 minutes, or until the fish is tender. The bones should separate easily from the meat. Stir in 1 teaspoon gelatin, softened in a little cold water, and cool. When cold, remove the bone from the center of each piece of eel and cut the meat lengthwise into filets. Put the fish in a serving dish, strain the cooking liquid over it, and chill in the refrigerator. Sprinkle with paprika just before serving.

*Escabèche
de Poisson*

USE small whole fish, such as smelts, or cut fish filets into small pieces about the size of smelts. Clean the fish and flour them lightly. Fry the fish in hot deep fat (370° F.) for 2 to 3 minutes or until golden, drain thoroughly, and put them in a deep earthenware dish. Sauté 1 carrot and 1 onion, both sliced, and 5 or 6 cloves of garlic in 1/2 cup hot olive oil until the onion begins to turn golden. Add 1 cup vinegar, 1/2 cup water, 1 teaspoon salt, a little pepper, a little thyme, 1 bay leaf, and 1 pimiento, chopped. Bring the liquid to a boil and simmer for 10 to 15 minutes. Pour the marinade over the fish and marinate for 24 hours before serving.

MARINATED HERRING

*Harengs
Frais
Marinés*

CLEAN 18 to 24 fresh herring and arrange them in a saucepan. In another saucepan bring to a boil 3 cups white wine and 1 1/2 cups vinegar with 1 teaspoon salt, 1 carrot, and 2 onions, both thinly sliced, 1 shallot, finely chopped, a little thyme, 1 small bay leaf, a little sage, 4 sprigs of parsley, and 8 peppercorns. Simmer this marinade until the onions and carrots are tender, pour it over the herring, and simmer for 10 to 12 minutes longer. Transfer the herring to a deep dish, cover them with the marinade, and chill thoroughly. Serve the fish garnished with slices of carrot and raw onion, slices of lemon from which the rind has been removed, and enough of the marinade to keep it moist.

COLD MUSSELS

*Moules
Froides*

SCRUB mussels thoroughly and steam them in a small amount of water for a few minutes until the shells open. Remove the mussels from the shells, cut away the beard of fringe around the edge, and chill the mussels thoroughly. Serve the mussels very cold, on chilled plates, with mayonnaise mixed with mustard and a little cream or with *sauce moutarde à la crème*, cream mustard dressing.

CUCUMBERS STUFFED WITH OYSTERS OR MUSSELS

*Concombres
Farcis
aux Huîtres
ou aux
Moules*

CUT cucumbers into pieces about 1 inch long and remove enough of the seedy center from each piece to form tiny baskets large enough to hold a mussel or an oyster. Poach fresh oysters in their own juice for a few minutes or steam mussels in a small amount of water and drain. Cool them and trim the edges. Cook the liquor until it is reduced to almost nothing and mix it with a little chili sauce. Roll the oysters or mussels in the sauce, place them in the baskets, and sprinkle with chopped parsley.

The sea-food cocktail is an American contribution to the list of possible hors-d'oeuvre. These recipes were devised to please our American guests at the Ritz in New York.

LOBSTER COCKTAIL À LA RITZ

Cocktail de Homard à la Ritz

REMOVE the meat from 2 boiled lobsters, weighing 1 1/4 to 1 1/2 pounds each, and cut it into small pieces. Add 1 heart of celery, diced, and 1 heart of lettuce, chopped. Make a dressing by mixing together 3 tablespoons each of mayonnaise and Russian dressing, 1 tablespoon each of chili and Worcestershire sauce, 1 tomato, peeled, seeded, and chopped, and 1 teaspoon each of chives and parsley, both chopped. Combine the dressing with the lobster mixture and serve the mixture on beds of lettuce.

LOBSTER COCKTAIL

Cocktail de Homard

CUT cooked chilled lobster into pieces of any desired size. Serve in either of the following ways: Arrange finely crushed ice on chilled plates and place 2 leaves of lettuce on it. Put a small glass of cocktail sauce à la Ritz and a wedge of lemon on the center, and arrange the lobster on the lettuce. Or put coarsely shredded lettuce in the bottom of glass cocktail dishes and fill the dishes with lobster mixed with the sauce. Garnish with a wedge of lemon.

Cocktail Sauce à la Ritz COCKTAIL SAUCE À LA RITZ

Mix together thoroughly 1 cup tomato catsup, 1/2 cup chili sauce, 1 tablespoon vinegar, 1 teaspoon each of Worcestershire sauce and grated horseradish, the juice of 1 lemon, 1/4 teaspoon celery salt and 5 drops Tabasco sauce.

SHRIMP COCKTAIL

SERVE cooked, well-chilled shrimp as you would lobster, above, with cocktail sauce à la Ritz.

Cocktail de Crevettes

SPICY SHRIMP

IN A kettle combine 2 quarts water, 5 or 6 stalks of celery, and some celery tops, 24 allspice berries, 2 blades of mace, 9 cloves, 1 pod of red pepper, a little cayenne pepper or Tabasco, a faggot made by tying together 5 sprigs of parsley, 1 bay leaf, and a little thyme, and enough salt to make the broth quite salty. Simmer the court bouillon for 30 minutes to extract the flavors of the ingredients. Add the shrimp and cook 5 minutes. Cool the shrimp in the broth, shell, and remove the intestinal veins. Arrange them on a bed of cracked ice and garnish with parsley. Serve with cocktail sauce, if desired.

Crevettes Pochées

CRAB MEAT BOUCHÉES

COMBINE picked-over crab meat with enough mayonnaise to bind it. Stuff *petites bouchées*, little patty shells, with the mixture, cover each with a small piece of smoked salmon, curl an anchovy filet in a ring on top, and fill the anchovy ring with caviar.

Petites Bouchées à la Ritz

Cold Meat

CALVES' OR LAMBS' TONGUES

IN A saucepan combine 2 tablespoons flour, 2 to 3 tablespoons vinegar, and the juice of 1 lemon. Add 2 quarts water, 1 tablespoon salt, and the calves' or lambs' tongues. Bring the water to a boil and cook the tongues for about 1 hour, or until they are tender. Cool the tongues in the liquor,

Langues de Veau ou d'Agneau

skin them, cut into thin slices, and arrange in a serving dish. Spread sliced or chopped sour pickles and chopped hard-cooked eggs over the slices. Moisten with vinaigrette sauce and sprinkle with chopped parsley and chives.

Rillettes de Porc

PORK RILLETTES

DICE 1 1/2 pounds each of lean pork and fresh pork fat. Sprinkle the dice with a little pepper and 1 1/2 teaspoons salt mixed with 1/4 teaspoon Parisian spice or poultry seasoning, put them in a heavy pan, and add 1 cup boiling water and 1 bay leaf. Cook the pork very slowly, stirring it occasionally, until the water has cooked away. Continue cooking until the fat dice start to brown, but do not let the meat become dry. Remove the pan from the heat, lift the meat and fat dice into a strainer, and let the fat drain into the fat remaining in the pan. Discard the bay leaf. Grind the dice or chop very fine, put in a bowl, and gradually mix in all but 1 cup of the hot fat. Pack the meat mixture into small jars or crocks and pour the reserved fat over the top 1/2 inch deep. Store the *rillettes* in the refrigerator until ready to use. Remove the fat before serving. Use as a spread on toast, crusty bread, or rolls.

The Elegant

Hors-d'Oeuvre

A GREAT DINNER deserves an hors-d'oeuvre of classic importance, usually chosen from among these few: pâté—often *pâté de foie gras*—caviar, oysters, or smoked salmon, and served by itself and with great elegance. (Pâtés and terrines, so unmistakably French, have been put in the chapter on French *spécialités*.) Of the elegant hors-d'oeuvre, caviar is perhaps the most frequently used.

TRADITIONALLY, caviar is served either in its original container or in a bowl buried in a larger bowl of finely chopped ice. A porcelain or ivory spoon for service will spare crushing of the grains. Chopped hard-cooked eggs, chives or onion, or sour cream, served in separate dishes, may accompany caviar, and freshly made toast or slices of rye or whole wheat bread should be provided. Caviar is also served with melted butter and *blinis*, small, thin Russian buckwheat pancakes. On French menus this dish is called *crêpes de sarrasin*.

At the old Ritz we often baked special tiny brioches, éclairs, or puff paste shells for caviar. Or we placed the delicate roe in a cleaned oyster shell and decorated the edge with mimosa garnish. What is the most suitable beverage with caviar? Many gourmets believe that the only fitting wine for such a rare delicacy is the driest of Champagnes. In my early days in this country, when the Ritz was considered the last word in sophistication, small fortunes were spent at New Year's Eve festivities in our various dining rooms for thousands of servings of caviar and Champagne.

In my day at the Ritz hotels in Paris and London, and in my early years at the New York Ritz, we always had a special refrigerator for our most highly prized foodstuff: the fresh Molossol caviar ordered by the hundred pounds from Russia. It was gray, large grained, and not very salty because a little benzoate of soda had been added to it as a preservative. The use of this chemical is now strictly limited by law, and caviar, which therefore must be preserved only with salt, is sometimes *too* salty for true connoisseurs.

Nowadays, little fresh caviar is served in America. Instead you see the glistening black, small-grained, salty variety, which comes in tins and jars and is mostly used for canapés. And more and more use is made of red salmon caviar, which is less expensive and more plentiful.

PROFITEROLES WITH CAVIAR

Profiteroles au Caviar

MAKE little *profiteroles*, using half the recipe for *pâte à chou*, cream puff and éclair paste. Let the *profiteroles* cool.

Cut the tops from the *profiteroles*, fill the centers with fresh caviar, and decorate the edges with a border of mimosa, finely chopped hard-cooked egg and parsley. Replace the cover so that it rests halfway over the top yet shows the filling of caviar and the mimosa border. Place each *profiterole* on a plate lined with small leaves of lettuce and garnish with a small wedge of lemon.

OYSTERS WITH CAVIAR

Huîtres au Caviar

OPEN and drain well 6 oysters for each serving. Reserve and clean the deep shells. Lay an oyster in each deep shell. Rim the oyster with caviar and lay a thin serrated slice of lemon on each. Serve the oysters with a dish of finely chopped parsley.

Raw Oysters

To OBTAIN the choicest flavor from an oyster, you should open it just before it is served. Raw oysters are served very cold, usually on their own half shells embedded on cracked ice. They are accompanied with a sharp, acid sauce. In this country it is usually a cocktail sauce—like cocktail sauce à la Ritz—with a tomato base or lemon juice and horse-radish or just lemon juice. In France, they prefer *sauce mignonnette* made of vinegar, shallots, and finely crushed pepper, and serve thin slices of buttered whole-grain bread with the oysters. Oysters can also be cooked, chilled, and marinated to make a kind of salad.

Alcohol with Oysters

Raw oysters, or those cooked very lightly, are probably one of the most easily digested of the solid foods we eat. But they have one peculiarity—they are quickly toughened by alcohol. If you drink anything with oysters, make it a dry white wine, which makes a very delightful combination.

MARINATED OYSTERS

Huîtres Marinées

MAKE a marinade by combining in a saucepan 1 cup each of white wine and water, 1 1/2 tablespoons vinegar or 1 teaspoon lemon juice, 1 table-spoon olive oil, 1 onion and 1 carrot, both sliced, 4 sprigs of parsley, 1 stalk of celery, 1 clove of garlic, 1 teaspoon salt, 8 peppercorns, a little thyme, and 1 bay leaf. Bring the mixture to a boil, simmer it for 1 hour, and strain it. Pour the marinade over 3 to 4 dozen raw oysters with their juice, bring the liquid to a boil, and remove immediately from the heat. Let the oysters cool in the marinade. Serve them in an hors-d'oeuvre dish and pour over them enough marinade to keep them moist. Sprinkle the oysters with parsley and chives, both chopped, and garnish them with lemon slices. Cocktail sauce à la Ritz may be served separately.

OYSTERS WITH COLD SHALLOT SAUCE

Huîtres Mignonnette

MIX together 1/2 cup mild wine vinegar, 1 1/2 tablespoons finely chopped shallots, 1/4 teaspoon salt, and some finely ground black pepper or mignonnette pepper, very finely crushed. Serve the sauce with the oysters on the half shell.

SMOKED salmon is arranged on the serving dish in a neatly overlapping row of paper-thin slices. Lemon wedges, capers, and freshly ground pepper are the usual seasonings, and thin slices of dark bread, small rolls, or toast, along with sweet butter, the usual accompaniment.

Smoked Salmon

Hot Hors-d'Oeuvre

SPREAD oblongs, squares, triangles, or circles of buttered toast or spread dry crackers with savory mixtures such as those below. Reheat the prepared canapés in a moderate oven (350° F.) or under the broiler just before serving them. Take care that they do not burn.

Canapés Écossaise

REMOVE skin and bones from cooked smoked herring and chop the herring coarsely. To 1 cup herring, add 2/3 cup thick béchamel sauce, 1 tablespoon grated Parmesan cheese, and salt and pepper to taste. Heap on toast, sprinkle with more of the cheese, and brown in the oven or under the broiler.

Canapés Américaine

DICE 6 hard-cooked eggs and mix with 1/2 cup Mornay sauce. Spread on toast, cover each canapé with a slice of American cheese, sprinkle with paprika, and brown in the oven or under the broiler.

Canapés New England

MIX finely chopped cooked lobster and finely chopped cooked mushrooms with a little lobster butter and enough hot béchamel sauce to hold the mixture together. Spread on buttered toast and sprinkle with fine bread crumbs freshly sautéed in butter.

Canapés Jurassienne

MIX equal amounts of thick hot béchamel sauce and grated dry Gruyère or Swiss cheese. Add a little red pepper and some finely diced Gruyère cheese. Spread on toast and brown in the oven or under the broiler. Parmesan, Cheddar, or Holland cheese may also be used.

Canapés au Jambon

MIX very finely chopped cooked ham and a little chopped parsley with enough hot Madeira sauce to hold the mixture together. Spread on buttered toast, cover with a thin slice of cooked ham, and sprinkle with fine bread crumbs freshly sautéed in butter.

Canapés aux Sardines

MIX finely chopped hard-cooked egg with English mustard to taste and spread on buttered toast. Cover with skinless, boneless sardines and sprinkle the fish with fine bread crumbs freshly sautéed in butter. Reheat in the oven or under the broiler.

THE FIRST-COURSE hors-d'oeuvre is frequently a hot dish, often a savory sauced mixture served in a pastry shell, a *croustade*, a coquille, or the like. Although these sauced mixtures, called *salpicons*, vary widely in flavor, they consist basically of a mixture of cooked meat, poultry, fish, or shellfish with mushrooms, truffles, or other vegetables, in a smooth sauce. The mixtures can be varied easily and endlessly by using different combinations of these ingredients, and by changing the flavor of the sauce with curry, mustard, Worcestershire sauce, shallots, garlic, parsley, and similar seasonings. The cook's ingenuity need recognize no bounds except those of taste.

Salpicons

Small, bite-sized versions of these hors-d'oeuvre (as well as hot canapés, tiny croquettes, and other deep-fried savories and puffs) are eaten with cocktails. When a sauced mixture is used to fill tiny cocktail *profiteroles* and brioches that must be eaten with the fingers, it naturally cannot be as soft and fluid as if it were to be used for *bouchées* and *croustades*, which are eaten with a fork at the table. Make the sauce thicker (use 1/4 to 1/2 cup less liquid for 2 cups sauce), and chop the solid ingredients very, very fine. In fillings eaten at table, the pieces of meat, fish, or poultry in the sauce may be much larger. When these small hors-d'oeuvre are served at a cocktail party, the fillings should also be more highly spiced.

A sprinkling of paprika, sprigs of water cress or parsley, truffle cutouts, a border of golden-brown duchess potatoes piped through a pastry bag around a coquille—all these garnishes help to make hot hors-d'oeuvre as attractive to look at as they are delicious to eat.

Garnishes

Although the preparation of hot hors-d'oeuvre may seem to be more in a chef's repertoire than in that of a housewife, the fact is that the preparation of just one of the following interesting recipes—to be served at the table—is usually less time consuming than preparing a tray of fancy canapés.

Fortunately, most of the preparation for hot hors-d'oeuvre may be done in advance, so that the time needed for cooking at the last minute is very short. Sauces can be made early in the day; tart shells can be baked and ready to fill and brown; canapés can be spread for the broiler or the oven long before the guests arrive; croquettes or other mixtures for deep frying can be chilling in the refrigerator for hours.

Preparation in Advance

Hot Filled Hors-d'Oeuvre

Petits
Brioches

LITTLE BRIOCHES

BAKE brioche in tiny molds, cut off the round head of each to use as a cover, and remove the soft inside crumb. Fill the crusty shells with any savory sauced mixture, or *salpicon*.

Petites
Bouchées

LITTLE PATTY SHELLS

MAKE tiny patty shells of *pâte feuilletée*, or puff paste, and fill them with any savory sauced mixture, or *salpicon*.

Petites
Croustades

LITTLE BREAD CASES

CUT 2 1/2-inch cubes of bread and hollow out the centers so that the sides and bottom are about 1/2 inch thick. Or remove the crusts of thick slices of bread and hollow out the centers. Fry the cases in deep hot fat or brush with butter and brown in the oven. Fill with any savory sauced mixture.

Profiteroles

LITTLE CREAM PUFF SHELLS

MAKE *profiteroles* as described in the recipe for *pâté à chou*. Cut a small round from the top of each, for a cover. Or, while they are still hot from the oven, press down the center of each with the thumb to make an open shell like a *tartelette*. Fill the *profiteroles* with any savory sauced mixture, or *salpicon*. Garnish with parsley or a rim of mimosa.

Crêpes

LITTLE PANCAKES

SIFT together 1 cup flour and 1/4 teaspoon salt. Beat in with a wire whip 2 beaten eggs. Add 1 cup milk (or half milk and half broth) and mix well. Follow the directions for making crêpes, but make them quite small. Fill the crêpes with any *salpicon* or savory sauced mixture, and roll or fold them. Reheat them briefly in the oven.

FILLED PASTRY STRIPS *Allumettes*

CUT a strip of pastry 6 inches wide, place it on a baking sheet and spread 1/2 the length with any savory sauced mixture, or *salpicon*. Fold over the unspread half to make a strip 3 inches wide and press the edges firmly together. Cut across the folded strip to make pieces 1 inch wide but do not separate them. Bake the *allumettes* in a moderately hot oven (375° F.) until they are brown. Separate them as you remove them from the pan.

FRIED PASTRIES *Rissoles*

CUT pastry into small circles and fill the centers with any *salpicon* or savory sauced mixture. Fold the circles in half and press and seal the edges together. Fry the *rissoles* in deep hot fat as described in the section on deep frying.

Salpicons: Hors-d'Oeuvre and Croquette Mixtures

CHICKEN AND SWEETBREADS *Financière*

COMBINE diced cooked chicken, diced cooked sweetbreads, sliced cooked mushrooms, and pitted olives with Madeira sauce. Garnish with sliced truffles.

CHICKEN AND TRUFFLES *Princesse*

COMBINE finely chopped cooked chicken and chopped truffles with hot thick cream sauce. Garnish with 2 or 3 very short asparagus tips and a rim of mimosa.

CHICKEN AND ONION *Seville*

COMBINE chicken mousse with very finely chopped onion that has been cooked in a little butter and season with paprika.

Reine CHICKEN BREAST AND MUSHROOMS

COMBINE equal quantities of finely minced cooked chicken breast and finely chopped cooked mushrooms with thick *velouté* sauce. Add a little finely chopped truffle.

Strasbourgeoise GOOSE LIVER

COMBINE finely diced goose liver and finely diced truffles with hot thick Madeira sauce.

Louisiane SHRIMP

COMBINE finely diced cooked shrimp and finely diced cooked mushrooms with hot Newburg sauce.

Dieppoise SHRIMP AND MUSSELS

COMBINE diced cooked shrimp, diced cooked mussels, and sliced cooked mushrooms with white wine sauce.

Américaine LOBSTER

COMBINE diced cooked lobster and sliced cooked mushrooms with *sauce américaine*. Garnish with a cooked shrimp.

Cape Cod OYSTERS AND SCALLOPS

POACH small oysters and bay scallops, or sea scallops that have been cut in quarters, each in their own liquor for 2 to 3 minutes. Cook sliced mushrooms in a little water with a few drops of lemon juice for 5 minutes. Drain each. Combine the shellfish cooking liquors and mushroom liquor and cook the mixture until it is reduced to 2/3 the original quantity. Combine with an equal amount of hot thick cream sauce. Add a little of the sauce to a slightly beaten egg yolk and return the egg to the pan. Cook the mixture, stirring constantly, until it reaches a boil. Remove it from the heat, add the oysters, scallops, and mushrooms, reheat briefly, and add chopped parsley and chives.

ANCHOVY AND EGG　　　　　　　　　　　　　　　　　*Anchois*

COMBINE equal amounts of finely diced anchovy filets and finely chopped hard-cooked egg with very thick béchamel sauce.

SPINACH　　　　　　　　　　　　　　　　　　　*Florentine*

CHOP enough spinach very fine to make 1 cup, firmly packed. Cook it in butter until all the moisture is cooked away. Add 3 to 4 tablespoons very thick béchamel sauce and 2 tablespoons grated Parmesan. If *allumettes* are filled with this mixture, bake them until they are half done, then sprinkle with grated Parmesan and continue baking. If used in crêpes, sprinkle them with cheese before reheating them in the oven.

LITTLE ROUND OR OVAL TARTS　　　　　　　*Tartelets et Barquettes*

LITTLE open tarts filled with savory mixtures, browned in the oven and served hot, are called *tartelets* or *barquettes*. The round ones are *tartelets* and the oval ones, *barquettes*. Roll out *pâte à tourte* until quite thin and cut it into the right size and shape for the shallow little molds, either fluted or plain. These should be about 1 1/2 inches in diameter or length. Fit the pastry into the molds and press it firmly against the bottom and sides. Prick the pastry, cover with wax paper, and fill the molds with rice or dried beans so the dough won't rise out of shape during baking. Bake in a moderately hot oven (375° to 400° F.) for 12 to 15 minutes. Remove the rice or beans (they can be used over and over again) and the wax paper. Unmold and fill the pastry shells with any *salpicon*, or savory sauced mixture. Sprinkle with fine bread crumbs and brown in a hot oven (400° F.).

OYSTERS BOURGUIGNONNE IN BARQUETTES　　*Barquettes d'Huîtres à la Bourguignonne*

POACH small oysters in their own liquor for 2 minutes and drain them well. Put them in pastry shells and cover them with the garlic butter for snails with garlic butter. Sprinkle with fine water-cracker crumbs and brown in a hot oven (450° F.) or under the broiler.

Barquettes de Moules à la Poulette MUSSELS POULETTE IN BARQUETTES

STEAM 18 to 20 well-scrubbed mussels with 2 finely chopped shallots or 1 small white onion and 1/2 cup white wine for 6 to 8 minutes, or until the shells open. Remove the mussels from their shells, draining all the liquor from them into the wine in the pan. Cook the liquor until it is reduced to about 1/3 and thicken it with *beurre manié* made by creaming together 2 tablespoons butter and 1 tablespoon flour. Add 1 teaspoon chopped parsley and 4 or 5 cooked mushrooms, thinly sliced, combine the sauce and mussels, and fill the baked pastry shells. Sprinkle with fine bread crumbs, dot with butter, and brown in a hot oven (450° F.).

Tartelets Rachel MUSHROOM AND TRUFFLE TARTLETS

MIX together equal parts of finely diced cooked mushrooms and truffles and add enough hot cream sauce to hold the mixture together. Fill small pastry shells, sprinkle with fine bread crumbs sautéed in butter until golden brown, and place a small slice of sweetbread sautéed in butter on top of each. Heat thoroughly in a hot oven (400° F.).

Tartelets au Fromage CHEESE TARTLETS

LINE *tartelets* or *barquette* molds with *pâte à tourte*. Slice thinly 1/2 pound Swiss cheese and spread it over the pastry. Combine 1 1/2 cups hot milk, 3 beaten eggs, 1/2 teaspoon salt, and 1/8 teaspoon each of paprika and ground nutmeg and divide the mixture among the cheese-lined molds. Bake the *tartelets* in a moderately hot oven (375° F.) for 10 to 15 minutes, or until the custard is set and the top is brown. Serve warm.

Barquettes de Jambon HAM BARQUETTES

FOLLOW the recipe for *tartelets au fromage,* but use finely chopped ham instead of cheese.

QUICHE LORRAINE

LINE an 8-inch pie pan or a 10-inch flan ring with *pâte à tourte*. Broil 6 not-too-thin bacon slices and arrange the pieces over the bottom of the pastry shell. Cut 6 ounces Swiss cheese into small, thin slices and arrange on top of the bacon. Beat together 3 eggs and 1 yolk with 1 tablespoon flour, 1/2 teaspoon salt, and a pinch of nutmeg and add 2 cups rich milk or milk and cream and 1 tablespoon melted butter cooked until it is a little brown. Pour the mixture over the bacon and cheese and bake the *quiche* in a moderately hot oven (375° F.) for 30 to 35 minutes, or until the custard is set and the top is brown. Serve warm. This amount will make 2 to 3 dozen *tartelets*, depending on their size.

Quiche Lorraine

FILLED BAKED SHELLS

USE real scallop shells or shells of ovenproof pottery or glass. Fill with any *salpicon*, or savory sauced mixture. Pipe a narrow border of duchess potatoes around the edge and brown in the oven or under the broiler. For 6 shells, prepare about 2 cups of duchess potatoes.

Coquilles

CHICKEN AND MUSHROOMS IN SHELLS — *Coquilles de Volaille à la Parisienne*

MIX together small thin slices of cooked chicken and sliced cooked mushrooms. There should be about 2 cups. Prepare 1 1/2 cups Mornay sauce. Put a narrow border of duchess potatoes around the edge of 6 baking shells and fill the centers with the chicken mixture combined with 1 cup of the sauce. Add 1 or 2 tablespoons whipped cream to the remaining sauce and spread it over the filling. Sprinkle with grated Parmesan, brown in a hot oven (450° F.) or under the broiler, and serve immediately.

SWEETBREADS AND SPINACH IN SHELLS — *Coquilles de Ris de Veau à la Florentine*

DICE enough cooked sweetbreads to make 1 cup and heat them in 1/2 cup cream sauce. Heat about 1/2 cup cooked, drained spinach in a little butter. Pipe a narrow border of duchess potatoes around 6 baking shells and brown in a hot oven (450° F.) or under the broiler. Arrange spinach in the center of each shell and cover with the hot creamed sweetbreads. Sprinkle with finely chopped cooked ox tongue or cooked ham.

481

Coquilles de Poissons Diverses   FISH WITH MORNAY SAUCE IN SHELLS

CUT enough cooked fish in small pieces to make 1 1/2 cups. Prepare 1 1/2 cups Mornay sauce. Pipe a narrow border of duchess potatoes around 6 baking shells and fill the centers with the fish mixed with 1 cup of the Mornay sauce. Add 1 or 2 tablespoons whipped cream to the remaining 1/2 cup of sauce and spread it over the filling. Sprinkle with grated Parmesan and brown in a hot oven (450° F.) or under the broiler.

The sauce may be sharpened, if desired. Melt 1 1/2 tablespoons butter, stir in 1 teaspoon English mustard, and add the mixture to the cup of Mornay sauce to be mixed with the fish.

Coquilles d'Huîtres et de Crevettes   OYSTERS AND SHRIMP IN SHELLS

POACH oysters in their own juice for 2 minutes, allowing 2 or 3 for each serving. Cook 1 or 2 shrimp for each serving. Drain. Make 1 1/2 cups Mornay sauce. Pipe a narrow border of duchess potatoes around 6 baking shells. Arrange oysters and shrimp in each shell with 2 tablespoons of sauce. Add 1 or 2 tablespoons whipped cream to the remaining sauce and spread it over the filling. Sprinkle with grated cheese, brown in a hot oven (450° F.) or under the broiler, and serve immediately.

Deep-Fried Hors-d'Oeuvre

MANY hot hors-d'oeuvre are deep fried, and of these, croquettes are perhaps the most popular. Croquette mixtures, which you will find in the section on deep frying, are also used to make *subrics* and *cromesquis*. *Salpicons*, the sauced mixtures used to fill *bouchées*, *profiteroles*, *tartelettes*, and the like, are also used to make croquettes and can be used interchangeably with them. Just be sure the mixture is not too fluid. Use about 2 cups of solid food to 1 cup sauce. The techniques for cooking croquettes and other fried delicacies are included in the section on deep frying.

Garnish platters of fried hors-d'oeuvre with fried parsley. These hors-d'oeuvre are served without sauce, of course, unless they are eaten with a fork, at table.

LITTLE CROQUETTES

To MAKE little croquettes, chill any croquette mixture or any *salpicon* and shape it into balls or ovals about the size of plums, following the directions for croquettes in the section on deep frying. Coat the croquettes *à l'anglaise,* fry them in deep hot fat (390° F.) until they are golden brown, and drain them on absorbent paper.

CHEESE CROQUETTES
Croquettes de Fromage

IN A saucepan melt 2 tablespoons butter, add 3 tablespoons flour, and cook the *roux* until it starts to turn golden. Gradually add 1 1/2 cups hot milk and cook the sauce, stirring constantly, until it thickens. Add 3/4 cup Swiss cheese or 1/2 cup Parmesan, finely diced, and stir until the cheese melts. Add a little of the mixture to 2 beaten egg yolks, mix well, and return it to the saucepan. Simmer briefly over very low heat until the egg yolks are thoroughly blended, and correct the seasoning with salt. Spread the mixture about 3/4 inch thick on a flat pan, cool it, and chill it in the refrigerator. Cut it in rectangles 3/4 inch by 1 1/4 inches or 3/4-inch cubes. Coat the croquettes *à l'anglaise* and fry them in deep hot fat (390° F.) until they are golden brown.

LITTLE SAUTÉED CROQUETTES

SHAPE croquette mixtures into small balls, coat them *à l'anglaise* and sauté in butter, rolling and shaking them carefully in the pan to brown them evenly all over.

CROQUETTE ROUNDS

SHAPE croquette mixtures into small round flat cakes, coat them *à l'anglaise,* and sauté in butter or fry in deep hot fat (390° F.) and drain.

For more detailed instruction on making these little fritters, read the section on beignets. *All entrée* beignets *are suitable for hors-d'oeuvre, if they are kept small.*

Beignets

CUT cooked meat, fish, poultry, or vegetables into bite-sized pieces and marinate them about 1/2 hour in 1 to 2 tablespoons salad oil with a few drops of lemon juice or vinegar, salt and pepper, and a little finely chopped parsley. Dip piece by piece into fritter batter. Or shape croquette mixtures into small balls or ovals and coat them with fritter batter instead of *à l'anglaise*. Fry the *beignets* in deep hot fat (390° F.) until they are golden brown and drain them on absorbent paper.

Beignets Soufflés

COMBINE finely chopped cheese, fish, or other cooked food—about 3/4 cup—with *pâte à chou*, cream puff and éclair paste. Season the mixture with salt. Drop it by teaspoonfuls into deep hot fat. *Beignets soufflés* must cook a little longer than *beignets* because the cream puff paste is uncooked and also because, if they are not sufficiently cooked, they will collapse before they can be served. Therefore the fat should not be quite as hot, about 350° F. instead of the 375° to 390° F. used for *beignets*. Cook the *beignets soufflés* until they are brown on both sides and drain them.

Attereaux

THREAD on short skewers small pieces of cooked meat, fish, shellfish, or poultry with mushrooms and cooked vegetables such as artichoke bottoms and celery knob. Roll the skewers in very thick Villeroy sauce or tomato sauce and chill thoroughly. Coat *à l'anglaise*, fry in deep hot fat (390° F.) until golden brown and drain.

Hot Stuffed Eggs
ANY and all of the hot stuffed eggs found in the section on eggs—deviled, Chimay, and so on—make appetizing hors-d'oeuvre.

Hot Oysters
There are many oyster-lovers who scorn to eat them any way but raw; on the other hand, cooked oysters have their fanciers, and such hors-d'oeuvre as oysters Casino or *bourguignonne* or Portia are very popular. Indeed, almost any recipe for cooked oysters that you find in the chapter on shellfish is appropriate for hors-d'oeuvre.

LE BUFFET

The Cold Buffet

THE SUMMER we opened the Roof Garden at the Ritz, I set up there a cold buffet, and the buffet table greeted the guests as they came in. On its three great round tiers, each packed with ice, we arranged the beautifully decorated buffet platters. Set in the top tier there was even a small fountain with a sculptured figure of a little boy. On a side table we had one elegant hot food, served from a *tortue*, a huge silver dish with an enormous dome, like a turtle.

Surely there is no more practical and agreeable way to serve a large number of guests than the buffet, where the guests help themselves, or are helped by a waiter, from an array of dishes displayed on a handsomely arranged table. This kind of service has the further advantage of being versatile. It can be adapted to any occasion, from the very informal to the very formal with which we concern ourselves here.

The formal cold buffet achieved its first great fame in France in the days of the *cuisine artistique* of the great chef Carême, during the early years of the nineteenth century, and was characterized by elaborately conceived and fantastically embellished *pièces montées* in sugar and in aspic. But by the time I arrived in Paris to make my debut as a chef, these extravagantly executed showpieces—better to look at than to eat— were already out of fashion.

Pièces
Montées

That is not to say that aspic was also out of fashion. Cold jellied dishes have always been popular in great European houses where eating is a fine art, and even the most humble *charcuterie* has its jellied meats. Aspic does more than make food attractive; it serves to keep fish, poultry, meat, eggs, and vegetables fresh and moist, and contributes a delightful flavor and texture of its own.

Jellied dishes were part of the cuisine at the Ritz Hotels in Paris and in London. We may not have been expected to deck out a lobster to represent the spirit of the sea, or some such fanciful notion in the Ca- rême tradition, but on special occasions we did produce some startling effects.

I remember one outstanding party directed by Monsieur Malley, our *chef des cuisines*, for the distinguished Monsieur Sebastopoulo, who was first secretary of the Russian embassy. The guest list included the entire diplomatic corps of London, as well as all the members of Europe- an and Asiatic royalty, nobility, and aristocracy who were in London for the " season. " The rooms were decorated to resemble a Russian winter, with artificial snow and ice, and intricate lighting effects. For the late supper that followed the entertainment and dancing, Monsieur Sebastopoulo had ordered a sumptuous buffet, including *truite en gelée*. We molded the trout in jelly and presented them handsomely on silver servers. Monsieur Sebastopoulo was not pleased. He waved our platters away. Expense? *N'importe !* The trout were to be very tiny; they should be molded in a crystal-clear aspic flavored with Chablis; and they should be so presented in great shallow glass bowls that they would look as if they were swimming about in an aquarium. The success of this tour de force was *magnifique*.

I have in one of my old notebooks the menu for another of these collations. The list may seem long—and the dishes complicated—but it is typical of a pre-World War II buffet supper. The *spécialités* included: two lobsters *en belle vue*, facing each other; *poularde soufflé Vendôme* and *poularde rose de mai*; duckling Montmorency and duckling *soufflé rouennaise garni à l'orange*; mousses of chicken, of ham, and of *foie gras*; vegetables in aspic; halibut or turbot; filet of sole *à l'orientale* and filet of sole Bayard; ox tongue *à l'écarlate*; braised beef and roast filet of beef, chilled and garnished with vegetables; ham; galantine; *fricandeau de veau*; terrine of duck *rouennaise* and terrine of game in season; *pâté maison* and pâté of game in season. In addition, there were hors-d'oeuvre consisting of stuffed tomatoes, hard-cooked eggs stuffed with caviar, vegetables in season, cucumbers, and salads all dressed with appropriate cold sauces. The desserts served were fairly simple, as befits a lavish buffet: *brioche à la parisienne*; pastries; *petits fours*; compote of fruit and macédoine of fruit.

Your formal buffet need not be this elaborate, of course. It may include only as many dishes as the number of guests indicates will be required. For instance, for 25 guests, plan on 5 entrées and salads, each dish made with a recipe for 12. This allows each guest to help himself at the buffet twice, and leaves a margin of safety. A typical menu might include a whole salmon mayonnaise, a ham mousse, cold roast poultry, a jellied vegetable salad, and a pâté. Tiny buttered rolls or bread-and-butter sandwiches are usual. For dessert, simple preparations of fruit go best with the rich entrées, and *petits fours* or small pastries should accompany the fruit.

A buffet must be as appetizing to look at as it is to eat; beautiful linens, silver and crystal serving dishes, lighted candelabra, and flowers—such an affair calls for the best table appointments the house affords. The platters and other serving dishes should be of moderate size, and should be refilled as necessary from the kitchen. Jellied dishes should be made in several small molds, rather than in one large mold, so that the extra dishes can be kept cold and firm in the refrigerator until they are needed.

One custom still survives from the old days of *la cuisine artistique*, the use of *attelets*. These are long silver brochettes or skewers with large, elaborately designed finials. *Attelets* are purely decorative; you will see them effectively used for this purpose in the photograph of *chapon truffé*.

Almost any dish that does not have to be served at once, as does a soufflé, may be served at a buffet, but this chapter deals with the aspics

Attelets

that are characteristic of the formal buffet. The making of pâtés and terrines, indispensable to the buffet table, is taken up elsewhere.

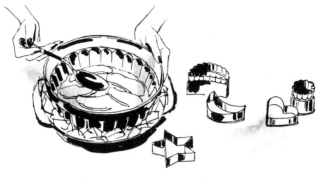

The Use of Aspic

A N ASPIC may be made in several ways. The simplest way, of course, is to add unflavored gelatin to canned consommé or bouillon. Most gelatin today comes in small envelopes that contain enough to congeal from 1 3/4 to 2 cups liquid. First soften the gelatin for 5 minutes in cold liquid, then dissolve it in boiling hot liquid. If you use a canned consommé or bouillon, soften the gelatin in 1/4 cup cold water and dissolve it in 1 1/2 cups boiling bouillon.

The professional chef always makes his own aspic, of course, from soup stock. To ensure that the stock will jelly to the desired stiffness, he should put into the soup kettle something, such as calf's feet, that is richer in gelatin than ordinary bones. However, if these are unavailable, he may substitute 2 or 3 veal shinbones for each calf's foot specified. Or he may use 6 or 7 chicken feet, which have the gelatin content of 1 calf's foot.

Before they are added to the pot, the veal bones should be split and parboiled, and the chicken feet scalded and skinned.

If neither calf's feet nor chicken feet are available, test the aspic by chilling a little on a cold saucer. If it does not stiffen, soften 2 envelopes or tablespoons unflavored gelatin in 1/2 cup cold consommé and dissolve it in 3 1/2 cups hot consommé. If it is somewhat firm, add 1 tablespoon gelatin.

Aspic jelly must be completely transparent, so clear that it sparkles, and should be a very pale golden color that sets off food and its decorations to best advantage. If it is to be transparent the aspic must be completely free of particles of solid matter. To achieve this clarity and at the same time add richness to the flavor of the aspic, the professional chef uses egg white and chopped beef. Egg white alone will serve almost as well. Strain the stock and allow it to cool so that every trace of fat may be removed from the surface. Stir in the chopped beef mixed with the well-beaten egg whites and slowly bring the stock to a boil, stirring only until the boiling point is reached. Simmer the stock without disturbing it further. As the mixture coagulates, it attracts the solid bits floating in the stock. The beef is lifted out with a skimmer, and the stock is strained through a sieve lined with muslin wrung out of cold water.

To Clarify Aspic

ASPIC JELLY

Gelée de Viande

BRING to a boil in a kettle the following ingredients: 1 1/2 pounds each of beef bones and veal shinbones, 3 calf's feet and a leek, an onion, and a carrot, all sliced, a stalk of celery, 6 peppercorns, 1 tablespoon salt, and 4 quarts water. Cover the kettle and simmer the mixture for 4 to 5 hours. Skim off the scum that rises to the surface, frequently during the first half hour and as necessary thereafter. Strain the stock and discard the bones and vegetables. Cool the stock, remove the fat which hardens on the surface, and stir in 3 egg whites, well beaten, mixed with 1/2 pound chopped beef. Add a faggot made by tying together a sprig each of tarragon and chervil, a bay leaf, and 3 sprigs of parsley, and bring the stock slowly to the boiling point, stirring it constantly. Simmer it without stirring for 30 minutes and strain it through a sieve lined with damp muslin. Makes about 6 cups.

WINE ASPIC: SHERRY OR MADEIRA   *Gelée au Vin : Xérès ou Madère*

ASPIC jelly is usually flavored with wine; 1/2 cup Sherry or Madeira is added to the above amount after it is strained.

CHICKEN ASPIC   *Gelée de Volaille*

ADD a fowl to the ingredients for aspic jelly, and use chicken feet instead of or in addition to the calf's feet.

To Cool Aspic THE trick in using aspic successfully is to have it just on the point of setting, but still liquid, and to chill the other ingredients and the utensils until they are all very cold. Do not cool aspic in the refrigerator. The outside will congeal, the center will still be too liquid. Pour hot aspic into a metal bowl, set the bowl in another bowl of cracked ice, and with a metal spoon stir the aspic constantly until it is about to congeal. This is the point at which to use it. It may soon congeal too much, but congealed aspic can be remelted and cooled again and again.

To Line a Mold To line a mold with aspic, chill the mold thoroughly and set it deep in a pan of ice. Pour in a small amount of very cold, thick aspic and roll and turn the mold until it is coated. The jelly will set almost immediately. To make a thicker lining, add successive coats of aspic, allowing each to set before another is added. **To Decorate a Mold** To decorate the mold, arrange a design of cutouts of egg white, olives, tarragon leaves or whatever you wish to use between aspic layers. Fix each in place with a few drops of aspic. When this aspic sets, the covering layer of aspic can be applied over all. The salad or other mixture is added, and usually more aspic to fill the mold to the top.

To Unmold an Aspic To unmold an aspic, slip a small knife around the top edge to loosen it. Dip the mold into very hot water and remove it, in and out in one smooth operation. If the mold does not immediately slip out when it is turned over on a plate, repeat the dipping, a little more quickly this time. Hold the serving plate upside down on the mold and turn plate and mold together.

To Apply Aspic Coating When aspic is used to coat something like a chicken or a fish, the food to be coated must be very cold and should be kept in the refrigerator between steps. A thin coat of aspic poured over the food and allowed to set will hold the decorations. A second thin coat can be spooned over the decorations, and as many more as are necessary to achieve the desired thickness, a layer at a time. When the aspic is thoroughly set, the food can be safely lifted from the preparation platter to a serving dish. However, some foods, such as salmon, cannot be lifted and should be coated and decorated on the serving dish. Small items like eggs can be arranged on a rack; the aspic that drips off them onto the plate beneath can be reused. All aspic dishes should be returned to the refrigerator until servingtime.

To Make Aspic Garnish Aspic that is to be used as a decoration—cut into shapes or stirred with a fork or chopped with a knife into diamond-like crystals—is poured into a shallow pan to set.

Meat in Aspic

PARSLEYED HAM IN ASPIC

Jambon Persillé en Gelée

PUT a 10- to 12-pound ham in a large kettle, cover well with fresh water, and add 2 pig's knuckles or a piece of pork shoulder and a few pork or veal bones. Parboil the ham for about 1 hour. Taste the water and, if it is salty, discard it and cover the ham with fresh water. Add 2 onions, each studded with a clove, 1 clove of garlic, 1 carrot, sliced, 2 leeks, and a faggot made by tying together 2 stalks of celery, 6 sprigs of parsley, 1 bay leaf; and a little thyme. Bring the water to a boil, simmer the ham for 4 hours, then leave it in the water until it is cool enough to handle.

Remove the ham from the kettle and save the cooking liquor. Take off the skin from the top of the ham in one piece and save it to cover the ham later. Trim off the surplus fat from the top of the ham and discard it. Trim off any remaining skin and any of the lean meat at the edges that has darkened in cooking. Combine these trimmings with the skin of the pig's knuckles or pork shoulder and run them through a meat chopper. Measure this mixture and add to it an equal quantity of chopped parsley, 1 clove of garlic, minced, 1 teaspoon chopped shallot or onion, a little freshly ground black pepper, a little grated nutmeg, and 1 1/2 tablespoons good wine vinegar. Mix thoroughly.

Carefully remove the bones from the cooked ham so that the meat is left in a few very large pieces. Strain the reserved cooking liquor, taste it and, if it is too salty, add a little unsalted white stock; if not seasoned enough, add salt. Chill a little of the liquid to make sure it will become firm when cold. The pig's knuckles usually supply enough gelatin but if there is any doubt, add 1 tablespoon gelatin softened in 3 tablespoons water for every pint of liquor, and bring to a boil to dissolve the gelatin. Let the liquid cool.

Use a ham-shaped mold, a large oval mold, or an oval roasting pan. If a canned ham is used, use the can the ham was packed in. Spread over the bottom of the mold about 1/2 inch of the ground stuffing, which will be green from the parsley. Add a layer of ham pieces and pack stuffing down around the ham, against the sides of the mold. Repeat until all is used. The top layer should be stuffing. Add cooking liquor to fill the mold and cover it with the reserved ham skin. Place a board on top of the mold and weight it down. Chill thoroughly.

To serve, remove the ham skin, unmold the ham on a chilled serving platter, and coat it with a layer of aspic. Cut several slices and arrange them around the ham. They will alternate pink sections of ham and bright green stuffing. Put a 1/4-inch layer of aspic in a shallow pan and let it set. Add a layer of stuffing and chill. Turn the aspic out and cut it in triangles. Garnish with these and with tomato roses.

Boeuf
à la Mode
en Gelée

JELLIED BRAISED BEEF

PREPARE *boeuf à la mode*, or braised beef, and remove it to a board. Cover it with another wooden board and weight the board down. Reduce the pan gravy to 3 cups, strain it, and flavor it with 1/2 cup Madeira. Cool the sauce until it is very thick, but still liquid. Arrange the cold beef on a serving platter. Garnish the platter with small glazed onions, rounds of cooked carrots, and, if desired, crisp squares of bacon or sautéed fat pork dice. Spoon the sauce over meat and garnishings and chill until the sauce is jellied. Cover all with clear aspic.

Braised veal may also be prepared this way.

Mousse
de Jambon
Norvégienne

HAM MOUSSE NORWEGIAN STYLE

GRIND 1/2 cup chopped cooked ham through a food chopper 2 or 3 times and then press it through a fine sieve. Mix this ham purée with 1/2 cup thick béchamel sauce and add 1/2 cup each of meat stock and tomato juice, and 1/2 teaspoon paprika. Bring the mixture to a boil and add 1 tablespoon unflavored gelatin, softened in 2 tablespoons cold water. Stir until the gelatin is thoroughly combined, rub the mixture through a fine sieve, and cool, stirring occasionally. Beat 1 cup heavy cream stiff and carefully fold in the cooled ham mixture. Stir in 1 tablespoon Sherry.

Have ready 2 cups cool but still liquid chicken aspic. Coat a chilled mold and decorate the mold with truffle slices. Set it in a bowl of cracked ice and when the aspic is firm, fill the mold with the ham mousse. Chill it thoroughly. To serve, invert the mold on a chilled serving dish. The mousse may also be poured into a china or glass serving dish and the top covered with aspic and decorated with truffles. Serve it from the dish.

OX TONGUE WITH PORT WINE ASPIC

Lange de Boeuf en Gelée au Porto

SOAK a smoked ox tongue for 3 or 4 hours or overnight. Drain and boil it until it is tender when tested with a fork. Cool it in the stock. Remove the skin and trim away the butt end with the bones. Chill. Put the tongue on a rack and coat it with clear aspic jelly flavored with a little Port, and colored with a few drops of red coloring. Chill the tongue well. Coat a serving dish with aspic, place the tongue on it and decorate the platter with truffles and hard-cooked eggs cut in fancy shapes.

PORT WINE ASPIC

Gelée au Porto

PUT into a saucepan 3 cups chicken consommé, 1 cup Port wine, 1 tablespoon tarragon vinegar, 2 tablespoons dry white wine, 3 envelopes of gelatin, salt and pepper to taste, and the crushed shells and beaten whites of 2 eggs. Heat the mixture slowly, stirring constantly, until it boils up in the pan. Remove from the heat, let it stand for 10 minutes, and strain it through a sieve lined with cheesecloth wrung out of cold water. Port wine aspic may also be made by simply adding Port to liquid aspic.

Sea Food in Aspic

SALMON IN ASPIC PARISIENNE

Saumon Glacé à la Parisienne

BOIL a whole salmon as described in the recipe for boiled salmon. Remove the string, open the cloth, and scrape off the skin and the dark flesh on the top side of the fish. Carefully turn the fish onto a platter and do the same to the side that is now uppermost. Chill thoroughly. Spoon a coat of cold aspic over the fish and arrange on the aspic whatever decorations you fancy. Tarragon or parsley leaves and chopped egg white or sliced eggs are usually included among the decorations. Apply several more coats of aspic, chilling well between coats. Just before servingtime, garnish the platter with tomatoes stuffed with diced cucumbers moistened with French dressing, stuffed eggs, lettuce nests filled with mixed cooked vegetables tossed with mayonnaise, and green and black olives.

To Carve Salmon in Aspic

Carve the salmon with a thin, sharp knife dipped into warm water. Holding the flat side of the blade parallel to the platter, slit the fish just above the backbone, working from the tail to the center and the head to the center until the separation is complete, but the flesh is not at all disarranged. Cut in slices about 2 inches wide and lift the portions carefully from the bone. When the top filet has been served, lift off the bones and set them aside. Slice and serve the bottom filet in the same way.

A 4- to 5-pound piece of halibut may be prepared and decorated like the whole salmon for the buffet. Allow about 20 to 25 minutes poaching time, according to the thickness of the fish.

Fish may be coated with an aspic made from fish stock, although the flavor of this aspic is not as generally liked as that of the usual meat or chicken aspic.

FISH ASPIC

Gelée de Poisson

COMBINE 2 pounds chopped uncooked fish bones and trimmings with 2 onions and 1 carrot, all chopped, a few sprigs of parsley, 5 or 6 peppercorns, 1/2 teaspoon salt, and 1 quart dry white wine and 1 1/2 quarts water. Bring the liquid to a boil and let it boil gently for 30 minutes. Strain this stock through a fine sieve. There should be 2 quarts or less.

Fumet de Poisson or Fish Stock

Add 1/2 pound finely chopped cod or whiting mixed with 3 egg whites, a leek, finely chopped, and a few sprigs of parsley. Bring the mixture to a boil. Soften 4 tablespoons gelatin in 1/2 cup cold water and dissolve it in the hot stock, off the heat. Skim the stock and keep it hot, without allowing it to boil, for 30 minutes. Strain the aspic through a sieve lined with damp muslin and cool it.

TROUT JELLIED IN WHITE WINE

*Truite
en Gelée
au Vin Blanc*

POACH 6 cleaned trout for 10 to 15 minutes in the court bouillon used for *truite au bleu*, blue trout. Remove the trout from the court bouillon, cool them, and peel off the skins. Arrange the trout on a serving dish and decorate each with tarragon leaves, sprigs of chervil, and sliced hard-cooked eggs. Coat carefully with cool but still liquid *gelée de poisson*, fish aspic, to fix the decorations. Chill until the aspic is set and cover with the remaining fish aspic. Garnish the platter with tomatoes and cucumbers.

FILETS OF SOLE ORIENTAL IN ASPIC

*Filets de Sole
à l'Orientale
en Gelée*

SPREAD 1 tablespoon butter in a large baking pan, add 1 tablespoon chopped shallot or onion and arrange in the pan 6 filets of sole, sea bass, or other fish, seasoned with a little salt and pepper. Add 1/2 cup each of white wine and fish stock. Lay on the fish a circle of wax paper with a tiny hole cut in the center, cover the pan, and cook the fish for about 10 minutes, or until they are done. Remove the filets to a rack to cool.

Reduce the liquid in the pan to 1/3 the original quantity and add a generous pinch of chopped saffron and 1 tablespoon gelatin softened in 1/4 cup cold water. Peel, seed, and chop 3 tomatoes and cook them until they are soft. Add 1 cup tomato purée, cook 5 to 10 minutes, and add 1 tablespoon finely chopped parsley and tarragon, mixed, and 1 teaspoon chopped chives. Correct the seasoning with salt and add a little freshly ground pepper. Combine this sauce with the gelatin mixture and chill it. When the mixture begins to congeal, coat the fish filets. Arrange the filets in a serving dish, garnish the dish with cooked lobster claws or with shrimp, and cover all with clear fish aspic. Garnish the platter with marinated cucumbers in lettuce nests.

In addition to the clear, transparent aspic, another kind of jelly is used on the buffet froid, *which has all the advantages of aspic plus additional flavor and color. This is mayonnaise* chaud-froid, *a jellied mayonnaise used to coat fish and lobster and to bind vegetable salads and other foods that are improved by mayonnaise, which at the same time offers a gleaming background to set off the decorations.*

Mayonnaise
Chaud-Froid

JELLIED MAYONNAISE

Soften 2 tablespoons gelatin in 1/2 cup cold water for 5 minutes and dissolve it over hot water. Add the dissolved gelatin to 2 cups mayonnaise and stir well.

Filets de Sole
Bayard

FILETS OF SOLE WITH JELLIED MAYONNAISE

POACH 6 filets of sole, or other fish, in court bouillon for 5 to 6 minutes, or until they are done. Remove the filets to a rack and chill them. Coat them thickly with mayonnaise *chaud-froid*, jellied mayonnaise, using about 1 to 1 1/2 cups. Decorate the fish with tarragon leaves and with vegetables or hard-cooked egg cut in fancy shapes and coat with cool but still liquid clear aspic. Chill. Arrange the filets on a bed of mixed cooked vegetables cut in fine dice and mixed with mayonnaise *chaud-froid*. Decorate the platter with chopped clear aspic.

Soufflé
Froid
de Homard

COLD LOBSTER SOUFFLÉ

REMOVE and crack the claws of 2 live lobsters weighing 1 3/4 to 2 pounds each. Cut the tail sections from the bodies and cut the tails crosswise into 3 slices. Split the body sections lengthwise and discard the intestinal veins and stomach sacs. Sauté the lobster meat and the shells in 1/4 cup hot olive oil for 6 minutes, or until the shells turn red. Remove the meat from the tails and claws and reserve it.

Remove the remaining lobster meat from the shells and pound it very fine, or put it through the finest blade of the food chopper. Add 1 cup béchamel sauce, 3 tablespoons sweet butter, and 1 cup liquid aspic. Force the mixture through a fine sieve into a bowl, place the bowl in a pan of crushed ice, and blend it well. Fold in 1 cup cream, whipped stiff. Cut off a few thin slices of the tail meat and reserve them. Dice finely the remaining tail meat, and fold the dice into the lobster-and-cream mixture.

Fold a sheet of wax paper in half lengthwise and butter one side. Tie the paper around the top of a soufflé mold, butter side inside, so that about 3/4 inch of paper stands above the rim of the mold. Fill the mold to the top of the paper. Chill the soufflé in the refrigerator for 2 hours, or until it is set. Carefully remove the paper collar: the soufflé will stand above the rim of the mold, as a hot one does. Garnish the top of the soufflé with the reserved claw meat and slices of tail meat, coat them lightly with clear aspic, and chill the soufflé in the refrigerator again until the aspic sets.

COLD LOBSTER FIGARO

Homard Figaro

BOIL 3 medium lobsters in court bouillon for 15 minutes and cool them in the liquid. Drain the lobsters well, split them in half lengthwise, and discard the intestinal veins and stomach sacs. Remove the tomalleys and reserve them, and discard the gray fringe from the upper body. Cut off the claws, crack them, and remove the meat. Remove the meat in each of the tail sections and cut in 2 strips, trim the edges to give them shape, and reserve both the tail strips and the trimmings. Finely chop the claw meat and tail trimmings and add the reserved tomalleys, 1 cup crab meat, and 2 tablespoons mixed chives, chervil, and tarragon. Add 3 tablespoons chili sauce and 6 tablespoons mayonnaise. Fill the lobster halves with this mixture, arrange the strips of tail meat on them, and garnish the lobsters with thin strips of pimiento, anchovy filets, and capers. Coat the stuffed lobsters with clear aspic and serve them with mayonnaise or green sauce.

RING OF SHELLFISH IN ASPIC

Turban de Crustacés en Gelée

COAT a ring mold with aspic. When the aspic begins to set, arrange slices of hard-cooked egg around the sides of the mold and garnish the bottom with capers and sliced ripe olives. Chill well. Add 1 teaspoon prepared mustard, 1/4 teaspoon Worcestershire sauce, 1 tablespoon chopped parsley and 1/2 teaspoon mixed chopped tarragon, chervil and chives to 2 cups mayonnaise *chaud-froid*.

Combine this with 1/3 cup cooked shrimp cut in pieces, 1/3 cup diced lobster and 1 cup lump crab meat. Fill the mold with the seafood salad and cover the salad with a layer of clear aspic. Chill until thoroughly set. Spread a thin layer of clear aspic on a serving dish and chill it until set. Unmold the salad on the dish and garnish it with tomatoes stuffed with cucumber salad.

Poultry in Aspic

Poularde Rose de Mai

CHICKEN WITH TOMATO MOUSSE

TIE the legs and wings of a cleaned and singed 4- to 5-pound capon, or large roasting chicken, close to the body. Poach the capon in chicken broth only until the meat is tender and a fork inserted in the second joint brings no red juice; the skin and bones should be firm. This will take 1 hour or longer, depending upon the bird's size. Let the bird cool in the stock, then drain it thoroughly. With a sharp knife, detach all the breast meat. With kitchen scissors, carefully cut away the breastbones, leaving wings and legs attached to the back with their skin intact, but the breast cavity open.

Put the bird on a rack to steady it and stuff the cavity with tomato mousse, rounding it up to re-form the shape of the bird. Trim the skin from the breast meat, slice the meat neatly, and arrange the slices carefully on either side of the exposed rounded part of the mousse.

Blanch some tarragon leaves in boiling water for a minute, chill in cold water, and drain well. Decorate the surface of the mousse in an attractive pattern with the tarragon leaves, fresh chervil, and small crescent-shaped slices of truffle. Chill the chicken thoroughly. Spoon cold but still liquid aspic over the chicken so that it makes an even coating. If the bird is very cold, the aspic will congeal almost immediately. Pour a layer of aspic on a cold serving dish and arrange the chicken on it. Chill well and, when ready to serve, garnish the platter with cherry tomatoes, slices of ripe red tomatoes, and small tomatoes stuffed either with whipped cream mixed with horseradish or with a mixture of thinly sliced cucumbers, whipped cream, and horseradish.

TOMATO MOUSSE *Mousse Froide de Tomates*

PEEL 8 large, ripe tomatoes. Cut them in halves and press out the juice and seeds. Chop the tomato flesh and press it through a fine sieve to make a fine purée. Mix 1 cup of the purée with 1 cup tomato juice and season the mixture to taste with about 1 teaspoon salt. Soften 2 tablespoons gelatin in 1/3 cup cold water, then stir it over hot water until the gelatin is dissolved. Stir the gelatin into the tomato mixture and again press through a fine sieve. Stir in 1 1/2 cups heavy cream whipped stiff.

JELLIED WHITE SAUCE *Chaud-Froid Blanc*

SOFTEN 2 tablespoons gelatin in 1/2 cup cold water. Bring 2 cups *sauce velouté* to a boil and dissolve the gelatin in the sauce. Add 1 cup heavy cream and correct the seasoning with salt. Strain the sauce through a fine sieve. Just before it congeals, use the sauce to coat cold chicken, eggs and other foods suited to a jellied white sauce.

CHICKEN BREASTS WITH GOOSE LIVER MOUSSE *Suprêmes de Volaille Jeannette*

CLEAN and truss a 4-pound chicken and simmer it until it is tender. Cool and remove the breast meat. Cut each breast lengthwise to make 3 servings. Flatten and trim each a little to make a neat shape. Spread each one with a heaping tablespoon *mousse de foie gras*, goose liver mousse, smoothing the surface. Chill in the refrigerator. Soften 1 tablespoon gelatin in 1/4 cup cold water for 5 minutes and dissolve it in 2 cups hot chicken *velouté*, and add 1/2 cup cream. Let the sauce cool. Or use 2 1/2 cups mayonnaise *chaud-froid*. Place the breasts on a rack and when the sauce is just ready to congeal, coat the breast pieces well. Chill and then decorate with truffles cut in fancy shapes and tarragon leaves. Place the chicken breasts on a serving dish and spoon over each some clear chicken aspic.

GOOSE LIVER MOUSSE *Mousse de Foie Gras*

USE the following proportions: 3 parts *pâté de foie gras*, 1 part creamed sweet butter, and 1 part heavy whipped cream. Beat the *foie gras* in a saucepan set on ice and then slowly work in the butter, seasoning to taste with salt and a little pepper. Fold in the whipped cream and work all together until the mousse reaches a creamy consistency.

Poularde Virginie

CHICKEN WITH HAM MOUSSE

PREPARE a capon as for *poularde rose de mai*, chicken with tomato mousse. Restore the bird to its original shape by filling the cavity with ham mousse prepared as for ham mousse Norwegian style. Round up the mousse to reshape the bird.

Remove the skin from the breasts and slice the meat neatly. Arrange the slices on each side of the rounded surface of the ham mousse. Decorate with tarragon leaves that have been parboiled for a few seconds, then put in cold water and drained, and with chervil leaves and slices or small designs of truffle. Chill thoroughly and coat with clear aspic. Pour a 1/2-inch layer of aspic in a cold serving dish and place the chicken on it. Let all congeal. Garnish with small cornucopias of sliced Virginia ham stuffed with grated horseradish mixed with whipped cream, and with cucumber salad in tiny lettuce nests.

Poulet à l'Estragon en Gelée

JELLIED CHICKEN WITH TARRAGON

CLEAN and singe a 3-pound chicken. Remove the leaves from 5 or 6 stalks of tarragon and set them aside for garnishing. Put the tarragon stems into the cavity of the chicken, truss it for roasting, and sprinkle it with salt. Lay the bird on its side in a roasting pan and spread it with 2 tablespoons butter. Add 1/4 cup hot water to the pan. Roast in a moderately hot oven (375° F.) for 20 to 25 minutes, turn the bird, and roast it for 20 to 25 minutes longer to brown both sides. Baste the bird frequently with the pan juices and add a little more water if necessary. Turn the chicken on its back to brown the breast. When the chicken is done drain the juices from the cavity into the pan.

Remove the bird to a platter. To the pan add 1/4 cup liquid aspic. Bring the mixture to a boil and skim the fat from the surface. Season the liquid with salt, strain it, and cool it.

Blanched Tarragon

Plunge the reserved tarragon leaves into boiling water for a few seconds. Drain them, plunge them into ice water, and dry them on a towel. When the chicken has cooled, detach the legs and the breast and take out the small bones. Reshape the bird on a rack and coat it with the cool but still liquid pan juices. Chill the bird well, place it on a serving dish, and decorate it with the tarragon leaves. Finish with a coat of clear aspic.

JELLIED CHICKEN MOUSSE

Mousse de Volaille en Gelée

CUT up enough freshly poached breast of chicken to make 2 cups and put the chicken through the finest blade of the food chopper with 1 cup thick *sauce velouté* made with chicken stock. Rub the mixture through a fine sieve and cool it. Gradually add to it 2 cups chicken aspic. If the aspic does not jell, reheat it and add 1 tablespoon gelatin softened in 1/4 cup cold water. Cool until it starts to set. Fold in 1 cup heavy cream, whipped stiff, and season the mixture to taste. Coat the inside of a large mold (or individual molds) with clear aspic and decorate it with truffles cut in fancy shapes. Chill until the aspic is set, and coat again with more aspic. Chill until the second coat of aspic is set, fill the mold with the chicken mixture and chill thoroughly. To serve, unmold on a chilled serving dish.

JELLIED SQUAB CHICKEN WITH GRAPES

Poussin à la Véronique en Gelée

HAVE the butcher bone 6 squab chickens weighing about 1 pound each. Or remove the feet and the wing tips and bone the squabs as follows: Cut down the back to open the bird. With a very sharp small knife detach the rib bones and other bones from the meat, keeping meat and skin intact. Remove the breast bones, still working from the inside, push back the flesh around the second joint, and carefully cut the meat away from the second joints and legs and pull the bones out. Remove the wing bones the same way.

Spread the boned birds flat on a board, skin side down, and season them with a little salt. Spread the center thickly with *mousse de foie gras*, goose liver mousse, and fold both sides over the filling to form a kind of roll. Tie the birds with soft string, tying the legs and second joints close to the body. Roast in a moderately hot oven (375° F.), basting often with butter, for about 35 or 40 minutes. Add a little water if the butter starts to scorch in the pan. Remove the birds to a platter and cool them.

Discard the fat from the pan and add 1/4 cup Sherry or Madeira, 2 tablespoons meat extract, and 1 1/2 cups aspic. Boil the sauce for a minute or two, stirring to combine all ingredients, and strain and cool it. Discard the trussing strings, arrange the birds on a serving dish, and coat them lightly with the cool but still liquid sauce. Garnish the dish with seedless white grapes. Chill well and coat with another layer of sauce.

Caneton à la Montmorency en Gelée

Goose Liver and Rouennaise Mousse

DUCKLING IN ASPIC WITH CHERRIES

TRUSS the legs and wings of a 5-pound duck close to its body. Roast the duck in a moderate oven (350° F.) for about 1 3/4 hours, or until it tests done, turning it from side to side and basting it every 15 minutes. Let the duck cool, remove the breasts and cut them in thin slices.

Prepare *rouennaise* with 1 cup chicken livers. Combine the *rouennaise* with an equal amount of sweet butter that has been worked until creamy and 3 times the amount of purée of goose liver as follows: Work the goose liver with a wooden spoon until it is very light, then gradually work in the *rouennaise*. Pass the mixture through a very fine sieve into a bowl set in a bed of cracked ice. If the mousse is to be eaten right away, add about the same amount of whipped cream as butter. The mousse can be kept for a few days, but in this case the cream should be omitted.

Fill the carcass with the mousse and cover the outside where the breasts were removed with the same mixture, reconstructing the the duck to give it its natural form. Then carefully lay the thin slices of breast meat over the mousse, overlapping them neatly to cover it. When well set, cover with chicken aspic flavored with Port or Madeira and colored light pink with a drop or two of vegetable coloring. Arrange the duck on a flat oval serving platter, surround it with chopped aspic, and decorate it with pitted red cherries and slices of orange.

Or the mousse can be arranged in a mound in an entrée dish and the slices of duck placed on it, then the whole coated with aspic and garnished with cherries.

ENTREMETS

Desserts

MANY EUROPEAN gourmets prefer hot desserts to cold. Mr. Albert Keller, who was president of the Ritz-Carlton in New York, was a connoisseur of international reputation, and to him the perfect end for a distinguished meal was *croûte aux fruits flambés*, the flaming fruit mélange served in a ring of brioche. Mr. Keller was not the only gourmet who understood and appreciated hot desserts. Our experience indicated that emphasis on frozen desserts and French pastries may be the easy way for a hotel to deal with the dessert problem, but it is not always the answer to public demand. I know that men, particularly, are fond of hot desserts, and that the fame of many restaurants in this country rests on their skill with *les entremets flambés*. Furthermore, I maintain that many desserts usually eaten cold taste much better when they are freshly cooked and still warm—among them fruit pies, rice puddings, and baked apples.

The hot dessert is not purely a French tradition, although the dessert soufflés, *beignets*, and crêpes—all dealt with in other sections of this book—and the fruit charlottes of France are superb examples of the genre. I learned in England how much hot puddings mean to the British, and how bare a British Christmas table would be without the flaming plum pudding to crown it. Typical of America's favorite hot desserts are apple brown betty and the fruit cobblers. But in many families, as in most restaurants, dessert is almost always ice cream, cold pudding, or pastry, and the special savor of a hot dessert, its sweet richness enhanced by the piquancy of a burning liqueur, is, sad to say, unfamiliar.

Most hot desserts are served with a sauce, either a fruit sauce, a hard sauce, vanilla sauce, or a sabayon sauce. Charlottes are decorated with fruits cooked in heavy sugar syrup. If you use canned fruit, avoid further cooking that will make it too soft; merely add it to the hot syrup and reheat it. The fruit may be garnished with glacéed cherries and angelica. Sometimes a hot dessert is simply coated with a hot apricot sauce to give it color, luster, and additional flavor. The techniques of flambéing are discussed elsewhere.

Puddings

Croûtes
aux Fruits
Flambés

FLAMING FRUIT RING

CUT stale brioches or sweet buns or coffee cake into thin slices. Place the slices in a baking pan, sprinkle them with a little sugar, and bake in a hot oven (400º F.) until golden brown.

Prepare a macédoine of fruit, using pears, apples, peaches, oranges, cherries, pineapples, strawberries or any desired combination, combining fruits of different colors to make the dish more attractive. Have the large fruits cut into uniform pieces. Make a light sugar syrup by combining 1 1/2 cups water and 1/2 cup sugar and boiling for 5 minutes. Add about 1 quart of mixed fruit and cook for just a minute or two—not long enough for the fruit to become soft. Add enough apricot sauce to give the juice a saucelike consistency and flavor the sauce with rum or kirsch.

Arrange the slices of browned brioche in a ring on a serving dish and fill the center with the hot fruit mixture. Pour hot rum over the top, ignite, and serve flaming.

CHOCOLATE PUDDING

Pouding au Chocolat

IN a warm bowl work 1/4 cup butter with a wooden spoon until it is creamy. Add 1/2 cup powdered sugar and 1/4 teaspoon vanilla extract or a few seeds scraped from a split vanilla bean and continue to cream the mixture until it is fluffy. Work in 6 egg yolks, one at a time. Melt 1/4 pound bitter chocolate over hot water and add it to the creamed mixture with 3 tablespoons flour and 2 tablespoons arrowroot or cornstarch. Fold in 5 egg whites, beaten stiff. Butter and flour a 1 1/2-quart round or oblong mold and fill it with the pudding mixture. Set the mold in a pan of hot water and bake the pudding in a moderate oven (350° F.) for about 45 minutes. Let the pudding stand for 10 or 15 minutes before unmolding it on a serving dish. Serve warm with chocolate sauce.

BREAD PUDDING FRENCH STYLE

Pouding au Pain à la Française

SCALD 1 quart milk with a piece of vanilla bean. Add 6 cups soft bread crumbs and 1 cup sugar. Rub the mixture through a fine sieve. Beat together 4 eggs and 6 yolks and combine them thoroughly with the bread crumb mixture. Fold in 4 stiffly beaten egg whites. Butter a tall 2-quart cylindrical mold, sprinkle it with fine dry bread crumbs, and fill it with the pudding mixture. Set the mold in a deep pan of hot water and bake the pudding in a moderate oven (350° F.) for about 40 to 45 minutes, or until it is firm. Let the pudding stand for about 15 minutes before unmolding it. Serve it hot or warm with vanilla sauce or a fruit sauce.

*Pouding
Stéphanie*

BREAD AND FRUIT PUDDING

SAUTÉ 2 cups bread cut into small dice in 3 tablespoons butter, tossing them in the butter until they are golden on all sides. Add 1 1/2 cups hot milk. Peel and core 2 tart apples, cut them in dice, and put them in a bowl with 1/4 cup finely chopped candied orange peel, 1/2 cup each of powdered almonds, seedless raisins, and sugar, and the grated rind of 1 lemon. Add the milk and bread and mix all together. Add 3 beaten egg yolks and fold in 3 egg whites, beaten stiff. Butter a 1-quart mold and fill it with the mixture. Set the mold in a pan of hot water and bake the pudding in a moderate oven (350° F.) for 45 minutes. Let the pudding stand for about 15 minutes before unmolding it on a serving dish. Serve with red wine sauce.

*Charlotte
de Pommes*

APPLE CHARLOTTE

CUT bread from which the crusts have been removed into enough 1/4-inch slices to cover the bottom and sides of a charlotte mold or deep casserole. Dip the sliced bread in melted butter and line the bottom and sides of the mold by overlapping the slices to give the finished pudding more rigidity.

Peel and quarter enough apples to fill the mold and cook in a little butter until they are soft and thick and all surplus juice is cooked away. Add a little sugar or a little lemon juice, depending on the taste of the apples. Fill the mold with apples and bake it on a baking sheet to prevent the bottom from browning too much in a hot oven (425° F.) for 40 to 45 minutes, or until it is golden brown. Let the mold stand for 5 to 10 minutes after removing from the oven, then invert it on a warm serving dish. Serve the charlotte with hot apricot sauce.

*Christmas
Plum
Pudding*

CHRISTMAS PLUM PUDDING

MIX together 2 cups finely chopped beef kidney suet, 5 ounces each of Malaga raisins, sultana raisins, and currants, 3 ounces of finely chopped mixed lemon peel and citron, 2 ounces of chopped, blanched almonds, 3/4 cup each of fine dry bread crumbs and flour, 1 teaspoon mixed ground cinnamon, nutmeg, and mace with a very little clove, 3 beaten eggs, 1 cup brown sugar, and 1/2 teaspoon salt. Add the grated rind and juice of

1 lemon. Mix all together well and moisten with 6 ounces each of ale and stout and 3 ounces each of rum and brandy.

Fill a well-buttered bowl 3/4 full and tie a heavy muslin cloth securely over the top. Place the bowl on a rack in a large kettle with boiling water about halfway to the top of the bowl. The water should not be high enough to boil over into the bowl. Or put the bowl in a steamer. Cook for 3 hours. Cool the pudding and store in a cold dry place.

To reheat it, put the bowl in a kettle, add cold water to the halfway mark, and bring the water to a boil. Cook for an hour or more to heat it thoroughly.

When ready to serve it, remove the muslin from the top, unmold the pudding on a serving dish, and sprinkle it with sugar. Then pour 2 or 3 ounces of warm rum or brandy over it and ignite. Serve flaming, with sabayon, vanilla, or hard sauce. Or decorate the top with hard sauce piped through a pastry tube. This pudding will serve 12, but it may be divided and cooked in smaller bowls.

CHERRY PUDDING FRENCH STYLE

Pouding de Cerises à la Française

MAKE a syrup by bringing to a boil 3/4 cup sugar and a generous 1/2 cup red wine. Add 2 cups pitted cherries and simmer for 10 to 15 minutes. Drain the cherries, reserving the juice for the sauce. Rub 1 cup dry bread crumbs through a fine sieve and put in a bowl with 1/2 cup butter. Cream together until thoroughly mixed and add the seeds scraped from a 1-inch piece of vanilla bean and 1/2 cup sugar. When well combined, add the yolks of 3 eggs, 1 at a time. Fold in the drained cherries and then 5 stiffly beaten egg whites. Put this into a pudding mold which has been buttered and lightly dusted with fine dry bread crumbs. Set in a pan of boiling water and bake in a moderately hot oven (375° F.) for 35 to 40 minutes. Unmold in a deep serving dish. Add 2 tablespoons apricot jam or sauce and 1/4 cup kirsch to the cherry juice and pour around the pudding.

Custards

H ERE are the procedures to follow for making custards successfully: Use a double boiler to scald milk unless you have a very heavy saucepan and use very low heat. Milk scorches easily, and when scorched it should be discarded. Beat eggs or egg yolks or a combination of the two with a wire whip or a beater, then add sugar gradually and continue whipping until it is thoroughly mixed in.

Soft Custards

In making soft custards, there are two crucial points. One comes when the hot milk is combined with the eggs and sugar; the other comes during the cooking. Never add eggs directly to a hot mixture. Always pour some of the hot liquid into the eggs, or eggs and sugar, stirring briskly, then return this warmed mixture to the remaining hot liquid in the pan. From that time, stir the custard constantly—over the low heat already mentioned—until it acquires body. You can test the custard by letting it run off the back of the spoon; if a light coating clings to the spoon, the custard is done. The French call this consistency *à la nappe*. With experience, you " feel " when the custard has cooked enough. Now remove it immediately from the heat, strain it into a cold bowl, and stir it briskly a few times to dissipate some of the heat. Stir the custard occasionally as it cools, to prevent a surface skin from forming. When it is cool, chill it in the refrigerator.

Crème à l'Anglaise

SOFT CUSTARD

S CALD 1 1/2 cups milk with a 1-inch piece of vanilla bean, and let it stand for 10 minutes to absorb the vanilla flavor. Beat 3 egg yolks light, gradually add 1/3 cup sugar, and beat until the mixture is smooth and creamy.

Stir in 1 teaspoon flour. Pour the scalded milk gradually into the egg mixture, stirring constantly. Return to the pan and cook the mixture over low direct heat or in the top of a double boiler over simmering water, stirring constantly, until it coats the back of the spoon. If cooked over direct heat, remove it from the heat the moment it reaches the boiling point. Remove the vanilla bean, strain the custard into a cold bowl, and stir it briskly. Cool the custard, stirring occasionally; and chill it.

VANILLA BEANS *Vanilles*

VANILLA bean is used in two ways. For soft custard, sauces, and pastry cream, from which it can be removed after cooking, an inch-long piece of bean is split and cooked in the liquid. After the bean is strained out, wash it in cold water and dry it. It can be used again.

After the bean has been used twice, it can be dropped in a jar of sugar to make vanilla sugar to flavor puddings, fruit, and so on. The jar should be tightly closed. Or the pods can be pounded with a few spoonfuls of sugar and sieved with the sugar, to get the last bit of flavor. *Vanilla Sugar*

An extract of vanilla bean can be made by putting 2 split beans into an 8-ounce bottle of Cognac. The alcohol will absorb much of the flavor in a few days.

The trick in making a successful meringue, needed for desserts like floating island, is to beat the whites until they begin to form peaks, then gradually add the sugar. Continue to beat all the while, until the meringue forms firm peaks and all traces of graininess from undissolved sugar have disappeared. To achieve greatest volume, have egg whites and utensils at room temperature. Be sure that there is no trace of egg yolk or other fatty substance on the beater or whisk, for any fat will make the meringue fall. When the meringue reaches the desired stiffness, use a spatula to fold in chopped nut meats, flavorings, or any other ingredient, cutting through the mixture lightly and carefully. Never try to beat them in. Meringue

FLOATING ISLAND *Île Flottante*

MAKE a meringue with 4 egg whites and 1/2 cup sugar. Carefully fold in 1/2 teaspoon vanilla and, if desired, 6 tablespoons roasted almonds or almond praline pounded to a powder, and turn the mixture into a 1-quart or round mold, buttered and sugared, or coated with caramel. Place the mold in a pan of hot water and bake the meringue in a very slow oven (275° F.) for 20 to 25 minutes, or until it is firm. Cool the meringue, unmold it in a glass bowl, and pour *crème à l'anglaise* around it. Decorate with whole toasted almonds.

Oeufs à la Neige — SNOW EGGS

MAKE a meringue with 4 egg whites and 3/4 cup sugar. Using a wet spoon, form the meringue into egg-shapes and slip them off the spoon into a shallow pan of simmering water. Poach for about 2 minutes, turn them and poach them on the other side for 2 minutes. Remove the snow eggs from the water with a skimmer and dry them on paper towels.

Make soft custard with 4 egg yolks, 1/2 cup sugar, and 2 cups milk. Float the meringues on it and sprinkle with grated chocolate or caramel glaze. Or put sliced fruit or berries in a dish and arrange the meringues on the fruit. Pour cold vanilla sauce around the meringues and sprinkle with toasted slivered almonds or grated chocolate.

Baked Custards

THE FRENCH call baked custard *crème renversée*. When it is baked in a mold coated with caramel, which is very popular, it becomes *crème renversée au caramel*. When the dish is simply buttered, it is *crème renversée à la française*. These custards are often served with a chocolate or a fruit sauce. Delicate, smooth and nicely chilled baked custard is delightful.

Baked custards are cooked in a slow oven, 300° F. or less, with the dish set in a pan of hot water. To keep the water in the pan from boiling, a little cold water is added to it occasionally. A baked custard full of tiny holes, or one that separates into a very firm curd floating in a great deal of liquid, has been cooked at too high heat or too long. Use high heat only if the cooking time is very short.

Crème Renversée à la Française — VANILLA CUSTARD

SCALD 3 cups milk with a 1-inch piece of vanilla bean and cool it slightly. Beat 4 eggs, 4 egg yolks and 1/2 cup sugar until light and lemon-colored and add the milk, stirring constantly. Strain the mixture through a fine sieve into a buttered baking dish or individual custard cups. Set the dish or cups in a pan of hot water, cover, and bake in a slow oven (325° F.) until the custard is set and a knife inserted near the center comes out clean. Allow 45 to 50 minutes for a large custard or 20 to 25 minutes for the small ones.

CHOCOLATE CUSTARD

Crème Renversée au Chocolat

COOK 1/2 cup water and 1/4 pound grated sweet chocolate over low heat, stirring constantly, until the mixture is smooth. Combine with 2 1/2 cups scalded milk to make 3 cups of liquid and follow directions for *crème renversée à la française*, vanilla custard.

To make coffee custard, combine 1/2 cup strong coffee with 2 cups scalded milk and follow the directions for *crème renversée*.

Coffee Custard

CARAMEL CREAM CUSTARD

Crème Renversée au Caramel

SCALD 1 cup cream and 1 cup milk with a 1-inch piece of vanilla bean. Beat together until well blended 3 eggs, 2 egg yolks and 1/2 cup sugar. Cool the milk slightly and pour it gradually into the egg mixture, stirring constantly. Strain through a fine sieve.

Melt 1 cup sugar in a heavy skillet over a moderate fire. Gradually add 1/2 cup water and let the mixture boil until the caramel is well blended and brown. Pour the caramel into a 3-cup mold, turning the mold around and around until the inside is well coated. Cool until the caramel is set, pour the custard into the mold and put the mold in a pan of hot water. Bake in a moderate oven (350° F.) for about 45 minutes, or until the custard is set and a knife inserted near the center comes out clean. Cool and chill the custard and unmold it onto a serving dish. If the custard is baked in individual cups, bake for only 25 minutes.

VANILLA CREAMS

Petits Pots de Crème à la Vanille

SCALD 2 cups cream with a 1-inch piece of vanilla bean and 1/2 cup sugar and cool it slightly. Beat 6 egg yolks until they are light and lemon-colored and add the cream, stirring constantly. Strain the mixture through a fine sieve into small earthenware pots or custard cups. Set the pots in a pan of water, cover the pan and bake in a moderately slow oven (325° F.) for about 15 minutes, or until a knife inserted near the center comes out clean. Serve the *pots de crème* chilled.

Chocolate Creams To make chocolate creams, substitute 4 ounces sweet chocolate, melted, for 1/2 the sugar. Serve with heavy cream, plain or whipped.

Fruit Desserts

IN FRANCE, fruit in one form or another is the usual climax to an everyday meal. Peaches, pears, or apples are served whole—washed, well dried, chilled or at room temperature, and arranged in a serving dish or basket. They are eaten gracefully with knife and fork. This is the simplest procedure for serving fruit. Sometimes several fruits are cut up and combined, perhaps enhanced with a little kirsch or other liqueur, a combination that is called a macédoine if the fruit is fresh, a compote if it is stewed. Many fruits go into puddings and tarts, or serve as garnish for other desserts.

Apples grow practically everywhere in France. But the place best known for them is Normandy; an apple tree in bloom with a cow lazily browsing under its foliage is the symbol of the province. More dishes with apples in them appear in the Normandy cuisine than in any other, many dishes that are renowned all over France and in other parts of the world. Normandy cider and Calvados, both made from apples, are the equally renowned thirst-quenchers of that section. Calvados, in fact, has been called " l'âme et le cœur de Normandie. " *Whenever you see* normande *attached to the name of a dish, you can be quite sure either that apples are included in it or that Calvados is the liquor that flavors it. Even the crêpes in Normandy are basted with flaming Calvados.*

For baking, where color and shape are important, choose a red-skinned, firm-fleshed fruit that is neither too sweet nor too tart. The mealy Rome Beauty is a typical baking apple. For sauce, soft-fleshed, very juicy apples of varying sweetness are good; the McIntosh and Cortland are examples. The sour greening is a perfect choice for pies and other dishes where slices of the fruit are cooked in a sweet sauce. The greening has a distinctive taste; it is not at all mealy but firm-fleshed enough to hold its shape in cooking.

POMMES BONNE FEMME

Baked Apples

SELECT 6 large firm-fleshed apples and remove the core without puncturing the skin at the base and leaving about 1/2 inch of apple there to hold in the filling. Make an incision straight around the center part of each apple by slitting the skin with a sharp knife to release the steam without bursting the skin and thus keep the apple in shape. Arrange the apples in a baking dish and fill each center with 1 or 2 tablespoons sugar and 1 teaspoon butter. Put enough water in the pan to keep the fruit from scorching on the bottom and bake in a moderate oven (375° F.) until the fruit is soft and the outside golden brown. Serve with the juice from the pan or combine the juice with some apricot sauce, cook it down a little, and spoon it over the tops of the apples. Serve either warm or cold.

APPLESAUCE

Sauce aux Pommes

THERE are two kinds of applesauce, both of them popular. The first is a very smooth purée, the second a soft sauce that resembles crushed cooked fruit.

For a smooth sauce, remove the black blossom end and the stem of the fruit, and cut the apples into quarters. It is not necessary to peel the fruit, and red-skinned apples will give an attractive, pinkish tinge to the finished sauce. Put the apples in a saucepan with just enough water to prevent scorching and cook the fruit until it is soft, stirring often. Rub the fruit through a sieve or a food mill and discard the skins and pits. Return the purée to the pan, sweeten it to taste, and cook, stirring, until the sugar dissolves. The amount of sugar depends upon the natural tartness of the fruit and the use to which the sauce will be put—it should be less sweet if it is to be served with meat or poultry than as a dessert.

To make a sauce with more texture, peel and core the apples and cut them into eighths. Put the fruit in a saucepan with just enough water to prevent scorching and cook it, stirring occasionally, until it softens and breaks up. Add sugar to taste and cook until the sugar dissolves.

STEWED APPLES

Pommes Pochées

MAKE a light syrup by boiling for 5 minutes a mixture of 2 cups water, 3/4 cup sugar, the juice of 1/2 lemon, and a piece of vanilla bean. Peel and core 4 to 6 apples and cut them in half, in quarters, or in thick slices. Poach the fruit gently in the syrup, basting occasionally or turning carefully, until it is just tender.

CROWN OF APPLES BRILLAT-SAVARIN

Turban de Pommes Brillat-Savarin

MAKE a Savarin ring, that is, baba dough baked in a ring mold. Fill the center with a mixture of equal parts of *crème pâtissière*, pastry cream, and applesauce. Set around the ring apples that have been peeled, cored, cut in halves, and briefly stewed in light syrup containing a piece of vanilla bean and the juice of 1/2 lemon. Drain and dry the apple halves well before arranging them around the Savarin ring. Coat the apples with apricot sauce and decorate the top of the ring with toasted almonds and glacéed cherries. Serve with a vanilla sauce flavored with rum, to which a little whipped cream has been added.

APRICOTS WITH ALMOND CREAM

Abricots Bourdaloue

BAKE a spongecake in a ring mold and remove it from the pan to cool. Drain canned or stewed dried apricot halves and dry them on a paper towel. Overlap them on top of the cake and fill the center with *crème Bourdaloue*, almond cream. Sprinkle with chopped almonds or macaroon crumbs and a little melted butter and brown the dish under the broiler flame. Spread the apricots with apricot sauce and decorate with maraschino or glacéed cherries.

To make the cream, blanch 1/2 pound shelled almonds, discard the skins, and dry the nuts very thoroughly. Crush them or run them through a food chopper, adding very gradually 2 cups water until the liquid becomes milky colored and almond flavored. Strain through cheesecloth. Or 1/3 cup almond paste can be used instead of the crushed blanched almonds, but the almond milk will be less white.

Mix together 1 whole egg, 2 egg yolks, and 3/4 cup sugar. Stir in 3 tablespoons rice flour. Scald the almond milk and add it, little by little, to the egg mixture. Return the mixture to the saucepan and cook, stirring constantly, until it reaches the boiling point. Turn off the heat and stir briskly for 2 minutes. Stir in 2 tablespoons butter and 1 tablespoon kirsch.

APRICOT MOLD

*Abricots
Hélène*

Soak 1/4 pound stale ladyfingers in 1 1/2 cups hot milk for about 10 minutes. Press the mixture through a sieve and add 4 tablespoons sugar and 4 well-beaten eggs. Pour the batter into a buttered and sugared mold and bake in a pan of hot water in a moderate oven (350° F.) for 30 to 40 minutes, or until the pudding is set. Unmold on a serving dish and arrange well-drained canned or stewed dried apricot halves, rounded side down, around the pudding. Fill the hollow of each apricot with a piece of glacéed *marron* or cherry and coat with apricot sauce.

CHERRIES WITH KIRSCH

*Cerises
au Kirsch*

Pit 2 pounds cherries. Crack 2 dozen of the pits and tie them in a cheesecloth bag. In a saucepan put 2 cups dry red wine, 1 cup sugar, and the bag of pits, bring to a boil, and cook for 5 minutes. Add the cherries, cover the pan, and simmer for 8 to 10 minutes. Remove the cherries with a skimmer to a serving bowl and cool. Cook the syrup until it is reduced to 1 1/2 cups, strain through a fine sieve, and cool. Add 3 tablespoons kirsch to the sauce and pour over the cherries. Serve with vanilla ice cream.

Compote de Cerises au Vin Rouge

CHERRY COMPOTE WITH RED WINE

MAKE the following syrup: bring to a boil 2 cups red wine with 1 cup sugar to which a little lemon peel has been added and cook for 5 minutes. Add 2 quarts sweet cherries and simmer for 10 to 15 minutes. Remove the cherries and reduce the syrup to about 2/3 the original quantity. Mix 1 teaspoon arrowroot or cornstarch with 1 tablespoon cold water and add to the syrup. Simmer for a few minutes longer and flavor to taste with kirsch. Pour the syrup over the cherries and cool.

Cerises Los Angeles

CHERRIES LOS ANGELES

PLACE cooked cherries on orange ice, cover with *sauce parisienne*, and decorate the top with spun sugar and crystallized violets.

Cerises Laurette

CHERRIES LAURETTE

ARRANGE cooked cherries on raspberry ice, cover with Cardinal sauce, and decorate with whipped cream and spun sugar.

Bananes Flambées

FLAMING BANANAS

PEEL 6 bananas, cut them in half lengthwise, and sprinkle with sugar. Dip the pieces in flour, in beaten egg, and again in flour. Sauté them in 3 tablespoons hot butter until lightly browned on both sides. The bananas should be soft but not mushy. Arrange them side by side on a warm serving platter and sprinkle them with sugar. Pour over them 3 ounces of warm kirsch, ignite the spirit, and serve blazing.

Poires des Vignerons

PEARS IN RED WINE

PEEL, core, and slice 5 or 6 apples. Cook until soft in 1 tablespoon butter with 1/4 cup sugar and a piece of stick cinnamon. Discard the cinnamon and add 3 tablespoons chopped walnuts. Bring to a boil 2/3 cup red wine, 1 cup sugar, a small piece of stick cinnamon, and a piece of lemon rind.

Peel 6 pears and poach them in the wine syrup until soft. Put the apple mixture in a serving bowl and arrange the pears on it. Cook the syrup until it is reduced to about 1/2 the original quantity, strain, and pour it over the pears. Just before serving, pour over the pears 1/4 cup warmed rum or Cognac and ignite at the table.

MACÉDOINE OF FRUITS WITH KIRSCH

Macédoine de Fruits au Kirsch

CUT fresh fruits, such as pineapple, grapefruit, oranges, apples or pears into slices or chunks. Add sugar to taste, a few drops lemon juice, about 1/2 cup orange juice and 1 or 2 tablespoons kirsch. Set the fruit in a cool place to marinate in the liquid. At servingtime, decorate the top with sections of orange and grapefruit, and a few strawberries or pitted cherries. Serve with cookies that are not too sweet.

CUSTARD RING WITH FRUIT

Crème Sainte-Cécile aux Fruits

SCALD 3 cups milk with a piece of vanilla bean, then leave the bean in the milk for 15 minutes. Mix together 4 whole eggs and 4 yolks, and 1/2 cup sugar until the mixture is smooth. Remove the vanilla bean from the milk, add 3 tablespoons finely crushed almond praline, stir this slowly into the egg mixture, and pour into a well-buttered ring mold. Set the mold in a shallow pan of hot but not boiling water and bake it in a slow oven (325° F.) about 45 minutes, or until the custard is set, adding a little cold water occasionally to keep the water below the boiling point. The custard is done when a small pointed knife inserted near the center comes out clean. Let the custard stand until it is lukewarm.

In the meantine, prepare a macédoine of mixed cooked fruit cut in dice or slices, using any desired combination—pears, pineapple, peaches, cherries, oranges, and so on. Drain the juice from the fruit. To each cup juice, add 1 teaspoon cornstarch or arrowroot mixed with 2 tablespoons cold juice, and cook, until it thickens slightly. For each cup of fruit add 1 tablespoon kirsch, Cointreau, or Grand Marnier, 2 tablespoons puréed stewed dried apricots and the thickened fruit juice. Keep this fruit mixture warm. Invert the custard ring on a serving dish and unmold it. Fill the center of the ring with fruit and pour the remaining juice around the ring. Pour over a little heated kirsch, rum, or Cognac and ignite it.

Les fraises des bois, *as the woodland strawberries are called, grew profusely in the part of France where I was raised. And May was* le mois des fraises *because spring came early to our Bourbonnais countryside.*

Our berries were somewhat larger than the wild strawberries I have had in this country, and more fragrant and flavorful, too, unless my memory tricks me into thinking so. I feel sure, though, that whoever has eaten French fraises des bois *cannot forget how luscious they were. The French themselves have affectionately called them* la petite reine des desserts, *the little queen of desserts.*

We also had cultivated strawberries, which were certainly big and sweet. At my home they came from strawberry plants bordering the garden.

In England and on the Continent straw is usually spread on the ground under the plants to prevent the damp soil from causing spots of decay before the plants are fully mature and also to keep the soil from washing up onto them during rains. Consequently, the berries require very little cleaning. But in this country, where a straw baffle is seldom used, they are sometimes quite sandy. Then cleaning is very important, because there is nothing much worse than getting even the slightest bit of grit in the mouth.

To Clean Strawberries *I clean strawberries this way: Remove the stems and put the berries in a colander or large strainer. Dip this in very hot water for 2 seconds and follow with a quick dip in a pan of cold water. Then give them a final rinse in cold water and drain them thoroughly.*

Strawberries have such a superb flavor that they should be prepared in ways that will best emphasize it and never overpower it by other too-pronounced flavors.

Fraises au Crème d'Isigny

STRAWBERRIES WITH HEAVY CREAM

SELECT large, fully ripe strawberries, wash them if necessary, but do not remove the stems. Put a generous serving of heavy cream in the center of each plate and arrange the berries, sprinkled with a little powdered sugar, in a circle around the cream. Eat the berries with the fingers, picking up one at a time by its stem and dipping it in the cream.

One of the most usual ways of serving strawberries in France, but less usual elsewhere, is au vin. *A light, pleasant wine is preferred. At home we used* les vins du pays, *local wines with a low alcoholic content.*

STRAWBERRIES WITH RED WINE

Fraises au Vin Rouge

SPRINKLE 1 quart cleaned whole strawberries with 3 tablespoons sugar and pour 1/2 cup red wine over the fruit, using a shallow bowl so that they will all be covered. Chill for a few hours before serving.

A more elegant way of serving strawberries with wine, often seen in the de luxe hotels and a pleasant change for a sophisticated party, is with Champagne.

STRAWBERRIES WITH CHAMPAGNE

Fraises au Champagne

SPRINKLE cleaned whole strawberries with sugar and chill. When ready to serve, put them in individual glass dishes and pour Champagne over them.

STRAWBERRIES IN PINEAPPLE SHELL

Fraises à la Créole

SLICE off the top of a large ripe pineapple and take out the fruit, leaving the shell intact. Discard the core. Chill the shell in the refrigerator. Cut the pulp in small dice and mix with an equal quantity of cleaned strawberries. Sprinkle with sugar and a little kirsch and chill. When ready to serve, fill the pineapple shell with the fruit, replace the top, and arrange on a serving dish surrounded by crushed ice. Or slice the pineapple in half from top to bottom, remove the core, and follow directions for the whole pineapple.

STRAWBERRIES JUBILEE

Fraises Jubilé

BOIL 1 1/2 cups water with 1/2 cup sugar for 5 minutes, flavoring with a slice of lemon or a piece of vanilla bean. Mix 2 tablespoons arrowroot or 1 tablespoon cornstarch with a little cold water, add to the syrup, and cook until slightly thickened. Add 1 quart cleaned whole strawberries, bring to the boil, and turn the strawberries and syrup into a serving bowl. When ready to serve, pour over them a glass of kirsch and ignite. This is usually served flaming as an accompaniment to an ice cream *bombe* or a fruit ice.

Rice Desserts

Rice can be used as the base of many cold desserts as well as of hot desserts, and for both I prepare a kind of rice custard that is creamy and light and that lends itself to croquettes, molded puddings, and many other dishes. The dessert is much more delectable than is ever possible when plain boiled rice is the base. In making this foundation, called rice for *entremets*, or desserts, the trick is to cook the rice partially and then rinse it to remove surplus starch that might make the final mixture gummy or sticky. When finishing the cooking in milk, either use a heavy pan and turn down the heat very low or cook the rice in the top of a double boiler to prevent scorching.

*Riz pour
Entremets*

RICE FOR DESSERTS

Wash 1 cup rice in cold water, put it in a saucepan, and add cold water to cover generously. Bring to a boil, turn off the heat, and let it stand for 5 minutes. Drain the rice in a sieve, rinse it with cold water, and drain it. Return the rice to the pan or put it in the top of a double boiler with 2 1/2 cups scalded milk, 6 tablespoons sugar, 1/2 teaspoon salt, and a piece of vanilla bean. Bring to a boil and add 1 tablespoon butter. Cover the pan and simmer very gently for about 1/2 hour or cook in the top of a double boiler for about 45 minutes, or until the rice is tender. Remove the vanilla bean. Toss the rice with a fork to separate the grains and add 3 egg yolks mixed with 2 tablespoons cream, tossing all together carefully with a fork. Spread the mixture on a platter to cool.

RICE CROQUETTES WITH JAM

PREPARE rice for *entremets*, cool it, and shape it into small balls putting 1/2 teaspoon apricot jam in the center of each. Roll the balls in flour, dip them in beaten egg, and roll in fine fresh bread crumbs. Fry in deep hot fat (370° F.) until golden brown and drain on absorbent paper. Serve on hot plates with sabayon or fruit sauce.

Croquettes de Riz au Confiture

APPLES WITH RICE AND MERINGUE

PREPARE rice for *entremets*, cool it, and spread it in an ovenproof serving dish. Peel 6 apples, remove the cores, and cut the apples in halves. Poach them in a syrup containing a piece of vanilla bean and the juice of 1/2 lemon. Drain and dry the apple halves and arrange them on the rice. Beat 3 egg whites stiff but not dry, adding 3/4 cup powdered sugar, a little at a time, to make a stiff meringue. Heap the meringue attractively over the apples or use a pastry bag. Sprinkle with powdered sugar and bake in a hot oven (400° F.) until delicately browned. Decorate the depressions of the meringue with red currant jelly or thick apricot sauce, using a tube.

Pommes Meringuées au Riz

RICE AND APPLESAUCE TIMBALE

PREPARE rice for *entremets* using 2/3 cup rice, 3 cups water, 1 1/2 cups milk, 4 tablespoons sugar, a piece of vanilla bean, 1/2 tablespoon butter, and 2 egg yolks, but no cream.

Fill an unbaked 9-inch pie shell 2/3 full with thick applesauce and bake the pie in a hot oven (425° F.) for 20 minutes, until the shell is lightly browned. Fold into the rice mixture 2 egg whites, beaten stiff. Spread the rice on the applesauce and sprinkle it with sugar. Bake the pie in a moderately hot oven (375° F.) until browned. Serve hot or warm.

Timbale Paysanne

RICE MOLD WITH CARAMEL

WASH 1/2 cup rice in several changes of cold water and put it into a saucepan with 3 cups cold water. Bring the water to a boil and cook the rice for 3 or 4 minutes. Drain the rice and put it in a deep baking dish.

Gâteau de Riz au Caramel

Scald 2 cups milk with a piece of vanilla bean, remove the bean, and pour the milk over the rice. Cover the dish tightly and bake the pudding in a moderate oven (350° F.) for 1/2 hour. Do not stir the mixture.

Cream 2 tablespoons butter with 1/2 cup sugar and add 3 beaten egg yolks. Add the cooked rice and milk, tossing the mixture well with a fork. Coat the bottom and sides of a mold with caramel glaze and fill it with the rice mixture. Set the mold in a pan of hot but not boiling water and bake the pudding in a slow oven (325° F.) for 30 to 40 minutes. Add a little cold water as needed to keep the water in the pan below the boiling point. Remove the pudding from the oven and let it stand for 10 to 15 minutes. Unmold it on a serving dish. Pour a little caramel syrup around the pudding and serve it warm.

PARISIAN HOT RICE PUDDING

Pouding au Riz à la Parisienne

WASH 1/2 cup rice in several changes of cold water and put it into a saucepan with 3 cups water. Bring the water to a boil, turn off the heat, cover the pan, and let the rice stand for 5 minutes. Drain the rice. Scald 2 cups milk and add the rice, 2 tablespoons sugar, a pinch of salt, and 1 teaspoon butter. Cover the pan and simmer the rice gently for 1/2 hour, until it is very tender. Add 3/4 cup *crème pâtissière*, pastry cream, and toss the mixture with a fork. Spread the rice in a shallow heatproof dish, sprinkle it with powdered sugar, and brown it lightly under the broiler. Serve the pudding warm with light cream or thin vanilla sauce.

RICE IMPERATRICE

Riz à l'Impératrice

PREPARE *crème à l'anglaise collée* using the following proportions: 1 1/2 cups milk, a piece of vanilla bean, 4 egg yolks, 1 cup sugar, and 1 tablespoon gelatin softened in 1/4 cup cold water. Prepare rice for *entremets* using the following proportions: 1/2 cup rice, 1 1/4 cups milk, a piece of vanilla bean, 3 tablespoons sugar, and 2 egg yolks. Remove the pieces of vanilla bean and combine the two mixtures. Chill the mixture until it is just beginning to set and fold in 1 cup cream, whipped stiff. Pack into an oiled mold, preferably a ring mold, and chill until set. Unmold on a serving dish and surround it with a sauce made by beating with a fork 1 cup currant jelly and 3 tablespoons rum. Garnish with mixed glacéed fruits.

Gelatin Desserts

WHEN A custard has gelatin added to it we call it *crème à l'anglaise collée*, or jellied English custard. Elaborate molded French desserts called *crèmes* are made with this basic mixture by adding whipped cream, fruit or fruit purées, ladynngers, macaroon crumbs and other ingredients. These must be added after the gelatin has started to thicken the custard but before it begins to actually set. Unless the custard has started to jell, the added ingredients will not be evenly distributed; if it has been allowed to set, the finished dessert will have lumps and streaks of jellied custard through it. It is important to watch a gelatin custard carefully as it cools to catch it at the right stage for folding in other ingredients. If despite your vigilance the *crème* becomes too firm, set the bowl in a pan of warm water and stir the mixture until it softens.

Gelatin Custard Desserts

Rinse the mold in cold water before pouring in a gelatin mixture. It will slip out more easily when unmolded. Chill it for several hours. When the dessert is thoroughly set, loosen the edges with a small knife and turn it out on a chilled platter. If a molded *crème* does not slide out at once, wrap the mold for a minute or two with a cloth wrung out of hot water. Unmold gelatin desserts just before serving them. If they must stand on a buffet for a large party, make 2 small molds rather than 1 large one, keeping one in the refrigerator until the other has been eaten, since the more delectable mixtures soften rapidly at room temperature.

JELLIED ENGLISH CUSTARD

SCALD 1 cup milk with a 1-inch piece of vanilla bean, and let it stand for 10 minutes to absorb the vanilla flavor. Beat 2 to 3 egg yolks lightly,

Crème à l'Anglaise Collée

depending upon the size of the eggs. Gradually add 1/2 cup sugar, and beat until the mixture is smooth. Pour the scalded milk gradually into the egg mixture, stirring constantly. Cook the mixture over low direct heat or in the top of a double boiler over simmering water, stirring constantly, until it coats the back of the spoon. If the cream is cooked over direct heat, remove it from the heat the moment it reaches the boiling point. Remove the vanilla bean, strain the cream into a chilled bowl, and add 1/2 tablespoon gelatin softened in 2 tablespoons cold water and dissolved over hot water. Stir the cream briskly, cool it, and chill it until it just begins to thicken and hold its shape.

VANILLA BAVARIAN CREAM

*Bavarois
à la Vanille*

WHIP 1 cup heavy cream until it is stiff, and fold it into *crème à l'anglaise collée* when the *crème* just begins to thicken and hold its shape. Pour the Bavarian into a lightly buttered mold and chill it for 3 hours, or until it is set. Unmold it on a serving dish and pass a fruit sauce.

CHOCOLATE BAVARIAN CREAM

*Bavarois
au Chocolat*

PREPARE *crème à l'anglaise collée*, adding 1/4 pound grated sweet chocolate to the hot milk and stirring it until the chocolate is thoroughly combined. Follow directions for vanilla Bavarian cream and serve with *crème Chantilly*.

STRAWBERRY BAVARIAN CREAM

*Bavarois
aux Fraises*

CLEAN 1 quart strawberries, mash them, and rub them through a fine sieve or food mill. Add 3/4 cup powdered sugar and the juice of 1 lemon. Stir until the sugar is dissolved. Add 1 or 2 drops red vegetable coloring. Soften 1 1/2 tablespoons gelatin in 1/2 cup cold water, place over hot water, and stir until the gelatin is dissolved. Add to the strawberry mixture. Chill until it starts to become thick and syrupy and then fold in 1 cup heavy cream that has been whipped stiff. Pour into a mold that has been rinsed in cold water and chill until set. To serve, unmold it on a serving dish, and garnish with whole strawberries.

WINE CREAM

Crème au Vin

BRING to a boil 1 cup each of sugar and white wine, and the juice and grated rind of 1/2 lemon and 1 orange, and add 1 tablespoon cornstarch dissolved in 1/4 cup of the same wine. Cook the mixture for 1 minute longer, stirring constantly. Warm 6 beaten egg yolks by mixing them with a little of the hot mixture, then add them to the pan. Cook over low heat, stirring constantly, until the mixture just reaches the boiling point. Strain the cream into a chilled bowl, cool it, and chill it. At servingtime, fold in 2 stiffly beaten egg whites.

CHESTNUT CREAM

Plombières aux Marrons

MAKE 1 cup sweet chestnut purée (with chestnuts cooked in milk and water) and combine with 2 cups warm *crème à l'anglaise collée*. Blend well and cool the mixture until it begins to thicken. Fold in 1/2 cup heavy cream, whipped stiff. Sprinkle 6 ladyfingers with 1 tablespoon rum. Put 1/3 of the *crème aux marrons* in the bottom of an oiled mold, arrange 3 ladyfingers in it, add 1/2 the remaining *crème*, 3 more ladyfingers, and finally the remaining *crème*. Chill until set. Unmold on a serving dish and serve with sabayon sauce to which a little rum has been added.

Blanc manger *has been a popular French dessert for more than two centuries. It is made with gelatin, not with cornstarch or arrowroot, and always with almond milk, a water extraction of finely ground fresh almonds. Flavored with a little rum or kirsch, it is a favorite of French gourmets.*

FRENCH MILK PUDDING

Blanc Manger à la Française

Almond Milk

PREPARE almond milk as follows: Grind 1 cup blanched almonds and 2 or 3 blanched bitter almonds in a mortar with a pestle until they are completely crushed. Work in 2 cups water, a very little at a time. Continue to grind and crush until the water is very milky. Strain the milk through fine muslin, squeezing firmly. Combine the almond milk with 3/4 cup milk, 1/4 cup cream, 1/2 cup sugar, and 1 1/2 tablespoons gelatin softened in 1/4 cup cold water. Bring the mixture slowly to the boil, stirring constantly to dissolve the sugar and the gelatin. Do not allow it to boil. Add

1 tablespoon rum or kirsch. Cool the *crème* and pour it into an oiled mold. Chill, unmold on a chilled serving dish, and serve plain or with cooked fruit.

Cold Soufflés and Mousses

CERTAIN classic desserts are made of mixtures in which whipped cream and whipped egg whites and fruit purées in varying proportions are held in suspension by the use of gelatin in much the same way as in a *bavarois*. These formulas similar to *bavarois* are often called mousses or cold soufflés. One exception is the popular chocolate mousse, and cooks make it in different ways. Some use eggs and no cream, others use whipped cream and only the whites of eggs. A cold soufflé—like a frozen one, a *soufflé glacé*—is usually molded in a traditional soufflé dish with a rim of waxed paper tied around the top, as described in the soufflé chapter. When the paper is removed, the chilled and set soufflé looks like a hot one that has risen above the top of the dish.

COLD SOUFFLÉ RUSSE

Soufflé Froid à la Russe

MAKE a vanilla Bavarian cream: Soften 1 envelope gelatin in 1 cup cold water and dissolve it over hot water. Beat 3/4 cup sugar with 8 egg yolks until the mixture is very thick. Combine the dissolved gelatin with the sugar and egg yolks and add 1 teaspoon vanilla extract. Cool the mixture until it starts to thicken and fold in 2 cups cream, whipped stiff. Line the sides of a soufflé mold with large dry ladyfingers 1/2 inch taller than the mold. Stand the ladyfingers on end, close together. Fill the mold with the Bavarian cream and chill it until the cream sets. Just before serving, decorate the " soufflé " with whipped cream flavored with kirsch and piped through a pastry tube. Garnish the whipped cream with candied cherries and angelica.

CHOCOLATE MOUSSE

Mousse au Chocolat

MELT 1/4 pound sweet chocolate in the top of a double boiler. Combine 1/2 cup sugar with 1/4 cup water and cook together until a little syrupy. Pour this slowly into the chocolate, stirring briskly. Add 4 egg yolks, one at a time, beating vigorously after each addition. Remove from the heat and add 1 tablespoon rum or Cognac. Beat 4 egg whites stiff and fold them into the mixture. Heap the mixture in a serving bowl or in individual serving dishes or in a soufflé dish and chill overnight.

CLEAR gelatins are less often seen on French tables than in this country but they are not unknown. However, they are usually prepared with lemon and orange and flavored with a complementary liqueur or a wine, the *gelée* taking its name from the name of the liqueur or wine used. If a bright color is wanted, add a few drops of red or orange coloring. *(margin: Clear Gelatin Desserts)*

An attractive way of molding clear gelatin is to use several flavors and colors and set them in even layers in the mold, called *gelées rubannées*.

When fruit is combined with clear gelatin, a layer of the flavored gelatin is allowed to set in the bottom of the mold, then the fruit is arranged on it in a pattern and set with enough gelatin to hold it in place. Another layer of the clear gelatin is added and allowed to set and so on until the mold is filled. This is called *gelée à la suédoise*.

Sometimes the *gelée*, allowed to chill only until it becomes syrupy, is whipped until it is light and foamy. If it is flavored with kümmel this is called *gelée à la russe*.

GELATIN WITH LIQUEUR

(margin: Gelée au Liqueur)

PUT the juice of 1 lemon and 1 orange in a quart measure and add enough water to make 3 1/4 cups. Sprinkle in 2 tablespoons gelatin and stir until the gelatin is dissolved. Pour this into a saucepan and add the grated zest of the lemon and orange and 1 cup sugar. Bring the mixture to a boil. Remove from the heat and strain through a double thickness of cheesecloth. When cool add 1/3 cup liqueur such as kirsch, maraschino, anisette, or Grand Marnier, or rum. Mold the gelatin as desired and chill it until it is set.

WINE GELATIN

(margin: Gelée au Vin)

FOLLOW the recipe for gelatin with liqueur, using 2 3/4 cups fruit juice and water and 1 cup wine such as Champagne, Marsala, Madeira, Port, or Sherry.

Frozen Desserts

A FRENCH hostess planning to serve an *entremet glacé*, a frozen dessert, at a party in her own home orders an elaborate *bombe* from the neighborhood *pâtisserie*. Not for her packages of vanilla ice cream and orange ice, *mais non*. Rather an elegant *bombe Elysée* made by lining a high decorative mold with orange ice, then filling it with a vanilla mousse dotted with raisins soaked in Cognac. The shop will probably send one of their eager young *apprentis* to unmold their *bombe* on her silver platter and to garnish it with loops and rosettes of *crème Chantilly*. In this country, where ice cream is so readily available, it is served by many, even at a party, with chocolate or fruit sauce. In France, where ice cream is far from an everyday dessert, one would be more apt to combine fruit with an ice cream or an ice and mask it with a rich, liqueur-flavored sauce to make a dish like *poires belle dijonnaise*.

The elegant frozen desserts *à la française* are the *bombes*, coupes, *coeurs* and *soufflés glacés*.

Bombe   A *bombe* combines water ice with ice cream or a mousse, or ice cream with a mousse. These have complementary flavors and colors. The metal ice cream mold is lined with the water ice and the center is filled with the mousse or ice cream. Mousses are light, delicate mixtures that are not sold in many places, as ice creams are, so you have to make them at home. But mousses are simple enough to make and can be frozen in the automatic refrigerator or home freezer although not quite so well as when they are buried in an ice and salt mixture.

Coupe   Coupes combine ice cream or ices, fruit, sauces, and whipped cream. When served in tall slender glasses, they resemble parfaits; when served in shallow glass dishes they are more like American sundaes.

A *coeur* is a mousse, again homemade, frozen in individual heart-shaped molds. They are served with a sauce and decorated with fruit, chocolate leaves, praline, or whatever will add a touch of elegance.

A *soufflé glacé* is merely a mousse frozen in a traditional soufflé dish. However, before the mousse is poured in, a rim of waxed paper is tied around the top of the dish so that the mixture can extend about an inch or so above the rim. When the mousse is frozen and the paper removed, the height above the dish makes it look like a hot soufflé. I sometimes stand a second rim of paper inside the dish and pour the mousse only between the sides of the dish and the paper ring, leaving the center empty to be filled with fruit after this shell is frozen.

A VERY simple *bombe* can be made at home by lining an ice cream mold with orange or raspberry ice and filling the center with a mousse made on a base of vanilla ice cream. To make the mousse, leave the ice cream in a bowl at room temperature until it is just soft enough to handle, then fold in 1/2 the amount of whipped cream.

The first step in preparing a *bombe* is to have the mold thoroughly chilled and the water ice used for lining it very firm. Spread the ice on the bottom and sides of the mold in an inch-thick layer. Then pack the mousse or ice cream into the center to the very top and cover it with a piece of wax paper and the lid. If the cover of the mold fits tightly, there is little chance of salt water seeping in. An extra precaution is to dip a strip of cheesecloth into melted shortening and wrap 2 or 3 thicknesses around the seam. The cold hardens the fat, thus sealing the mold. Bury the mold in a mixture of 2 parts ice and 1 part rock salt—also called ice cream salt. Or put it in the coldest part of the home freezer or the freezing compartment of the automatic refrigerator. Allow a minimum of 2 to 2 1/2 hours for the mixture to become firmly frozen.

In unmolding the frozen *bombe* on the serving dish, you may need to wrap a cloth wrung out of hot water around the outside of the mold to release the *bombe*. Be careful not to let the metal get hot enough to cause the contents to melt. And have the plate well chilled. *Bombes* are usually quite lavishly decorated with swirls and rosettes of whipped cream, berries, larger fruits poached in a heavy syrup and then drained well, glacéed fruits, or tiny rosettes of meringue. It is an elegant dessert and it must look like one.

Use any 2 complementary flavors and colors. Here are a few particularly popular combinations. *Andalouse*—Apricot ice and vanilla mousse. *Alsacienne*—Pistachio ice cream with chocolate mousse. *Caprice*—Tangerine ice and strawberry ice cream. *Créole*—Pineapple ice and maraschino mousse. *Georgette*—Pineapple ice and praline ice cream. *Lucette*—Raspberry ice and kirsch mousse containing diced, mixed glacéed fruit in kirsch. *Napolitaine*—Strawberry ice cream and praline ice cream with diced glacéed fruits in kirsch. *Olympia*—Peach ice cream and brandy-flavored peach mousse containing diced peaches soaked in brandy. *Sans Gêne*—Apricot ice and kirsch mousse containing white grapes in kirsch. *Traviata*—Strawberry ice cream and lemon ice containing diced glacéed fruits.

French Mousse THE traditional French way to make a mousse is with either a *pâte à bombe* foundation or an *appareil à mousse*. *Pâte à bombe* is a cooked mixture of egg yolks and sugar syrup to which whipped cream and flavoring are added. *Appareils* can be either cooked or uncooked mixtures of egg yolk and sugar to which whipped cream and flavoring are added. The advantage of the cooked mixture is that when the egg yolks and syrup are cooked, they keep in the refrigerator for 2 or 3 days. Then cream and flavor can be added when you are ready to make the mousse. The uncooked egg and sugar mixture, however, must be frozen immediately.

Starting with any of the mousse recipes given below or even starting with sweetened whipped cream, flavors of all kinds can be added. If fruit is used it should be forced through a food mill or sieve to make a purée, and if liqueur is used it must be added with restraint because too much prevents complete freezing.

PÂTE À BOMBE AND MOUSSE

Pâte à Bombe
Pet Mousse BRING 3/4 cup sugar and 1/2 cup water to a boil and cook for 5 minutes. Let the syrup cool. Blend 4 egg yolks in the top of a double boiler and add the sugar syrup gradually. Add some of the fine seeds from the inside of a vanilla bean for flavoring. Cook over hot but never boiling water, stirring constantly, until the mixture becomes creamy and thick. Rub this paste through a fine sieve and cool it quickly, preferably set on ice, whipping it constantly.

For a vanilla mousse, whip 1 pint heavy cream until stiff, flavor with vanilla, to taste, and fold it into the above amount of *pâte à bombe*.

Or omit the vanilla and fold in: 1/2 cup melted and cooled semi-sweet chocolate for chocolate mousse; coffee extract to taste for coffee mousse; or flavor to taste with a sweetened fruit purée—strawberry, peach, and so on—or with a liqueur.

UNCOOKED MOUSSE

Appareil à Mousse I

STIR the yolks of 6 eggs until they are broken up and add gradually 1/2 cup sugar. Beat together until creamy. Whip 1 1/2 cups cream until stiff and fold into the egg yolk mixture. Flavor with the seeds scraped from the inside of a vanilla bean, or with 1/2 cup melted chocolate, or with coffee extract, or with sweetened fruit purée or a liqueur to taste.

COOKED MOUSSE

Appareil à Mousse II

MAKE a vanilla sauce as follows: Scald 1/2 cup milk and 1/2 cup light cream with a piece of vanilla bean in the top of a double boiler. Beat 2 egg yolks light, add 1/4 cup sugar, and combine with the hot liquid. Cook over boiling water, stirring constantly until the mixture has a custardlike consistency. Strain through a fine sieve and cool. Fold in 1 cup heavy cream whipped stiff.

Here are examples of coupes, which show how fruits are combined with ices and ice creams.

Coupes

FRUIT BEATRICE

Fruits Béatrice

PLACE fresh berries or fruit on raspberry ice, cover with *sauce riche* flavored with anisette, and decorate with crystallized violets.

*Figues
Santa Clara*

FIGS SANTA CLARA

PLACE fresh figs, fruits, or berries on apricot ice and cover with apricot sauce flavored with kirsch. Decorate with sweetened whipped cream put through a pastry bag with a fancy tube.

*Pêches
Frisson*

PEACHES FRISSON

REMOVE the pits from stewed peaches and stuff the fruit with vanilla ice cream. Place them on raspberry ice and cover with whipped cream. Sprinkle with chopped praline and, if desired, veil with spun sugar.

*Poire
ou Pêche
Mary
Garden*

PEAR OR PEACH MARY GARDEN

PLACE a well-drained poached pear or peach on a large macaroon. On one side put a small mold of vanilla ice cream and on the other side one of raspberry water ice. Coat with apricot sauce flavored with kirsch. Decorate the top with crystallized violets.

*Poires
Geraldine
Farrar*

PEARS GERALDINE FARRAR

BOIL 2 cups water, 1 1/4 cups sugar, and a 2-inch piece of vanilla bean for 5 minutes. Peel, halve, and core 6 uniform pears and poach them in the syrup until they are tender but not soft. Cool them in the syrup, drain them, and chill them. In individual dessert dishes arrange 2 pear halves with a serving of orange ice between them. Mask the pears with apricot sauce and decorate with whipped cream.

*Fraises
Fedora*

STRAWBERRIES FEDORA

CUT off the top of a huge, very ripe pineapple. Discard the core and cut the pulp into small slices or dice. Mix it with an equal amount of strawberries. Add sugar to taste and flavor with kirsch. Let the fruit stand in the refrigerator for a few hours. When ready to serve, put a layer of orange ice in the bottom of the pineapple shell, then a layer of fruit, a layer of orange ice, one of fruit, and so on until the pineapple is filled. Replace the top and, if desired, veil with spun sugar.

STRAWBERRIES OR RASPBERRIES WILHELMINE

Fraises ou Framboises Wilhelmine

ARRANGE individual servings of orange ice and place cleaned whole strawberries or raspberries on top of each. Mix 3/4 cup cream, whipped, with 1/2 cup crushed raspberries and decorate the top of each serving.

PEARS DIJON STYLE

Poires Belle Dijonnaise

BOIL 1 quart water with 1 1/2 cups sugar and half a vanilla bean for 5 minutes. Skim. Peel 6 pears, leaving them whole, and brush them with lemon juice. Put the pears in the boiling syrup and simmer until they are cooked but are firm, not soft. If a clean napkin or a piece of heavy cheesecloth is placed on top of the fruit (to hold it down under the surface of the liquid), it will prevent the part of the fruit that rises out of the liquid from darkening. Let the pears cool in the syrup.

Fill a ring mold with raspberry ice and put it in the freezing compartment or freezer. When ready to serve, unmold the ice and arrange the pears around or in the center of the ice. Coat with *sauce riche* flavored with prunelle liqueur instead of kirsch. Decorate with crystallized violets and, if desired, with spun sugar.

HEART OF CREAM WITH STRAWBERRIES

Coeur Flottant Merveilleux aux Fraises

BEAT 6 egg yolks with 1/2 cup sugar until the mixture is very thick and pale in color. Flavor with vanilla extract or add the seeds from the inside of a 1-inch piece of vanilla bean. Fold in 3 cups whipped cream. Fill a heart-shaped mold and place it in the refrigerator freezing unit or home freezer. Macaroons or ladyfingers sprinkled with a liqueur may be put in the center of the cream in the mold. When ready to serve, dip the mold for an instant in hot water, turn out the cream into a rather deep serving plate, and decorate it with a chocolate leaf or leaves. Surround the cream with strawberries, washed, hulled, and sprinkled with kirsch, and serve a rich vanilla custard sauce separately.

533

Coeur
Flottant
à la Ritz

MOLDED PRALINE MOUSSE

PREPARE a *pâte à bombe* using the following proportions: 3 cups sugar, 1 1/2 cups water, a piece of vanilla bean, and 5 egg yolks. Discard the vanilla bean and add 1/2 cup almond praline. Fold in 2 cups cream, whipped stiff. Soak a few dice of spongecake in any liqueur and put them in the center of a heart-shaped mold or individual molds. Fill the mold with the mousse and freeze it in the refrigerator freezing unit or the freezer.

When ready to serve, invert the mousse on a serving dish and surround with vanilla sauce combined with a few berries or pieces of fruit. Place chocolate leaves around the heart and sprinkle it with chocolate trimmings. If desired, the dish may then be masked in spun sugar.

Ice Creams and Ices

FINE COMMERCIAL ice creams and ices are available almost everywhere, but homemade ice creams offer great rewards in flavor and variety for the trouble they take. You will need a churn freezer, for the smoothness of these frozen desserts depends upon constant agitation while they freeze. A 2-quart freezer, powered by electricity if possible, is ideal for the average family. Directions for using the freezer come with it, but I would like to emphasize the rules on which really fine results depend. Never fill the metal freezer can more than 2/3 full; the mixture expands during the freezing. Use 3 to 4 parts ice to 1 part rock salt or ice cream salt. Chop the ice rather finely and pack the ice and salt mixture firmly around the can. If you have a hand-powered freezer, turn the crank smoothly and at a regular tempo until it becomes too difficult to turn at all. Then carefully remove the cover, being sure that no salty water is allowed to seep into the ice cream, remove the dasher, and pack the ice cream down firmly. Put a cork in the hole of the cover to seal it and cover the can. Drain off as much water as possible, repack the tub with fresh ice and salt, and cover it with a thick insulating layer of burlap or newspapers. Allow the frozen dessert at least an hour to mellow.

A beaten egg white is frequently added to water ices halfway through the freezing. If whipped cream is to be folded into ice cream, this operation is performed after the dasher has been removed.

If ice creams or ices are to be molded, they can usually be packed in the molds immediately, without standing in fresh salt and ice. The molds should be chilled, to keep the lining mixture from melting.

Too much sugar will hamper freezing, as will too much alcohol, so liqueurs must be added discreetly. For a more distinct liqueur flavor, soak macaroon crumbs in the liqueur and stir them into the frozen cream after you remove the dasher.

To achieve a fruit-flavored ice cream, rather than a plain ice cream studded with icy lumps of fruit, crush the fruit, sugar it, and let it stand until the sugar is absorbed.

VANILLA ICE CREAM

Glace Vanille

BRING to a boil 1 1/3 cups milk and 2 2/3 cups cream with a piece of split vanilla bean. Beat 8 egg yolks and 1 cup sugar with a wire whip until the mixture is smooth and creamy. Pour the hot milk mixture over the egg yolks, stirring briskly, then cook over very low heat until the custard almost reaches the boiling point. Be careful that it does not boil or it will curdle. Strain the custard through a fine sieve and chill quickly. Freeze as described above. If desired, 1 cup cream, whipped, may be folded into the ice cream after the dasher is removed.

Glace au Chocolat—CHOCOLATE ICE CREAM. Make vanilla ice cream with 6 egg yolks. Stir 1/4 cup each of cocoa and grated sweet chocolate into the scalded milk and stir the mixture well.

Glace aux Pêches—PEACH ICE CREAM. Make vanilla ice cream, adding to adding to the mixture before it is frozen 1 pint strawberries, crushed and mixed with 1/4 cup sugar and allowed to stand for 1 hour.

Glace aux Fraises—STRAWBERRY ICE CREAM. Make vanilla ice cream, the mixture before it is frozen 1 pint fresh peaches, crushed and mixed with 1/4 cup sugar and allowed to stand for at least 1 hour.

Glace au Praliné—PRALINE ICE CREAM. Make vanilla ice cream, adding to the mixture before it is frozen 1 cup finely crushed praline.

ORANGE ICE

Glace à l'Orange

DISSOLVE 1 cup sugar in 2 cups water, bring the mixture to a boil, and cook the syrup for 5 minutes. Add 3 cups orange juice and 1/4 cup lemon juice. Cool the mixture and freeze it in a churn freezer as described above. When the mixture is half frozen, add 1 egg white, beaten stiff.

Glace au Citron—LEMON ICE. Follow the directions for orange ice, but use 2 cups sugar, 5 cups water, and 1 cup lemon juice.

Glace à l'Ananas—PINEAPPLE ICE. Follow the directions for orange ice, but use 1/2 cup sugar, 2 1/2 cups water, and 2 1/2 cups crushed fresh or canned pineapple, and 2 tablespoons lemon juice.

Glace aux Framboises ou aux Fraises—RASPBERRY OR STRAWBERRY ICE. Follow the directions for orange ice, cooking 1 1/2 cups sugar in 3 cups water and adding 3 cups fruit purée, made by crushing the fruit and rubbing it through a sieve, and 2 tablespoons lemon juice.

FROZEN TANGERINE DESSERT

Mandarines Givrées

ALLOW 1 tangerine for each serving. Cut off a slice from the tops and reserve them. Remove all the pulp from the shells with a spoon and reserve the shells. Put the juice of 3 oranges into a 2-cup measure, add the juice squeezed from the tangerine pulp and enough more tangerine juice to make 2 cups. Cut off the zest (the very thin surface skin without any of the white underneath part) from 4 tangerines and 2 oranges. Dissolve 2 cups sugar in 1 1/2 cups water, bring to the boil and cook for 5 minutes, add the zest and let it cool. Add the fruit juice and, if desired, 1 or 2 drops red and yellow coloring. Strain the mixture and freeze. When frozen fold in 2 egg whites beaten stiff with 2 tablespoons sugar. Fill the tangerine shells with the ice, place the tops on them and put in a freezer until ready to serve. Or arrange them carefully in a rather shallow pan that can be tightly closed and pack about an inch of ice and salt around them.

BAKED ALASKA

Omelette Norvégienne en Surprise

FIRMLY pack a 1-quart mold with any desired flavor, or 2 flavors, of ice cream, and leave it in the freezer until it is very hard. Beat 5 egg whites until they form peaks and gradually beat in 1 1/4 cups confectioners' sugar, a tablespoon at a time. Cover a wooden board with brown paper and on it place a layer of spongecake 1 inch thick and 1 to 1 1/2 inches larger than the mold of ice cream. Unmold the ice cream onto the center of the spongecake. If desired, the sides and top of the ice cream may also be covered with pieces of spongecake cut to fit. Cover ice cream and cake carefully with a thick layer of meringue. Quickly pipe the remaining meringue through a pastry tube. Dredge the meringue with granulated sugar and bake the Alaska in a very hot oven (450° F.) for 5 minutes, or until the meringue is delicately brown. If necessary, turn the board to brown the meringue evenly. Quickly slide the baked Alaska onto a chilled platter and serve.

Dessert Sauces

CATERING to the American taste for sweets requires an agile hand with *les entremets riches et délicieux*, and with the sauces that are the final flourish for so many of these dessert masterpieces.

Fortunately, one can approach French sweet sauces as one does the entrée sauces: when the basic types have been mastered, the variations offer few problems.

The first of the sweet sauces is the simple, smooth one called soft custard sauce or vanilla sauce in English and *sauce vanille* in French. Its outstanding characteristic, a uniquely velvety smoothness, depends upon its being made correctly, and I suggest that you read the directions given for *crème à l'anglaise,* that is, soft custard, in the section on desserts before you make *sauce vanille* for the first time.

Sauce Vanille   SOFT CUSTARD SAUCE OR VANILLA SAUCE

SCALD 1 cup milk, 1 cup cream, and a 3-inch piece of vanilla bean in a double boiler. Beat 4 or 5 egg yolks and 1/2 cup sugar together until light and combine them with the hot milk and cream, stirring vigorously with a whip. Cook the mixture over gently boiling water, stirring constantly, until it is thick enough to coat the spoon. Strain the sauce through a fine sieve and cool, stirring occasionally. For a thicker sauce add 1/2 teaspoon flour to the sugar and egg yolks. This sauce can be kept for one or two days in the refrigerator. For a lighter and richer sauce, fold in, just before serving, 1/4 cup cream, whipped. Do not store the sauce after the cream is added.

Many sauce recipes call for rum or liqueur, but be careful not to overdo. A little liqueur goes a long way as flavoring; too much can ruin the sauce.

Sauce Riche   RICH SAUCE

MIX 1/2 cup vanilla sauce with about 1/4 cup any desired cordial or liqueur and fold in 1/2 cup cream, whipped.

Sauce Rhum   RUM SAUCE

FOLLOW the recipe for *sauce riche,* using rum instead of liqueur.

Sauce Grand Marnier   GRAND MARNIER SAUCE

FOLLOW the recipe for *sauce riche,* using Grand Marnier.

PARISIAN SAUCE   *Sauce à la Parisienne*

MIX 1/2 cup vanilla sauce with 1/2 cup puréed fresh strawberries (wild strawberries, if possible) and add 1/4 cup maraschino liqueur. Fold in 1 cup cream, whipped, and add a drop of red vegetable coloring to tint the sauce pink.

Coffee flavor for sauce moka *can be quickly achieved by using bottled coffee extract or a little instant coffee dissolved in a tablespoon of hot water. But for coffee flavor that is delicate and definite at the same time, use coffee beans.*   Coffee Flavor

COFFEE SAUCE   *Sauce Moka*

HEAT 2 tablespoons roasted coffee beans in a hot oven (450° F.) for 3 to 4 minutes—just long enough to heat them through and release their flavor. Crush the hot beans coarsely and add them to 1 cup milk and and 1 cup cream. Bring the milk to a boil and strain it. Use this liquid to make vanilla sauce but omit the vanilla bean.

RUM COFFEE SAUCE   *Sauce Moka au Rhum*

ADD 2 tablespoons rum to *sauce moka* and when it is cold, fold in 1/4 cup cream, whipped.

Although there are scores of different chocolate sauces only 2 kinds are regularly used in French cuisine. The first one, made with sauce vanille, *is served cold with such desserts as vanilla soufflé or* bavarois. *The other, a thin mixture of chocolate, sugar, and water, is served warm on profiteroles or ice cream.*

THICK CHOCOLATE SAUCE   *Sauce au Chocolat I*

DISSOLVE 3 to 4 ounces sweet cooking chocolate or 2 ounces baking chocolate in 2 to 3 tablespoons hot water; 2 tablespoons sugar may be added to the baking chocolate, if desired. Mix well and add slowly to 2 cups vanilla sauce. Serve cold.

Sauce au Chocolat II THIN CHOCOLATE SAUCE

ADD 2 cups water to 1 pound grated sweet cooking chocolate. Bring the liquid to a boil and cook it, stirring until the chocolate melts. Rub the sauce through a fine sieve. Serve warm.

Sabayon is served as a dessert, as well as a dessert sauce. In Italy, it is called zabaglione, *and is perhaps better known by its Italian name. Sabayon requires the same care in the making as does* sauce hollandaise, *to prevent curdling.*

Sabayon SABAYON SAUCE

IN the top of a double boiler, over cold water, whip together 4 egg yolks and 2/3 cup sugar until the mixture is very light and fluffy. Stir in 1 cup white wine or marsala. Cook over moderate heat, stirring constantly with a whip, until the water in the bottom reaches the boiling point or until the mixture becomes creamy and thickened. Add about 1 tablespoon rum or kirsch. Serve hot with pudding soufflé, English plum pudding, or any other warm pudding dessert. Or set the pan in a bowl of chopped ice, stir the mixture until it cools, chill, and serve as a dessert with ladyfingers.

For the starchy desserts like rice puddings and beignets soufflés *and also for cooked fruits, fruit sauces made with fruit purée or with fruit juice thickened with arrowroot or cornstarch are preferred. The most important and versatile of the fruit sauces is apricot sauce.*

Apricot sauce is used as a dessert sauce and in scores of ways. It makes an excellent glaze for fruit tarts and other fruit desserts, and it improves other sauces by giving them du corps *or body.*

I learned the importance of apricot sauce early in my career. And learned, too, the hazards of making it. The hot, syrupy paste must be stirred constantly as it cooks, for it is so thick and heavy that it can scorch in a second and ruin the flavor of the entire batch. The newest boy in the restaurant kitchen was always given the task of pushing the wooden spatula around the big copper pan, and inevitably received his baptism when the paste jumped out of the pan in thick, hot bubbles.

Apricot sauce can be made either from apricot jam or from dried apri-

cots. It may be flavored with liqueur, and it will keep for several weeks in a closed jar if the surface is always kept covered with a little of the same liqueur.

APRICOT SAUCE I   *Sauce à l'Abricot I*

RINSE 1/2 pound dried apricots and soak them in water to cover for several hours. Bring the water to a boil and simmer the apricots until they are soft. Rub the fruit through a sieve and add 1/2 cup sugar. Return the pan to the heat and cook until the sugar is dissolved. If the mixture is too thick, stir in a little water and continue to cook the sauce until it is smooth.

APRICOT SAUCE II   *Sauce à l'Abricot II*

MIX together 1 1/2 cups apricot jam, 1/2 cup water, and 2 tablespoons sugar. Bring the sauce to a boil and cook it for 5 to 10 minutes, stirring it to keep it from scorching. Rub the sauce through a sieve and add 1 to 2 tablespoons kirsch, brandy, or any liqueur.

RED WINE SAUCE   *Sauce au Vin Rouge*

BOIL 1 cup red wine with 2 tablespoons sugar for 2 or 3 minutes and add 3 tablespoons thick purée of cooked dried apricots or apricot jam. Serve the sauce warm.

FRUIT SAUCE   *Sauce aux Fruits*

COMBINE 2 cups of any desired fruit juice with 1 teaspoon lemon juice and 2 teaspoons cornstarch mixed to a paste with a little cold fruit juice. Simmer the sauce until it is thick and clear, about 5 minutes, and add sugar to taste.

RASPBERRY
OR STRAWBERRY SAUCE   *Sauce aux Framboises ou aux Fraises*

BRING to a boil equal parts of raspberry or strawberry juice and melted red currant jelly. Thicken by adding 1 teaspoon cornstarch or arrowroot mixed with a little cold juice for each cup of mixed fruit juice. Boil until the sauce is clear and thickened.

Sauce Cardinale   CARDINAL SAUCE

MIX together 1 cup mashed raspberries and 1 cup mashed strawberries.·
Add 1 cup sugar mixed with 1 teaspoon cornstarch. Bring the sauce
to a boil and cook it until it is thickened. Rub through a fine sieve.

Sauce Jubilé   CHERRY SAUCE

COOK 1 cup of the syrup from canned black Bing cherries until it is reduced to 3/4 cup. Thicken with 1 teaspoon arrowroot or cornstarch
mixed with a little cold juice. Boil the sauce until it is clear and thick
and pour it over the cherries. Add 1/4 cup warmed Cognac or kirsch at
servingtime and ignite it.

*Hard sauces are always served on hot desserts. They should be chilled so
that the butter becomes very firm, thus taking longer to melt.*

Beurre au Cognac   HARD SAUCE

CREAM 1/2 cup sweet butter and add gradually 1 cup confectioners' sugar.
Flavor with a few drops of any desired liquor for flavoring: brandy, Co-
gnac, rum, Bénédictine, Sherry, cherry brandy, Cointreau, and so on.
Chill before serving.

Whipped cream and crème Chantilly, *often used with desserts, are dealt with
in the section on cake and pastry decoration.*

Caramel syrup, used to coat the molds in which crème renversée *and
similar desserts are baked, is also described in that section. When the
dessert is unmolded, the caramel coating serves as a sauce. Its burnt-
sugar flavor makes it a perfect contrast for the blandness of custards
and rice puddings. Puddings not baked with caramel syrup are sometimes served with caramel sauce.*

Sauce Caramel   CARAMEL SAUCE

ADD a little water to caramel syrup and cook it, stirring constantly, until
the sauce is well blended and thickened.

PAINS, PÂTISSERIES, ET GÂTEAUX

Bread, Pastries, and Cakes

THE MOST IMPORTANT citizen of a French community is, I sometimes think, not the mayor, or the doctor, or even the *curé*, but
the baker. Do you remember the film of several years ago, *The
Baker's Wife*? It describes the desperate predicament of a small town
when the baker, unhappy because of his wife's infidelity, goes on strike.
The townspeople rally to set the baker's affairs straight so they can persuade him to return to his ovens. The story is perhaps a little exagger-
ated, but I cannot imagine what we should do without the long, narrow
loaves and the crusty dinner rolls of *le boulanger*.

In rural areas far from the towns, each farm has a large brick oven, constructed outdoors. To save fuel, always a problem in France, only one oven is heated each week, on an alternating schedule, and all the families in the area bring their bread to be baked together. But in the towns, practically all baked goods are purchased at the shops.

When I was a boy in Montmarault, my mother sent me almost every day to buy a pound or a half pound of bread, and I remember with what fascination I watched the *boulanger* slash the huge, round country-style loaf with his knife, and then cut a notch in the stick I carried to record each purchase. At the end of the month, my mother would pay for each notch, and the baker acknowledged receipt by rubbing the stick smooth with coarse sandpaper. It was perhaps a quaint way of keeping books, but it served our purpose.

You will not find bread and cakes in the same shop in France. The two professions are jealously kept separate. A *boulanger* may make *brioche* and *croissants*, but a *pâtissier*, a pastry chef, makes only *gâteaux, petits fours*, tarts, and other sweet pastries, and has nothing at all to do with bread.

Larger *pâtisseries* are also catering establishments, and make forcemeat for quenelles, game pâtés, frozen mousses and *bombes*, filled *vol-au-vent* and *bouchées* of puff paste, and other specialties for important parties. La Maison Calondre in Moulins, where I commenced my apprenticeship as a chef, was that kind of *pâtisserie*.

The shop was on rue de l'Evèché (and, as a matter of fact, it is still there), its doorway flanked by sparkling window displays of enticing sweet goods. Inside, the shop was furnished with marble counters, round marble-topped tables and little iron chairs. It gleamed with mirrored walls and shining nickel plate and was very elegant indeed. Madame Calondre was in charge of the shop. She had been born and raised in Moulins and knew all the local gentry. In fact, she would "*tutoyer*" even the highest of the *haut monde*: that is, she used the more intimate "*tu*" instead of the formal "*vous.*" It was she who advised customers on the selection of foods for their parties, and directed the two apple-cheeked country girls who helped in the shop. Madame was the front.

But in back of this retail shop was our big *laboratoire*, the kitchen where we apprentices worked. This was the domaine of Monsieur Calondre, our instructor. It boasted a row of the best ranges, a gas-driven mixing machine, fine long work counters, and shelves galore on which were stacked hundreds of large and small baking tins and molds, and tubes of every shape and size for the pastry bags. All the equipment one could need for fine cooking was there, and my father could not have chosen a better place for me to begin my studies as a chef.

I learned the many kinds of baking—the breads, pastries, and *gâteaux*—in no logical order. An apprenticeship is a working arrangement, and I began by learning to make whatever was most in demand. But to help you to understand and follow the recipes, I have divided the subject of baking into several parts: yeast doughs, pastry doughs or *pâtes*, *gâteaux grands* (large cakes, sponge roll, and meringues), and *gâteaux petits* (small cakes, cookies, and tarts). As in other fields of cookery, when one has mastered the fundamental rules and skills, the variations are easy to learn.

Yeast Doughs

MAKING YEAST DOUGH requires a special skill, *mais oui*. But what is more important is acquiring the " feel " of what you are doing. For example, it is next to impossible to give exact measurements or weights for the flour needed in certain recipes because flours vary so greatly. Therefore the amount specified is only approximate, usually a little less than will probably be needed. The " feel " of the dough—how it sticks to the hands or board—must tell you whether or not to add more. How long to knead is also judged by the " feel " of the dough; it has been worked enough when it is smooth and springy and no longer sticks to the board.

The ingredients for yeast doughs are few and simple. For plain bread and rolls only 3, yeast, flour, and a liquid, are essential, but usually small amounts of sugar and shortening are included. Richer yeast products, such as sweet buns, Danish pastry, brioches, *croissants, savarins,* and *babas,* use more shortening and sugar, and usually eggs, plus raisins, spices, nuts, and the like.

Yeast dough differs from other flour mixtures in that it is kneaded, and must be left covered in a warm place long enough for it to rise and become light. There are various ways to knead. I believe the simplest is to toss the ball of dough onto a lightly floured board, pull it toward you with the fingers of both hands, and then push it down hard and away from you with the heels of your hands; turn it quarter way around and repeat; and continue doing this until the ball feels smooth and springy and no longer sticks to the board, about 8 to 10 minutes. Sprinkle the board with more flour as necessary. The harder you work the dough the better it is.

Various flours may be used in making bread and rolls but because wheat contains a high proportion of gluten it is possible, through kneading, to develop the texture we want in a good dough. If flour from other grains is used it is usually combined with some wheat flour.

Yeast   I believe anyone who knows what yeast is and understands how it works will make better breadstuffs. Yeast is a living organism that grows when placed in warm moist mixtures and creates bubbles of gas which make the mixture light and porous and greatly increased in size. Excessive heat will kill yeast and this must not happen until it is put into the oven to bake. Also, if the dough is allowed to rise too long it will fall and even turn sour. Yeast dough should be allowed to rise until it doubles in bulk, and at this point it should be punched down, shaped, or baked. In order to help the dough capture the gas and distribute it evenly through the mass, the mixture must be kneaded or beaten, a process which makes the dough elastic and gives it body.

There are 2 kinds of yeast on the market, a foil-wrapped, moist cake that requires refrigeration and a granulated, dry yeast in a sealed foil pack that does not have to be refrigerated. Both kinds work equally well, but experts recommend that the temperature of the water in which the dry yeast is dissolved be slightly warmer than that for the moist cake.

A Sponge   Before yeast can be combined with other ingredients, it must first be dissolved in warm water. Very often the next step is to make a sponge. Add enough flour to the dissolved yeast to make a soft ball, and allow the ball to rise in a warm place. Many French bakers cut a cross on top of the ball to encourage it to rise and drop it into a deep bowl or pitcher of warm water. When the sponge is ready to go into the dough it rises to the surface of the water. I prefer this method for very rich doughs.

It seems to me that everyone who bakes wants to learn to make "French" bread, with its light, porous crumb and tender crisp crust. The only way I know to make this kind of loaf is to use the special flour used by French bakers and to bake the bread in a brick-lined steam oven. These ovens are heated by steam until the bricks have absorbed so much heat that they retain it through the whole baking process. The following recipes for bread, rolls, and *croissants* were used in the old New York Ritz-Carlton, which had such a specially built steam oven. These bread-stuffs are not quite the same when they are made with all-purpose flour and baked in an ordinary household oven, but they will still be delicious. Richer doughs can be made just as well in a home kitchen as in a baker's shop.

FRENCH BREAD

Baguette

DISSOLVE 2 cakes of yeast or 2 envelopes of active dry yeast in 1/4 cup warm water. Scald 1/2 cup milk with 1 cup water and add 1 tablespoon each of sugar and butter or shortening and 2 teaspoons salt. Let it cool to warm and add the yeast and water. Gradually stir in about 5 cups flour and mix well. Toss the dough onto a floured board and knead it until it is smooth and springy and does not stick to the board, adding more flour if needed. Place the dough in an oiled bowl, oil the top, cover the bowl and let the dough rise in a warm place until it doubles in bulk, about 1 1/4 hours. Test the dough by touching it firmly with your fingers. When it is fully risen the imprint of your fingers will remain and the dough will start to fall. Punch it down, pull the edges into the center making a firm ball, cover the dough and let it rise again. When the dough has doubled in bulk, about 30 minutes, toss it onto the board again and divide it into 3 or 4 parts. Shape each part into a long cylinder about 1 1/4 inches in diameter. Place the loaves on a greased baking sheet, cover them with a towel, and let them rise in a warm place until they double, about 30 minutes. Cut 6 or 7 diagonal slits 1/4 inch deep in the top of each loaf when it is half risen. Brush them with milk and bake them in a hot oven (400° F.) until the crust is brown and the bread done, about 20 to 25 minutes.

Petits Pains DINNER ROLLS

MIX and knead the dough for French bread. After the second rising divide the dough into quarters and cut each quarter into 6 or 8 pieces. Roll each piece into a round ball and then into a cylinder with pointed ends. Arrange the rolls on an oiled baking sheet about 2 inches apart, cover them with a towel and let them rise in a warm place until they double, about 30 minutes. Cut 2 or 3 diagonal slits 1/4 inch deep in the top of each roll when they are half risen. Brush the rolls with milk and bake them in a very hot oven (425° F.) until they are brown and done, about 12 to 15 minutes.

Petits Pains au Lait MILK ROLLS

DISSOLVE 1 cake of yeast or 1 envelope of active dry yeast in 1/4 cup warm water and combine the liquid with 1/2 cup flour. Form this dough into a ball, cut a cross on the top and drop the ball into a deep bowl filled with warm water. When the sponge rises to the surface it will be ready to mix with the other ingredients. Into a bowl sift 1 1/2 cups flour with 1/2 teaspoon salt and 1 tablespoon sugar. Knead 1/4 pound butter to remove any water in it and to soften it. Heat 1 cup milk to lukewarm. Add the butter and some of the milk to the flour and work the dough with the hands until it is elastic, adding enough milk to make a rather soft dough. Add the sponge that has risen to the surface of the water to the dough in the bowl, cutting and folding it in. Working the mixture at this point would destroy its elasticity. Form it into a ball, cover it with a towel and let it rise until double in bulk. Toss it onto a board and punch it down, pulling the edges into the center and making a large ball. Cut the dough into pieces about as large as walnuts. Roll each ball on a floured board to make a small thumb-sized roll and arrange the rolls about 1 1/2 inches apart on a buttered baking sheet. Cover and let the rolls rise in a warm place until double in bulk. Brush them with *dorure* and bake them in a very hot oven (450° F.) until they are brown.

Dorure DORURE

TO MAKE this glaze for breads and pastries, beat an egg or an egg yolk with 1 tablespoon water.

Brioche

DISSOLVE 1 cake of yeast or 1 envelope of active dry yeast in 1/2 cup warm water and combine this liquid with 1 cup flour to make a ball of dough. Cut a cross on the top of the ball—to encourage it to swell—and drop it into a deep bowl filled with warm water. When the ball rises to the surface, it is ready to mix with the other ingredients.

Meanwhile, mix and sift into a very large bowl 3 cups flour, 1 teaspoon salt, and 1 tablespoon sugar. Make a well in the center of the flour and into it drop 4 eggs. Mix the eggs into the flour (chefs use their hands for this operation) and work the dough by raising it and slapping it against the sides of the bowl until it becomes elastic—that is, until it develops what is called *du corps*, or body, changing from a limp mass to a springy ball of dough. Work in 2 more eggs, one at a time. Knead 1/2 pound butter well with the hands to remove any water in it and to soften it. Work the butter into the dough and add 1/4 to 1/2 cup milk, or just enough to make a rather soft dough.

When the ball of sponge has risen to the surface of the water, add it to the dough in the bowl, cutting and folding it in. Work the dough into a large ball, sprinkle it lightly with flour, cover it with a towel, and leave it at room temperature for 2 or 3 hours. When the dough is double in bulk, punch it down, pull in the edges, punch them into the center with the fist, and shape the dough again into a ball. Sprinkle it lightly with flour, cover it, and put it in a cold place overnight, or for at least 6 or 7 hours. Doughs so rich in butter cannot be shaped when warm.

Punch down the dough again and pinch off pieces to half fill small or large round brioche molds. Fluted molds are the most usual. Cut a cross in the top and crown the brioche by pushing down into the opening a small ball or head. The brioche may also be baked in a ring mold, or in a loaf pan with a twisted strip of dough for a topping. Let the brioche rise in a warm place for 15 to 30 minutes, or until it has increased in bulk by about 1/3. Brush it with *dorure*, a mixture made of 1 egg beaten with 1 tablespoon milk, applying it very lightly and carefully with a pastry brush so as not to disturb the risen dough. Bake the brioche in a very hot oven (450° F.) for 15 to 20 minutes, depending upon the size, until it is well browned. Test with a steel skewer. If it comes out clean the brioche is done.

To make a brioche ring, roll about half the dough into a long piece (like shaping dough for French bread) and form it into a ring on a buttered baking sheet, joining the two ends together. Let the ring rise in a warm place until it has increased 1/3 in bulk and brush it with *dorure*. With scissors, clip the top evenly and diagonally all the way around the ring to make a crisscross pattern. Bake the ring at once in a very hot oven (450° F.) for about 15 minutes.

Croissants

DISSOLVE 2 cakes of yeast or 2 envelopes of active dry yeast in 1/3 cup warm water, add 1 cup flour and form the dough into a ball. Cut a cross in the top and drop the ball into a deep bowl of warm water. Sift 3 cups flour, 1/2 teaspoon salt and 1 tablespoon sugar onto a wooden pastry board. Make a well in the center of the flour and add gradually 1 1/2 cups warm milk, stirring and mixing it in. Work the mixture until it becomes elastic. The dough for *croissants* should not be as soft as a brioche dough. When the ball of sponge has risen to the surface of the water, add it to the dough, cutting and folding it in. Working the dough at this point destroys its elasticity. Cover the dough with a towel and let it stand for 30 minutes.

Meanwhile, knead 1/2 pound butter with the hands until it is soft and free of water. Roll the dough out about 1/2 inch thick. Form the butter into a flat cake and place it in the center of the dough. Fold one third of the dough over the butter in the center and fold the other third of the dough on top to make 3 layers. Turn the folded dough so that one of the open ends faces front. Roll it out again into a long rectangle, fold over as before and turn it. This classic procedure is called a turn. Make another turn and put the dough, wrapped in wax paper, in the refrigerator for several hours or overnight.

Next day, roll out the dough, fold it and turn. Repeat this operation, making 2 more turns. Chill the dough in the refrigerator for 1 hour.

Cut the dough into 4 equal parts and roll out each part, one at a time, into a circle 1/8 inch thick and about 12 to 14 inches in diameter. Cut the circle, pie-fashion, into 8 triangles. Starting with the base of the triangle, roll each section of dough loosely to form a cylinder thicker at the center than at the ends. Shape the rolls into crescents and place them on a lightly floured baking sheet. Cover the sheet with a towel and let the *croissants* rise in a warm place for 30 minutes. Brush them with *dorure* and bake them for 5 minutes in a hot oven (400° F.). Reduce the temperature to moderate (350° F.) and bake the *croissants* for 15 to 20 minutes longer, or until they are well browned.

DANISH CRESCENTS

DISSOLVE 1 cake of yeast or 1 envelope of active dry yeast in 1/4 cup warm water and add 1/2 cup flour to make a ball of sponge. Cut a cross on top of the ball, drop it into a bowl of warm water and leave it until it rises to the surface. Mix together 3 1/2 cups flour, 1/2 cup warm milk, 1 egg, 2 tablespoons sugar and 4 tablespoons soft butter. Knead the dough until it is smooth and elastic. When the ball of sponge has risen to the surface of the water add it to the dough and work it in. Return the dough to the bowl, sprinkle it lightly with flour, cover it with a towel and let it stand for 1 hour at room temperature. Roll out the dough in an oblong shape and put in the center 3/4 cup soft butter, shaped into an oblong cake. Make 2 turns, as for *croissants*, and refrigerate the dough overnight. Make 2 more turns. Roll out the dough into circles about 1/8 inch thick, as for *croissants*, and cut it into wedges. Put some almond filling and a few raisins on each wedge and roll them up like *croissants*. Let the crescents rise on a buttered baking sheet until they are double in bulk. Brush them lightly with beaten egg and bake them in a moderately hot oven (375° F.) for about 15 minutes, or until they are golden brown.

Work 1/2 pound almond paste with 1/2 cup granulated sugar and 3 eggs until the mixture is thick and creamy. Add 1 cup softened butter, 1 tablespoon cornstarch, and a little vanilla or lemon extract.

SAVARIN DOUGH

DISSOLVE 1 cake of yeast or 1 envelope of active dry yeast in 1/2 cup warm water. Sift 1 1/2 cups flour into a warm bowl, add the dissolved yeast, 2 large (or 3 small) eggs and 1/4 to 1/2 cup lukewarm milk. Work the mixture until it is elastic, adding enough milk to make a very soft dough, much softer than brioche dough. Cover the dough with a towel, put it in a warm place and let it rise until double in bulk, about 45 minutes. Knead 1/4 pound butter until it is as soft as heavy cream. When the dough rises, punch it down and add the butter, 1/2 teaspoon salt and 1 tablespoon sugar. Mix all together well. Turn the dough into a large, buttered ring mold. The mold should be about half full. Put the sa-varin in a warm place to rise. When it has risen almost to the top of the mold, bake it in a hot oven (425° F.) until it is brown, or for about 18 to 20 minutes. As soon as the cake is done, loosen it from the sides of the mold with a small sharp knife and remove it from the mold.

Make a light syrup by cooking 1 cup sugar with 1 cup water for 5 minutes. Add 2 or 3 tablespoons kirsch or rum and pour and spread this syrup over the warm cake. Sprinkle another tablespoon or two of the same spirit over the cake and decorate it to taste with almonds and candied fruit. The top may be spread with apricot sauce. Serve warm.

Pâte à Baba   BABA DOUGH

FOLLOW the recipe for savarin, adding to the dough 2 tablespoons dried currants and 1 tablespoon raisins. *Babas* may be made in deep individual molds or in popover pans.

Gannat   GANNAT

SIFT 1 cup flour into a bowl and make a hole in the center. In the hole put 1 cake of yeast or 1 envelope of active dry yeast dissolved in 1/4 cup warm water, and mix together into a firm dough, adding a little more warm water if necessary. Shape the dough into a ball, cut a cross on top, and put the ball in a deep bowl filled with warm water to rise.

Sift 3 cups flour with 1/2 teaspoon salt into another bowl, make a hole in the center, and add 1 cup butter, 4 to 5 tablespoons Cognac, and 6 eggs and 6 yolks beaten together. Mix to a soft dough and work in 1 cup diced Swiss cheese.

When the sponge rises to the surface of the water, remove it and work it gently into the egg dough. Put the dough in a large bowl, cover it with a towel, and set it in a warm place to rise until double in bulk. Punch the dough down, put it in a buttered round baking pan with sides from 1 1/2 to 2 inches high, and let rise again until it doubles in bulk. Brush the dough with *dorure* and bake it in a hot oven (425° F.) for 40 to 50 minutes, or until golden brown. Or put the dough in narrow loaf pans to rise and bake. Slice cold *gannat*, toast it, and serve for hors-d'oeuvre.

KUGELHOFF DOUGH

DISSOLVE 1 cake of yeast or 1 envelope of active dry yeast in 1/4 cup warm water, add 1/2 cup flour and form the dough into a ball. Sift over this ball 1 1/2 cups flour and let the dough stand in a warm place until the ball of sponge rises up through the flour. Then work in 2 eggs, 1/3 cup butter, kneaded to remove the water and to soften it, 1/2 teaspoon salt, 1 tablespoon sugar and about 1 cup warm milk, or enough to make a soft dough. Work the dough until it is elastic. Add 1/4 pound seedless California or Malaga raisins. Butter an 8- or 9-inch *Kugelhoff* mold—a fluted, round cake tin with a tube in the center—sprinkle the sides with chopped blanched almonds and decorate the bottom with almond halves. Put the dough in the mold (the mold should be only about half full) and leave it in a warm place to rise. When the dough rises almost to the top of the mold, bake the cake in a hot oven (400° F.) for about 40 to 45 minutes, until it is nicely browned and tests done.

*Pastry Doughs
or Pâtes*

IN THE spring of 1899, when my father left me in Moulins, to start my apprenticeship as a chef, I was away from my family for the first time in all my fourteen years. For months—even years—I had been pleading to be permitted to train to be a chef. Now that I had my certificate from our local school and the decision had been made, I was actually on the threshold of a career. But it was a very homesick, very shy youngster trying desperately to appear unconcerned who unpacked his bag in the dormitory to be shared for nearly two years with five other *apprentis*.

All that kept me from bolting was my determination to succeed and my self-confidence. I thought—I *knew*—that I was a good cook. *Mais oui*! Hadn't I watched and helped my gifted mother for years, and *grand-mère*, too, in her big farm kitchen? I was considered quite an expert, especially with soup, the good leek and potato soup which my family liked so well. "*Ah*," they would say appreciatively, "*nôtre petit Louis, comme il est un bon chef!*"

Next morning I donned my new chef's coat and the blue apron which signified that I was an *apprenti*, and stalked proudly into our kitchen workshop prepared to demonstrate my facility at the soup kettle. It was, to say the least, somewhat unnerving to be informed that I would begin my course by making éclairs!

I had eaten éclairs, of course, but they had been purchased—as is usual in France, where *petits fours*, *gâteaux* and pastries are the province of the *pâtisserie*. I had no idea how the crusty little shells were achieved, or by what magic trick the sweet, creamy filling was hidden inside them.

But éclairs it was, for every day of that first week, and many more times as the months rolled by, until my clumsy hands could line up row after row of perfectly shaped éclairs varying hardly an iota in size, glossy with vanilla, coffee, or chocolate frosting, and with not a drop of cream showing to reveal how the filling found its way inside.

Of course, not every cook wants to make pastries. And some cooks are simply not suited to this kind of cookery. The hand that wields a cleaver cannot always manage the tiny paper *cornet* that decorates an inch-square cake. And few chefs can switch successfully from huge soup kettles or mammoth roasting ovens to the delicate pastry tube. In pastry making, one must work deftly, quickly, and with what is called a light hand. The standards for pastry baking are very exacting; variation in the browning of a bird or in the color of a consommé may go unnoticed, but in delectable little cakes even a slight variation may be unacceptable. The aspiring pastry cook must have infinite patience, must be willing to go through every process over and over again until he learns the feel of the mixture at each step.

There are two major differences between the French pastries of this country and those of France. In France there is greater variety in shapes, fillings, icings, and decoration, the pastry chef working as creatively and artistically as a jeweler does in fashioning his metals, stones, and enamels. The second difference is in their size. French gourmets believe that large pastries are the work of a chef of poor taste and inexpert craftsmanship. I remember how infuriated Madame Ritz used to be if the pastries on her tea tray were one iota larger than the size established by the Ritz as being *de rigueur*. And Robert W. Goelet, who built and owned the old New York Ritz and who had lived a great part of his life in Paris, was as adamant about this as Madame Ritz. In the best establishments in France, éclairs are never larger than your middle finger; *napoléons*, *dartois*, and other puff paste tidbits are a mere 3 inches long, fruit *tartelettes* only a trifle bigger than a silver dollar, *petits chaussons* (fruit turnovers) about 2 inches at their longest point. Cream puffs and little iced cakes shaped in squares, rounds, or triangles are just bite size, like a bonbon.

In France, the term "pastry" covers all the sweet cakes, tarts, *petits fours*, *friandises*, and *gâteaux* served at a tea or a soirée, or with desserts, particularly frozen desserts. In America, "pastry" usually refers to a pie or tart of some sort, while other baked sweets are called cakes, cookies, and so on. The French word for the uncooked dough with which tarts are made is *pâte*, or paste, and a French chef thinks in terms of tart paste puff paste, and so on. Incidentally, do not confuse a *pâte* with a pâté, which is a delicately seasoned meat or fish paste. Pâtes

The first *pâte* we shall deal with is the *pâte à chou*—the dough that makes cream puffs.

Chou *paste is one of the easiest and most widely used of all* pâtisserie *mixtures. From it one makes éclairs and cream puffs and all the desserts involving them, such as the* profiteroles au chocolat *and the* beignets soufflés—*sometimes called French crullers in this country. An hors-d'oeuvre called* gougère *is made of* chou *paste combined with finely chopped Swiss cheese, and tiny nuts of* chou *paste are baked to use as a consommé garnish. The famous* croquembouche, *gâteau* Saint-Honoré *and* religieuses *are all made with* chou *paste.*

The pastry tube can be mastered without too much difficulty, and chou *paste is a particularly good choice to practice with, since it is less delicate than whipped cream, for instance, yet not so heavy as some other mixtures. The paste may also be shaped with a spoon, which is simple enough in making cream puffs, but may be more complicated with éclairs. But remember that* chou *paste puffs in baking to four or five times its original size.*

Bake chou *paste in a hot oven, so that it puffs immediately. To discourage overbrowning, the heat may be reduced after 12 to 15 minutes. The puffs must be baked until they are thoroughly dry and feel light in the hand. A puff that is brown outside but still moist inside will collapse as it cools. If necessary, cover the puffs with paper to keep them from browning too much.*

Cream puffs and éclairs are filled with sweetened whipped cream or pastry cream (which in French are called crème Chantilly *and* crème pâtissière) *or with* crème Saint-Honoré, *which includes beaten egg whites and a small amount of gelatin. The shells must be thoroughly cooled before they are filled. To fill them the professional way, put the cream filling in a pastry bag, use the point of a knife to cut a tiny hole in the side of the éclair or cream puff, and force the filling through the little hole. It may be easier, in dealing with large éclairs and puffs, to slit the shell and fill it with a small spoon. Tiny puffs can also be pushed in at the top with a finger to make little tartlets, which are filled with a mound of* crème pâtissière *and glazed with caramelized sugar.*

Traditionally, cream puffs are finished with confectioners' sugar (sometimes the sugar is caramelized by passing a red-hot iron rod like a poker over it). Éclairs are iced with a fondant icing. The flavor of the icing is usually the same as that of the filling—vanilla, chocolate, or coffee.

Pâte à Chou   CREAM PUFF AND ÉCLAIR PASTE

IN a small saucepan, bring to a boil 1 cup water, 1/2 cup butter, 1/2 teaspoon salt and 1 teaspoon sugar. Add all at once 1 cup flour and cook the paste over low heat, beating it briskly and constantly until the ingredients are thoroughly combined and the mixture rolls away from the sides of the pan. Remove the pan from the heat, cool a minute or two, and beat in 4 eggs, one at a time. If the eggs are unusually small, add an extra one.

Cream Puffs To form cream puffs, drop the paste from a teaspoon or tablespoon, or force it through a pastry bag into balls onto a greased baking sheet, allowing space for expansion between the shapes.

Éclairs To make éclairs, use a pastry bag with a plain round tube. Force the mixture through the bag to make strips 3 1/2 to 4 inches long and 1 inch wide or 2 inches long and 1/2 inch wide, depending upon the size desired.

Profiteroles To make *profiteroles*, drop the paste in small balls, about the size of small walnuts.

Ring To make a ring, shape the paste on the baking sheet with a spoon.

To glaze the top, brush it with *dorure*. Bake the shells in a hot oven (425° F.) for 15 to 18 minutes, reduce the heat to moderate (375° F.) and bake until they are golden brown and feel light in the hand.

IN la cuisine française, *different* pâtes *are used for different types of pies and tarts, not the same "flaky pie dough" for everything, as is often the practice of American cooks. The* pâtissier *chooses a sweetened pastry for very juicy fruits because it absorbs less moisture.* Tourtes, *as double-crust pies are called, use another kind of pastry and meat pies and* pâtés *still another. But it is puff paste that is the pride of all French pastry cooks, a pastry that swells into a light, unbelievably delicate, flaky crispness and that has almost as many uses as it has layers. Puff paste is called* pâte feuilleté, feuilletage, *or* mille-feuille. *The word* feuille *means leaf.* Napoléons, *tarts, fancy* petits fours, bouchées—*tiny puff paste shells--and* vol-au-vent—*large shells for sauced meats and sea foods—all are made of puff paste. The rule followed by pastry chefs is not to use puff paste for heavy fillings such as fruits with sugar or heavy meat mixtures, particularly if they are to be baked in the crust, because their weight would crush the delicate flaky layers. Puff paste shells are first baked and then filled with light pastry creams, sometimes topped with fresh fruit.*

There are 3 important points in making puff paste: the ingredients must always be cold, a minimum amount of water should be used, and the mixture must be handled very, very lightly and as little as possible.

Be sure to follow the recipe meticulously and be especially careful about chilling the paste as indicated in the recipes. And do not discard even a scrap of the trimmings—they can be used to make wonderful little "extras." Roll them lightly into a ball and use them to make tartelette *shells, meat-pie crusts, or palm leaf cookies. Or cut the puff paste into exquisite little crescents or diamond shapes, and use them to garnish elaborate* plats.

PUFF PASTE

Pâte
Feuilleté

SIFT 4 cups flour and 1 teaspoon salt into a bowl or in a mound on a pastry board, make a well in the center, and add 1 cup very cold water. Mix together carefully and gently, taking care not to "work" the dough, and add another 1/2 cup water or as much more as is needed to make a fairly firm paste, which must not have any elasticity but should be moist enough to permit rolling it out easily without having to force or work it. Form the paste into a ball and chill it for 15 minutes.

Knead 1 pound sweet butter with the hands, working it in a bowl of ice water if it starts to soften. Squeeze out all the water. The butter should be pliable and waxy, not soft or creamy, and should be the same consistency as the dough. Put the chilled ball of dough on a lightly flour-ed board and roll it into a square about 1/4 inch thick. Put the butter in the center of the square, flattening it slightly. Fold all four sides of the dough over the butter to encase it completely. Wrap the package in a towel or plastic wrap and chill it in the refrigerator for 25 minutes. Roll the dough into a rectangle 20 inches long and 1/2 inch thick. Fold the rectangle into thirds and turn it so that the open edge faces you. The dough must always be in this position for rolling. Roll the folded dough into a rectangle again. This operation of folding, turning and rolling

Turn out is called a "turn." Fold the dough into thirds once again, refriger-ate it for 25 minutes, and roll it out into a rectangle, fold it, and roll and fold it again, thus completing 2 more turns, or 4 in all. Wrap the paste and chill it for 25 minutes in the refrigerator.

In order to finish the puff paste, 2 more turns will be required. If the pastry is to be baked right away, the last 2 turns are made at this point. However, the paste can be made up ahead and be stored in the refrigerator for several days before it is baked. If this is to be done, wrap the dough very closely in plastic wrap and put it in the refrig-erator. Make the final 2 turns when you are ready to shape the pastries. After the final 2 turns, roll the dough to a thickness of 1/8 to 1/4 inch, depending upon how it is to be used. For baking, use a very heavy pan, lightly moistened. Cut the paste into the desired shape. Flip each piece when placing it on the pan, so that the side that was uppermost is face down on the moistened pan. Let the paste stand for 15 minutes and bake until brown on the lowest rack of a hot oven (425° F.).

The secret of a tender tart paste is to add as little water as possible, just enough to hold the particles of flour and butter together, and to handle the mixture as little as possible. The ingredients and utensils should be chilled, and the dough should be chilled before it is rolled out and again before it is baked. Tart pastes are always baked at a high temperature until the dough is firm and set.

TART PASTRY

*Pâte Sucrée
ou Pâte
à Flan*   SIFT 1 cup flour into a bowl or in a mound on the pastry board. Make a well in the center and put in it 1/4 cup creamed butter, 5 tablespoons sugar, a little salt and 1 egg. Mix all together by gradually pulling the

flour into the ingredients in the center. If the mixture is too stiff to roll out, add a few drops of water. Chill the paste for several hours before using it. For an open 9-inch tart.

PASTRY FOR TWO-CRUST PIES

Pâte à Tourte

CUT 5 tablespoons butter and 5 tablespoons lard (or other shortening) into 2 cups of flour sifted with 1/2 teaspoon salt, mixing the butter and lard in with the finger tips or with a pastry blender. Add 6 or 7 tablespoons cold water, or enough to make a firm dough, handling it very gently. Chill the dough for several hours before using it.

The *pâte à tourte* resembles the standard American pie pastry. Notice that the recipe specifies half lard and half butter—lard for flakiness, butter for flavor.

PASTRY making was one of my early culinary loves, but when the time came to write about it I was beset by doubt. Some kind American friends offered me their kitchen as a workshop, a typical American kitchen, they assured me, not French, like my own, with equipment Americans use. It would be a perfect way to test myself.

Utensils for
Making Cakes

I was delighted to find in my friends' kitchen the heavy baking pans I prefer; cakes bake more evenly and rise better in a heavy pan. I found also the essential measuring cups and spoons, a good flour sifter, a wooden mixing spoon, a flexible spatula, and pastry bags equipped with several kinds of tubes. I like pastry brushes for oiling pans and for glazing the tops of some pastries, and, for cooling the cakes, I like wire racks which allow the air to circulate evenly around them. My friends had an efficient electric mixer, a great work saver for many purposes. And to my delight, as I worked, all that I knew about pastry making seemed to come back— the look and feel of the *pâtes* were utterly familiar.

Chemical leavenings like baking powder do not belong to the classic cuisine of France. Lightness achieved with eggs gives French cakes a slightly different texture from that of the usual American layer cake. Eggs do cost more than baking powder; but, on the other hand, these cakes require less butter, and the fillings and icings may be omitted altogether without sacrificing the deliciousness of the cake.

Gâteaux raised with eggs are basically simple mixtures. The main ingredients are eggs, sugar, and flour, or eggs, sugar, flour, and butter. Vanilla or lemon may be used as a flavoring, and sometimes almond powder is an additional ingredient.

Different recipes vary the proportions of these basic ingredients or the way they are combined, or they use a different pan and different icing and filling. But the basic *pâtes* are essentially unaltered.

Beating Cake Batter The first and most important step in making these egg-raised *pâtes* is incorporating enough air to make them light by the beating of the sugar and eggs. In some recipes the whole eggs are beaten with the sugar, in others only the yolks are beaten with the sugar, and the whites, beaten separately, are folded in at the last. One precaution is never to use very cold eggs. Take them from the refrigerator an hour before you begin to mix the cake. Beat the mixture in a warm bowl. Most French chefs wrap a metal mixing bowl in a large towel wet with very hot water. A porcelain or glass bowl may be rinsed with hot water beforehand and set in a second bowl of hot water. Then beat the eggs and sugar until the mixture is lukewarm, and very light and fluffy. When only the yolks are used, the mixture should flow from the beater in ribbons, and be almost white. Then let it cool, but keep on beating it. This procedure takes from 20 to 30 minutes with a hand whip, and about 5 or 6 minutes with an electric beater.

Having beaten all this air into the batter, be very careful not to lose it. Flour, egg whites, if they are added separately, and butter, if it is used, must be folded, not stirred, into the batter with a spatula, cutting through the mass of beaten egg and sugar and folding it over and over the added ingredients until they are evenly distributed. Work carefully, with a very light touch, never using one unnecessry stroke. Melted butter requires special attention, because it is likely to slip to the bottom of the bowl and remain there in a little pool, not to be discovered until the moment when you pour the batter into the pan. To prevent this, slide the spatula over the bottom of the bowl as you fold the butter in, literally lifting the butter into the batter.

A French pastry chef weighs his ingredients, and many recipes call for a certain number of grams of arrowroot or rice flour or potato flour in addition to fine wheat flour. Realizing how impractical this would be in most American kitchens, I have transposed all the weights into measurements and suggest that you use fine cake flour. Since fine flour is apt to pack or settle unevenly in the package, sift the flour, then measure.

To prepare the baking pans, butter them or brush them with oil, using the pastry brush, and dust them lightly with flour. For some cakes, the pan may be lined with wax paper or with heavy white paper. French cakes are not usually baked in separate layers; a layer cake is made from a single cake split horizontally into 2 or 3 slices.

Preparing
Baking
Pans

The *biscuit de Savoie*, or spongecake, is baked in a high mold, the large copper molds you see often in antique shops, not in the tube pan used for American spongecakes.

Although there are some exceptions, most of these cakes should bake at a low temperature, and they rise better on the lower racks of the oven. When the cake is done it shrinks slightly from the sides of the pan, and a skewer thrust into the center of the cake comes out dry and clean. Press the top lightly with a finger; a well-baked cake springs back at once.

I have gathered for you the traditional basic recipes that should be in every pastry cook's repertoire. The cakes made without butter are very light; when butter is added, they have a closer texture. Almond powder, which is added to some cakes, adds firmness and moisture. Layer cakes and *petits fours* are usually cut from butter and almond cakes, since these slice more easily than spongecakes.

One last word before I begin the recipes: have all the ingredients measured and ready before you begin to combine them. Light the oven before you begin to mix the cake. Read the recipe carefully, and reread it if necessary, until you are thoroughly familiar with every step.

SPONGECAKE

Biscuit de Savoie

BEAT 8 egg yolks, 1 1/2 cups sugar, and 1/2 teaspoon lemon (or orange or vanilla) flavoring in a warm bowl with a hand whip or an electric beater until the mixture is thick and creamy. Add 1 whole egg and continue to beat until the sugar is dissolved and the mixture is very light and fluffy. Measure 1 3/4 cups sifted cake flour (or use 1 1/2 cups sifted flour and 1/4 cup cornstarch) and fold it into the mixture in 3 portions with a metal spatula.

Beat 8 egg whites until they are stiff and cut and fold them into the batter. Butter a deep pan or fancy mold, sprinkle it with sugar, and fill it about 2/3 full. Bake the *biscuit* in a slow oven (300° F.) for 45 to 50 minutes, or until the cake is a light brown and tests done.

Pâte à Biscuit au Beurre

BEAT 4 egg yolks and 1/2 cup sugar in a warm bowl with a hand whip or electric beater until the mixture is very light and fluffy and almost white. Measure 1 cup less 2 tablespoons sifted cake flour and fold it into the mixture in 3 portions with a metal spatula. Beat 4 egg whites until they are stiff and cut and fold them into the batter with the spatula. Add 4 tablespoons butter, melted over low heat and cooled, gradually cutting and folding it in with the spatula.

Pour the batter into a pan that has been buttered and sprinkled with flour. Fill the pan to a depth of 3/4 inch to 2 inches, depending upon how the cake is to be used. Bake the cake in a moderate oven (325° to 350° F.) for 25 to 35 minutes, or until it tests done. Turn it out on a wire rack to cool. Split it to make 2 or 3 layers and spread pastry cream or jam between the layers. Spread apricot jam or purée very thinly over the top and sides and then cover the cake with fondant icing. Decorate it with glazed fruit.

Biscuit Roulé

BEAT 4 egg yolks and 1/3 cup sugar in a warm bowl with a hand whip or electric beater until the mixture is very light and " ribbons " as it runs off the beater or a spoon. Sprinkle 1/3 cup sifted flour on the egg mixture, cutting and folding it in a little at a time with a metal spatula. Beat 3 egg whites until they are stiff but not dry and cut and fold them in with the spatula. Fold in 2 tablespoons butter, melted and cooled. Line a large flat jelly-roll pan with wax paper. Butter the paper well and spread the batter evenly on it, about 1/3 inch thick. Bake the cake in a hot oven (400° F.) for 7 to 9 minutes, or until it tests done. Turn the cake out onto a board dusted with confectioners' sugar, remove the paper, and roll the cake. Cool it. Unroll it and spread with jelly, pastry cream, or whipped cream, and roll it again. Or cut it into 3 equal strips and arrange the strips in layers, with jelly, whipped cream, or pastry cream.

Génoise *has butter in it, and although it is light like spongecake, it has a firmer, moister texture. As a consequence it cuts and slices more easily than sponge.* Génoise *batter is baked about 1 inch deep in shallow pans, and split into layers. As many layers as desired are built up and filled with one of the pastry creams or with jam or jelly. The sides and top are finished with a fondant icing. Or batter is baked 3/4 inch deep in a large flat pan, and the cake is cut into small squares, triangles, or diamonds which are iced and fancifully decorated.*

Always cool génoise *by removing it from the baking pan to a wire rack. If the cake is allowed to cool in the pan it becomes damp and heavy.*

LIGHT BUTTER CAKE

Pâte à Génoise

IN a bowl combine 4 eggs, 1/2 cup plus 1 tablespoon sugar and 1/2 teaspoon vanilla extract. Set the bowl in a second bowl filled with fairly hot water and beat the mixture until it is lukewarm, very light and fluffy, and has doubled in bulk, about 20 minutes with a hand whip or 5 minutes with an electric beater. Remove the bowl from the hot water and continue to beat the mixture until it is cool. Measure 1 cup less 2 tablespoons sifted cake flour and cut and fold it into the mixture in 3 portions with a metal spatula. Fold in 7 tablespoons melted and cooled butter.

Pour the batter into a buttered and floured pan to a depth of 3/4 inch to 2 inches, depending upon how the cake is to be used. Bake the cake in a moderately slow oven (325° to 350° F.) for 25 to 35 minutes, until it tests done. Turn the cake out on a wire rack to cool. This recipe makes one 10-inch square cake or two 8-inch layers or an 8- or 9-inch round high cake. If you wish to cut the cake into small fancy shapes and ice them to make *petits fours*, bake the cake in a 10- by 12-inch sheet.

ALMOND CAKE

Pain de Gênes

CRUSH 1/2 pound blanched almonds into powder. Combine the almond powder with 6 tablespoons fine sugar and 2 eggs, and beat the mixture well with a hand whip or an electric beater. Add 6 tablespoons sugar and another egg, and continue to beat until the mixture is very light and fluffy. Put 6 tablespoons butter into a warm bowl and work it with a wooden spoon until it is very creamy, but not oily. Using a metal spatula, cut and fold the softened butter into the first mixture. Fold in 1/2 cup cake flour sifted with 1/4 teaspoon salt, and 1 tablespoon kirsch. Pour the batter into a shallow 8- or 9-inch pan that has been lined with heavy wax paper and well buttered. Bake the cake in a slow oven (300° F.)

for 35 to 40 minutes. Turn the cake out on a rack to cool. Remove the paper and serve the cake plain or with a dusting of confectioners' sugar.

Cakes

IN FRANCE, *les gâteaux grands*, the great cakes, are elaborate confections that may combine two or three different kinds of *pâtes* with various creams, fruits, nuts, and sometimes icing. A classic example of this genre is the *gâteau Saint-Honoré*, which is composed of a ring of *pâte à chou* baked on a circle of tart pastry, surmounted by tiny cream puffs filled with whipped cream and dipped into caramel syrup. The center of the ring is then filled with a rich pastry cream.

Needless to say, in France such *gâteaux* are seldom made at home. But every town, no matter how small, has access to a fine *pâtisserie*, a pastry shop whose proprietor is usually a skilled cook well trained in the arts of fine baking.

In this country, where it is often impossible to find a *pâtissière* who is capable of making such *gâteaux*, we have no choice except to make them ourselves. The *gâteaux* given here can soon be mastered by anyone who wishes to take the trouble. In fact, I think that the only *pâte* that is truly difficult to make is puff paste. But even in making puff paste, if the recipe is followed carefully all one then needs for success is a light hand and a good oven—and, of course, patient practice.

ST. HONORÉ CAKE

Gâteau Saint-Honoré

ROLL out tart pastry 1/8 to 1/4 inch thick and from it cut a circle 9 or 10 inches in diameter. Lay the circle on a greased baking sheet. Using a pastry bag with a plain round tube, make a border of *chou* paste about as thick as a thumb around the edge of the pastry circle. Brush the paste with *dorure*. Bake the tart in a hot oven (425° F.) for 20 to 25 minutes, or until the *chou* paste edge puffs and the tart is brown. Meanwhile, make 18 small cream puffs from balls of *chou* paste about the size of walnuts. Cool the puffs and make a small hole in the side of each with a small kitchen knife. Using a pastry bag with a small tube, fill the puffs through this hole with *crème pâtissière* or whipped cream. Dip the puffs in warm caramel syrup and arrange them around the edge of the cake. Fill the center of the cake with *crème Saint-Honoré*.

MECCA CAKE

Pain de la Mecque

WITH a pastry bag form a large round of *chou* paste on a greased baking sheet, starting at the center and going around in a spiral. Sprinkle the round with granulated sugar and bake it until it is brown and light in the hand. When it is cool, split it and fill it with whipped cream, *crème Saint-Honoré*, or preserved fruit.

CONVERSATION

Conversation

ROLL out 2 separate pieces of puff paste, one piece 1/8 inch thick and the other 1/4 inch thick. Cut them into 8-inch circles, using a plate as a guide. Turn the thinner layer onto a moistened baking sheet. Spread the center with pastry cream leaving a clear border about 1 1/2 inches wide around the edge. Moisten the edge with water, place the other layer on top and press the two edges together to seal them. Make tiny nicks with a small knife around the edge to give a decorative scalloped effect.

Make a smooth paste with confectioners' sugar and 1 egg white and spread this over the top. Cut very narrow strips of puff paste, brush them with *dorure* and arrange them in a pattern on top of the cake. Bake it in a moderately hot oven (375° to 400° F.) for 25 to 30 minutes.

To make individual *conversations*, line individual tart molds with puff paste, prick the bottoms, and fill the molds just to the top with pastry cream. Moisten the edge of the pastry with water and cover the tarts with circles of puff paste. Trim the edges and seal them. Finish the tarts as you would the large *conversation* and bake them for 15 to 18 minutes.

Napoléons

NAPOLEONS

ROLL out puff paste into a sheet 1/8 inch thick and about 14 by 12 inches. Lay the sheet on a buttered baking pan and prick it all over with a fork. Bake it in a hot oven (400° to 425° F.) until it is golden brown. The cake should be light but not puffy. With a very sharp knife, cut it into three strips, each 4 by 14 inches. Form a 3-layer cake, using pastry cream between the layers. Brush the top layer with apricot purée and ice it with white fondant icing. Put a little melted chocolate in a tiny paper cornucopia and make stripes across the icing. Lightly cut across the chocolate stripes with a small knife and pull it carefully to make the conventional wavering design used for *napoléons*. With a sharp knife dipped in boiling water slice into pieces 1 1/2 inches wide.

Mille-Feuille

MILLE-FEUILLE

FOLLOW the recipe for *napoléons*, filling the layers with thick apricot purée mixed with the pastry crumbs left from cutting the baked strips. Or fill the layers with whipped cream and sprinkle the top with powdered sugar.

Gâteau Moka

MOCHA CAKE

MAKE a *génoise* or a *biscuit au beurre* and slice it horizontally into 2 or 3 layers. Spread *crème au beurre au moka*, mocha butter cream, between the layers and cover the cake with *crème au beurre au moka*. To decorate the top, pipe the cream through a pastry bag with a fancy tube. Cover the sides of the cake with chopped toasted almonds. Before cutting the cake chill it until the *crème au beurre* is firm.

Gâteau Jalousie

JALOUSIE CAKE

ROLL out 2 oblongs of puff paste 12 inches long and 4 1/2 to 5 inches wide, one piece 1/8 inch thick, the other 1/4 inch thick. Lay the 1/8-inch-thick oblong on a moistened baking sheet. Spread the center with red currant jelly or raspberry jam (or a mixture of the two), leaving a border about 3/4 inch wide all around the rectangle. Fold the thicker oblong in half lengthwise and, starting 1 1/2 inches from each end, make parallel cuts, 1/4 inch apart, across the fold to within 1 1/2 inches of the side. Moisten the edges of the bottom layer, unfold the cut layer, and cover the bottom layer with it. Seal the edges well. With a sharp knife make tiny nicks, 1/2 inch apart, along the edges to give a scalloped effect. Brush the top of the cake with *dorure* and prick the edges in a few places with a fork. Bake in a hot oven (400° F.) for about 20 minutes. Brush the top with thick apricot purée or jam and sprinkle the edges with granulated sugar or chopped almonds. The *gâteau jalousie* may be served uncut or it may be cut crosswise into 1 1/2-inch slices.

AMBASSADOR

Ambassadeur

MAKE and cool a high (3 to 4 inches) *génoise* or *biscuit au beurre*. Slice off the top of the cake and scoop out the inside, leaving a shell about 3/4 inch thick on the sides and 1/2 inch thick on the bottom. Prepare a macédoine of mixed, diced fresh fruits, including some strawberries, sweeten it with a little powdered sugar, and flavor it with 1 or 2 tablespoons kirsch. Fill the hollowed-out cake with this mixture and replace the top. Brush the cake with apricot jam and sprinkle it with chopped toasted almonds.

Galettes are a favorite pastry for the home cook in France. They are hardly more than sheets of pastry baked in shallow round or square pans. They resemble puff paste, but are not quite so light and flaky. Galette doughs are rich with butter or shortening, which gives them a special crispness and an appetizing golden-brown color. Cut in wedges or squares, they are eaten warm or cold with jam or jelly.

GALETTE DES ROIS

Galette des Rois

SIFT 2 cups flour and 1/4 teaspoon salt into a bowl or in a mound on a board, make a well in the center and put into it 3/4 cup butter and 3/4 cup water. Mix the ingredients together with the finger tips, handling the mixture as lightly as possible. Form the dough into a ball and chill it for 1 hour. Roll the dough as you would puff paste, making 4 turns in all and chilling it after the second turn. Roll the paste into a round or oblong shape about 1/2 inch thick, lay it on a buttered baking sheet, brush the top with *dorure* and prick it well with a fork to form a design. Let the *galette* stand for 10 minutes and bake it in a hot oven (400° to 450° F.) for 20 to 25 minutes, or until it is brown. Serve cool or lukewarm.

When this cake is served at a Twelfth-night party, a very tiny metal doll or an almond is pressed into the dough as a symbol of *l'Enfant*, the Christ Child. Whoever finds the token in his piece of *galette* becomes the king (or queen) of the evening's festivities and leads the games at the party.

Little Cakes

LES GÂTEAUX PETITS—little cakes—are known in this country by the name *petits fours*. The French call them by several names which are variously defined by different pastry chefs. Usually *petits fours* is a general term for all the small cakes, tarts, and cookies; *milanaises* refers to the very tiny ones; and *friandises* and *gourmandises* to the more elaborate of these last. There is no end to the possible kinds of *petits fours*. Ladyfingers, macaroons, tiny cream puffs and éclairs, iced tidbits made with *pâte à génoise* (described in the section on cake and pastry decoration), puff-paste dainties with various fillings, tiny cookies, some sweet and short, some dry and crisp, and tarts can all be varied—and are—according to the chef's skills and the materials he has available.

Profiteroles

PROFITEROLES

MAKE *profiteroles* as described in the recipe for *pâte à chou* and when the tiny puffs are baked and cooled, fill them with whipped cream or vanilla ice cream. Serve from 2 to 4 puffs to a portion and spoon hot chocolate sauce over them.

DARIOLES

LINE 6 *baba* molds with puff paste or tart paste, prick the bottoms with a fork and put 1/2 teaspoon butter in each. Fill the baba molds 3/4 full with the following mixture: Beat 2 eggs with 1/2 cup sugar until they are light and add 2 tablespoons flour and 1 cup cold milk. Flavor with a little orange-flower water. Bake the *darioles* in a moderately hot oven (375° to 400° F.) for 15 minutes.

MIRLITONS

LINE 12 individual deep tart molds with puff paste and prick the paste well with a fork. Put 1/2 teaspoon apricot jam in each mold and fill the shells with the following mixture: Beat 2 eggs with 1/2 cup sugar until they are light and fluffy, flavor with a little vanilla and add 4 or 5 dry macaroons, crushed to make very fine crumbs. Sprinkle the tarts lightly with chopped almonds and bake them in a moderately hot oven (375° to 400° F.) for 12 to 15 minutes.

PALM LEAVES

ROLL puff paste 1/8 inch thick, 10 to 15 inches long and 4 1/4 inches wide. Sprinkle the strip with granulated sugar. Fold over the long sides so that they meet in the center and sprinkle the strip again with granulated sugar. Fold over the long sides so that they meet in the center. You now have a long strip 1 inch wide and 1/2 inch thick. Cut the strip crosswise into slices 1/4 to 1/2 inch wide. Lay the slices, cut side down, on a buttered baking sheet and spread them open to make a small V. Bake the *palmiers* in a hot oven (425° to 450° F.) until the bottom is caramelized and brown, then turn them over to caramelize and brown the other side.

Cocktail *palmiers* are made with grated cheese instead of sugar.

LADYFINGERS

PUT 6 egg yolks and 3/4 cup sugar into a warm bowl and beat the mixture until it is creamy, fluffy, and almost white. Add 1 teaspoon orange-flower water or vanilla. Add 1/2 cup sifted cake flour, cutting and folding it in about a third at a time with a metal spatula. Beat the 6 egg whites until stiff and cut and fold them into the mixture. Cover a baking sheet with heavy white paper. Put the mixture into a pastry bag with a medium-large, plain round tube in it. Force the mixture onto the paper in fingers about 3 inches long and 1 1/4 inches wide. Sprinkle the tops very lightly with powdered sugar. Bake in a slow oven (300° F.) until light brown. Remove from the paper while still warm by lifting each one carefully with a thin metal spatula. When cold put them together in pairs to prevent their drying out.

Fedora au Chocolat

CHOCOLATE FEDORA

BEAT 3 egg whites until they are stiff. Mix together 1/4 cup each of almond powder and hazelnut powder, 1/2 cup vanilla-flavored powdered sugar, and 1 tablespoon sifted flour. Add this to the egg whites, cutting and folding it in with a metal spatula. Put the mixture in a pastry bag with a medium-sized plain round tube. Force the mixture onto a buttered and floured baking sheet making cookies the size of half dollars but oval in shape. Bake in a hot oven (450° F.) for 4 or 5 minutes or until lightly browned. Remove from the pan before they cool. When cool put together in pairs with the following filling: Melt 3 tablespoons grated sweet chocolate and combine with 3 tablespoons heavy sweet cream and 1/2 cup confectioners' sugar. Cool before spreading it, adding more sugar if the mixture is runny.

Madeleines

MADELEINES

PUT 4 eggs and 1/2 cup sugar in a warm bowl. Place it in another bowl of water that is almost hot and beat the mixture until it has become lukewarm and is light and fluffy. Remove the bowl from the hot water and continue beating the mixture until it is cool. Add 1 cup sifted cake flour, a third at a time, cutting and folding it in with a metal spatula. Melt 6 tablespoons butter over low heat, let it cool, and gradually cut and fold it in with the spatula. Add 1 tablespoon rum if desired. Put it in small buttered and floured *madeleine* molds or other tiny individual molds and bake in a hot oven (400° F.) for about 10 minutes.

SABLÉS

MIX together 6 tablespoons butter, 5 tablespoons sugar, a pinch of salt, the grated rind of 1/2 a lemon and the yolks of 2 hard-cooked eggs that have been forced through a fine sieve. Add 1 cup sifted flour 1/3 at a time, combining it thoroughly with the other ingredients. Cover it and chill it for 1 1/2 to 2 hours. Roll out 1/8 inch thick on a lightly floured pastry board. Cut the dough into any desired shapes and lift onto a buttered baking sheet. Make a design on the top of each one with a fork or a cork pressed into the surface. Bake in a hot oven (425° F.) for 7 to 8 minutes. Remove from the pan before they cool.

FOR almond *sablés*, follow the recipe but increase the butter to 7 tablespoons and the sugar to 6 tablespoons and add 1/4 cup almond powder. Before baking them brush with *dorure* instead of making a design.

Almond Sablés

LITTLE ALMOND COOKIES

CREAM together 2/3 cup butter and 1/2 cup sugar. Gradually mix in 2 cups sifted flour to which 1/2 teaspoon baking powder has been added. Add 2 eggs and either 1/2 teaspoon vanilla extract or a little grated orange rind. When well combined, form the mixture into a ball and let it stand in a cool place for about 1 hour. Roll it out 1/4 inch thick on a lightly floured board, cut it in strips 1 1/2 inches wide and place it on a buttered baking sheet. Brush the tops with beaten egg and sprinkle with sugar and finely chopped blanched almonds, pressing them into the surface. Score the strips every inch. Bake in a moderate oven (375° F.) for 15 to 20 minutes. When they have cooled break the strips apart where they are scored to make little oblong cookies.

SMALL DRY COOKIES

SIFT 2 cups flour into a bowl and make a well in the center. Put in this well 2/3 cup sugar, 2/3 cup creamed butter, 2 eggs, and 1 tablespoon orange-flower water or vanilla. Mix them together well, pulling the flour into the mixture with the hands or a wooden spoon. Continue mixing until all the ingredients are well combined. Form it into a ball, wrap it in a towel, and let it stand for 2 hours in a cold place. Roll out 1/4 inch thick on a lightly floured board and cut with a fancy cooky cutter. Place on a baking sheet that has been moistened with a little water. Decorate the tops with almonds or candied fruit. Bake in a slow oven (300° to 325° F.) for about 15 minutes, or until brown. Brush immediately with sweetened milk made by dissolving 2 tablespoons sugar in 1/2 cup hot milk. These cookies will keep for several weeks.

Florentines

MIX in a saucepan 2 tablespoons butter, 1 cup sugar, 1/4 cup unsifted flour, the grated rind of 1 lemon, 1/2 pint heavy cream, 1/2 pound slivered almonds, and 1/2 pound candied orange peel or a combination of lemon peel and orange peel cut in fine slivers. Stir over very low heat until the mixture is well blended. Drop by spoonfuls (about 1 tablespoon) onto a baking sheet that has been buttered and very lightly floured, allowing at least 2 inches between them to allow for spreading. Flatten each one with a moistened fork or spatula. Bake in a slow oven (300° F.) for about 10 to 12 minutes, or until the cookies are brown. Remove from oven and let cool 3 or 4 minutes, then lift off carefully with a thin metal spatula. If removed too soon they will not hold their shape. If left too long on the pan they will stick to it; if that happens put the pan back in the oven for a minute to loosen them.

Meringues, as the French use them, are not so often the finish on a pie but rather the base of a dessert. The meringue mixture, made merely of egg white and sugar, is formed, usually with a pastry bag, on white paper placed on a baking sheet. It is baked slowly to make pielike or tartlike shells which are served filled with fruit, pastry cream, or ice cream, or a combination of fruit and one of the crèmes or whipped cream. Or the meringue mixture may be formed into ovals about twice the size of an egg. After baking, the underside of each is pressed in a little with the thumb to provide a cavity that can be filled with ice cream. They are then put together in pairs and served with a fruit sauce and decorated with whipped cream swirls. Meringue shells will keep several weeks if stored in a box with a tight cover and kept in a dry place.

MERINGUE SHELLS

Meringues

BEAT 4 egg whites until stiff, and, as they begin to become light, gradually add 1 cup sugar and continue beating until the mixture has no undissolved grains of sugar in it. Shape on white paper laid on a baking sheet, using a pastry bag or a spoon. Make into a pie shell or small nest-like tart shells or into ovals about twice the size of a small egg. Allow space between them. Bake in a very slow oven (250° F.) about 25 minutes or until they take on a very little color. Raise the paper from the baking sheet, sprinkle a little water underneath and lift off the meringues with a spatula. Serve them filled with ice cream, pastry cream, fruit, or a combination of these and topped with whipped cream.

Fruit Tarts

UNLIKE THE more elaborate *gâteaux*, fruit tarts are often made at home, particularly in country places where people grow their own fruit and berries.

Apples go so well with pastry that some form of pie or tart made with apples is one of the most popular desserts wherever apples are grown. The double-crust pie, which in France is called a *tourte*, is most popular in the United States; the baked apple dumpling in which a whole apple is encased in the dough is a favorite in England; and in France the apple tart made with a combination of applesauce and sliced apples competes for first place with the *gâteau normand*, which adds an icing and chopped nuts to the top crust.

Tarte
aux Pommes

APPLE TART

MAKE *pâte à flan*, tart pastry, for fruit, using an egg. Roll this pastry into a circle about 1/4 inch thick, place it on a tart pan, and shape up the edge to make a rim about 1 inch high to hold in the fruit. Prick the bottom of the pastry. Spread generously with applesauce and then arrange thin apple slices on top, overlapping them in an orderly fashion. Sprinkle with powdered sugar and bake in a moderate oven (350° to 375° F.) for 35 to 40 minutes. Spread with thinned apricot sauce.

Gâteau
Normand

APPLE TART NORMANDY STYLE

ROLL out tart pastry 1/8 to 1/4 inch thick and line a shallow oblong pan with it. Spread it with a 3/4-inch layer of very thick applesauce. Cover the top with the same pastry and seal the edges together. Spread over the top a very thin layer of *glace royale* and sprinkle it with chopped almonds. Bake in a hot oven (400° F.) for about 30 minutes, or until the top is crusty and starting to brown. Serve in slices.

Chausson
aux Pommes

APPLE TURNOVER

PEEL, core and slice 1 pound apples. Melt 2 tablespoons butter in a saucepan and in it sauté the apple slices until they begin to soften. Add 2 tablespoons sugar, or more to taste, and cook until the mixture is thick. Add a little vanilla or a few drops of lemon juice or 1 tablespoon of rum. Cool the apples. Two tablespoons of raisins may be added, if desired.

Roll puff paste 1/4 inch thick and cut it into an 8- or 9-inch circle, using a plate as a guide. Spread the center with the apple slices or thick applesauce, leaving clear a 1 1/2-inch rim all around. Moisten one half of this rim with water and fold it over the other half to make the circle into a half-moon. Seal the edges together and make tiny nicks with a small knife around the curved edge to give a decorative scalloped effect. Brush the top with *dorure* and prick it in several places with a fork. Lay the *chausson* on a moistened baking pan and bake it in a hot oven (400° to 425° F.) for 30 to 35 minutes. About 5 minutes before taking it from the oven, sprinkle the turnover with powdered sugar; this gives it an attractive glaze. Serve cool or lukewarm.

LITTLE TURNOVERS

FOLLOW the recipe for *chausson aux pommes*, apple turnovers, but make tiny individual turnovers. Fill them with the apple mixture or with jam or pastry cream and bake them for 12 to 15 minutes in a hot oven (425° to 450° F.).

Petits Chaussons

CHERRY TART COUNTRY STYLE

LINE a pie pan with tart pastry, forming a good edge that will hold in the filling. Mix together 3 tablespoons flour, 1/2 cup milk, 1 egg, 1 tablespoon sugar, and a pinch of salt. Remove the stems from 2 cups sweet cherries and pit them. Fill the tart shell with the cherries and pour the batter over them. Bake in a moderately hot oven (375° F.) for 30 to 35 minutes, or until the top is delicately browned.

Millas aux Cerises à la Bourbonnaise

DRIED PLUM TART

COOK 12 to 15 prunes slowly in 1 1/2 cups red wine to which a scant 1/2 cup sugar and 1 or 2 slices of lemon have been added. Cool the prunes and remove the pits. Line a pan with tart pastry, forming a good edge that will hold in fruit and juice. Fill it with the fruit and cover the top with strips of the pastry. Brush the pastry with *dorure* (1 egg beaten with 1 tablespoon milk). Bake in a hot oven (450° F.) for about 15 minutes, or until the pastry is browned.

Tarte aux Pruneaux

STRAWBERRY TART

LINE a pie pan or individual tart pans with tart pastry and prick the bottom well. Put a piece of wax paper on the dough and fill the pan with dried beans or lentils. Bake in a hot oven (425° F.) for 18 to 20 minutes. Discard the beans and the paper. Cool the shells and fill them with strawberries. Glaze them with melted currant jelly.

Or cover the bottom of the baked tart shell with whipped cream or *crème pâtissière* and arrange whole strawberries on top. Glaze the surface with a little melted currant jelly.

Tarte aux Fraises

*Chausson
aux Fraises*

FOLLOW the directions for *chausson aux pommes*, apple turnovers, but instead of using apples spread 3 or 4 crushed macaroons or ladyfingers over the paste and over these put 1 cup strawberries, washed and thoroughly dried, and 2 teaspoons red currant jelly.

Icing and Decoration

IN FRANCE cakes that are to be decorated for a confirmation, a christening, or a saint's day party are almost never baked in what we here call layer-cake pans. They are customarily baked in a deep springform pan, or a charlotte mold, or sometimes in a deep rectangular or square pan. The cake is then split horizontally with a serrated knife into as many layers as are desired. The layers are notched, much as dress patterns are notched, and when they are filled and must be reassembled, the notches serve as a guide. If your cake pans are no more than 2 inches deep, you can easily transform them into deep, French-style pans. Simply cut a 4-inch-wide strip of heavy brown paper and stand the strip like a collar around the inside of a buttered and floured layer pan, doubling the height of the pan.

Decorated
Petits Fours

The tiny decorated cakes that appear among the *petits fours* on the tray of French pastries are almost always made of *génoise* cake. The batter for the cake is poured 3/4 inch deep in a large square or oblong pan and the baked sheet of cake is cut into diamonds, squares, circles, or any desired shapes with a cooky cutter. Each small cake is dipped into luke-warm fondant. When the fondant base icing begins to harden, the cakes are decorated with patterns in royal icing or with chocolate or candied fruits. Colored fondant for the base icing should be very delicately tinted; the most appetizing colors are very pale yellow, pink, and green.

Pastry tubes of many sizes are generally available. They are identified by number. Number 1, Number 2, Number 3, and Number 4, for instance, are round tubes of graduated size; Number 2 and Number 3 are most popular for lettering and general use. The beginner's repertoire should include rosettes, shell borders, and simple push flowers, and for these you will need Number 30, a small star tube, and Number 190, a large star tube. For more ambitious cake decorators, the Number 67 tube is used to shape leaves, and Number 104, along with Numbers 1, 2, 3, and 4, for experimenting with more elaborate flowers. These numbers are used in both France and America, and the tubes may be ordered by number.

Pastry
Tubes

The large decorators' tubes are used with a cloth pastry bag to make borders and decorations of *duchesse* potatoes, and other garnishes, and to shape éclairs, but icings must be pressed through cones made of non-absorbent paper. Parchment paper is ideal material, but if parchment is not available, heavy freezer paper may be used, with the moistureproof waxed side inside. Use a clean cone for each new icing.

Before you begin to fill the cake, brush away any crumbs from the layers. A thin coating of jelly helps to keep more crumbs from coming off and also keeps the cake moist, as well as adding to its flavor. When the layers have been spread with filling and assembled, put the reshaped cake on a turntable. The household Lazy Susan makes an excellent substitute for the professional chef's turntable. Use a straight-sided, long spatula to apply the icing, holding the knife still while the cake turns. Keep a glass of hot water on hand to dip the spatula into occasionally. This trick helps to make the icing smooth and keeps it from thickening too quickly.

If a turntable is not available, put the cake on a board or flat plate for icing. It can be transferred to the serving platter after it is iced by slipping under it 2 wide knives or spatulas, crisscrossed.

Some cakes are simply sprinkled with powdered sugar, sometimes through a stencil, such as a paper doily.

Before applying the frosting, brush the crumbs again from the reshaped cake. Brush it with jelly or apply a thin first coat of icing before applying the final coat. This undercoating prevents crumbs from marring the fin ished cake.

If a thin icing of the fondant type is used, pour it over the top of the cake and spread it evenly on top and sides. Soft icings like whipped cream or butter cream are applied to the sides first and the top last.

For the simplest kind of decoration, cut a zigzag pattern out of cardboard and draw this comb over the icing, leaving a pattern of lines. Or with a pastry cone apply large rosettes of butter cream or whipped cream and finish with a border made with a smaller star tube.

To decorate a cake with fresh fruit, shape large rosettes of whipped cream and set a slice of fruit or a whole berry in the center of each flower.

To Make Pastry Cones

To make a cone to hold a large tube, cut a 15- to 16-inch square of parchment or freezer paper and cut the square into 2 equal triangles. Hold the triangle with the thumb and third finger at the center of the long side. Bring the left corner to the top and hold these points together with the right hand. Bring the right-hand corner to the left, over and around to meet the other 2 corners at the top. Be sure the sides are perfectly aligned down the middle of the cone. Fold the 3 points down inside the cone to hold it in shape. Clip off the bottom of the cone to allow the tube to be inserted, and slip the tube in from the inside. Fill the cone no more than 2/3 full, press the top together to close the cone, and fold the top over to seal it.

Make the top fold down far enough to expel most of the air in the cone. Press the cone with one hand to force the icing out through the tube and use the other hand to guide the tube. The pressure should come from the top of the cone, so that the part of the cone around the tube is always full of icing.

Even the newest hand at cake decorating can make simple icing flowers. I suggest that you practice on the back of a cake tin first (the icing can be scraped up and used again).

Icing Flowers

To make a rosette, the most useful of all decorations, use a Number 30 star tube. Gently press out a spiral, beginning at the center and raising the tube as you press. To finish the rosette with a graceful swirl, stop pressing the cone, but continue to move the tube. Large rosettes are made with Number 190.

To make simple push flowers, hold the Number 30 tube against the surface of the cake, squeeze quickly, and pull the tube away abruptly. If you turn the tube slightly as you pull it away, a different effect is achieved.

Lettering—writing "Happy Birthday" and such messages on a cake—requires one of the small round tubes, such as Numbers 2 or 3. Guide the cone by holding it very close to the cake, at a 45° angle. This permits you to write firmly and eliminates wavering lines.

WHIPPED CREAM   *Crème Fouettée*

THE pure whiteness, velvety texture, and rich delicate flavor of whipped cream make it a delightful decoration for cakes and desserts. It can be spooned or spread on, but professionals always use a pastry bag and tube. A star tube of medium size is usual, both for making a single rosette or swirl on an individual tart and for a row of rosettes on *gâteaux*, mousses, and other desserts, as well as for narrow decorative borders, plain or with loops and scallops.

Whipped cream is not easy to handle in a pastry tube unless it is both light and firm—light enough to stand up attractively and firm enough to hold the pattern made by the tube. Only heavy cream will make whipped cream of this consistency. Cream doubles in bulk when it is whipped, so judge the amount accordingly. The cream must be very cold. Put it into a large, thoroughly chilled bowl. The bowl may be set in a pan of chopped ice. The whip should be thoroughly chilled as well. Most chefs prefer a wire whip to a rotary beater, which may require less labor but produces a less fluffy *crème fouettée*. Be careful not to beat the cream too long, or you will have butter for your pains.

Crème fouettée *becomes* crème Chantilly, *a garnish for desserts, when it is sweetened and flavored. Sweetening whipped cream is a delicate matter. If too much sugar is added, or the sugar is beaten in too forcefully, the cream may lose its lightness and fall. The best way to add sugar is to sprinkle it over the cream and fold it in cautiously with a spatula.*

SWEETENED WHIPPED CREAM   *Crème Chantilly*

WHIP heavy cream in a chilled bowl until it is thick but not stiff and on the verge of turning to butter. Into each cup of whipped cream fold 1 to 1 1/2 tablespoons vanilla sugar. If vanilla extract is used for flavoring, add a few drops during the final moments of whipping, then add unflavored sugar.

579

In addition to whipped cream, 5 icings are used to frost cakes: royal icing, fondant, confectioners' sugar icing, butter cream made with egg yolks, and meringue frosting.

Royal icing provides a very hard, mat-finish surface that is an excellent background for lettering and designs. Since it is pure white, it can be accurately tinted in pastel colors. It goes on smoothly, hardens quickly, and helps to protect the freshness of the cake.

Glace Royale ROYAL ICING

SIFT 1 pound confectioners' sugar through a fine sieve. Combine 3 egg whites in a bowl with about 1/3 of the sugar. Mix and beat the mixture with a wooden spoon until it is smooth and creamy. Add 1/2 teaspoon cream of tartar and the remaining sugar, a little at a time, and continue to beat the icing until it is thick as heavy cream. If a single coat of royal icing does not cover completely, ice the cake twice, allowing the first coat to harden slightly before adding the second. To finish the cake with rosettes of royal icing, thicken the icing with more confectioners' sugar.

In an emergency, a simple confectioners' sugar icing may be substituted for fondant. For general use, however, it is worth taking the trouble to make cooked fondant, which can be stored almost indefinitely, and can therefore be made in substantial quantities.

To use the fondant, melt the required amount in a small saucepan. Add a little water or simple syrup to facilitate the melting. Do not allow the fondant to get too hot or it will lose its shine. It should be lukewarm, just liquid enough to spread easily.

Fondant FONDANT

COMBINE in a small saucepan 2 cups sugar, 2/3 cup water, and a pinch of cream of tartar or 1 tablespoon white corn syrup. Bring the mixture to a boil and cook it rapidly until it reaches the soft-ball stage, (238º F. on a candy thermometer). Pour the syrup at once onto an oiled platter or a marble slab to cool until it is barely warm to the touch and will not stick to the fingers when it is lightly tapped. Work the mixture with a spatula, scraping it up from the bottom, folding it over and pulling in the edges, until the mass is creamy white. Put the fondant in a jar or bowl and cover it with a damp cloth. The fondant should ripen for 2 days before it is used. Fondant icing may be colored with a drop or two of vegetable coloring, to produce a pastel shade.

Fondant may be variously flavored. To 1/2 cup warmed fondant, add 1 tablespoon warm, strong coffee or 2 ounces melted unsweetened chocolate or 1 tablespoon kirsch or other liqueur.

Coffee
Chocolate
Liqueur

CONFECTIONERS' SUGAR ICING   *Glace à l'Eau*

SIFT 2 cups confectioners' sugar and beat in 1 teaspoon lemon juice and, very gradually, flavoring and water, using about 1/4 cup liquid in all. Beat the icing for at least 10 minutes, until it is thick enough to spread. Confectioners' sugar icing may be flavored with any liqueur or with vanilla or almond extract. If it is to be flavored with coffee extract or with chocolate, omit the lemon juice.

Crème au beurre au sirop is very rich, but not too sweet. It stays soft, stores well, and keeps the cake moist. It can be applied thickly, and can be easily forced through a pastry tube. Crushed praline or chopped nuts can be added to crème au beurre au sirop.

WHIPPED BUTTER CREAM   *Crème au Beurre au Sirop*

IN A heavy saucepan stir 9 tablespoons sugar, 1/4 cup water, and 1/8 teaspoon cream of tartar until the sugar is dissolved. Cook the syrup over high heat until it spins a light thread (238° F. on a candy thermometer). Beat 5 egg yolks for 1 minute and add the hot syrup gradually, beating until the mixture is stiff and almost white. Still beating, add in small pieces 1/2 to 3/4 pound softened sweet butter. Chill slightly if the mixture seems too soft. If it separates, beat in 1 tablespoon melted butter. Flavor the cream with any desired liqueur or essence or with chocolate. The frosted cake may be finished with rosettes of the same mixture forced through a pastry tube.

Meringue   MERINGUE FROSTING

COMBINE in a saucepan 1 cup sugar, 1/3 cup water and 1/4 teaspoon cream of tartar. Stir until the sugar is dissolved and cook the mixture over high heat without stirring until the syrup spins a thread, or to 240° F. on a candy thermometer. Beat 4 egg whites until they are almost stiff, and pour the boiling syrup into the egg whites, beating constantly, until all the syrup is added. Continue beating the frosting until it is firm enough to spread. Flavor and color as desired. Spread on the top and sides of the cake with a spatula.

For decorating frosted cakes, a variation of royal icing and a simple butter cream are most generally used.

Royal icing for decorating hardens quickly and will not run or smear. If it seems too stiff to force through a small pastry tube, thin it with water or with more egg white. Since it is pure white, it can be tinted to any desired shade. Add the coloring matter very carefully ; a little goes a long way.

Glace Royale pour Décorer les Entremets   ROYAL ICING
                                                 FOR DECORATING

To 1 egg white add a few drops of lemon juice and enough confectioners' sugar to make a thick smooth paste. Continue to work the paste with a wooden spoon until it loses its translucency and is stiff enough to hold its shape.

Butter cream icing is widely used in this country for making flowers with a pastry tube. It has one disadvantage; its natural color is creamy, rather than pure white, and subtleties of color are difficult to achieve. But it is soft and easy to work with, and has good flavor. To make the color light as possible, use sweet butter, or substitute vegetable shortening for part of the butter. The longer the icing is beaten, the lighter the color.

Crème au Beurre pour Décorer les Entremets   BUTTER CREAM
                                                 FOR DECORATING

CREAM 1/2 cup softened butter and gradually add 1 3/4 cups sifted confectioners' sugar. Beat the mixture until it is very pale, with an electric mixer if possible. In hot weather, use slightly more sugar, about 2 cups.

Flavor with a few drops of almond or vanilla extract, if desired, and tint by working in a drop or two of coloring liquid with a small spatula.

Crème pâtissière is a rich filling that holds its shape when it is cold, yet is soft and never stiff. In France, a vanilla bean is used to obtain the vanilla flavor. If you do not have vanilla bean, you may substitute vanilla extract, adding to the finished cream about 1/2 teaspoon for each pint of milk.

PASTRY CREAM   *Crème Pâtissière*

BEAT together 4 to 6 egg yolks, depending upon the size of the eggs, and 3/4 cup sugar until the mixture is very pale and light. Add 1/3 cup flour and beat just until the mixture is smooth. Scald 2 cups milk with a 1-inch piece of vanilla bean and remove the bean. Pour the flavored milk slowly onto the egg mixture, stirring constantly. Add a pinch of salt and cook, stirring vigorously with a wire whisk, until the sauce almost reaches the boiling point. Continue to cook the cream for 2 or 3 minutes, but do not let it boil. Strain the cream. Let it cool, stirring it occasionally to prevent a crust from forming.

    To make *crème au chocolat*, add 2 squares or ounces melted and cooled unsweetened chocolate to the scalded milk.   *Chocolate*

    To make *crème au moka*, flavor 1 cup *crème au chocolat* with 1 tablespoon hot, triple-strength coffee.   *Mocha*

    To make *crème au café*, flavor 1 cup plain *crème pâtissière* with 1 tablespoon hot, triple-strength coffee or 1/2 teaspoon instant coffee dissolved in 1 tablespoon hot water.   *Coffee*

ALMOND CREAM   *Crème d'Amandes*

BLEND 1/2 egg white or 2 egg yolks with 5 ounces almond paste. Add gradually 2/3 cup *crème pâtissière* and mix all together thoroughly. Add gradually 3 tablespoons softened butter and mix all together well. If desired, flavor the cream with a little vanilla or with 1 tablespoon rum or kirsch. Use for filling.

St. Honoré cream is a delicate mixture made with crème pâtissière *lightened with egg whites and held together with gelatin.*

Crème Saint-Honoré
ST. HONORÉ CREAM

ADD to 2 1/2 or 3 cups hot *crème pâtissière* 1 envelope gelatin softened in 2 tablespoons cold water. Stir until the gelatin is completely dissolved in the *crème*. Cool the *crème* and fold into it 4 egg whites beaten stiff with 3 tablespoons confectioners' sugar, added during the last minutes of beating. Use for filling.

Frangipane
ALMOND PASTRY CREAM

MIX together 3/4 cup sugar, 1/3 cup flour, and a pinch of salt. Add 1 whole egg and 1 egg yolk and when well combined add another whole egg and 1 egg yolk. When thoroughly combined add, little by little, 2 cups milk that has been scalded with a piece of vanilla bean. Stir the mixture until it is very smooth, return to the pan in which the milk was scalded, bring back to the boiling point, and cook about 2 minutes, stirring vigorously all the time. Remove from heat, take out the vanilla bean, or, if it was not available, add 1/2 teaspoon vanilla extract. Add 2 tablespoons butter and either 3 or 4 finely crushed macaroons or 2 tablespoons almond paste. Cool, stirring occasionally, to prevent crust from forming on top.

A very rich butter cream filling for cake is made by combining butter with crème pâtissière, *pastry cream. The* crème pâtissière *should be cold, and the butter thoroughly creamed until it is very fluffy and satiny in appearance. The* crème *must be added a little at a time, and each bit incorporated thoroughly before more is added. Otherwise the mixture tends to curdle or separate.*

Crème au Beurre
BUTTER CREAM FILLING

CREAM 6 tablespoons cold butter well with 1/2 tablespoon sugar. Blend the butter thoroughly and very slowly with 1/2 cup cold *crème pâtissière*, added a bit at a time.

Mocha

To make *crème au beurre au moka*, add 1 tablespoon triple-strength coffee at the end.

Chocolate

To make *crème au beurre au chocolat*, add 1 square melted and cooled unsweetened baking chocolate.

Nuts are a favorite cake decoration, as well as a cake ingredient. Hazelnuts and almonds are the most commonly used nuts; for decorative purposes, they are blanched and skinned, and used whole, shredded, or chopped. Chopped pistachios are also used.

ALMONDS AND HAZELNUTS   *Amandes et Noisettes*

BLANCH almonds as follows: Soak shelled almonds in boiling water for 2 or 3 minutes, until the skins loosen. Drain the nuts, plunge them into cold water and rub off the skins. Chop the nuts, sliver them, or slice them into flakes, while they are hot, spread them on a shallow pan and dry them thoroughly in a 250° F. oven. Cool the nuts and put them through a food chopper, using the finest blade. The almonds may take on a little color during the drying, but they should not be allowed to darken. This is not toasting, but drying.

> To Blanch Almonds
>
> To Cut Up
>
> Almond Powder

Toast almonds in a moderate oven (350° F.) until they are golden, stirring frequently.

> To Toast Almonds

To skin hazelnuts, toast them in the oven until the skins begin to pucker, then rub them in a coarse towel until the skins come off.

> To Skin Hazelnuts

ALMOND PRALINE   *Pralin aux Amandes*

MIX equal quantities of blanched almonds and sugar, and heat the mixture in a heavy skillet until it is well caramelized, stirring to brown it evenly. Add a few drops vanilla extract. Cool the praline on a heatproof platter until it hardens. Crush the praline to a powder by chopping it and pounding it with a heavy rolling pin.

ALMOND PASTE   *Pâte d'Amandes*

GRIND blanched almonds and pound them to a smooth paste, using a pestle and mortar. To sweeten the paste, use half granulated sugar and half confectioners' sugar, to taste.

CANDIED CHESTNUTS   *Marrons Glacés*

THESE dry candied chestnuts, used in pastries and desserts, are usually imported and almost never made in the home kitchen. The process is too time-consuming and tedious.

Glace du Sucre   CONFECTIONERS' SUGAR DECORATION

IN FRANCE, many cakes that do not require the additional richness of icing or frosting are decorated with a dusting of confectioners' sugar. A pattern can be made by laying a paper doily on the cake or by making a stencil pattern of ordinary paper. Sift confectioners' sugar heavily over the unprotected areas and carefully remove the paper, leaving the design intact.

Fruits Glacés   CANDIED FRUIT DECORATIONS

GLACÉED fruit—cherries, angelica, lemon, pineapple, citron—make colorful decorations. The fruit can be cut into any desired shapes and used to create flowers and other designs. To make the fruit flexible, wrap it in a damp towel. If the cake to be decorated is first spread with a layer of jam or jelly, the fruit decorations will adhere firmly. Blanched whole nuts are frequently used with glacéed fruits.

Caramel   *Caramel syrup is used to glaze certain tortes and cakes. The syrup is poured over cakes, but smaller cakes or filled cream puffs may be dipped into caramel glaze. It dries to a thin crackling coating with a high shine.*

Caramel   CARAMEL SYRUP

DISSOLVE 1 cup sugar in 1 cup hot water and cook, watching carefully until the syrup is a rich golden color. Keep the syrup hot. It hardens

Glaze   quickly on cooling. To make caramel glaze, use only 1/2 cup water.

In elegant hotels and restaurants, spun sugar is a favorite decoration for elaborate desserts. The lacy cloud is not as difficult to form as it looks; with a little practice, anyone can learn to achieve this spectacular result.

SPUN SUGAR   *Sucre pour Décorer les Entremets*

SPINNING sugar simply consists of drawing the hot sugar, which has been boiled to a hard crack, into fine strands which will harden immediately and retain their form.

Dissolve 4 cups sugar in 2 cups water while heating and stirring. Cook to 280° F., or to the soft-crack stage, then add a pinch cream of tartar and 1 teaspoon white corn syrup and continue cooking to 310° F., or to the hard-crack stage. Remove quickly from the heat and, to prevent the sugar from becoming dark, set the pan in cold water. A few drops vegetable coloring may be added. Remove the pan and set it in warm water.

Oil a rolling pin or the blade of a large knife and hold it out straight with the left hand. With the right hand dip a warm spoon into the syrup and shake it backward and forward over the rolling pin. The sugar will fall across the pin in long threads. Continue the operation until enough spun sugar is obtained, then trim off the ends and press it into molds or shapes.

Another method of spinning sugar is to oil the handles of two wooden spoons and fasten them in drawers or under weights with the ends projecting over the edge of a table. Cover the floor underneath with clean paper or several baking pans. Then dip into the syrup a large fork or a wire whisk. Move the fork quickly back and forth over the handles of the spoons. The threads may be made fine or coarse by moving the fork quickly or slowly.

Some cakes, particularly those decorated with fruit and nuts, are finished with a transparent icing that gives cake and decorations an attractive high shine.   **Clear Glaze**

TRANSPARENT ICING   *Glace Transparente*

MAKE a thick syrup by boiling 1 cup sugar in 1/2 cup water, without stirring, until the syrup spins a thread (220° F. on a candy thermometer). Pour the syrup very slowly in a thin stream into a bowl, working it constantly with a wooden spoon until it becomes clear and thick. Add 1 teaspoon rum and continue to work the icing until it is lukewarm. Pour the icing over the decorated cake.

Chocolat CHOCOLATE

DARK sweet or semisweet chocolate, grated or shredded or shaped into fat curls, is a simple and very attractive finish for a frosted cake. To make chocolate curls, melt the chocolate over hot water and pour it out to cool on a flat plate or a marble slab. While the chocolate is still soft enough to be flexible, draw a knife across the top and shape the curls. Cones or cornets may be shaped in the same way. When these harden, they may be filled with butter cream or whipped cream, with the aid of a pastry tube, and arranged on or around the cake. Hard chocolate may be grated or shredded with a knife or on a kitchen grater.

Glace pour Tartes aux Fruits Divers GLAZE FOR FRUIT TARTS

THE lovely gloss that you may have admired on a French chef's fruit tarts comes from the application of melted jelly. Strawberries and other dark or red fruits are glazed with currant jelly; peaches, bananas, and other light-colored fruits are glazed with apricot jam. The clear jelly need only be melted, stirred with a fork, and thinned with a little hot water. The apricot jam should be thinned and strained. Or apricot sauce may be used for this purpose.

Fruit tarts are frequently finished with rosettes of whipped cream, and a border of chopped green pistachios, or of chopped almonds, is sometimes added.

SPÉCIALITÉS FRANÇAISES

French Specialties

PÂTÉS TO WINES IN COOKING

T HERE are scores of dishes that are as French as the *fleur-de-lis*, and almost exclusively French. The appearance, flavor, and savory subtle aroma of pâtés, for instance, always evokes thoughts of French cooking and France. No one who has not eaten the Frenchman's beloved *escargots* can claim to know *la cuisine française*, and the black truffle of

589

Perigord is symbolic of that section of France because it is considered an almost priceless foodstuff by some gourmets. The list of such peculiarly Gallic foods is long. Special consideration is given to a few of them in this chapter, and to the subject of wine and liqueurs in cooking, in the use of which the French have always been masters.

Pâtés and Terrines

PÂTÉS MAY seem to some, perhaps, a kind of special " extra, " but to a Frenchman pâté is an ever-present foodstuff—part of everyday meals and important social occasions, and an indispensable part of *haute cuisine*. *Pâté de foie gras* opens a fine dinner; *pâté de foie de porc* goes along in the huntsman's *pique-nique* luncheon basket, and *pâté maison* is the pride of any French restaurant, anywhere in the world, because it reflects the owner's or chef's skill in blending meats and seasonings. It would take a social revolution to remove the pâté from the French scene.

It has become customary to describe as a pâté any of the finely ground hors-d'oeuvre mixtures made with pork, veal, fowl, game, and liver, variously combined and seasoned according to the demands of the particular mixture. Technically speaking, however, most of these mixtures are not pâtés but terrines. The basic meat mixture remains exactly the same *Terrines* for both, but when the meat is baked in a casserole lined with fat pork, *Pâtés* it becomes a terrine; when it is baked in a crust, or, as the French say, *en croûte*, it becomes a pâté. If the mixture is made from a fowl, or a *Galantines* game bird, and steamed instead of baked, it is called a galantine.

Except in farm homes, where the ingredients come from the farm itself, most people in France do not make their own pâtés, for the simple reason that they can easily buy such good ones. Every city has scores of *charcuteries*, the shops that specialize in making pâtés, terrines, galantines, and all the other hors-d'oeuvre specialties.

Pâté mixtures fall into two basic groups. One group consists entirely of ground meats combined with other finely chopped ingredients and is, I believe, the one most familiar to Americans because it includes the *pâté maison* found in French restaurants. The second group of pâtés combines the ground ingredients with strips of meat cut into large julienne, long strips about 1/2 inch square. These are marinated in seasoned wine and arranged in the center of the ground mixture. Pieces of truffles, if available, also go in with the julienne. When the finished pâté is cut and served, each slice has an attractive mosaic pattern. The ground mixture—and it always includes considerable fat to make it smooth and rich—is called the *farce*, or stuffing. The marinated strips of meat, the **Farce** fat pork, and the truffles are the *garniture*, or garnish.

The crust in which pâtés are baked may vary, according to taste, **En Croûte** from a yeast-raised brioche to a fine, flaky pastry. The kind most commonly used, however, is rather firm, but short and rich. Most chefs prefer this crust for a good reason. A pâté is often kept for at least a week, to be served as the first course of several meals or possibly as the entrée for light luncheons, and the crust just described remains fresh longer than flaky pastry or puff paste. The latter kinds, so excellent when freshly baked, become limp and unattractive after a few days.

The importance of aspic in pâtés should be stressed. If you make **Aspic in** a terrine, the final trick is to place a board or flat plate on top of it and **Pâtés** weight it down as it cools. As the terrine shrinks in cooling, this weight compresses it just enough to eliminate the tiny air holes that would make it difficult to slice. The slices must be firm, and must not fall apart under the pressure of the knife. But when you bake a pâté in its crust, you can't, of course, weight it down. Therefore you pour in the aspic to fill the tiny holes formed during baking, and to bind the mass together. The aspic also fills the space created by shrinkage during the baking process. Furthermore, a savory aspic improves the flavor of the final dish, adding what is called a *fumet*.

Terrines are usually baked in heavy pottery baking dishes, round or oval, that have straight sides and covers with a small hole to vent the steam. The chef lines the bottom and sides of the dish with thin slices of fat salt pork. To get larger pieces that cover more surface, cut the slices at least 1/4 inch thick, put them between 2 pieces of wax paper, and pound them with a wooden mallet to about 1/8 inch thickness. Or ask your butcher to do it for you. Some recipes call for fat fresh pork. To substitute fat salt pork—more easily obtained—pound it thin and then parboil it for a minute or two, if necessary, to remove excess salt.

Terrines should always be baked surrounded by a water bath, like a baked custard. Choose a roasting pan that permits the water to be about 1/3 as deep as the sides of the baking dish. The oven heat should be a little slower than the temperature suitable for roasting meat, but high enough to maintain constant steam around the casserole. *Pâtés en croûte* are more often baked in oblong casseroles. But you can use a loaf pan,

Pâté Mold — the kind suitable for pound cake. A true pâté mold has no bottom; the sides are hinged at one side and closed at the other with a metal pin. When the pin is removed, the sides open and the pâté can be removed from the mold without breaking. The mold must be put on a baking sheet so that the pâté may be put into the oven without being disturbed. If the pan is metal, line it with foil so that the crust will not be overcooked before the meat filling is done. Traditionally, the top of the crust is decorated with overlays of pastry cut in fancy patterns and intricate scorings made with a sharp pointed knife.

It takes about 30 to 35 minutes per pound to cook either a terrine or a pâté. A professional chef can tell when the pâté is done by inserting a long kitchen needle or skewer into the center, leaving it there for a minute, and then touching it to the tongue as soon as it is withdrawn. The heat of the metal tells him whether cooking should be continued. But the novice will find it easier to examine the fat which rises up in the small paper funnel usually inserted in the top of the pâté crust. It serves the double purpose of venting the steam and providing a place for the

To Test
Baked Pâtés
and Terrines fat that rises to the surface as the pâté cooks. When this fat is perfectly clear, with no trace of cloudiness, all the meat juices have been completely absorbed and thoroughly cooked, which means that the pâté is done. In other words, the fat looks clear because no uncooked juice remains to make it cloudy.

In baking a terrine, you can remove the cover of the baking dish and see whether the fat on the surface is clear or cloudy. This fat, incidentally, is all reabsorbed during the cooling period and contributes to the final excellence of the pâté.

Pâtés and terrines should be slowly cooled after baking and should not be refrigerated until they have reached room temperature. In all, they should have 12 to 24 hours of cooling and chilling before they are sliced. After you have sliced them, cover the cut surface with fat or with a piece of foil before returning them to the refrigerator. And a whole uncut terrine or pâté mixture without a crust that is to be stored for future use should be completely covered with a thick coating of fat. Pork fat, melted and cooled, is the best choice.

Pâté recipes do not vary radically, as the procedures of mixing and cooking remain much the same. The differences lie in possible combinations of meats and seasonings that give the individual touch. Thus, anyone can evolve his own *spécialité*. For example, a liver pâté may be made entirely with poultry livers, entirely with pork liver, or with a combination of the two, in any desired proportion. Or it may be made with pork and veal, or game, either furred or feathered. However, the first named will be the most delicate. The more delicate the mixture, the lighter the spice, so that game mixtures usually demand more piquant seasoning. Many cooks like to add a spoonful of Cognac for each pound of pâté mixture.

As for the aspic, any good consommé will serve as a base, and it is customarily flavored with Sherry or Madeira. For game mixtures, the bones of the animal or bird should be used in making the stock. It is wise to make sure that the aspic will set by chilling it thoroughly and remelting it for use in the pâté. If it fails to set, strengthen it by adding 1 envelope gelatin softened in 2 tablespoons cold water for each pint of boiling aspic.

The secret of making a successful pâté lies in the fine grinding of the ingredients. In the old days, the meats were finely chopped by hand or pounded in a mortar and then forced through a sieve. But mechanical food choppers have happily eliminated that chore. Running the mixture through the food chopper a second time or more, using the finest blade, insures a beautifully smooth result.

PORK LIVER PÂTÉ

Pâté de Foie de Porc

CUT in pieces 2 pounds pork liver, cover the pieces with milk, and soak them for at least 1 hour. Drain the liver, rinse it with cold water, and dry it well. Mix with 3/4 pound each of lean pork and fat pork, both diced, and put all through the food chopper twice. Add 1 1/2 tablespoons flour and, with a wooden spoon, work the mixture for about 5 minutes. Add

2 eggs, one at a time, mixing them in well. Add 1 teaspoon chopped parsley, 1/2 teaspoon salt, a pinch each of ground thyme and Parisian spice or poultry seasoning, 1 bay leaf, powdered, and 2 shallots or 1 small onion, finely chopped.

Line a baking dish or a loaf pan with thin slices of salt pork, pack in the pâté mixture, and cover the top with slices of salt pork. Cover the baking dish, set it in a pan of boiling water, and bake the pâté in a moderate oven (350° F.) for 1 3/4 hours. Remove the cover, place a plate on top of the pâté, and put a weight on it to flatten the top as the pâté cools. Chill the pâté and unmold it. Garnish with parsley.

TERRINE DE CHAGNY LAMELOISE

Chicken Liver and Sausage Pâté

CHOP 1 1/2 pounds fresh chicken livers very finely and mix well with 1 pound fresh sausage meat. Season with 1 teaspoon salt and a pinch of poultry seasoning. Add 1/4 cup good Madeira or Sherry, 2 tablespoons Cognac, and 3 eggs, well beaten, and beat thoroughly with a wooden spoon. Line the bottom and sides of a heavy casserole with thin slices of fat salt pork and fill with the meat mixture. Cover with thin slices of fat salt pork and lay a bay leaf on top. Cover the casserole and seal the edge with a stiff dough, made by mixing flour and water together. Set the casserole in a pan containing about 2 inches of boiling water and bake in a hot oven (400° F.) for about 1 1/2 hours, adding more boiling water to the pan as the water evaporates. Remove the casserole from the oven and cool. Remove the cover and discard the bay leaf and fat salt pork from the top of the pâté. Chill the pâté and serve it from the casserole. Madeira aspic may be poured over the top before chilling.

TRUFFLED GOOSE LIVER PÂTÉ WITH PORT WINE ASPIC

Terrine de Foie Gras Truffé au Porto

DIVIDE in half a firm 2-pound goose liver and trim each half to make regular-shaped pieces. Save the trimmings. Make a hole in each half with a skewer and insert a piece of truffle. Season the liver with 1/2 teaspoon salt mixed with a pinch of poultry seasoning, place it in a bowl, and sprinkle with 3 tablespoons Cognac. Let it marinate for 2 hours, turning occasionally. Cut 3/4 pound lean fresh pork and 1 pound fat fresh pork in pieces, mix with the trimmings of the goose liver, and run through a meat grinder, using the finest blade. Add 1/4 to 1/2 cup truffles cut into small dice, season with 1/2 teaspoon salt mixed with a pinch of poultry seasoning and add 1/2 cup Madeira or Sherry. Mix well.

Line the bottom and sides of a terrine with very thin slices of fat salt pork, and cover the bottom with the ground seasoned pork mixture, using about 1/3 of it. Place one of the pieces of seasoned goose liver on this and cover with another layer of the pork mixture. Put the other piece of seasoned goose liver on top and cover with the remaining pork mixture. Cover with thin slices of fat salt pork. Put a small bay leaf on top and a little thyme, a sprig of fresh thyme if available. Cover the terrine and seal the edges with a roll of dough made by mixing flour with enough water to make a firm dough. Place the terrine in a shallow pan of boiling water and cook in a moderately hot oven (375° F.) for 1 1/2 hours, or until steam comes out of the hole in the cover and the fat that boils out is clear and colorless. Remove the dough, take off the cover, and place a stack of 4 or 5 plates on top of the mixture to compress it as it cools. Let it stand overnight. Unmold the pâté by dipping the outside of the terrine in hot water to melt the fat, then loosen the inside edges with a knife, and invert the pâté on a dish. Remove the slices of fat pork, clean the terrine, and return the pâté to it. Fill the terrine with Port wine aspic and chill until the aspic is set.

PÂTÉ MAISON

Pâté Maison

MAKE a marinade by mixing together 1 cup dry white wine, 4 tablespoons each of brandy and olive oil, 2 teaspoons salt, and a generous pinch of poultry seasoning. Cut 1/2 pound each of veal and pork, well trimmed, into strips about 1/2 inch square. Put the strips in a bowl and cover them with half the marinade. Put twice through the finest blade of the food chopper 1 pound pork, containing a high proportion of fat, and 1/2 pound veal (the trimmings from cutting the strips can be used), put the ground meat in another bowl, and cover it with the remaining marinade. Top the marinade in each bowl with 1 onion, sliced, 2 cloves of garlic, and a sprig of parsley, cover the bowls, and let the meat marinate in the refrigerator overnight or for 12 hours.

Prepare a pâté dough as follows: Sift together 4 cups flour and 1 teaspoon salt, and add 1 cup each of butter and shortening, cutting them in with a pastry blender or with 2 knives. Add 1 beaten egg and about

Pâté Dough

1/2 cup very cold water, or enough to make a firm dough, and mix the dough well, handling it lightly. Wrap the dough in wax paper and chill it overnight or for 12 hours.

Roll out part of the dough 1/8 to 1/4 inch thick, in a rectangle large enough to line the bottom and sides of a pâté mold or loaf pan.

Line the mold or pan, letting the dough hang over about 3/4 inch around the top edge. Discard the onion, garlic, and parsley from both bowls of meat and stir the marinade with the meat. Spread half the ground pork mixture on the dough in the pan and arrange on the pork the meat strips, laying them parallel and lengthwise to make an attractive pattern. For a richer pâté, strips of cooked ham, goose liver, and truffles may also be added.

Cover the strips with the remaining ground pork mixture. Divide the remaining dough in half and roll it out into two pieces, large enough to cover the pâté. Roll them a little thinner than the piece used to line the pan. Lay one piece on top of the pâté, moisten the edges, and fold over the 3/4-inch edge of the bottom, sealing the dough by crimping the edges. Cover the top with the second piece of dough, pressing it down firmly. Cut a 1/2-inch round hole in the center and insert a small paper funnel. If desired, decorate the top with pastry flowers or score it with a small sharp knife in an attractive pattern. Bake the pâté in a hot oven (400° F.) for 15 to 20 minutes, reduce the heat to moderately hot (375° F.), and bake the pâté for 1 1/2 to 1 3/4 hours more, or until the fat rising in the paper funnel is clear. Let the pâté cool partially, pour in through the hole in the top 1 cup Madeira aspic, and let it cool to room temperature. Chill the pâté thoroughly before serving it.

CHICKEN GALANTINE

Galantine de Poularde

SPLIT a chicken down the back and open it out flat, skin side up. Using a very sharp knife, start at the neck and carefully cut the skin away from the flesh, removing it in one piece. Trim the skin at the wings and legs, leaving enough skin to fold over the openings.

Remove the breasts and the tenderloins under them and cut the meat lengthwise in 6 strips from each side. Cut into 6 strips each a 1/4-pound slice leg of veal and 1/4 pound fresh pork loin or tenderloin, and cut into 12 strips 1/2 pound fat pork. The strips should be of uniform size. Place the strips in a shallow bowl with 1 tablespoon shallot or onion, finely chopped, 1 teaspoon salt, a pinch of poultry spice, 3 sprigs of parsley, 1 bay leaf, a pinch of thyme, and 3 tablespoons Cognac or 4 tablespoons Madeira. Cover the bowl and marinate the meat in the refrigerator for several hours or overnight.

Cut 4 thin slices from a 1-pound piece of fat salt pork and keep the slices. Combine the remainder of the pork fat with 1/4 pound each of veal and pork, both lean, and all the remaining meat from the chicken bones, cut the meat in pieces, and run all together twice through the finest blade of the food chopper. Add to the ground meat 1 teaspoon salt, a pinch of poultry spice, and 2 beaten eggs. Drain the marinade from the meat strips, and strain it into the ground meat. Mix all together well. Cut into 6 strips each 1/4 pound cooked ham and 1/4 pound cooked ox tongue.

When starting to form the galantine, you should have the whole skin of the chicken, a bowl of seasoned ground meat mixture, the strips of meat and pork fat drained from their marinade, the strips of cooked ham and ox tongue, and 4 slices fat pork.

Lay the 4 slices fat pork on a towel and cover the fat pork with the chicken skin, outside down. Spread 1/4 the ground meat mixture on the skin and on it arrange 1/3 the meat strips, alternating the different kinds so that each slice of the finished galantine will contain a mosaic pattern. Continue to make alternate layers of 1/4 the ground meat mixture and 1/3 the strips, finishing with the ground meat mixture. Add thick slices of truffle, if desired, distributing them through the farce.

By lifting the towel, gently shape the arrangement into a roll, enclosed firmly in the skin. Sew the skin the length of the roll and at the ends, then roll the galantine securely in the towel. Tie the ends tightly. Lower the galantine into a kettle containing 3 quarts boiling chicken stock (which can be made from the chicken bones). Cook the galantine slowly for 1 3/4 hours. Remove the galantine from the broth and let it stand until it is cool enough to handle. Remove the towel and roll the galantine in another towel, tightening it again and tying the ends securely. Lay it on a platter, place a board on top, and weight the board with about 5 plates, or enough to press the galantine a little, but not enough to squeeze out the juice. Cool the galantine to room temperature, remove the towel, and chill it. The galantine will keep for a week. To keep it for 2 weeks, spread it thickly with pork fat. To serve, cut the galantine in slices.

Timbales

TIMBALES remind me of England's Edward VII. They were one of his favorite dishes, and I cannot recall a single royal menu that did not include a timbale. In fact, almost every elaborate menu in those days included a timbale. In the early days of the old Ritz in New York, these elegant pastry shells, filled with succulent sauced foods, still appeared regularly on menus in both the public dining rooms and for private parties.

I can remember standing in the kitchen of the house on Grosvenor Square, where Edward conducted his personal life apart from public duties, and hearing the butler ask, " Is the timbale ready for His Highness ? The fish course has been served. " Into his white-gloved hands I would put the silver server with its shining dome, under the dome perhaps a *timbale de ris de veau à la régence*, which the king liked especially.

Those were years of royal opulence, at the turn of the century, when the gourmet king gave famous dinner parties for 6 or 8 close friends. They were *dîners par excellence*, because the king's friends, for the most part, were among the world's greatest connoisseurs of food and wine. I, a *sous-chef* at the Ritz in London, had come to Grosvenor House because of the king's devotion to my employer, César Ritz, and to the cuisine of the Ritz Hotels.

My acquaintance with King Edward began when I arrived in Paris at the end of the century, and found a place in the kitchens of the Hotel Bristol. Edward, then Prince of Wales, frequently visited the Bristol. But when the Ritz opened its doors on the Place Vendôme, Edward transferred his Paris headquarters to it at once. " Where Ritz goes, I go, " he has been quoted as saying. Rumor has it that Monsieur Morlock, the owner of the Bristol, never again spoke to Monsieur Elles the manager of the Ritz, after this terrible *coup*.

I myself was at that time at the bottom of the ladder, a poor *potager* struggling in the kitchen with gallons of stock and soup bubbling in copper pots. I could not have imagined that one day I would be entrusted with the preparation of *les dîners intimes* for Edward VII, at a time when Great Britain was at the peak of her power and glory and her king set a high standard in the art of fine living. (Nor could I know I would watch from a window of the London Ritz his impressive funeral procession, with its poignant touch—the king's little dog trotting behind the great flag-draped coffin in the slow-moving cortege.)

The custom of having a special staff to handle the fine cookery for special functions, rather than the regular staff of a household, is a typically French one. Monsieur Malley, my colleague at the Paris Ritz and later my superior in charge of the kitchens at the London Ritz, knew that since I had served my apprenticeship in the château section of France, I knew the fine points of catering to the French aristocracy. Chef Malley had every reason to believe that I would know how to handle the special dinner parties at Grosvenor House, so when he was called upon to cater parties there, he asked for my assistance.

In common with many other London mansions, Grosvenor House had a fine kitchen. There was all the equipment one could want to work with, and everything was in perfect order, immaculate from the tiled floors to the warming ovens on the ranges. There was a fireplace in which to broil meat and fish and a spit for roasting meat and poultry. Not the least of the advantages of the royal kitchen were the rosy-cheeked English kitchenmaids, always three or four of them dancing attendance on us, fetching this, fixing that, cleaning up here, offering the help of a pair of hands there. It was in a pleasant atmosphere, you can see, that I made the timbales for the king.

In our culinary language, the word "timbale" has two meanings. It means an ovenproof clay, porcelain, or metal mold, either round or oval, with straight sides, and it also means a pie shell that is baked in one of these molds, in which exquisitely sauced mixtures of chicken, sweetbreads, mushrooms, truffles, and so on are served. This shell, however, is not served from the mold in which it is baked, like an American chicken pie or an English beef and kidney pie. A pastry timbale is unmolded and placed on a serving platter and is filled just before it is sent to the table. A true gourmet likes to eat the crust. In some ways the timbale can be more delicious than a puff paste *vol-au-vent*. Its crust is slow to absorb the filling and thus lose its crispness.

I think it is too bad that more people do not try their hands at timbales, because a timbale can quite properly be the main dish of a simple dinner or luncheon—and a very good and hearty main dish. In elaborate menus it is the first entrée, served after the fish course. However, if the timbale has a fish filling, it can take the place of both fish course and first entrée.

Pâte
à Timbale

PASTRY FOR TIMBALES

MIX 1/2 cup butter, 1 tablespoon sugar, 1 teaspoon salt, and 1 egg. Cut this mixture into 2 cups sifted flour and add just enough cold water, about 4 or 5 tablespoons, to hold the mixture together. Work this dough as little as possible; too much handling toughens it.

To Line a
Round or Oval
Mold with
Dough

To shape the timbale, roll out a circle of dough about 1/4 inch thick and large enough to cover the bottom and sides of the mold. Sprinkle lightly with flour and fold the sheet of dough in half, but do not crease the fold. With the open edges facing forward, pull the two ends towards you to form what looks like a skull cap, in French, *la calotte de pâte*. Stretch the dough gently to get a bowl-shaped piece when the halves are opened. Fit this into the well-buttered mold, working it into the edges so that the finished timbale will have the exact shape of the mold. A decoration on its sides will, of course, show on the finished timbale.

Let about 1/2 inch of dough lap over the edge of the mold like a flange and decorate with a pastry wheel or pastry leaves or pinch it neatly. Line the mold with wax paper and fill it with dried beans to weight down the pastry and keep it from puffing up and out of shape as it bakes. Bake in a hot oven (400° F.) until the shell is golden brown. Discard the beans, remove the wax paper, and carefully unmold the timbale. Let dry in a warm place until ready to fill and serve.

For a pastry cover, roll out a piece of the dough and cut it to fit nicely over the top of the timbale, resting on the 1/2-inch flange. Decorate the edge of the cover like the flange. Leaves are usually cut from the pastry and arranged in a kind of wreath around the top of the cover and 3 small circles of dough, graduated in size, are placed in the center, one on top of the other, for a knob. Bake the cover on a flat pan or cooky sheet.

Timbale molds vary in height from 2 1/2 inches to 7 or 8 inches. Any straight-sided mold can be used, a charlotte mold, a deep pie dish, or a casserole. Usually covers are made only for the very high timbales, and when the timbale is covered, the contents of the timbale are not elaborately garnished. When the timbale is not high, the filling is garnished and the mixture is piled up a little higher than the edge of the timbale. The pastry cover is then omitted. In France one can buy a dome-shaped, high silver cover to place over the open timbale.

FILLINGS FOR TIMBALES AND VOL-AU-VENT

Garnitures pour Timbales et Vol-au-Vent

IN FRENCH a timbale or a *vol-au-vent* is said to be "*garnie*," or garnished, when it is filled. The richly sauced fillings for the two are interchangeable and are often combinations that can also be served simply with rice. In the section on variety meats you will find several combinations that go well in a timbale or *vol-au-vent*: *ris de veau Toulousaine*, sweetbreads with chicken quenelles and mushroom caps, for example, and *ris de veau à la crème*, creamed sweetbreads. The *salpicons*, or fillings, for hot hors-d'oeuvre are also appropriate for timbales. Cut the pieces of chicken, mushroom, fish, and so on into large pieces; do not chop them fine as you would for hors-d'oeuvre. An important point to remember is not to put the filling into the timbale crust or *vol-au-vent* until just before it is served.

Because timbales and *vol-au-vent* are elegant dishes, the special garnishes arranged on the filling take on added importance. Mushrooms, for example, are always turned. (Turning mushrooms, incidentally, was one of the first things we *apprentis* were taught. Before we could be trusted with making the sauces for the fillings or the pastry for the crust of a timbale, we had the job of making garnishes.) Quenelles and *mousselines* of chicken, veal, or fish, truffles, and cockscombs, which you will find in the section on garnishes, often appear in traditional timbales, such as this one of sweetbreads *à la régence*.

TIMBALE OF SWEETBREADS REGENCY

Timbale de Ris de Veau à la Régence

BLANCH 3 pairs of sweetbreads and braise them *à blanc*.

Make a good *sauce suprême* by adding to 1/2 cup chicken broth the stems and peelings of the 12 mushrooms used for the garnishing, the liquid in which they were cooked, and a little truffle juice. Boil this rapidly until it is reduced to 1/2 its original quantity. Add 1 cup *sauce velouté*, combine well, and add 1 cup heavy cream. Correct the seasoning with salt and thicken the sauce with 2 egg yolks mixed with a little cream. Heat the sauce just under the boiling point and strain it through a fine sieve.

In another saucepan put 12 turned and cooked mushrooms, 12 cockscombs, and 12 to 15 small *mousselines* of chicken decorated with truffles cut in half-moon shapes. Heat them with 1/4 cup dry Sherry or Madeira and 1/2 cup of the sauce.

Place a baked pastry timbale ·3 to 3 1/2 inches deep on a serving platter and spread some of the sauce in the bottom. Arrange the sweetbreads over it and place the mushrooms, cockscombs, and *mousselines* of chicken over and around them. Add more sauce and serve immediately.

Vol-au-Vent and Bouchées

THE TERMS "*vol-au-vent*" and "*bouchée*" are not, I believe, familiar to many people in this country. But everyone knows what a "patty shell" is. *Eh bien*, a *bouchée* is a patty shell, and a *vol-au-vent* is the same thing, a patty shell, but one large enough to serve several people. In France, you can order either from any *pâtisserie*, but here only the small patty shells are generally available. These light, flaky cases, served with the sauced fillings described above, can be the main dish of a luncheon or supper or the *petite entrée* of an elaborate dinner. Very tiny *bouchées* (really just mouthfuls, the literal translation of the word) are served as hot hors-d'oeuvre.

Vol-au-vent and *bouchées* are made from puff paste, which you will find in the section on pastry. You can make the paste several days before it is used. In this case, it is given only 4 of the 6 "turns" required. The thick folded square of paste, well dusted with flour, is wrapped securely in plastic wrap or aluminum foil to prevent the surface from drying out. When the shells are to be served, the paste is given the final 2 "turns," cut, and baked.

LARGE PUFF PASTE SHELL

Vol-au-Vent

ROLL out puff paste 3/4 inch thick and cut out two 8-inch circles. Moisten a baking sheet with water and lay one circle on it, top side down. Cut out a 6-inch circle inside the second 8-inch circle, and remove the inner circle, leaving a 1-inch rim. Reserve the 6-inch circle for another use or bake it for a cover. Moisten the border of the first circle to the width of 1 inch. Lay the cutout rim, top side down, on the first circle so that it fits exactly over the moistened border. Press the rim down lightly on the circle. With a knife score the outside of the shell at half-inch intervals—cut in about 1/4 inch, and at an angle—for a scalloped effect. Chill the shell in the refrigerator for about 15 minutes before baking. The dough should be ice cold.

Brush the top only of the shell with *dorure*—1 egg beaten with 1 tablespoon water. Do not let the *dorure* run down inside or outside the shell. It will prevent the pastry from rising evenly. Bake the *vol-au-vent* in a very hot oven (450° F.) for 10 minutes, or until the shell is well puffed and lightly browned. Reduce the oven temperature to moderately hot (375° F.) and bake for 25 to 30 minutes longer.

PUFF PASTE PATTY SHELLS

Bouchées

ROLL out puff paste 1/2 inch thick and cut it with a round scalloped cooky cutter about 2 1/2 inches in diameter. Place the scalloped circles top side down on a baking sheet moistened with water. Brush the tops with *dorure*—1 egg yolk beaten with 1 tablespoon water. With a round sharp-edged cooky cutter about 1 1/2 incles in diameter, press halfway down into the paste to mark a 1/2-inch rim. Or, if preferred, the paste can be rolled thinner and a rim laid on each circle, as in making *vol-au-vent*. Chill the paste in the refrigerator for about 10 minutes.

Bake in a hot oven (425° to 450° F.) for about 10 minutes, then reduce the heat to moderately hot (375° F.) and bake the patty shells until they are golden brown, for about 20 minutes. Remove from the oven and cut around the scored circles with a small sharp knife. Lift out the inner circles to use as covers. If there is any soft, partly cooked dough inside the patty shells, lift it out and discard it. Use patty shells the same day they are baked, if possible. Reheat them briefly, fill them, and put on the covers.

*Vol-au-Vent
ou Bouchées
à la Reine*

CREAMED CHICKEN IN PUFF PASTE SHELLS

To 2 cups hot cream sauce, add 2 tablespoons of the water in which 1/4 pound mushrooms have been cooked and stir in 2 egg yolks lightly beaten with 3 tablespoons heavy cream. Dice enough leftover white meat of chicken to make 1 cup and combine it with the cooked and diced mushrooms, and if desired 1/4 to 1/2 cup leftover sweetbreads and 1 truffle, both diced. Heat the meat and vegetable mixture in a saucepan with 1/4 cup dry Sherry or Madeira for 5 to 6 minutes, add the hot sauce, and keep hot over hot water until ready to serve. Serve in *bouchées*, patty shells, or in a *vol-au-vent*. It is important to have plenty of sauce in proportion to chicken because the crust of the patty shells or the *vol-au-vent* will absorb some liquid.

Cassoulet

THERE are as many different recipes for *cassoulet* as there are for bouillabaisse. Goose, game, pork, or another meat—or a combination of these—may go into a *cassoulet*, but whatever the meat or poultry used, the base of every *cassoulet* is beans. It is a kind of bean stew. Garlic is essential, and usually tomatoes are included.

*Cassoulet
d'Oie
Toulousaine*

CASSOULET OF GOOSE TOULOUSAINE

SOAK 3 pounds dried white beans in water for a few hours and drain them. Put them in a large kettle, cover them with fresh water, and add 1 carrot, 1 onion studded with 2 cloves, 1 clove of garlic, crushed, 1 tablespoon salt, a little pepper, 1/2 pound garlic pork sausage, and a faggot made by tying together a stalk of celery, 2 sprigs of parsley, 1 bay leaf, and a little thyme. Cook slowly for 1 hour, or until the beans are soft. Remove the sausage after 35 minutes and reserve it. Leave the beans in a warm place.

In another saucepan, melt 1 tablespoon butter, add 1 large onion, finely chopped, and cook until the onion is lightly browned. Add 3 tomatoes, peeled, seeded, and chopped, 1/2 cup tomato sauce, and 1 tablespoon chopped parsley. Cook the sauce for about 5 minutes.

Drain the beans and remove and discard the carrot, onion, and faggot. Correct the seasoning with salt. Slice the meat from a small roast goose and slice 2 pounds roast lamb or pork—freshly cooked or leftover—and the cooked sausage. Add the gravy from the roast goose to the beans.

Spread a layer of beans in an earthenware casserole, rubbed with a clove of garlic, add a layer of the mixed sliced meats, and repeat until the beans and meats are used. Spread the top with fine bread crumbs, dot with butter, and brown in a moderately hot oven (375° F.). Sprinkle with chopped parsley, if desired, and serve very hot.

Frogs' Legs

WE FRENCHMEN are noted for our love of frogs' legs. For French boys, catching frogs can be a combination game and business, a sport from which pocket money can be realized. Frogs are quite stupid and very easy to catch. One easy way is to go out at night with a lantern and attract them to the water's edge with the light. They can then easily be pulled into a net, but the method is perhaps a bit unsportsmanlike.

Fresh frogs' legs are so perishable that you must order them in advance at most fish markets, and they should not be kept longer than overnight. The frozen ones must be prepared as soon as they are defrosted. A strong odor tells you when frogs' legs have been kept too long and must be discarded. Frogs' legs vary in size; the medium size, which I prefer, ranges from 8 to 12 legs to the pound. Larger legs are likely to be old and tough. Very small ones, ranging from 18 to 20 to the pound, are usually very tender, but of course there's not much to eat on the leg. The meat is extremely delicate and very delicious. It tastes something like the white meat of a small squab chicken. There is no way that I know of to tell whether frogs' legs will be tender or not, although frogs raised in captivity are more likely to be uniform in tenderness as well as in size. But when you cook them, it is very easy to predict how tender they will be, because as soon as a tough stringy leg is touched by the heat, it stiffens out straight in the pan. Tender legs remain relaxed and supple.

Frogs purchased in the market are already skinned; but if you catch them yourself, you must skin them and cut off the feet with a pair of kitchen scissors. Then you should soak them in cold water for about 2 hours, changing the water occasionally. This makes the flesh white and plump. Allow 3 pairs or more for each serving, depending on the size of the legs.

Sautéed Frogs' Legs — Dry the legs well on a towel if you plan to sauté them. Otherwise they won't brown and have the characteristic crusty surface. Heat the fat very hot, put in the legs, and cook them quickly. Allow 7 or 8 minutes for small legs, 10 to 12 for large ones, turning them as they cook, to brown them on all sides. A frog's leg is just about as easy to cook as a piece of bacon.

Grenouilles à la Meunière

FROGS' LEGS WITH BROWN BUTTER

SOAK 2 pounds frogs' legs in cold water to cover for 2 hours and drain and dry them thoroughly. Dip them in milk, then in flour, and shake off the surplus flour. Cover the bottom of a skillet generously with clarified butter or oil, heat it well, add the frogs' legs, and brown them on all sides, turning them in the butter. This takes about 7 to 10 minutes, depending on how heavy the legs are.

Transfer the legs to a serving dish and season them with salt, a little freshly ground pepper, and a few drops of lemon juice. Discard the oil in the pan and add 1/2 tablespoon butter for each serving. Cook the butter until it is nut brown, pour it over the frogs' legs and sprinkle all with finely chopped parsley. Garnish with slices of lemon sprinkled with finely chopped parsley.

Grenouilles Amandine

FROGS' LEGS WITH ALMONDS

FOLLOW the recipe for *grenouilles à la meunière*, frogs' legs with brown butter, adding blanched, slivered toasted almonds to the brown butter.

FROGS' LEGS WITH SAUTÉED POTATOES

SAUTÉ frogs' legs as for *grenouilles à la meunière*, frogs' legs with brown butter. In another pan sauté raw potatoes cut in small dice until they are golden brown. Combine the potatoes with the cooked frogs' legs and season with salt, a little freshly ground pepper, and a few drops lemon juice. Finish with brown butter.

Grenouilles à la Parmentier

FROGS' LEGS WITH GARLIC BUTTER

DIP 2 pounds frogs' legs in milk, then in flour and sauté them quickly in a mixture of half olive oil and butter until golden brown. Turn the frogs' legs into a serving dish and sprinkle them with salt and pepper, a few drops of lemon juice, and chopped parsley.

Cook 6 tablespoons butter until it is hazelnut brown, add 1 tablespoon minced garlic, and pour the garlic butter over the frogs' legs.

Or peel, seed, and chop 1 or 2 tomatoes and cook them quickly in a shallow pan until most of the moisture is cooked away, add 1 teaspoon finely chopped garlic, and pour this sauce over the frogs' legs with the brown butter.

Grenouilles à la Provençale

FRIED FROGS' LEGS

SOAK 2 pounds frogs' legs and drain and dry them thoroughly. Beat 2 whole eggs lightly, season them with a little salt, pepper, and grated nutmeg and add 2 tablespoons cream. Dip the frogs' legs in this mixture and in fine, fresh bread crumbs. Fry the legs in deep hot fat or oil to a golden brown. Drain them on absorbent paper. Serve with tomato sauce to which a few drops of lemon juice have been added.

Grenouilles Frites

FROGS' LEGS POULETTE

SOAK 2 pounds frogs' legs and drain and dry them thoroughly.

Clean and slice 1/2 pound fresh mushrooms and put in a saucepan with 1 tablespoon chopped shallots or onion and 1 tablespoon butter. Add the frogs' legs and 1/2 cup white wine. Bring the liquid to a boil

Grenouilles à la Poulette

and cook the legs for 10 to 12 minutes, or until they are tender. Remove the frogs' legs and mushrooms to a serving dish and reduce the liquid in the pan to not more than 1/2 cup. Add 1/2 cup cream, boil the sauce again, and cook it for 2 or 3 minutes. Thicken with *beurre manié* made by creaming 1 tablespoon butter with 1 teaspoon flour, and cook, stirring constantly, for a few minutes. Season with salt and a little freshly ground pepper, and if desired a few drops of lemon juice. Pour the sauce over the frogs' legs and sprinkle with 1 tablespoon finely chopped parsley.

Snails

SNAILS ARE FOUND in various parts of Europe, but I don't believe that they are eaten with the same gusto outside France. In France the best snails come from the wine-growing sections. But even there fresh snails are not a year-round food, because it is only after they have receded into their shells, closing themselves in for winter hibernation from the first of November through March, that they are prime. The rest of the year canned snails are served; and snails, fortunately, are excellent when canned. The seasonal situation does not affect us at all here in this country, because all the snails we eat here are canned and imported from France.

Preparing fresh snails involves a tedious process that includes many washings in water with salt and vinegar and cooking in court bouillon for 4 hours. I won't go into these details because you will be using canned snails, and I am sure that you will be more interested in knowing how the canned ones are sold. Two sizes are canned, the average sized snails and extra large ones. The former are packed 2 dozen and 4 dozen to the can for households and 100 to the can for restaurants, the latter 18 and 24 to the can for households and 72 for restaurants. The shells are packed separately in cartons that contain 48 shells for regular-sized snails or 36 for the large size. There is also a special package for the housewife that contains a can of 24 snails, a carton of 24 shells, and seasonings for the butter sauce. Snails are served by the dozen or half dozen.

Canned snails are the easiest fare in the world to prepare. They have already been thoroughly cooked, and the shells have been cleaned and sterilized so that after the special butter and the snails are put into the shells they need only be thoroughly heated. Always serve them very, very hot. To eat snails in the conventional way, pick up the shell with a holder made for this purpose and dig out the snail with a tiny two-tined snail fork.

SNAILS WITH GARLIC BUTTER

Escargots à la Bourguignonne

FOR 36 snails prepare butter as follows: Cream 1 1/4 cups butter and add to it 1 teaspoon finely chopped shallots, 2 cloves of garlic, crushed, 1/2 tablespoon finely chopped parsley, 1 teaspoon salt, and a little pepper. Put a little of this butter in each of 36 shells, put a snail in each shell, and cover the snails with the remaining butter. Pour 2 tablespoons white wine in a flat baking dish or use the special small pans with indentions for 6 or 12 snails that may be obtained at gourmet shops. Arrange the shells in the dish and sprinkle them with fine bread crumbs. Bake the snails in a very hot oven (450° F.) or put the dish under the broiler until the crumbs are golden brown. Serve immediately, from the baking dish.

An unusual recipe for snails which does not require the use of the shell is a spécialité of the Burgundy countryside, where both snails and red wine are at their best.

SNAILS IN RED WINE

Escargots au Vin Rouge

PARBOIL 1/4 cup fat salt pork, diced, for 5 minutes and drain it. Melt 1 tablespoon butter in a heavy pan or casserole and in it sauté the pork dice until golden brown. Add 1 1/2 cups red wine, 12 small white onions, 1 large clove of garlic, crushed fine, and a faggot made by tying together 3 sprigs of parsley, 1 stalk of celery, 1/2 bay leaf and a little thyme. Bring the liquid to a boil, cover the pan and cook the mixture slowly for about 1 hour. Add 36 canned snails and heat them for 5 minutes. Discard the herbs and thicken the sauce by swirling in *beurre manié* made by creaming together 1 tablespoon butter and 1/2 tablespoon flour. Add 1 tablespoon brandy and sprinkle the snails with chopped parsley.

Truffles

I N THE section on trüffle stuffings, I mentioned that it was from Monsieur Jules Tissier, in the kitchens of the Bristol in Paris, that I first learned how to truffle-stuff a bird. Before I tell you now something more about truffles, I would like to tell you something more about the Bristol.

The scope and quality of the cuisine of the Bristol can be appreciated only when one understands the kind of hotel it was. In the first place, it was Paris headquarters of the élite of the world—such well-known persons as King Edward of England, King Leopold of Belgium, Queen Amelia of Portugal, Pierpont Morgan of this country.

In the second place, although its kitchens, appointed and equipped as they were to take care of any and every request, produced some of the finest dishes ever eaten by man, the Bristol had no public dining rooms. Every suite, of course, had its own dining room where our guests entertained on a smaller scale, a more intimate one, albeit several chefs would be assigned for a whole day to the preparation of one meal served to a small party, turning out dishes that were utterly perfect. This was at the turn of the century, you must remember, and a public eating room in the place where one lived was still considered a bit bourgeois. When the *haut monde* dined in public, it was in the ultrasmart restaurants.

The Bristol had no menus as we know them today with long lists of soups, entrées, and so on. The maître d'hôtel discussed with the *chef des cuisines* the foods in season and received his suggestion for the day and for functions that were being planned by guests. Then he discussed with the guests the meals and entertaining problems in much the same way that their own butlers did when they were at home. There were times, however, when a guest would set his heart on something special that required foodstuffs not on hand in the kitchen. And then what a hurrying and scurrying around Paris to get them. The newest chef—and for too long that seemed to be me—would be pulled off his work and sent bustling to the rue St. Honoré or other market area with the inevitable " *Vite, vite* " ringing in his ears.

But the running of errands was a small price to pay for learning from Monsieur Tissier, a chef trained in the classic tradition. Later, I became still more experienced under two other equally famous chefs of the era, Monsieur Gimon of the Paris Ritz and Monsieur Malley of the London Ritz, as I moved on at the opening of each of these hotels. By the time I arrived in New York, I was certainly well versed in handling truffles, as in most of the other aspects of the culinary arts.

In dealing with truffles, the first thing to understand is how to handle them—and rather a temperamental comestible they are. I speak of fresh truffles, which unfortunately too few Americans have ever seen or tasted due to the fact that their occurrence in nature is so limited and their deterioration so rapid.

Truffles are a sort of underground fungus whose whereabouts are discovered by trained truffle pigs—and sometimes dogs—which root them out of the ground. They are a rare delicacy because they have a unique and very volatile aroma which exudes from the truffle to permeate and richly flavor everything it is cooked with. They are found in only a few sections of France and Italy, and these limited sources of supply are still further narrowed down when one considers that there is only one truly epicurean variety, the black truffle of Périgord. The soil, climate, or whatever it is that influences truffle culture, gives those of Périgord an unusual quality and flavor lacking in the ones found in Normandy, Burgundy, and other parts of France. Those of Italy are apt to have a slight garlic taste and so are used only for dishes which that flavor enhances. In Périgord truffles are not just another foodstuff. They dominate the section, their subtle scent permeating every breath you draw and their captivating flavor every bite you eat. Only in Périgord will you find peasants in the smallest villages enjoying as a regular treat the hot truffles that come out of their roasted turkeys. Only in Périgord will the scent of truffles come upon you while you are still hundreds of feet away from the market where the baskets are on sale. If you ever have the opportunity of buying fresh truffles, consider the ones of Périgord first.

The season for fresh truffles is rather short, and so the surplus is canned. That is how their use is spread throughout the year and how we purchase them in this country. You will find that both the peeled and unpeeled are canned. In Paris they come into the market packed in baskets in their own earth which holds in their flavor. As soon as they are pulled out of this covering of earth, they should be used as quickly as possible or their finest characteristics are lost. I recall my keen disappointment in attempting to serve *dindonneau truffé* (truffle-stuffed young turkey) made with fresh truffles when we first opened the Ritz-Carlton. It was December, holiday time, truffle time, and I had planned to have them shipped by fast boat from France. But the fastest boat took six to seven days, and that was too long for this fragile commodity. *Zut, alors!* When I opened the package I found I had something as tasteless as a piece of sponge. The *parfum* had completely disappeared.

The average truffle is about the size of a small egg, occasionally smaller, sometimes larger. Its skin is rough and full of irregular ridges in which the moist soil collects as it grows. Cleaning one, therefore, must be thorough with brush and water in order to get all the soil out of these crevices. They are peeled before using, but even the peeling of a truffle is too precious to be discarded. Instead it is always finely chopped and used. You will find more details in the stuffing and garnish chapters.

Garlic

THIS STRANGE little bulb is used in most of the cookery along the Mediterranean, and in France it is often called *la vanille de Marseille*. It has a strong flavor, as anyone knows who has ever tasted such things as garlic butter or *aïoli* sauce, a flavor of great character and robustness. But it can also impart a flavor so subtle as hardly to be detected. The point is to use it properly, whether in small or large amounts.

Seasoning New Casserole   Apart from its virtues as a flavoring, garlic is considered indispensable in France for curing a new casserole—the traditional kind made of brown clay with an unglazed outer surface. The theory is that when the casserole is rubbed inside and out with cut pieces of garlic, the oil penetrates the clay and toughens it. The casserole is then filled with water to which are added celery leaves, onion skins, leek tops, chopped carrots, and parsley stems. With an asbestos pad protecting the casserole from the direct heat, the water is brought to a boil and the mixture simmers for at least 2 hours. Then it is discarded. The French consider the casserole " seasoned " —there is no taste of clay when it is used—and made more durable by the garlic.

Many French dishes would almost lack their *raison d'être* if the garlic were omitted—*bouillabaisse marseillaise*, for one, *escargots* with garlic butter, for another. A trace of garlic improves any number of sauced dishes like beef or lamb stew, oxtail ragout, *coq au vin*, eggplant dishes, and specialties made with tomatoes. Indeed, tomatoes and garlic, or garlic alone, indicate the mode of preparation known as *provençale*.

In using garlic remember three basic facts. First, the heavy flavor that offends some people will evaporate, leaving only a pleasing pungency, if the garlic is crushed. Second, this same heavy flavor disappears when garlic cooks in a liquid. Third, garlic acquires a bitter taste if it cooks long enough in butter and oil to take on color. In making butter sauces, add the crushed garlic to butter heated through or lightly browned just before you pour the sauce over the meat, fish, or vegetable.

I prefer to crush garlic, even for a stew or sauce, but if the clove is left whole, be sure to take it out at the end of cooking. Anyone biting into it will still get the flavor full strength. One way of using garlic combines parboiling the cloves a few minutes and then crushing them. Chopping garlic does not do quite the same thing as crushing it. In any case, garlic is always peeled.

To Crush Garlic

The chef does chop it on the board first, but then he takes the flat side of a big, heavy knife and slaps it down sharply, crushing the garlic completely—that is, if he is using a small amount. (French recipes often say *une pointe d'ail*, which means a very little crushed garlic, just as much as can be picked up on the tip of a small pointed kitchen knife.) If a number of cloves of garlic are to be crushed, he puts them in a mortar and pounds them with a small pestle. Of course, you can buy one of the popular little gadgets called a garlic crusher. It does the job well but must be carefully washed after using. Clean thoroughly the boards, knives, or other utensils used with garlic, because a lingering garlic flavor on kitchen equipment is far from desirable.

Here are a few favorite ways of using garlic in French cookery: in a brown butter sauce made by cooking butter to hazelnut brown and adding a little crushed garlic and some finely chopped parsley (sautéed eggplant or frogs' legs are delicious this way and simple to prepare); as part of a mixture of fine bread crumbs, a small amount of crushed garlic, and some finely chopped parsley on foods to be broiled (the crumbs on tomato halves absorb the moisture of the tomatoes and the garlic perfumes them); and finally as a flavoring for roasts. Anyone who likes garlic invariably uses it in roasting mutton or lamb. Insert slivers of it in little slits cut in the meat. Or chop and crush the garlic with salt and pepper and rub this mixture over the surface of the roast. Or rub it with garlic oil.

Those who don't like garlic in anything else seem to like a trace of its flavor in tossed green salad. The section on green salads tells you ways for achieving this flavor, including the use of the little garlic-imbued crusts called *chapons*. Let me just remind you: a slice of garlic lost in the greens of a salad will always get into someone's mouth and make an unhappy situation. Use one of the other methods instead.

Huile d'Ail

GARLIC OIL

PARBOIL 12 cloves of peeled garlic for 2 or 3 minutes, drain, and crush in a mortar. Add 1 1/2 to 2 cups olive oil and strain through fine cheesecloth. Use the oil for seasoning lamb and for making salad dressings.

Canapés à l'Ail

GARLIC CANAPÉS

PARBOIL 6 cloves of garlic for 2 or 3 minutes and drain and crush them. Combine the garlic with the yolks of 6 hard-cooked eggs and mash all together until it is thoroughly blended. Add 3 tablespoons butter, mix well, and rub the mixture through a fine sieve. Spread on small rounds of toast.

Sauce à l'Ail

GARLIC SAUCE

PARBOIL 6 to 8 cloves of peeled garlic, drain, and crush in a mortar. In a saucepan melt 2 tablespoons butter, add 1 teaspoon chopped onion. and cook until the onion is soft, but not brown. Add 2 tablespoons flour and cook, stirring, until the *roux* turns golden. Add gradually 1 1/2 cups hot milk, stirring vigorously until the sauce is smooth and thickened. Add 1/8 teaspoon salt and cook over a gentle flame for about 20 minutes, or until the sauce is reduced to 1 cup, stirring frequently. Add the crushed garlic, cook for 10 minutes longer, and strain the sauce.

GARLIC SOUP PROVENÇALE

Soupe à l'Ail à la Provençale

IN A soup kettle put 2 quarts water, 15 to 18 small cloves of garlic, 1 sprig of thyme, 1 clove, a pinch of sage, 1 tablespoon salt, and a little pepper. Bring the water to a boil and simmer for 20 to 25 minutes. In an oven-proof casserole or soup tureen put about 20 small slices of French bread, strain the garlic bouillon over the bread, and sprinkle with grated Parmesan or dry Swiss cheese and about 2 tablespoons olive oil. Put the tureen in a hot oven (450° F.) for a few minutes until the cheese is melted.

Leeks

LEEKS ARE for soup, and no Frenchman thinks he can make a really excellent soup without them. *Potage Parmentier* or vichyssoise may be made with onions instead of leeks and still be a perfectly good soup, but it will lack a recognizable refinement of flavor.

The flavor of leeks, while similar to that of onion, is more delicate and subtle, enhancing rather than overpowering the other flavors in the soup. You must distinguish between the two parts—the white section at the base and the coarser green tops. The white part should be used for white soup stock and for the more delicate soups, such as chicken or vichyssoise, while the green part is only put into darker or stronger soups. The bright green tops of leeks are especially good in *potage Saint-Germain*, or pea soup, because they not only add flavor but also improve the color. A good trick with leeks is to add one when cooking vegetables for the purée base of cream soups. This gives a sophisticated, almost unidentifiable flavor.

Another leek *spécialité* is as an hors-d'oeuvre. If they are simmered gently and not too long in the soup, they can be removed without falling apart. There is plenty of good flavor still in them, and they can be chilled and served with vinaigrette sauce.

Care must be taken in cleaning leeks, which are very sandy. To remove the grit, split the leeks lengthwise or quarter them and flush the pieces thoroughly under fast-running water.

Eels

I N FRANCE, eels are used in making matelote, are always included in bouillabaisse, and almost always appear in *hors-d'oeuvre variés*. In this country home cooks like to sauté them, and in restaurants they often appear with a vinaigrette sauce on the hors-d'oeuvre tray.

The best eels always come from swiftly running water and all eels should be cooked as soon after they are caught as possible. Naturally, people have personal preferences among the many varieties of eels, and a recipe may sometimes specify the use of a certain kind of eel. Old large eels require a precooking in court bouillon or other liquid to cook out some of their great quantity of fat, which makes them less digestible than small eels. In *haute cuisine*, cooks use only small tender eels.

Eels bought at market will be skinned. Those you catch, you must skin yourself. Cut off the head and pull the skin back and off the eel in one piece. If this proves too difficult, cut the eels in 1- to 1 1/2-inch pieces and broil or fry the pieces in very hot fat until the skin loosens and puffs up. It can easily be peeled off. Clean as you would other fish.

Anguilles Sautées

SAUTÉED EELS

CUT 2 very young, skinned eels in 1 1/2- to 2-inch pieces, season them with salt and pepper and dip them in milk, then in flour. Heat salad oil in a skillet until it is very hot, add the eels and cook them 6 to 7 minutes on each side, or until they are golden brown and tender. Remove them to a serving dish and sprinkle them with lemon juice and parsley. Pour off the oil from the pan and discard it. Add 3 tablespoons butter to the pan, cook it until it is hazelnut brown, and pour it over the eels.

Anguilles Vinaigrette

EELS VINAIGRETTE

CUT a 2-pound skinned eel into 1 1/2- to 2-inch pieces and season them with salt and pepper. Put 1 tablespoon salad oil or butter in a saucepan,

add 1 onion and 1 carrot, both sliced, 1 clove of garlic, crushed, and a faggot made by tying together a stalk of celery, a sprig of parsley, a piece
of bay leaf, and a little thyme. Place the sections of eel on the vegetables
and add equal parts of white wine and water to cover them. Bring the liquid to a boil, cover the pan, and cook the eel for 20 to 25 minutes, or
until it is tender. Cool it in the cooking liquid. Skim the fat from surface,
remove the eel to a serving dish, and moisten it well with vinaigrette
sauce.

 *Shallots*

A FRENCHMAN considers shallots as important for certain sauces
as he does leeks for certain soups. When I first came to this country, very few markets sold shallots, but now they have become much more
familiar and more readily available, at least in large cities.

Shallots look something like onions, but they are much smaller—
never bigger than a small fig, often only the size of an olive—and more
pear-shaped. Their skin is a little browner than that of a yellow onion
and also a little thicker, and the inner layers have a purplish cast. Shallots
grow as garlic does, in a compact group of individual " cloves " attached
to a common base.

They are easy to grow in a kitchen garden and thrive in the same
soil and climate as onions. You plant the same kind of bulbs as are used
for cooking, placing them about 2 inches deep in light rich soil and about
4 inches apart. When the slender hollow leaves die at the end of summer,
it is time to dig up the new bulbs. Each bulb planted produces a clump
of about 5 or 6 new shallot bulbs. If thoroughly dried and stored in
ventilated baskets in a cold dry place, they will keep all winter.

The flavor of shallots resembles that of onions, but it is mellower,
more subtle, and less sweet. Although onions may be substituted in a
recipe when shallots are unavailable, a true gourmet can recognize the
difference. Because of their subtlety, they are preferred for sauces used
with delicate foods such as chicken, fish, and veal, and with some broiled
meats. They have a special affinity for wine and are always included in
such sauces as *poulette* and *chasseur*, but less frequently in sauces strongly
flavored with herbs, spices, garlic, or other ingredients that would overwhelm their delicacy. In cookery, shallots are always peeled and very

finely chopped. Use only a small quantity, and do not let them brown when cooking, or the sauce will have a slightly bitter taste.

Wines and Spirits in Cooking

HAUTE CUISINE in America survived the hardships and restrictions of the first World War without serious distress. A well-trained chef could cope with "wheatless days" and "meatless days" so long as there were other starches and enough fish and poultry. But prohibition dealt fine cookery a blow from which it recovered only slowly and painfully. To one schooled in the tradition of enhancing the flavors of fine foods with wines and spirits, it was unthinkable to expect the same effect without wine. The salt-laden "cooking Sherry" that we were allowed had to be used with infinite caution—and even so, the results were frequently *épatant*. Occasionally, during those unhappy days, a guest would bring me a cherished bottle of wine from his private stock, so that I could prepare for him an authentic *coq au vin* or sabayon—and gratefully accept his invitation that I make enough for myself at the same time.

Eh bien, everything comes to an end, even prohibition, and the day came when once more I had only to ask to obtain any wine I needed from the cellars hewn and blasted out of the rock beneath the old Ritz, cellars protected by walls so thick that the vibrations of traffic never penetrated them and the temperature remained constant through the seasons.

If you are puzzled about how to buy wines and spirits for cooking, let me advise you first to find a wine merchant you can trust, and depend upon him for advice. Beware of bargains in wine, and never use in cooking a wine you would not drink. This does not mean marinating a shoulder of venison in a precious, expensive vintage Burgundy, which deserves to be enjoyed in a glass, where it can be fully appreciated.

But there are many wines, domestic and imported, which are both pleasant to drink and reasonably priced for cooking.

In France, the wine we drank and also cooked with was a local wine, a *vin du pays*. This was, of course, a *vin ordinaire*, usually low in alcoholic content, that was not exported or even transported any distance. Such wines are usually stored in casks and do not follow the life cycle of bottled wines, which " live, " ripen, and grow in quality, then begin to age, sicken, and die. *Vins ordinaires* are used too quickly.

Vins
Ordinaires

There was always a bottle of wine on the table in my mother's kitchen. It was tightly stoppered, although it bore no label, and like the widow's cruet, it never seemed to be empty. It was years before I realized that the bottle was constantly being replenished from two casks of local wine, one white, one red, that were stored in our cool cellar. *Maman* would add a little wine from the bottle to the stew bubbling on the stove and pour some of the same wine into *papa's* glass when she served the stew.

The wine *maman* used in cooking, and that the family drank at every meal, was sometimes red, sometimes white, but both whites and reds were dry, that is, not sweet. There are only a few instances when a touch of sweetness is not out of place in meat cookery—the Madeira sauce served with ham and tongue, for example. The color of the wine is a factor, of course, and white wine is usual for fish and poultry dishes. Red wine will add a dark color to a meat gravy or to coq au vin.

Wine is added to foods to enhance natural flavor, not to overwhelm it, so moderation is the key to successful use. When wine is cooked, the alcohol evaporates, leaving only the flavor of the fruit. Why, then, you may ask, use wine? Why not use unfermented fruit juices? The answer to that question is a simple one: It is the process of fermentation, the process of turning grape juice into wine, that makes possible otherwise unobtainable subtleties and nuances of flavor, aroma, and bouquet.

Wine has three major uses in cooking, other than its use in desserts.

First, it is used with herbs and spices as a marinade, to season and tenderize meat before long braising. The marinade is used in the cooking, as well, and becomes part of the sauce. In cooking fish, wine is part of the liquid for poaching, and also becomes part of the sauce. In both these cases, the wine is subjected to considerable cooking and thus reduced, so that it need not be of the highest quality, although it should be, like all " cooking wines, " good enough to drink.

The second use of wine in cooking is to make pan sauces. The wine is used to deglaze the pan in which meat, fish, or poultry was roasted or

Deglazing sautéed, that is, to dissolve the brown juices that cling to the pan. The pan should be very hot when the wine is added. This hastens the deglazing and the evaporation of the alcohol. The sauce is reduced a little and poured over the waiting food. This quick cooking does not cause the wine to lose its bouquet completely, and a wine of slightly better quality than that used for marinades should be chosen.

The third use of wine in cooking is as a final flavoring, in which case it is added at the very last of the cooking process, or just before serving. The sauce is not brought to a boil after the wine is added. Wines for this purpose are usually fortified, that is, strengthened with brandy, and the Sherry, Madeira, or Port used in this fashion should have excellent flavor.

I would like to warn you not to use more wine than is specified in a recipe on the theory that if a little wine is good, more will be better. On the contrary, too much wine can spoil a dish irreparably.

The remainder of a bottle of wine used in cooking can be served with the meal. Or the bottle can be tightly corked and laid on its side in the refrigerator until it is needed again for cooking, but it must be used within a few days. Wine tends to turn to vinegar rather quickly once it has been exposed to air. However, if your leftover wine turns, use it for making salad dressing—it need not go to waste.

Wine and Spirits in Desserts

WINE is used less frequently than liquor in desserts, but the fortified wines, particularly, have some special uses. Macaroon or cake crumbs soaked in Sherry brighten soufflés and cream desserts, frozen or not. Fruit is poached in a wine syrup and fresh fruit is sprinkled with it or macerated with it. Butter cakes are flavored with Madeira, and fruit cakes are moistened with Madeira or Sherry as well as with brandy and rum.

Wine is used to good advantage in many dessert sauces, of both the custard and fruit variety. Your own experience with wine in the dessert recipes given in this volume will lead you to further experiments, I am sure. Remember the warning I have repeated so often in these pages, and use wine discreetly and cautiously to enhance the flavor of your dessert, not overwhĕlm it.

The purpose of flambéing desserts—of finishing them just before they are served with blazing spirits—is twofold: First, but least important, is the dramatic presentation it makes possible. Second is the intriguing flavor left by the burning of the spirit, for as the alcohol burns away, only the intrinsic flavor of the fruit remains.

Flambéing Desserts

To make sure of a brilliant and long-lasting flame—a sight that invariably charms diners—heat the brandy or Cognac in the spoon to the igniting point and touch it with a match. Or tilt a tiny pan of warmed brandy toward the flame of the chafing dish lamp until it catches fire. Then pour it blazing over the food, continuing to baste the food with the flaming sauce until the spirit burns out. If you sprinkle a steamed pudding or crêpes lightly with sugar before ladling the blazing spirits over them, the flame will burn longer and more brightly.

Wines are less important than liquors in flavoring desserts because the small amounts that can be added as a flavoring would have little effect compared with the intensity of flavor that can be derived from an equal amount of rum, brandy, or a liqueur. The simplest way of using liquors to flavor desserts is to add them to puddings, sauces, or whipped cream, or sprinkle them over fresh or cooked fruit or over ice cream or ices. One ingenious dessert is made by scooping the seeds and fibre from a ripe melon through a small plug and filling the melon with kirsch, the cherry-flavored liqueur. When the melon is chilled and served, its flesh is permeated with the liqueur flavor. Ladyfingers soaked in Grand Marnier are added to the famous *soufflé Grand Marnier*. As the soufflé bakes, the flavor of the liqueur is released to spread throughout the mixture. Again I remind you: use liqueurs in cooking as you do wine—discreetly. Too much liqueur added to an ice cream or ice mixture will prevent it from freezing; too much liqueur added to anything can make the dish taste of nothing but the liqueur.

Liquors in Desserts

Flaming desserts are a familiar sight to anyone who has ever eaten in a fine French restaurant. The uses of flambéing in the kitchen are

Flambéing
Entrées

perhaps less known, although they are no less important. The chef blazes such foods as lobster, chicken, and game birds with brandy or Cognac after they are sautéed at the beginning of their preparation. The mellowing and flavoring effect of the flambéing then persists throughout the entire cooking process. Heat the liquor in a small deep pan and pour it flaming over the hot food, or if pan and food are hot enough the spirit can be poured directly over the food in the pan, and encouraged to blaze, if necessary, by tipping the pan slightly toward the flame.

Wines and Spirits for the Kitchen

THE EXTENT of any householder's wine cellar depends upon his tastes and his pocketbook, and this is also true to a degree of his kitchen wine-and-spirit shelf. For successfully making the recipes in this volume, however, certain wines and spirits are indispensable, and I strongly advise that you have these on hand as a beginning.

You will need two kinds of wines, reds for cooking dark meats and game and whites for fish and poultry dishes. Both kinds should be dry wines. For flaming, you should have Cognac or another brandy. A Sherry and a Madeira of excellent quality are useful for flavoring everything from soups through desserts. And for other dessert uses, have on hand dark rum, kirsch (cherry brandy), and one of the liqueurs, such as Grand Marnier, Cointreau, or Curaçao.

When you have become accustomed to using these basic wines and spirits in your kitchen, you will want to try others and add them, too, to your kitchen wine and spirit shelf.

INDEX

INDEX

All recipes, unless otherwise noted, are for six persons. When reference is made within a recipe to a second recipe, consult the index.